RESEARCH HANDBOOK ON EMPIRICAL STUDIES IN INTELLECTUAL PROPERTY LAW

RESEARCH HANDBOOKS IN INTELLECTUAL PROPERTY

Series Editor: Jeremy Phillips, *Intellectual Property Consultant, Olswang, Research Director, Intellectual Property Institute and co-founder, IPKat weblog*

Under the general editorship and direction of Jeremy Phillips comes this important new *Research Handbook* series of high quality, original reference works that cover the broad pillars of intellectual property law: trademark law, patent law and copyright law – as well as less developed areas, such as geographical indications, and the increasing intersection of intellectual property with other fields. Taking an international and comparative approach, these *Research Handbooks*, each edited by leading scholars in the respective field, will comprise specially commissioned contributions from a select cast of authors, bringing together renowned figures with up-and-coming younger authors. Each will offer a wide-ranging examination of current issues in intellectual property that is unrivalled in its blend of critical, innovative thinking and substantive analysis, and in its synthesis of contemporary research.

Each *Research Handbook* will stand alone as an invaluable source of reference for all scholars of intellectual property, as well as for practising lawyers who wish to engage with the discussion of ideas within the field. Whether used as an information resource on key topics, or as a platform for advanced study, these *Research Handbooks* will become definitive scholarly reference works in intellectual property law.

For a full list of Edward Elgar published titles, including the titles in this series, visit our website at www.e-elgar.com.

Research Handbook on Empirical Studies in Intellectual Property Law

Edited by

Estelle Derclaye

Professor of Intellectual Property Law, School of Law, University of Nottingham, UK

RESEARCH HANDBOOKS IN INTELLECTUAL PROPERTY

Edward Elgar
PUBLISHING

Cheltenham, UK • Northampton, MA, USA

Published by
Edward Elgar Publishing Limited
The Lypiatts
15 Lansdown Road
Cheltenham
Glos GL50 2JA
UK

Edward Elgar Publishing, Inc.
William Pratt House
9 Dewey Court
Northampton
Massachusetts 01060
USA

A catalogue record for this book
is available from the British Library

Library of Congress Control Number: 2023937058

This book is available electronically in the **Elgar**online
Law subject collection
http://dx.doi.org/10.4337/9781802206210

ISBN 978 1 80220 620 3 (cased)
ISBN 978 1 80220 621 0 (eBook)

Printed and bound by CPI Group (UK) Ltd, Croydon, CR0 4YY

To all past, present and future intellectual property scholars doing legal empirical research, with thanks for the inspiration

Contents

Contributors

Mateo Aboy, Professor, Principal Research Scholar, Centre for Law, Medicine and Life Sciences (LML), Faculty of Law, University of Cambridge, UK

Christoph Antons, Professor, Macquarie Law School, Australia

Jane Cornwell, Senior Lecturer in Intellectual Property Law, University of Edinburgh, UK

Ben Depoorter, Max Radin Distinguished Professor of Law, University of California, Hastings College of the Law; Affiliate Scholar, Stanford Law School, Center for Internet and Society; Director, CASLE, Ugent

Estelle Derclaye, Professor of Intellectual Property Law, School of Law, University of Nottingham, UK

Dr Louise C. Druedahl, Post-doctoral researcher, Centre for Advanced Studies in Biomedical Innovation Law (CeBIL), University of Copenhagen, Denmark

Ilanah Fhima, Professor of Intellectual Property Law and Co-director, Institute of Brand and Innovation Law, Faculty of Laws, University College London, UK

Deborah R. Gerhardt, Reef C. Ivey II Excellence Fund Term Professor of Law, University of North Carolina, USA

Branislav Hazucha, Professor of Intellectual Property Law, The Hokkaido University Graduate School of Law, Japan

Dr Vicki Huang, Associate Professor of Law, Deakin University, Melbourne, Australia

Emily Hudson, Professor, Dickson Poon School of Law, King's College London, UK

Jon J. Lee, Professor of Practice, School of Law, University of Minnesota

Mark P. McKenna, Professor of Law, UCLA School of Law, Faculty Co-director, UCLA Institute for Technology, Law & Policy, Los Angeles, California, USA

Timo Minssen, Professor of Law at the University of Copenhagen (UCPH), Denmark, Founding Director of UCPH's Center for Advanced Studies in Biomedical Innovation Law (CeBIL)

Pinai Nanakorn, Professor of Private Law, Thammasat University, Thailand

Dianne Nicol, Distinguished Professor Emerita, Faculty of Law and Centre for Law and Genetics, University of Tasmania, Australia

Jane Nielsen, Associate Professor, Faculty of Law and Centre for Law of Genetics, University of Tasmania, Australia

Dr Kylie Pappalardo, Queensland University of Technology, Brisbane, Australia

Jason Rantanen, David L. Hammer and Willard L. "Sandy" Boyd Professor and Director, Innovation, Business & Law Center, University of Iowa College of Law, USA

Michael Risch, Vice Dean and Professor of Law, Villanova University Charles Widger School of Law

Jessica Silbey, Professor of Law and Yanakakis Law Faculty Scholar, Boston University School of Law, Boston, Massachusetts, USA

Amrithnath Sreedevi Babu, Doctoral researcher, Macquarie Law School, Australia

Cameron Stewart, Professor, Sydney Law School, The University of Sydney, Australia

William van Caenegem, Professor of Law, Bond University, Queensland, Australia

Esther van Zimmeren, Professor of Intellectual Property Law & Governance, University of Antwerp, Belgium

Runhua Wang, Associate Professor of Law, University of Science and Technology Beijing

Xianwei Zhang, Assistant Professor, College of Law, Shenzhen University, China

Introduction
Legal empirical studies – Where does intellectual property law stand and what does the future hold?

Legal empirical research in the field of intellectual property (IP) law has been off to a slow start but is finally b(l)ooming. In 2015, Ilanah Fhima and Catrin Denvir could only find five articles with the key words "empirical" (title) and "intellectual property" (text) on the legal database Hein Online.[1] A few years later, there were 39 in a combined Hein Online and Westlaw search.[2] Of course, these databases are not comprehensive and there must have been a bit more such research but it gives a flavour of the relative lack of such studies in the field of IP law. Legal empirical research is not new and there are several books dedicated to the field generally. However, there are none specifically on the topic of IP law. While this book aims to fill this gap, this is not its only aim, and arguably not even the most important. I believe legal empirical research is extremely important for obtaining a better understanding of IP law in practice and to help both policymakers to achieve the best laws and litigants to achieve the best outcome for their clients. Legal empirical research also furthers academic debate and opens new avenues of research and can change and even revolutionise IP law. Legal empirical research is an indispensable complement to economic research in the field of IP law, which is far more abundant but also oftentimes based on the decried Posnerian law and economics approach.

My first legal empirical output was a book chapter titled "A historical journey of the linguistic influences in Belgian copyright law: From united to lost in translation?" in Ysolde Gendreau and Abraham Drassinower's edited collection *Language and Copyright* published by Y. Blais in 2009. The empirical bug caught me and since then I have been increasingly interested and passionate about legal empirical research. When the editors of the International Review of Intellectual Property and Competition Law asked me to write an editorial in 2016, I made a passionate case for more such research, as well as inter-, cross-, pluri- and multi-diciplinary research, which empirical research often requires.[3] It is always difficult to determine the impact of editorials, but since then the UK government[4] and European Commission[5] have increasingly acknowledged the relevance and importance of legal empir-

---

[1]   Ilanah Fhima and Catrin Denvir, 'An Empirical Analysis of the Likelihood of Confusion Factors in European Trade Mark Law' [2015] I.I.C. 310, 313, note 19.

[2]   Oliver Church, Estelle Derclaye and Gilles Stupfler, 'An Empirical Analysis of the Design Case Law of the EU Member States' [2019] I.I.C. 685–719.

[3]   Estelle Derclaye, 'Editorial: Today's Utopia is Tomorrow's Reality' [2017] I.I.C. 1–3.

[4]   UKIPO, 'Guide to Evidence for Policy', available at https://assets.publishing.service.gov.uk/ government/uploads/system/uploads/attachment_data/file/510985/Guide_to_evidence_for_policy.pdf (last accessed 31 October 2022).

[5]   See e.g. Commission Staff Working Document, 'Evaluation of EU Legislation on Design Protection', Brussels, 6 November 2020, SWD(2020) 264 final, available at https://ec.europa.eu/ docsroom/documents/43705 (last accessed 31 October 2022).

ical research. In any case, it is great to see that many IP scholars are increasingly embracing legal empirical research and producing fascinating outputs.

I am very fortunate to have been able to assemble such a great and diverse group of legal empirical researchers from many continents for this book, both junior and seasoned. I wanted the book to be wide in both geographical and material scope, covering the main IP rights and important jurisdictions. That said, space was constrained so unfortunately, South America and Africa are not represented. I hope another book will address legal empirical research in IP from those parts of the world. This book's contributions are a mix of legal empirical research on specific topics (e.g. Jason Rantanen on US patents, Michael Risch on US trade secrets, Jane Cornwell on EU designs and Ilanah Fhima on EU trade marks), some literature reviews on legal empirical research in IP law (e.g. Mateo Aboy, Louise Druedahl and Timo Minssen's and Ben Depoorter's chapters) or a mix of the two (Mark McKenna and Jessica Silbey's chapter). Chapters employ many different methods, both qualitative (surveys, interviews) and quantitative (descriptive and inferential statistics).

The following briefly summarises the different chapters.

Starting with patents, in Part I of the book, **Jason Rantanen** provides very refined statistics on appeals in US patent cases for over 20 years. He analyses US patent litigation data in a very detailed way, making links between different datasets including the district courts and appellate docket datasets and appellate decisions dataset. His descriptive statistics give a very rich picture of the situation. Among others, he calculates the time it takes for a decision on an appeal and it shows differences with the type of court and how many cases come from which courts to the federal circuit. It shows that the federal circuit affirms 78% of the time, adding the 9% of affirmed in part it makes for a high 87%. Decisions from other appellate courts show similar percentages except for one court which is higher (91%) and one lower (68%) and offers explanations for these differences. His results also show that decisions from some courts are appealed more often than those of others. His methodology has vast possibilities as it can be used in other fields.

Esther van Zimmeren's chapter gives a "tour d'horizon" of the vast legal empirical literature on patenting practices and patent licensing practices as well as the methods used in such studies, especially in the field of life sciences and biopharmaceutical sector. This includes research on patent pools, patent pledges and compulsory licences. One of the main takeaways coming out of her chapter is that even if there is anecdotal evidence that the volume and value of patent licensing, and the number of empirical studies on them, have expanded over the last decades, because licensing agreements are typically confidential, the empirical patent licensing literature has not been able to follow the pace of the more general patenting literature. She highlights the three main challenges associated with empirical research in the realm of patent licensing in addition to the difficulty in obtaining quality patent licensing data: (1) it requires significant scientific expertise related to the patented inventions concerned and thus an experienced interdisciplinary team, (2) it necessitates a lot of funding, (3) identifying the journal where to publish the results of such interdisciplinary research can sometimes be difficult too. Her chapter ends with a "call for more collaboration to enable more empirical research regarding patent licensing practices to enable evidence-based law- and policymaking processes".

Jane Nielsen, **Dianne Nicol** and **Cameron Stewart** analyse bioprinting and gene editing patenting in Australia. The chapter gives statistics on applicants by country and type (public v private) and the analysis is complemented by interviews with Australian researchers to find out why there is little or no patenting in these fields. These interviews reveal a "sizeable disconnect" between Australian universities' pressures and expectations and their ability to commercialise/capitalise on their researchers' inventions. Whereas there are relatively few freedom-to-operate issues at the moment, they note it may become an issue in the future.

Christoph Antons and **Amrithnath Sreedevi Babu** write about the challenges of empirical research on plant variety protection in India and Indonesia. They argue that in methodological terms, it is essential to combine fieldwork, statistical analysis and analysis of secondary sources to research this area. Their results show that farmers have played a very small role and so far, have not gained much from plant variety protection. This is so despite the governments' rhetoric to favour local and traditional plant varieties. They also note that more empirical research can be done in this field, for instance studying the impact of laws on the domestic plant breeding industry and on public sector research agencies in developing countries.

Part II then moves on to trade secrets. After summarising the history of patent protection software at the US Supreme Court and the recent trend with the *Alice* decision to not allow computer programs to be protected by patents because they are often abstract ideas, **Michael Risch** performs sophisticated statistical analysis on litigation data to show whether software developers now rely more heavily on trade secrets than patents. His hypothesis "that software patent plaintiffs, product company plaintiffs, and especially software product company plaintiffs would be more likely to assert trade secret claims along with their patent claims in the time following the change in patentable subject matter rules" is confirmed. He concludes cautiously (because the causal inference is likely but still uncertain) that the *Alice* decision has probably changed the behaviour of litigants. His chapter also reveals some interesting data about the litigating behaviour of non-practising entities.

In their chapter, **Mateo Aboy**, **Louise Druedhal** and **Timo Minssen** present different types of empirical research that can be done with patent and trade secret data, how to do them insisting on transparency, quality and reproducibility of the results, and provide a helpful guide to researchers. It also shows that it is better to use different methods for patents and trade secrets, for instance interviews are better for trade secrets as data is difficult to obtain for obvious reasons. They also summarise some of the previous research to show that empirical studies are really important for judges and policymakers to take the right decisions; the example of the US *Myriad* case is illuminating in that respect. Had the court had access to the empirical research on isolated DNA patents, they would probably have decided the case differently.

Runhua Wang's chapter reviews all public judicial decisions regarding the misappropriation of technical secrets in China between January 2013 and December 2021 and shows that despite efforts by courts to strengthen trade secret protection, there are deficiencies in the legislation which the courts also reinforce. After presenting the succession of amended Chinese anti-unfair competition law, her chapter makes a thorough analysis of the courts' reasons for rejecting or accepting breaches of trade secrets. The analysis shows among other things that having criminal litigation precede civil litigation increases the level of damages awarded in civil cases. However, it is also a matter of concern because criminal litigation in China often lacks due process.

In Part III, which deals with copyright, **Ben Depoorter** provides a literature review of legal empirical literature in US copyright law on the infringement test, fair use defence, remedies, ideology in litigation and copyright enforcement. The review shows that most studies on fair use find that transformative use will strongly predict a finding of fair use. Among the interesting findings that his chapter summarises some are quite striking, especially on how courts apply the fair use defence: "the market impact of an unauthorized use on the copyrighted work (factor four) is most highly correlated with a fair use verdict" and "the application of the fair use test by courts is far more consistent and predictable than conventional wisdom suggests". Also, the proportion of transformative use decisions in fair use decisions in US courts jumped over 30% one year after the Supreme Court endorsed transformative use in the famous *Campbell v. Acuff-Rose* case. And of all the courts holding there was transformative use, 94% of them held that the fair use defence was applicable. Later research also confirms that transformative use is key in the courts' application of the fair use defence. Another interesting finding is that in the fair use decisions, the judge's copyright ideology did not influence the outcome. However, in copyright litigation at the level of the Supreme Court, it did. One finding is that "the more conservative a justice is, the more likely he or she is to vote in favor of recognizing and enforcing rights to intellectual property".

Emily Hudson's empirical research gives a rich and enlightening narrative on how copyright exceptions are used in practice compared to the law on the books. She draws from several years of interviews with countless cultural institutions on the way they digitise works and use copyright limitations and exceptions. Based on this research, she does not propose the adoption of a fair use exception in the UK at least not now and not in isolation, even if it is seen by most interviewees using the exception (US cultural institutions) as predictable and easy to use. Instead, she thinks it is best to have "expanded fair dealing". Two main reasons are that her empirical work shows that changes in the law pertaining to Canadian and Australian exceptions have not really made much difference in practice. Sometimes, even new practices emerged without legislative changes. More empirical work with users of copyright works in the UK should be done before a fair use exception is introduced in the UK. And of course, the same goes with any country who would wish to change their exceptions. As she says, "a major lesson from the empirical work is that meaningful changes can often be achieved without *any* change to the law".

Kylie Pappalardo showcases two case studies in Australia to highlight the importance of empirical research for evidence-based policy but more specifically the combination of both quantitative and qualitative research for the best such policy which will meet the needs of everyone affected by copyright law; creators, producers, distributors and users alike. Her qualitative research on what creators want from copyright law shows that many are not in most part motivated by economic rewards unlike what classical economic theory propounds. Her chapter goes into the detail of her methodology before summarising her results. In the second case study, she looked at whether the market for digital products, mainly audio-visual ones, is functioning or not in Australia. The evidence is that Australians have access to less audio-visual content than consumers in other markets. After explaining her methodology, she shares some of her main findings such as that "Australians had access to about 65 percent of movie titles and 75 percent of TV titles that were available to their US counterparts". She finishes with a summary of the research she is currently doing on how copyright structures influence the distribution of film and television content in Australia. She uses both quantitative data on digital markets and qualitative data (interviews with various stakeholders including producers and filmmakers). She concludes that "qualitative work allows us to test the theories and assumptions underlying the law" and "qualitative data can help us to see the bigger picture". Both types of empirical research are necessary to "properly understand the full scope of copyright law".

In his chapter, **Branislav Hazucha** empirically examines, via a survey using vignettes based on real decided cases, how the public views the use of user-generated content on social networks in France, Germany, Japan and the USA, specifically what kind of sanctions should be imposed namely disgorgement of profits, damages, injunction and apology. The countries were chosen because of different legal, social and cultural environments and traditions. The results show that there are indeed differences between countries where the US and Japan are the extreme (personal individual freedom so less prone to sanction versus a long and strong tradition of communitarianism so more prone to sanction) and France and Germany in between. There were also differences depending on gender and age. His results show that "although respondents deemed disgorgement of profits an appropriate remedy in certain cases, it was not as important as several other remedies" and "the more wrongful the presented vignette was perceived by a respondent, the higher was the chance that disgorgement of profits was deemed a suitable remedy". There were again cultural differences between the four countries on this point. The results also show that copyright law is based on moral foundations in social norms recognised by the general public.

Part IV is then concerned with trademarks. The story of US Patent and Trademark Office (USPTO) trademark data by **Deborah R. Gerhardt** and **Jon J. Lee** first sets the scene on how trademarks are protected in the US and how to apply for them at USPTO. It then retraces some of the prior empirical, both economic and legal, trademark research. The authors analyse 40 years of trademark data at the USPTO to show that trends in trademark applications are clearly influenced by changes in the law (e.g. a sustained spike of intent to use applications once it was allowed). Some of the very interesting results show among others that applicants who have registered their trademark abroad and rely on these registrations to register in the US have more chance of having their trademark registered in the US than those applying in the US directly, that trademark applicants were more likely to succeed to publication and registration if they were assisted by legal counsel, and that the success rates were even higher if the applicant's lawyer was very experienced.

Ilanah Simon Fhima analyses decisions of the European Union Intellectual Property Office (EUIPO) on shape marks to see which grounds of refusal are most used and finds that, rather counterintuitively, it is not the absolute grounds specifically relating to shapes of the goods under Article 7(1)(e) of the EU trade mark regulation but lack of distinctiveness which top the charts. She offers possible explanations for this including a reluctance to tackle these grounds because of their complexity. The chapter shows that "the time is ripe for an examination of whether the exclusion is doing what it is meant to do particularly in terms of protecting competition". The chapter also finds that the "more black and white marks are refused registration than colour marks and likewise that more marks without non-3D features are refused registered than those with". Importantly, her chapter leads to several new interesting questions to research further.

Pinai Nanakorn's chapter reveals that the Thai Trade Marks Board, a quasi-judicial appellate body reviewing registrars' orders in some important cases including refusal of registration, is very strict and often refuses trade marks for lack of distinctive character whereas they are not entirely descriptive. Indeed, the same marks for the same goods were registered in other jurisdictions. An example is combinations of letters and numerals. The Thai courts have, however, often reversed the Trade Marks Board's decisions and prompted the Manual of Trade Mark Registration to be changed. His chapter also analyses decisions on trade marks refused for being contrary to public order or morality which serve as a ground for refusing marks registered in bad faith as the Thai Trade Marks Act does not have such ground. The data shows a high number of decisions using this ground to remedy this problem and proves the law needs to be changed to add an absolute ground of refusal for bad faith.

William van Caenegem draws general guidelines from his experience doing different types of empirical research in different fields including geographical indications of origin (GIs) and fashion designs and can serve as a bridge between the parts of the books dealing with these two IP areas. The main takeaway of the chapter is that qualitative empirical research is well worth it despite the drawbacks (mainly doubts about legitimacy and ability to draw inferences especially from small samples) as it gives very rich data and can still inform policymaking, especially as an alternative or complement to surveys which have their own limitations. The important things are to not overclaim and clearly indicate the limitations of the research done to the reader. The added benefits of doing such research with others is that it helps to strengthen the conclusions reached because they are subject to active discussion between the several collaborators testing their validity. To illustrate these findings, he summarises the ways he proceeded with interviews leading to five different research outputs, naming the pitfalls but also the interesting aspects of doing such qualitative research.

Last but not least, Part V of the book deals with designs. US professors **Jessica Silbey** and **Mark McKenna** study designers, using mainly the qualitative method (interviews) and shed light on some puzzles in design law. They describe in detail how they did their interviews, e.g. why they did, how many they did and stopped, how their method led to the snowball effect (leading to more interviews with other designers). They trace the journey of their research and it is very helpful as a guide for similar research by other researchers. Thus, their chapter is not only interesting for the results they find but for the whole methodology. Their chapter includes interesting quotes from their interviews which reveal how designers see the evolution of design over time as creating experiences rather than products and finding design problems rather than solving them. Their chapter is only a small sample of questions that future work will analyse with the data and it will be fascinating to see what results their future research reveals for the world of design and intellectual property.

In her chapter, **Jane Cornwell** reviews invalidity decisions at EUIPO to show that it may be advisable for the European Commission, in its forthcoming design reform, to consider *ex ante* examination of substantive design law. It shows that at least 50% of designs are found invalid during litigation at EUIPO in every year bar one and that there is merit in putting some sort of *ex ante* examination at least for novelty and individual character (which are by far the main reasons for which the designs are invalidated). She also points out that there has been little research on "strategic design filing" so more research would be welcome to see if there is abuse of the system and whether or not such *ex ante* examination would be helpful, or some halfway house solution, to tackle the massive proportions of invalid designs.

Vicki Huang shows that even with changes in the 2003 Australian Design Act, very few designs are applied for and mostly by foreigners. A recent report from IP Australia shows designers do not apply nor rely much on designs and find it costly to enforce. Her chapter examines the 15 design infringement cases where there is a substantive discussion at first instance since the entry into force of the 2003 Act until June 2022. The win rate is quite high at 80% and the three cases which went on appeal were all affirmed. She compares this result with the litigation under the previous Act for the same amount of time, i.e. 18 years, and finds that under the new Act courts find designs infringed more often. She also finds that additional damages claims are often granted by courts which, coupled with the high infringement rate, could act as an incentive to apply for designs and sue for infringement, all in all good news for designers, domestic and foreign alike.

Finally, **Xianwei Zhang** analyses thousands of court decisions on designs in China. The results show that the number of design registrations has steadily increased since 2015 and that in the vast majority of cases in both administrative and civil disputes (ca. 90%) second instance courts confirm the first instance courts' verdicts. On the legal interpretations, courts are still grappling with concepts such as "average consumer" which is the standard to judge design infringement in China but they also increasingly implicitly refer to each other's decisions to decide the disputes, showing therefore a growing body of case law slowly interpreting the statute harmoniously.

In conclusion, these chapters offer a diverse range of methods and perspectives on the several IP rights, giving rich insights into IP practices and litigation, including rulings of intellectual property offices and how changes in legislation affect (or not) IP owners and users. In addition, many chapters also comment on the methodologies chosen, the reasons why they were chosen, the researcher journeys, the challenges, the pitfalls to avoid and provide examples of good practice and advice to follow and further avenues for research. I can see a time soon where these studies will lead to more empirical research in all these areas. For instance, the empirical research done by these authors could be replicated in other countries. It would be useful if inferential statistics could be performed on the data in some of the chapters (e.g. that of Jason Rantanen). This shows the importance of interdisciplinary teams including statisticians, and the difficulty in finding them, a challenge also highlighted by Esther van Zimmeren in her chapter.

As Aboy, Druedhal and Minssen conclude in their chapter, the time is ripe for IP scholars to engage in more empirical research. These chapters will hopefully provide inspiration, helpful guidance and encouragement to yet more IP scholars to embark in the exciting world of legal empirical studies in IP law.

Having said that, more often than not, combining both quantitative and qualitative research is important and doing legal empirical research does not mean leaving aside doctrinal, black letter law research altogether, as many contributors in the book highlight (e.g. van Zimmeren, Antons). Every methodology brings something to the table and a healthy combination of all adds to the evidence for good policymaking.

It is my hope that the book helps legislatures in the UK, EU and around the globe, in their policy- and law-making in view of the increased interest and importance in evidenced-based policymaking. I trust the book will also be valuable to authors, designers, inventors, traders, companies, practitioners and judges to help them make appropriate decisions. The information provided in many chapters will enable them to predict the outcome of cases relevant to them, and/or give them interesting insights so they can better decide, advise and/or litigate.

Last but not least, I would like to record my grateful thanks to all the contributors for their interesting and timely contributions and to the Elgar Team especially Laura Mann for helping along the way.

Estelle Derclaye
Nottingham, 3 November 2022

PART I

PATENTS AND PLANT
VARIETY RIGHTS

1. Studying patent infringement litigation

Jason Rantanen[1]

1. INTRODUCTION

Conventional studies of intellectual property litigation in the United States are dominated by studies of patent infringement cases that primarily approach the study of cases in one of two ways: either by studying just one layer of litigation, such as trial court cases, or by focusing on a cohort of cases and pursuing those cases to their final conclusion through extensive hand-coding.

This chapter describes a more comprehensive approach to studying patent infringement litigation that visualizes infringement litigation as a system composed of interrelated components, describing how to link together and analyze datasets containing information about those components. The example used in this chapter involves patent litigation, but this approach can be expanded to empirical analysis of other types of intellectual property litigation, or even legal disputes more generally.

Drawing upon this systems approach allows for new insights into the composition of appeals in patent litigation in the United States. Among other findings, this analysis reveals that:

- Approximately 85% of appeals to the Federal Circuit that originate in the district courts arise from patent infringement cases.
- While 6% of patent infringement cases filed in the district courts result in an appeal, this percentage varies widely by district from 2.4% for cases filed in the Eastern District of Texas to 11% for cases filed in the Southern District of New York.
- The time from appeal to decision varies substantially by origin and the form of the decision, with summary affirmances from some origins taking longer than opinions.

2. BACKGROUND

Studying litigation is difficult, especially with a topic as procedurally and substantively complex as patent law. Despite the challenges, over the past few decades numerous research-

[1] David L. Hammer and Willard L. "Sandy" Boyd Professor and Director, Iowa Innovation, Business & Law Center, University of Iowa College of Law. Thanks to Connor Williams, Allison Williamson, Sara Liebee, Claire Poeckes, Meddie Demmings, Ryan Meger, Charles Neff, Brenna Kingyon, Matt Fuentes, Dan Kieffer, Kallee Hooley, and many former research assistants who have helped develop the Federal Circuit Dataset Project. Thanks also to David Schwartz, Paul Gugliuzza, and Ted Sichelman for providing helpful feedback and comments on earlier drafts, as well as the attendees at the Intellectual Property Scholars Conference 2022. Data and code associated with this chapter is available at Rantanen, J., Replication Data for Studying Patent Infringement Litigation (2022) https://doi.org/10.7910/DVN/LQVVAK, Harvard Dataverse, V1, UNF:6:Ra8LmqnaBWzY1y3//PDW2g== [fileUNF].

ers have studied a variety of attributes of patent litigation.[2] Given the volume of modern patent litigation, with thousands of infringement cases and hundreds of appeals filed each year, these studies typically take one of a few approaches: study a single layer of patent litigation, such as district court cases, employ a cohort-based approach in which cases filed in one or two years are examined, or focus on a subject-matter constrained set of decisions that can be obtained from a commercial data source.

The quintessential example of these approaches are the groundbreaking studies conducted by John Allison and Mark Lemley, later joined by David Schwartz. The initial Allison & Lemley study, *Empirical Evidence on the Validity of Litigated Patents*, studied final patent validity decisions issued by federal courts between 1989 and 1996.[3] As the authors recognized, however, a limitation of this study was that it encompassed only published decisions, of which about half were appellate court decisions.[4] Sixteen years later, these authors undertook a new study that encompassed all patent infringement cases filed in 2008 and 2009 – over 5,000 lawsuits with 949 merits decisions.[5] Two of the authors spent hundreds of hours coding the dockets, including tracking the cases through to appeals and appellate decisions.[6] These studies illustrate the immensity of the task, and how researchers typically approach studying patent litigation by focusing on a particular subset of the overall whole, such as a limited type of decision or a narrow slice of time.

More recently, large-scale publicly accessible datasets spanning a long period of time have become available. However, these datasets are limited to only a single layer of litigation.[7] Two examples of single-layer databases of patent-related cases are the United States Patent and Trademark Office (USPTO) Patent Litigation Dataset and the Federal Circuit Dataset Project.

At the district court level, the USPTO Patent Litigation Dataset provides data on patent infringement cases filed in district courts. This dataset was created through a joint project between the USPTO and the University of San Diego Law School. The authors drew on PACER (acronym for Public Access to Court Electronic Records) to collect information about all patent litigation at the district courts from 1963–2015. A 2019 update added cases filed in 2016 and additional hand-coded fields.[8] In total, the dataset contains 81,350 unique *district court* patent litigation records.

---

[2]   For literature reviews of the many studies of patent infringement litigation, *see* Menell, P. & Schwartz, D., Research Handbook on the Economics of Intellectual Property Law, Volume 2: Analytical Methods (Edward Elgar 2019).

[3]   Allison, J. & Lemley, M., *Empirical Evidence on the Validity of Litigated Patents*, 26 AIPLA Q.J. 185 (1998).

[4]   *See* Allison, J., Lemley, M. & Schwartz, D., *Understanding the Realities of Modern Patent Litigation*, 92 Tex. L. Rev. 1769, 1770 (2014); Allison, J., Lemley, M. & Schwartz, D., *Our Divided Patent System*, 82 U. Chi. L. Rev. 1073 (2015); Allison, J., Lemley, M. & Schwartz, D., *How Often Do Non-Practicing Entities Win Patent Suits?*, 32 Berk. Tech. L. J. 235 (2017).

[5]   For comparison, the dataset in Allison & Lemley (1998) contained 300 final validity decisions over an 8-year period.

[6]   Allison, Lemley & Schwartz (2014) at 1774.

[7]   As discussed below, there are commercial databases for conducting legal research such as WestLaw and Lexis, as well as commercial services for lawyers such as DocketNavigator and LexMachina. However, these systems are suboptimal for empirical research due to a lack of transparency, restrictions on archiving and sharing data, and changing interfaces.

[8]   Marco, A., Tesfayesus, A. & Toole, A., *Patent Litigation Data from US District Court Electronic Records (1963–2015)*, USPTO Economic Working Paper No. 2017-06 (available at https://ssrn.com/

At the appellate court level, the Federal Circuit Dataset Project provides a resource for empirical studies of the United States Court of Appeals for the Federal Circuit.[9] The Federal Circuit Dataset was initially created to provide a publicly available dataset of information about all decisions[10] released by the Federal Circuit on its website.[11] The dataset contains all Opinions by the court since late 2004 and all summary affirmances under Federal Circuit Rule 36 since late 2007, along with some other important court orders.[12] The resulting public dataset, named *The Compendium of Federal Circuit Decisions*, was released in 2018 accompanied by an article describing the methodology for creating the dataset and providing descriptive statistics about the Federal Circuit's decisions.[13] The *Compendium* website (empirical.law.uiowa.edu) contains a description of the dataset, copies of the codebook describing the fields in the dataset, and an application providing a searchable and downloadable copy of the dataset. In addition, the dataset is archived on the Harvard Dataverse.[14] Since its launch, the *Compendium* dataset has since been used in multiple studies of the court.[15] The second generation of the *Compendium* was released in June 2019. This version added a substantial number of new fields, including links to copies of the documents stored in a cloud repository.

A limitation of these datasets is that they only provide information on a specific layer of litigation. For example, the USPTO Litigation Dataset provides information on patent infringement litigation at the trial court, while the Federal Circuit Dataset provides information on appellate decisions at the Federal Circuit. Currently, there is no easy way to link these two datasets.

---

abstract=2942295); Schwartz, D., Sichelman, T. & Miller, R., USPTO Patent Number and Case Code File Dataset Documentation (2019) USPTO Economic Working Paper No. 2019-05 (available at https://papers.ssrn.com/sol3/papers.cfm?abstract_id=3507607).

[9]   The United States Court of Appeals for the Federal Circuit is a federal appellate court that hears appeals from specified administrative agencies as well as appeals from federal district courts involving patents. Decisions of the Federal Circuit may be reviewed by the Supreme Court of the United States, although in practice such review occurs only in a tiny fraction of cases.

[10]   Consistent with previous practice for the dataset, we refer to Opinions and Rule 36 summary affirmances collectively as "decisions." Rantanen, J., *The Landscape of Modern Patent Appeals*, 67 AM. U. L. REV. 985 (2018); but see Rantanen, J., *Missing Decisions and the United States Court of Appeals for the Federal Circuit*, 17 U. PENN. L. REV. ONLINE 73 (2022) (describing other types of appeal terminations).

[11]   Rantanen, J., *The Landscape of Modern Patent Appeals*, 67 AM. U. L. REV. 985 (2018).

[12]   *Id.*

[13]   *Id.*

[14]   Rantanen, J., Federal Circuit Document Dataset (2021) (available at https://doi.org/10.7910/DVN/UQ2SF7, Harvard Dataverse, V2, UNF:6:QBIhjCxH5VOp8d+QxaZ6ow== [fileUNF]).

[15]   These include Rantanen, J., *Administering Patent Law*, 104 IOWA L. REV. 2299 (2019); Rantanen, J., *The Future of Empirical Legal Studies: Observations on Holte & Sichelman's* Cycles of Obviousness, 105 IOWA L. REV. 15 (2020); Gugliuzza, P. & Lemley, M., *Can a Court Change the Law by Saying Nothing?*, 71 VAND. L. REV. 765 (2018); Gugliuzza, P., *Elite Patent Law*, 104 IOWA L. REV. 2481 (2019); Semet, A., *Specialized Trial Courts in Patent Litigation: A Review of the Patent Pilot Program's Impact on Appellate Reversal Rates at the Five-Year Mark*, 60 B. C. L. REV. 519 (2019); Wasserman, M. & Slack, J., *Can There Be Too Much Specialization: Specialization in Specialized Courts*, 115 NW. U. L. REV. 1405 (2021); Gugliuzza, P. & Rebouché, R., *Gender Inequality in Patent Litigation*, 100 N. C. L. REV. (forthcoming) (available at https://ssrn.com/abstract=3871975); Rantanen, J., Kriz, L. & Matthews, A., *Studying Nonobviousness*, 73 HASTINGS L. J. 667 (2022); Anderson, J., Gugliuzza, P. & Rantanen, J., *Extraordinary Writ or Ordinary Remedy*, WASH. U. L. REV. (forthcoming).

Commercial databases such as Westlaw and Lexis containing both trial and appellate court decisions, and links between these decisions, exist. However, while these traditional legal research platforms are highly advanced toolsets that provide access to a multitude of judicial opinions, there are numerous drawbacks to using them for quantitative analysis of judicial decisions. These platforms restrict access to their data through paywalls and licenses, provide minimal methodological transparency, and use interfaces that are routinely updated, thus imposing a barrier to future attempts to replicate the methods used in earlier studies.[16] In addition, they do not contain the full universe of judicial decisions.[17]

3. LINKING DISTRICT COURT AND APPELLATE COURT DATASETS

Given the lack of a publicly accessible dataset containing both district court cases and Federal Circuit opinions, it was necessary to develop a way to link the existing datasets. To accomplish this, we employed identifying information present in both datasets to automatically match individual records. We used the widely available statistics software program STATA, for this task. The challenge revolved around (1) understanding and resolving instances in which a single record in one dataset is associated with multiple records in another dataset, and (2) standardizing (and in some cases collecting) the identifying information so that correct matches can be established. This section introduces readers to the concept of relational data through the example of civil cases then provides an explanation for how this data can be put into a form that allows users to work with it.

3.1 Understanding the Relational Nature of Civil Cases

In theory, linking cases at the district courts and appeals at the appellate courts should be a simple matter of matching up district court cases to Federal Circuit appeals. In practice, however, linking these datasets is substantially more complicated due to many-to-many relationships between cases, appeals, and decisions. This required us to first develop a relational model of the data.

Relational data models are based on the concepts of "entities," "entity types," "entity instances," and relationships between entities.[18] An "entity" is something that the data system will maintain data about.[19] For example, in our environment appellate Opinions and Rule 36 summary affirmances are both entities. An "entity type" is the set of entities with a particular property.[20] Continuing this example, both Opinions and Rule 36 summary affirmances are types of documents in which the court issues its decision on the appeal. An "entity instance" is a single instance of one entity – for example, a particular Opinion or a specific Rule 36

---

[16]   Rantanen (2018); Wheeler, R., *Does WestlawNext Really Change Everything: The Implications of WestlawNext on Legal Research*, 103 L. Libr. J. 359 (2011).

[17]   McAlister, M., *Missing Decisions*, 169 U. Pa. L. Rev. 1101 (2021); Engstrom, D., *The Twiqbal Puzzle and Empirical Study of Civil Procedure*, 60 Stan. L. Rev. 1203 (2013).

[18]   See Hoffer, J., Ramesh, V. & Topi, H., Modern Database Management, 10th edition (Prentice Hall 2011), at 68.

[19]   *Id.*

[20]   *Id.*

affirmance.[21] We refer to this as a "record" or "record unit." Using these terms, it's possible to visualize a typical dataset of Federal Circuit decisions as consisting of the court's decisions, each being a separate record on a single table with rows (the individual decisions) and columns providing some piece of information about the decision (such as the document type, or its date, or the judge who wrote the decision). These columns are referred to as "attributes" or "fields."[22]

The relational component comes into play when working with multiple tables of data that relate to each other.[23] For example, in addition to the table of decisions, we might also have a separate table of judges. Each judge may have certain information associated with them such as their dates of service, prior work experience, and which president appointed them. There is thus a relationship between the table of decisions (which contains a field that indicates which judge authored the opinion) and the table of judges (which contains information about each judge). In this scenario, there is a one-to-many relationship: each opinion has only a single author, but each judge authors multiple opinions.

To illustrate how this applies to the context of linking district court and appellate datasets, consider the idea of a legal "case." A "case" is a nebulous construct that is not uniquely linked to either a docket or a document. A single patent infringement "case" might consist of multiple separate lawsuits that relate to one another; however, each would have its own docket at the district court. On the other side, a single docket will have numerous documents in it; some consisting of party filings, others consisting of court orders. And it is possible for a single decision to resolve multiple docketed cases.[24] There is thus a many-to-many relationship among dockets and decisions at the district court level.

A similar challenge exists at the appellate level. A single opinion or order can decide the merits of multiple docketed appeals, while a single docketed appeal can have multiple terminating opinions or orders.[25] For example, an opinion issued in an appeal might be replaced by a corrected opinion, or replaced after a panel rehearing, or a rehearing en banc, or even after a decision by the Supreme Court vacating the initial decision.

Another challenge is that a single civil action at the district court may be appealed multiple times. For example, a party may appeal the grant of a motion for summary judgment. Should the appellate court reverse and remand, the case would go back to the district court for further proceedings such as a trial on the merits.[26] That could result in further appeals. Another example is an appeal that follows a decision on the merits that is then followed by an appeal of

---

[21]   *Id.*

[22]   *Id.* at 157.

[23]   *Id.*

[24]   *See, e.g.,* Ranbaxy Labs., Ltd. v. Abbott Laboratories, 2005 WL 305068 (involving N.D.Ill. Civil Actions 04-C-8078 and 05-C-1490).

[25]   An example is Castillo v. United States, Appeal No. 2019-1158, which involved an initial panel opinion issued on February 20, 2020 (uniqueID 26848) and a modified opinion issued on March 6, 2020 (uniqueID 26981).

[26]   An example is John Bean Techs. Corp. v. Morris & Associates, Inc., 887 F.3d 1322 (Fed. Cir. 2018) (appeal decided in 2018 involving affirmative defenses of equitable estoppel and laches) and John Bean Techs. Corp. v. Morris & Associates, Inc., 988 F.3d 1334 (Fed. Cir. 2021) (appeal decided in 2021 involving equitable intervening in rights and prosecution laches).

the entry of attorneys' fees.[27] The result may be two "appeals" that are in rapid succession and which, fundamentally, may involve the same core issues.

First, at the district court level the record unit consists of the district court docket number (i.e.: civil action). Second, at the appellate docket level, the record unit consists of each appeal docket number. Finally, at the appellate decision level, we limit the analysis to the final panel decision. Thus, for instances in which an opinion or terminating order has been replaced by a newer document by the court, we treat the newer document as the decision of record.[28] The consequence of this is that each docketed appeal has only a single terminating opinion or order.

While this substantially reduces the complexity, it doesn't eliminate it because a single district court docket may still result in multiple appeals, and a single appellate decision can decide multiple docketed appeals. The diagrams at Figures 1.1–1.3 illustrate typical examples of the relationships. We explain how these permutations are addressed below.

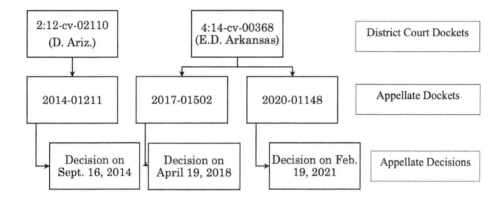

Figure 1.1   *Example 1 of trial court and appeal docket relationships*

---

27   PODS, Inc. v. Porta Stor, Inc., 484 F.3d 1359, 1365 (Fed. Cir. 2007) (holding that the merits of the case could be appealed before the motion for attorney's fees was resolved); Robert Bosch, LLC v. Pylon Mfg. Corp., 719 F.3d 1305, 1315 (Fed. Cir. 2013) (en banc); Mondis Tech. Ltd. v. LG Elecs. Inc., 6 F.4th 1379, 1382 (Fed. Cir. 2021) (holding that a judgment is final and appealable when all liability issues have been resolved and only the decision of damages is unresolved).

28   The exception are appeals in which the Federal Circuit took the decision en banc or the Supreme Court granted certiorari. These rare cases are excluded from the primary analysis and are treated as special cases.

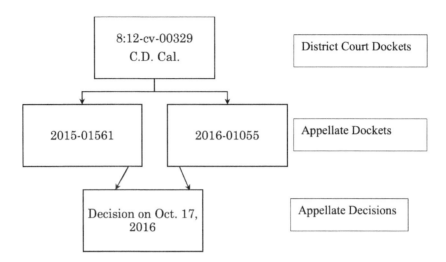

Figure 1.2   Example 2 of trial court and appeal docket relationships

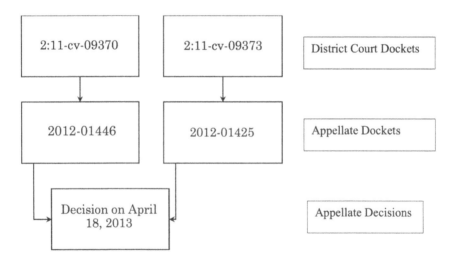

Figure 1.3   Example 3 of trial court and appeal docket relationships

3.2   Preparing the District Court Dataset

The district court patent litigation dataset that we used was the updated version of the USPTO patent litigation dataset. Details on the construction of the original dataset are provided in Marco et al. (2017), and information on the updated information is provided in Schwartz et al.

(2019).[29] This dataset contains detailed patent litigation data on over 80,000 district court cases filed between 1963 and 2016.

We began with the "cases" file, which contains information about individual civil actions.[30] The accompanying documentation explains that each unique record unit consists of the case's docket number and the court name. One observation that we made while working with this data is that the uniqueness of district court cases requires the entire docket number including the division prefix. In addition, rather than use the court_name field, which contained inconsistent formatting, we instead used the district_id field, which contains a standardized version of the court that the case was filed in or transferred to.[31] Using this combination, there were 76 non-unique records. Visual observation of these records indicated that they were duplicate records involving the same cases. To maintain the uniqueness of the dataset, duplicates of these records were dropped. The result was a dataset that was unique with respect to case_number + district_id.

3.3   Preparing the Appeal Docket Dataset

Although litigation researchers have historically treated judicial opinions as the corpus of appellate decisionmaking, appeals can be terminated in other ways.[32] For example, appeals may be dismissed by a judicial order or voluntarily terminated by the parties.[33] In addition, a single decision may decide multiple appeals. Thus, in order to understand the relationship between appeals and appellate decisionmaking, researchers need to employ a dataset of appeals in addition to decisions. This dataset should contain information that allows for linking to both appellate decisions and district court cases. For appeals in federal court, this information can be obtained directly from PACER with relatively minimal effort as described below.

3.3.1   Initial construction of the docket dataset

The Federal Circuit docket dataset was constructed by collecting tables of information from PACER for cases opened between October 1, 1999 and July 31, 2021. To obtain this information, a query was run on PACER for all dockets created in a given period.[34] This resulted

---

[29]   Marco, A., Tesfayesus, A. & Toole, A., *Patent Litigation Data from US District Court Electronic Records (1963–2015)*, USPTO Economic Working Paper No. 2017-06 (available at https://ssrn.com/abstract=2942295); Schwartz, D., Sichelman, T. & Miller, R., *USPTO Patent Number and Case Code File Dataset Documentation* (2019) USPTO Economic Working Paper No. 2019-05 (available at https://papers.ssrn.com/sol3/papers.cfm?abstract_id=3507607).

[30]   Marco et al. (2017).

[31]   Schwartz et al. (2019).

[32]   McAlister (2021).

[33]   Rantanen (2022).

[34]   This footnote provides further technical details on the methodology for obtaining this information. In 2012, the Federal Circuit transitioned to a new version of PACER that resulted in older dockets being maintained in a legacy system. According to PACER, cases after March 1, 2012, are searched in one place, while cases filed before March 1, 2012 are obtained in another place. The reality is more complex. In practice, we found dockets created as late as April 22, 2013 in the "legacy" system, while dockets created before March 1, 2012 but with activity after March 1, 2012 also appeared in the newer system. Due to the constraints of the search fields, we employed the appeal number query to obtain the list of dockets in the legacy system. We searched for appeal docket numbers within the range 0001 to 9999 for each financial year. Specifically, the query involved using each two-digit year from 00 to 14 as the prefix

in a table listing all dockets for that year along with some additional information about the appeals. The table was copied over to Microsoft Excel and then parsed to separate out distinct fields.[35]

The result was a complete dataset of all Federal Circuit dockets that exist on PACER as of December 31, 2021. Docket numbers were standardized to the formats ####-0#### and ##-#### but can easily be converted to other formats. In these formats, the number before the hyphen (which we refer to as the prefix) indicates the financial year of the docket[36] and the number after the hyphen (which we refer to as the suffix) indicates the unique number within that year. For example, docket number 2020-01403 is an appeal docketed in FY 2020 with the suffix "01403" (or "1403").

To assess whether the docket dataset contained all Federal Circuit appeal dockets, we compared a theoretical set of all possible docket numbers to the dockets actually available in PACER. We observed that all of the dockets available in PACER fell within contiguous sequential ranges that were complete except for an occasional gap. Specifically, the analysis involved: (1) generating a theoretical set of docket numbers using a range of 2000-2020 for the first part of the docket number and a range of 0001-9999 for the second part of the docket number. For example, the theoretical set contained docket numbers with a range of 2000-0001 to 2000-9999, 2001-0001 to 2001-9999, etc. (2) Merging the theoretical docket dataset with the PACER docket dataset. The merged dataset was sorted by docket_year and docket_end. (3) Conducting manual review of the actual docket dataset against the theoretical docket dataset to identify the endpoints of contiguous ranges with an existing PACER appeal docket number.[37] Table A.1 in the Appendix shows the number of missing docket numbers from the PACER docket dataset from within the contiguous ranges.

Based on this analysis, the actual data from PACER matched up nearly exactly with the expected contiguous ranges. Except for a small number of missing docket numbers, which samples typed directly into PACER indicated were under seal or otherwise not available, all of the docket numbers that we would expect to find within the contiguous ranges were, in fact, present.[38]

---

and 01 to 9999 as the suffix. For appeal dockets in the newer PACER system, we were able to use the Advanced Search functionality, which allows for a search based on when the docket was created. This method allowed us to generate a table for appeals filed during each calendar year. In addition, by running the search for all appeal dockets created in a given calendar year, we were able to obtain information from the more-comprehensive newer system for legacy dockets with activity after March 1, 2012. Data from all years was combined into a single dataset and duplicate dockets resulting from overlap due to the 2012 PACER changeover were resolved in favor of records from the newer system.

[35]   Dockets were sometimes in both systems due to activity that occurred after the changeover. For documents in both systems, the data from the more modern system was used because it contains more information.

[36]   The Federal Circuit uses a financial year system that runs from October 1 to September 30.

[37]   Currently, the court appears to be sequentially numbering all new appeals in order, with a separate track for miscellaneous matters. However, in the past the court used different ranges to reflect different origins. For example, all appeal docket numbers in the 5000's involved appeals from the Court of Federal Claims.

[38]   Due to the small apparent number of the dockets that are missing from the contiguous ranges, their confidential nature, and the likely confidential nature of any court decisions relating to these dockets, they are not included in the dataset at the present time.

One limitation of this approach is that we cannot determine whether the Federal Circuit is maintaining a separate set of dockets in a noncontiguous range that are not publicly available. We are only able to observe dockets that are available on PACER. With this caveat, however, the docket dataset contains a set of all docket numbers for appeals to the Federal Circuit and miscellaneous matters docketed at the court, with a handful of exceptions for cases under seal.

The docket dataset contains several types of information about each appeal docket, including the date the appeal was docketed and information about the origin of the appeal. The amount and quality of the information for a given record in the docket dataset depends on whether the docket number was collected from legacy PACER or the current version. Data from appeals that are only in legacy PACER is more limited than data from appeals that are in the current version. All dockets contain the docket number, docket title, generation of PACER that the data is from, date and calendar year the appeal was docketed in the Federal Circuit, the originating case number from PACER, whether the docket is a miscellaneous docket, and the financial year in which the docket was filed. Records for appeals that are in the current version of PACER also include the originating tribunal. The consequence is that currently there is origin data for all appeals filed in calendar year 2011 and later.

While the table information from PACER provided the docket number for the originating tribunal for appeals filed in 2011 and later, it was reported in a variety of different formats. We standardized these numbers through a series of algorithmic formatting steps.[39] District court docket numbers were standardized to the format [division number]:[fiscal year of case]-[type code]-[five-digit suffix]. An example is 3:09-cv-03239. In total, the docket dataset contains 30,609 dockets filed between October 5, 1999 to December 31, 2021.

3.4   Preparing the Appellate Decision Dataset

For the appellate decisions dataset, we used the *Compendium of Federal Circuit Decisions*. The methodology for creating this dataset is described in Rantanen (2018).[40] At present the decisions dataset contains all documents made available on the Federal Circuit's website through March 31, 2022, totaling 18,624 records.[41]

The document dataset currently contains over 50 fields, described in more depth in the dataset Codebook.[42] Each document has a unique ID number to allow for easy reference. For all documents, the dataset indicates the date of the document, the document title, the document type, the general origin of the appeal, whether the document is categorized as "Precedential" by the court, and the appeal docket numbers associated with the document. For documents classified as an "Opinion" or "Rule 36" (which we refer to collectively as a "decision"), the document dataset contains much more information, including the judges on the panel, the authors of majority and separate Opinions, detailed information on the origin of the appeal,

---

[39]   A small number of docket numbers from the appellate dataset could not be algorithmically standardized. Most of these were hand-coded using information from decisions deciding these appeals or by review of the docket itself. Twenty-five appeals arising from the district courts could not be hand-coded; these almost entirely consisted of miscellaneous matters, such as petitions for writs of mandamus.

[40]   Rantanen (2018).

[41]   Note that these datasets are updated multiple times a year with new dockets and decisions. If seeking to replicate the results in this chapter with a more recent version of the dataset, limit documents to only those with a document date (docDate) prior to January 1, 2022.

[42]   All versions of the Codebook, including the most recent, are available at empirical.law.uiowa.edu.

and more. In addition, for decisions originating from the United States Patent and Trademark Office (USPTO) and federal district courts, the document dataset provides information on the nature of the dispute being appealed and the general disposition of the appeal.[43] For decisions involving patents, the dataset contains the numbers of the patents in suit, issue coding for substantive patentability/validity issues, and the type of appellants. Finally, almost all records in the dataset contain the link where the document can be found on the Federal Circuit's website and a link to a copy of the document in a Google cloud repository.[44] A list of all of the data fields contained in the document dataset is provided in the Codebook in the data repository.

In order to construct the relationship between the data in the appellate decisions dataset, the appellate dockets dataset, and the district court datasets, we needed to accomplish two tasks. First, we needed to obtain identifying information that matched the information in the other datasets. Second, we needed to develop a record unit for each dataset that eliminated as much duplication as possible so as to minimize the many-to-many relationships.

3.4.1   Docket data

First, we needed to develop a field in the appellate decisions dataset that could be used to match to data within the other datasets. We accomplished this through the use of the Appeal_Dockets field.[45]

To obtain the Appeal_Dockets information, we applied an automated technique combined with manual review. Because the appeal docket information was coded for only around 2,000 documents in the original dataset, we wrote a Python script to extract the appeal docket number text from the text of the documents. This script was used to extract appeal docket numbers for the remaining documents in the dataset. We also conducted a manual review of every record in the dataset, except the 326 records for which no document was available.[46]

---

[43] By "disposition," we mean whether the decision of the tribunal being reviewed was affirmed, affirmed-in-part, reversed, or vacated, or the appeal was dismissed.

[44] For some documents, the Federal Circuit's website contained a record but no linked document. In addition, we have recently begun adding terminating decisions that are not available on the court's website by collecting them from PACER. The source of document collection is indicated by the Source field.

[45] In addition, the document dataset contains manually coded information on the district court docket numbers associated with that decision. However, for many older decisions, the division information is not present in the decision itself, thus limiting its utility. While it is possible to use this information to identify additional matches going forward, that will require additional manual coding. Consequently, we did not use the district court docket information from the document dataset for this study.

[46] As indicated above, the document link did not work for all documents on the Federal Circuit's website. In addition, as discussed in Rantanen (2018) and below, some records from 2012 and 2013 have since vanished from the Federal Circuit's website. While we collected many of these documents as part of an earlier project before they vanished, and have now collected additional decisions from the Internet Archive, in some cases we have only the record entry for these decisions. We obtained the actual decision from PACER for all Opinions and Rule 36 affirmances for which we had a record but not a document; this was possible for those decisions that pre-dated the 2013 PACER update. We have kept the record for the nine decisions that are no longer available through PACER, the 310 Orders, and the seven instances in which the document type is unknown.

We did not use the appeal number from the Federal Circuit's website unless absolutely necessary because the Federal Circuit only provides one appeal number per document and some documents relate to multiple appeal dockets. The only documents that we used this number for were Orders and Errata.

For these 326 records, we used the appeal number provided on the Federal Circuit's website.[47] The human review resulted in corrections being made to 2.9% of the records in the dataset.[48] The final document-to-docket correspondence was 99.9%, meaning that 99.9% of the docket numbers in the Appeal_Dockets field in the document dataset matched to a docket number in the docket dataset constructed using PACER.[49]

3.4.2   Replaced decisions

The second project involved identifying decisions in the document dataset that were subsequently replaced, thus resulting in two or more entries for the same appeal docket in the document dataset.[50] This issue is a concern because it can lead to a situation in which the same "decision" may be counted twice in statistical analyses.

A common (although infrequent, as the data below indicate) reason for a decision to be replaced is that the panel subsequently issued a "corrected," "revised," or "modified" version of the decision.[51] In other cases, a nonprecedential decision is made precedential; this, too, results in a new document. In other instances, a panel decision taken by the court en banc and the original decision is withdrawn. Or certiorari may be granted by the Supreme Court, which typically results in a new panel decision on remand.

To identify possible replaced decisions, we first identified instances where multiple decisions were associated with the same appeal number.[52] All together, we identified 133 appeal dockets with two decisions in the dataset, 13 with three decisions, and four with four decisions. For comparison, 13,788 appeal dockets had only a single version of a decision. We then manually reviewed these documents to determine whether the original document was replaced and, if so, the circumstances for that replacement. In total, we identified 47 decisions in which the original decision was replaced in some form by the panel directly, 20 for which there was a subsequent en banc review,[53] 15 for which there was a subsequent grant-vacate-remand by

---

[47]   We recommend avoiding the use of the appeal number on the court's website because it only reflects one appeal number associated with the document and a non-negligible number of documents are associated with multiple appeal dockets.

[48]   In total, the human review identified 511 records out of 17,854 records reviewed that required correction of the set of appeal numbers for the document, typically because one or more numbers were missing. New records now go through a double-check process in which the original number is first coded by the Python script, then reviewed by the initial document coder, and finally is checked by a review coder.

[49]   Nineteen docket numbers from the document dataset did not match with a docket number in the docket dataset while 16,220 matched. The non-matches are discussed in more detail below.

[50]   Note that these situations do not involve true duplicates, which we define as an identical document that is in the dataset more than once. We previously tracked true duplicates using the "duplicate" field; these have now been removed from the dataset entirely.

[51]   In some instances this is because there is a minor correction, such as to the spelling of someone's name, while in other instances this is the result of a petition for panel rehearing.

[52]   Due to the wide variation with which the court has made non-dispositive Orders available on its website, we did not see any value in going through this process with Orders, with the exception of Orders classified as terminating Orders in miscellaneous dockets (the court always decides the issues in a miscellaneous docket in an "Order" rather than an "Opinion"). Terminating Orders for miscellaneous dockets were reviewed in connection with a project focusing specifically on miscellaneous dockets.

[53]   Astute observers will note that the Federal Circuit has issued more than 20 en banc decisions between 2005 and 2021. In fact, the dataset actually contains 47 full or partial en banc decisions. There are two reasons for this difference. First, sometimes the Federal Circuit grants en banc review on the first

the Supreme Court, and 16 for which there was a subsequent Supreme Court decision followed by a decision on remand by the Federal Circuit. These documents can now be treated accordingly depending on the type of analysis being performed. Generally, we recommend excluding documents that have been directly replaced by the panel and using the final version of the decision.[54] Depending on the analysis, it may also be appropriate to either exclude or only focus on extraordinary decisions, such as those for which the court granted rehearing en banc or the Supreme Court granted certiorari.

3.5   Linking the District Court Docket Dataset to the Appellate Docket Dataset

We employed STATA to link the district court dockets to the appeal docket dataset, matching on the combination of district court docket number (case_number) and originating district (district_id). This information was unique at the district court level but not unique at the appeal level because a single district court case could be the subject of multiple appeals. In total, 2,760 civil actions matched to an appeal docket (not including matches to miscellaneous dockets, which typically involve petitions for a writ of mandamus or permission to appeal). Of those, 854 civil actions involved more than one appeal.

Table 1.1 indicates the number of Federal Circuit appeal dockets arising from the district courts that corresponded with a district court docket in the USPTO patent litigation dataset. We have excluded miscellaneous appeal dockets from these numbers.

In total, out of the 3,076 total appeals docketed at the Federal Circuit from 2011 through 2016[55] that arose from the district courts, 2,791 matched a district court docket in the USPTO patent litigation dataset. In other words, approximately 91% of the Federal Circuit appeal dockets arising from the district courts matched to a district court docket in the USPTO dataset. However, the USPTO dataset contains some patent litigation types beyond patent infringement suits, including false marking suit and inventorship and ownership disputes.[56] Limited to only infringement litigation case types (categories 1–4), 2,628 appeal dockets for appeals filed from 2011–2016 arising from the district courts matched to a case type 1–4 docket in the USPTO dataset. In other words, approximately 85% of the Federal Circuit appeal

---

instance. *See, e.g.,* Procopio v. Wilkie, 913 F.3d 1371 (2019). Second, the Federal Circuit appears to have at various times removed "withdrawn" decisions from its website, possibly because en banc review was granted. An example is the original panel decision in CLS Bank International v. Alice Corporation Pty. Ltd., appeal no. 11-1301. The original panel decision issued on July 9, 2012, and was published in the Federal Reporter at 586 F. 1341. On October 9, 2012, rehearing en banc was granted and the panel Opinion was withdrawn. On May 10, 2013, the Federal Circuit issued its en banc Opinion, published in the Federal Reporter at 717 F.3d 1269. (The Supreme Court ultimately granted certiorari and issued Alice v. CLS Bank, 573 U.S. 208 (2014).) While the court's website contains the order granting rehearing en banc and the court's en banc Opinion, as of June 18, 2021, it no longer contains the original panel decision. Because data collection for the document dataset took place at various points in time, it did not capture documents that had been removed from the website during the intervening period.

54   For example: Replaced=="Yes".

55   These cutoffs were selected because the district court docket numbers in the appeal dockets dataset are incomplete prior to 2011 and because the USPTO Patent Litigation Dataset ends with cases filed in 2016.

56   Schwartz et al. (2019).

Table 1.1   *Federal Circuit appeals arising from district courts, 2011–2021*

Year the appeal was docketed at the CAFC	Appeal did not match to a patent infringement docket at the district court	Appeal matched to a patent infringement docket at the district court	Yearly total
2011	59	372	431
2012	50	433	483
2013	52	466	518
2014	36	513	549
2015	42	551	593
2016	46	456	502
2017	69	427	496
2018	146	233	379
2019	178	129	307
2020	209	87	296
2021	246	40	286
Total	1133	3707	4840
Total 2011–2016	285	2791	3076

Table 1.2   *Cases in USPTO dataset associated with an appeal to the Federal Circuit*

	No appeal	Appeal	Total	
2011	3,934	288	4,223	6.8%
2012	5,477	341	5,818	5.9%
2013	6,025	379	6,404	5.9%
2014	4,792	297	5,089	5.8%
2015	5,610	242	5,852	4.1%
2016	4,373	198	4,571	4.3%
Total	30,211	1,745	31,956	5.5%

dockets arising from the district courts arose from patent infringement litigation, a figure consistent with other measures.[57]

Measured in terms of the number of appeals relative to the number of district court cases, about 6% of cases in the USPTO litigation dataset initiated between 2011 and 2016 were associated with an appeal at the Federal Circuit.

Table 1.2 shows the dramatic effect of the 2011 America Invents Act, which amended the joinder provision to limit the circumstances in which parties may be joined as defendants.[58] This resulted in an overall increase in the number of actions filed because infringement suits against multiple defendants now typically needed to be filed as separate actions rather than naming multiple defendants in a single civil action.

We also observe that the rate at which district court cases are appealed fell over this period. Whereas around 6.8% of cases filed in 2011 were associated with at least one appeal, only 4.3% of cases in 2016 were associated with an appeal. We explored the possibility that this

---

[57]   Rantanen, J., *Missing Decisions and the United States Court of Appeals for the Federal Circuit*, *supra* note 10; Rantanen et al., *Who Appeals (and Wins) Patent Cases*, Hous. L. Rev. (forthcoming).

[58]   Miller et al., *Who's Suing Us: Decoding Patent Plaintiffs since 2000 with the Stanford NPE Litigation Dataset*, 21 Stan. Tech. L. Rev. 235 (2018).

could be due to data truncation (i.e.: a case filed in 2011 has had ten years for an appeal to be filed while a case filed in 2016 has had only five years). However, an examination of appeal rates over a long period of time reveals that over 95% of first appeals in a case are filed within six years of case filing[59], indicating that the decline in appeal rates is not due simply to data truncation.

3.6   Linking the Appellate Docket Dataset and the Appellate Decisions Dataset

We next used STATA to link the combined district court/appeal docket dataset to the appeal document dataset. To simplify analysis, we limited the appeal documents to only Opinions and Rule 36 summary affirmances. An "Opinion" is a term of art that refers to a document containing the court's decision accompanied by a written explanation of the court's reasoning.[60] In addition, Federal Circuit sometimes affirms the lower tribunal's decision without any explanation, a practice permitted by Federal Circuit Rule 36.[61] While these do not constitute the entire universe of dispositions,[62] at the Federal Circuit "Opinions" and "Rule 36 summary affirmances" comprise nearly all decisions on the merits of an appeal.[63]

If a decision was replaced, we used only the final version of the decision. Consequently, both the appeal docket dataset and appellate decisions dataset were unique with respect to appeal docket numbers. In addition, each appeal docket number was associated with a single district court docket number + district_id (although multiple appeal docket numbers were associated with the same district court docket number). However, some decisions in the document dataset decided multiple appeals (and thus could potentially, although not necessarily, involve multiple civil actions).

When linking the appellate docket dataset and the appellate decision dataset, each record in the document dataset matched to at least one record in the docket dataset with the exception of 13 docket numbers appearing on documents but not present in the docket dataset.[64] However, the reverse is not true: not every appeal docket number is associated with an Opinion or Rule 36 affirmance in the document dataset.

Table 1.3 shows the number of appeal dockets that matched with a decision, as well as the number of decisions on appeals filed in each year.

Beginning with appeals docketed in 2008, the court has consistently decided about 60–65% of appeals through an Opinion or Rule 36.[65] The percentage of appeals with decisions drops off in 2020 and 2021, as it typically takes over a year from case filing to decision. The remaining 35–40% of appeals are terminated for other reasons, including that the appeal was filed too late, failure to prosecute, lack of appellate jurisdiction, and voluntary dismissal.[66]

---

[59]   Rantanen et al. (forthcoming).

[60]   *See* McAlister, *Missing Decisions, supra* note 17; Rantanen, *Missing Decisions and the Federal Circuit, supra* note 10.

[61]   *See* FED. CIR. R. 36.

[62]   *See* McAlister, *supra* note 17.

[63]   *See* Rantanen, *supra* note 10.

[64]   A manual search of PACER for these 13 docket numbers confirmed that they are not available on PACER, with the more recent docket numbers returning the result "Case Under Seal."

[65]   The starting point for this table is 2008 because the earliest Rule 36 affirmance in the document dataset is in 2008.

[66]   Rantanen (2022).

Table 1.3   *Federal Circuit appeals arising from the district courts with and without merits decisions*

Year appeal filed	Appeal with no decision in dataset	Appeal with decision in dataset	Total	Percent of dockets with decision	Number of decisions
2008	537	794	1,331	60%	680
2009	485	712	1,197	59%	633
2010	446	679	1,125	60%	579
2011	490	753	1,243	61%	651
2012	474	785	1,259	62%	624
2013	470	820	1,290	64%	655
2014	557	899	1,456	62%	724
2015	547	1,134	1,681	67%	846
2016	644	1,183	1,827	65%	833
2017	547	1,063	1,610	66%	703
2018	582	885	1,467	60%	653
2019	604	829	1,433	58%	659
2020	897	681	1,578	43%	535
2021	1,236	76	1,312	6%	64
Total	8,516	11,293	19,809		
2011–2019	4,915	8,351	13,266	63%	6,348

Columns 2–4 in Table 1.3 use appellate dockets as the record unit. Column 5 reports the number of decisions. There are fewer decisions than appeals with a decision because a single decision can address multiple docketed appeals. Figure 1.4 illustrates the relationship of the different components.

Using the resulting datasets, we are able to provide more comprehensive descriptive statistics of Federal Circuit decisions and their relation to appeals. The following sections describe (1) characteristics of appellate decisions relative to appeals, and (2) characteristics of appeals of patent infringement decisions relative to district court cases.

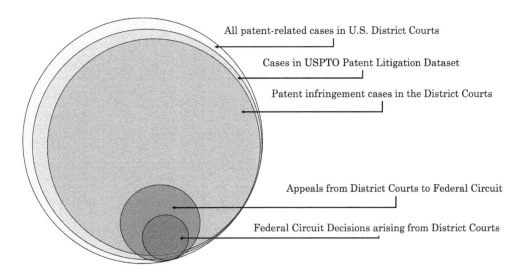

All patent-related cases in U.S. District Courts

Cases in USPTO Patent Litigation Dataset

Patent infringement cases in the District Courts

Appeals from District Courts to Federal Circuit

Federal Circuit Decisions arising from District Courts

Figure 1.4   *Relationship of dataset components*

4.   DESCRIPTIVE STATISTICS ON FEDERAL CIRCUIT APPEALS GENERALLY

Understanding appeals in patent infringement cases requires understanding appeals at the Federal Circuit generally. This section draws on the combined appellate dockets and decisions data to provide information about the origin of appeals at the Federal Circuit, the relationship of appeals to decisions, and the time from appeal to decision-by-decision type, and outcomes of appeals.

4.1   Appellate Docket by Origin and Year

Table 1.4 provides information on the origin of appeals filed at the Federal Circuit. While the current version of PACER provides information on the origin of the appeal in tabular form, the legacy version of PACER does not. Consequently, comprehensive data on the origin of appeals is not available through the docket dataset for appeals filed prior to 2011 that did not have activity after March 1, 2012.[67]

The highest number of appeals arise from the district courts, the PTO, the Merit Systems Protection Board (MSPB), the Court of Federal Claims, and the Court of Appeals for Veterans' Claims. However, the number of appeals arising from the PTO has grown dramatically since 2013, while the number of appeals from the MSPB and district courts have fallen.[68]

Table 1.4   Origin of Federal Circuit appeals

Year appeal docketed at CAFC	Tribunal of origin										
	No information	BCA	CAVC	CFC	CIT	DCT	ITC	MSPB	Other	PTO	Total
2008	1,286	0	1	5	0	10	0	1	0	0	1,303
2009	1,143	1	1	5	0	15	0	2	0	0	1,167
2010	746	5	50	43	9	136	4	55	1	28	1,077
2011	3	20	201	131	35	431	12	241	1	128	1,203
2012	0	16	175	148	46	483	22	205	2	131	1,228
2013	0	14	152	146	52	518	17	195	8	147	1,249
2014	0	20	127	152	40	549	12	217	17	260	1,394
2015	0	17	95	154	52	593	11	232	10	472	1,636
2016	0	20	109	177	38	502	18	229	21	684	1,798
2017	0	14	124	171	40	496	16	142	18	536	1,557
2018	0	14	67	162	35	379	20	113	21	609	1,420
2019	1	22	115	160	47	307	22	128	12	591	1,405
2020	12	14	138	294	44	296	26	123	11	566	1,524
2021	0	19	120	168	62	286	14	129	7	402	1,207

Legend: CAVC=Court of Appeals for Veterans Claims; CFC=Court of Federal Claims; CIT=Court of International Trade; DCT=District Court; ITC=International Trade Commission; MSPB=Merit Systems Protection Board; PTO=Patent and Trademark Office. "Blank" indicates that the source is the legacy version of PACER, which does not provide origin information in the tabular view.

---

[67]   In contrast, data on the origin of all Opinions and Rule 36 affirmances is available in the docket dataset because this data came from the document itself.

[68]   Thanks to Paul Gugliuzza for pointing out that this is likely because the MSPB hasn't had a quorum since January 2017 and currently has zero members. *See* https://www.mspb.gov/FAQs

4.2   Decisions by Year and Origin

Table 1.5 indicates the general origin for Federal Circuit "decisions" (i.e.: Opinions and Rule 36 summary affirmances). In contrast with Table 1.4, it treats a decision (rather than an appeal) as the record unit. This data excludes miscellaneous dockets because the court uses Orders to decide almost all of these proceedings (which are docketed with a number under 1,000). Much more granular data on origin, including specific district courts and administrative agencies, is available in the dataset. Note that the year for this table is the year of the decision, rather than the year the appeal was docketed. Information on the origin of the appeal is drawn from the document dataset, which contains information on the origin of all decisions.

Table 1.5 indicates that most decisions issued by the Court of Appeals for the Federal Circuit (CAFC) arise from the District Court, the PTO, the Court of Federal Claims, and the Court of Appeals for Veterans Claims (CAVC). Historically, a large number of appellate decisions were in cases arising from the MSPB; that has declined in recent years as appeals from the MSPB have declined as noted above. Decisions in appeals arising from the PTO, on the other hand, have increased dramatically since the passage of the America Invents Act in 2011 created the inter partes review mechanism.

Table 1.5   Federal Circuit decisions by origin and year

Year of Decision	BCA	CAVC	CFC	CIT	DCT	ITC	MSPB	Other	PTO	Total
2008	11	102	90	34	215	6	223	13	25	719
2009	11	86	80	29	152	7	217	8	51	641
2010	10	68	70	28	191	10	148	8	45	578
2011	8	104	86	27	167	8	114	7	48	569
2012	9	87	91	22	193	7	151	7	89	656
2013	8	131	74	27	193	10	146	3	66	658
2014	2	90	84	41	231	7	101	1	85	642
2015	15	76	104	25	218	8	129	4	138	717
2016	9	76	95	22	219	2	159	8	196	786
2017	9	65	85	19	206	11	119	4	229	747
2018	10	66	107	23	183	5	50	8	231	683
2019	9	58	89	31	180	12	60	7	251	697
2020	13	78	88	26	196	6	72	4	205	688
2021	14	95	77	21	140	8	73	2	220	650
Total	138	1182	1220	375	2684	107	1762	84	1879	9431

4.3   Time from Appeal to Decision

Next, we calculated the time from appeal to decision. While the court itself reports statistics on the time from filing to disposition following oral argument or submission,[69] it provides limited details on the data that it uses or how the calculation is performed, it also does not differentiate between type of decision.

_Absence_of_Board_Quorum_Feb_10_2021_508.pdf.
   [69]   https://cafc.uscourts.gov/wp-content/uploads/reports-stats/disposition-time/06_Med_Disp_Time_MERITS_table.pdf.

Table 1.6   Average number of days from appeal filing to decision

| | Average number of days to decision | | |
	Overall	Opinion	Rule 36
DCT	404	437	333
CAVC	292	280	351
PTO	401	435	362
CFC	335	340	317
MSPB	265	252	342

Drawing on the dataset constructed above, we calculated that the average time from the first appeal filed to the decision was 356 days (standard deviation 174 days) for appeals decided since 2008. For all origins, the average time was 360 days (standard deviation 191 days) for decisions made in an Opinion and 345 days (standard deviation 118 days) for decisions made in a Rule 36 summary affirmance – a surprisingly small difference given that Rule 36 affirmances are typically issued shortly after oral argument in an appeal and Opinions take time to write. However, there is substantial variation in this time when broken down by origin. Table 1.6 shows the average time to a decision for a Rule 36 summary affirmance versus an Opinion for the five most frequent origins for appeals docketed in 2008 and later.

While decisions made in an opinion that arise from the district courts and USPTO take substantially longer than summary affirmances, decisions made in an opinion for appeals arising from the MSPB and CAVC are issued substantially *earlier* than decisions made in a Rule 36.

One possible explanation is that the court issues an opinion if the parties in an appeal from the CAVC or MSPB forgo oral argument, which typically takes time to calendar, but affirm through a summary affirmance if there is an oral argument and affirmance is appropriate. This explanation is consistent with previous research on the court's practice with appeals from origins such as the MSPB and with respect to pro se appellants.[70]

4.4   Outcomes

The following tables summarize outcome data for the decisions in the document dataset. The record unit for these tables is the individual Federal Circuit decision. As a reminder, this chapter defines a "decision" as an Opinion or Rule 36 summary affirmance. The year is the year that the court issued the decision, rather than the year the appeal was filed.

Table 1.7 shows overall general disposition rates for all decisions in the database from 2008–2021. Not including dismissals or "other" dispositions, the Federal Circuit affirms-in-full about 78% of the time, affirms in part about 9% of the time, and reverses or vacates the remaining 13% of the time.

Table 1.8 breaks out the numbers of dispositions by origin while Table 1.9 shows affirmance rate calculations by origin. For both tables, the record unit is Federal Circuit decisions. The

---

[70] *See* Shaw, B., *Please Ignore This Case: An Empirical Study of Nonprecedential Opinions in the Federal Circuit*, 12 Geo. Mason. L. Rev. 1013 (2004) (finding that, in a sample of a two-month calendar from the Court, arguments were heard in 39% of MSPB appeals whereas 61% of MSPB appeals were decided on the briefs); *accord* Brean, D. H., *Pro Se Patent Appeals at the Federal Circuit*, 20 Stan. Tech. L. Rev. 1 (2017) (conducting a study of pro se patent appeals at the Federal Circuit and finding that "The Federal Circuit almost always wrote an opinion in its pro se patent appeals, generally reserving its Rule 36 judgments for the small number of cases argued orally").

Table 1.7   *Federal Circuit disposition in Opinions and Rule 36 summary affirmances,*
                   2008–2021

DispGeneral	Freq.	Percent
Affirmed	6,855	72.72
Affirmed-in-part	806	8.55
Dismissed	579	6.14
Other	43	0.46
Reversed	636	6.75
Vacated	507	5.38
Total	9,426	100

Table 1.8   *Federal Circuit disposition in Opinions and Rule 36 summary affirmances by*
                   origin, 2008–2021

Origin	Affirmed	Affirmed-in-part	Dismissed	Other	Reversed	Vacated	Total
BCA	105	10	3	0	16	4	138
CAVC	559	54	456	5	51	55	1,180
CFC	959	89	13	1	118	40	1,220
CIT	266	34	2	2	47	24	375
DCT	1,801	415	32	11	245	179	2,683
ITC	74	12	1	1	14	4	106
MSPB	1,563	38	36	3	45	76	1,761
Other	55	3	7	15	3	1	84
PTO	1,473	151	29	5	97	124	1,879
Total	6,855	806	579	43	636	507	9,426

Table 1.9   *General dispositions in Federal Circuit decisions, 2008–2021*

Origin	Percent affirmed	Percent affirmed-in-part	Percent reversed or vacated
BCA	78%	7%	15%
CAVC	78%	8%	15%
CFC	80%	7%	13%
CIT	72%	9%	19%
DCT	68%	16%	16%
ITC	71%	12%	17%
MSPB	91%	2%	7%
Other	89%	5%	6%
PTO	80%	8%	12%
Total	78%	9%	13%

denominator for the affirmance rate calculations in Table 1.9 is the sum of affirmances, affirmances in part, reversals and vacates (i.e.: it does not include dismissals or "other" dispositions).

Tables 1.8 and 1.9 show wide variation in the rate at which the Federal Circuit affirms the decisions it reviews. Whereas appeals from the Merit Systems Protection Board involved a full affirmance over 90% of the time during this time period, decisions reviewing appeals arising from the district courts affirmed in full only 68% of the time.

There are important limitations and caveats to these figures, however, and care should be used when discussing them. One contextualization is that appeals from the district courts sometimes involve cross-appeals, which may increase the likelihood of an affirmance in part.

Another aspect of appeals from district courts is that they may involve multiple issues, and an appellant may prevail on some but not others.[71] In addition, settlement may produce selection effects.[72] Finally, standards of review – particularly, limitations on the reviewability of facts – may affect affirmance rates. For example, while the Federal Circuit appears to affirm appeals arising from the CAVC relatively less often, it also dismisses many appeals as it affirms on the basis that it cannot review challenges to factual determinations or to a law or regulation as applied to the facts of a particular case.[73]

5.   CHARACTERISTICS OF FEDERAL CIRCUIT APPEALS RELATIVE TO DISTRICT COURT PATENT LITIGATION

Incorporating the district court patent infringement dataset allows for a more contextualized picture of appeals in these cases.

5.1   Appeals by Origin

The record unit for this analysis is appeal dockets. This analysis focuses on district court patent infringement cases with at least one appeal.

Table 1.10 shows the number of patent infringement cases filed in each jurisdiction between 2011 and 2016, as well as the number of those cases with an appeal. At the top is a surprising flip: while almost 30% of patent infringement cases were filed in the Eastern District of Texas, only about 12% of appeals originate from those cases. On the other hand, while the District of Delaware has had 15% of patent infringement case filings, appeals from those cases constitute 22% of all appeals.

One reason for the difference may be the different types of patent litigation occurring in these districts. Examining the composition of patent asserter types for cases filed in 2008 and 2009, Allison, Lemley & Schwartz found that decisions involving operating companies made up a much larger proportion of adjudicated district court decisions in Delaware than cases involving non-practicing entities, while the reverse was true in the Eastern District of Texas.[74] If operating companies are more likely to consist of lawsuits between competitors, it may be that these cases are more likely to be appealed all the way to a decision at the Federal Circuit.[75] Consistent with these prior findings over 8% of patent infringement cases filed in Delaware

---

[71]   Lemley, M., *The Fractioning of Patent Law*, in INTELLECTUAL PROPERTY AND THE COMMON LAW, Shyamkrishna Balanesh, ed., Cambridge University Press (2012).

[72]   Allison et al. (2017).

[73]   *See* Dowd, M., *No Claim Adjudication Without Representation: A Criticism of 38 U.S.C. 5904(C)*, 16 Fed. Cir. Bar J. 53, 60 (2006) ("The Federal Circuit has limited jurisdiction to review decisions of the CAVC. The Federal Circuit may review and decide a challenge to the validity or interpretation of a relevant statute or regulation … however, the Federal Circuit may not review a challenge to a factual determination or 'a challenge to a law or regulation as applied to the facts of a particular case").

[74]   *See* Allison et al. (2017); Miller et al. (2019).

[75]   *Accord* Miller et al. (finding that the average time to termination at the district court for cases filed by Category 1 patent asserters was 327 days as compared with 443 days for product company patent asserters; *see also* Cotropia, C.; Kesan, J.; & Schwartz, D., *Heterogeneity Among Patent Plaintiffs: An Empirical Analysis of Patent Case Progression, Settlement, and Adjudication*, 15 J. OF EMP. LEG. STUD. 80 (2018)).

Table 1.10   *Cases and appeals by originating district*

All patent infringement cases filed 2011–2016			Patent infringement cases with appeals			
district_id	Freq.	Percent	district_id	Freq.	Percent	Percent of district court cases with an appeal
txed	8,699	28.9%	ded	384	21.9%	8.3%
ded	4,651	15.4%	txed	206	11.7%	2.4%
cacd	2,065	6.9%	cand	169	9.6%	10.6%
cand	1,601	5.3%	cacd	164	9.4%	7.9%
njd	1,240	4.1%	njd	91	5.2%	7.3%
ilnd	1,202	4.0%	nysd	86	4.9%	11.0%
nysd	785	2.6%	casd	57	3.2%	8.4%
flsd	755	2.5%	ilnd	50	2.9%	4.2%
casd	679	2.3%	vaed	47	2.7%	10.8%
flmd	443	1.5%	mad	46	2.6%	10.5%
Other	7,995	26.5%	Other	454	25.9%	5.7%
Total	30,115		Total	1,754		5.8%

Abbreviations: txed: Eastern District of Texas; ded: District of Delaware; cacd: Central District of California; cand: Northern District of California; njd: District of New Jersey; ilnd: Northern District of Illinois; nysd: Southern District of New York; flsd: Southern District of Florida; casd: Southern District of California; flmd: Middle District of Florida; vaed: Eastern district of Virgnia; mad: District of Massachusetts.

between 2011 and 2016 had an appeal, as compared with 2.4% of cases filed in the Eastern District of Texas.

Table 1.10 provides another insight: while the overall appeal rate for patent infringement cases filed between 2011 and 2016 was 5.8%, that figure is substantially affected by the Eastern District of Texas, which had almost a third of all cases but a much lower appeal rate for those cases. Excluding the Eastern District of Texas, the appeal rate for the period was 7.2% – with several districts having a higher rate.

5.2   District Court Cases with Multiple Appeals

Most patent infringement cases have only a single appeal. A portion, however, involve multiple appeals. Sometimes, a party will file multiple appeals in rapid succession. Typically, these appeals will be consolidated and resolved in a single appellate decision. Other times, a party might file an appeal, obtain a reversal, and then later on, after further district court proceedings, a party will file a new appeal.

We calculated both the frequency of multiple appeals as well as the rate at which multiple appeals led to multiple decisions in the same underlying civil action. First, we calculated the number of cases with more than one docketed appeal. In order to capture as many instances of multiple appeals as possible, and in light of our finding in section 4.3 above, we limited the time period to cases filed between 2011 and 2015. Out of the 1,555 cases with an appeal, 1,127 (72%) had a single appeal, 306 (20%) had two appeals, 84 (6%) had three appeals, and the remainder had four or more appeals.

However, often multiple appeals end up being decided as a group in the same appellate decision. Thus, we calculated the number of distinct *decisions* for a single civil action – in other words, how many different Federal Circuit decisions involved the same originating civil action.

Only a small number of civil actions with an appeal had multiple appellate decisions arising from subsequent appeals. Out of the 1,044 infringement cases from this time period that had at least one appellate decision, 955 (91%) had only a single decision associated with them while another 86 (8%) had two decisions. Only three cases had more than three appellate decisions associated with them. As a reminder, the decisions dataset was limited to only final panel decisions for each appeal; thus, this does not reflect revised opinions issued upon rehearing or subsequent opinions issued by the court sitting en banc.

5.3   Outcomes by Origin

Finally, we examined whether there are differences in the Federal Circuit's affirmance rate by district of origin (see Table 1.11). The record unit for this analysis is on a per-decision basis. Cases were filed between 2011 and 2016. This data consists of appeals in patent infringement cases.

Table 1.11   Federal Circuit outcomes by origin

District_id	Total affirmed, reversed or vacated	Percent affirmed	Percent affirmed-in-part	Percent reversed or vacated
ded	168	72%	12%	16%
cand	93	73%	13%	14%
cacd	87	76%	14%	10%
txed	84	65%	14%	20%
nysd	47	72%	11%	17%
njd	34	71%	15%	15%
ilnd	32	69%	9%	22%
mad	29	62%	14%	24%
vaed	28	79%	4%	18%
flsd	24	63%	17%	21%
Other	297	72%	14%	13%
Total	923	71%	13%	15%

Affirmance-in-full rates range from 62% (District of Massachusetts) to 79% (Eastern District of Virginia), with the overall rate at 71%. However, these districts had the fewest appellate decisions in the set.

Another observation on this data is that the Eastern District of Texas falls to fourth in frequency when the data is looked at the per-appellate decision level. In addition, its affirmance rate is the lowest of the top-five courts, at 65%. Put another way, appeals from the Eastern District of Texas were relatively rare, but they were successful in obtaining at least a partial reversal more often than districts with a much higher percentage of appeals.

6.   CONCLUSION

The picture presented by the multi-layered data above is complex, but provides a foundation for further research into the relationship between trial and appellate courts. By systematically

linking district court cases to appeals to appellate decisions, it is possible to identify characteristics of appellate litigation that were previously difficult to observe.

There are several possible avenues for further research using this dataset. One possible use
is to replicate previous studies of patent litigation, both at the district court and appellate level,
and assess whether findings for previous time periods remain true. Another possible use is to
observe whether case characteristics at the district courts affect appellate decision-making –
such as the type of party asserting the patent.[76]

In addition, the matching methodology we employed here can be used to link other types
of cases to appellate datasets. For example, using this methodology it is possible to link inter
partes review decisions to the corresponding Federal Circuit appeal. The key components are
a unique identifier that is present in both datasets and is standardized in the same way, and an
understanding of the interrelationships between records at each level. Keeping these components in mind will make it possible to conduct multi-level studies of judicial decisionmaking.

---

[76]   *See* Rantanen et al., (forthcoming).

APPENDIX

Table A.1   *Comparison between theoretical docket numbers and actual docket numbers within contiguous ranges*

Docket year	Actual versus theoretical docket number			
	Theoretical-only	Actual-only	Present in both	Total
2000	0	46	1361	1407
2001	0	12	1367	1379
2002	0	8	1673	1681
2003	0	8	1424	1432
2004	0	3	1475	1478
2005	0	1	1415	1416
2006	0	1	1642	1643
2007	0	8	1437	1445
2008	0	1	1347	1348
2009	0	2	1216	1218
2010	0	3	1119	1122
2011	0	1	1265	1266
2012	0	4	1286	1290
2013	0	2	1199	1201
2014	0	11	1429	1440
2015	0	15	1644	1659
2016	0	0	1776	1776
2017	0	3	1675	1678
2018	0	8	1488	1496
2019	0	6	1476	1482
2020	0	3	1400	1403
2021*	1279	0	0	1279
Total	1279	146	30114	31539

Note: * 2021 was not matched.

2. Legal empirical studies of patenting and patent licensing practices

Growth versus a tenacious gap?

Esther van Zimmeren[1]

1. INTRODUCTION

In a fascinating recent article by Keestra et al. (2022), the authors investigated measures taken by the top 35 publicly funded UK universities to ensure global equitable access to COVID-19 "health technologies" (January–end of October 2020).[2] The authors sent Freedom of Information (FOI) requests and analyzed universities' websites, to "(i) assess institutional strategies on the patenting and licensing of COVID-19-related health technologies, (ii) identify all COVID-19-related health technologies licensed or patented and (iii) record whether universities engaged with the Open COVID pledge, COVID-19 Technology Access Pool (C-TAP), or [the US] Association of University Technology Managers (AUTM) COVID-19 licensing guidelines during the time period assessed". Despite – or perhaps actually due to – the very prominent nature of the patents and licenses of the health technologies in the pandemic and despite the non-profit nature of universities, it has not been easy to get detailed information on the licensing practices of the universities concerned. In particular the University of Oxford argued that "[it] is our view that disclosure would be likely to prejudice the commercial interests of Oxford University Innovation (OUI) and/or the University, because the information would weaken the bargaining position of the OUI/University in negotiating similar agreements with potential licensees in future."[3] This statement clearly reflects how complex it generally is to carry out empirical studies in the area of patent licensing practices. The more so, when it comes to an empirical analysis of the patent licensing practices adopted by commercial actors.

Organizations such as the Licensing Executives Society International (LESI),[4] AUTM[5] and the European Association for Knowledge Transfer (ASTP)[6] do collect data related to knowledge transfer and patent licensing, which are very interesting and valuable, but the

---

[1]   Professor of Intellectual Property Law & Governance, Faculty of Law, Research Groups Government & Law and Business & Law, GOVTRUST Centre of Excellence, University of Antwerp.

[2]   S Keestra et al., 'University patenting and licensing practices in the United Kingdom during the first year of the COVID-19 pandemic' (2022) 17(5) *Global Public Health*, 641–651.

[3]   Ibid, 645.

[4]   https:// www .lesi .org. In addition, LESI publishes a journal, les Nouvelles, where often practice-based articles related to licensing practices are published, see https://www.lesi.org/publications/les-nouvelles/les-nouvelles-online/.

[5]   https://autm.net/. For more information on the AUTM annual survey, see: https://autm.net/surveys-and-tools/surveys.

[6]   https://www.astp4kt.eu/. For more information, see e.g. *ASTP 2020 survey report on knowledge transfer activities in Europe* (ASTP, 2020), available at: https://www.astp4kt.eu/assets/resources/impact/ASTP%202020%20Survey%20Report%20on%20KT%20Activities%20in%20Europe.pdf.

results are generally reported in an aggregated manner and some (more detailed) information may only be available for members of those organizations. Obviously, also some fascinating studies related to knowledge transfer, licensing and licensing performance are carried out by scholars in economics, yet the data they analyze are typically not focused on a detailed qualitative empirical analysis of the contractual arrangements and their licensing clauses.[7] The Organisation for Economic Co-operation and Development (OECD) has also carried out some surveys, the results of those studies are interesting, but again do not allow for a more detailed systematic analysis of licensing practices and common licensing clauses. As a result common assumptions about licensing strategies often fail to capture the nuances and complexities of patent licensing and technology transfer. In some cases, this may lead to (seemingly) bold claims by academics, advisory committees, parliamentarians or policymakers about the lack of access to key inventions or to pinpointing to particular actors and/or patent owners who are allegedly responsible for restrictive licensing practices. However, as the negotiations and the license information are confidential and only limited information is available, it is very hard to ascertain the truth behind any such statements and to reveal and fully understand the cause in cases of limited access to particular patented inventions.

For instance, regarding access to COVID-19 mRNA-based vaccines some experts argue that if compulsory patent licenses would have been granted in a timely manner, global access to those vaccines could have been ascertained. Others claim that this argument ignores the complexity of those vaccines and the relevance of trade secrets, access to materials and manufacturing capacity, which would still have led to a stalemate. In a very different sector, the sector for mobile phones, consumer electronics and Internet of Things, patent owners and so-called 'implementers' of Standard Essential Patents (SEPs), i.e. patents which protect a technology that forms part of a technical standard, such as for instance the "G" mobile communication standards (3G, 4G, 5G, …), are aggressively litigating and debating the setting of the FRAND licensing terms; terms that are supposedly fair, reasonable and non-discriminatory. What is fair and reasonable and non-discriminatory is highly debatable and depends on the side you are on. Different proposals have been made to determine what "FRAND-licensing" really means, including the calculation of (fair, reasonable and non-discriminatory) royalties. At present, judges in such cases rely heavily on confidential inside information provided by the parties on allegedly "common" or "comparable" licensing practices.[8] Clearly, transparency regarding those practices is basically non-existing and license information is regarded as

---

[7]   Actually, extensive literature by economists exists related to patent practices, knowledge transfer and licensing, here I include only a few recent and less recent examples to give an impression: K-B Min et al., 'The impact of the timing of patent allowance on technology licensing performance: evidence from university invention commercialization' (2022) 52(4) *R&D Management*, 633–649; A Radauer & T Dudenbostel, 'PATLICE Survey: survey on patent licensing activities by patenting firms', Report for the Directorate-General for Research and Innovation by Technopolis, part of the study *Measurement and analysis of knowledge and R&D exploitation flows, assessed by patent and licensing data* (Publications Office of the European Union, 2013); MI Leone & T Reichstein, 'Licensing-in fosters rapid invention! The effect of the grant-back clause and technological unfamiliarity' (2012) 33(8) *Strategic Management*, 965–985; K Motohashi, 'Licensing or not licensing? An empirical analysis of the strategic use of patents by Japanese firms' (2008) 37(9) *Research Policy*, 1548–1555.

[8]   See for instance this study: C Pentheroudakis & JA Baron, *Licensing Terms of Standard Essential Patents: A Comprehensive Analysis of Cases*, Joint Research Centre (JRC) Science for Policy Report (Publications Office of the European Union, 2017). Whereas the title on first face may seem to suggest a systematic empirical overview of licensing practices, the report is mainly a review of selected court

highly confidential.[9] For some authors, this has been a reason to suggest that arbitration may be a more appropriate approach in SEP/FRAND disputes.[10] Although, a shift towards the use of alternative dispute resolution (ADR) may have considerable benefits for the parties concerned, it will undoubtedly lead to even less public insights into licensing practices.

Recent legal scholarship demonstrates increased attention to empirical research in the design and evaluation of law and the policies and practices of legal actors. In the past, legal scholarship was traditionally heavily dominated by normative analyses of the law, i.e. by "black letter law". The trend towards more and more quantitative and qualitative empirical research can also be observed in the area of intellectual property law. In particular, in patent law during the last decades, we have seen an emergence of quantitative and qualitative empirical studies. Some of

---

cases and academic literature like many other reports, articles, book chapters, policy documents, etc. in the area.

[9]   See e.g. this very interesting review article: JL Contreras, 'Technical Standards, Standards-Setting Organizations and Intellectual Property: A Survey of the Literature (With an Emphasis on Empirical Approaches)' in PS Menell & D Schwartz, *Research Handbooks on the Economics of Intellectual Property Law, Vol 2 - Analytical Methods* (Edward Elgar, 2019), also available as a research paper at SSRN: https://ssrn.com/abstract=2900540, which concludes: "In addition, more public data is needed regarding patent licensing and royalty rates for standardized technologies. The data that currently exists is gleaned largely from public sources such as litigation records, government licenses and public securities filings. This data, however, represents only the tip of the iceberg. The largest and most meaningful accumulation of data concerning patent licensing is locked within the files of private firms, subject to strict confidentiality restrictions, and beyond the reach of researchers, policy makers, enforcement agencies and courts. Greater public access to this data has the potential to lower licensing transaction costs, reduce the number of disputes regarding FRAND royalty rates, improve the accuracy of judicial damages determinations, inform agency enforcement decisions, and improve policy making. As such, it is in the interest of all participants in the standardization ecosystem to contribute to the growing public data resources in this important area of economic activity."

[10]   PG Picht, 'Arbitration in SEP/FRAND Disputes' in S Kolpschinski & MR McGuire (eds.), *Research Handbook on Intellectual Property Rights and Arbitration* (Edward Elgar, 2023 (forthcoming)), available at SSRN: https://ssrn.com/abstract=4214738. Apart from the confidentiality of arbitration proceedings, authors that favor arbitration over court procedures for such disputes tend to refer to the multi-jurisdictional nature of most of the SEP/FRAND disputes, the flexibility of arbitration, the potential time-savings (depends on the jurisdiction(s) where the cases would otherwise be litigated), the expertise of the arbitrators, the risks involved in the trend towards the use of "anti-(anti-)(anti-)(anti-)suit injunctions" by way of which the parties try to prevent each other from bringing claims or anti-suit injunctions in other jurisdictions. Moreover, in their SEP/FRAND case-law both the European Commission and the USFTC have mandated the use of alternative dispute mechanisms (Press Release, European Commission, 'Antitrust: Commission Accepts Legally Binding Commitments by Samsung Electronics on Standard Essential Patent Injunctions' (April 29, 2014), http://europa.eu/rapid/press-release_IP-14-490_en.htm and Decision and Order in the Matter of Motorola Mobility LLC and Google Inc., File No. 121-0120, Dkt. No. C-4410 (USFTC, 2013). The Commission has also confirmed the advantages of using ADR for SEP/FRAND disputes in its SEP communication (European Commission, Communication from the Commission, 'Setting out the EU approach to Standard Essential Patents', November 29, 2017, COM(2017) 712 final) and the CJEU (C-170/13 Huawei/ZTE, ECLI:EU:C:2015:477, para. 68) does not seem to exclude this possibility either. In practice several FRAND arbitrations were carried out, for instance between Nokia/Samsung, Nokia/LG, InterDigital/Huawei, Ericsson/Huawei, see R Vary, 'Arbitration of FRAND Disputes in SEP Licensing' in JVH Pierce & P-Y Gunter, *The Guide to IP Arbitration* (Law Business Research, 2021), 161, 163. Furthermore, WIPO is actively promoting ADR options for FRAND dispute management and solution and has reported "more than 60 WIPO mediation cases relating to FRAND licensing negotiations", see https://www.wipo.int/amc/en/center/specific-sectors/ict/frand/.

these studies have been drafted and published by global, regional and national IP offices, such as the World Intellectual Property Organization (WIPO), the European Patent Organization (EPO), the United States Patent and Trademark Office (USPTO), the UK Intellectual Property Office (UKIPO), the Japan Patent Office (JPO) and IP Australia.[11] Others have been prepared by commercial actors that deliver free – or partially free – patent landscapes in a particular field of technology area to showcase their expertise and experience.[12] Finally, during the last two decades in several universities interdisciplinary research groups or teams have been established with high-level expertise in carefully drafting patent landscapes, in particular in the biopharmaceutical sector,[13] but also beyond that.[14]

Notwithstanding this increase in empirical studies regarding patent landscapes and patent practices, due to the confidential nature of patent licensing negotiations and licensing agreements the licensing literature has not followed this pace of the patent literature.[15] The gap regarding patent licensing data seems to be tenacious. Already in 2016 Contreras et al. proposed a carefully designed study aimed "to provide researchers, litigants, judges, policymakers, regulators and the public with previously unavailable information regarding commercial patent licensing practices, including royalty rates, in a manner that does not compromise firm-level confidential information".[16] Despite its careful design (starting with one sector[17] and a small pilot study), it appears that this proposal has not garnered sufficient uptake by the industry and the gap regarding patent licensing data appears to be persistent.

---

[11]   See for instance: WIPO, 'COVID-19-related vaccines and therapeutics – Preliminary insights on related patenting activity during the pandemic' (WIPO, 2022), available at https://www.wipo.int/edocs/pubdocs/en/wipo-pub-1075-en-covid-19-related-vaccines-and-therapeutics.pdf; EPO, European Space Policy Institute, European Space Agency, 'Space-borne sensing and green applications: Patent insight report' (EPO, October 2022), available at https://documents.epo.org/projects/babylon/eponet.nsf/0/043B2CF6909AA8BEC12588CA00555E33/$File/Space-borne%20sensing%20and%20green%20applications%20report.pdf; USPTO, https://developer.uspto.gov/visualizations; JPO, 'Recent Trends in AI-related Inventions – Report' (JPO, July 2020), available at https://www.jpo.go.jp/e/system/patent/gaiyo/ai/document/ai_shutsugan_chosa/report-2020.pdf; Australian Government – IP Australia, 'Patent Analytics on Low Emission Technologies' (Patent Analytics Hub, September 2022), available at https://www.ipaustralia.gov.au/tools-resources/publications-reports/patent-analytics-low-emission-technologies.

[12]   See for instance IP Studies, 'CRISPR Patent Analytics', https://www.ipstudies.ch/crispr-patent-analytics/ or Clarivate, https://clarivate.com/products/ip-intelligence/patent-intelligence-software/innography/.

[13]   A Colaianni et al., 'Impact of gene patents and licensing practices on access to genetic testing and carrier screening for Tay-Sachs and Canavan disease' (2010) 12(1) *Genetics in Medicine*, S5–S14; B Verbeure et al., 'Analysing DNA patents in relation with diagnostic genetic testing' (2006) 14 *European Journal of Human Genetics*, 26–33 and M Aboy et al., 'Mapping the European patent landscape for medical uses of known products' (2021) 39(11) *Nature Biotechnology*, 1336–1343.

[14]   For instance, M Aboy et al., 'Mapping the Patent Landscape of Quantum Technologies: Patenting Trends, Innovation and Policy Implications' (2022) *53 IIC – International Review of Intellectual Property and Competition Law*, 853–882.

[15]   See for a very similar statement: L Pressman et al., 'The licensing of DNA patents by large U.S. academic institutions: an empirical survey' (2006) 24(1) *Nature Biotechnology*, 31.

[16]   JL Contreras et al., 'Study Proposal – Commercial Patent Licensing Data' (2016) *University of Utah College of Law Research Paper No. 164*, available at: https://ssrn.com/abstract=2755706.

[17]   Actually, the proposal was focused on the SEP/FRAND context, but it is also applicable to other contexts and sectors.

The objective of this chapter is to first briefly explore the growth in academic empirical research regarding patenting practices and the methods used in such studies (Section 2). This is followed by a non-exhaustive overview of empirical research regarding licensing practices, both regarding voluntary and compulsory licensing, bilateral and collaborative licensing (Section 3). In Section 4, I identify a number of challenges for further developing the academic literature regarding patenting and patent licensing and potential ways out. Finally, I end this chapter with some comments and a call for more collaboration to enable more empirical research regarding patent licensing practices to enable evidence-based law- and policymaking processes.

2.   EMPIRICAL PATENT RESEARCH – OBJECTIVES, SCOPE, METHODS AND SOME RESULTS

As indicated in the introduction to this chapter, several IP offices (WIPO, USPTO, EPO, UKIPO, JPO, IP Australia) engage in large-scale patent landscaping to assist companies and government agencies that set science and technology policies or funding strategies. These IP offices are particularly and uniquely well-positioned to provide such landscapes to guide firm strategies and national industrial policy. They have access to internal databases and to highly qualified technical staff with the required scientific knowledge, expertise and experience with the patenting process and the necessary skills to interpret patent claims and emerging patent terminology.[18]

Next to these highly specialized IP offices, the last decade a few interdisciplinary teams of scientists, legal researchers and patent practitioners have been created, who have been actively engaged with similar – although generally more limited in scope – patent landscaping activities. The composition of such teams tends to include both scientists with in depth expertise in the particular technology field and an interest in patent law, patent practitioners with elaborate skills in patent analytics and legal scholars concerned by safeguarding access to key technologies. Bubela et al. have observed that despite the growing prevalence and importance of patent landscapes, serious inconsistencies persist in landscaping techniques, which may create obstacles in assessing the patent landscape concerned and in comparing, combing and extending multiple landscapes.[19] Therefore, they developed recommendations for developing consistent and transparent landscaping practices.[20] Some of the more recent academic patent landscaping studies explicitly refer to these recommendations.

The empirical studies carried out by such academic teams of researchers described in this chapter were mainly focused on the life sciences. However, also some studies have been done

---

[18]   T Bubela et al., 'Patent landscaping for life sciences innovation: toward consistent and transparent practices' (2013) 31 *Nature Biotechnology*, 202–206.

[19]   *Ibid*, p. 202.

[20]   *Ibid*. Figure 1 in their paper gives a clear overview of the iterative process of patent landscaping, including stages to (1) assess time and costs constraints; (2) define purpose and scope of landscape; (3) consult with information and technical specialists; (4) design search strategy (identify databases and develop search algorithm); (5) data cleaning and curation (merge data sets, define degree of error tolerated, remove irrelevant documents); (6) augment data sets with additional fields of manual coding; (7) expert validation; (8) output: descriptive statistics, visualization of trends and higher-order analytics (importance/value, relationships between documents, impact of documents on innovation).

that go beyond the scope of the biopharmaceutical sector.[21] Several studies were prompted by the global controversy regarding so-called "gene patents" and particularly by the Myriad case, which internationally led to serious concerns about the potentially hampering effects of Myriad's patenting and restrictive licensing practices on access to genetic diagnostic tests for breast and ovarian cancer.[22] Many later studies were triggered by the US Supreme Court's Mayo and Myriad decisions[23] that limited patent eligibility (35 U.S.C. §101) or similar cases in other jurisdictions. As these concerns were originally especially raised by anecdotal evidence, various authors called for empirical data to provide evidence for such hampering effects.[24] The aim of the empirical studies is to identify whether the patent landscape or changes in the relevant case-law had actually adversely affected research and development (R&D) of a particular product or access to particular services or would likely affect it. Overall, the studies that have been reviewed for this chapter have a rather limited geographical scope and focus generally on the US and Europe. Many of these studies used state of the art patent analytical tools and software, a few carried out surveys or interviews and case studies.

---

[21]   See e.g. M Aboy et al., 'Mapping the Patent Landscape of Quantum Technologies: Patenting Trends, Innovation and Policy Implications' (2022) 53 *IIC – International Review of Intellectual Property and Competition Law*, 853–882.

[22]   The literature on gene patents and the Myriad case is abundant and it goes beyond the scope of this chapter to provide an exhaustive overview of it. This chapter only includes a snapshot of the literature focusing on several national reports issued by advisory councils, empirical papers and some comparative reviews. See e.g. Nuffield Council on Bioethics, *The ethics of patenting DNA: a discussion paper* (Nuffield Council on Bioethics, 2002), available at: http://www.nuffieldbioethics.org/fileLibrary/pdf/theethicsofpatentingdna.pdf; Ontario Ministry of Health, *Genetics, testing and gene patenting: charting new territory in healthcare* (Ontario Ministry of Health, 2002), available at: http://www.health.gov.on.ca/english/public/pub/ministry_reports/geneticsrep02/report_e.pdf; UK Public Health Genetics Unit, *Intellectual property rights and genetics* (Public Health Genetics Unit, 2003); Australian Law Reform Commission, *Report 99 – genes and ingenuity: gene patenting and human health* (Australian Law Reform Commission, 2004) available at: http://www.austlii.edu.au/au/other/alrc/publications/reports/99/; Danish Council of Ethics, *Patenting human genes and stem cells* (Danish Council of Ethics, 2004) available at: http://www.etiskraad.dk/sw475.asp; World Health Organization (WHO), *Genetics, genomics and the patenting of DNA: review of potential implications for health in developing countries* (World Health Organization, 2005) available at: http://www.who.int/genomics/patentingDNA/en/; US National Research Council, *Reaping the benefits of genomic and proteomic research: intellectual property rights, innovation and public health* (US National Research Council, 2006), available at: http://www.nap.edu/catalog.php?record_id=11487; OECD, *Guidelines for the licensing of genetic inventions* (OECD, 2010), available at: http://www.oecd.org/dataoecd/39/38/36198812.pdf. For a comparative review of the Myriad case, see: E van Zimmeren et al., 'The BRCA patent controversies: an international review of patent disputes' in S Gibbon et al. (eds.), *Breast Cancer Gene Research and Medical Practices: Transnational Perspectives in the Time of BRCA* (Routledge, 2014), 151–174.

[23]   Mayo Collaborative Servs. v. Prometheus Labs., Inc., 566 U.S. 66 (2012) and Association for Molecular Pathology v. Myriad Genetics, Inc., 569 U.S. 576 (2013). Basically, the Mayo case ended the USPTO practice of granting patents on medical relationships between molecules and health outcomes when implemented using conventional scientific techniques, whereas the Myriad case ended the USPTO practice of granting patents on isolated genomic DNA. In parallel to the US case, similar challenges to the patents of Myriad have happened in Europe and Australia.

[24]   T Caulfield et al., 'Evidence and anecdotes: an analysis of human gene patenting controversies' (2006) 24 *Nature Biotechnology*, 1091–1094.

At the start of the 21st century I had the pleasure to be part of such an interdisciplinary team at the KU Leuven, while I was writing my PhD thesis.[25] Even though I was not personally involved in drafting the patent landscape analyses, it was a wonderful interdisciplinary learning environment. I actually learnt a lot about the methodology and software tools that were being used, the various stages and quality checks in the studies,[26] the pros and cons and the key challenges in carrying out such analyses. Apart from the (common) challenges related to data collection, data analysis and interpretation and data visualization, it was clear that this type of empirical research is very time-consuming and requires significant funding for the interdisciplinary team. Ensuring the continuity that will allow the team to build, develop and maintain the required expertise, apply it to different fields of application and to – ideally – also carry out longitudinal analyses is a major challenge. In this light, my overview of a (non-exhaustive) collection of empirical patent landscaping studies published during the last two decades in the life sciences shows that this has led to a kind of "relay race-effect", where one academic team seems to pass on the "stick" to a next team after several years of investing in conducting such patent landscapes.

When I joined the interdisciplinary team in Leuven, the Myriad case was still in an early phase. We closely followed the Myriad case at the EPO and had many conversations with the patent attorneys involved in that case. We were also involved in giving advice on a study by the European Society of Human Genetics related to patenting and licensing in genetic testing[27] and the development of licensing guidelines for genetic inventions by the OECD.[28] We co-authored several articles that focused more on legal mechanisms that are designed to render patented genetic inventions accessible to further use in research, and to diagnosis and/or treatment, including the research exemption, voluntary bilateral and collaborative licensing (e.g. patent pools and clearinghouses) and compulsory licensing.[29] Some of our research on the licensing mechanisms will be analyzed in somewhat more detail in the next section of this contribution. My colleagues who did the patent landscapes examined in particular the implications of gene patents on genetic diagnostic testing. Verbeure et al. strongly argue in favor of the need for systematic empirical studies in the field and describe a pilot study on 11 selected hereditary disorders and the two tools developed to facilitate the study. These tools consist of an advanced search strategy to find the relevant patents and a claim classification template to assist the user in the assessment of the subject matter covered by the patent claims and in creating a comprehensive overview of the patent landscape in the field.[30] These tools were also used in later studies published by the team. Huys et al. conclude on the basis of a patent land-

---

[25] E van Zimmeren, 'Towards a new patent paradigm in the biomedical sector? Facilitating access, open innovation and social responsibility in patent law in the US, Europe and Japan' (Leuven, 2011).

[26] See e.g. *supra* the stages identified in Bubela et al. (2013).

[27] E.g. G Matthijs & S Ayme (eds.), 'Patenting and licensing in genetic testing' (2008) 16 *European Journal of Human Genetics*, S1–S50.

[28] OECD (2010).

[29] G Van Overwalle et al., 'Models for facilitating access to patents on genetic inventions' (2006) 7 *Nature Reviews Genetics*, 143–148; B Verbeure et al., 'Patent pools and diagnostic testing' (2006) 24(3) *Trends in Biotechnology*, 115–120; E van Zimmeren et al., 'A clearinghouse for diagnostic testing: the solution to ensure access to and use of patented genetic inventions?' (2006) 84(5) *Bulletin of the World Health Organization*, 352–359.

[30] B Verbeure et al., 'Analysing DNA patents in relation with diagnostic genetic testing' (2006) 14 *European Journal of Human Genetics*, 26–33.

scape analysis of 22 common genetic diagnostic tests, that they identified substantially fewer claims on genes per se than initially suggested. At the same time in their opinion significant issues existed that resulted in legal uncertainty as to the patent claims' scope[31] and the use of method claims.[32]

In parallel at the Center for Public Genomics (CpG) at Duke University, a team led by Robert Cook-Deegan was analyzing how patenting (and licensing) was affecting clinical access to genetic testing in the United States.[33] The research was requested by the Secretary's Advisory Committee on Genetics, Health, and Society (SACGHS). In mid-2006, SACGHS appointed a task force to address the impact of patenting and licensing on clinical access to genetic testing, chaired by James P. Evans of the University of North Carolina. A report of 2006 by the National Research Council[34] had reviewed several cases of clinical genetic testing, but it mainly addressed whether patents affected genomic and proteomic research. SACGHS wished to delve more deeply into the effects on clinical access to genetic testing. As these case studies involved significant empirical research, the team relied on substantial support by students: in January 2007 the task force became the client of the graduate and professional student capstone section of Duke's Health Policy Certificate program. In addition, the CpG-SACGHS project depended on the work of many people over several years leveraging a network of experts associated with the SACGHS grant and organizing many meetings to discuss the preliminary results of the case studies. From late 2006 until March 2009, several CpG researchers began working almost exclusively for SACGHS and its task force. Conditions studied by the team together with the students were breast and ovarian cancers, colon cancers, Alzheimer's disease, cystic fibrosis, hearing loss, hereditary hemochromatosis, Long QT syndrome, spinocerebellar ataxia, Tay-Sachs disease and Canavan disease. The CpG case studies were released in March 2009 as a 300-page appendix to the "Public Consultation Draft Report on Gene Patents and Licensing Practices and Their Impact on Patient Access to Genetic Tests." The report was discussed at the SACGHS's October 8th–9th meeting in 2009, when the case studies were referred to during the debate.

The CpG team also closely followed later developments in the US case-law and the US Congress and the implications for genetic testing.[35] Moreover, an interesting case study by Baldwin & Cook-Deegan shows that the debate about gene patents and the Myriad litigation was not only – or even mainly – about the patents.[36] The case study compares the development of Herceptin® (Genentech) with Myriad's development of BRACAnalysis®. Baldwin &

---

[31]   I Huys et al., 'Legal uncertainty in the area of genetic diagnostic testing' (2009) 27(10) *Nature Biotechnology*, 903–909.

[32]   I Huys et al., 'Gene and genetic diagnostic method patent claims: a comparison under current European and US patent law' (2011) 19(10) *European Journal of Human Genetics*, 1104–1107.

[33]   R Cook-Deegan & C Heaney, 'Gene Patents and Licensing: Case Studies Prepared for the Secretary's Advisory Committee on Genetics, Health, and Society' (2010) 12 (https://www.sciencedirect.com/science/article/pii/S1098360021019924) *Genetics in Medicine*, S1–S2.

[34]   National Research Council, *Reaping the benefits of genomic and proteomic research: intellectual property rights, innovation and public health* (National Research Council, 2006) available at: http://www.nap.edu/catalog.php?record_id=11487.

[35]   R Cook-Deegan & A Niehaus, 'After Myriad: Genetic Testing in the Wake of Recent Supreme Court Decisions about Gene Patents' (2014) 2 *Current Genetic Medicine Reports*, 223–241.

[36]   See also: E van Zimmeren et al., 'The BRCA patent controversies: an international review of patent disputes' in S Gibbon et al. (eds.), *Breast Cancer Gene Research and Medical Practices: Transnational Perspectives in the Time of BRCA* (Routledge, 2014) 151–174.

Cook-Deegan convincingly show that some of the assumptions that the cause of the problems underlying the debate are inherently due to patents and that eliminating gene patents will solve those problems ignore the impact of the broader business practices. Patents contribute to and enable business practices, but many genes have been patented that did not lead to the same problems.[37]

In Canada another interesting case study was carried out, which examined how Twitter was used in the context of the controversy about gene patents triggered in Canada by a patent case filed by the Children's Hospital of Eastern Ontario (CHEO) to invalidate patents for five genes associated with Long QT Syndrome (LQTS), a rare disorder of the heart's electrical activity that may cause sudden, uncontrollable and dangerous arrhythmias. The authors collected 310 English-language tweets that contained the keyword "gene patents", conducted a content analysis of the messages to establish the Twitter users' perspectives on both CHEO's court challenge and the broader controversy over the patenting of human DNA.[38]

Moreover, with new scientific advances new challenges emerged with respect to other patented technologies, such as non-invasive prenatal testing.[39] In addition the emergence of big data highlighted the need to regulate practices for sharing and curating data, analytical algorithms, interpretive frameworks and patient re-contact.[40]

At present, a team of researchers at Copenhagen University and Cambridge University seems to have taken over the "empirical stick". In an impressive number of legal and empirical papers mostly published in the high-impact journal *Nature Biotechnology*, the team has critically examined the fundamental implications of the Mayo and Myriad cases (and later follow-up case-law) on patent drafting practices and patent prosecution strategies of applicants and patent granting practices of the USPTO. Firstly, they delved into the questions of whether the Myriad case has resulted in "drafting around" the legal principles set out by the Myriad decision or in claim amendments,[41] the impact of the case on gene patents[42] and beyond[43] and precision medicine.[44] They also examined Mayo's impact on patent applications related to

---

[37]   AL Baldwin & R Cook-Deegan, 'Constructing narratives of heroism and villainy: case study of Myriad's BRACAnalysis® compared to Genentech's Herceptin®' (2013) 8 *Genome Medicine* 5, https://doi.org/10.1186/gm412.

[38]   L Du et al., 'The gene patent controversy on Twitter: a case study of Twitter users' responses to the CHEO lawsuit against Long QT gene patents' (2015) 16 *BMC Medical Ethics*, 55.

[39]   A Agarwal et al., 'Commercial landscape of noninvasive prenatal testing in the United States' (2013) 33(6) *Prenatal Diagnosis*, 521–531 and N Hawkins et al., 'The continuing saga of patents and non-invasive prenatal testing' (2019) 39(6) *Prenatal Diagnosis*, 441–444.

[40]   JY Cheon et al., 'Variants of uncertain significance in BRCA: a harbinger of ethical and policy issues to come?' (2014) 6 *Genome Medicine* 121.

[41]   M Aboy et al., 'After Myriad, what makes a gene patent claim "markedly different" from nature?' (2017) 35(9) *Nature Biotechnology*, 820–825.

[42]   M Aboy et al., 'Myriad's Impact on Gene Patents' (2016) 34(11) *Nature Biotechnology*, 1119–1123.

[43]   M Aboy et al., 'Was the Myriad decision a "surgical strike" on isolated DNA patents, or does it have wider impacts?' (2018) 36(12) *Nature Biotechnology*, 1146–1150. Contrary to some of the early predictions that the decision would be a narrow "surgical strike" carving out isolated gDNA from patent eligibility, the study finds that 85% of the Myriad-based rejections have been directed to non-isolated DNA patent claims.

[44]   M Aboy et al., 'How does emerging patent case law in the US and Europe affect precision medicine?' (2019) 37(10) *Nature Biotechnology*, 1118–1125.

biotechnology, diagnostics and personalized medicine[45] and claim drafting techniques to overcome Mayo-based rejections.[46] Finally, recently Aboy et al. also mapped the European patent landscape for medical uses of known products.[47]

In these studies the team generally uses automated searching combined with human expert review, but Liddicoat et al. also carried out an interview-based study (2020) focusing on whether the Mayo and Myriad judgments of the US Supreme Court had adversely affected the development of molecular tests in the US and Europe.[48] The study showed that US organizations have been more affected by these case-law developments than European organizations, even though both types of organizations file for US patents. In particular half of the US university technology transfer offices that were interviewed decided not to develop tests, and many other organizations explained that the legal uncertainty created by the cases has been problematic.

Another interesting empirical research method used within the patent context relates to scenarios' research. This method is noteworthy because of its forward-looking and explorative approach. The EPO's Scenarios for the future,[49] which contains the results of a two-year project in which the EPO interviewed around 150 key players – including critics – from the fields of science, business, politics, ethics, economics and law, seeking their opinions on how intellectual property and patenting might evolve over the next 15 to 20 years. Four scenarios[50] – relevant and plausible stories about the future – were developed in a series of workshops based on the answers obtained. This is not a method which has been employed very often, but in my view the current wicked problems related to climate change, inequality, mobility, inflation and the push for economic "degrowth" rather than growth and for inclusivity and

---

[45]   M Aboy et al., 'Mayo's impact on patent applications related to biotechnology, diagnostics and personalized medicine' (2019) 37(5) *Nature Biotechnology*, 513–518. The authors conclude that the biggest problem related to the Mayo case is the extensive degree of legal uncertainty. This legal uncertainty was already identified by other authors, but has been confirmed by the empirical results. Smaller companies with limited budgets and access to experts are likely to be hardest hit, and also in greatest need of patent protection to get a foothold in the life sciences industry.

[46]   M Aboy et al., 'One year after Vanda, are diagnostics patents transforming into methods of treatment to overcome Mayo-based rejections?' (2020) 38(3) *Nature Biotechnology*, 279–283.

[47]   M Aboy et al., 'Mapping the European patent landscape for medical uses of known products' (2021) 39(11) *Nature Biotechnology*, 1336–1343. The study shows a substantial upward trend in the past 10 years (since 2010) for patents with claims to new medical indications of existing compounds. Such patents are granted to large pharmaceutical companies as well as to universities and publicly funded research institutes. Some experts have criticized Articles 54(4) and (5) of the European Patent Convention (EPC) for harming repurposing activity rather than promoting it by allowing it to be patent protected. Differently, Aboy et al. show that the provisions in the EPC appear to encourage early disclosure of new medical uses in the first patents claiming novel products (to avoid third parties acquiring rights to certain uses of the product) and, thus may also support the public interest by disseminating new scientific knowledge through the disclosure function of the patent system.

[48]   J Liddicoat et al., 'The Effects of Myriad and Mayo on Molecular-Test Development in the United States and Europe: Interviews from the Frontline' (2020), 22 *Vanderbilt Journal of Entertainment and Technology Law* 785, available at: https://scholarship.law.vanderbilt.edu/jetlaw/vol22/iss4/5.

[49]   S Elahi et al., *Scenarios for the future* (EPO, 2007), available at: https:// documents .epo .org/ projects/ babylon/ eponet .nsf/ 0/ 63A 726D28B589 B5BC12572D B00597683/ $File/ EPO _scenarios _bookmarked.pdf.

[50]   The four scenarios are the following: (1) Grey Scenario: Market Rules; (2) Red Scenario: Whose Game?; (3) Green Scenario: Trees of Knowledge; and (4) Blue Scenario: Blue Skies.

well-being rather than an economic concept such as consumer welfare, would justify an iteration of the Scenarios study by the EPO.

3. EMPIRICAL PATENT LICENSING RESEARCH – OBJECTIVES, SCOPE, METHODS AND SOME RESULTS

A patent license is a contractual agreement by which the patent holder authorizes another party to use its invention under the conditions elaborated in the agreement. License agreements generally contain a wide variety of conditions and clauses related to the exclusive, non-exclusive or sole nature of the license, its material scope, its geographical scope, the licensing fee or royalty rates, specific milestones, guarantees and liabilities, confidentiality provisions, monitoring and accountancy, provisions on the right to sub-license, improvements to the licensed technologies, the applicable law, ADR clauses, the competent court, etc.

Information on the practices related to such clauses would especially be worthwhile to collect, analyze and compare. For legal researchers it would be very interesting to get a better understanding of the strategic considerations in patent licensing and the common use of particular clauses in licensing agreements. This could be relevant from a policymaker perspective as well, as at various occasions, attempts have been made to impose licensing guidelines in specific sectors or for particular types of inventions to influence market behavior and to stimulate knowledge exchange ensuring access to key technologies.[51] Nonetheless, as indicated above, generally it is very challenging to collect the detailed patent licensing data required for a science-based recommendation, both with respect to licensing practices adopted by commercial actors and those by public actors, including universities and public research institutes.[52]

Anecdotal evidence suggests, however, that the volume and value of patent licensing has expanded over the last decades.[53] This phenomenon has been attributed to changes in the modes of innovation (a shift towards so-called "open innovation" and co-creation), globalization and strengthened market competition.[54] Increased competition, shorter product life-cycles and technological developments are forcing companies to innovate more rapidly and to focus their R&D expenditures. This requires then access to complementary knowledge from the public and private sector. Innovative firms are increasingly dependent on external sources of knowledge rather than conducting in-house research. As a result, the industry research is less centered on the individual firm and has gradually become more based on knowledge exchange,

---

[51] See e.g. OECD (2010).

[52] For instance, for the PhD research project of Arina Gorbatyuk we had initially foreseen a systematic analysis of R&D and licensing agreements. As it turned out to be basically impossible to collect an appropriate sample of agreements, in the end she carried out almost 60 interviews to collect the relevant qualitative information for her PhD project on the Allocation of IP Ownership of Jointly Developed Knowledge: her dataset consists of 56 semi-structured interviews conducted with representatives of various organizations (i.e. companies, technology transfer offices and research institutions). The interviews are systematically transcribed and coded using NVivo software. For more information, see A Gorbatyuk, *Rethinking IP ownership in the context of open innovation*, May 2019 (supervisors G Van Overwalle & E van Zimmeren).

[53] MP Zuniga & D Guellec, *Who licenses out patents and why? Lessons from a business survey*, STI Working Paper 2009/5, Statistical Analysis of Science, Technology and Industry (OECD, 2009), 6.

[54] S Kamiyama et al., *Valuation and Exploitation of Intellectual Property*, STI Working Paper (OECD, 2006).

public-private research collaborations, networks and technology markets with an increased role for intermediaries.

Open innovation is enabled by spinning in and out, licensing in and out and through R&D collaborations. From a social welfare perspective this dynamic nature of the technology market, including licensing, has many potentially positive but also possibly some negative effects. In terms of the positive impact, licensing of patents will generally increase the diffusion of technology, it facilitates vertical specialization and the division of tasks between companies and prevents R&D duplication. Moreover, licensing can boost downstream competition by reducing barriers to entry related to R&D and licensing revenues can be invested in further innovation. Finally, licensing facilitates the exploitation of a technology at a larger scale than if the patentee would refuse to license and would decide to exploit the patent by itself. Licensing will allow commercialization of the patented technologies across industries and jurisdictions where the patent owner otherwise would not operate. On the other hand, licensing can also have negative effects as it may result in collusion between companies, and hence may reduce competition and ultimately innovation. Therefore, national and European authorities active in innovation and IP policy and competition authorities have a strong interest in monitoring and assessing licensing practices. The OECD has been gathering evidence on licensing and has been particularly active in promoting conferences and information exchange between authorities regarding the interface between competition law and IP law and relevant licensing practices.[55]

Still relatively little is known on licensing practices from an empirical quantitative and qualitative perspective: their volume, the profile of companies involved, the sectors where they are more prevalent, the motives for the firms involved, their economic effects, difficulties encountered, strategic considerations (e.g. use of milestones, transparency and access obligations) and the licensing conditions used. Whereas anecdotal evidence may be available for all these issues and organizations such as for instance LESI, AUTM, ASTP and the OECD have been collecting some survey data, in most sectors no systematic quantitative or qualitative empirical studies are carried out. Data collected are often quite generic and do not provide detailed information on the licensing clauses. For instance, in 2009, Zuniga & Guellec from the OECD published a report[56] on a business survey carried out by the OECD, the EPO and the University of Tokyo on the licensing-out of patents. The goal of this study was to investigate the intensity of licensing to affiliated and non-affiliated companies, its evolution, the characteristics, motivations and obstacles met by companies doing or willing to license. In the report they show that patent licensing is indeed widespread among firms that own patents in Europe and Japan. Small firms and large firms are more likely to license out their patented inventions. One third of "young" (recently established) European firms deemed patents as quite or very important to convince private investors and venture capitalists to provide them with funds.[57] However, according to this report in Europe small to medium sized enterprises (SMEs) have more difficulties to license out their patents than large firms. The major perceived barrier to licensing out relates to the lack of information for the identification of potential partners. The lack of transparency in technology markets is hence not only problematic from the research and policymaking perspective, which I am highlighting in this chapter, companies also

---

[55]   See e.g. https://www.oecd.org/daf/competition/licensing-of-ip-rights-and-competition-law.htm.
[56]   Zuniga & Guellec (2009), see footnote 53 above.
[57]   *Ibid.*

encounter problems due to the "patent notice failure"; the failure of the patent system to ensure not only the adequate disclosure of (patented) inventions, but also the adequate disclosure of the owners of the patents.[58]

In Sections 1 and 2, I have mentioned briefly that WIPO and the EPO have been actively collecting empirical data regarding the patent landscapes for different technologies. Unfortunately, they have not taken up an equally active role to collect systematic (and preferably also longitudinal) data regarding licensing practices for different technologies/in different sectors. This seems to be a missed opportunity. For the EPO this may be more logical in view of its relatively limited patent-based mandate,[59] but WIPO seems particularly well-placed to carry out such systematic, longitudinal studies. In fact, WIPO has also been involved in the promotion of the use of collaborative licensing schemes (see below) for instance to promote knowledge transfer regarding green technologies to facilitate access to patented inventions.

To a certain extent, some academic scholarly work has tried to fill the tenacious patent license data gap, in particular in the life sciences. As indicated above, the CpG team at Duke University was involved in an extensive, four-year-long study of the effects of patenting and licensing practices on clinical access to genetic testing. However, these studies involved significant funding by SACGHS and human resources. An intense (US and global) policy debate about gene patents and access to clinical genetic testing services had justified the extensive financial support. The studies focused on the US, just like many other key empirical studies described in this chapter.

Cook-Deegan, who played a crucial role in the success of the SACGHS case studies, was also involved in a fascinating study about the patent history and licensing practices related to polymerase chain reaction (PCR),[60] nowadays well known by the general public due to COVID-19 PCR tests, but also a key research tool for many different types of life sciences research. This important technology was discovered, developed and patented in an industry setting. According to Fore et al. (2006), PCR has earned approximately $2 billion in royalties for the different rights-holders while also becoming an essential research tool. They show that the technology was subject to patent protection and strict licensing terms, but was still made widely available through the use of "business partnerships and broad corporate licensing, adaptive licensing strategies, and a 'rational forbearance' from suing researchers for patent infringement".[61] Therefore, their analysis suggests that, at least in the case of PCR, patenting of genomic research tools need not impede their dissemination, provided that the technology is made available through appropriate business practices.

Another US-based paper on a survey of licensing practices of DNA patents by large US academic institutions highlights that common assumptions about licensing practices often fail to capture the nuances and complexities of technology transfer in practice.[62] This finding empha-

---

[58] See also: A Gorbatyuk & A Kovacs, 'Patent Notice (Failure) in the Era of Patent Monetization' (2022) 53 *IIC*, 506–542.

[59] Nonetheless, the EPO did publish a review report on compulsory licensing, see below in footnote 83.

[60] J Fore et al., 'The effects of business practices, licensing, and intellectual property on development and dissemination of the polymerase chain reaction: case study' (2006) 3(1) *Journal of Biomedical Discovery and Collaboration*, 7.

[61] *Ibid.*

[62] L Pressman, 'The licensing of DNA patents by large U.S. academic institutions: an empirical survey' (2006) 24(1) *Nature Biotechnology*, 31–39.

sizes the importance of combining quantitative and qualitative empirical research (combination of web-based survey with open-ended policy questions followed up by semi-structured telephone interviews) to get a better understanding of licensing practices and their potential implications. In the paper, they describe the academic DNA patent landscape and present the results of a federally funded survey of licensing practices at 19 of the 30 US academic institutions that – by then – had received the largest number of DNA patents. Their analysis showed how large US academic institutions were very actively participating in DNA patenting and licensing. Furthermore, their patenting and licensing practices appeared to be "designed pragmatically to accommodate both economic goals, such as revenue generation and new company formation, and social goals, such as ensuring utilization and availability of federally funded inventions".[63] The authors provide some valuable insights as to the implications of certain nuances in licensing practices, for instance in terms of the exclusive or non-exclusive nature of a license.[64]

Unfortunately, the global CRISPR patent dispute between the Broad Institute and Berkeley University over the foundational patent rights to CRISPR-Cas9 gene-editing technology tells us that in some cases large US research institutes seem to be playing the "wrong ballgame". CRISPR is one of the recent patent cases that has garnered widespread interest of the global research community, the patent community, industry, investors, and also the general public to a certain extent. Contreras & Sherkow[65] describe that – despite the fact that patent ownership is still being disputed – the institutions behind CRISPR have capitalized on the enormous market for this groundbreaking technology by entering into a series of licensing agreements with commercial enterprises. Actually, both key CRISPR patent holders have granted exclusive rights to a spinoff or what the authors refer to as "surrogate company" formed by the institution and one of its principal researchers with respect to human therapeutics and treatments, a potentially very profitable market. This type of technology transfer model, in which a university basically outsources the licensing and commercialization of a valuable patent portfolio to a private company, is not uncommon, particularly in the US, but also in other jurisdictions. The authors express, however, concerns that the use of such a model could rapidly become a key bottleneck for the use of CRISPR technology to discover and develop useful human therapeutics.[66]

Contrary to what the Myriad and CRISPR examples may suggest, overall policymakers and competition authorities are convinced of the advantages of licensing, such as stimulating R&D, prevention of duplication of R&D and promoting dissemination of the licensed technology, as described at the start of this section. Such pro-competitive effects are also acknowl-

---

[63]   *Ibid.*
[64]   *Ibid.* For instance an invention which is licensed only once is not necessarily the object of an exclusive license, and some exclusive licenses are restricted by field of use or in terms of their duration or they may be terminated by one party or the other. Moreover, technologies can remain available for licensing, while exclusively licensed, if the exclusivity is for a particular field of use, or if research or humanitarian use exemptions have been included in the license. In addition, licenses are not simply static legal instruments: an exclusive license may, under certain circumstances, be renegotiated to be nonexclusive and if allowed by the license the licensee may sublicense.
[65]   JL Contreras & JS Sherkow, 'CRISPR, Surrogate Licensing, and Scientific Discovery' (2017) 355(6326) *Science*, 698–700.
[66]   *Ibid.*

edged by competition authorities in their technology transfer or IP licensing guidelines.[67] Such (voluntary) licensing mechanisms can be bilateral, one-on-one, license contracts between a licensor and a licensee or more complex cross-licenses, in which both parties operate as licensor and licensee. In addition, in some sectors, patent owners have engaged in even more "collaborative" licensing mechanisms, such as patent pool arrangements or clearinghouses.

A patent pool is an agreement between two or more patent owners owning patents relating to the same technology to license one or more of their patents to one another, or to license them as a package to third parties. Several authors have explored the potential of patent pools to ensure access to genetic inventions and diagnostics.[68] They draw from experiences with patent pools in other sectors, most notably the mobile communications and consumer electronics sector for explaining the concept and mechanisms of patents pools, their strengths and weaknesses, incentives, etc.[69] Recently, patent pools have also been recommended within the context of the Internet of Things.[70] The World Health Organization (WHO) Expert Advisory Committee on Developing Global Standards for Governance and Oversight of Human Genome Editing has expressed an interest in patent pools to deal with the fragmented ownership for genome editing technologies.[71] Finally, the WHO supports the use of the patent pool model to secure access to essential COVID-19 related inventions.[72] Nonetheless, apart from a few successful cases (e.g. Medicines Patent Pool[73]) patent pools are relatively uncommon beyond the mobile communications and consumer electronics sectors.

---

[67] See for instance the EU Technology Transfer Block Exemption Regulation and the associated Technology Transfer Guidelines (2014), the USDoJ and USFTC Antitrust Guidelines for the Licensing of Intellectual Property (2017) and the JFTC Guidelines for the Use of Intellectual Property under the Antimonopoly Act (2005).

[68] D Matthews et al., 'The Role of Patents and Licensing in the Governance of Human Genome Editing: A White Paper' (2021) Queen Mary Law Research Paper No. 364/2021, available at SSRN: https://ssrn.com/abstract=3896308; B Verbeure et al., 'Patent Pools and Diagnostic testing' (2006) 3 *Trends in Biotechnology*, 115–120; G Van Overwalle (ed.), *Gene Patents and Collaborative Licensing Models: Patent Pools, Clearinghouses, Open Source Models and Liability Regimes* (Cambridge University Press, 2009); G Van Overwalle et al., 'Models for facilitating access to patents on genetic inventions' (2006) 7 *Nature Reviews Genetics*, 143–148; E van Zimmeren, 'Patent Pools and Clearinghouses in the Life Sciences' (2011) 29 *Trends in Biotechnology*, 569–576; E van Zimmeren, 'Towards a new patent paradigm in the biomedical sector? Facilitating access, open innovation and social responsibility in patent law in the US, Europe and Japan' (Leuven, 2011).

[69] In this context, a discussion related to patent pools is, thus, often closely interlinked with questions related to SEPs and FRAND licensing.

[70] European Commission's Group of Experts on Licensing and Valuation of Standard Essential Patents 'SEPs Expert Group' (E03600) – Contribution to the Debate on SEPs (2021), available at https://ec.europa.eu/docsroom/documents/45217.

[71] World Health Organization (WHO) Expert Advisory Committee on Developing Global Standards for Governance and Oversight of Human Genome Editing, *Human Genome Editing: Recommendations* (WHO, 2021), available at: https://www.who.int/publications/i/item/9789240030381 and D Matthews et al. (2021).

[72] WHO COVID-19 Technology Access Pool; E Billette de Villemeur et al., 'Pool patents to get COVID vaccines and drugs to all' (2021) 591 *Nature*, 529.

[73] For more information, see https://medicinespatentpool.org/; S Morin et al., 'The economic and public health impact of intellectual property licensing of medicines for low-income and middle-income countries: a modelling study' (2022) 7(2) *Lancet Public Health*, e169–e176; E Burrone et al., 'Patent pooling to increase access to essential medicines' (2019) 97 *Bull World Health Organ*, 575–577; E Burrone, 'Patent Pooling in Public Health' in *The Cambridge Handbook of Public-Private Partnerships,*

In the literature regarding pools, also some other collaborative licensing mechanisms tend to be included, such as clearinghouses.[74] Clearinghouses can be depicted as platforms or intermediaries bringing together owners and users of goods, services and information to lower transaction costs. There are many types of clearinghouses ranging from mere databases of information to technology exchange platforms and royalty-collecting organizations performing many functions. The clearinghouse operates as a neutral intermediary or platform for a wide variety of licensable technologies (a type of "supermarket" for licensable technologies) with substantial expertise in licensing. It matches patent owners and licensees by delivering standard or one-stop-licenses.

Both patent pools and clearinghouses are licensing mechanisms which may be helpful to overcome situations where the patent landscape is very fragmented. To address a given public interest problem, an initiative could be taken to negotiate with the patentees for joint licenses. Nevertheless, patent pools and clearinghouses are typically voluntary measures and thus rely on the goodwill of the parties involved. Typically the goodwill to contribute patents to a patent pool is higher when (1) the need for third party technology is reciprocal and (2) it is a generic part of the final product and/or (3) none of the parties have a product in development covered only by the relevant patent.[75] Some quantitative empirical research has been carried out in Europe and Australia in order to better understand the relatively limited use of pools and clearinghouses in the life sciences.[76] It appears that patent owners are often not willing to engage in the establishment of such models as they would lose control regarding potentially very valuable patented technologies and regarding the establishment of the licensing conditions, including the setting of the royalties. Moreover, the interests of the heterogenous players in the life sciences are rarely aligned, which is required for the smooth operation of such collaborative licensing mechanisms.[77] For the study in Europe, we managed to gain significant "moral" support of the European Commission, LESI and ProTon Europe, which has helped to get feedback on an early pilot study and to get attention from stakeholders in the survey. Nonetheless, the sample size (177 respondents) of the survey remained relatively modest despite this moral support.

Apart from these more exotic collaborative licensing models, researchers have also been quite attracted to so-called "patent pledges" as another tool for dealing with fragmented patent landscapes. Patent pledges are public commitments to limit the enforcement or other exploita-

---

Intellectual Property Governance, and Sustainable Development (Cambridge University Press, 2018), 93–108 and LX Wang, 'Global drug diffusion and innovation with the medicines patent pool' (2022) 85 *Journal of Health Economics*, 102671.

[74]   E van Zimmeren et al., 'Patent Pools and Clearinghouses in the Life Sciences' (2011) 29 *Trends in Biotechnology*, 569–576; E van Zimmeren at al., 'A clearinghouse for diagnostic testing: the solution to ensure access to and use of patented genetic inventions?' (2006) 84 *Bulletin of the World Health Organization IP Theme Issue*, 352–359.

[75]   E van Zimmeren et al., 'Patent Pools and Clearinghouses in the Life Sciences' (2011) 29 *Trends in Biotechnology*, 569–576.

[76]   E van Zimmeren et al., *Dwanglicenties voor dure geneesmiddelen: juridische en economische afwegingen,* (Federaal Kenniscentrum voor de Gezondheidszorg (KCE), 2022), KCE Reports 356A. DOI : 10.57598/R356AS, available at: https://kce.fgov.be/nl/dwanglicenties-voor-dure-geneesmiddelen -juridische-en-economische-afwegingen (also available in English).

[77]   E van Zimmeren et al., footnote 75 and JL Nielsen et al., 'Sharing the Burden in Australian Drug Discovery and Development: Collaborative Trends in Translational Research' (2014) 3 *Intellectual Property Quarterly*, 181, available at: https://ssrn.com/abstract=2509581.

tion of one's patent rights.[78] Such arrangements have been increasing in popularity in a range of market sectors from telecommunications and software to biopharma and green technology. Over time, patent pledges have become more complex and a wider variety of motivations seem to be leading firms to pledge patents.[79] Moreover, increased attention is given to the role that patent pledges may play in innovation, the governance of collective pledges, and a trend toward democratization and internationalization of pledge behavior.[80] Ehrnsperger & Tietze[81] have explored those motivations in a qualitative empirical study consisting of 30 expert interviews, including people directly involved in the decision to initiate and to execute patent pledges. In addition, they analyzed 50 public patent pledge statements with respect to their underlying motivations. They found 13 distinct motivations belonging to three general categories, the primary motive being "driving technology diffusion".

Generally patent owners can decide whether they are willing to license their patented invention or not and if so under which conditions. However, under compulsory licensing and government use mechanisms the government or a court can compel a patent holder to license the rights. The Paris Convention for the Protection of Industrial Property[82] (hereinafter "Paris Convention" (PC)) of 1883 already provided a legal basis for Member States to grant compulsory licenses (art. 5A(2) PC). Article 31 of the WTO Agreement on Trade-Related Aspects of Intellectual Property Rights (TRIPs) also affirms the right of Member States to grant compulsory licenses; it implicitly confirms their autonomy to determine the legal grounds on which such licenses can be granted and sets a detailed list of conditions and limitations that need to be respected by WTO Member States. Various studies have made a systematic comparison of compulsory licensing mechanisms in national patent acts.[83] Even though the legal bases for compulsory licenses are quite common, overall the number of actual granted compulsory licenses is relatively low, in particular in high-income countries.[84] In many countries, potential licensees have applied for compulsory licenses, but often they did not succeed.[85] 't

---

[78]   JL Contreras, 'The Evolving Patent Pledge Landscape' Centre for International Governance Innovation (CIGI), International law research program working paper series, 2017, available at: https://ssrn.com/abstract=3067095.

[79]   *Ibid.*

[80]   *Ibid.*

[81]   JF Ehrnsperger & F Tietze, 'Motives for Patent Pledges: A Qualitative Study', Centre for Technology Management working paper series, No. 2019/11 (2019).

[82]   Paris Convention for the Protection of Industrial Property (1883) (as amended on September 28, 1979), available at: https://wipolex.wipo.int/en/treaties/textdetails/12633.

[83]   CMS, *The Compulsory Licensing eGuide, 2021*, CMS Compulsory Licensing Global E-Guide, 2021 https://cms.law/en/media/expert-guides/files-for-expert-guides/cms-compulsory-licensing-global-expert-guide-feb-2021; WIPO, *Database on Flexibilities in the Intellectual Property System*, https://www.wipo.int/ip-development/en/agenda/flexibilities/search.jsp?field_id=2343&type_id=2349&territory_id=; WIPO, *Survey on Compulsory Licenses Granted by WIPO Member States to Address Anti-Competitive Uses of Intellectual Property Rights*, CDIP/4/4 Rev./Study/Inf/5 October 4, 2011 https://www.wipo.int/edocs/mdocs/mdocs/en/cdip_4/cdip_4_4_rev_study_inf_5.pdf; EPO, *Compulsory licensing in Europe: A country-by-country overview* https://documents.epo.org/projects/babylon/eponot.nsf/0/8509F913B768D063C1258382004FC677/$File/compulsory_licensing_in_europe_en.pdf (Munich, 2018).

[84]   E Van Zimmeren et al. (2022) – legal part of the report (see footnote 76).

[85]   Some notable exceptions are compulsory licenses in Brazil related to Efavirenz, an anti-retroviral drug. In Denmark three cases have been reported, two of which are in the pharmaceutical sector. For Germany, two key compulsory licenses cases related to drugs are reported. Between 2006 and 2008,

Hoen et al. (2018) show, however, that the use of the flexibilities included in the WTO TRIPs Agreement to access lower-priced generic medicines, including compulsory licenses, is much more frequent than is commonly assumed. They identify 100 compulsory licenses/public non-commercial use licenses, including two granted by developed countries.[86]

A review study on the actual economic consequences in terms of financial gains or losses, the potential impact on wealth, health and well-being of the population of compulsory licenses has shown no conclusive evidence. In view of the limited empirical evidence base predominantly focused on the use of compulsory licenses in low- to middle-income countries, most of these effects remain uncertain, open for speculation and highly dependent on the specific context (e.g. the country, the product, the companies involved, etc.). For most of the economic consequences, there is no consensus in the literature about the magnitude or even the direction of the consequences listed. Therefore, the economic impact of issuing a compulsory license must always be evaluated on a case-by-case basis. Moreover, compulsory licenses can be issued in a variety of forms and modalities each with different expected economic consequences. These modalities will affect the purported costs and benefits of the system. Finally, many of the "side-effects" of compulsory licenses can be mitigated through careful design.[87]

4.   CHALLENGES FOR EMPIRICAL RESEARCH ON PATENTING AND PATENT LICENSING PRACTICES

Even though this chapter may have revealed to you that a larger amount of empirical research related to patenting and patent licensing practices is available than you initially expected, I have also highlighted a number of challenges. First, not uncommon for research in the area of patent law, empirical research in this domain definitely involves significant scientific expertise related to the patented inventions concerned. This may not be uncommon in this domain, but in particular, the preparation of a patent landscape will require more than that and involves complex patent analytics and experience with working with advanced algorithms to provide sustainable and replicable research results.

Second, patent landscaping studies and systematic quantitative and qualitative studies regarding licensing practices will generally necessitate long-term funding and a stable funding base, which supports the investment in a highly-qualified interdisciplinary team. The more so, because the methods used often also involve the use of expert patent databases and survey research or interview results will likely only be published by high-level peer reviewed journals if a significant response-rate and sample of respondents or interviewees has been secured. In this respect, close collaboration with various organizations and their "moral" support will be helpful.

---

the government of Thailand granted a series of compulsory licenses to allow the import of generics equivalents of seven drugs that were patent protected and used in the treatment of HIV/AIDS (Efavirenz (marketed as Sustiva by Merck) and lopinavir/ritonavir (marketed as Kaletra by AbbVie, then Abbott Laboratories)).
[86]   EFM 't Hoen et al., 'Medicine procurement and the use of flexibilities in the Agreement on Trade-Related Aspects of Intellectual Property Rights, 2001–2016' (2018) 96 *Bulletin of the World Health Organization*, 185–193.
[87]   Van Zimmeren et al. (2022) – economic part of the report (see footnote 76).

Third, different from patent databases, no easy, systematic access to high-quality patent licensing data is currently available. Although one may be able to collect some information from court and competition law cases, it would be desirable to be able to compare licensing clauses across a wide variety of licensing agreements and a wide variety of actors to safeguard a nuanced understanding of the dynamics of patent licensing negotiations and contract drafting.

Fourth and more general for interdisciplinary research, the interdisciplinary team will likely face some challenges within the team to overcome differences and barriers and use of disciplinary jargon. Such challenges can relatively easily be overcome by following trainings offered by other faculties, working closely together on the various studies and by all being involved in the various stages of the paper drafting process. Nonetheless, identifying an appropriate journal to publish this type of interdisciplinary research may sometimes be daunting. In the life sciences, a number of high-impact peer-reviewed journals such as *Science*, *Nature Biotechnology* and *Trends in Biotechnology* has shown substantial interest in publishing this kind of empirical studies. For now, the geographical scope of these studies has mostly been limited to the US and Europe, sometimes including or referring to Australia, Canada, India, Brazil or South Africa for specific topics (e.g. compulsory licensing). It would be desirable to secure a more diverse geographical scope in future empirical studies.

5.   CONCLUDING REMARKS

For the design and evaluation of patent law and patent governance a good evidence-based understanding of patent landscapes and patent licensing practices is essential. Without such a good understanding, shifts in the case-law and modifications of patent legislation (i.e. limiting patent eligibility, raising the bar of patentability requirements, the introduction of new compulsory licensing mechanisms) and the introduction of responsible licensing policies and obligations may have unanticipated effects or may be unnecessary, inappropriate and/or ineffective in the long-term.

In the past, legal scholarship was traditionally heavily dominated by normative analyses of the law, i.e. by "black letter law" and involved "doctrinal analyses" aimed at better understanding the (in)coherence of the law or the "best" balance of rights and obligations within the framework defined by law often inspired by sources from moral, legal and political philosophy. This scholarship was building its analysis around normative questions of what ought to be. Whereas many legal scholars – although they have been criticized by colleagues from other disciplines for doing so – have not dropped this normative dimension, we see a shift towards an increased use of empirics next to the normative dimension. A "healthy" combination of more traditional doctrinal legal research with experimentation with various methods of empirical research seems to be a well-grounded, forward-looking research approach.

However, in order to do so in a systematic and ideally also longitudinal manner, the confidential nature of the license information is problematic. Moreover, conducting such studies requires an interdisciplinary team with extensive scientific expertise of the patented inventions, access to and experience with advanced patent analytics software, a stable funding base and human resources. In this respect, such studies rely on "moral support" from key national, European or international advisory bodies and policymakers combined with (substantial) research grants by public or private bodies (e.g. US SACGHS, WHO, WIPO, European Commission) and the collaboration with other organizations (e.g. LESI, AUTM, ASTP).

Although this chapter is not meant to be exhaustive, I tried to collect and describe studies that employ a wide variety of quantitative and qualitative empirical methods. Depending on the research question, different methods can be useful. Nonetheless, unfortunately the challenges raised here and in Section 4 will apply to most of those methods. One step, which would make it easier to conduct empirical research regarding licensing practices, would be if data on licensing practices would be more easily available. Therefore, I would like to recall the proposal of Contreras et al. mentioned in my introduction and launched in 2015, but which did not receive the required support. The Contreras et al.-proposal was focused on SEP/FRAND licensing data, but it does reflect a much wider, tenacious gap in the availability of patent licensing data.

Some public data may be available in certain countries,[88] but not necessarily in a wider group of countries, which would be desirable to enable effective comparative empirical analysis as well. Patent legislation in various jurisdictions requires patent offices to track changes of patent ownership. A recently published study by Gorbatyuk & Kovacs (2022) shows that although the patent offices they covered in their analysis (the EPO, the USPTO, the JPO, the INPI, the DPMA and the UKIPO) "impose strict requirements concerning the identification of initial patent applicants, they do not impose and/or enforce such strict requirements with respect to the disclosure of the identity of subsequent owners, following a change of ownership".[89] In the context of promoting open innovation, technology markets rely to a great extent on the effectiveness of the patent system's notice function, which has also been recognized by Zuniga & Guellec (2009).[90] Gorbatyuk & Kovacs make a balanced proposal to address the flaws of the current patent provisions concerning the disclosure of patent ownership information with a number of minimal requirements that future initiatives by patent offices should impose to warrant a more adequate, accurate and timely disclosure of patent ownership information. Other intellectual property scholars have gone beyond that and have called upon national patent offices, the EPO and WIPO to provide more support to the scientific community in collecting licensing data.[91] I fully support this ambitious call. However, although I am an optimistic person by nature, I am rather skeptical that this call will be realized anytime soon.

---

[88]   See for instance the sources mentioned in the Contreras et al. proposal with respect to the US (2015): (1) licensing agreements that have been disclosed in judicial proceedings, (2) agreements that are filed as exhibits to public company filings with the U.S. Securities and Exchange Commission (SEC), (3) licenses offered by patent pools, (4) licenses of government funded inventions, (5) licenses that have been recorded at the US Patent and Trademark Office (6) data from patent assertion entities collected by the U.S. Federal Trade Commission.

[89]   A Gorbatyuk & A Kovacs, 'Patent Notice (Failure) in the Era of Patent Monetization' (2022) 53 *IIC*, 506–542.

[90]   See footnote 53 above.

[91]   A recent example of such a call occurred by various economic and legal scholars at the EPIP2022 conference in Cambridge during a panel where many of these patent offices were represented. This initiative was loudly applauded by the audience present at the plenary session.

3. The Australian 'Valley of Death'? Australian research and patenting practices in bioprinting and genome editing

Jane Nielsen, Dianne Nicol and Cameron Stewart

1. INTRODUCTION

In the 1990s and early 2000s, much was written about the role of intellectual property (IP) (particularly patents) in facilitating and/or impeding innovation.[1] In the context of biomedicine, there were particular concerns that patents claiming rights to foundational technologies could slow the pace of innovation and negatively impact on access to healthcare.[2] A body of evidence (as well as a large number of anecdotes) emerged that lent support to these concerns.[3] There was other evidence, however, that was more equivocal.[4]

This evidence base could be a powerful driver for policy reform in the context of research, innovation and IP. However, one of the issues with this evidence base is that it comes almost entirely from the United States (US) and western Europe. Recognising that biomedical innovations have global reach, the innovation landscape is, nevertheless, highly susceptible to local conditions, including but not limited to researcher and research laboratory capacity, public and private support for innovation, and the regulatory and healthcare environments within which biomedicine is situated. Shaping domestic research, innovation and IP policy reform based on evidence from distant climes is unlikely to result in outcomes that best serve the local community. As such, it is vital that evidence-based policy reform is informed by a local evidence base.

Our earlier work has shown how influential a local evidence base can be in shaping policy reform. In 2002–03 we undertook a study of patenting and patent licensing in Australian medical biotechnology.[5] Coincidentally, the Australian Law Reform Commission (ALRC)

---

[1]   Some of the classic literature includes Robert P Merges and Richard R Nelson, 'On the complex economics of patent scope' *Columbia Law Review* 90, 839 (1990); Susan Scotchmer, 'Standing on the shoulders of giants: cumulative research and the patent law' *Journal of Economic Perspectives* 5, 29 (1991); Robert Mazzoleni and Richard R Nelson 'The benefits and costs of strong patent protection: a contribution to the current debate' *Research Policy* 27, 273 (1998).

[2]   Michael A Heller and Rebecca S Eisenberg, 'Can patents deter innovation? The anticommons in biomedical research' *Science* 280, 698 (1998).

[3]   Timothy Caulfield, Robert M Cook-Deegan, F Scott Keiff and John P Walsh, 'Evidence and anecdotes: an analysis of human gene patenting controversies' *Nature Biotechnology* 24, 1091 (2006).

[4]   John Walsh, Ashish Arora and Wesley Cohen, 'Effects of research tool patents and licensing on bio-medical innovations', in Wesley Cohen and Stephen Merrill (eds), *Patents in the Knowledge-Based Economy. National Research Council Committee on Intellectual Property Rights in the Knowledge Based Economy* (National Academies Press, 2003) 285.

[5]   Dianne Nicol and Jane Nielsen, *Patents and Medical Biotechnology: An Empirical Analysis of Issues Facing the Australian Industry* (Centre for Law and Genetics Occasional Paper No. 6, Hobart; 2003).

was given a reference to examine the impact of patents on human health in 2003. The final report from the ALRC inquiry cited our work extensively.[6] The subsequent introduction of an experimental use exception in Australian patent law also cited our work in the Explanatory Memorandum.[7] Yet our study remains one of the few examples of local analysis of the impact of patents and patent licensing in biomedicine outside of the major blocs of the US and western Europe.

Innovation in biomedicine continues at a rapid pace. For instance, techniques such as genome editing and bioprinting are rapidly becoming de rigueur in biomedical research laboratories globally. Indeed, it is difficult to imagine a laboratory without a bioprinter on the bench, or a genome editing specialist on the team. These techniques are slowly being adopted in the clinical environment as well, but only after safety concerns have been addressed, regulatory hurdles have been satisfied and funding is secured. It is a long road to product development. The emergence of these and other technological innovations has been accompanied by much hype about the promise they may offer in alleviating suffering caused by disease, but also by a slew of patents and other commercial interests.

Admittedly, there has been some tinkering with patent law and research and innovation policy in the intervening period since questions were first being asked about the role of patents in biomedical innovation. One notable example is judicial recognition in Australia and the US that naturally occurring DNA, even when isolated, does not constitute patentable subject matter.[8] However, there remains much that still needs to be debated in the policy context, with each new technological innovation creating its own particular set of issues. As such, there remains an ongoing need for evidence of the impact of patents and patent licensing, and a need for local evidence to help drive local policy reform.

The study reported in this chapter examines the research, patent and innovation landscape for bioprinting and genome editing in Australia. It uses mixed methods, including both patent mapping and qualitative interviews. The chapter starts with some context setting, broadly describing key features of Australian research and innovation, and core aspects of the debate about the impact of patents and patent licensing on biomedicine. The global innovation and patent landscapes for bioprinting and genome editing are also briefly described. The chapter then turns to the empirical study itself, reporting on methodology, results and potential policy outcomes. Our aim is to draw this evidence together to assess whether levels of patenting in the areas of bioprinting and genome editing accord with international trends for each of these technologies, and Australian trends in other biomedical fields. We then attempt to evaluate whether patents in these areas are positively or negatively impacting on Australian research and downstream innovation.

---

[6]   Australian Law Reform Commission (ALRC), *Genes and Ingenuity: Gene Patenting and Human Health*, Report No 99 (2004).

[7]   Explanatory Memorandum, Intellectual Property Laws Amendment (Raising the Bar) Bill 2011.

[8]   *Association for Molecular Pathology v Myriad Genetics, Inc.*, 569 U.S. 576 (2013); *D'Arcy v Myriad Genetics, Inc* [2015] HCA 35.

2.   THE AUSTRALIAN CONTEXT

Australia has always boasted a robust fundamental research base, accounting for 3.8% of the world's medical research publications, a figure that exceeds expectations given Australian research expenditure comprises 1.1% of global figures.[9] Australia has a long history of bio-medical research in its publicly funded institutions. Most of the patents granted by IP Australia (the body that administers the Australian patents system) are in the fields of biomedical sciences and pharmaceuticals.[10] Expenditure on Australian government-conducted research totalled $3,618 million during the 2020–21 financial year, while funding on private non-profit organisations totalled $1,399 million. Business expenditure totalled $18,171 million during the 2019–20 financial year.[11] The greatest proportion of the public spend ($614 million) was on health research, while private health research expenditure accounted for $1,664 million of total business R&D expenditure.[12] Health research represents the highest proportion of public R&D funding.[13]

With such significant investment in health research, substantial returns on research might be expected. However, there are many impediments to research translation in Australia (and elsewhere)[14] particularly in the biomedical sphere.[15] These obstacles have been widely acknowledged.[16] Improvement of poor translational and commercial outcomes has been identified as a priority strategy.[17] Persistent themes are an Australian patent system that grants patents too readily,[18] coupled with a preponderance of ownership of Australian patents by non-Australian inventors. While the number of Australian companies patenting in the medical and pharmaceutical sectors is climbing,[19] domestic ownership of Australian patents is still

---

[9]   Access Economics, *Exceptional Returns: The Value of Investing in Health R&D in Australia II*, Australian Society for Medical Research, Canberra (2008).

[10]   IP Australia Report, 2022 https://www.ipaustralia.gov.au/ip-report-2022.

[11]   Australian Bureau of Statistics, *Technology and Innovation* https://www.abs.gov.au/statistics/industry/technology-and-innovation.

[12]   Ibid.

[13]   Ibid.

[14]   Zoe Slote Morris, Steven Wooding and Jonathon Grant, 'The answer is 17 years, what is the question: understanding time lags in translational research' *J R Soc Med* 104, 510 (2011) doi 10.1258/jrsm.2011.110180; Malcolm R Macleod, Susan Michie, Ian Roberts, Ulrich Dirnagl, Iain Chalmers, John P A Ionnidis, Rustam Al-Shahi Salman, An-Wen Chan, and Paul Glasziou, 'Biomedical research: increasing value, reducing waste' *Lancet* 383(9912), 101–104 (2014); Pmid:24411643.

[15]   Tracy Robinson, Helen Skouteris, Prue Burns, Angela Melder, Cate Bailey, Charlotte Croft, Dmitrios Spyridonidis and Helena Teede, 'Flipping the paradigm: a qualitative exploration of research translation centres in the United Kingdom and Australia' *Health Research Policy and Systems* 18, 111 (2020) https://doi.org/10.1186/s12961-020-00622-9.

[16]   Australian Government, *Australian Medical Research and Innovation Strategy 2016–2021* (2016); Australian Government, Department of Education, Department of Industry (2014) *Boosting the commercial returns from research*.

[17]   MTP Connect, *Medical Technology, Biotechnology and Pharmaceutical Sector Competitiveness Plan* (Department of Industry, Science, Energy and Resources, 2022) ('MTP Connect'), 28, 31; CSIRO Futures, *Medical Technologies and Pharmaceuticals: A Roadmap for unlocking future growth opportunities for Australia* (2017), 10, 76.

[18]   See, eg, Productivity Commission (2016) *Intellectual Property Arrangements, Inquiry Report No 78* (Commonwealth of Australia, Canberra).

[19]   MTP Connect, above n17, 11, 16.

outstripped by foreign ownership. Australia's ranking in global innovation indices indicates strong performance in terms of innovation inputs, offset by less impressive performance in terms of knowledge and technology outputs (particularly patent filings).[20] Recent comments by the newly sworn-in Commonwealth Minister for Industry and Science recognised this fact and stressed a focus of Australia's new government was to finally ensure Australian researchers were 'makers' and not 'takers'.[21]

The fastest growing technology fields over the 2020 period in terms of international patent filings were medical technology, pharmaceuticals and biotechnology.[22] Data from IP Australia, Australia's patent office, indicates that the four leading technology classes in Australia (in terms of absolute patent numbers) all relate to the biomedical sciences,[23] and each of these areas has experienced significant growth over the previous 12-month period (most notably Pharmaceuticals with a growth rate of 27%).[24] There has been a concomitant exponential increase in foreign-owned patents in these growth areas.[25] These figures on Australian patent ownership in these technology areas are broadly consistent with patenting trends worldwide.

3.   PATENTS AND FREEDOM TO OPERATE

Patents that include broad claims to core aspects of bioprinting and genome editing technologies could facilitate innovation and development of new healthcare products by encouraging financial and other investment in product development. However, they could also compromise follow on innovation if they create impediments to research and product development. This could occur if patentees refuse to grant licences allowing others to use their patented technology, or if they impose onerous licence conditions. Effectively such actions could block off whole areas of research and product development.[26]

Even with less exclusive licensing practices, impediments to innovation could also arise if the patent landscape is so complex that it would be impossible to license in all necessary technology to secure freedom to operate (FTO), or, even if it were possible, cumulative licensing obligations make it highly unattractive. A so-called 'anticommons' could be the inevitable consequence.[27] Stacking of royalty obligations is a particular problem if each licence carries with it an obligation to share a percentage of profits made on downstream product sales. Such eventualities could have social as well as economic consequences, because they could deter research and delay public access to new healthcare developments. As such, licensing to secure

---

[20]   Soumitra Dutta, Bruno Lanvin, Lorena Rivera Leon and Sacha Wunsch-Vincent (eds), *Global Innovation Index, 2021: Tracking Innovation through the COVID-19 Crisis* (WIPO, 2021: 14th ed) ('WIPO Global Innovation Index 2021') Table 5, 30, 47.

[21]   https://www.minister.industry.gov.au/ministers/husic/speeches/address-science-and-technology -australia-gala-dinner.

[22]   WIPO Global Innovation Index 2021, above n20, 15.

[23]   IP Australia, *2022 Australian Intellectual Property Report*, Chapter 2: Patents. These technology classes are, in descending order, Pharmaceuticals, Medical technology, Biotechnology, Organic fine chemistry and Computer technologies.

[24]   Pharmaceuticals: 27%; Medical technology: 6%; Biotechnology: 9%; Organic fine chemistry: 1%.

[25]   IP Australia, above n23, 9.

[26]   Walsh et al, above n4, 332–335.

[27]   Heller and Eisenberg, above n2.

FTO presents an acute challenge for biomedicine both in Australia and globally. Ways in which any negative impacts might be addressed have vexed Australian policymakers.

Our previous research suggests that, despite ongoing concerns about the impact of patents claiming biomedical technologies on research and development, ways are being found to work around these impediments in Australia.[28] Our study reported liberal licensing of some key patented upstream technologies within the Australian biomedicine sector. However, the study concluded that increasing complexity of the patent landscape will inevitably create difficulties for Australian biomedicine in the future. Our study identified the following challenges: onerous and expensive searching obligations, negotiating difficulties, restrictive licence terms, refusals to license and stacking of royalties. Similar research in other countries suggests that market solutions are also being found to work around these impediments, including licensing, inventing around, ignoring 'bad' patents and challenging validity.[29]

From the patentee perspective, maintaining and enforcing strong patent rights continues to be seen as crucial for attracting downstream licensing partners and for securing venture capital, public equity and other sources of funding.[30] Nevertheless, finding partners and negotiating suitable licensing arrangements for such patents is equally as costly and time consuming for the patentee and licensor as it is for their licensee. There may also be inequality of bargaining power, particularly where public sector organisations or small upstream biotechnology companies have to deal with large pharmaceutical companies. In addition, enforcement of patents claiming biomedical research tools is particularly difficult because use generally occurs in secret behind laboratory doors.

On the one hand, then, without patents, there is a risk that important biomedical innovations may never reach the marketplace. But on the other hand, it seems that patents claiming rights over biomedical technologies have the capacity to create impediments in the development of new healthcare products instead of facilitating their development. There is a risk that the complexity of the patent landscape and the difficulties involved in negotiating patent licences will create holdups both for upstream innovators in disseminating their new technological developments and for downstream innovators in securing FTO. These issues are explored below in the particular contexts of bioprinting and genome editing. The rationales for selecting these technologies are also explored below.

4.   A BRIEF OVERVIEW OF THE RESEARCH AND PATENT LANDSCAPES IN BIOPRINTING AND GENOME EDITING

4.1   Bioprinting

From the development of the first bioprinter in the early 2000s, researchers have been progressively pushing the bounds of tissue engineering using 3D printing technologies. Bioprinting involves the production of human tissue using various 3D printing techniques, through the process of printing bioinks: a medium containing human cells (usually stem cells) and bio-

---

[28]   Nicol and Nielsen, above n5, particularly at 251–256.
[29]   See particularly on the US perspective: Walsh et al, above n4.
[30]   Dianne Nicol, *Patent Licensing in Medical Biotechnology in Australia: A Role for Collaborative Licensing Strategies* (Centre for Law and Genetics Occasional Paper No. 7, Hobart, 2010) 63.

compatible materials (hydrogels to support the cells and growth factors). Because the growth of tissue can be controlled to accurately conform with 3D scans of patients and to produce internal architectures that accurately simulate native tissue structures,[31] it has the potential to transform tissue engineering for the purposes of transplantation, drug screening and disease diagnosis.[32] The technology has been broadly defined as:[33]

> ...the automated generation of biologically functional products with structural organization from living cells, bioactive molecules, biomaterials, cell aggregates such as micro-tissues, or hybrid cell-material constructs, through bioprinting or bioassembly and subsequent tissue maturation processes.

Like much research in biomedicine, a significant amount of bioprinting innovation initially emerged from publicly funded institutions, with institutional researchers active in building bioprinting machines, and in developing bioinks[34] and generating application-driven bio-printed products and processes.[35] A number of leading private bioprinting companies (for example, Organovo) emerged from public laboratories.

A recent review aimed at assessing concentration of bioprinting research activity shows that Australia ranks ninth globally in terms of scholarly output and author affiliations, with Australia's leading publications focusing primarily on biofabrication of tissue and organs.[36] Just two Australian-based authors, both based at the University of Wollongong, are comprised in the list of leading authors. The University of Wollongong is the leading (and most established) Australian public institution in biofabrication,[37] although a number of other Australian institutions are also involved in bioprinting research, some of which were identified in the Santoni review (St Vincent's Hospital, University of Melbourne and Queensland University of Technology).[38]

Significant public funding, both federal and state, has been dedicated to Australian research and development of bioprinting technologies and products with practical application. Relative

---

[31]   Patrick Thayer, Hector Martinez and Erik Gatenholm, 'History and trends of 3D bioprinting' in Jeremy M Crook (ed), *3D Bioprinting: Principles and Protocols, Methods in Molecular Biology*, vol 2140 https://doi.org/10.1007/978-1-0716-0520-2_1 (Springer Science+Business Media LLC, 2020) 3, 7.

[32]   IA Otto, CC Breugen, J Malds and AL Bredenoord, 'Ethical considerations in the translation of regenerative biofabrication technologies into clinic and society' *Biofabrication* 8, 042110 (2016); Anthony Atala and Gabor Forgacs, 'Three-dimensional bioprinting in regenerative medicine: reality, hype and future' *Stem Cells Transl Medicine* 8(8), 744–745 (2019).

[33]   Jürgen Groll, Thomas Boland and Torsten Blunk et al, 'Biofabrication: reappraising the definition of an evolving field' *Biofabrication* 8(1), 013001 (2016).

[34]   Patrick Thayer, Hector Martinez and Erik Gatenholm, 'History and trends of 3D bioprinting' in Jeremy M Crook (ed), *3D Bioprinting: Principles and Protocols, Methods in Molecular Biology*, vol 2140 https://doi.org/10.1007/978-1-0716-0520-2_1 (Springer Science+Business Media LLC, 2020) 3, 4–5.

[35]   Silvia Santoni, Simone G Gugliandolo, Mattia Sponchioni, Davide Moscatelli and Bianca M Colosimo, '3D bioprinting: current status and trends – a guide to the literature and industrial practice' *Bio-Design and Manufacturing* 5, 14–42, 19 (2022).

[36]   Ibid, 23–25.

[37]   See Australian Centre of Excellence for Electromaterials Science (ACES), https://electromaterials .edu.au/about/ (visited 27 June 2022). ACES received funding as an Australian Research Council Centre of Excellence from 2005 to 2020, and was founded by Professor Gordon Wallace, a world-renowned expert in materials science.

[38]   Santoni et al, above n35, Supplementary file S2.

to the world-leading countries (in terms of research affiliations), the Australian contingent comprises few institutions. Worldwide, bioprinting research outputs are certainly concentrated among a number of leading institutions, although there are a far greater number of these institutions (and affiliated authors) in the US, China, South Korea, Germany, the United Kingdom, Singapore and Canada.[39] Australia is a small but important player in the international bioprinting research landscape, with a vast majority of Australia's bioprinting innovation emerging from public research institutions and hospitals.[40]

There is also an increasingly strong private presence in global bioprinting research. Interestingly, Santoni et al found a majority of bioprinting companies to be involved in the manufacture of bioprinters and bioinks, with some 63% of companies involved in the bioprinting market producing printers and/or bioinks. The remainder were generally involved in producing bioprinting services (37%)[41] or research partnerships and product development (1%). It is likely that these figures under-represent the growing number of start-ups and spin-offs that are emerging in response to a flourishing university research culture in bioprinting. Again, Australian companies account for a relatively low percentage (1%) of bioprinting companies worldwide as identified by Santoni et al,[42] a figure commensurate with Australia's global academic bioprinting profile.

The question is how much of the bioprinting innovation being generated is protected through patents. Santoni et al found that using Espacenet, most new bioprinting patents now being sought relate to bioinks and specific applications, including bioprinting methods for particular functions.[43] Approximately two thirds of these patents were being sought by academic institutions and/or unaffiliated scientists.[44] The rate of patent grants overall is increasing exponentially.[45] The data presented by Santoni et al suggests that internationally, Australian researchers based in public institutions are involved in some patenting activity, albeit on a relatively limited basis.[46] There is no jurisdictional breakdown presented in their analysis. The data presented in this chapter fills that gap in terms of Australian patentability, recognising that not all patentees applying for patents in the US and Europe will patent in Australia given that Australia is not a major market for many inventors. It has traditionally been common practice, however, for Australian inventors to file in Australia in order to ensure FTO and provide capacity to commercialise in Australia.[47]

4.2 Genome Editing

Like bioprinting, genome editing is one of the most significant recent developments in bioscience. It has broad applications, including in agriculture, for such things as modifying the ways that plants and animals adapt to disease and to changes in the climate. It also has diverse applications in humans, including to prevent or alleviate the symptoms of certain diseases and

---

[39] Ibid, 22–26.
[40] https://3dprint.com/291649/inventia-snags-3-2m-in-new-funding-to-commercialize-bioprinter/.
[41] Defined to include CAD modelling, tissue or cell constructs, scaffolds, grafts or consulting.
[42] Santoni et al, above n35, Figure 8b, 29.
[43] Ibid, 31.
[44] Ibid, 31.
[45] Ibid, 31–32.
[46] Ibid, 33.
[47] Nicol and Nielsen, above n5, 80.

for diagnostic purposes.[48] There is much discussion about the promise of genome editing to treat diseases that are not currently treatable.[49]

Techniques have existed for almost 50 years that allow the introduction of foreign DNA into living cells. In plants and animals, for example, genetically modified organisms have been created with different characteristics from those existing in nature, both to repair naturally occurring defects and to introduce new (enhanced) traits. In humans, the term "gene therapy" is generally used instead of "genetic modification". Gene therapies that can be inherited by future generations are not currently regarded as safe or ethically acceptable in humans.[50] To date, only three gene therapies have been approved for non-heritable use in Australia. These are Kymriah, for treatment of a type of leukemia, Luxturna, for treatment of retinal dystrophy, and Zolgensma, for treatment of spinal muscular atrophy.[51] More recently, various new techniques have emerged with names like CRISPR, TALENS, Zinc Fingers, prime and base editing.[52] These new technologies offer significant advances over earlier gene therapy techniques. The technique known as CRISPR is particularly notable.[53] It involves making very precise cuts to the two strands of DNA within the nucleus of a cell, which are then either allowed to heal naturally or are guided in the healing process.[54]

To date, no form of human genome editing has been approved for use in medical care in Australia, or globally for that matter. A number of genome editing clinical trials are, however, currently under way, including in Australia.[55] Many of these clinical trials are for hereditary diseases and cancers.[56] One of the features of these clinical trials is that they involve ex vivo application of the genome editing construct to cells removed from the body and then reinserted back into the body.[57] In vivo applications, in contrast, require delivery of the genome editing construct into the human body using viral or other delivery systems. Fewer clinical trials have commenced for in vivo applications of genome editing, given the additional safety considera-

---

[48]   Hongyi Li, Yang Yang, Weiqi Hong, Mengyuan Huang, Min Wu and Xia Zhao, 'Applications of genome editing technology in the targeted therapy of human diseases: mechanisms, advances and prospects' *Signal Transduction and Targeted Therapy* 5, 1 (2020).
[49]   David B Turitz Cox, Randall J Pratt and Feng Zhang, 'Therapeutic genome editing: prospects and challenges' *Nature Medicine* 21, 121 (2015); Morgan M Maeder and Charles A Gersbach, 'Genome-editing technologies for gene and cell therapy' *Molecular Therapy* 24, 430 (2016); Matthew Porteus, 'Genome editing: a new approach to human therapeutics' *Annual Review of Pharmacology and Toxicology* 56, 168 (2016).
[50]   Patrick D Hsu, Eric S Lander and Feng Zhang, 'Development and applications of CRISPR-Cas9 for genome engineering' *Cell* 157, 1262 (2014).
[51]   Samantha L Ginn, Anais K Amaya, Ian E Alexander, et al., 'Gene therapy clinical trials worldwide to 2017: an update' *Journal of Gene Medicine* 35, e3015 (2018); Jane Nielsen, Lisa Eckstein, Dianne Nicol and Cameron Stewart, 'Integrating public participation, transparency and accountability into governance of marketing authorisation for genome editing products' *Frontiers of Political Science* 3, Article 747838 (2021), doi: 10.3389/fpos.2021.747838.
[52]   Li et al, above n48, 1–2.
[53]   Jennifer Doudna and Emmanuelle Charpentier, 'Genome editing: the new frontier of genome engineering with CRISPR-Cas9' *Science* 46, 1077 (2014); Hsu et al, above n50.
[54]   Michael R Lieber, 'The mechanism of double-strand DNA break repair by the nonhomologous DNA end joining pathway' *Annual Review of Biochemistry* 79, 181 (2010).
[55]   Lisa Eckstein and Dianne Nicol, 'Gene editing clinical trials could slip through Australian regulatory cracks' *Journal of Law and Medicine* 27, 274 (2001).
[56]   Li et al, above n48.
[57]   Ibid, Table 2.

tions involved in delivery of constructs directly into the human body. Most progress has been made in the in vivo treatment of eye disease,[58] which has the advantage that the eye is closed off from the rest of the body. Aside from therapeutic interventions, genome editing techniques also hold promise medically in the diagnosis and treatment of viral infections.[59] CRISPR has also been described as an 'indispensable tool in biological research'.[60]

Although the translation of genome editing techniques into the clinic may be in its infancy, there has been significant interest in the adoption of these techniques in research laboratories and in the commercial sector. For example, Jefferson et al estimate that since 2012, there have been more than 25,000 scholarly works published, and over 20,000 patents filed globally on one particular form of CRISPR, known as CRISPR-Cas9 (noting that their analysis covers all applications of this technology, including in agriculture as well as medicine).[61]

Jefferson et al acknowledge that the fact that the majority of filed patents are still in the application phase and that most filings are recent shows that the development of the technology is still in an early stage.[62] The fact that the most common category of patents is for technical improvements further illustrates this point.[63] Indeed, Martin-Lafon et al describe the CRISPR field as 'a technology field still in the quest of technology improvements'.[64] Despite its infancy, the CRISPR commercial landscape is already highly competitive, as illustrated by the fierce contest over patent rights to the core technology,[65] together with the sheer number of patent licences that have been publicly disclosed.[66] It should be noted that these disclosed patent licensing arrangements are likely only the tip of the iceberg, with many others remaining confidential. These activities are themselves leading to a burgeoning collection of scholarly works addressing IP and technology transfer issues in genome editing.[67]

---

[58]   Ibid, 15.
[59]   See, for example, Uyanga Ganbaatar and Changchun Liu, 'CRISPR-based COVID-19 testing: toward next-generation point-of-care diagnostics' *Frontiers in Cellular and Infection Microbiology* 11, Article 663949 (2021), doi: 10.3389/fcimb.2021.663949.
[60]   Mazhar Adli, 'The CRISPR tool kit for genome editing and beyond' *Nature Communications* 9, 1911 (2018), 1911.
[61]   Osmat Azzam Jefferson, Simon Lang, Kenny Williams, et al, 'Mapping CRISPR-Cas9 public and commercial innovation using The Lens institutional toolkit' *Transgenic Research* 30, 585 (2021), 586. See also Knut J Egelie, Gregory D Graff, Sabina P Strand and Berit Johansen, 'The emerging patent landscape of CRISPR–Cas gene editing technology' *Nature Biotechnology* 34, 1025 (2016); Katelyn Brinegar, Ali K Yetisen, Sun Choi, et al, 'The commercialization of genome-editing technologies' *Critical Reviews in Biotechnology* (2017) doi.org/10.1080/07388551.2016.1271768; Raphael Ferreira, Florian David and Jens Nielsen, 'Advancing biotechnology with CRISPR/Cas9: recent applications and patent landscape' *Journal of Industrial Microbiology & Biotechnology* 45, 467 (2018); Jacqueline Martin-Lafon, Marcel Kuntz and Agnès E Ricroch, 'Worldwide CRISPR patent landscape shows strong geographical biases' *Nature Biotechnology* 37, 613 (2019), noting each of these studies undertakes slightly different patent landscaping inquiries.
[62]   Jefferson et al, above n61, 590.
[63]   Ibid, 595.
[64]   Martin-Lafon et al, above n61, 615.
[65]   Jacob S Sherkow, 'Inventive steps: the CRISPR patent dispute and scientific progress' *EMBO Reports* 18, 1047 (2017); Jacob S Sherkow, 'Immaculate conception? Priority and invention in the CRISPR patent dispute' *CRISPR Journal* (2022) doi.org/10.1089/crispr.2022.0033.
[66]   Jefferson et al, above n61, 587.
[67]   Ibid, 588. See also Edison Bicudo, Michael Morrison, Phoebe Li, et al, 'Patent power in biomedical innovation: technology governance in biomodifying technologies' *Journal of World Intellectual*

As might be expected for any country investing in genomics research, Australian research-ers have adopted genome editing as part of their toolbox, and are contributing to the scholarly literature on this topic. Jefferson et al's global analysis puts Australia as the tenth most prolific country when it comes to scholarly works relating to CRISPR-Cas9.[68] They also list Australia as one of the top countries where patents are published.[69] However, it is clear from the work of Jefferson et al, Martin-Lafon et al, Brinegar et al and others that filings for CRISPR-related patents in the US and China far outnumber those in other countries and the vast majority of applicants also reside in those two countries.[70]

Brinegar et al point out one notable feature of the CRISPR patent landscape: unlike other forms of genome editing, the majority of CRISPR patents were filed by academic institutions.[71] This feature, together with the emergence of genome editing spin-out companies, is described by Brinegar et al as 'a shift in entrepreneurship strategies that were previously led by the indus-try'.[72] Whilst academic-led innovation of this nature might provide the opportunity to embrace more ethical approaches to patent licensing,[73] it also carries the risk that universities may act as surrogates for commercial entities.[74]

The fact that the most significant patent dispute that is currently on foot is between academic institutions[75] illustrates the highly competitive nature of this movement towards academic-led innovation. Some CRISPR tools and associated patents are being freely shared for academic purposes through intermediaries like Addgene.[76] Yet because subsequent commercial use requires renegotiation of licence terms, any research group with an eye to commercialising their research needs to have a FTO strategy in mind. If their negotiations are with commercial entities or their surrogates, they are likely to be faced with more aggressive and exclusive tactics than they would with academic institutions.[77]

5.   PATENT GRANTS IN THE AREAS OF BIOPRINTING AND GENOME EDITING IN AUSTRALIA

One broad aim of this study was to examine the patent landscape in Australia. As such, the search strategy involved searching IP Australia's database, AusPat. A similar strategy for searching was undertaken in relation to bioprinting and genome editing.

Property 1 (2022) 1, noting that they examine patenting and patent enforcement strategies in genome editing, bioprinting and stem cell technologies.

[68]   Jefferson et al, above n61, 589.
[69]   Ibid, 593.
[70]   Ibid; Martin-Lafon et al, above n61; Brinegar et al, above n61.
[71]   Brinegar et al, above n61, 1.
[72]   Ibid, 1.
[73]   Christi Guerrini, Margaret A Vurnutte, Jacob S Sherkow and Christopher T Scott, 'The rise of the ethical license' *Nature Biotechnology*, 35, 22 (2017).
[74]   Jorge L Contreras and Jacob S Sherkow, 'CRISPR, surrogate licensing, and scientific discovery: have research universities abandoned their public focus?' *Science* 355, 698 (2017).
[75]   Sherkow (2017), above n65; Sherkow (2022), above n65.
[76]   Jane Nielsen, Tania Bubela, Don Chalmers, et al, 'Provenance and risk in transfer of biological materials' *PLOS Biology* (2018), doi.org/10.1371/journal.pbio.2006031.
[77]   Bicudo et al, above n67.

5.1   Methodology: Bioprinting and Genome Editing Patent Landscaping

Comprehensive analyses of the bioprinting and genome editing patent landscapes in Australia were undertaken using search terms derived from examining published journal articles, existing patent landscapes and iterative consideration of patent documents (particularly claims and abstracts). Keyword strings of the relevant search terms were entered together with operators 'AND/OR' and where necessary, wildcard '*' into the AusPat search query box. Root words were marked with an asterisk to allow for all potential suffixes to be discerned within the search query.

Accepted, ceased, lapsed, filed and granted patents were searched with no time limit on application date to maximise the likelihood of ensuring a comprehensive search. The search period ended in January 2022.

Bioprinting and genome editing are relatively 'young' technologies, and so the resulting number of applications to manually consider was manageable. Searches involving the search terms elucidated returned approximately 2,872 patent documents. However, most of the search results comprised duplicates or obviously non-bioprinting related documents which were able to be discounted from analysis. This search process was repeated iteratively until the search returned a set of results that could be stated with confidence to comprise all relevant patents[78] in Australia at that point in time. The title, abstract, claims and specification of the data set were screened to establish relevance of patent documents for inclusion into the final data set for analysis.

Primary filter criteria for bioprinting were bioprinter types; compositions and types of bioprinting matrices/materials; cell and/or tissue culture and/or engineering; methods of manufacturing tissue models for disease treatment, drug screening and/or research purposes; and methods for fabricating tissue for regenerative medicine or for making implants. Cross-deduplication in the form of further manual review was then conducted to determine if remaining patent applications were sufficiently on-topic. Applications which made no reference to bioprinting, additive manufacturing or cell/organ printing or simply mentioned a tentative application of bioprinting in the embodiment section were omitted from the final data set. The data set was narrowed down to 172 patents for detailed analysis.

For genome editing, our searches focused on CRISPR patent applications on the basis that we surmised that CRISPR is currently the dominant genome editing technique used in Australia. Many of the patent claims analysed did not include specific mention of potential applications of CRISPR-based gene-editing tools or methods, whether in humans, plants or animals. At the same time, some applications/patents referred to potential applications of CRISPR in transgenic non-human multicellular organisms alongside humans. The primary filter criteria were therefore CRISPR-based gene-editing methods; tools; and components/compositions in humans. Applications strictly limited to agriculture or to animals were excluded from analysis. Patent documents with vague applications were included as part of the landscape given their potential application in humans. A total of 1,072 applications were identified and reduced to 314 after the elimination of duplicates and off-topic applications, and a final search was conducted to ensure that relevant applications/patents had not been overlooked.

---

[78]   Rodríguez-Salvador, Rio-Belver and Garechana-Anacabe, 'Scientometric and patentometric analyses to determine the knowledge landscape in innovative technologies: the case of 3D bioprinting' *PLoS one* 12(6), 1, 4 (2017), https://journals.plos.org/plosone/article?id=10.1371/journal.pone.0180375.

Although the search terms chosen to conduct this patent landscape exercise were common denominators of most bioprinting and genome editing literature and patent documents, it is possible that the final data set in this analysis is not an exhaustive list of all patent applications filed in Australia given that in some cases, there may not have been any indication of claims to these technologies in the title, abstract and claims. However, given the trends and breadth of results observed in the data set, we are confident that the data set examined is generally representative of the bioprinting and genome editing fields in Australia.

5.2   Results: Bioprinting and Genome Editing Patent Landscaping

The results of our patent landscaping showed marked divergence between technologies in terms of local patent activity. Patent numbers for these two technology areas paint an interesting picture in that patent numbers generally are higher for genome editing despite the fact that genome editing products are further from market than bioprinting products (see Figure 3.1).

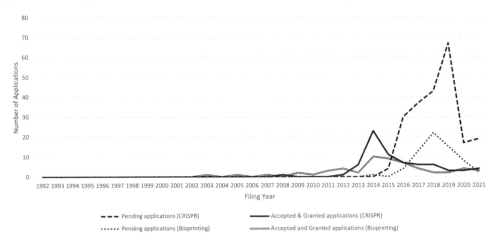

Figure 3.1   *Trends in Australian patent application status across CRISPR and bioprinting fields*

Another important variable examined was the geographical origin of applicants. As expected given the general trends of patent filings with intellectual property Australia, a common trend across these two technology areas is that overseas applicants are the primary patentees in each area. One marked difference between the technology areas, however, is that while Australian patentees sit in tenth position for patentees in the bioprinting area, there were no Australian patent applicants, at the time our searches were conducted, in relation to CRISPR technology (see Table 3.1).

Breaking these figures down into technology areas, it is evident that the nature of technologies being patented have expanded over time. Early patents in bioprinting focused primarily on bioprinters and materials, and on more fundamental tissue engineering research. This patent environment has expanded to include claims over clinical applications, claims over bioprinting methods, and greater development of tissue models for research and diagnostic purposes (see Figure 3.2).

Table 3.1   Geographical affiliation of Australian patent applicants in the bioprinting and CRISPR technology areas

Countries of Origin	Number of Applications	
	CRISPR	Bioprinting
USA	215 (68.47%)	88 (51.16%)
Switzerland	23 (7.32%)	8 (4.65%)
China	12 (3.82)	7 (4.07%)
Korea	6 (1.91%)	4 (2.33%)
Denmark	5 (1.59%)	0
Germany	5 (1.59%)	4 (2.33%)
UK	5 (1.59%)	5 (2.91%)
Australia	0	21 (12.21%)
Canada	0	11 (6.40%)

Similarly, in genome editing, patenting of CRISPR applications has increased as the technology has evolved, and we are now seeing more applied research in the CRISPR landscape leading to patents over CRISPR applications. Nevertheless, general CRISPR applications and technical improvements remain the dominant class of patent filings. This is pretty much as expected, given the findings from other patent landscaping analyses discussed earlier in this chapter (see Figure 3.3).

Finally, affiliations of patent applicants were noted. Universities, research institutes and teaching hospitals have applied for a significant proportion of patents in the bioprinting field. This no doubt represents the strong academic research baseline in additive manufacturing and materials science both in Australia, and internationally. US applicants form the greatest percentage of applicants from publicly funded institutions.

The strong presence of publicly funded institutions was exceeded, however, by patent applications filed by for-profit companies. Not surprisingly, an increasing number of private entities are entering the bioprinting ecosystem as years of basic research begins to reap dividends. Again, US companies feature heavily in this number, followed, encouragingly, by Australian and Canadian companies. Somewhat surprisingly, a limited number of patent applications have been filed by university spin-off companies, or by public-private partnerships. This tends to indicate that universities are very reliant in assigning patents to private companies to commercialise, and that very few spin-off companies are emerging from the public system to translate research. There also appear to be relatively few public-private collaborations that are resulting in patent applications (see Figure 3.4).

The CRISPR patent landscape looks considerably different. A disproportionate number of patents have been applied for by public entities, particularly US institutions. Predictably, a significant number of these CRISPR patent applications have been filed by Harvard University and MIT. Outside these patents, however, most patent applications have been filed by for-profit companies, again, many of which are located in the US. Swiss company CRISPR Therapeutics AG features heavily in this number. This marks a change from earlier patent landscape analyses, which tended to show an overwhelming preponderance of academic patenting. However, the recent study by Bicudo et al aligns with our findings, also showing a shift to the for-profit sector.[79]

---

[79]   Bicudo et al, above n67.

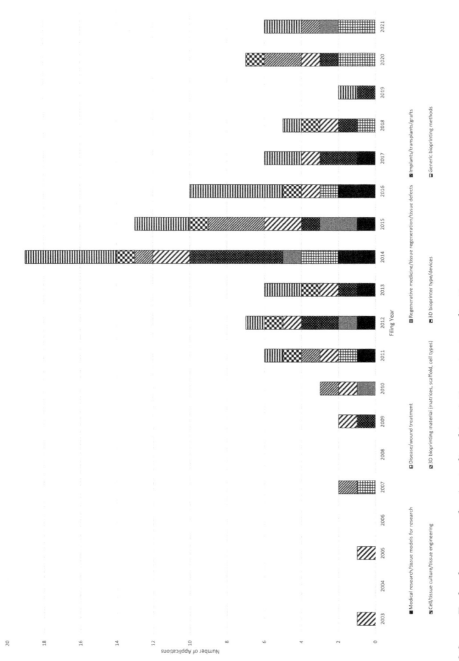

Figure 3.2   Technology areas for Australian bioprinting patent applications

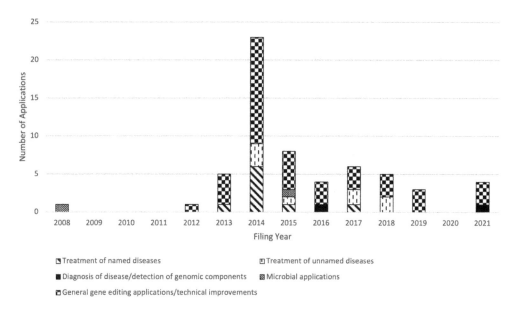

Figure 3.3   Technology areas for Australian CRISPR patent applications

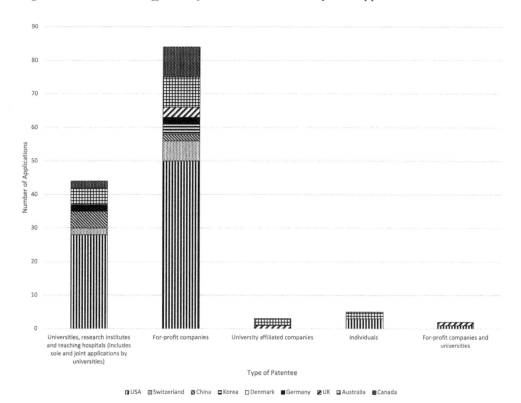

Figure 3.4   Institutional affiliations of Australian patent applicants in bioprinting

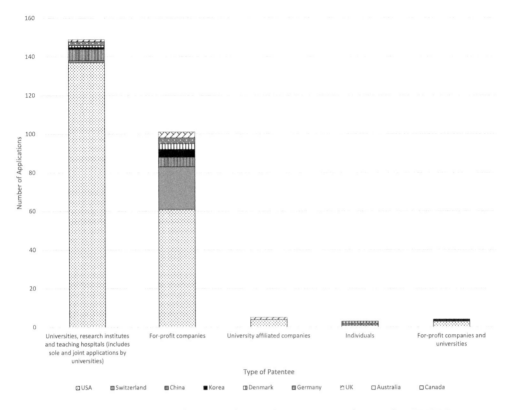

Figure 3.5   Institutional affiliations of Australian patent applicants for CRISPR

Similar to bioprinting, there is a decided lack of patent activity through public-private collaborations in respect of CRISPR technology. This is likely to be because the leading public
institutions are 'going it alone', and have been uncompromising in filing for patents and in litigating to establish the validity of those patents. There seems little appetite for private-industry
linkages in terms of the foundational technologies (see Figure 3.5).

For both bioprinting and genome editing, the current scheme paints a picture of a technology area where several dominant players have featured, and the number of patent applications
filed by these parties has proliferated. Table 3.2 summarises the leading patent applicants for
each technology area.

*Table 3.2   Leading patent applicants in the bioprinting and CRISPR technology areas
in ascending order*

	Applicants
Bioprinting	Organovo Inc (USA); Wake Forest University (USA); Harvard College (USA); Inventia Life Science Pty Ltd (Australia); Octane Biotech Inc (Canada); Aspect Biosystems (Canada); Cellularity Inc (USA); Advanced Solutions Life Systems LLC (USA); Bioprinting AS (N/A); New South Innovations Pty Ltd (Australia)
Genome Editing (CRISPR)	MIT/Harvard/Broad Institute* (USA); Harvard College (USA); CRISPR Therapeutics AG (Switzerland); MIT/Broad Institute (USA); The General Hospital Corporation (USA); Bayer Healthcare/CRISPR Therapeutics AG (USA/Switzerland); Editas Medicine Inc (USA); The Regents of the University of California (USA); Integrated DNA Technologies Inc (USA)

To give some context, in the bioprinting area, Organovo has filed 19 patent applications in Australia (nine of which are now granted patents) while Wake Forest has filed 10 (three of which have been granted). Harvard College has filed six (two granted). Organovo has therefore filed a significantly larger volume of patents than other applicants.

In the CRISPR area, MIT/Harvard/The Broad Institute (as joint applicants) have filed 30 patent applications (resulting in 10 accepted/granted patents) and Harvard has filed 28 (13 accepted/granted patents). MIT/The Broad Institute (as joint applicants) have filed 18 applications (six granted patents) and CRISPR Therapeutics AG has filed 19 applications (none of which have yet been granted). The General Hospital Corporation has filed 13 applications (six granted patents) and Bayer Healthcare/CRISPR Therapeutics have filed nine applications (no granted patents). The University of California has eight applications but no granted patents as yet.

6.   THE QUALITATIVE DATA: IS RESEARCH TRANSLATING INTO PATENTS?

6.1   Methodology: Interviews with Bioprinting and Genome Editing Practitioners

A qualitative methodology was employed to ascertain whether Australian researchers are actively involved in translating their research by seeking patent protection, and to assist in determining whether patents are proving to be an obstacle to FTO for Australian researchers. As the previous section has demonstrated, Australian inventors are more active in patenting in the bioprinting space in Australia, but active in both genome editing and bioprinting research.

During 2020 and 2021, we conducted interviews with leading Australian researchers and researcher/clinicians, in these technology areas. Interviewees were identified by conducting searches of Web of Science literature in the fields of bioprinting and genome editing, using search terms designed to identify scholarly output in basic and applied research by Australian scholars. For genome editing, search terms were broad in scope and focused on genome editing technologies,[80] but results that indicated researchers were involved in plant sciences, mycology or biochemistry, or molecular biology were excluded. For bioprinting, search terms were similarly broad in scope.[81] A list of publications containing these search terms was compiled. These publications were examined and a list of authors for both technology areas was constructed. In both technology areas, we reached a point where our researcher lists were comprehensive, and we were adding no additional researchers upon examination of publications with more peripherally relevant search results.

Interviews were requested with researchers on the resultant researcher lists. Twenty-six researchers agreed to be interviewed: in one case, two interviewees from one university were interviewed, resulting in a total number of 25 interviewees. The interviews can be broken down as in Table 3.3.

The researchers interviewed were involved in research at publicly funded institutions and the research they undertook in all cases was directed to human health applications. The cli-

---

[80]   (CRISPR OR "gene edit*" OR "zinc finger*" OR "talens") AND ADDRESS: (Australia).
[81]   ("bioprint*" OR "bio-printing" OR "3D-bioprinting" OR "additive manuf*" OR "biofab") AND ADDRESS: (Australia).

Table 3.3   Breakdown of interviewees by technology area

Technology Area	Researcher	Clinician/Researcher	Other
Bioprinting	11	4	1
Genome editing	5	4	0
Total	16	8	1

nician/researchers all had clinical and research appointments. Areas of specialty ranged from ophthalmic, to orthopaedic, to cardiac. The interviewee who fell into the category of 'Other' was involved in regulatory consultancy/private enterprise. Although not a large number, we are confident that data saturation was reached in relation to issues associated with patenting, IP more generally and FTO. We focused our analysis on researchers for public institutions given Australia's strength in fundamental research, and the FTO issues we sought to examine. In a vast majority of cases, the researchers we identified through our search methodology identified researchers engaged in public sector institutions.

We also reviewed extensive literature in the area, which enabled us to construct a conceptual framework for interview questions/themes and to undertake iterative data analysis. Interviews were conducted in a semi-structured format and informed iteratively. This format of data collection provided us with the capacity to inductively conceive relevant concepts rather than generalisable concepts.[82] Interview transcripts were coded and analysed using latent content analysis techniques.[83]

6.2   Results: Interviews with Bioprinting and Genome Editing Practitioners

6.2.1   Patent ownership

Of all the interviewees we questioned, just two were named on patents generated from their current research projects. Twelve interviewees in total indicated they had been involved in at least one granted patent. Eight of these were involved in bioprinting research and four were from our genome editing cohort. Of the bioprinting applicants, just three bioprinting researchers were named on patents that clearly related to the technology area of bioprinting (note these researchers had also been inventors on patents in earlier research projects). The remainder had been named on patents relating to previous research that could not be classed as bioprinting. Similarly, those genome editing interviewees who had been named on patents indicated these patents related to research that predated their genome editing research. As we expected, none were involved in patents related to genome editing (see Table 3.4).

Table 3.4   Patent grants and applications among interview cohort

	Bioprinting	Genome Editing
Granted Patents – bioprinting and genome editing	3	0
Granted Patents – previous research	5	4
Current Filed Applications	0	1
Rejected applications	2	0

[82]   Jane Ritchie et al, 'Designing and selecting samples' in Jane Ritchie et al (eds), *Qualitative Research Practice: A Guide for Social Science Students and Researchers* (Sage Publications, 2014: 2nd ed).
[83]   Maria J Mayan, *Essentials of Qualitative Inquiry* (Left Coast Press, 2009).

A number of these interviewees had been named on multiple patents (one bioprinting, two genome editing) and one had been involved in development through to a successful commercial product. One genome editing researcher indicated they had been involved in 18 patents. A majority, however, had been named on just one or two applications, some of which had lapsed.

Two interviewees indicated they were named on applications yet to be assessed, and two had been named on an application that had been rejected. These interviewees were involved in the same research project and referring to the same patent application. Essentially the patent failed on novelty grounds, on the basis of previous publications on the part of the applicants. At least three other interviewees indicated they were close to filing patent applications, all of whom are involved in genome editing research, all in the genome editing area. Three further interviewees (two bioprinting, one genome editing) were developing technologies or products that had definite patenting potential.

What was it about those applicants who had granted patents, that had led to their decision to patent? While some acknowledged that their technologies were unlikely '… to stand the test of time', others had been very successful. Essentially, it seems to have come down to the fact that the patented technologies were strong and had commercial potential, and in a number of cases were licensed. There was clear division between researchers who patented due to pressure placed on them by personnel at their institution, and those who clearly had patenting at the forefront of their minds from an early stage of their research. The genome editing researcher who had patented 18 times commented that they had '… never made a cent out of it'.

Even those who were advocates of patenting acknowledged that patents are 'a double-edged sword' in that '… they allow you to protect something you can sell or license, but they also prevent you from publishing for some time'. The issues were aptly summarised by one genome editing interviewee with patenting experience:

> Without IP we can't really move to the next step because we don't have the money or the support to do anything. I think that's a major hurdle because we are pushed to find something that will make money … commercial partners are only interested in co-funding if there is some type of money coming back to the[m] … The real risk is that work will stop here. We are a small country … The Americans are doing way better than we do. So is China, Japan. So we're taking a huge risk here by being so focused on patents when we find that work will happen elsewhere before us. It doesn't make sense to me that we are funded by the public system but then pushed to seek IP rights.

A more detailed exposition of the grounds on which interviewees (both those who had patented and those who hadn't) had encountered difficulties in the patent process is discussed below.

Finally, one successful bioprinting researcher commented that confidential information was 'absolutely core' to universities, and that 'patents are worth it if they lead to external investment and an immediate return'. The fact that they rarely lead to an immediate return means they are not always attractive to academics.

6.2.2   University expertise
Interestingly, few of these interviewees had entirely positive views of the patent application process. Despite pressure to patent, often there was little support provided to these researchers. Eight interviewees who had successfully patented questioned the adequacy of universities to translate research:

Strategy needs to be thought through in advance – having a patent is one thing, there are then decisions around whether to do a PCT, how many countries. [You're] looking at a million or two over the lifetime of a patent. Filing patents just to get patents out means wasted resources. A lack of expertise in universities is a weakness in the system – there are not many universities that are resourced enough to understand IP strategy.

Even the interviewee who had had a commercially successful product was critical of the lack of expertise in universities with regard to patenting, and their inability to recognise commercial potential early in the research lifecycle:

The systems within universities are not agile – if you find something you need to act quickly, not have an internal bitter war over who owns what.

At the core of these complaints was the under-resourcing of university commercialisation offices, leading to a misunderstanding of patent strategy. One bioprinting researcher who has previously patented commented that Australian universities '… need to have more support on that [in order to compete internationally]'. Further, many universities will only pursue patent protection if a commercial partner has been identified early. This creates a conflict because commercial parties require the certainty of patent protection prior to investing in a product or technology. As commented by a bioprinting researcher/clinician, '… in my opinion universities should be facilitating the translation of research, not trying to become venture capitalists and sourcing money'. They stated that the translational process is easier where universities spin-out companies. Another bioprinting researcher commented that they had had difficulties with university administration in that all commercialisation needs to 'pass through' the university: '… the commercial pathway will be dictated by where the intellectual property sits'. This highlights the importance of making the right decisions early in a product's lifecycle.

Compounding these issues, universities play a limited role in the translation of products once patents have been obtained. Two interviewees, in particular, commented on this. The interviewee who had filed a patent application commented that it was likely to be up to them to seek commercial partners, and that they didn't anticipate the university would do it.

Another researcher (the researcher who had developed a successful commercial product) who spoke of these issues was more scathing of universities:

But universities are really dumb at patenting. They'll often patent the wrong thing. The commercialisation imperative is problematic because not everything can be translated and everything's a pyramid and they're completely eroding our knowledge. Tech transfer offices tend not to know what they're doing even once you have a patent, basically once the costs of the patent have been recovered. They won't help translate.

This tension concerning the role of universities in translating research is something that requires resolution if translational pathways for Australia's leading researchers are to be improved. Australian public funding bodies now place great emphasis on university/industry linkages in grant application processes.[84] This 'linking' of public research and private investment would not appear to have been successfully converted through university commercialisa-

---

[84]   See, notably, https://www.health.gov.au/initiatives-and-programs/medical-research-future-fund/all-mrff-initiatives; https://www.arc.gov.au/funding-research/funding-schemes/linkage-program.

tion practices, with a number of universities, interviewees spoke of, offering limited support to researchers aside from ensuring patent applications were filed and investment returned.

Notably, this concern was picked up by a number of our interviewees who are successful researchers, but who have not yet successfully patented with the following comment being typical: 'Commercialisation offices in universities are under-resourced and under-expertised … researchers tend to give up.'

The obvious resolution to these issues is significantly greater funding for translation of university innovation, and the fostering of expertise within university commercialisation offices.

6.2.3   Lack of private investment or other funding

The impacts of a lack of private investment funds for Australian research have been well documented.[85] A number of interviewees corroborated that this is an issue for researchers, noting that limited options exist for researchers to translate products even once patents have been obtained.

One bioprinting interviewee emphasised the importance of fostering university understanding of the imperatives of private entities. Building on the issues with commercialisation by universities identified above, this interviewee stated:

> Patent offices in universities are under-resourced and have a lack of expertise. They are trying to do too much. They manage the patent portfolio and make decisions as to whether to go through PCT or national-phase filing. If they don't support progressing to national-phase filing because they believe there's not enough commercial interest you've got to accept that. Often they don't understand how an industry partner might view things or how the market works.

A genome editing interviewee who had 18 patents said that they always contemplated patents because they feel they have to: there is pressure from funding bodies to have commercial partners.

> [We contemplate] patents because we feel we have to – there is pressure from funding bodies to have commercial partners … Without IP we can't really move to the next step because we don't have the money or the support to do anything. I think that's a major hurdle because we are pushed to find something that will make money … commercial partners are only interested in co-funding if there is some type of money coming back to them.

Seven interviewees (four bioprinting, one genome editing) in total discussed the role commercial funding had played or would play in translating their research. Indeed, it was evident from comments made by four of the interviewees with granted patents that the involvement of commercial entities was critical to the translation of their patented research: one bioprinting researcher/clinician set up a company to fund translation; one (a bioprinting researcher) always develops fundamental research with an industry partner; and two genome editing researchers have explored possible commercial partners once patents have been obtained. Interestingly, of these researchers, just one (genome editing researcher) has had a successful commercial product while the two bioprinting researchers have patents in force and product in

---

[85]   See, eg, Australian Government (2014) *Boosting the commercial returns from research*, above n16, 16.

an early stage of development. The final genome editing researcher[86] has not had any products translated despite these patents and efforts to take the products forward.

The remaining four researchers are seeking to implement similar strategies, with two bioprinting researchers seeking involvement of commercial parties early in the development of a product, and two bioprinting researchers looking to spin-out a company to commercialise patented technology.

Notably, seeking commercial interest from particular parties is not without its problems, as the genome editing interviewee with a successful product noted:

> Often universities have partnered with particular companies so they narrow their focus and patent the wrong thing. One issue was a potential patent the university chose not to pursue. They gave it back to the inventor. He's now doing clinical trials with this in Europe.

This same researcher commented on his experience that companies are not interested in backing a product unless it is in Phase II–III trials, which in his opinion demonstrates a lack of innovation of the part of those companies.

Finally, two interviewees (one bioprinting, one genome editing) indicated they would be more likely to seek further public funding than funding from private entities, one (genome editing researcher) on the basis that the institute he worked for was very risk averse to spinning off small companies, and didn't tend to invest in IP or spin-offs. It is evident from our discussions with our interviewees that many Australian researchers rely on ongoing public funding to continue particular research projects, given the dearth of private investment available, and the difficulty in navigating the private investment environment.

6.2.4   Freedom to operate

As we have identified, a primary concern when Australian patents are foreign owned is that Australian inventors will encounter issues with FTO. Our interviewees were divided when it came to considering whether patents held by others create FTO issues for them, but generally, there were few identifiable issues created by patents for bioprinting and genome editing research at this stage.

In total, 16 interviewees commented on whether patents had created any issues for them in terms of FTO. The results of these discussions are summarised in Table 3.5.

A number of interviewees (six bioprinting, six genome editing) expressly stated they were either neutral in relation to whether patents caused FTO issues, or that they had encountered IP in the course of their research, but it had not proved to be a barrier in any way. They had either not encountered patent issues, or accepted that they needed to check whether there were any patents that might impede their research at an early stage of that research. This was

Table 3.5   Views of interviewees in respect of freedom to operate

	Neutral/No barrier	Changed research direction	Stopped research	Approached for infringing
Bioprinting	6	3	0	0
Genome editing	6	1	0	0
Total	12	4	0	0

---

[86]   This is the genome editing researcher with 18 patents.

simply part of doing their research. There was acceptance that others held patents, and that it was important to identify these patents early. At the same time, two bioprinting researchers and a number of genome editing researchers indicated that they licensed in patents or used commercial products in their research. In the case of the genome editing researchers, this was most often CRISPR patents licensed through Addgene.

In most cases, interviewees indicated that this was because their research could be classified as upstream research, or alternatively, because it determined at a very early point which direction their research took. In this sense, there had not been a change in direction in respect of an established research project. For example, one genome editing researcher commented that they had had '… no real problem getting other patents in because we are developing our own tools … We are buying in cell lines and modifying.' This raised no problems for this researcher because their research is so far upstream.

One leading bioprinting researcher commented that FTO had not been a major issue, and that they knew many researchers in the field. Genome editing researchers in this category generally commented that licensing IP from others where necessary had generally not been problematic. Several interviewees from both bioprinting and genome editing commented on the importance of seeking the advice of specialist patent attorneys, although some interviewees also stated that they do their own patent searches. This may become more difficult as the patent fields become more cluttered, but one bioprinting researcher indicated that he conducted his own searches because the university he worked for did not have adequate expertise or funding to pay patent attorneys.

Any barriers that were identified by those in this group of interviewees tended to be associated with patent ownership, for example, one interviewee identified university ownership of patents as a barrier to being able to develop research in the way they wanted it to proceed. And interestingly, one bioprinting clinician/researcher in this group identified that infringement occurs frequently in the conduct of surgical procedures, when clinicians modify existing products to suit clinical need: 'Surgeons respond to clinical need all the time and there is a real issue in relation to IP ownership … Surgeons often modify … IP infringement is a big conversation 3D printing's opened up.'

Four interviewees (three bioprinting, one genome editing) had changed research direction due to existing patents. One bioprinting researcher stated that although conducting fundamental research hadn't been problematic, they had encountered some issues with translational research:

> … we either stopped, but two or three times, it made us think so hard that we went back, did some more fundamental research, found some more mechanisms and then brought it back to the translation side and could bypass this IP.

Another bioprinting researcher acknowledged that:

> I don't think there's any project we were involved in that hadn't encountered some sort of, not conflict, but running into an awareness that we need to avoid that area if we're going to have a clear path going through.

The final bioprinting researcher made a similar comment:

[FTO] hasn't been a major consideration for us. Only when we've done prior art and … when it impacts on the current IP applications that we're putting in. We haven't worried about infringing or licensing or anything like that because I think we're just not at that stage yet; we're not proposing any products yet … The number of patents around bioink formulations and things have exploded in the last five years … that has influenced the direction of our research away from certain formulations. When we're aware of that kind of protection by other people, then we make strategic decisions about where we're going.

The genome editing clinician/researcher who commented on the impact of patents on research direction made some observations on the practices of a competitor well known to them. This interviewee said that his team has done work themselves to determine FTO rather than rely on the university commercialisation office. Their competitor has filed a broad class-based patent application: the interviewee's research, if the patent is granted, will fall within the class rather than the specific claims. This interviewee described the competitor's filing as that competitor starting to 'ring-fence' and file to protect disease-specific applications. Of course, much will hinge on whether the patent in question is granted.

Clearly, changing research focus had not been a major issue for any of these researchers. Further, none of our interviewees had had to stop research projects, or had received cease-and-desist letters.

On the CRISPR patent dispute, a number of our genome editing interviewees commented on the implications of the dispute for their research. While making it clear that this is not the only IP that needs to be considered, all of these researchers had a keen interest in the outcomes of the Broad-Berkeley patent dispute. As one researcher observed:

But the technology has evolved, … we have so many different enzymes, it makes it truly bizarre … Either the Broad or Berkeley do have now [a] clear [right to] licensing on these enzymes.

Our interviewees indicated they had chosen to 'back' one of the parties to the dispute over the other, and recognised that at some point, the resolution of the dispute might cause problems for them:

The CRISPR patent dispute is very relevant to any thought given to commercialisation. The patent battle will … interfere to the extent that you wonder which of those warring parties you're going to go to.

Another described the patent dispute as 'a bit like a farce at the moment'. They have been using Broad products but it may be that they have backed the wrong horse. Another researcher opined that CRISPR patents have the potential to be an obstacle to research in this field on the basis that it had led to institutional roadblocks for researchers. The patent dispute between Broad and Berkeley has been a problem because:

… there's a fear that there will be lawsuits for people using CRISPR without a licence … I've been running into resistance to any basic research with CRISPR because of that … So far I've been able to get around it, but this university has not officially approved that we're allowed to use CRISPR.

This researcher's experience was that IBC approvals are being blocked randomly because they are using CRISPR. University counsel are concerned about them infringing CRISPR patents to a greater extent than patents over other technology.

Finally, one genome editing researcher considered that the Broad-Berkeley dispute has been overstated:

> The patent dispute is not of any significance for us at the end of the day – it might be if you operate more in a commercial space. We were a little bit cautious for a while there but it didn't slow us down. This is not the only IP we have to worry about. Each of Broad and Berkeley have different sequences, one not better than the other. Then there are other labs that have created their own libraries that are all different. IP doesn't change what we do.

This comment is encouraging to the extent that fundamental research appears to be proceeding relatively unhindered. It remains to be seen whether commercialisation of research is negatively impacted in years to come. Most researchers we spoke to appear to be (not surprisingly given the patent application numbers presented earlier) using Addgene products.

7.   DISCUSSION

A number of observations can be made about the evidence presented. First, the low propensity to patent by Australian researchers is following a similar path to that followed in terms of previous health and medical research areas. This is despite the fact that Australia has strong research capability in both bioprinting and genome editing, particularly in public sector institutions. A vast majority of applications and granted patents in both of these technology areas are foreign owned. This is particularly acute in the CRISPR area, but in bioprinting too, there is evidence of a lack of leadership when it comes to translating fundamental Australian research into practice. Australian public sector researchers are not patenting basic research. Internationally, we see universities patenting and enforcing patents as aggressively as private companies, particularly in relation to CRISPR patents. There is little difference, practically speaking, between public and private patent ownership in the context of these technologies. However, Australian public institutions *do not feature* or feature to a very limited degree in this picture.

There is undoubtedly an issue of capacity at play here. The impediments to translation of Australian biomedical research are well documented, and include, most notably, very limited private funding available to take products through to clinical trials.[87] Many of our interviewees commented that private investors require proof of commercial promise (that is, patent protection over the products of research and in some cases products in at least Phase II trials) prior to committing to investing. Even once patents have been obtained, securing ongoing commercial funding is difficult. Some interviewees admitted that unless they could successfully obtain further public funding for their research, projects would likely stall. Australian universities appear reluctant to spin-out companies to aid commercialisation, an averseness that is out of step with US and European trends.[88] Neither researchers nor their institutions are equipped to assess the potential patentability of inventions, nor to conduct prior art searches; a number of researchers were particularly critical of the unrealistic expectations placed on university

[87]   See, eg, Australian Government (2014) *Boosting the commercial returns from research*, above n16, 11–16.
[88]   See, eg, Tom Hockaday, *University Technology Transfer: What it is and How to Do it* (Johns Hopkins University Press, Baltimore, 2020).

administrators to comprehend and work within the requirements of the patent system. The costs of obtaining patent protection are formidable, and therefore strategic decisions as to which research to focus resources on is imperative.

There is currently a sizeable disconnect between broad policy statements on what needs to happen in order to facilitate translation of public sector research, and the proficiency of institutions in engaging with this process. The considerable government investment currently being made in early stage biomedical research[89] must be accompanied by mechanisms to ease the burden of translation. These might include the establishment of organisations to facilitate public-industry collaboration and transfer.[90] Greater training for researchers and university administrators in patent awareness is also key to fostering understanding, awareness and pro-activity. In terms of targeting Australia's areas of research strength, there have been strategies implemented to tailor grant opportunities to encourage research-industry collaboration.[91]

As to whether evidence of an overwhelming foreign presence in patent applications in the technology areas examined is leading to an anticommons or other FTO issues, there is limited evidence that research is being permanently stymied. The issues communicated to us are not so much about FTO, but lost opportunity. Although some changes to research focus have been necessary as a result of patents held by competitors, the impacts of foreign-owned patents have been minimal to date. The effect of patents held by others has been felt to a slightly greater extent by bioprinting researchers, no doubt due to the fact that bioprinting has progressed to a pre-clinical phase while genome editing is at an earlier stage in the research-development continuum.

Many researchers know others in the field, and are better equipped to conduct patent searches than the administrators in the institutions they work for. One genome editing clinician/researcher was cognisant of a broad class-based patent that will impact their research, and regarded this practice as 'ring-fencing'. Of course, there are issues with applications of this type in that the breadth of their claims may result in their rejection. Just how broad claimed CRISPR applications are likely to be remains an open question.

Genome editing researchers reported having encountered few issues with accessing CRISPR technologies, and were ambivalent about the patent dispute on foot. Any issues researchers identified were concerned with whether they had 'backed the right horse'. A key factor militating against CRISPR patents impinging on FTO is that they have been broadly and non-exclusively licensed. This practice of extensive and open licensing ameliorates the impact of broad patents over foundational technologies.[92] Whether FTO becomes an issue will depend on how foundational the patents are, how easy patents are to invent around, and how broadly they are being licensed. To some extent the continuation of FTO in these technology areas will depend on patentees engaging in non-exclusive and 'ethical' licensing.[93] Whether such open licensing practices can continue once CRISPR research moves more into the applied phase, and there is more engagement with commercial partners, remains to be seen.

---

[89]   See Medical Research Futures Fund, https://www.health.gov.au/initiatives-and-programs/medical-research-future-fund.

[90]   Australian Government (2014) *Boosting the commercial returns from research*, above n16, 13.

[91]   See, eg, https://www.health.gov.au/initiatives-and-programs/medical-research-future-fund/all-mrff-initiatives.

[92]   Nicol and Nielsen, above n5, 208–210.

[93]   E Richard Gold, 'The Fall of the Innovation Empire and its Possible Rise through Open Science' *Research Policy* 50, 104226 (2021).

It should also be remembered that we have been dealing here with two very different technologies. Genome editing is very much a foundational research tool accompanied by many ethical and safety issues because the technology manipulates the genome. By contrast, bioprinting is essentially a new method of tissue engineering, an established technology with a well-explored safety and ethical profile. In the case of bioprinting, it is the development of new materials and methods that poses challenges.

The technologies also evidence very different patent topographies. The CRISPR landscape is characterised by two litigious parties aggressively defending their patent portfolios. The patents at stake protect foundational research tools, which have the capacity to impede research if for some reason, the patentees discontinue their current practice of licensing widely. By contrast, many bioprinting researchers develop their own research tools,[94] and are arguably less reliant on circumventing patents. Unlike research using CRISPR, there is no single core technology. Ultimately, this is likely to mean that there are fewer patent impediments for bioprinting researchers going forward.

8.   CONCLUSION

Our aim in conducting this research was to assess the Australian patent landscape for two technology areas – bioprinting and genome editing. The purpose of doing so was twofold: to consider whether Australia's strong research base in these areas of research excellence is being successfully translated (recognising that patents are not the only path to commercialisation), and to consider whether Australian researchers are encountering issues associated with FTO. We expected low levels of patenting by Australian patentees, in line with trends across publicly funded biomedical research in Australia. In fact, our data demonstrated exceedingly low levels of patenting, and highlighted some persistent obstacles to translating research. Addressing these impediments is critical to ensure the important biomedical research being undertaken by Australian researchers, and funded by public money, is capitalised on.

It was also evident that FTO has not been a significant issue to date, but there is capacity for this issue to become more prominent. As research becomes more applied, and research fields become more cluttered, working around patents may become an imperative for bioprinting researchers. For those researching in the genome editing space, the outcome of the CRISPR patent litigation will be keenly observed, as this issue has the capacity to shape applications of CRISPR technology.

---

[94]   Elizabeth Webster and Paul H Jensen, 'Do patents matter for commercialisation' *Journal of Law and Economics*, 54, 431 (2011).

4. Plant variety protection and farmers' rights in India and Indonesia

Christoph Antons and Amrithnath Sreedevi Babu

1. INTRODUCTION: THE CHALLENGES OF EMPIRICAL RESEARCH ON PLANT VARIETY PROTECTION IN DEVELOPING COUNTRIES

Plant variety legislation in the developing world has been mushrooming over the last two decades. That this spectacular growth began around the turn of the century is primarily due to the WTO Agreement on Trade-related Intellectual Property Rights (TRIPS). Article 27.3.b TRIPS required WTO member states to protect plant varieties either through patents or a *sui generis* system or a combination of the two systems. In view of the difficulties with patent protection for an area of vital importance for food security,[1] it is hardly surprising that – with very few exceptions[2] – the world's low- and middle-income economies, in the politically more correct and more accurate recent terminology of the World Bank,[3] opted for *sui generis* protection.[4] Much more surprising is perhaps that such countries have made relatively little use of their freedom under the WTO TRIPS Agreement to design their own *sui generis* systems.[5] Instead, they have largely opted for laws in accordance with the standards of the International

---

[1]   C. Antons, 'Article 27(3)(b) TRIPS and Plant Variety Protection in Developing Countries', in H. Ullrich, R. M. Hilty, M. Lamping and J. Drexl (eds), *TRIPS plus 20: From Trade Rules to Market Principles* (Springer 2016), 389–414.

[2]   Such exceptions in favour of patent rights and an elimination of the choice of Article 27.3.b TRIPS are often the result of Free Trade Agreements with the United States. They involve countries such as Morocco, Bahrain, Jordan, Oman and Singapore, see Antons (n 1) 394–395 with further references. Many of these are, however, high income economies in the more recent classification of the World Bank, see https://data.worldbank.org/country/XD accessed on 25 January 2023.

[3]   Apart from the problematic nature of concepts such as "development", see I. Wallerstein, 'Development: Lodestar or illusion', in L. Sklair (ed), *Capitalism and Development* (Routledge 1994), 3–20, the continued possibility for high income economies such as Singapore to self-identify as "developing" countries in WTO terms, see https://www.wto.org/english/tratop_e/devel_e/d1who_e.htm accessed on 13 April 2023, has been controversial due to their special and differential treatment, see C. Antons, 'Intellectual property in plant material in the ASEAN countries', *Southwestern Journal of International Law* (28(2) 529–549, at 531); C. Yong, 'Singapore does not exploit WTO provisions for developing nations', *The Straits Times*, 28 July, 2019.

[4]   Antons (n 1) 394.

[5]   C. M. Correa, *TRIPS-Related Patent Flexibilities and Food Security: Options for Developing Countries* (Quaker United Nations Office (QUNO) and International Centre for Trade and Development (ICTSD) 2012), 3. For studies on the wide range of options see D. Leskien and M. Flitner, *Intellectual Property Rights and Plant Genetic Resources: Options for a Sui Generis System* (IPGRI 1997) and C. M. Correa with S. Shashikant and F. Meienberg, *Plant Variety Protection in Developing Countries: A Tool for Designing a Sui Generis Plant Variety Protection System: An Alternative to UPOV 1991* (APBREBES 2017).

Union for the Protection of New Varieties of Plants (UPOV). As Aoki has pointed out,[6] UPOV has been widely regarded as a model of what an "effective" *sui generis* system should look like,[7] although it falls short of the TRIPS standard in some respects. It has also been criticised for not protecting traditional farmer varieties and for not helping to meet the goals of the Convention on Biological Diversity (CBD).[8]

Developing country membership in UPOV has increased very substantially as a result of TRIPS with many of those countries introducing UPOV-conforming laws also taking the further step of joining UPOV.[9] Others have experimented with modifications and *sui generis* approaches different from UPOV and meant to better suit local conditions, meet the goals of the CBD and accommodate the interests of farmers. This chapter will examine two examples of such approaches drawn from two very large lower middle-income economies with similar concerns and policies in relation to agriculture. Both India and Indonesia have very diverse economies, in which agriculture still holds a substantial share. Agriculture, forestry and fishing accounts for 18.3 percent of GDP in India and for 13.7 percent of GDP in Indonesia.[10] Of the approaches of these two countries to plant variety protection, the Indian one is the much better known and has been frequently discussed as an influential model.[11] Empirical research into the workings of the laws in India and Indonesia, however, is still relatively limited, in spite of the strong interest in the Indian model in particular. Exceptions are a few studies relying on statistical evidence,[12] fieldwork[13] or a combination of the two.[14]

---

[6]   K. Aoki, *Seed Wars: Controversies and Cases on Plant Genetic Resources and Intellectual Property* (Carolina Academic Press 2008), 82 fn 101.

[7]   UNCTAD-ICTSD, *Resource Book on TRIPS and Development* (Cambridge University Press 2005), 394.

[8]   Aoki (n 6).

[9]   C. Antons, 'Intellectual Property in Plant Material and Free Trade Agreements in Asia', in K.-C. Liu and J. Chaisse (eds), *The Future of Asian Trade Deals and IP* (Hart Publishing 2019), 237.

[10]   https://data.worldbank.org/indicator/NV.AGR.TOTL.ZS accessed 13 April 2023.

[11]   R. Kanniah and C. Antons, 'The regulation of innovation in agriculture and sustainable development in India and Southeast Asia', in C. Antons (ed), *Routledge Handbook of Asian Law* (Routledge 2017), 287–309; T. Winge, R. Andersen and A. Ramanna Pathak, 'Combining Farmers' Rights and Plant Variety Protection in Indian Law', in R. Andersen and T. Winge (eds), *Realising Farmers' Rights to Crop Genetic Resources: Success Stories and Best Practices* (Routledge 2013), 54–61; S. Ragavan and J. Mayer, 'Has India Addressed Its Farmers' Woes? A Story of Plant Protection Issues', *Geo. Int'l Envtl. L. Rev.* (2007) 20, 97. For frequent reference to provisions in Indian law and relevance for Indonesia see also S. Ghimire, N. Barizah, I. Soeparna and K. Van der Borght, 'Plant variety protection law and farmers' rights to save, exchange and breed seeds: the case of Indonesia', *Journal of Intellectual Property Law and Practice* (2021) 16(9), 1013–1025.

[12]   Kanniah and Antons (n 11); S. Kochhar, 'How Effective is Sui Generis Plant Variety Protection in India: Some Initial Feedback', *Journal of Intellectual Property Rights* (2010) 15, 273–284; S. Rani, S. Singh and S. Bhattacharya, 'Impact of India's Plant Variety Protection Act: Analytical Examination Based on Registrations under the Act', *Journal of Intellectual Property Rights* (2020) 25, 131–139; R. R. Hanchinal, R. C. Agarwal, R. Prakash, T. Stephen and J. Jaiswal, 'Impact of awareness programmes and capacity building in Farmer's Plant Variety Registration under the PPV&FR Act', *Journal of Intellectual Property Rights* (2014) 19, 347–352; K. Lushington, 'The Registration of Plant Varieties by Farmers in India: A Status Report', *Review of Agrarian Studies* (2012) 2(1), 112–128.

[13]   Ghimire et al. (n 11).

[14]   K. Peschard, 'Farmers' rights and food sovereignty: critical insights from India', *The Journal of Peasant Studies* (2014) 41(6), 2014, 1085–1108; K. Peschard, 'Seed wars and farmers' rights: Comparative perspectives from Brazil and India', *The Journal of Peasant Studies* (2017) 44(1), 144–168;

It should perhaps not surprise that empirical research into this field of intellectual property is more difficult than research into trade mark, copyright or patent law. Because of the complicated testing requirements before plant variety rights are granted, plant variety protection tends to be the responsibility of agricultural ministries rather than the justice, trade or technology ministries, which are usually responsible for other fields of intellectual property law. In those countries where this is the case, it separates discussions about plant variety rights from more general discussions about intellectual property and innovation policies. It also means that statistical evidence must be collected from plant variety protection (PVP) units within agricultural ministries rather than from intellectual property offices, which have greater experience in publishing filing statistics that can be easily compared with those elsewhere. With regards to fieldwork, there are very diverse groups of actors and stakeholders, from government branches and institutions over state- and privately-owned plant breeding businesses of different sizes to farmers with large-scale, medium-size and small-scale operations. As the consumers and users of new varieties of plants are mostly outside of the big cities, arranging for fieldwork with them can be challenging. Research into the practices of even more remote living farmers, e.g. those from indigenous or tribal communities,[15] presents even greater difficulties.

The research presented in this chapter was conducted in the context of the Australian Research Council funded project "Food security and the governance of local knowledge in India and Indonesia",[16] which includes research team members from the disciplines of law, anthropology, agricultural science and political science. Because of the context and approach of this project, our focus will largely be on the impact of plant variety legislation on farmers, although insights from statistics will be presented with regards to foreign and domestic agribusinesses as well as public sector research.

As will be explained in the following, in carrying out research on knowledge epistemologies in countries such as India and Indonesia, the picture is not complete if one confines oneself to neatly separated fields of intellectual property law such as plant variety rights. Fieldwork confined in this way yields relatively few results outside of government and agribusiness circles, as there is yet relatively little understanding of the details of intellectual property rights in agriculture among farming communities or, indeed, the media and wider public and the new laws have not yet been widely enforced. In local perceptions and in the implementation of the laws, plant variety rights overlap and are often confused with other intellectual property rights such as patents, copyright and geographical indications as well as with seed laws and biodiversity laws, which often promise compensation and recognition to farmers for their contributions to the development of new varieties or to biodiversity conservation. At least for small-scale farmers, seed laws can be of greater immediate concern than intellectual property laws, the impact of which seems still more remote. Therefore, while our chapter is focused on plant variety rights, we will briefly discuss these overlaps, whenever they become relevant.

M. Blakeney, J. Krishnankutty, R. K. Raju and K. H. M. Siddique, 'Agricultural Innovation and the Protection of Traditional Rice Varieties: Kerala a Case Study', *Front. Sustain. Food Syst.* (2020) 3, 116 https://www.frontiersin.org/articles/10.3389/fsufs.2019.00116/full accessed on 11 June 2022.

[15]   The terminology in much of Asia and Africa with regards to the concept of "indigenous peoples" remains contested, see e.g., G. Benjamin, 'Indigenous peoples: Indigeneity, indigeny or indigenism', in C. Antons (ed), *Routledge Handbook of Asian Law* (Routledge 2017), 362–377.

[16]   Australian Research Council Discovery projects funding scheme, project number 170100747.

Our insights are based on fieldwork carried out with anthropologists from the University of Indonesia in Java and Sumatra between 2017 and 2019[17] and on statistical material made available by the Plant Variety Protection Centre of the Indonesian Ministry of Agriculture. As far as India is concerned, reliance has been placed on the statistical evidence and data collected from the Protection of Plant Varieties and Farmers' Rights Authority in India on applications and registrations along with secondary sources focusing on the same. We will argue that in methodological terms, a combination of fieldwork, statistical analysis and analysis of secondary sources is essential. We conclude that among the various aims and purposes of the plant variety legislation, the desire to establish a national seed industry and foster rural development is paramount and that, despite the rhetoric in favour of local and traditional varieties, farmers play only a symbolic and subordinated role and so far have gained little from the new forms of intellectual property protection.

2.   PLANT VARIETY PROTECTION IN INDIA

2.1   History and Political and Economic Background of Plant Variety Protection in India

Plant varieties were not protected in India until 2001 since the Indian Patents Act 1970 expressly excluded plants, seeds and varieties from patentable subject matter. To comply with Article 27.3.b TRIPS, India opted for a *sui generis* system. Plant varieties are now protected under the intellectual property regime through the Protection of Plant Varieties and Farmers Rights Act 2001 (PPVFR). However, patents are granted for biotechnological inventions which include microorganisms. Thus, a biotechnological invention can be embedded in a plant variety and in such a case, a patent can subsist simultaneously with the plant variety protection.

India has a unique legislation that protects farmers' rights under the same law as breeders' rights. Along with the protection accorded individually to farmers' varieties, farmers are also considered breeders. The PPVFR was supposedly implemented by India in response to TRIPS commitments, but as we will see in this section, there were other policy considerations, political bargains, and proposals to pass such a legislation notwithstanding TRIPS. It is necessary to examine the historical evolution of agricultural policies and priorities prior to the introduction of the PPVFR in order to comprehend the factors that led to its passage.

---

[17]   Some of the results are published in C. Antons, Y. T. Winarto and A. F. Prihandiani, 'Farmer-plant-breeders and the law on Java, Indonesia', *Critical Asian Studies* (2020) 52(4), 589–609; C. Antons, Y. T. Winarto, A. F. Prihandiani and S. Uli, 'Farmers as Researchers: Government Regulation of Farmers' Local Knowledge in Indonesia', in M. Blakeney and K. H. M. Siddique (eds), *Local Knowledge, Intellectual Property and Agricultural Innovation* (Springer 2020), 117–151.

Agriculture in India is said to have evolved in the period during the Neolithic age[18] and has its reference in the *Rigveda*[19] as well.[20] Highly effective traditional farming was practised. Extensive studies on these practices were conducted by Indian as well as foreign scientists.[21] Despite the benefits associated with traditional agriculture, such as an increase in genetic diversity, Indian policy documents, particularly the five year plans, promoted modern varieties.[22] There are various social and political reasons for this preference.

India has been always prone to famines both before and after independence. Some of these famines are said to be manmade[23] but some others are due to natural causes. The majority of the famines are regarded as being the result of severe droughts whereas other reasons include low crop yields, crop failure, rising population and the world wars.[24] It is no wonder that independent India's first government focused on ending famines and starvation.[25] In 1950, faced with an acute food shortage, the Indian Government requested food aid in the form of grain from the United States (US). The US agreed to this request, not because of humanitarian concerns but due to communist upheavals in Asia which they wanted to prevent from spreading to India.[26] The two countries signed a treaty for a Technical Cooperation Programme in 1952 which paved the way for the US promoting agricultural research and education in India.[27] The agreement led to India importing more fertilisers but the traditional varieties in India were not responding to these chemical fertilisers. Central Rice Research Institute (CRRI) scientists were of the opinion that varieties which respond to fertilisers had to be introduced through breeding programmes in order to increase the crop yield rather than focusing on traditional varieties.[28]

The introduction of the first official crop improvement programme by the Indian Council of Agricultural Research (ICAR) in 1957 demonstrates this tendency.[29] During that time, India experienced famines owing to natural disasters, prompting it to request subsidised wheat from the US.[30] The supply under Public Law 480 lasted from 1956 to 1966, when the US demanded

---

[18]   Vishnu-Mittre, 'Origins and history of agriculture in the Indian sub-continent', *Journal of Human Evolution* (1978) 7(1), 31–36, 31.

[19]   Rigveda (Sanskrit: "The Knowledge of Verses"), also spelled Ṛgveda, is the oldest of the sacred books of Hinduism, composed in an ancient form of Sanskrit about 1500 BCE, *Encyclopaedia Britannica* https://www.britannica.com/topic/Rigveda accessed on 11 June 2022.

[20]   M. Kochupillai, *Promoting Sustainable Innovations in Plant Varieties* (Springer 2016), 81. An exact period is not agreed to by scholars but there are references to agricultural practices in various ancient documents.

[21]   See generally A. Howard, *An Agricultural Statement* (OUP 1940) which studied traditional agricultural practices in India and endorsed them.

[22]   Kochupillai (n 20).

[23]   V. Mishra et al., 'Drought and famine in India, 1870–2016', *Geophysical Research Letters* (2019) 46(4), 2017–2083, 2081.

[24]   Ibid.

[25]   M. Saha, 'The State, Scientists, and Staple Crops: Agricultural "Modernization" in Pre-Green Revolution India', *Agricultural History* (2013) 87(2), 201–222, 202.

[26]   Ibid, 204.

[27]   Agreement Between the Government of India and the Government of the United States of America Relating to Technical Cooperation Programme, Ministry of External Affairs, Government of India https://mea.gov.in/bilateral-documents.htm?dtl/7218/Agreement+regarding+Technical+Cooperation accessed on 13 June 2022.

[28]   Saha (n 25) 214.

[29]   Kochupillai (n 20).

[30]   Ibid.

a "package deal" in which India was required to promote new agricultural techniques and inputs in exchange for the US delivering wheat.[31] These political pressures prompted India to adopt self-sufficiency measures, which culminated in the "Green Revolution".[32] India established agricultural universities in every state as well as research institutes in the public sector to promote research on agriculture. The Seeds Act 1966 was adopted in response to the push for modern varieties that employ chemical fertilisers for high yields, as well as the necessity to ensure seed quality and nurture a seed industry. The Government of India established the Seed Review Team (SRT) in 1967 to recommend short-term and long-term measures in light of rapid changes in new seed consumption and problems in the country. The SRT recommended, among other things, the introduction of a breeders' rights system and mandatory seed registration in India.[33]

The clamour for the recognition of breeders' rights and plant variety protection is attributable to the rising importance and growth of the private sector in India during the 1980s, as well as the gradual commercialisation of seed.[34] Until then, the public sector used to herald the seed sector in India. The provision of breeder seed by the public sector to the private sector is one of the efforts that contributed to this growth.[35] The Indian seed industry was de-reserved in 1987 when the government changed its industrial licensing policy, allowing private companies to produce and market seeds.[36] Also, in 1988, the New Policy on Seed Development (NPSD) was put in place. This policy focused on importing high-quality seeds by giving tax cuts and giving incentives in the form of tax rebates to encourage the domestic seed industry. The New Industrial Policy[37] in 1991 paved the way for considerable foreign investment in numerous areas, including the seed sector. All of these policy initiatives have contributed to the growth of the private seed industry, establishment of breeding programmes by the private sector[38] and the entry of multinational seed corporations into joint ventures with Indian seed companies.[39]

---

[31]   Video: CGIAR System Organization (2011), "The Start of CGIAR", https://www.youtube.com/watch?v=eP41jc8xJk8 accessed on 11 June 2022.
[32]   The term "Green Revolution" was conferred in 1968 by US Agency for International Development (USAID) administrator William Gaud. N. Cullather, *The Hungry World: America's Cold War Battle Against Poverty in Asia* (Harvard University Press 2010).
[33]   Government of India, *Seed Review Team Report*, https://archive.org/details/dli.ministry.22540 accessed on 11 June 2022. Even though such a recommendation was given, the team was of the view that introduction of such a regime in 1968 would not be practicable and that it would be applicable to public agencies only.
[34]   S. Seshia, 'Plant Variety Protection and Farmers' Rights: Law-Making and Cultivation of Varietal Control', *Economic and Political Weekly* (2002) 37(27), 2741–2747, 2743.
[35]   V. Shiva and T. Crompton, 'Monopoly and Monoculture: Trends in Indian Seed Industry', *Economic and Political Weekly* (1998) 33(39), 137–151, 141.
[36]   D. E. Kolady, D. J. Spielman and A. Cavalieri, 'The Impact of Seed Policy Reforms and Intellectual Property Rights on Crop Productivity in India', *Journal of Agricultural Economics* (2012) 63(2), 361–384, 364.
[37]   Statement on Industrial Policy 1991, Ministry of Industry, Government of India, https://dpiit.gov.in/sites/default/files/IndustrialPolicyStatement_1991_15July2019.pdf accessed on 22 June 2022.
[38]   C. Niranjan Rao, 'Indian Seed System and Plant Variety Protection', *Economic and Political Weekly* (2004) 39(8), 845–852, 848.
[39]   J. Kaur Plahe, 'TRIPS Downhill: India's Plant Variety Protection System and Implications for Small Farmers', *Journal of Contemporary Asia* (2011) 41(1), 75–98, 77. Also *see* Seshia (n 34).

The growth of the private seed sector and the significance placed on it by policymakers led to its formation as an organisation. The Seed Association of India (SAI)[40] represents medium to large foreign and domestic companies. One of their objectives is policy advocacy by engaging with government and scientific entities in enabling a favourable policy environment and furthering the stakeholder's interest.[41] They were able to acquire participation in governmental committees as a result of their declared goal and the increasing influence of being an organisation, which provided them with preferential access to policymakers and a platform to influence policy.[42] These and other events had a significant effect on how India drafted its plant variety protection legislation.

Since 1978, India has been under constant pressure to sign the International Union for the Protection of New Varieties of Plants (UPOV) treaty.[43] India was hesitant to pass legislation since plant breeding was restricted to the public sector, and there was little demand for IPR protection.[44] However, changes in policy during the 1980s and the emergence of the private seed industry altered the situation, resulting in calls for IPR protection. In 1989, SAI in association with the Ministry of Agriculture (MoA) held a two-day seminar titled "Plant Variety Protection: Pros and Cons", that is believed to have influenced the formulation of the Bill to protect plant varieties.[45] Representatives from the private seed industry, officials from the MoA, UPOV and the American multinational seed industry attended the seminar. The seminar focused on plant variety protection in various countries and whether patents or plant variety protection are preferable for India, rather than whether India needs a plant variety protection (PVP) law.[46] The seminar's main recommendation was to implement plant breeders' rights in India, modelled after the UPOV convention.[47] However, the recommendation of the seminar should not be seen as the only reason why India adopted plant breeders' rights. India had evaluated the legislation of a number of UPOV nations and maintained an ongoing information and scientific knowledge exchange with the UPOV authorities.[48] The Indian Government commissioned the UN Food and Agriculture Organisation (FAO) in 1989 to examine the "desirability and feasibility" of establishing plant breeders' rights law in India.[49] The Indian Council of Agricultural Research (ICAR) also recommended plant breeder's rights for hybrid varieties in

---

[40]   Currently, National Seed Association of India (NSAI).
[41]   What We Do, https://nsai.co.in/about-us accessed on 22 June 2022. It is achieved through brain storming sessions/roundtables/conferences and seminars.
[42]   Seshia (n 34) 2744.
[43]   Minutes of Dissent, Report of the Joint Committee on the Protection of Plant Varieties and Farmer's Rights Bill, 1999, Lok Sabha Secretariat, https://eparlib.nic.in/bitstream/123456789/757682/1/jcb_13_2000_farmers_crop_protection.pdf accessed on 22 June 2022.
[44]   N. S. Gopalakrishnan, 'An "Effective" Sui Generis Law to Protect Plant Varieties and Farmers' Rights in India', *J. of World Intell. Prop.* (2002) 4, 157–172, 158.
[45]   Seed Association of India (1990) Plant variety protection: Pros and cons. Proceedings of the Second National Seed Seminar, 13–14 March 1989. Seed Association of India, New Delhi, 161. As *quoted* in Seshia (n 34) 2742 *and* R. K. Arora, R. S. Paroda and J. M. M. Engels, 'Plant Genetic Resources Activities: International Perspective', in R. S. Paroda and R. K. Arora (eds), *Plant Genetic Resources Conservation and Management Concepts and Approaches* (International Board for Plant Genetic Resources, Regional Office for South and Southeast Asia, Malhotra Publishing House 1991).
[46]   Ibid.
[47]   Ibid.
[48]   Seshia (n 34).
[49]   Seshia (n 34).

1991. But the sub-committee cautioned that if such a protection is granted to varieties other than hybrids, the ability for farmers to utilise their own seed must be guaranteed.[50]

In case of farmers' rights provisions as well, there were some defining incidents which led to their recognition. The liberalisation of the economy raised concerns in the agriculture sector, leading to protests in India over fears that multinational corporations would enter the market and begin selling seeds. Karnataka Rajya Raitha Sangha (KRRS), a farmers' organisation in the state of Karnataka, is one of the largest farmers associations in India. They started a movement for "Seed Satyagraha" or seed freedom in December 1992 against multinational companies fearing that farmers may be prohibited from selling and multiplying seeds.[51] As part of the movement, members of KRRS, whose philosophy is founded on Gandhian ideals, invaded the headquarters of Cargill Seeds India, a subsidiary of the American multinational corporation, and destroyed office equipment and documents.[52] Similar protests followed, with the most notable being a march of between 18,000 and 200,000 Indian farmers against the Dunkel Draft in Delhi.[53] A four-day dialogue on Farmers' Rights, organised by the M S Swaminathan Research Foundation (MSSRF) in January 1994 recommended recognition of local communities in the conservation of plant genetic resources.[54] These protests, as well as the engagement of civil society organisations, garnered widespread support for India's farmers' rights provisions.[55]

The aforementioned events indicate that the TRIPS agreement and India's resulting obligation to enact laws to protect plant varieties are not the primary reasons for India's PVP law. In combination with other factors, stakeholder industry demands and international political pressures contributed to the formulation of the bill. This is evidenced by the fact that the MoA proposed the first PVP bill in 1993, prior to the conclusion of the TRIPS agreement.[56] Community rights and farmer's rights to sell seeds, but not branded ones, were included in the original draft of the bill.[57] This was widely criticised for being too similar to the UPOV model and unsuitable for Indian agriculture.[58] The SAI strenuously opposed granting farmer's rights to sell seeds,

---

[50]   ICAR (Indian Council of Agricultural Research) (1991) Indian Council of Agricultural Research Report of the Group on Gene Patenting and Plant Breeders' Rights. New Delhi: ICAR. As *quoted* in A. Ramanna and M. Smale, 'Rights and Access to Plant Genetic Resources under India's New Law', *Development Policy Review* (2004) 22(4), 423–442.

[51]   C. Pionetti, 'Protecting Farmers Rights and Livelihood: The Experience of Karnataka Rajya Ryota Sangha', http://base.d-p-h.info/en/fiches/premierdph/fiche-premierdph-4116.html accessed on 11 June 2022.

[52]   Seshia (n 34) 2745.

[53]   Ibid. The "Dunkel draft" is a 500-page document prepared by Arthur Dunkel, former Director General of the GATT which worked as a breakthrough in the negotiations which led to the establishment of the WTO. It led to fierce protests in developing countries especially in India because of concerns regarding its impact on agriculture due to introduction of biotechnological patents and plant variety protection. See JM, 'GATT, the Dunkel Draft and India', *Economic and Political Weekly* (1992) 27(4), 140–142, 140.

[54]   M. S. Swaminathan Research Foundation, 'Thirty Years of MSSRF: Influencing Policy Change' http://59.160.153.188/library/sites/default/files/30%20Years%20of%20MSSRF%20Policy%20Change .pdf accessed on 11 June 2022; Seshia (n 34) 2746.

[55]   Seshia (n 34) 2745.

[56]   Plahe (n 39) 79.

[57]   Ramanna and Smale (n 50) 427.

[58]   D. Rangnekar, 'Tripping in Front of UPOV: Plant Variety Protection in India', *Social Action* (1998) 48(4), 432–451, https://www.iatp.org/sites/default/files/Tripping_in_Front_of_UPOV_Plant _Variety_Protec.htm accessed on 11 June 2022.

arguing that the purpose of plant variety protection would be compromised if farmers were permitted to sell seeds.[59] Numerous NGOs raised significant opposition to the bill because it lacked provisions for farmers' rights. In August 1996, the MoA circulated a second draft that incorporated provisions for seed multiplication by farmers to an expert panel comprised of M. S. Swaminathan, Suman Sahai and B. K. Keayla.[60] A third draft was released in April 1997, and for the first time, the words "farmer's rights" were used in the title.[61] A fourth draft was introduced in 1999 and forwarded to a Joint Parliamentary Committee (JPC), which held extensive discussions with stakeholders around the nation. The JPC recommended various amendments to the bill and produced a revised draft in 2000, which was mostly accepted and became law in 2001.

The PPVFR grants exclusive rights to those persons who register a new variety, extant variety, farmer's variety and essentially derived variety. One of the unique features of the Act is including a farmer within the definition of breeder. A farmer can register a new variety, in a similar way as a plant breeder, and a farmers' variety as a farmer. A farmer who is engaged in the conservation of genetic resources of land races and wild relatives of economic plants and their improvement through selection and preservation shall be entitled in the prescribed manner for recognition and reward from the National Gene Fund. Benefit sharing is intended to be achieved through the fund. A farmer shall be deemed to be entitled to save, use, sow, resow, exchange, share or sell his farm produce including seed of a variety protected under PPVFR in the same manner as he was entitled before the coming into force of this legislation thereby recognising the traditional practices of farming.

2.2   Application of the Distinct, Uniform and Stable Criteria for Farmers' Variety

Farmers' variety is defined as a variety which has been traditionally cultivated and evolved by the farmers in their fields; or as a wild relative or land race of a variety about which the farmers possess the common knowledge.[62] It is clear that the aim is to protect traditional varieties which the farmers have selected and bred on the basis of physically observable traits. The PPVFR also upholds this by exempting the farmers' variety from the application of the distinct, uniform and stable (DUS) test which is otherwise applicable to all other varieties. It is a test modelled on the DUS testing protocol of the UPOV convention and is followed in the majority of countries with a plant variety protection legislation.

---

[59]   Ramanna and Smale (n 50).

[60]   Rangnekar (n 58). M. S. Swaminathan is an Indian geneticist and international administrator, renowned for his leading role in India's Green Revolution. From 1972 to 1979 he was Director General of the Indian Council of Agricultural Research, and he was Principal Secretary of the Indian Ministry of Agriculture and Irrigation from 1979 to 1980. He served as Director General of the International Rice Research Institute (1982–88) and as President of the International Union for Conservation of Nature and Natural Resources (1984–90); Suman Sahai is founder Chairperson of the Gene Campaign which is a leading research and advocacy organisation, working on issues relating to food, nutrition and livelihoods. Dr Sahai chaired India's Planning Commission Task Force on 'Agro biodiversity and Genetically Engineered Organisms', for the XIth Plan; B. K. Keayla was the trustee and Secretary General of the Centre for Study on Global Trade System and Development and convener of the National Working Group on Patent Laws.

[61]   Ramanna and Smale (n 50) 428; Rangnekar (n 58).

[62]   Section 2(l) PPVFR.

The relevant provisions in the PPVFR which clarify said exemption are sections 15 and 18. Section 15(1) clearly lays down that a new variety shall be registrable if it conforms to the criteria of distinctiveness, uniformity and stability. Section 15(3) further elaborates on when a new variety may be deemed to satisfy the above said criteria. A farmers' variety is different from a new variety. Further, section 18(1) provides the details which should be included in the form of an application for registration which invariably in clause (f) states that the form must be accompanied by a statement containing a brief description of the variety and its characteristics of novelty, distinctiveness, uniformity and stability. The proviso to the same sub-section clarifies that in the case of a farmers' variety application nothing contained in clauses (b) to (i) shall apply in respect of the application. The combined reading of these provisions makes it abundantly clear that DUS criteria are not to be applied to a farmers' variety registration application.

However, since the establishment of PPVFR authority, the exemption seems to have been ignored in subordinate legislation. From the time the authority commenced accepting applications for registrations, the same form was being used for all varieties including farmers' varieties (or FVs). It was only in 2013 that an application form was notified specifically for FVs and the DUS criteria were removed from it. However, the new application form does not seem to have brought much change to the approach taken by the authority towards FVs. A perusal of the plant variety journal makes it clear that DUS characteristics of farmers' varieties are also published in the passport data while inviting objections to the application. Further, Regulation 5 of the Protection of Plant Varieties And Farmers Rights (Criteria For Distinctiveness, Uniformity And Stability For Registration) Regulations 2009 specifically lays down DUS criteria for the registration of farmers' varieties. Sub-regulation (2) of regulation 5 provides that wherever the distinctness of the variety is required to be verified, field tests will be conducted for DUS in the test centres. It is really unfortunate that the salutary provisions and objective of the statute are undermined through subordinate legislation and by the statutory body. While the statute recognises the efforts put in by farmers for generations, the PPVFR authority seems to undermine the objective and makes the process difficult for farmers. It is essentially a violation of statutory provisions and an exercise of arbitrary powers by the Central Government and PPVFR authority.

2.3   PPVFR and Farmers' Variety Applications

The body established under the PPVFR to implement the legislation is the Protection of Plant Varieties and Farmers' Rights Authority (authority). The authority started accepting registration applications from 2007 onwards and in the initial years farmers' variety applications were very small in numbers. Commentators have identified as reasons for the small numbers lack of awareness among farmers and departments like the National Agriculture Research System (NARS), non-governmental organizations (NGOs) and Krishi Vigyan Kendras (KVKs) not being conversant with the Act.[63] Farmers' variety applications saw a steady increase since 2012–13 and have consistently been the highest among all other variety applications since then. It's a curious case as to how such an increase happened. The overall number of registra-

---

[63]   Hanchinal et al. (n 12) 348.

tions for farmer varieties is also the greatest in comparison, although, the ratio of applications to registrations is lowest for farmer varieties, at around 12 percent.[64]

The increase in applications can be attributed to a variety of factors. The key reason is the awareness programmes undertaken by different stakeholders including the PPVFR authority. According to research undertaken by PPVFR authority officials, the authority's awareness programmes and the Plant Genome awards and recognitions given to farmers as well as communities have led to an increase in applications and subsequently registrations.[65] It is true that awareness programmes would have had an effect, given that past impact assessment studies indicated a lack of awareness as the cause of fewer applications.[66] The review of year-by-year statistics about the number of awareness programmes undertaken and the number of farmer variety applications received reveals an uneven pattern. As these programmes also emphasised training at the grassroots level, it is reasonable to assume that they had a positive effect. However, this cannot be the primary explanation for the significant increase in applications, since the number declined in consecutive years after reaching its peak in 2016–17, which was not proportional to the number of awareness programmes (Figure 4.1).

Section 15(2) of the PPVFR specifies that an extant variety[67] shall be registered within a specified period if it conforms to the DUS criteria. Rule 24(1) of the PPVFR Rules 2003 stipulated that all extant varieties must be registered within three years. However, due to the lack of applications for farmers' varieties since 2007, the aforementioned rule was amended in 2009 to provide that every farmers' variety must be registered within five years from the date of crop species notification, thereby extending the term. In the initial years and even later, the bulk of farmers' variety applications submitted for registration were for the crop "Rice". This may be due to the fact that rice is a staple crop. Rice as a crop for registration was notified on 1 November 2006, therefore the high number of applications for rice may also be due to the time restriction established by rule 24. The deadline stipulated in rule 24 was supposed to expire on 31 October 2011, however, the PPVFR authority continued to accept the maximum number of farmers' variety applications for "rice" until 2017–18. The proviso to rule 24 provides the registrar with the discretionary power to register the farmers' variety after five years, but the registrar must record the reasons in writing. An examination of the plant variety registrations reveals that there was a rush of farmers' variety applications until 31 October 2011 continuing beyond for a period of one year as well. Since June 2015,[68] farmers' variety applications for rice have been submitted and registrations have been granted based on a public notice issued by the PPVFR authority extending the time limit for registration to 6 years for extant varieties and 10 years for farmers' varieties from the date of expiry of the original time limit.

Another factor for the rise in applications for farmers' variety and other registrable varieties is the increase in number of notified registrable crops. As of the most recent notification, dated

---

[64]   Rani et al. (n 12) 134.

[65]   Hanchinal et al. (n 12).

[66]   S. Kochhar, 'How Effective is Sui Generis Plant Variety Protection in India: Some Initial Feedback', *Journal of Intellectual Property Rights* (2010) 15, 273–284, 282.

[67]   Extant variety includes existing varieties. It is defined in Section 2(j) as follows:
   j) "extant variety" means a variety available in India which is—(i) notified under section 5 of the Seeds Act, 1966 (54 of 1966); or (ii) farmers' variety; or (iii) a variety about which there is common knowledge; or (iv) any other variety which is in the public domain.

[68]   Rule 24 was omitted by Protection of Plant Varieties and Farmers' Rights (Amendment) Rules, 2015.

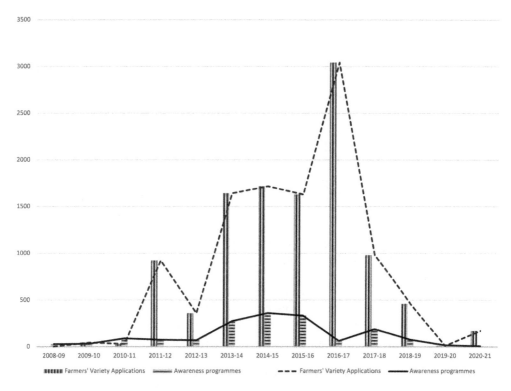

Figure 4.1   *Chart depicting the number of farmers' variety applications received and awareness programmes conducted by the PPVFR authority from 2008–9 to 2020–21*

21 March 2022, the number of crops eligible for registration has increased to 156 from 12 in the initial notification. A crop-wise examination of applications for farmers' variety demonstrates a proportional rise in applications to the number of notified crops. In 2012–13, farmers' variety applications were received for 11 crops; by 2016–17, that number had risen to 84, the highest ever. Evidently, 2016–17 was the year in which the greatest number of FV applications were submitted.[69]

The systemic practice of intermediaries in the farmer's market in India is seen to have crept into the farmer's variety registration process as well.[70] They are referred to as IP facilitators who act as intermediaries between the farmer and the PPVFR authority assisting or encouraging the farmer to make an application for registration. There are NGO and retired agricultural scientists among them, and some of them demand a nominal consulting fee for their services.[71] The PPVFR under section 16(1)(e) provides that an application for registration may be made by any person authorised, in prescribed manner, to make the application on behalf of the

---

[69]   Number of Crops for which applications were received year-wise: 11 in 2012–13, 37 in 2013–14, 54 in 2014–15, 62 in 2015–16, 84 in 2016–17, 75 in 2017–18, 57 in 2018–19.

[70]   S. Bhutani, 'Role of Agricultural Intermediaries: IPRs for Farmers', *Economic and Political Weekly* (2015) 50(32), 18–20, 19.

[71]   Ibid.

farmer. The form PV-1 in the first schedule is prescribed under Rule 25 for the same. The PPVFR authority also promotes this process by instituting a reward and recognition system for facilitators. Facilitators from the National Agricultural Research System (NARS) and NGOs facilitating at least 100 applications at a time in different crops are rewarded with a recognition certificate, citation and cash award of INR 10000 (equivalent to US$ 127).[72] Interestingly, the staff of the authority are also entitled to this reward for more than 500 applications at a time.[73] Even while there is no clear evidence that these facilitators have contributed to the increase in applications, it is reasonable to assume that they have had a significant influence.[74] The surge in numbers in certain years is not due to an increase in applications from the entire nation, but rather to a concentration of applications from a single state. Such a trend is observed for multiple years, and it is reasonable to assume that it is the result of a facilitator's involvement. For instance, because of the assistance provided by the State Commissionerate of Agriculture in 2011, 939 farmers' variety applications were received from the state of Odisha alone in 2011.[75]

The registration of a farmers' variety (FV) culminates in the granting of certain exclusive rights. These rights include the right to produce, sell, market, export or import the variety.[76] Section 26 of the PPVFR provides the option for submitting benefit sharing claims to the authority with respect to a registered variety if the genetic material of the claimant is used in the development of the variety. If the claim is successful, the breeder will be required to deposit the determined amount into the National Gene Fund, from which it will be awarded to the claimant. Even though, such laudable provisions are available under the PPVFR, it seems that in reality the purposes of the Act are not being achieved.

In this context, it is necessary to examine what transpires once these FVs are registered. The highest number of registrations awarded by the PPVFR to date are for FVs, albeit representing just 12 percent of the applications filed. It is the lowest compared to other varieties' application-to-registration ratios. As far as the effect of registration is concerned, there is no evidence that a licensing agreement has been signed nor that royalties have been paid to the owners of FVs. Regarding benefit sharing, there has not been a single instance in which the National Gene Fund established for this purpose has awarded any benefits.[77] Even though the PPVFR authority and the government are encouraging farmers to apply for FVs, no FVs have been put into the seed distribution system of the Government of India.[78]

The Government of Kerala, the southernmost state in India, has introduced a special scheme called Wayanad Package Scheme to promote the specialty scented rice varieties Jeerakasala

---

[72]   Minutes of the 21st Meeting of the Authority held on 31 October 2015 at NASC Complex, Delhi, https://plantauthority.gov.in/sites/default/files/twentyone.pdf accessed on 11 June 22.
[73]   Ibid. In the 22nd Meeting of the Authority held on 17 April 2015, the reward was extended to Zonal Project Directors who facilitate more than 500 applications at a time through NARS, organize at least two biodiversity fairs and promote community seed banks in tribal and agro-biodiversity-rich regions.
[74]   Lushington (n 12) 121.
[75]   Hanchinal et al. (n 12) 349.
[76]   Section 28(1) PPVFR.
[77]   S. Bhutani, 'Plant Breeder Rights on the Table, Farmers' Rights for the Chair', *The Wire*, 9 June 2018, https://thewire.in/agriculture/plant-breeder-rights-on-the-table-farmers-rights-for-the-chair accessed on 11 June 2022.
[78]   Ibid.

and Gandhakasala rice.[79] These two varieties are registered as FVs under PPVFR. However, the scheme promotes these varieties because they are also registered as Geographical Indications (GIs) and includes assistance for cultivation of these varieties and marketing them as specialty rice. Interestingly, these FVs are registered as GIs by persons other than the owners of FVs.[80] These GI registered varieties and FVs are sold by different brands as well in the commercial market including on ecommerce websites.[81] On their packaging, however, none of these brands recognise them as registered GIs or FVs. In this regard, it is unclear whether these brand owners who are selling these varieties have obtained authorisation from the proprietors of the GIs or the FVs.

Farmers' rights emerged as a response against the intellectual property regime that protected the rights of plant breeders, but farmers have never asked for IP protection. One of the purposes of PPVFR is to protect and recognise the rights of farmers in conserving plant genetic resources. This purpose is being served in theory through the legislation's benefit sharing provisions and plant genome saviour awards. Another objective is to protect plant breeders' rights to stimulate investment for research and development, for the development of new plant varieties and for accelerated agricultural development in the country. As a farmer is also considered as a breeder, the recognition of FV is regarded as a realisation of the objective in relation to plant breeders under the PPVFR. In that regard, it is a pertinent question as to what benefit accrues to farmers from the IP protection through the FV registration. When we examine who registered these FVs, we find that the majority are individuals and the remainder are panchayat organisations,[82] farmer community groups and NGOs. Those who registered the FVs don't seem to be in a position to commercialise them without support from either the government or private sector. Some of these registrants do not intend to commercialise it and only want to get recognition.[83] The situation of FV owners can be seen from SEED Care in Wayanad district of Kerala state in India. Farmers' rice varieties were registered by Seed Care in order to ensure their availability to farmers, instil pride in the farmers by gaining scientific validity for their varieties, and finally, to attract breeders who would benefit from accessing the scientifically validated varieties and reaping the benefits for farmers.[84]

---

[79]   Circular TA (1) 15876/18, Directorate of Agricultural Development & Farmer's Welfare, https://keralaagriculture.gov.in/wp-content/uploads/2019/01/circular_ps_2018-19_15876_01.pdf accessed on 22 June 2022. These are scented speciality rice varieties found in the Wayanad district of State of Kerala, India. They are mainly cultivated and preserved by tribal communities in the district.

[80]   Gandhakasala (57/2013) and Jeerakasala (59/2013) rice varieties are registered as farmers' varieties in the name of "Seed Care" under the PPVFR. Wayanad Jeerakasala Rice (186/2009) and Wayanad Gandhakasala Rice (187/2009) are registered as Geographical Indications under the Geographical Indications of Goods (Registration and Protection) Act 1999 in the name of Kerala Agricultural University and Wayanad Jilla Sugandha Nellupadaka Karshaka Samithi as registered proprietors.

[81]   https://www.amazon.in/Double-Horse-Jeerakasala-Rice1kg-Biriyani/dp/B08L1TK964 accessed on 22 June 2022.

[82]   Panchayat is a village council in India. Panchayats promote the farmers by taking the initiative for the registration of farmers' varieties in the village.

[83]   Blakeney et al. (n 14).

[84]   Ibid.

2.4   The Pepsi Co Suit and Its After-effects

Pepsi Co, the multinational food and beverage company, entered India in 1989 by launching their agribusiness.[85] The company started contract farming operations in India in the same year with tomatoes.[86] Contract farming for potatoes followed from 1995.[87] Gujarat is one of the top potato producing states in India and the company supplies farmers with seeds.[88] There are local seed markets and grey markets as well from where farmers are able to obtain seeds.[89] Pepsi Co India Holding Pvt Ltd (Pepsi Co) has registered two potato varieties FL 1867[90] and FL 2027[91] under the PPVFR. The registration grants them exclusive rights to produce, sell, market, distribute, import or export the varieties.[92] On the basis of these rights and under section 64 of the Act,[93] Pepsi Co filed suit against four farmers and others for infringement of the exclusive rights granted to Pepsi Co. An *ex parte* ad interim injunction was passed by the court and the farmers were asked to appear in the subsequent hearing.

Farmers were unaware about IP rights as they procured the seeds from local markets and through exchange and they had been growing them for more than four years.[94] Pepsi Co subsequently offered an out of court settlement wherein the farmers were supposed to either join the company's contract farming programme or sign an agreement that they will refrain from growing the FL 2027 variety.[95] The offer of settlement was largely seen as a result of fierce protests of farmers organisations which erupted around the country against the actions of Pepsi Co, which prompted the Government of Gujarat to intervene in the matter.[96] Before the farmers were able to inform the court of their decision not to accept the out of court settlement, Pepsi Co withdrew the suit and issued a public statement that they had taken this decision after discussions with the government.[97]

---

[85]   About us, Pepsico India website, http://www.pepsicoindia.co.in/company/pepsico-india/about-us accessed on 21 June 2022.

[86]   P. Kaur, 'Contract Farming of Potatoes: A Case Study of PEPSICO Plant', *International Journal of Scientific and Research Publications* (2014) 4(6), 2, https://www.ijsrp.org/research-paper-0614/ijsrp-p3040.pdf accessed on 21 June 2022.

[87]   S. Singh, 'Contract farming for agricultural diversification in the Indian Punjab: A study of performance and problems', *Indian Journal of Agricultural Economics* (2000) 55(3), 283–294, 286.

[88]   S. Bhutani, 'The "Farmers' Rights" Law Lays the IPR Trap', https://spicyip.com/2019/04/the-farmers-rights-law-lays-the-ipr-trap.html#_ftn6 accessed on 21 June 2022.

[89]   Ibid.

[90]   Reg. No. 50 of 2016.

[91]   Reg. No. 59 of 2016.

[92]   Section 28(1) PPVFR.

[93]   Section 64 of the Act:
64. Infringement.—Subject to the provisions of this Act, a right established under this Act is infringed by a person—(a) who, not being the breeder of a variety registered under this Act or a registered agent or registered licensee of that variety, sells, exports, imports or produces such variety without the permission of its breeder or within the scope of a registered licence or registered agency without permission of the registered licensee or registered agent, as the case may be.

[94]   'PepsiCo offers out of court settlement to farmers it sued', https://indianexpress.com/article/india/pepsico-offers-out-of-court-settlement-to-farmers-it-sued-5697060/ accessed on 21 June 2022.

[95]   L. Jishnu, 'Farmers' rights are a hot potato', *Down to Earth*, Tuesday 14 May 2019, https://www.downtoearth.org.in/news/agriculture/farmers-rights-are-a-hot-potato-64535 accessed on 22 June 2022.

[96]   Ibid.

[97]   'Pepsi withdraws Indian potato farmer lawsuits after political pressure', https://www.reuters.com/article/us-india-pepsi-farmers-idINKCN1S817I accessed on 22 June 2022.

The pertinent issue which comes to the fore is the farmer's rights provisions under the PPVFR and especially section 39(1)(iv) which clearly lays down that a farmer shall be deemed to be entitled to save, use, sow, resow, exchange, share or sell his farm produce including seed of a variety protected under PPVFR in the same manner as he was entitled before the coming into force of this Act. The farmers and farmers organisations in the Pepsi Co case have been citing the purpose of this section and demanding the government to emphasise its importance in traditional agriculture. A plain reading of the section makes it clear that it would have squarely been applicable in the case had it proceeded to the trial stage. Even section 64 starts with the saving clause "subject to the provisions of this Act" which makes it clear that infringement proceedings are subject to section 39.

2.5   Seed Law and PPVFR

India's seed market is regulated by the Seeds Act 1966. The objective of the Seeds Act 1966 (the Act) is to regulate the quality of certain notified seeds to be sold for the purposes of agriculture. It achieves the objective by fixing minimum standards of germination, purity and other quality factors; testing seeds for quality factors at the seed testing laboratories to be established by the Central Government and the State Government; creation of seed inspection and certification services in each state and grant of licences and certificates to dealers in seeds; compulsory labelling of seed containers to indicate the quality of seeds offered for sale; and restricting the export, import and inter-state movement of non-descript seeds.[98] The Seeds Act 1966's fundamental limitation is that it applies only to notified varieties of seeds. No germination or purity criteria is applied to any seed or crop variety that is not a notified variety. Even the criteria, as they pertain to notified varieties, are self-certified claims made by seed dealers, which merely have to be placed on the label. Dealers desiring certification can approach the certification body and get certification for their varieties, which can then be included on the label. This is a completely self-supporting endeavour and is not mandatory under the Act. Even though not expressly stated in the objective, the Act and subsequent policies introduced by the Government of India aimed at developing a seed industry in India. In that regard, there is an express overlap with the PPVFR. The preamble to the PPVFR states that plant variety protection will facilitate the growth of seed industry in the country which will ensure the availability of high-quality seeds and planting material to the farmers. The PPVFR also considers a variety notified under the Act to be an extant variety.

In order to replace the Seeds Act 1966, the Seed Bill 2004 was introduced by the government which was again reintroduced as the Seeds Bill 2019. The 2019 bill incorporated some of the recommendations of the Standing Committee on Agriculture which considered the Seeds Bill 2004. If the 2019 bill becomes a law, there may be some overlaps with the PPVFR. The 2019 bill prescribes mandatory registration of all seed varieties, and they must satisfy the minimum germination and purity standards as well. Farmers and their varieties are exempted from the applicability of this provision thus streamlining it with the PPVFR provisions. Registration does not grant any exclusive IP rights, but only the right to sell after registration.

---

[98]   Statement of Objects and Reasons, The Seeds Act 1966.

3.   PLANT VARIETY PROTECTION IN INDONESIA

3.1   Changing Discourses and Competing Paradigms

Developments with regards to intellectual property in agriculture in Indonesia are internationally less well known and discussed than those in India. While the farmers' rights provision in the Indian legislation are rather elaborate, Indonesia is one of several Southeast Asian countries which have enacted a largely UPOV confirming legislation with some modifications.[99] In accordance with UPOV 1991, Law No. 29 of 2000 on the Protection of Plant Varieties protects varieties that are new, distinct, uniform and stable, extends to essentially derived varieties[100] and includes a narrow, if ambiguously drafted seed saving privilege,[101] which excludes use for commercial purposes and further distribution to accommodate the needs of a group of people.

Yet another reason for the greater interest in Indian developments is simply that English language publications on the topic from India have been available for many years, whereas writing in English has only in recent years assumed greater importance in Indonesia, where much of the discussion has been and still is carried out in the national language Bahasa Indonesia.[102] Further, there have been authoritarian periods in both countries that impacted also on agricultural transformation. But while Indira Gandhi's declaration of the state of emergency in the mid-1970s was relatively short-lived and led, according to some observers, to an emergence of a new rights culture,[103] the military-backed government of Indonesia's second President Suharto stifled the emergence of a strong civil society in the country for over 35 years until the end of the 1990s. However, following the onset of what is known in Indonesia as the period of "reformation" (*reformasi*), a large number of civil society organisations has emerged, many of them concerned with agriculture and the plight of small-scale farmers. Many of them participated also in the 2012–13 landmark case in Indonesia's Constitutional Court challenging some key provisions on seed certification of the Suharto era Law No. 12 of 1992 on the Plant Cultivation System. The partly successful challenge was led by the Indonesian Human Rights Committee for Social Justice and joined by the Farmer Initiative for Ecological Livelihoods and Democracy (FIELD), the Alliance of Indonesian Farmers (*Aliansi Petani Indonesia*), the Sadajiwa Village Cultivation Foundation (*Yayasan Bina Desa Sadajiwa*), the People's Coalition for Food Sovereignty (*Koalisi Rakyat Untuk Kedaulatan Pangan*), the

---

[99]   Kanniah and Antons (n 11); C. Antons, 'Intellectual property in plant material in the ASEAN countries', *Southwestern Journal of International Law* (n 3).

[100]   Ghimire et al. (n 11) 1022–1023.

[101]   C. Antons and M. Blakeney, 'Intellectual Property, Farmers' Rights and Agriculture in the ASEAN countries', in C. Antons and M. Blakeney (eds), *Intellectual Property Law in South East Asia*, (Edward Elgar Publishing 2023) point out that UPOV may not be content with a seed saving provision prohibiting "use not for commercial purposes", because the further qualifications that this refers to the activities of individuals and farmers for their own needs and not for those of a group of people currently have to be collected from an explanatory memorandum accompanying the provision and are not to be found in the text of the law. Further, use for own needs does not make it plain that this use has to be confined to a farmer's own holdings.

[102]   For examples of recent publications in English see Ghimire et al. (n 11); N. Barizat, 'TRIPS Plus on Plant Varieties Protection under Indonesia-Japan Economic Partnership Agreement (JIEPA)', *Yuridika* (2009) 24(1), 1.

[103]   B. Stein (revised and edited by D. Arnold), *A History of India*, 2nd edition (Wiley-Blackwell 2010), 402–403.

Indonesian Farmers' Society for Integrated Pest Control (*Ikatan Petani Pengendalian Hama Terpadu Indonesia*), the Alliance of Oil Palm Farmers (*Ikatan Petani Kelapa Sawit*), the Coconut Watch Association (*Perkumpulan Sawit Watch*), the Union of Indonesian Farmers (*Serikat Petani Indonesia*) and the Alliance of the Agrarian Reform Movement (*Aliansi Gerakan Reformasi Agraria*) as well as individual farmers from the Kediri and Indramayu districts in East and West Java.[104]

Civil society organisations such as those listed above have succeeded in introducing a new discourse on "food sovereignty" (*kedaulatan pangan*) as a challenge to the internationally more established discourse on "food security" (*keamanan pangan*). Explaining the difference, McKeon points to the insufficient attention to political and structural causes of the food crisis and that it failed to answer important questions of "where food should be produced, how, by whom, under what conditions, for whose benefit, and under whose control".[105] The counter-discourse on food sovereignty is often associated with influential international peasant organisation La Via Campesina (LVC),[106] although earlier use of the concept by others has been documented.[107] Among the pillars of the concept of food sovereignty, as summarised by McKeon,[108] is local control over seeds and the rejection of the privatisation of natural resources through laws, commercial contracts and intellectual property rights. The food sovereignty concept has found support with the adoption in 2018 of the UN Declaration on the Rights of Peasants and Other People Working in Rural Areas (UNDROP), described as "a unique exercise in law-making from below" and "a new kind of people's diplomacy and an innovative, bottom-up process of building alliances, lobbying, and authoring international law".[109] Indonesian activists played a very important role in the negotiation of UNDROP with the chairman of the Indonesian Peasant Union (SPI), Henry Saragih, being also the Secretary General of LVC at the time,[110] who initiated the process within LVC after SPI had earlier adopted a similar declaration for Indonesia.[111] Hence, it is against this backdrop of competing paradigms and discourses that the discussion about plant variety rights protection in Indonesia has to be placed.

---

[104] For a detailed discussion of this case, see F. Utomo, *Bersemi dalam Tekanan Global* (Yayasan FIELD Indonesia 2013).

[105] N. McKeon, *Food Security Governance: Empowering communities, regulating corporations* (Routledge 2015) 75–76.

[106] https://viacampesina.org/en/ accessed 13 April 2023.

[107] McKeon (n 105) 77.

[108] Ibid., 78–79. The six pillars are: food for people (the right to food); valuing food providers; localising food systems; local control over territory, land, grazing, water, seeds, livestock and fish populations; building of knowledge and skills for localised food production and harvesting; and working with nature in diverse, agro-ecological production and harvesting methods.

[109] P. Claeys and M. Edelman, 'The United Nations Declaration on the rights of peasants and other people working in rural areas', *The Journal of Peasant Studies* (2020) 47(1), 1–2.

[110] J. Vidal, 'Interview: La Via Campesina's Saragih: We have no choice but to change the system', *The Guardian*, 17 June 2013, https://www.theguardian.com/global-development/2013/jun/17/la-via-campesina-henry-saragih accessed 13 April 2023.

[111] Saragih in Claeys and Edelman (n 109) 17.

3.2   Seeds at the Intersection of Seed Laws and Intellectual Property Rights

Field research for our project in Indonesia was carried out under the leadership of Professor Yunita Winarto and a group of anthropologists from the University of Indonesia in the provinces of West Java, Central Java, East Java, Banten and in Jakarta on the island of Java and in the province of Lampung on the island of Sumatra. Different from a recently published study carried out by Belgian and Indonesian legal researchers,[112] which focused on plant variety protection and inquired into the farmers' understanding of and experience with Law No. 29 of 2000 on Plant Variety Protection, our research question has been broader. We asked about farmers' knowledge and skills regarding plant breeding and selecting and exchanging the most suitable seeds and how laws support or hinder such processes. Our research revealed strong synergies between intellectual property and seed certification legislation, so that farmers' practices come under pressure from both government agencies seeking to enforce seed legislation in the furtherance of rural development objectives and private businesses seeking to enforce their intellectual property rights. There are numerous overlaps between the intellectual property and seed certification frameworks in Indonesia, some of which have meanwhile been revised, while others continue. The administration of both laws is the responsibility of the Ministry of Agriculture. Further, the examination process for seed certification and plant variety testing can be harmonised and carried out together and at the same time. In fact, until the revision of the regulation regarding the release of plant varieties in 2017,[113] release of a local variety could only occur after it had also been registered in the plant variety protection register and the certification requirements echoed the intellectual property criteria that the variety had to be "distinct, uniform and stable".[114] Under the 2017 regulation, these requirements were dropped for the seed certification process and an exempted "small farmers' breeding variety" was introduced,[115] but the possibility of joint testing for the purposes of variety release and the award of plant breeders' rights remains otherwise.

Our research took place from 2017 to 2019 during a period of intense discussions about a reform of Indonesia's law regulating seed certification and release, Law No. 12 of 1992 on the Plant Cultivation System. During this period, civil society organisations and most farmers saw the seed certification provisions of this law as most problematic, because of the ease with which they could be used to prosecute those who released non-certified seeds.[116] The Belgian-Indonesian study mentioned in the previous paragraph presented interviews from fieldwork carried out in 2018, in which farmers felt strongly and specifically threatened by the potential enforcement of plant variety rights.[117] This is not contradicting our findings, because of the specific focus of this study on farmers' experience with the PVP law.[118] Research for it was carried out in East Java, a province in which attempts had been made to charge farmers with violation of the plant variety legislation. These farmers had been experimenting with corn

---

[112] Ghimire et al. (n 11).
[113] Regulation of the Minister of Agriculture No. 40/Permentan/TP.010/11/2017 Concerning the Release of Plant Varieties, meanwhile replaced with Regulation of the Minister of Agriculture No. 38 of 2019 on the Release of Plant Varieties.
[114] Antons et al., 'Farmers as Researchers' (n 17) 127.
[115] Ibid., 145.
[116] Utomo (n 104) 74–75.
[117] Ghimire et al. (n 11) 1020–1021.
[118] Ibid., 1019.

seeds. According to statistics presented by Professor Erizal Jamal, Director of the Center for Plant Variety Protection and Agricultural Permits at the Ministry of Agriculture, corn is the food crop which attracts the highest number of PVP applications in Indonesia.[119] Involved as complainant in these earlier cases in East Java according to Utomo[120] was Thai majority owned seed provider PT BISI, which has its headquarters in the province and has the greatest market share in Indonesia in hybrid corn seeds.[121] According to the findings in Ghimire et al.,[122] the company continues to exert pressure on farmers based on its intellectual property rights.

Although trade mark violations were raised in the prosecution of the farmers in East Java,[123] convictions were handed down on the basis of Law No. 12 of 1992 on the Plant Cultivation System, perhaps also because the distribution of non-certified seeds was regarded as easier to prove than intellectual property violations.[124] Thus, the challenge in the Constitutional Court, mentioned in the previous section of this chapter, focused on key provisions of the 1992 Law on the Plant Cultivation System, which were regarded as the main restrictions on the freedom of farmers to operate. The Court agreed that two provisions were unconstitutional, which respectively made the search and collection of germplasm dependent on permits and the release of varieties the prerogative of the government, in both cases without making exemptions for small farmers. Both had to be amended to exempt small farmers and the release of varieties by them.[125]

In spite of this decision, the harassment of farmers initially continued, because of lack of awareness among police and other government agencies of the Constitutional Court decision and its implications. One of the farmers in East Java was rearrested and farmers in West Java were questioned by authorities as to whether their plant breeding practices and products had been officially permitted.[126] In a case in North Aceh in 2019, the head of a village was arrested and charged as director of a village enterprise selling uncertified seed under the 1992 Plant Cultivation Law. This case concerned rice seeds obtained from the Indonesian Farmers Association for Seed Bank and Technology (AB2TI – *Asosiasi Bank Benih dan Teknologi Tani Indonesia*) in Bogor, West Java, and sold under their label. Again, the Constitutional Court's reinterpretation of the 1992 law was not mentioned or discussed.[127]

In 2019, a new Law on the Sustainable Agricultural Cultivation System[128] replaced the controversial 1992 law. This revision removes the insecurity around the exemptions for small farmers mandated by the Constitutional Court by now codifying them. Interestingly, it also adopted the "food sovereignty" terminology, which civil society organisations had popularised. However, while implementing the Constitutional Court decision, it also introduced some new requirements. Farmers are now exempted from licensing requirements for the search for

---

[119] See E. Jamal, 'The PVP System of Indonesia: Plans for the Future, https://ipkey.eu/sites/default/files/ipkey-docs/2021/IPKeySEA_jan2021_Erizal-Jamal_The-PVP-System-of-Indonesia-Plans-for-the-Future.pdf accessed 13 April 2023.

[120] Utomo (n 104) 62.

[121] https://bisi.co.id/en/index.php/2015/11/26/hybrid-corn-seeds-2/ accessed 13 April 2023.

[122] Ghimire et al. (n 11) 1021.

[123] Utomo (n 104) 61 fn. 45.

[124] Ghimire et al. (n 11) 1018–1019.

[125] Mahkamah Konstitusi, Decision No. 99/PUU-X/2012 of 9 July 2013, 124–129.

[126] Antons et al., 'Farmers as Researchers' (n 17) 132.

[127] Ibid., 132–133.

[128] Law No. 22 of 2019 on the Sustainable Agricultural Cultivation System.

and collection of genetic resources[129] and free from the requirements that results of their plant breeding have to be officially released by the government.[130] In both cases, however, they have to report to the central or regional government.[131] Further, while farmers felt free to distribute their cultivars nationwide after the Constitutional Court decision, Law No. 22 of 2019 restricts this freedom to circulation by small farmers within one regency (*kabupaten*) or city (*kota*).[132] Definition of small farmers as "subsistence farmers" is somewhat ambiguous and the fact that the law leaves all previous regulations accompanying the 1992 law in force as long as they are not contradicting the new law may well mean that the help of legally trained advisers in NGOs and farmers associations remains important. There are some further parts of the law, which could create difficulties for small farmers, because they could be extended to them in the absence of a clear exemption.[133]

In sum, while the new law has implemented the Constitutional Court decision, it has also brought some new restrictions. It is, therefore, too early to assume that seed certification legislation has become irrelevant as an alternative tool to intellectual property laws in regulating small farmers' plant breeding and seed exchange. In particular the geographical restriction to circulate seeds only within one regency or city may continue to create significant problems for those farmers distributing their seeds via social media networks or at fairs attended by farmers from different districts and provinces, for farmers' seed banks such as AB2TI[134] as well as for farmers living on the margins of districts, who would be prevented from exchanging seeds with farmers in towns and villages a short distance away, but across the district borders.

3.3   The Indonesian Plant Variety Protection Act and Farmers' Rights

The basic features of Indonesia's Law No. 29 of 2000 on Plant Variety Protection, which make it largely UPOV conforming, were discussed in the previous section. This section will discuss the efforts of the Indonesian government to include modifications from the UPOV standard model in the interest of farmers, local varieties and agricultural biodiversity. Indonesia is the largest of four ASEAN founding members and middle-income economies,[135] which have sometimes been examined together under labels such as "ASEAN 4" or "Second tier newly industrialised countries".[136] As India, they opted for *sui generis* legislation using modified UPOV standards to implement Article 27.3.b TRIPS by the deadline for developing countries in the year 2000.[137] As in India and these other ASEAN countries, Indonesia's agricultural

---

[129]   Article 27(2) Law No. 22 of 2019.

[130]   Article 29(2) Law No. 22 of 2019.

[131]   Article 27(3) and 29(2) Law No. 22 of 2019.

[132]   Article 29(3).

[133]   For a detailed analysis of Law No. 22 of 2019 see Antons et al., 'Farmers as Researchers' (n 17) 141–145. See also Antons et al., 'Farmer-plant-breeders' (n 17) 602–603.

[134]   For examples of such distribution networks see Antons et al., 'Farmers as Researchers' (n 17) 136–139.

[135]   The others being Thailand, Malaysia and the Philippines.

[136]   G. Felker and K. S. Jomo, 'New approaches to investment policy in the ASEAN-4' in K. S. Jomo (ed), *Southeast Asian Paper Tigers? From miracle to debacle and beyond* (Routledge Curzon 2003), 81–135; R. Rasiah, 'Manufacturing export growth in Indonesia, Malaysia and Thailand', in K. S. Jomo, 19–80.

[137]   Thailand introduced plant variety legislation in 1999, the Philippines in 2002 and Malaysia in 2004.

sector was transformed during the Green Revolution, which arrived in Indonesia during the early years of the military backed "New Order" government of Indonesia's second President Suharto.[138] Farmers were ordered during the so-called "mass guidance" (*Bimbingan Massal*) and "mass intensification" (*Intensifikasi Massal*) programmes to plant the new high yielding varieties, which they referred to as "government rice" (*padi pemerintah*) or "dwarf rice" (*padi pendek*).[139] Gradually, they lost their own local varieties in parts of Indonesia.[140] In West Java, farmers in a district on the North Coast were rediscovering them in the early 2000s, when they learned to be plant breeders in Farmer Field Schools for Participatory Plant Breeding led by scientists from Wageningen University in the Netherlands and the NGO FIELD Indonesia.[141] Such a scientific approach used by farmers and based on local crop germplasm from once "lost" local varieties [142] raises important questions about the appropriateness of the dichotomy, common in intellectual property discourses, between "traditional" and "scientific" knowledge.

Farmers involved in the plant breeding field schools also learned about intellectual property rights from facilitators, state plant breeders, NGO staff and district agricultural officials. Although they initially did not understand the details and discussed possible IP rights in their cultivars in terms of patents or copyright,[143] some of those farmers who had become plant breeders thought that they should now also be earning royalties and that intellectual property rights could be used to prevent seed companies from appropriating their seeds.[144] One farmer attempted to establish a community register at village level[145] and, when this failed, started his own farmer field school, which he also used for dissemination of his cultivars in addition to social media.[146] Another farmer cooperated with a government research centre and achieved an official release of his variety, for which he received an award from the Ministry of Agriculture. Farmers know, however, how difficult it is to fulfill the requirements of formal legal processes, due to a frequent lack of documentation and the difficulties of providing the genealogies of their varieties.[147] Concern of violating the intellectual property rights discussed in the farmer field schools has intensified the search for local varieties, which are not yet subject to rights.[148]

The trajectory of agricultural transformation in Indonesia and the period of its introduction explains perhaps why Law No. 29 of 2000 has much less to say about farmers and their rights than the legislation in India. It is clear from the introductory part of the explanatory

---

[138]   Antons et al., 'Farmer-plant-breeders' (n 17) 590.

[139]   Antons et al., 'Farmer-plant-breeders' (n 17) 590, 598; Antons et al., 'Farmers as Researchers' (n 17) 133.

[140]   Y. T. Winarto, *Seeds of Knowledge: The Beginning of Integrated Pest Management in Java* (Yale Southeast Asia Studies 2004), 75; Antons et al., 'Farmer-plant-breeders' (n 17) 597.

[141]   Antons et al., 'Farmer-plant-breeders' (n 17) 598; Y. T. Winarto, 'Kembalinya Benih dan Pengetahuan Lokal dalam Budi Daya Padi', in Y. T. Winarto, *Bisa Dèwèk: Kisah Perjuangan Petani Pemulia Tanaman di Indramayu* (Gramata Publishing 2011), 201–229.

[142]   Antons et al., 'Farmer-plant-breeders' (n 17) 598.

[143]   I. Ardhianto, 'Benih Milik Saya, Kami atau Mereka? Tumbuh Kembang Pranata Kepemilikan Benih Kultivar', in Y. T. Winarto, *Bisa Dèwèk*, 307–325. In this fieldwork, farmers' terminology alternates between patent and copyright.

[144]   Antons et al., 'Farmers as researchers' (n 17) 134.

[145]   Ardhianto (n 143).

[146]   Antons et al., 'Farmers as researchers' (n 17) 134.

[147]   Antons et al., 'Farmers as researchers' (n 17) 134–135.

[148]   Winarto, 'Kembalinya Benih' (n 141) 209.

memorandum[149] that the legislator in 2000 did not think of farmers as plant breeders. The only time "small farmers" are mentioned in this introduction is in connection with the seed privilege, explaining that small farmers should have a chance to use "new varieties" for their own purposes. "Local varieties" are mentioned and defined in the explanation to Article 7 as already existing varieties cultivated over generations by farmers and "owned by the community". Farmer varieties other than these traditional varieties are not contemplated. The focus in the explanation of the aims of the law is on the use of Indonesia's natural wealth for the creation of "superior varieties" (*varietas unggul*) to support the economic development of the agricultural sector in particular and national development more generally. To achieve this, the integrated development of agribusiness and seed industry, which will join the ongoing efforts of government research bodies, is regarded as important.

Law No. 29 of 2000 nevertheless makes a few concessions to the concerns of farmers and agro-biodiversity considerations. The ambiguously structured seed privilege in Article 10(1) of the Plant Variety Protection Act was already mentioned in the previous section of this chapter. The actual text allows for use of a portion of the harvest if it is not for commercial purposes. However, this broad wording is immediately narrowed down in the explanatory memorandum (*penjelasan*) to the legislation, which is of great importance in Indonesia and almost has the same status as the law itself. It explains that the article concerns "the activities of individuals and small farmers in particular for their own needs" and does not allow further distribution to accommodate the needs of a group of people. As explained in the previous section, this seed saving provision is unlikely to be narrow enough to satisfy UPOV,[150] nor is it broad enough to accommodate the seed saving and exchange practices of farmers.

Article 7 of the Plant Variety Protection Act regulates local varieties (*varietas lokal*). It states that "local varieties owned by the community shall be under the control of the state".[151] What the provision means becomes clearer if one reads it in conjunction with the implementing Government Regulation No. 13 of 2004 on the Naming, Registration and Use of the Initial Variety for the Making of Essentially Derived Varieties. Depending on the location of the variety, the Government Regulation empowers the Governor of a Province or District, the Mayor of a city or, where a variety is found in several provinces, the Plant Variety Registration Office to represent the community and register the local variety on its behalf.[152] Those using the local variety for the production of an essentially derived variety then must conclude an agreement with the registered administrative authority, which could include a reward for the variety owning community.[153] If such reward is agreed upon, it should be used for raising the prosperity of the variety owning community and for the conservation of the local variety and germplasm preservation efforts in the location of the local variety.[154] The explanatory memorandum to Government Regulation No. 13 of 2004 clarifies that it is in principle the right and

---

[149]   Penjelasan Undang-Undang Republik Indonesia Nomor 29 Tahun 2000 Tentang Perlindungan Varietas Tanaman.

[150]   See n 101.

[151]   R. Kanniah and C. Antons, 'Plant Variety Protection and Traditional Agricultural Knowledge in Southeast Asia', *Australian J. Asian L.* (2012) 13, 3 point out (at 16) that the Indonesian term "*milik masyarakat*" is subject to interpretation and can refer to "community property" as well as "public ownership".

[152]   Article 5 and 7 Government Regulation No. 13 of 2004.

[153]   Article 9 Government Regulation No. 13 of 2004.

[154]   Article 10 Government Regulation No. 13 of 2004.

authority of the variety owning community to agree on the use of a local variety, but that they are represented by government authorities, because due to the large number of community members, individual identification was difficult and there was often a lack of understanding of rights and how to secure them.[155] The explanation to Article 10 of the Government Regulation stresses specifically the conservationist concerns with regards to the potential for overexploitation of local varieties.

Besides local varieties, Government Regulation No. 13 of 2004 also encourages the registration of "varieties resulting from plant breeding", even if they are not granted plant variety protection under Law No. 29 of 2000.[156] A similar reward system applies to these registered varieties, except that the agreement is concluded with the registered owner of the variety and if the registered owner is not identical with the breeder, a reward for the breeder has to be included in the agreement.[157] In theory, this system could be used by farmer-plant-breeders to register their varieties, which have difficulties complying with the DUS criteria of Law No. 29 of 2000. In practice, however, and for the reasons explained in the previous section, they would find it difficult to document the identity of their cultivars, as required in Article 12(2) of Government Regulation No. 13 of 2004. The notarial deed required in Article 16 of the Government Regulation for any agreed reward would be another obstacle.

3.4   Statistics and Further Outlook

The Plant Variety Protection Centre[158] maintains in addition to the different registers mentioned above a further one for horticultural varieties. Statistics of PVP applications presented by Professor Erizal Jamal based on data up to 31 October 2020[159] show a majority of private domestic applicants (at 57%),[160] followed by the government (17%),[161] private overseas applicants (13%), national universities (5%), individual applicants (4%), research institutes (3%) and local governments and research institutes (1%). As for granted PVP rights, Kanniah calculated that foreign actors accounted for only 4.4 percent of granted certificates. She suggests that a possible explanation is that "in Indonesia, many international companies have domestic subsidiaries or local joint venture partners" and that this may distort the classification.[162] Such joint ventures are sometimes easy to identify when they bear the name of a foreign multinational company or when the group structure is explained on their websites.[163] An examination of granted PVP rights between 2007 and 2017 shows among the PVP rights holders several multinational companies such as Bayer, Dupont, Monsanto and Dole, but also many compa-

---

[155] Penjelasan atas Peraturan Pemerintah Republik Indonesia Nomor 13 tahun 2004 Tentang Penamaan, Pendaftaran dan Penggunaan Varietas Asal Untuk Pembuatan Varietas Turunan Esensial.

[156] Article 12 Government Regulation No. 13 of 2004.

[157] Article 16 Government Regulation No. 13 of 2004.

[158] http://pvtpp.stjen.pertanian.go.id/ accessed 12 August 2022.

[159] Jamal (n 119).

[160] Presumably these are corporations as there is separate data about individual applicants.

[161] Presumably the national government as there is separate data about local government applications.

[162] R. Kanniah, 'Implementation of the plant variety protection laws of Indonesia, Malaysia and the Philippines', in K. Adhikari and D. J. Jefferson (eds), *Intellectual Property, Law and Plant Protection* (Routledge 2020) 79–80.

[163] As with PT Dupont Indonesia, https://www.dupont.com/locations.html, or PT BISI International, https://bisi.co.id/en/index.php/2015/10/17/group-structure/ respectively, both accessed 13 April 2023.

nies with majority foreign ownership from different countries.[164] Clearly domestic companies are also well represented, however, as are government research institutes. Two universities hold several certificates and there are several individual rights holders. A different picture emerges from the register of varieties resulting from plant breeding. Government research organisations are in the majority here in comparison with the private sector, both domestic and foreign, and there is a larger number of universities and individuals among the registrants. What is clear from the statistics is that an Indonesian seed industry has emerged, but more research is required with regards to the question how competitive it is vis-à-vis the foreign invested companies and multinationals.

A revised version of the plant variety protection legislation is currently in preparation. On the one hand, concept descriptions[165] of both the Peoples' Representative Council (*Dewan Perwakilan Rakyat* – DPR) and the Regional Representative Council (*Dewan Perwakilan Daerah* – DPD) in a section on "background and drafting purpose" repeat many of the criticisms of the law that have been raised by farmers' organisations. On the other hand, the section on "range and direction of the regulation" repeats the industry positions on superior varieties and optimalisation of the technology and speaks of pushing and providing opportunities to the business world in the development of the agricultural sector. In the section on "targets desired for realisation", the DPR concept paper repeats the support for the business world and for the development of a national seed industry, while the DPD concept paper mentions the protection of the rights of farmer-plant-breeders together with those of plant varieties. Improvement and revision of the PVP law is also mentioned in Professor Erizal Jamal's presentation,[166] held in 2020, which sees Indonesia's long-term future as a UPOV member by 2023–24 and suggests that a national convention could be held on this controversial issue. Indonesia has already promised in Economic Partnership Agreements with Japan and the EFTA countries to comply with the provisions of UPOV 1991.[167] It also suggests harmonisation of seed and PVP regulation and a simplification of the regulation on the release of varieties.

4.   CONCLUSION

The explanatory memorandum to the Indonesian PVP Act shows that such laws were written at the height of neoliberal policies and globalisation enthusiasm based on the Washington consensus prevalent at the time.[168] Times have changed, but the laws remain, and recent bi-lateral agreements concluded by Indonesia require that the intellectual property rights put in place should be strengthened further. Middle-income countries such as Indonesia and India have tried to combine ambitious plans for their own agribusinesses and biotech industries lobbying for intellectual property rights with attempts to isolate their still substantial small-scale farming sectors from these developments. India's PPVFR Act is often discussed in this context

---

[164]   Antons and Blakeney (n 101).

[165]   https://www.dpr.go.id/uu/detail/id/97 accessed 12 August 2022.

[166]   Jamal (n 119).

[167]   This obligation is modified in the EPA with the EFTA countries, however, as being without prejudice to Indonesia's rights to protect its local plant varieties, see Antons, 'Intellectual Property in Plant Material' (n 9) 248–249.

[168]   See the contributions in C. Antons, *Law and Development in East and Southeast Asia* (Routledge 2003).

as a model for other countries of how to achieve this difficult harmonisation of conflicting policies. Our analysis suggests, however, that small-scale farmers have gained few material benefits from such mixed approaches. Success for them is to keep spaces open for their operations, but the pressure to close these spaces is mounting. Political campaigns and public interest litigation have shown some success in both countries, as is visible in the Pepsi Co case in India and in the preference of seed companies in Indonesia to complain to the authorities about seed certification rather than intellectual property violations. Interesting in this context is also the emergence of regionalised intellectual property rights such as GIs and provincial level intellectual property regulations in Indonesia.[169] Depending on their implementation, such schemes may open up some opportunities for communities to link up with local governments and enhance their bargaining powers.

Hence, there remain many questions in this field, which require further empirical research. Our focus in this contribution has been on the small-scale farming sector. Because this grass-roots level research is different from research in other fields of intellectual property law, where activities are concentrated in the big cities, a combination of fieldwork, ideally in collaboration with experienced social scientists, statistical analysis and study of secondary sources is in our view the most promising. Further, we have adopted an actor and stakeholder centred perspective and believe that in this approach, other areas of regulation, which interact with and impact on the way intellectual property law is administered, should not be ignored. However, the introduction of plant variety legislation can be approached from many different angles, which we cannot explore further within the limited space of this contribution. For example, further research on the impact of the laws on the domestic plant breeding industry and on public sector research agencies as well as on the relationship of PVP laws to GIs and regional intellectual property regulation will be of great interest and could further enhance the understanding of this field of law in the context of developing countries such as India and Indonesia.

---

[169] C. Antons, 'Geographical Indications, Heritage and Decentralization Policies: The Case of Indonesia', in I. Calboli and W. L. Ng-Loy (eds), *Geographical Indications at the Crossroads of Trade, Development and Culture* (Cambridge University Press 2017), 485–507.

PART II

PATENTS AND TRADE SECRETS

5.   From patents to trade secrets

Michael Risch

1.   INTRODUCTION

Trade secrets are on the rise, or so we're told.[1] The offered reasons vary. Some point to a generalized trend toward confidentiality.[2] Others are concerned about overzealous counterespionage efforts.[3] Still others argue that trade secrets have been overpropertized.[4] And some argue that recent legal changes that deny patenting of abstract ideas will cause inventors to protect their creations with trade secrets rather than patents.[5]

But how do we show trade secrets are on the rise? After all, we would expect IP cases simply to increase with population and/or innovation.[6] Further, even if trade secret litigation is increasing beyond some historical baseline, proving which of the proffered reasons (among others) caused the increase can be difficult. This chapter seeks to test one of the theorized causes of increased trade secret litigation, particularly the last one: that changes to patent law have caused inventors to shift enforcement of their inventions to trade secrets.

Traditionally, companies use patent law to protect inventions, copyright law to protect expression, and trade secret law to protect nonpublic information. Each legal framework allows developers to extract value from information that would otherwise be freely copied by competitors. While copyright protects the specific expression, protecting the idea and functionality of novel processes has typically fallen to patent or trade secret.[7] Software developers, especially, have always faced a tradeoff in how to protect the inventive aspects of their software.[8] They can use trade secrets and even copyrights to maintain the value of the hidden parts of their products: trade secret and copyright law generally protect source code.

---

[1]   David S. Almeling, *Seven Reasons Why Trade Secrets Are Increasingly Important*, 27 BERKELEY TECH. L.J. 1091 (2012).

[2]   David S. Levine, *Confidentiality Creep and Opportunistic Privacy*, 20 TUL. J. TECH. & INTELL. PROP. 11 (2017); Charles Tait Graves & Sonia K. Katyal, *From Trade Secrecy to Seclusion*, 109 GEO. L.J. 1337 (2021).

[3]   Rochelle Cooper Dreyfuss & Orly Lobel, *Economic Espionage as Reality or Rhetoric: Equating Trade Secrecy with National Security Business Law Fall Forum: Workplace Secrets, Loyalty, and Theft*, 20 LEWIS & CLARK L. REV. 419 (2016–2017).

[4]   Amy Kapczynski, *The Public History of Trade Secrets*, 55 UC DAVIS L. REV. 1367 (2021–2022).

[5]   Edmund J. Sease, *Court Decisions and Recent Legislation Are Creating a "Perfect Storm" Incentive for Inventors to Rely on Trade Secrets, Not Patents*, 69 DRAKE L. REV. 53 (2021); Chris Palmer, *The Myriad Decision: A Move Toward Trade Secrets*, 22 THE NIH CATALYST (Mar.–Apr. 2014), https:// irp.nih.gov/catalyst/v22i2/the-myriad-decision-a-move-toward-trade-secrets, accessed April 8, 2023.

[6]   B. Zorina Khan, *Trolls and Other Patent Inventions: Economic History and the Patent Controversy in the Twenty-First Century*, 21 GEO. MASON L. REV. 825 (2013).

[7]   Michael Risch, *Hidden in Plain Sight*, 31 BERKELEY TECH. L.J. 1635 (2016).

[8]   Andrew Beckerman-Rodau, *The Choice Between Patent Protection and Trade Secret Protection: A Legal and Business Decision*, 84 JOURNAL PATENT & TRADEMARK OFFICE SOCIETY 371 (May 2020).

But copyright will not protect ideas at all, leaving the full burden on trade secrecy. Thus, developers might patent computerized functions if they fear either trade secret misappropriation or independent development. For many years protection for software shifted to patents, which steadily grew in number throughout the 1990s. These patents were spurred on by important court rulings in *In re Alappat*[9] and *State Street Bank.*[10] Recently, though, patenting software has lost much of its luster; obtaining and asserting a software patent today is far more difficult than it was less than a decade ago because the courts have enforced a ban on patenting abstract ideas.[11]

Left without the ability to patent protect software, developers allegedly look to the only form of intellectual property that will reliably protect algorithmic function: trade secrets.[12]

But is it true? And how do we prove it? Trade secrets are an extremely difficult area for empirical research because there is no single jurisdiction or database that collects cases.[13] Until recently, there was no federal cause of action, meaning that any cases available on federal dockets through PACER were available only through diversity or pendant subject matter jurisdiction. Furthermore, even if one could gather up all of the state court cases—which is technically possible and increasingly feasible as databases improve—causally testing a shift from patents to trade secrets would require some determination of which trade secret cases would have been patent cases, but for the change in law.

This chapter takes a different, novel approach to answer the question. It assumes that in the near-term aftermath of patent law changes, plaintiffs continued to hold and assert patents. Subject matter limitations did not reach into the U.S. Patent & Trademark Office (PTO) to invalidate patents—only a court could do that.[14] But we would expect that plaintiffs knew their patents were less likely to be enforceable, and so when they sued for patent infringement, this approach posits that they would be more likely to *also* sue for trade secret misappropriation. To be sure, not every case would give rise to a misappropriation claim—sometimes the parties have no prior contact with each other. Even so, we would expect aggressive plaintiffs to rely on trade secrets more often if it were true that protection was shifting from patents to trade secrecy.

Because of the apparent rise of trade secret claims generally, this chapter uses a difference-in-differences-in-differences methodology to test the hypothesis that changes to patent law *caused* a shift to trade secret law.[15] The diff-in-diff analysis assumes that before some treatment (or shock), two groups will have done something (here, asserted trade secret claims) at some baseline rate. The model then assumes that both groups *would have* continued along the same trend, but for the shock. The analysis then tests whether one of the groups leaves that

---

[9]   33 F.3d 1526 (Fed. Cir. 1994).

[10]   State St. Bank & Tr. Co. v. Signature Fin. Grp., 149 F.3d 1368 (Fed. Cir. 1998).

[11]   *See* Jasper L. Tran, *Two Years After Alice v. CLS Bank*, 98 J. PAT. & TRADEMARK OFF. SOC'Y 1, 3 (2016) (describing invalidations of software patents).

[12]   Michael P. Kahn & Matthew B. Weiss, *Trends in Patent and Trade Secrets Change Landscape of Innovation*, 255 NEW YORK LAW JOURNAL 255, 125 (Jun. 2016).

[13]   Michael Risch, *Empirical Methods in Trade Secret Research, in* RESEARCH HANDBOOK ON THE ECONOMICS OF INTELLECTUAL PROPERTY LAW 638 (Ben Depoorter et al. eds., Edward Elgar Publishing 2019).

[14]   The substantial number of patents invalidated after the law changed supports this assumption; if plaintiffs stopped filing patent suits then there would be no patents to invalidate.

[15]   Technically, *rejecting* the null hypothesis that there was *no* shift.

trend as compared to the other. The diff-in-diff-in-diff (DDD) model simply adds a third group to the analysis.

The first grouping separates cases that assert a software patent from those that do not assert any software patents. While a bar on abstract ideas affected all patents, it hit software patents especially hard.[16] The second group separates cases brought by those who practice their patents (companies that sell goods and services) from those brought by plaintiffs who primarily license patents for revenue. The latter group is unlikely to have contact with potential defendants and was therefore less likely to rely on trade secrets after patent law changed even if they wanted to.

The hypothesized result is that software patent plaintiffs, product company plaintiffs, and especially software product company plaintiffs would be more likely to assert trade secret claims along with their patent claims in the time following the change in patentable subject matter rules. And that's exactly what happened. The analysis shows that product companies with software patents were 50% more likely to include a trade secret claim in their patent case after patent law changed. All of the other groups asserted at essentially the same rate.

This chapter provides a more detailed introduction to the patent law changes, explains the data and methodology used, and then presents the results, including discussion of limitations in the robustness of the finding.

2.   BACKGROUND: FROM PATENTS TO TRADE SECRETS[17]

Protecting computer software with intellectual property invokes a long, tortuous history that will be briefly summarized here. In the beginning, there was only trade secret protection.[18] Even in the days of punch cards, improper access or use by another was actionable.[19] But this protection proved insufficient; it required both secrecy and wrongful appropriation or use. When a program was released into the wild, the developer could not stop others from examining it and using all the discernable—or, readily ascertainable[20]—features and functions.

2.1   Copyright

Protection gradually shifted from trade secrecy to copyright, but that protection did not come easily. It was initially unclear whether software could be subject to copyright protection at

---

[16]   *#AliceStorm in June: A Deeper Dive into Court Trends, and New Data on Alice inside the USPTO*, BILSKI BLOG, https://www.fenwick.com/bilski-blog/alicestorm-a-deeper-dive-into-court-trends-and-new-data-on-alice-inside-the-uspto (last visited Sept. 20, 2022). While diagnostic patents were also invalidated, they were not enforced anywhere near the scale of software patents, nor are they as likely to be secret given the role of academic publishing and FDA approval.

[17]   This section is drawn from Risch, *supra* note 7.

[18]   *See* David A. Rice, *Whither (No Longer Whether) Software Copyright*, 16 RUTGERS COMPUTER & TECH. L.J. 341, 342 (1990).

[19]   Telex Corp. v. Int'l Bus. Machs. Corp., 367 F. Supp. 258, 326 (N.D. Okla. 1973) (finding trade secret misappropriation for source code transferred via punch cards).

[20]   Unif. Trade Secrets Act § 1(4) (UNIF. LAW COMM'N 1985) [hereinafter UTSA] (defining trade secrets as information that is not "readily ascertainable").

all.[21] However, Congress eventually made clear that computer software could be protected by copyright and the courts began to apply Congress's mandate. But this did not end debate. While early cases found liability if one copied the entire source code of a program,[22] things grew more complicated when companies attempted to protect user interfaces—especially in cases involving non-literal copying of such interfaces.[23]

In general, user interfaces could be protected as a whole, even if their constituent parts were unoriginal.[24] An early exemplar of this approach is *Whelan Associates, Inc. v. Jaslow Dental Laboratory, Inc.*, in which the Third Circuit held that the only unprotected "idea" of a computer program is the program's purpose, and that the program constituted protectable expression when taken as a whole.[25] *Whelan*'s precedent has since been criticized thoroughly by many courts and commentators.[26] Despite criticism of the announced rule, a close reading of *Whelan* shows that the court was attempting to balance the incentives given to software authors and the ability to create in the future.[27]

By the mid-1990s, however, copyright protection in software—especially the functional aspects—narrowed. The first blow was in *Apple Computer, Inc. v. Microsoft Corp.*,[28] where the Ninth Circuit held that Apple could not protect functional elements in its desktop interface (like Apple's trash can) from being reused in functionally similar, but aesthetically different software by Microsoft (thus, a trash can would infringe but a recycle bin would not).[29]

The last influential case of that time came in 1996, when the First Circuit ruled that the Lotus 1–2–3 command structure was uncopyrightable as a method of operation.[30] The court likened the Lotus system to buttons on a VCR and ruled that even literal copying was accept-

---

[21]   Pamela Samuelson, *Reflections on the State of American Software Copyright Law and the Perils of Teaching It*, 13 COLUM.-VLA J.L. & ARTS 61, 61 (1988) ("[A]lmost all of the important questions about what copyright protection means for software have yet to be answered definitively."); C. Frederick Koenig III, *Software Copyright: The Conflict Within CONTU*, 27 BULL. COPYRIGHT SOC'Y U.S.A. 340, 341 (1979) ("Unfortunately just what the status of that law was on December 31, 1977, is extremely vague because of the total absence of statutory guidance in the Act of 1909 and the dearth of relevant cases dealing with this subject matter."); *see also* Atari Games Corp. v. Oman, 888 F.2d 878 (D.C. Cir. 1989) (reversing copyright office rejection of software based on lack of clarity in the rules applied).

[22]   Apple Comput., Inc. v. Franklin Comput. Corp., 714 F.2d 1240 (3d Cir. 1983).

[23]   *See* Jack Russo & Jamie Nafziger, *Software "Look and Feel" Protection in the 1990s*, 15 HASTINGS COMM. & ENT. L.J. 571 (1993) (discussing the definition and early history of "look and feel" protection).

[24]   Atari Games, 979 F.2d at 245–46 (holding that "breakout" game composed of geometric shapes may be protected by copyright).

[25]   797 F.2d 1222, 1236 (3d Cir. 1986).

[26]   Samuelson, *supra* note 21, at 63 ("Overbroad decisions, such as that of the Third Circuit in the *Whelan* case, have set off new rounds of litigation…"); *see also* Jack E. Brown, *"Analytical Dissection" of Copyrighted Computer Software—Complicating the Simple and Confounding the Complex*, 25 ARIZ. ST. L.J. 801, 814 (1993) (criticizing *Whelan*).

[27]   797 F.2d at 1235 ("[W]e must remember that the purpose of the copyright law is to create the most efficient and productive balance between protection (incentive) and dissemination of information, to promote learning, culture and development."); *see also* Michael Risch, *How Can* Whelan v. Jaslow *and* Lotus v. Borland *Both Be Right? Reexamining the Economics of Computer Software Reuse*, 17 J. MARSHALL J. INFO. TECH. & PRIVACY L. 511, 516 (1999) (arguing same).

[28]   35 F.3d 1435, 1442 (9th Cir. 1994), *cert. denied*, 513 U.S. 1184 (1995).

[29]   *Id.* at 1438 n.4.

[30]   Lotus Development Corp. v. Borland International, Inc., 49 F.3d 807, 814–15 (1st Cir. 1995), *aff'd by an equally divided Court*, 516 U.S. 233 (1996).

able given the system's functionality. It is telling that after the Supreme Court affirmed *Lotus v. Borland* by an equally divided court, and the issue has never been squarely presented to the Court again in the twenty-five years since.[31] The upshot, though, is that copyright is not a great way to protect functional aspects of computer software, especially when those aspects are inventive more than expressive.

2.2   Patent

Whether coincidentally or not, the mid-1990s marked a time of tremendous growth in software patents.[32] While there is no single reason for this growth, the historical narrative allows for a coherent, if not provable, story. Leading up to the 1990s, a triad of Supreme Court cases in the 1970s left uncertainty about what software could be patented. On the one hand, *Gottschalk v. Benson*[33] and *Parker v. Flook*[34] seemed to imply that algorithms were not patentable. But *Diamond v. Diehr*[35] implied that software might be patentable if combined with some generally useful process—in that case, manufacturing rubber. This uncertainty led to limited software patenting in the 1980s.

However, software patenting exploded in the 1990s. The early 1990s marked both the introduction of a commercialized internet and the World Wide Web. This created the incentive and means for a rapid expansion in software. Software was no longer limited to floppy (or compact) discs purchased at the store; every web site offered new products or services delivered over the internet, even if that service had previously been offered by traditional methods. Limitation in copyright protection surely spurred some movement to patent (but that is the topic of another study).

Thus, despite the uncertainty from earlier Supreme Court opinions, applicants began filing more and more software patent applications with the hope that they would eventually be affirmed. And they were: in 1994, *In re Alappat*[36] approved these software patents by ruling that general purpose computers become, in the eyes of the law at least,[37] a new machine when programmed with a new function. This opened the doors to many new machine patent claims: calculators on a computer, auctions on a computer, financial management on a computer, as if each computer running a program was some new device that had been invented.

---

[31]   Some might argue that *Oracle America, Inc. v. Google Inc.*, 872 F. Supp. 2d 974 (N.D. Cal. 2012), *rev'd*, 750 F.3d 1339 (Fed. Cir. 2014), later *rev'd Google, Inc. v. Oracle America, Inc.*, 530 U.S. __ (2021) came close.

[32]   *See* James E. Bessen, *A Generation of Software Patents*, 18 B.U. J. Sci. & Tech. L. 241, 253 (2012); *see also* Bronwyn H. Hall & Megan MacGarvie, *The Private Value of Software Patents*, 39 Res. Pol'y 994, 996 (2010).

[33]   Gottschalk v. Benson, 409 U.S. 63, 65 (1972).

[34]   Parker v. Flook, 437 U.S. 584, 589 (1978).

[35]   Diamond v. Diehr, 450 U.S. 175, 191 (1981).

[36]   *In re* Alappat, 33 F.3d 1526, 1545 (Fed. Cir. 1994).

[37]   This is, of course, a legal fiction—one that treats software as "structure" compared to the prior art. Without this fiction, a computer programmed to do X is the same as a program to do Y, because they both have all the same parts: microprocessor, RAM, etc. Michael Risch, Response Re: Request for Comments on Functional Claiming and Software Patents, Docket No. PTO-P-2012-0052 (March 12, 2013), http://www.uspto.gov/sites/default/files/patents/law/comments/sw-f_risch_20130312.pdf, accessed April 8, 2023 ("The easiest way to solve the functional claiming problem is to reverse the rule of *Alappat*, and recognize reality: machines do not become new simply because new software is loaded onto them.").

The Federal Circuit immediately began loosening up its restrictions, recognizing that the "new machine" fiction masked what was really going on: patenting novel ways of doing things on a computer. Thus, in *In re Beauregard*,[38] the court ruled that a computer program on a machine-readable medium was sufficient for a patentable claim, when ordinarily such a program would be unpatentable as inoperable printed matter.[39] Later, in *AT&T Corp. v. Excel Communications, Inc.*,[40] the court held that software was patentable whether it was claimed as a machine or a process, and in *State Street Bank & Trust Co. v. Signature Financial Group, Inc.*,[41] the court held that such a process need not be directed to manufacturing, and could encompass business methods so long as they yielded useful, tangible, and concrete results.

Thus, software patents proliferated during the 1990s. The desirability of this growth was vigorously disputed by scholars, practitioners, and programmers. Virtually every software engineer hates software patents, or thinks they are all obvious or otherwise defective.[42] Some scholars bemoan them.[43] Other scholars find benefits in them.[44] Some say it depends on who has them.[45]

The Supreme Court has since weighed in with its opinion, which is critical to this study. When the issue of patentable subject matter first returned to the Court in 2010, sixty-eight parties filed amicus briefs.[46] In *Bilski v. Kappos*, the Court issued a relatively short opinion.[47] The Court ruled that the useful, tangible, and concrete test of *State Street Bank* was insufficient to determine patent eligibility. However, the Court would not ban all business method or software patents. It noted that 35 U.S.C. § 100(b) defines a method as a new use for an existing machine.[48] Based on this definition, software patents make perfect sense: the software is a new use for the computer.

But the Court did not stop there: it ruled that even such processes must claim more than an abstract idea.[49] The patent at issue in the case essentially claimed the abstract idea of hedging,[50] and while the Court said machines were not required for patentability, it did not help that the claim mentioned no software or any new use for a machine.[51] Thus, the patent was barred as an abstract idea.

---

[38]   *In re* Beauregard, 53 F.3d 1583, 1584 (Fed. Cir. 1995).
[39]   *In re* Ngai, 367 F.3d 1336, 1339 (Fed. Cir. 2004) (citing *In re* Gulack, 703 F.2d 1381, 1387 (Fed. Cir. 1983)) (explaining that words, pictures, and other printed matter must have some functional relationship to the information's medium of display in order to create a "new" product).
[40]   AT&T Corp. v. Excel Communications, Inc., 172 F.3d 1352, 1355–56 (Fed. Cir. 1999).
[41]   State St. Bank & Tr. Co. v. Signature Fin. Grp., Inc., 149 F.3d 1368, 1375 (1998).
[42]   *See generally* GROKLAW, http://www.groklaw.net (last visited Aug. 23, 2017).
[43]   *See e.g.*, Bessen, *supra* note 32.
[44]   *See e.g.*, Michael Noel & Mark Schankerman, *Strategic Patenting and Software Innovation*, 61 J. INDUS. ECON. 481 (2013).
[45]   Iain M. Cockburn & Megan J. MacGarvie, *Entry and Patenting in the Software Industry*, 57 MGMT. SCI. 915 (2011) (arguing that patents benefit those who are able to use them in cross-licensing negotiations).
[46]   Michael Risch, *Forward to the Past*, 2009–2010 CATO SUP. CT. REV. 333, 337. The author discloses that he co-authored one of these briefs.
[47]   Bilski v. Kappos, 561 U.S. 593, 130 S. Ct. 3218 (2010).
[48]   *Id.* at 3222.
[49]   *Id.* at 3225.
[50]   Hedging is a risk mitigation strategy. In general, a party transacts with two groups with different risk profiles that roughly balance out—when one wins, the other loses.
[51]   For a more detailed critique of *In re* Bilski, *see* Risch, *supra* note 46.

In the immediate aftermath of the decision in *Bilski*, neither lower courts nor the Patent Office consistently interpreted the ruling. On the one hand, it seemed to rein in business methods patents; on the other hand, it had little to directly say about software patents. As a result, software patents received a bit more scrutiny, but they continued to issue and be successfully asserted.[52]

Any uncertainty disappeared three years later with the Court's decision in *Alice v. CLS Bank*.[53] In *Alice*, the patentee claimed a method of settling escrow accounts by keeping "shadow accounts" that tracked the results of accumulated transactions—sometimes one party spent more, sometimes the other party spent more. At the end of each day, the shadow accounts would be compared and reconciled, with any difference paid out of the actual escrow account. In practice, this was a relatively costly system to effectively implement, as it required high speed networks, databases, audit logs, and other software programming. It took the alleged infringer years to commercially implement after the idea was known.[54] As claimed, however, the system was remarkably simple: use two variables to track data and then compare them at some predetermined time. One amicus brief implemented what the author claimed was an infringing implementation in seven lines of BASIC code.[55]

The Supreme Court issued another relatively short opinion in *Alice*: the escrow patent was not different in kind from the hedging patent and was therefore an abstract idea.[56] The opinion added two important pieces to *Bilski*. First, there was a definite, "we really mean it" tone to the opinion that implied the lower courts had not heeded its prior opinion.[57] Second, the opinion provided a little more detail about how courts should go about determining if something is an abstract idea, though the framework the Court provided is extremely flexible.

The lower courts and Patent Office took the message in *Alice* to heart. In some technology fields, virtually every patent application was rejected for years. For example, district courts invalidated a large portion of challenged patents, and for the first two years after *Alice*, the time period studied in this chapter, the Federal Circuit invalidated almost all of the patents

---

[52] Kevin J. McNamee, *A View from the Trenches: Section 101 Patent Eligibility Challenges in the Post-*Bilski *Trial Courts*, N.Y. INTELL. PROP. L. ASS'N BULL. (Dec. 2013), https://www.mondaq .com/unitedstates/x/297550/Patent/A+View+From+the+Trenches+Section+101+Patent+Eligibility+ Challenges+in+the+PostBilski+Trial+Courts, accessed April 8, 2023 (describing outcomes of post-*Bilski* challenges).

[53] Alice Corp. v. CLS Bank Int'l, 573 U.S. 208, 134 S. Ct. 2347 (2014).

[54] Joe Mullin, *How Far Will the Supreme Court Go to Stop Patent Trolls?*, ARS TECHNICA (Mar. 31, 2014), http://arstechnica.com/tech-policy/2014/03/how-far-will-the-supreme-court-go-to-stop-patent -trolls/, accessed April 8, 2023. ("The systems used by CLS . . . are undoubtedly complex, but the bank itself is a classic example of an idea whose time had come—it was 'decades in the making,' as CLS' lawyers explain in their brief.").

[55] *Id.* This claim is a bit overstated. The patent claims "communications controllers," which would ostensibly allow "messages" to come from third parties (and for instructions to be sent back to those third parties). The seven lines of code use keyboard input and monitor output to add to internal variables as if that were messages coming over a network. Managing such data would be more complex than seven lines of code allows. Even so, the point is made that the claim is a broad one easily implemented, though one wonders if it could be implemented in seven lines of code, why it took decades to implement.

[56] *Alice*, 134 S. Ct. at 2357.

[57] *Id.* ("It is enough to recognize that there is no meaningful distinction between the concept of risk hedging in *Bilski* and the concept of intermediated settlement at issue here. Both are squarely within the realm of 'abstract ideas' as we have used that term.").

it considered on appeal.[58] The application of *Alice* has been so aggressive that many historic patents would be at risk today.[59] In short, the years after *Bilski* and then after *Alice* were not a great time for software patents, whether one disagrees with the trend or not.

2.3   Filling the Void: Trade Secrecy

Long before copyright and patent law were viable alternatives to protect software, courts consistently relied on trade secret law to protect software. The reason is straightforward: there is no definitional uncertainty in trade secret law. Indeed, functional and intangible information have unquestionably received trade secret protection since the dawn of software. The Restatement (First) of Torts defined a trade secret as "any formula, pattern, device or compilation of information which is used in one's business, and which gives" the secret holder "an opportunity to obtain an advantage over competitors who do not know or use it."[60] This included a "method of bookkeeping or other office management."[61]

Modern legislation frames trade secrets similarly to the Restatement. The Uniform Trade Secrets Act,[62] now adopted in forty-nine states, defines a trade secret as:

information, including a formula, pattern, compilation, program, device, method, technique, or process, that:
(i)   derives independent economic value, actual or potential, from not being generally known to, and not being readily ascertainable[63] by proper means by, other persons who can obtain economic value from its disclosure or use, and
(ii)   is the subject of efforts that are reasonable under the circumstances to maintain its secrecy.

Operation of a computer program, if it otherwise satisfies the requirements of the statute, falls squarely within the information, program, device, method, technique, or process portion of the definition. Unlike copyright, there is no exclusion for functionality. Unlike patent, there is no exclusion for abstract ideas. Instead, trade secrecy only requires that the information cannot be readily known or ascertainable, that it is subject to reasonable efforts to maintain secrecy, and that it evidences economic value *because* it is not known. It is therefore quite reasonable to think that software inventors would rely on trade secrecy as patentable subject matter changes limited protection in software.

---

[58]   Robert R. Sachs, *#AliceStorm: July is Smoking Hot, Hot, Hot...and Versata is Not, Not, Not*, BILSKI BLOG, https://www.fenwick.com/bilski-blog/alicestorm-july-is-hot-hot-hotand-versata-is-not-not-not (last visited Aug. 5, 2015).
[59]   Michael Risch, *Nothing is Patentable*, 67 FLA. L. REV. FORUM 45 (2015).
[60]   Restatement (First) of Torts § 757 cmt. b (AM. LAW INST. 1939).
[61]   *Id.*
[62]   UTSA § 1(4).
[63]   Some states, most notably California, omit the requirement that the information not be readily ascertainable from the definition. Cal. Civ. Code § 3426.1 (2012). Instead, the fact that information is "readily ascertainable" is a defense by the purported misappropriator, but only if the misappropriator actually "ascertained" the information in a legal way. Sargent Fletcher, Inc. v. Able Corp., 3 Cal. Rptr. 3d 279, 286–87 (Cal. Ct. App. 2003); ABBA Rubber Co. v. Seaquist, 286 Cal. Rptr. 518, 529 n.9 (Cal. Ct. App. 1991). In California, one may not obtain information contrary to the statute and then claim that the information would have been readily ascertainable if only the defendant had acted properly.

3.   MOTIVATION AND MODEL

There are generally two types of information associated with any product: non-revealing and revealing.[64] Non-revealing information cannot be gleaned by users who have the product in ordinary distribution.[65] Revealing information is information that can be discovered by use. This might include information that is easily visible or information that can be learned through reverse engineering.[66] Software contains a substantial amount of non-revealing information because of the source code involved. But many other products that are patented contain revealing information. It is this difference that creates two groups in the empirical analysis here. Even if patents cover the revealed aspects of each type of product, only the non-revealed aspects of software can *also* be protected by trade secrets.

Programmatic aspects that are non-revealing and not easily reverse engineered are the most easily protected by trade secret law.[67] Indeed, one of the primary justifications for the patent system—at least with respect to software—is to encourage disclosure of these non-revealed programmatic elements during the patent process rather than kept secret.[68] Thus, every software author faces a choice: use protection that requires disclosure or use protection that allows for secrecy. Patents usually force software authors to choose between secrecy and disclosure. In cases where software is patentable, the developer must choose whether to disclose in exchange for exclusive rights, or to hold the secret and risk independent development by competitors.[69] The choice typically depends on the likelihood that others will figure out the secret on their own, thus negating the value of a trade secret and increasing the value of a patent.[70]

However, if software is no longer patentable subject matter, logic dictates that developers will be incentivized to hide as much program functionality as possible. That includes information which would otherwise have been disclosed in the patent process. This result does not even depend on the existence of trade secret law, per se. In a world without forced disclosure, software developers would likely still attempt to rely on secrecy to minimize free-riding

---

[64]   *See* David A. Rice, *License with Contract and Precedent: Publisher-Licensor Protection Consequences and the Rationale Offered for the Nontransferability of Licenses Under Article 2B*, 13 BERKELEY TECH. L.J. 1239, 1244–45 (1998) (describing potentially self-revealing elements of software).

[65]   *See* J. Jonas Anderson, *Secret Inventions*, 26 BERKELEY TECH. L.J. 917, 956 (2011) (describing products that involve non-revealing information).

[66]   *See id.*

[67]   *See, e.g.*, Integrated Cash Mgmt. Servs. v. Dig. Transactions, 920 F.2d 171, 174 (2d Cir. 1990) ("The manner in which ICM's generic utility programs interact, which is the key to the product's success, is not generally known outside of ICM. Contrary to defendants' suggestion, the non-secret nature of the individual utility programs which comprise ICM's product does not alter this conclusion.").

[68]   *See* William M. Landes & Richard A. Posner, THE ECONOMIC STRUCTURE OF INTELLECTUAL PROPERTY LAW 294–333 (Belknap Press: Harvard University Press 2003).

[69]   A third choice often practiced is to disclose some information while keeping other information secret. Elisabetta Ottoz & Franco Cugno, *Patent–Secret Mix in Complex Product Firms*, 10 AM. L. & ECON. REV. 142, 143–45 (2008); Brian C. Reid, CONFIDENTIALITY AND THE LAW 64–65 (Waterlow 1986).

[70]   For a complete discussion on the tradeoffs between patent and trade secret, *see* Michael Risch, *Trade Secret Law and Information Development Incentives*, in THE LAW AND THEORY OF TRADE SECRECY: A HANDBOOK OF CONTEMPORARY RESEARCH (Rochelle C. Dreyfuss & Katherine J. Strandburg eds., Edward Elgar Publishing 2010).

effects from competitors, even if the law does not provide a remedy when others attempt to learn the secret.

This chapter's model is motivated by just this tradeoff—one faced primarily in the software area but to a much lesser extent in other areas. A legal shock to the system, namely changes to patentable subject matter protection in the *Bilski* and *Alice* cases, should disproportionately affect software developers. Whatever their varying rates of trade secret assertion, after it becomes harder to assert patents in software we would expect to see more reliance on trade secrets.

Now, that additional reliance could take the shape of more trade secret cases filed in state and federal court. Those cases are extremely difficult to gather, and even more difficult to categorize in any causal way, because one would need to somehow identify which cases involved patentable material that was no longer being asserted due to patent law changes.

The second best alternative is to consider whether current patent owners increased their reliance on trade secret cases. In theory, we would expect that every patent owner would be more likely to assert a trade secret when the scope of patents is reduced, and even more likely to do so in those technology areas most affected: software patents. This presents a straightforward application of difference-in-differences.

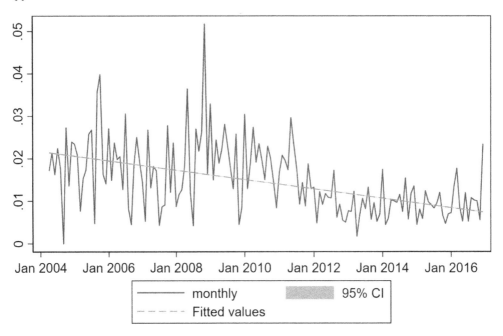

Figure 5.1   *Rate of patent cases that include trade secret claim by month*

As a first step, we consider the overall trend in trade secrets. Figure 5.1 is a graph showing the rate of trade secret filings in patent cases. That is, it shows the monthly percentage of patent cases that also includes a trade secret claim.

The graph is somewhat unexpected. Contrary to the conventional wisdom, the rate of trade secret claims not only fell over the twelve-year period, but also fell substantially.

Further consideration reveals the reason why. During this time period, there was a marked increase in case filings by non-practicing entities—that is, companies that do not sell a product or service (NPEs). The growth in NPE patent filings was substantial, literally thousands of additional cases each year. Further, the America Invents Act of 2011 required plaintiffs to file against each unrelated defendant separately rather than all at once. The number of lawsuits filed each year exploded overnight, as one case against ten defendants became ten separate lawsuits.

But most of those NPE lawsuits would not include a trade secret component. By and large, NPEs sue to enforce patents and obtain licenses. They rarely sue companies with which they have done business or that were otherwise likely to have misappropriated trade secrets because their business model does not include doing business with others (or often even having their employees develop the invention). Thus, we might expect that the *rate* of trade secret case filings will decrease even as the *number* of trade secret case filings increases.

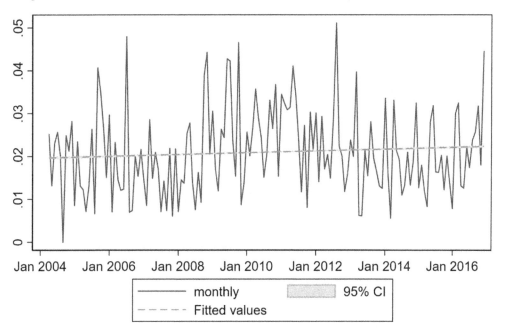

Figure 5.2   *Rate of patent cases that include trade secret claim by month, practicing plaintiffs only*

A revised trend graph confirms this intuition. Figure 5.2 shows that when limited to just traditional product and service companies, the rate of trade secret claims clearly grows over time, albeit slowly and with substantial monthly volatility.

The graph implies that any analysis must consider the type of plaintiff in addition to software patents. A graph of these two identified groups can provide further intuition about a difference-in-differences model. Figure 5.3 charts the rate of trade secret cases among product and service companies separating the cases between those asserting a software patent and those asserting only non-software patents.[71]

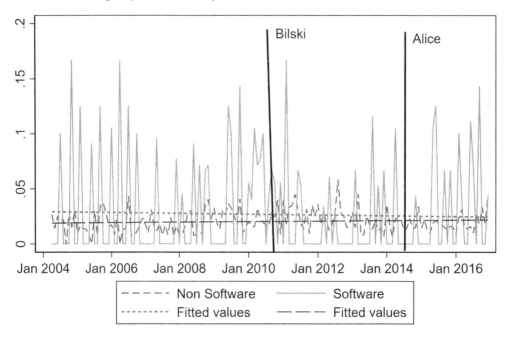

Figure 5.3   Trend of trade secret claims included in patent cases by month and type of patent – practicing plaintiffs only

Figure 5.3 shows that, among practicing companies, software patent cases saw an increased rate of trade secret claims while non-software patent cases remained steady or decreased. Interestingly, the non-software cases were less volatile from month to month, and had no months without any such cases at all, mostly due to a larger number of them. The fitted lines show the entire time period; regression analysis will test for whether the rates changed after the critical Supreme Court rulings.

The difference-in-differences model tested here is as follows:

$$\mathrm{Ln}\left(\frac{P}{1-P}\right) = \alpha + \beta x_i + \gamma y_i + \tau\left(x_i * y_i\right)$$

where x_i represents each group and y_i is 0 preshock and 1 postshock

This is a logistic model of the odds ratio. That is, the model estimates the log of the ratio between the likelihood of our event happening (a trade secret claim) and the likelihood of our event not happening. The coefficient of interest is τ, which represents the estimated effect of the interaction of the post-shock dummy and the treatment group on our logged odds ratio.

---

[71]   Methodology for making this classification is discussed below.

This model is non-linear, but best suited to binary outcomes. The interaction coefficient can be interpreted by direction; that is whether there is an increase or decrease in the odds of a trade secret claim being filed.[72] However, the magnitude of the effect—how much more likely it is for a trade secret claim to be filed—is not readily ascertainable from the estimated coefficient.[73]

A linear prediction model, which fits an ordinary least squares regression to binary dependent variables, would provide more interpretable coefficients. However, linear prediction models suffer from many theoretical drawbacks when applied to binary data. Most can be overcome, but one critical concern is that it can lead to estimated models that yield predictions both above one and below zero. When simply concerned with hypothesis testing for a single coefficient, this is usually not a problem. However, because the rate of trade secret claims is so small (ranging from 1% to 3%), any bias in the estimation near the extremes would overshadow the results. In short, linear probability models are not optimal for this chapter's problem and dataset.

Because there are two treatment groups—cases with software patents and cases with product companies—the difference-in-differences model must be extended to a difference-in-differences-in-differences (DDD) model. The model is similar but includes additional treatment terms.

$$\mathrm{Ln}\left(\frac{p}{1-p}\right)$$

$$= \alpha + \beta_1 x_{1i} + \beta_2 x_{2i} + \gamma y_i + \tau_1 \left(x_{1i} * y_i \right)$$

$$+ \tau_2 \left(x_{2i} * y_i \right) + \tau_3 \left(x_{1i} * x_{2i} \right)$$

$$+ \delta \left(x_{1i} * x_{2i} * y_i \right)$$

where x_{ni} represents each group n and y_i is 0 preshock and 1 postshock

Now, δ is the coefficient of most interest. It represents the change in logged odds of a trade secret claim for members of *both* treatment groups after the shock. In our case, it will include those product companies that assert software patents after the change in law. The τ coefficients also remain relevant for the sub-treatment groups.

Finally, control variables, time effects, and fixed effects variables may be included in the estimation. These additional coefficients serve to isolate any variation associated with factors unrelated to the shock but not randomly distributed among the groups.

---

[72]   Patrick A. Puhani, *The Treatment Effect, the Cross Difference, and the Interaction Term in Nonlinear "Difference-in-Differences" Models*, 115 ECONOMICS LETTERS 85 (Apr. 2012).

[73]   Pinar Karaca-Mandic et al., *Interaction Terms in Nonlinear Models*, 47 HEALTH SERVICES RESEARCH 255 (2012). To put it concretely, 50% of the treatment group plaintiffs could include a trade secret claim before the treatment shock, and 55% could include a claim after the shock (55/50=1.1=10%). The same odds ratio obtains if 77% of treatment group sues pre-shock and 70% sue afterward (77/70=1.1=10%). In both cases, the ratio shows a 10% change in odds, but the absolute values of the preferences generate different policy implications depending on which case applies. Given that trade secret claims are relatively rare, a relatively small absolute change can yield a relatively large odds ratio.

The treatment variable in a difference-in-differences analysis typically requires that the treatment be unexpected (hence, the "shock"). If the participants expect the treatment event, they might prepare in expectation of it. While lag variables might be used, it is best to have a clean break.

This chapter tests two different events. The Supreme Court's ruling in *Bilski v. Kappos* and the Court's ruling in *Alice v. CLS Bank*. Each of these cases had a significant effect on the enforceability of software patents. While *Bilski* could have been interpreted to bar software patents, lower courts continued to grapple with the law for four more years until *Alice* reiterated the sweeping nature of the Court's ruling.

These cases were very likely shocks. The sheer quantity of amicus briefing for *Bilski* implied that the case was hard fought. It was the first patentable subject matter case heard by the Court in nearly thirty years. There was no way to predict its outcome, which divided the Court. *Alice* was a shock in a different way; the evidence is relatively clear that *Bilski* was not taken as a fully formed rule, and so many must have believed that *Alice* could be decided to allow more patents than it did. In combination, *Bilski* moved the patentable subject matter needle partway, while *Alice* completed the turn toward non-protection of many software inventions.

4.   DATA GATHERING

Several sources provided data for this study. The primary dependent variable, trade secret claims in patent cases, came from two sources. First, the PTO is preparing a collection of patent case filings—complaints, motions, and orders—rendered into text form by optical character recognition, and kindly provided a preview of the data.

This yielded some 47,000 documents, far too many to review by hand. Natural language processing extracted a list of documents that included the words "trade", "secret", and "secrets." The software also counted the occurrences of each, as well as the occurrences of both "trade" and "secret" in the same document. A different algorithm tagged each of these documents, as well as every third document for review.

Reviewers then read each of the flagged documents and identified those cases in which the plaintiff brought both a trade secret claim and a patent claim. As such, declaratory relief cases were excluded, as were cases in which trade secrets were mentioned but not allegedly misappropriated. One of the reviewers (the author) randomly checked several dozen codings and found 100% concordance. The reviewers also read each of the randomly selected documents for trade secret cases to ensure that none were missed. Out of nearly 13,000 randomly selected documents, of those that did not include the words "trade" or "secret," only four involved a trade secret case.

Data from Lex Machina bolstered the PTO files. Lex Machina is an analytics service that collects and codes data about a variety of cases, including IP. A search for all patent cases that included a trade secret claim yielded 541 cases, most of which were already in the PTO data but some that were not. The two datasets were combined to create one list of all patent cases that also included a claim for trade secret misappropriation.

The PTO dataset on litigated cases provided additional case details, including a list of all litigated cases during the studied period, 2006–2016. These details include the date filed, the type of case (e.g. patent infringement or declaratory relief) as well as a list of all the patents asserted in the case. Only utility patent infringement cases were used.

The list of patents in the case were matched to the PTO's patent database, which provided information about the claims and technology class of each patent. The patent database provided the information necessary to identify software patents. The methodology used to define software patents is outlined by Hall & MacGarvie.[74] Following two papers and their own methodology, they consider any patent that falls into particular technology classes[75] or that contains particular words a software patent.[76]

Finally, patent owner data from the Stanford NPE Litigation Database[77] was merged with the litigation data. The NPE Litigation database also flagged declaratory judgment actions as a check on the PTO data. More important, the NPE database codes for thirteen different types of patent plaintiffs. Three of them are practicing plaintiffs: product and service companies, pre-product startups, and failed startups. The remaining are all some form of non-practicing entities: acquisition companies, R&D firms, inventor owned non-product companies, individual inventors, and so forth. These groupings were used to group plaintiffs into one of two treatment groups: product companies and non-product companies.

There were more than 41,000 cases in the studied time period that had data in all the sources. About 2,000 cases were omitted because they were not listed in one database or another. Examination of the distribution of those cases (and those that included trade secret claims) implies that it is a random assortment, and not one that is likely to bias the results in any direction.

5.   RESULTS AND IMPLICATIONS

Table 5.1 presents the results of four logistic DDD regressions. The first uses *Bilski* as the treatment shock date. The second lags *Bilski* by six months on the theory that it took time for plaintiffs to change their behavior. The third estimate uses *Alice* as the critical date and the fourth lags *Alice* by six months. The data began in January of 2006 and ended in December of 2016, the period for which the most complete data was available.[78]

Control variables included the month, so that any generalized trend in trade secret filings might be captured.[79] The estimates also include the number of patents, in case firms asserting

---

[74]   Hall & MacGarvie, *supra* note 32.

[75]   *Id.* at 998 n. 19 ("The groups included are G06F: 3,5,7,9,11,12,13,15; G06K: 9,15; H04L: 9"). Hall and MacGarvie also use additional classifications that they identify; however, their classes are tied to 2002 classifications, which were not readily available in the PTO dataset. Based on the discussion by Hall & MacGarvie, this omission likely leaves out some, but not a substantial number of software patents.

[76]   *Id.* at 998. Software patents "include the word 'software,' or the words 'computer' and 'program,' in the description and/or specification. Patents that meet these criteria and also contain the words 'semiconductor,' 'chip,' 'circuit,' 'circuitry,' or 'bus' in the title are excluded, as they are believed to refer to the technology used to execute software rather than the software itself. Patents containing 'antigen,' 'antigenic,' or 'chromatography' in the description/specification are also excluded." *Id.*

[77]   https://npe.law.stanford.edu/, accessed April 8, 2023.

[78]   Data prior to 2006 lacked much useful information because, despite the institution of nationwide electronic filing in 2003, many districts still did not require electronic filing of the complaint for several years. Further, six years before *Bilski* is likely too early to yield quality difference-in-differences results.

[79]   Alternative estimations used the month as a continuous variable and as a discrete fixed effects variable. Results did not differ materially.

Table 5.1   Logistic model of trade secret claims in patent cases title?

Variable	Bilski	Bilski-lag	Alice	Alice-lag
Month	-0.0047	-0.0026	-0.0054**	-0.0050*
No. of Patents	0.0398*	0.0384*	0.0447**	0.0449**
Is After Sup. Ct.	-1.2912***	-1.3384***	-0.6711*	-0.7384*
Is Product Co.	0.2840	0.4128	1.1077***	1.1573***
Is Software Patent	-0.4211	-0.1917	-0.6347	-0.6753*
Is Prod. Co. & SW	0.9963	0.7923	0.8290*	0.8334*
After Ct. & Prod Co.	1.5700***	1.4431***	0.7428*	0.6861
After Ct. & SW Pat.	-0.3622	-0.9578	-1.1161	-0.7949
After Ct. & Prod. Co. & SW Patent	-0.1958	0.3001	1.3407	1.2655
Constant	-1.5221	-2.8390	-1.8047	-2.1018
N	37946	37946	37946	37946
Chi^2(9)	172.1669	165.7508	179.1846	182.3254
p	0.0000	0.0000	0.0000	0.0000
Pseudo r-squared	0.0645	0.0658	0.0581	0.0578
	***p<.001	**p<.01	*p<.05	

more or fewer patents were systematically more likely to file a trade secret claim. Plaintiff fixed effects were unavailable due to computational limitations (there were some 15,000 different plaintiffs), but standard errors were clustered by plaintiff.

The results reflect much of what we know about patent litigation and the data already. As each month passed, all else equal a lower percent of patent cases included an attached trade secret claim. Additionally, the time after *Bilski* in 2010 indicated a reduced percentage of trade secret claims. Both of these findings are explainable by the massive growth in non-practicing entity patent assertions. Quite simply, after 2010 there were many more patent cases where the parties had no prior relationship than before. By 2014, this had somewhat evened out.[80]

Contrary to this trend, though, is the slightly positive increase in probability of filing a trade secret claim with every patent asserted in the case. One would expect that mass patent litigation would likely not include a trade secret claim. As a reminder, one must be cautious in reading these non-linear estimates. They do not directly indicate how much each month or patent will affect the probability of an included trade secret claim—only that the relationship is (very mildly) there.

The negative coefficients on both software cases standing alone as well as software cases after the Supreme Court ruling imply that software patent cases were less likely to include a trade secret claim, all else considered. This is a bit surprising at first blush, but explainable by the rest of the results. It likely means that there are many NPEs who brought patent claims for

---

[80]   The passage of the America Invents Act helps with this leveling out, as there was a spike in cases in 2011 based on joinder rule changes that required each patent defendant to be sued in a separate case, after *Bilski* but before *Alice*.

software patents. So many, in fact, that on average they drown out all the trade secret claims. This interpretation is verified by the positive coefficients on the product company/software patent interaction. Those companies were more likely to bring trade secret claims than the many NPEs asserting software patents.

Indeed, product companies, either with or without software patents, were more likely to include a trade secret claim. Interestingly, when the interaction effects were moved to the later date, product companies appeared to have a much higher likelihood of including a trade secret claim, all else equal (that is, both before and after *Alice*). This may seem like an anomaly but is pretty easily explained by the smaller value of the coefficient on the post-shock*product company interaction in the *Alice* estimates as opposed to the *Bilski* estimates. One explanation of this is that around 2010, product companies brought trade secret claims with a particular likelihood, but beginning in 2010, a lot more product companies brought such claims. By 2014, they were already bringing trade secret claims at the elevated post-*Bilski* rate, and so the increase after *Alice* does not appear to be so large.

This leaves the null hypothesis. Disproving the null hypothesis—that the Supreme Court's rule changes had no effect on product company assertions of trade secret claims in software cases—requires the final interaction coefficient (After*Product Company*SW Patent) to be positive. With respect to *Bilski*, there was no such effect. The coefficients at the time of *Bilski* and six months afterward run in opposite directions and the probability that the values are no different from zero are about 70%.

With respect to *Alice*, however, the results are different. Both after *Alice* and to a lesser extent (as we would expect) six months after *Alice*, product companies asserting a software patent were more likely to also include a trade secret claim. For each of these, the p-value was 25%. While these metrics are not individually statistically significant, within the context of the entire model, they infer a likely causal rejection of the null hypothesis.[81]

Figure 5.4 reflects the discussion above. Non-product company, non-software cases were unlikely to include a trade secret claim, and this became even less likely after *Alice* as the number of NPEs grew. Indeed, non-product company, software patent cases started and after *Alice* ended even less likely to include a trade secret claim. Thus, while changing patentable subject matter rules may have affected software patents, for those entities that were never in a position to make a trade secret claim, there was just no likelihood of doing so.

On the other hand, product companies that asserted non-software patents were already more likely to include a trade secret claim, and that probability increased just slightly. But product companies that asserted software patents—the key treatment group—increased the probability of asserting a trade secret claim by nearly a percentage point, and because the percentages are so small, this means a nearly 50% increase in likelihood that—after *Alice*—a software patent claim will be accompanied by a trade secret claim.

The effect appears to be substantial. But the causal inference is likely but uncertain. Like the p-value on the interaction coefficient, the probability change in the graph here has some overlap in 95% confidence intervals. In particular, the treatment group behavior is highly erratic, as shown generally in Figure 5.3; some months saw substantial trade secret claims

---

[81]   Ronald L. Wasserstein et al., *Moving to a World Beyond "p < 0.05,"* 73 THE AMERICAN STATISTICIAN 1 (Mar. 2019) (describing move away from rigid p-values to more holistic view of statisitical results).

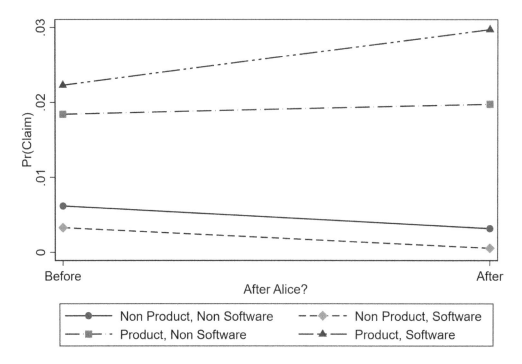

Figure 5.4   Predictive margins: product company/software patent interaction

while others saw none. This is likely due to fewer plaintiffs in the product group, which in turn leads to larger confidence intervals.

But this is not a sample study, where we are worried that our random sample has some unseen biased data. These are, with a few exceptions, all of the cases, more than 37,000 of them. The results are thus the actual likelihood of trade secret cases in the population. It is not surprising, then, that the results are stable. Probit regressions yield similar results. Changing the definition of product company to include other plausible companies (e.g., industry consortia and IP licensing subsidiaries of product companies) yields similar results. At minimum, the law likely caused a change in filing behavior.

6.   IMPLICATIONS AND CONCLUSION

The inclusion of trade secret claims in patent cases is but one component of the shift from patents to trade secrets which, in turn, is one component of the rise of trade secrets. This chapter has modeled trade secret claims in patent cases.

The results tell several stories. First, the story of the rise of NPEs as patent plaintiffs. After 2010, and especially after 2014, the percentage of cases that include a trade secret claim decreased in general, as a larger and larger number of patent plaintiffs entered the system with no prior relationship with their defendants. This is also reflected in a cohort of software patent cases that do not trend toward trade secrecy because they cannot.

Second, it appears that, after the Supreme Court narrowed the scope of software patents in the *Alice* case, the group of product companies were about 50% more likely to include a trade secret claim in their software patent cases. The absolute numbers are quite small, from about 2% to about 3%. Furthermore, because there are not that many of them, there is some uncertainty about how strong the effect is.

Third, the analysis here only answers part of the question. This chapter focuses on trade secret claims within patent cases because it is a convenient way to show a causal relationship between changes in patent law and trade secrets. But what the analysis cannot show is whether and how many companies left the patent system altogether (or at least stopped trying to enforce their patents) in favor of trade secrets.

On the one hand, we might think that the number is substantial, given the results shown in this chapter. If patent plaintiffs are adding trade secret claims to their cases then it stands to reason that even more companies who might have had patentable technology—but no longer do after *Alice*—are simply filing trade secret claims while bypassing the patent route. But this shift is cabined by the requirement that the trade secret defendant actually misappropriate the secret. That is, many previously patentable inventions may not be the type of technology that can be kept secret. More important, companies may not have contact with sufficient parties who misappropriate their information. Even so, to the extent that companies keep their inventions secret rather than patent them, the number of cases would likely increase simply because there is more to misappropriate.

Important questions about the trends of trade secret litigation: are cases growing and, if so, what is driving the growth? This chapter contributes a piece of the puzzle.

6.   Evidence-based IP research

Empirical studies in patent law & trade secrets

Mateo Aboy, Louise C. Druedahl and Timo Minssen

1.   INTRODUCTION

Qualitative and quantitative empirical methods are playing an increasingly important role in legal research. Complementing more traditional legal methods, empirical approaches allow an understanding of how the law operates in the real world, and this knowledge of *de lege lata* can be used to evaluate whether the law is working as intended. Such evaluations are important to analyse whether the desired outcomes of the law are being achieved, help inform policy, and advance new proposals for the law as it should be (*de lege ferenda*). The *Oxford Handbook of Empirical Legal Research* describes the contribution of empirical legal research to policy-making as two-fold:

1. Empirical evidence can reveal gaps in current legal provision, or weaknesses in the ways in which current law works. It can help identify new strategies for dispute resolution and more generally for increasing the impact of law on society. In short, empirical legal research can assist policy-makers in defining changes needed in law or legal process.
2. Empirical research on law can also be used to address policy areas where problems are not likely to be assisted by more legislation. Empirical research can challenge assumptions about the effectiveness of law as a regulatory tool. Those with experience of doing empirical research in law, who understand both the substance of current law and why it does not work, are well placed to suggest how sensible policy-making might not require the introduction of new law, but rather seek better use of existing legal provisions[1]

Empirical legal research is important for multiple areas of law, and it is particularly relevant when studying intellectual property (IP) law-related questions including inventive activity, subject-matter eligibility, incentives, and innovation.[2] In that regard, it should be borne in mind that many areas of IP law often rely on various assumptions about the expected behaviour of key stakeholders such as creators, inventors, entrepreneurs, and investors; how innovation markets function; or how the judicial system and legal profession are dealing with IP disputes.[3] But do all of these assumptions and beliefs hold true? And if not, what impact does this have on the underlying innovation incentives? What could and should be changed to

---

[1]   Martin Partington, 'Empirical Legal Research and Policy-making'. In: The Oxford Handbook of Empirical Legal Research (Oxford University Press: 2012). doi: 10.1093/oxfordhb/9780199542475.013.0042 . See also <https://academic.oup.com/edited-volume/35077> accessed 2 June 2022.

[2]   Chicago-Kent's Center for Empirical Studies of Intellectual Property, <https://www.kentlaw.iit.edu/institutes-centers/center-for-empirical-studies-of-intellectual-property> accessed 2 June 2022.

[3]   *Id.*

improve the functioning and beneficial impact of IP to promote sustainable innovation from a utilitarian, ethical, and societal perspective?

Empirical studies are increasingly useful to investigate the validity of IP law's assumptions and help propose reforms to existing IP and regulatory regimes with the goal of achieving desirable social outcomes. This is accomplished, for instance, by combining (1) empirical findings arising from the analysis of natural experiments emerging from legal and regulatory changes (e.g., Supreme Court decisions that change the law governing subject-matter eligibility and hence enabling researchers to conduct pre- and post-comparisons or comparisons across jurisdictions), (2) controlled experiments, (3) analysis of real-world data from increasingly rich and sophisticated IP-related databases involving real-world cases, and (4) semi-structured interviews with key stakeholders. Empirical legal studies also complement other types of legal research to provide evidence-based recommendations for increasing the effectiveness, efficiency, beneficial impact, and sustainability of the IP system[4] and the broader innovation ecosystem within which it operates.

This holds particularly true for the more specific areas of patent and trade secret law, because these rely on a quid pro quo that must be fair for inventors, entrepreneurs, investors, and society. Within IP law, the biotech and pharmaceutical sector provide a suitable example to elucidate the potential of empirical research. Due to the traditionally crucial importance of the patent and trade secrets systems for this sector, it is often referred to as the primary example for demonstrating the success of the IP system to provide necessary incentives in capital-intensive fields. Given the recent developments spurred by the combination of rapidly evolving medical and information age technologies (e.g., big data, artificial intelligence (AI), digital medicine, quantum simulation and computing), new societal threats such as the recent pandemic or antimicrobial resistance, and the resulting reactions in public perceptions and policy, the medicinal product and medical devices sector – with its rich ecosystem of affected stakeholders – provides an excellent example to illustrate the types of research questions that can be studied by empirical means.

This chapter is structured as follows: (1) Section 2 provides an overview of empirical studies in patent law, including a categorisation of these studies and methodological considerations, (2) Section 3 addresses similar aspects in connection with empirical studies involving trade secrets, (3) Section 4 includes selected case studies to illustrate the different types of empirical methodologies presented in Section 2 with reference to a selection of our published empirical IP studies, (4) Section 5 provides a discussion, and (5) Section 6 brief concluding remarks.

2.   EMPIRICAL STUDIES IN PATENT LAW

Evidence-based studies in patent law leverage the public nature of the patent disclosures. Patents are a valuable indicator of the pace and dynamics of innovation at the invention stage. Accordingly, empirical IP studies looking at the patenting activity can provide valuable evidence to help assess policy proposals related to intellectual property rights (IPRs), innovation, and regulation considering patent office data.[5]

---

[4]   *Id.*

[5]   Mateo Aboy, Timo Minssen, Mauritz Kop, 'Mapping the Patent Landscape of Quantum Technologies: Patenting Trends, Innovation & Policy Implications', forthcoming in IIC – International Review of Intellectual Property and Competition Law, 53, 6 (July 2022).

At the time of this writing, it is possible to search over 139 million global patent documents and conduct empirical studies based on these patent search results. The European Patent Office (EPO) patent information resource (Espacenet) provides free access to over 130 million patent documents from more than 80 different countries. Legal scholars can get started by using free educational resources, including e-learning tutorials and online seminars covering the advanced features of the EPO patent search engine.[6] Additionally, there are now publicly available resources such as the open web platform Lens.org[7] to help scholars search and analyse the global patent records to create patent landscape studies based on standardised data sharing protocols and open datasets of patents and scholarly works. IP scholars and practitioners have now free access to the global patent datasets, high-quality search tools, metrics, and analytics capabilities to study patenting trends across time and geographics, patent owners, citation graphs, inventive teams, and enriched metadata.

Depending on the level of analysis, empirical patent studies can be classified as (1) patent landscape studies or patent landscape reports (PLRs), (2) broad-level impact studies designed to answer questions regarding the large effects of legal decisions on patenting activity,[8] (3) claim-level studies designed to address questions regarding how claim practice and strategy changes and associated scope of protection, (4) prosecution-level studies designed to answer questions about the prosecution strategies and effects, and (5) secondary-impact studies. The World Intellectual Property Organization (WIPO) guidelines on patent landscaping state that:

> Patent Landscape Reports (PLRs) support informed decision-making and are designed to efficiently address the concerns associated with making high stakes decisions in various areas of technology, increasing the related degree of confidence [...] With the institution of patent analytics, and PLRs, it is possible for these critical decisions to be made with data-driven, evidence-based approaches that deliver informed choices, and mitigate the associated to the decision risks. The insight gained from the preparation of a patent landscape report can be applied to almost any organization engaged in the evaluation of technology, and its impact on society. Government agencies, as well as private enterprise can gain valuable perspective on a developing, or well-established field by generating a PLR. As an example, PLRs can be used as instruments to inform public policy makers in strategic decisions to related to R&D investment, prioritization, technology transfer or local manufacturing. Patent information can and is increasingly being used as a tool to inform public policy.[9]

Patent landscape studies are designed to answer questions such as: What has been the patenting trend over the past 20 years for a given technical field? Which countries and organisations are leading the particular technical field? What claim formulations are being used to protect these inventions? In what jurisdictions are they being protected? Without more evidence-based IP research to address these types of questions, it is often perilous for legal scholars and policymakers to presume they can propose reforms to existing IP and regulatory regimes with reasonable chances of achieving desirable social outcomes. This is especially the case in

---

[6]   EPO, 'Espacenet', <https://www.epo.org/searching-for-patents/technical/espacenet.html> accessed 9 May 2022.

[7]   The Lens, <http://lens.org> accessed 10 May 2022.

[8]   See e.g. Mateo Aboy, Kathleen Liddell, Cristina Crespo, I Glenn Cohen, Johnathon Liddicoat, Sara Gerke, Timo Minssen, 'How does emerging patent case law in the US and Europe affect precision medicine?', Nature Biotechnology, 37, 1118–1125 (2019) doi: 10.1038/s41587-019-0265-1. PMID: 31578504.

[9]   WIPO, 'Guidelines for Preparing Patent Landscape Reports' <https://www.wipo.int/patentscope/en/programs/patent_landscapes/> accessed 10 May 2022.

early-stage *deep tech* fields such as biotech and quantum technologies that require significant high-risk R&D investments and overcoming substantial scientific and engineering challenges.[10]

In addition to search results, patent landscape studies include analytics and visualisation of the findings. General PLRs often include: (1) analysis of the patent activity per year (i.e., the temporal distribution and growth rates) for the technology under study, (2) top patent owners (i.e., assignees), (3) citation analyses (e.g., forward and backward citation of the top patent portfolios), (4) analysis of the legal status of the various patent documents, (5) allowance rates, (6) top patent classes and temporal evolution of patenting activity per class, (7) patent term analysis and survivorship rates, (8) estimated expiration dates of patents, (9) concept landscaping, (10) technology breakdown by sub-classes or subfield, and (11) patent claim analysis.

Taking patent landscape studies as a starting point, the other types of empirical methodologies are aimed at analysing the impact of legal decisions involving patentability at four different levels of analysis:

- Broad-level impact analysis: before and after decision patent landscapes.
- Claim-level impact analysis: before and after decision claims, claim scope, claim strategies, claim formulations, and impact on business models.
- Prosecution-level analysis: before and after decision prosecution timelines, patent prosecutions strategies, effects of types of entities.
- Secondary impact studies: side effects, ripple effects, and unexpected consequences after a legal decision affecting patentability.

A key difference between these types of empirical patent studies relates to the nature of the source data. Patent landscapes are based on published patent applications and granted patents from the patent offices. Thus, the primary sources of authoritative patent data are the respective patent offices for each jurisdiction. In order to facilitate search and analysis across patent authorities, secondary patent databases have been developed. These include databases developed by patent authorities such as WIPO's PATENTSCOPE,[11] EPO's Espacenet,[12] publicly available databases and open-source tools such as Lens.org,[13] and commercial products. PATENTSCOPE, for instance, provides access to all Patent Cooperation Treaty (PCT)[14] applications from the 156 PCT contracting states in full text format on the day of publication.

While the primary source data for patent landscapes derive from the published patent documents (i.e., patent applications and the corresponding patent grants), prosecution-level studies require access to the internal communications between the patent authorities and the patent practitioners with power of attorney that represent the applicants during the patent examination process. Thus, the source data for these studies includes the internal office actions from the patent authorities such as non-final rejections, final rejections, advisory actions, as well as the corresponding responses from the applicant's patent attorney to overcome the rejections of record by arguing the patentability of the original or amended claims. The United States Patent

---

[10]   Mateo Aboy, Timo Minssen, Mauritz Kop, 'Mapping the Patent Landscape of Quantum Technologies: Patenting Trends, Innovation & Policy Implications', forthcoming in IIC – International Review of Intellectual Property and Competition Law, 53, 6 (July 2022).

[11]   WIPO, <https://www.wipo.int/patentscope/en/> accessed 12 May 2022.

[12]   EPO, <https://worldwide.espacenet.com> accessed 12 May 2022.

[13]   The Lens, <https://www.lens.org> accessed 12 May 2022.

[14]   WIPO, <https://www.wipo.int/pct/en/> accessed 12 May 2022.

Office (USPTO)'s Patent Application Information Retrieval (PAIR) provides web-based access to the office correspondence for published and issued patents. The USPTO documents contained in the patent file wrapper are downloadable in PDF form.[15] The primary source files for prosecution-level empirical studies are often based on the following USPTO document codes: CTNF (Non-Final Rejections), CTFR (Final Rejections), REM (Applicant Arguments/Remarks), CLM (latest version of the claims with indications of any amendments), and A (Amendments/Request for Reconsideration-After Non-Final Rejection). Prosecution-level studies focus on the rejections issued by the patent examiners to the patent applications, the corresponding arguments to overcome the rejections of record, the allowance rates, prosecution strategies, and prosecution timelines.

When conducting empirical patent studies involving several offices, it is advantageous to use a common patent classification scheme. Patent offices worldwide use the International Patent Classification (IPC) scheme, established by the WIPO-administered Strasbourg Agreement of 1971. The IPC provides a hierarchical system to classify patents according to different technical fields that is language independent. Various technologies are divided into eight broad sections and approximately 80,000 subdivisions. PATENTSCOPE enables searching of PCT patent applications by IPC class. Similarly, the EPO and USPTO jointly manage the Cooperative Patent Classification (CPC),[16] which extends the IPC by providing approximately 250,000 classification entries. The use of CPC in search strategies helps improve the specificity of search results because it leverages the manual classification conducted by USPTO and EPO patent experts to categorise each patent application and granted patent in the relevant CPC class, effectively combining the results of automatic search algorithms with manual expert reviews.

From a methodological standpoint, empirical patent studies should aim to achieve a high standard of quality by ensuring consistency, transparency, and reproducibility of results. Thus, it is beneficial that patent landscape studies follow scholarly recommendations to ensure consistency and transparency of patent landscaping,[17] as well as the checklist of information for patent landscapes to ensure reporting quality[18] and guidelines for preparing PLRs.[19]

Beyond patent landscapes, other types of empirical patent studies are often conducted with the goal of answering specific research questions (e.g., examining the impact of a given decision or change in examination guidance in a particular technical field) as opposed to providing a general patent landscape. In such narrower patent studies, not all the PLR reporting guidelines apply. That said, independently of the nature of the empirical patent study, disclosing the details of the patent search strategy (transparency) helps to ensure reproducibility and thus quality of the results and fosters follow-on research.

---

[15]   USPTO, <https://www.uspto.gov/patents/apply/checking-application-status/pair-resources> accessed 12 May 2022.

[16]   PCT, <https://www.cooperativepatentclassification.org/> accessed 12 May 2022.

[17]   Tania Bubela, 'Patent landscaping for life sciences innovation: toward consistent and transparent practices', Nature Biotechnology, 31, 202–206 (2013).

[18]   James Smith et al., 'The Reporting Items for Patent Landscapes', Nature Biotechnology, 36, 1043–1047 (2018).

[19]   WIPO, 'Guidelines for Preparing Patent Landscape Reports', <https://www.wipo.int/patentscope/en/programs/patent_landscapes/> accessed 10 May 2022.

3.   EMPIRICAL STUDIES IN TRADE SECRETS

Trade secrets are related to both IP and patents. Yet, they are often also regarded as a *sui generis* form of protection. In contrast to the disclosure requirement in patent law, however, trade secret protection would be forfeited if the protected information were to be disclosed.[20] The motivation is rather to keep information discrete, confidential, and secret to provide valuable protection. Hence, empirical studies in the law pertaining to trade secrets cannot rely on public databases or expect that interviewees or companies would willingly share the content of such information. This makes conducting empirical research in the field of trade secrets much more elusive and challenging compared to patents. However, from an innovation policy perspective and given the increasing importance of trade secrets in the medical innovation context, it is at least equally important to understand how trade secrets enable or hinder innovation and competitive advantages.

The literature on empirical legal trade secrets research is scarce exactly due to the secretive nature of trade secrets. However, in the body of research that exists, empirical trade secret studies have relied on three different types of methods: (1) case law, (2) quantitative questionnaire surveys, and (3) qualitative interviews.

Case law studies offer evidence of trade secrets from litigation related to alleged theft or violations of secrecy. One example of a trade secret case law study is by Rowe[21] who investigated trade secret damages following litigation. This type of knowledge is important, for example, to compare damages obtainable in trade secret versus patent cases. However, a limitation of using case law is that it is only possible to assess the trade secrets that surface when they get their validity tested in the courts.

Another body of work relates to investigations of trade secrets via questionnaire surveys, and examples of such research include Arundel and Kabla[22] and Cohen et al.[23] These surveys measured trade secret attractiveness in comparison to patents for different technology and product fields. In general, surveys have the advantages of being directly comparative between respondents, can typically involve a larger sample of respondents, and measuring quantifiable categories of knowledge.

A third method to study trade secrets is qualitative interviews which currently has been less applied but is gaining recognition. Qualitative interviews in empirical trade secret studies are useful because they allow access to perceptions, underlying rationales, and values related to protecting sensitive information. In general, qualitative methods can obtain knowledge on opinions, beliefs, or attitudes as well as experiences.[24] This is knowledge that is inaccessible to capture in-depth by the other methods. Therefore, the remainder of this section provides

---

[20]   See definition of trade secret (TS) in art 2 of TS directive. Must be kept secret. EU Directive 2016/943 https://eur-lex.europa.eu/legal-content/EN/TXT/PDF/?uri=CELEX:32016L0943&from=EN.

[21]   Elizabeth A. Rowe, 'Unpacking trade secret damages', Houston Law Review, 55, 155–198 (2017).

[22]   Anthony Arundel, Isabelle Kabla, 'What percentage of innovations are patented? Empirical estimates for European firms', Research Policy, 27, 127–141 (1998) doi: 10.1016/S0048-7333(98)00033-X.

[23]   Wesley M. Cohen, Richard R. Nelson, John P. Walsh, 'Protecting their intellectual assets: appropriability conditions and why firm patent and why they do not in the American manufacturing sector', NBER working paper, 7552 (2000).

[24]   Trisha Greenhalgh, Rod Taylor, 'Papers that go beyond numbers (qualitative research)', British Medical Journal, 315, 740–743 (1997).

a brief introduction on how to apply qualitative interviews as a method in empirical trade secret studies.

Individual interviews can access knowledge surrounding trade secrets and their use, but naturally not about the trade secret content itself. Thus, such empirical legal research can answer questions like: How do companies view the importance of trade secrets for innovation in their field? What scientific or technological aspects make it attractive to use trade secrets over another IP protection? For what reasons do companies expect an increase or decline in their use of trade secrets within a given field? Thus, it is possible to conduct interviews to shed light on, for example, companies' strategic use of trade secrets or their considerations and evaluations of the value of protection by trade secrets versus other types of IP for a given technology. It is possible from such insights and with the company's field of expertise in mind to interpret the competitive advantage of using trade secrets in the given technological field. For example, trade secrets are considered important for innovations within AI due to the rapid developments in the field and that may contain know-how which is undesirable to disclose in patents,[25] moreover, biological medicines have traditionally been protected with trade secrets.[26] However, as technology and science progress and evolve, the value of trade secret protection may change.[27]

Qualitative trade secret studies allow scholars and policymakers (1) to evaluate whether trade secrets *de facto* provide the intended protection according to trade secret holders, (2) to assess the appropriateness of the scope of trade secrets in, for example, the EU Trade Secret Directive and the US Uniform Trade Secret Act[28], and (3) to assess how different technologies rely on trade secret protection and the associated scientific and technological rationales. However, such studies are scarce and increasing research in this field will contribute to an understanding of interactions between science/technology and the use of trade secret protection.

To capture the subtleties and nuances of rationales and perceptions on when, how, and why to use trade secrets it is mostly adequate to use qualitative research methods. Individual interviews have an advantage for researching trade secrets because it is a one-on-one conversation between the interviewer and interviewee. However, as an interviewer, you can expect that formalities and ethics of interviewing are particularly important to interviewees when the topic is IP and especially trade secrets. Information about formalities and ethics should be provided in writing to the interviewee prior to the interview, and the essentials include but are not limited to written informed consent, anonymity, confidentiality, permission from institutional and/ or national review boards or committees, and jurisdictional or national rules for handling and processing as well as storage and management of data.

---

[25]   Quinn Emanuel Trial Lawyers, 'The rising importance of trade secret protection for AI-related intellectual property' https://www.quinnemanuel.com/media/wi2pks2s/the-rising-importance-of-trade -secret-protection-for-ai-related-intellec.pdf accessed 12 May 2022.

[26]   W. Nicholson Price, Arti K. Rai, 'Manufacturing barriers to biologics competition and innovation', Iowa Law Review, 101, 1023–1063 (2016).

[27]   Louise C. Druedahl et al., 'A qualitative study of biosimilar manufacturer and regulator perceptions on intellectual property and abbreviated approval pathways', Nature Biotechnology, 38, 1253–1256 (2020) doi: 10.1038/s41587-020-0717-7.

[28]   Directive (EU) 2016/943 of the European Parliament and of the Council. The protection of undisclosed know-how and business information (trade secrets) against their unlawful acquisition, use and disclosure, L157, and The Uniform Trade Secrets Act (UTSA) by the US Uniform Law Commission (ULC).

For conducting qualitative research, it is essential to have a firm methodological foundation and knowledge before initiating a study. The design of the study is the backbone of the data quality, and the design must be finalised before the study starts because it cannot be changed once the interviewing has started. Thus, a well-planned research design[29] with the 'right' number of interviewees[30] is needed to obtain high-quality data, which is vital to make strong research-based conclusions.

A typical pitfall for novice scholars when starting to conduct qualitative research is under-appreciation of the interview situation, which can have a profound influence on the data quality. It is important with early recognition that interviewing is more than 'just asking questions' and different from the typical lawyer-client conversation. Research interviews naturally have methodological overlaps with lawyer-client conversations such as the requirement for the lawyer/interviewer to conduct active listening and constant analysis of the content,[31] however, there are also essential differences. In lawyer-client conversations, the lawyer's purpose is to uncover the client's problem in a legal context and understand the client's desired outcome. On this basis, the lawyer will suggest and discuss possible actions or solutions in collaboration with the client. Ultimately, the client decides which way to proceed. Such conversation is typically outcome-driven and partial to the benefit of the client. In comparison, a research interview is a very different kind of conversation. The task of the interviewer in research interviews is overall to be impartial while shedding light on the interviewee's perspective on the research topic without the interviewer expressing their own views either directly or via comments. This requires the interviewer to have a high level of awareness and reflection both before, during, and after the interview to neither agree nor disagree with the interviewee. However, verbal and non-verbal cues to signal attention and listening to the interviewee and to express understanding of the logic behind the interviewee's perspective can naturally be used. Simplified, the interviewer is supposed to ask questions and probe to uncover the various facets of the interviewee's perspective on the research topic, including the interviewee's underlying preunderstandings and rationales.

For researching trade secrets with interviews, there is often an additional aspect to be aware of because the interviewees are likely to be experts in their fields. An expert has typically acquired the expert knowledge from one or more of the three factors: (1) education and experience, (2) the person's position and responsibility, or (3) a position in a process.[32] When

---

[29]   There are many facets to make a robust research design for qualitative research. It is recommended to begin by getting a methodological understanding and foundation for making qualitative research. For example, by reviewing methodological literature such as Barbara DiCicco-Bloom, Benjamin F. Crabtree, 'The qualitative research interview', Medical Education, 40, 314–321 (2006) doi:10.1111/j.1365-2929.2006.02418.x and Steiner Kvale, Svend Brinkmann, InterViews: Learning the Craft of Qualitative Research Interviewing (SAGE Publications, 2009).

[30]   A common consideration for planning a research interview study is how many interviewees are necessary for the study. The number of interviewees needs to be balanced towards the type of saturation that is strived for. For this reflection, it is recommended to read Benjamin Saunders et al., 'Saturation in qualitative research: exploring its conceptualization and operationalization', Qualitative Quantity, 52, 1893–1907 (2018).

[31]   Mark K. Schoenfield, Barbara P. Schoenfield, 'Interviewing and counseling clients in a legal setting', Akron Law Review, 11, 313–331 (2015).

[32]   Leo Van Audenhove, Karen Donders, 'Talking to people III: expert interviews and elite interviews'. In: The Palgrave Handbook of Methods for Media Policy Research (Cham: Palgrave Macmillan, 2019) 179–197 doi:10.1007/978-3-030-16065-4_10.

interviewing experts, it is crucial to be aware that the data quality can be affected by the interviewee's perceptions of the interviewer's status and competence. Therefore, it is important that the interviewer is well acquainted with the research topic before conducting expert interviews to reduce such potential influence on the collected data.[33] Nonetheless, qualitative interviews are recommended as a method for accessing expert knowledge[34] which further supports their use in empirical trade secret studies. An example of a qualitative study researching trade secrets by using expert interviews is described in section 4.6.

4.   EMPIRICAL PATENT AND TRADE SECRET CASE STUDIES

4.1   Patent Landscape Studies

An illustrative example of a broad-level impact study can be found in the article "Mapping the European patent landscape for medical uses of known products".[35] This empirical study was designed to examine the European patent landscape of first and further medical uses of known products.[36] Specifically, the article addresses the following patent landscape questions: (1) What activity has there been in the EPO for medical uses of known products over the last 30 years? How many of these patents are granted per year? and What is their allowance rate? (2) Which organisations are leading the patent activity for medical uses of known products? and (3) What types of claim formulations are being used to protect these inventions and what is their relative prevalence? Using a similar methodology, a targeted landscape study was conducted to investigate whether obtaining European patent protection for medical uses of known products was a key factor limiting drug repurposing activity. As an illustrative example, these empirical patent studies enabled us to find that there is: (1) an increasing number of medical use patents relative to the number of repurpose drug authorisations, (2) a relatively high grant rate for medical use patents indicating a clear legal basis for subject-matter eligibility, (3) diversity of patent owners obtaining these medical use patents (public and private), (4) diversity of jurisdictions where they are protected, and (5) coverage among the major therapeutic areas. In turn, these empirical findings provided relevant evidence to indicate that obtaining patent protection for medical use inventions at the EPO does not appear to be a major challenge and it is likely not hindering drug repurposing.[37]

Similarly, the article "Mapping the patent landscape for quantum technologies: patenting trends, innovation, and policy implications"[38] shows an example methodology and the results

---

[33]   Michael Meuser, Ulrike Nagel, 'The expert interview and changes in knowledge production'. In: Interviewing Experts (Basingstoke: Palgrave Macmillan, 2009) 17–42 doi:10.1057/9780230244276_2125.

[34]   Van Audenhove et al and Meuser et al (see n 32 and 33).

[35]   Mateo Aboy et al., 'Mapping the European patent landscape for medical uses of known products', Nature Biotechnology 39, 1336–1343 (2021).

[36]   EPO Guidelines for Examination, Section 7.1 'First or further medical uses of known products', <https://www.epo.org/law-practice/legal-texts/html/guidelines/e/g_vi_7_1.htm> accessed 9 June 2022.

[37]   Mateo Aboy et al., 'European patent protection for medical uses of known products and drug repurposing', Nature Biotechnology, 40, 465–471 (2022).

[38]   Mateo Aboy, Timo Minssen, Mauritz Kop, 'Mapping the Patent Landscape of Quantum Technologies: Patenting Trends, Innovation & Policy Implications', forthcoming in IIC – International Review of Intellectual Property and Competition Law, 53, 6 (July 2022).

of a study designed to map the patent landscape of quantum technologies. In particular, the article evaluates the real-world patenting trends over the last 20 years to determine: (1) the growth of quantum technology patents, (2) the technology breakdown and classification of patenting activity, (3) the choice of priority patent office, (4) the types of patent claims and strategies, (5) the subject matter of recently awarded patents, (6) the top patent owners and their characteristics, (7) the dominant patent portfolios in terms of forward citations, and (8) the geographical distribution of this patent activity.

The results of our patent landscape study for quantum technologies indicated: (1) the USPTO and EPO are currently granting around 2,000 patents per year related to quantum technologies, (2) the overall compound annual growth rate (CAGR) over the last 20 years has been 15.23%, and (3) approximately 50% of the patent disclosures published in the last 20 years are already in the public domain (including 4,536 granted patents that have now expired). Additionally, we found that (1) the majority of the granted patents relate to nanostructures, solid state devices, and their application, (2) the nature of the claims and claim drafting practice are similar to those found in the semiconductor patents that gave rise to the information technology revolution, (3) the increasing overlap between classical (e.g., sub 10 nm transistors used in current CPUs) and quantum technologies presents a challenge for proposals advocating for a *sui generis* quantum patent law regime. The results show that after a period of limited patenting activity (2001–2014), the field of quantum computing has experienced substantial growth recently with the number of granted patents increasing from 37 in 2014 to 435 by 2021 (CAGR = 42.2%). Notably, there is currently less concentration among the top quantum computing patent owners than in classical computing and IT markets. We found that in addition to well-known large cap companies, specialised SMEs, new ventures, universities, and government entities are featured among the top assignees, and the USPTO has been the patent office of choice in the last 20 years, accounting for 77.96% for the granted quantum technology patents by the EPO and USPTO.[39] These results help to illustrate the types of research questions and resulting findings that can be obtained from patent landscape studies.

4.2   Broad-level Impact Studies

Broad-level impact studies focus on the impact (i.e., before-and-after changes) of a legal decision or event. Thus, they often require evaluating the *changing* patent landscape. This can often be achieved by conducting two patent landscapes (before-and-after event under study) and comparing the changes. An illustrative example of a broad-level impact study can be found in the article "Myriad's impact on gene patents".[40] This empirical study was designed to provide evidence to the ongoing controversies and debates surrounding the potential broad-level impacts of the US Supreme Court *Myriad* decision. The key research question was: "What has been *Myriad*'s broad-level impact on gene patents?" The study presents a methodology for conducting broad-level empirical studies, and the results and discussion of a broad-level landscape study.[41] Based on this study it was possible to conclude that the *Myriad* decision did not result in a reduction of gene-related patenting activity. Except for

[39]   *Id.*
[40]   Mateo Aboy et al., 'Myriad's impact on gene patents', Nature Biotechnology, 34, 1119–1123 (2016).
[41]   *Id.*

isolated gDNA, general gene-related patents continued to be issued in increasing numbers (i.e., gene-related patents including SEQ IDs in the claims continue to increase post-*Myriad*). The empirical results indicated that there was a reduction in "isolated gene patent activity", but this reduction trend preceded the *Myriad* decision (i.e., the downward slope had been constant since 2010 and peaked back in 2001). Accordingly, there was strong evidence that the patent system was already "self-correcting" prior to the *Myriad* decision. The legal standards of novelty and especially non-obviousness (inventive step) had already been preventing further isolated gene patents from being issued.[42]

Figure 6.1 shows the number of granted patents by the USPTO with claims containing the limitation "isolated DNA". These updated results developed for this chapter (analysis patent data up to December 2021) confirm our previous hypothesis suggesting that even if *Myriad* had reached the opposite decision (and isolated gDNA patents were eligible subject matter), it is likely that very few of such patents would be granted by the time the *Myriad* case was declined since new patent filings (unless claiming priority back to the early 2000s) would not satisfy the non-obviousness requirement for patentability. Thus, our results based on real-world patent activity indicate that the legal standard of non-obviousness, as opposed to subject-matter eligibility, continues to be the main determinant of patent prosecution strategies.

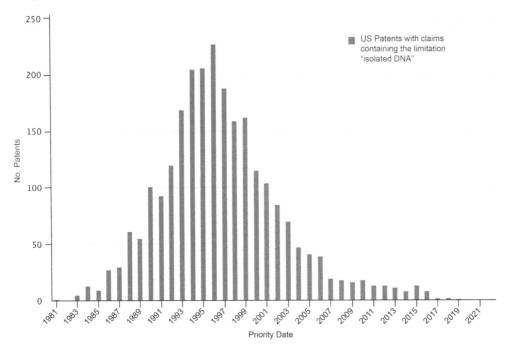

Note: Search conducted on June 9, 2022 by MA Source: USPTO Patent Grants.

Figure 6.1   *Number of granted patents by the USPTO with claims containing the limitation "isolated DNA"*

42   *Id.*

As previously noted, the relative importance of subject-matter eligibility versus non-obviousness may be studied by comparing filing, publication, and the corresponding priority dates of the patent applications and issued patents. Since patent applicants need to sacrifice valuable patent term in order to claim the priority benefits, the primary sound rationale to keep claiming early priority dates is to satisfy the increasingly high-bar of patentability due to the large amount of prior-art now available.[43] The results shown in Figure 6.1 provide further evidence that by the time the *Myriad* case was decided (2013), isolated DNA patents had been in decline for over 15 years. Contrary to the media and scholarly hype surrounding the case, the empirical results show that very few isolated DNA patents were being granted and those granted claimed priorities to around 10 years earlier (giving up their corresponding patent term). Had the US Supreme Court Justices had access to these type of empirical results[44] they may have decided the case differently since (1) the patent system had already self-corrected and isolated DNA patents were no longer being granted and (2) changing the law resulted in secondary (wider impact) effects that potentially undermined the patent system and innovation (*see* section 4.5).

4.3   Claim-level Impact Studies

While patent landscapes and broad-level impact studies can rely primarily on automatic search algorithm and analytics to summarise the results at the macro and meso levels of analysis, claim level studies often require more sophisticated algorithms to analyse the claim features, as well as manual expert review of the claims. The article "After *Myriad*, what makes a gene patent claim 'markedly different' from nature?"[45] provides an illustrative example of a claim-level impact study. This empirical study was designed to provide evidence to the expert debates surrounding the claim-level impacts of the *Myriad* decision such as: (1) What makes a DNA claim 'markedly different' from nature? and (2) Is it easy to 'draft around *Myriad*'? The article introduces an evidence-based methodology for claim-level empirical studies, and the results and discussion of a claim-level patent study designed to analyse *Myriad*'s impact on patent subject-matter eligibility and claim drafting strategies for DNA-based product inventions. The study presents typology to classify the amendments that, after *Myriad,* successfully transformed a simple isolated nucleic acid product claim into a patent-eligible claim. Aside from cancelling the isolated nucleic acid claims ($n = 183$), the results revealed that applicants are typically employing one of eight prosecution strategies: (1) amending to cDNA; (2) amending to nucleic acids with non-naturally occurring sequence variations; (3) amending to nucleic acids recombinantly linked with heterologous sequences; (4) amending to labelled nucleic acids; (5) amending to a nucleic acid in a vector; (6) amending to a nucleic acid recombined with a non-specific regulatory sequence; (7) amending with a Type-2 change and a negative-claim clause; and (8) amending to a short nucleic acid (so short that it does not naturally occur). Additionally, our empirical results indicated that in the years immediately after

---

[43]   *Id.*

[44]   Indicating that the standard of non-obviousness (inventive step) had already raised the standard of patentability for isolated DNA patents and consequently there were not thousands but only a very limited amount of patents with claims directed to isolated DNA being granted and with materially shortened patent terms.

[45]   Mateo Aboy et al., 'After *Myriad*, what makes a gene patent claim "markedly different" from nature?', Nature Biotechnology, 34, 820–825 (2017).

Myriad there has been much less amending activity than some commentators had expected. In over 79.2% of M1a cases, the simple isolated nucleic acid product claims were cancelled. Claim amendments were attempted and successful in less than 18.6% of the cases.[46]

4.4   Prosecution-level Studies

As noted in Section 2, prosecution-level studies require access to the internal communications between the patent authorities and the patent practitioners during the patent examination process to analyse non-final rejections, final rejections, advisory actions from the patent examiners, and the applicant responses. An illustrative example of a prosecution-level impact study can be found in the article "*Mayo*'s impact on patent applications related to biotechnology, diagnostics and personalized medicine".[47] The empirical study was designed to examine *Mayo*'s impact on patent applications related to biotech, diagnostics, and personalised medicine in the US. Specifically, we address the following research questions: (1) How many applications have received *Mayo*-based rejections over the last six years, and what has been the fate of these applications, were they eventually allowed, allowed with amendments, abandoned, or still pending? (2) What is the expected prosecution timeline of patent applications receiving a *Mayo*-based rejection? and (3) How has the prevalence of 35 USC §101 subject-matter eligibility rejections changed over the six years since *Mayo*? For example, has the prevalence of USPTO *Mayo*-based rejections reduced with the passage of time signalling that legal uncertainty surrounding the *Mayo* decision is declining? Using the same methodology, another prosecution-level study[48] was designed to analyse the impact of *Vanda*, including: (1) to what extent have legal arguments and claim amendments based on *Vanda* been effective in overcoming 35 USC §101 *Mayo*-based rejections? and (2) How are applicants transforming diagnostic patent claims into method of treatment claims to overcome *Mayo*-based subject-matter eligibility rejections? In this study, we identified 72,990 USPTO correspondence documents which contained a *Mayo* citation over the six years after the decision (March 20, 2012 to March 20, 2018). Of these, 33,878 were identified in Examiner Office Actions, 34,417 in Applicant Responses to Office Actions, and 4,695 in other correspondence such as Appeals. Analysis of the prosecution-level data enabled us to conclude that as of the sixth anniversary of *Mayo*: (a) 49.3% of the patent applications were rejected or abandoned, 27.6% were granted after overcoming a 35 USC §101 *Mayo*-based rejection, and 23.1% are still in active examination or prosecution; (b) the allowance rate for applications with *Mayo* rejections is 35.9%; (c) overcoming the rejections of record in the granted applications required more than one round of examination or prosecution and the need to file one or more RCEs in 45.8% of the cases (30.3% required two or more); and (d) the prevalence of 35 USC §101 rejections in key art units increased from 10.5% (pre-*Mayo*) to 55.5% (post-*Mayo*).[49]

---

[46]   *Id.*

[47]   Mateo Aboy et al., '*Mayo*'s impact on patent applications related to biotechnology, diagnostics and personalized medicine', Nature Biotechnology, 37, 513–518 (2019).

[48]   Mateo Aboy et al., 'One year after Vanda, are diagnostics patents transforming into methods of treatment to overcome Mayo-based rejections?', Nature Biotechnology, 38, 279–283 (2020).

[49]   Mateo Aboy et al., '*Mayo*'s impact on patent applications related to biotechnology, diagnostics and personalized medicine', Nature Biotechnology, 37, 513–518 (2019).

4.5   Secondary-impact Studies

Patent decisions and changes in examination guidance can have secondary and wider impacts that are often unexpected. An illustrative example of a broad-level impact study can be found in the article "Was the *Myriad* decision a 'surgical strike' on isolated DNA patents, or does it have wider impacts?" [50] This empirical study was designed to analyse the secondary effects and wider impacts of the *Myriad* decision. The article introduces the scholarly and practitioner legal debates surrounding the potential broad-level impacts of the *Myriad* decision, a fundamental research question that had not been previously addressed by other legal scholars related to prosecution impact and the scope of application of the decision, namely, "Has the *Myriad* decision been applied narrowly in a 'surgical strike' manner or broadly at the USPTO?". Additionally, it contains a methodology for an empirical study to address these types of research questions, and a prosecution-level study designed to analyse "*Myriad*'s Impact on Patent Subject-Matter Eligibility Beyond Isolated DNA Inventions". In particular, this empirical study examines the wider impacts of the US Supreme Court decision on subject-matter eligibility and patent prosecution for nature-based products beyond isolated DNA. Contrary to some of the early predictions that the decision would be a narrow "surgical strike" carving out isolated gDNA from patent eligibility, our study finds that 85% of the *Myriad*-based rejections have been directed to non-isolated DNA patent claims. A secondary contribution of the article is the illustration of a methodology for prosecution-level impact studies of patent decisions.

4.6   Trade Secrets Studies

Qualitative individual interviews can be used to study trade secrets empirically, and an illustrative example of this is the article "A qualitative study of biosimilar manufacturer and regulator perceptions on intellectual property and abbreviated approval pathways".[51] The research question was to investigate: What roles do scientific, legal, and regulatory challenges have in biosimilar manufacturing and development? The study was designed to answer this question by using semi-structured interviews. In total 25 experts were interviewed, all interviewees had experience and expertise in biologics either as EU national medicines regulators or as employees from the pharmaceutical industry. The interview guide consisted of questions related to, amongst others, the topics of establishing biosimilarity and a biosimilar manufacturing process, including the potential influence from trade secrets and patents. This case study description focuses on an overview of the results concerning trade secrets. Druedahl et al.[52] reported that the interviewees found that the science to establish biosimilarity and a biosimilar manufacturing process was challenging, but surmountable with the necessary expertise. Further, that such expertise exists independent of the originator companies. Moreover, the interviewees expressed that biosimilar development would not be eased by access to secrecy-protected knowledge of originator manufacturing parameters because such parameters would be

---

[50]   Mateo Aboy et al., 'Was the *Myriad* decision a "surgical strike" on isolated DNA patents, or does it have wider impacts?', Nature Biotechnology, 36, 1146–1149 (2018).

[51]   Louise C. Druedahl et al., 'A qualitative study of biosimilar manufacturer and regulator perceptions on intellectual property and abbreviated approval pathways', Nature Biotechnology, 38, 1253–1256 (2020) doi: 10.1038/s41587-020-0717-7.

[52]   *Id.*

exclusively applicable to the originator manufacturing facilities. Importantly, they found that manufacturing techniques for recombinant proteins had become standardised and, thus, they found it possible scientifically to work around trade secrets. For a more in-depth description of the methodology as well as the associated strengths and limitations, see Druedahl et al.[53] The research took place in the details of the intersection between law and science. This was possible from the interdisciplinary team of researchers that were enabled to tap into the important nuances between scientific knowledge and protection obtained from secrecy.

5.   DISCUSSION

The previous section provides illustrative examples of the types of research questions that can be addressed using empirical IP studies in patent law and trade secrets. As noted in Section 2, independently of the nature of the empirical patent study, transparency of the patent search strategy helps to ensure reproducibility and increase quality of the results and fosters follow-on research. For empirical patent studies, we recommend and encourage authors to disclose the patent search strategy including the specific search algorithms to generate the results and discuss the estimated sensitivity of the algorithm (true positive rate) to identify the relevant patents. It is also helpful to indicate the estimated specificity (true negative rate) of the patent search algorithm based on human expert review of a representative sample of the patent documents (to detect false positives), as well as clearly stating the inclusion and exclusion criteria and limitations of the study. In general, for patent studies at the macro (patent collection >10,000) it is recommended to optimise for specificity (e.g., >99.8%)[54] since – assuming lack of bias – the patent collection is sufficiently large to draw conclusions. Meso- (1,000–10,000) and micro-level (<1,000) studies require search algorithms with high specificity and sensitivity.

For reporting of qualitative interview or focus group research, we recommend following the COREQ-checklist[55] to ensure that transparent and sufficient descriptions of the research design are available to the readers. Further, it is good practice to evaluate the quality of the research by using quality criteria. The challenge of evaluating quality in qualitative research is that there is not one universally agreed standard of which quality criteria to use, but several authors (including Lincoln and Guba,[56] Malterud,[57] and Kitto et al.[58]) have published their views on what aspects to evaluate to assess quality. Reporting on empirical legal research of

---

[53]   *Id.*

[54]   To ensure that the algorithm has specificity >99.8% it is required to manually review a representative sample of at least 500 patents from the research results and conclude that the sample does not contain any false positives.

[55]   Allison Tong et al., 'Consolidated criteria for reporting qualitative research (COREQ): a 32-item checklist for interviews and focus groups', International Journal of Qualitative Health Care, 19, 349–357 (2007).

[56]   Yvonna S. Lincoln, Egon G. Guba, 'But is it rigorous? Trustworthiness and authenticity in naturalistic evaluation', New Directions for Program Evaluation, 73–84 (1986).

[57]   Kirsti Malterud, 'Qualitative research: standards, challenges, and guidelines', Lancet, 358, 483–488 (2001) doi:10.1016/S0140-6736(01)05627-6.

[58]   Simon C. Kitto et al., 'Quality in qualitative research', Medical Journal of Australia, 188, 243–246 (2008) doi:10.5694/j.1326-5377.2008.tb01595.x.

trade secrets must adhere to general quality criteria for the applied methodology. For example, using Kitto et al., the aspects that should be evaluated are: (1) Clarification and justification, (2) Procedural rigour, (3) Representativeness, (4) Interpretative rigour, (5) Reflexivity and evaluative rigour, and (6) Transferability. As an example, to evaluate transferability for an empirical legal study of trade secrets it would be relevant to assess whether the findings are applicable only, for example, to a particular technology (for example, AI/machine learning, quantum, or recombinant proteins) or in a particular jurisdiction.

Transparency about reporting and quality for both quantitative and qualitative research is essential to enable empirical legal research to make the best possible contributions to inform and impact policy. This must also entail a transparent reporting of the limitations of each study to support independent evaluation and interpretations of the data and conclusions, and to guide future research in the area. Empirical legal research for patent law and trade secrets is helpful for understanding the effects on innovation as well as to advance evidence-based policy proposals on *de lege ferenda*. This holds particularly true for capital intensive fields such as the pharmaceutical sector requiring risky R&D that can be relatively easy to reverse engineer. However, some legal scholars have been reluctant to engage in this type of research. There are various reasons for this reluctance, but three interrelated core challenges stand out at the conceptual, methodological, and practical levels. At the *conceptual* level, some legal scholars separate legal studies from empirical inquiries.[59] The *methodological* challenge relates to the required level of expertise needed by legal scholars to design and conduct evidence-based IP studies, including the tools and techniques to conduct empirical studies such as big-data analysis, programming, search algorithm design, natural language processing (NLP) for document analysis, visualisation, and statistics. Conversely, scientists and engineers with expertise in empirical research methods often lack a clear understanding and *design blueprints* that embed the legal and ethical status quo and implications. Finally, the *practical and infrastructural* challenge has been that until recently it was difficult to gain access to relevant datasets, either due to technical limitations, commercial fees to access proprietary databases, or due to confidentiality. Moreover, there are still relatively few legal journals focused on empirical-based research. That said, established IP journals have been increasingly publishing evidence-based studies. Additionally, high-impact science journals such as *Nature Biotechnology* now regularly publish empirical IP studies including "patent articles"[60] as features.

With the availability of new data-driven possibilities, open access databases such as Lens.org, new educational initiatives, and the increasing insight regarding the importance of empirical studies for well-informed and well-guided legal research on IP, the time is now ripe for effectively addressing these challenges. IP scholars can acquire the necessary methodological understanding and skills that go beyond the traditional legal methods. This is important because high-quality evidence-based IP research can improve the impact of scholarly contri-

---

[59]   Or they rely on empirical inquiries that do not sufficiently interact with laws or could be based on incomplete interpretations of applicable laws and their interactions since legal experts were not sufficiently involved in the design of the study. These conceptualisations obscure the actual interaction between the law, infrastructure, and the empirical context.

[60]   *Nature Biotechnology* in their publication Content Types defines such articles as: "A Patent Article offers our readership an expert insight and analysis of the legal issues that pertain to our field of science, including patenting, licensing, and technology transfer. Written by specialists in the field, patent articles are an informative guide to the legal aspects of research and industry", <https://www.nature.com/nbt/content> accessed 9 June 2022.

butions to help guide policy. A part of this is to avoid methodological pitfalls such as sampling bias, failure to account for key confounding variables, or not adjusting for selection effects.[61] Similarly, in qualitative research, it is important to plan the entire research design prior to the start and follow other best practices. Dissemination of empirical legal research should be inspired by the standards of reporting in science and engineering by including more in-depth descriptions of the applied methodology than what is typically reported in traditional legal studies to enable readers to assess the quality of the reported empirical legal study, as well as to access key supplementary information such as the data used to generate the results.

6.   CONCLUSION

This chapter provides an overview of evidence-based IP research methods with a focus on patent and trade secrets studies. It presented the key methodological considerations for several types of empirical studies including (1) patent landscape studies, (2) broad-level impact studies, (3) claim-level studies, (4) prosecution-level studies, (5) secondary-impact studies, and (6) trade secret studies. Additionally, it presented illustrative examples of each of these studies with reference to previously published research.

Given the proliferation of data-rich sources and the lower barrier of entry, we expect a continual increase in evidence-based IP research and multi-disciplinary collaborations. It is important to create an environment that appropriately acknowledges and rewards the value of competently conducted and well-informed empirical legal research. In turn, we expect that these empirical legal research contributions will further enhance the impact and utility of legal scholarship to help guide policy decisions.

ACKNOWLEDGEMENTS

The research for this contribution was supported by a grant from the Novo Nordisk Foundation for a scientifically independent Collaborative Research Programme in Biomedical Innovation Law (Grant agreement number NNF17SA0027784).

---

[61]   Daniel E. Ho, Larry Kramer, 'Introduction: the empirical revolution of law', Stanford Law Review, 65, 1195–1202 (2013).

7. Solving trade secret disputes in Chinese courts: some empirical evidence
Runhua Wang

1. INTRODUCTION

Developed countries including but not limited to the U.S. and the E.U. are increasingly struggling with the concerns about China's technology development relying on them under weak trade secret protection (Pooley 2020; The European Commission 2021). The toughest measures against trade secret thefts from China in history were adopted by the Trump administration. It issued the China Initiative targeting some research scientists tunneling trade secrets to the Chinese government, which was recently ended with many criticisms for civil rights (German & Liang 2022; Lucas 2022). Compared to this national security approach under criminal law, another direct but more useful approach is to initiate negotiations and agreements with China, which pushed China to revise its laws on trade secret protection, such as the latest revision of the Anti-Unfair Competition Law ("AUCL") in 2019 (Pooley 2020).

Before the 2019 AUCL strengthened trade secret protection further, however, China may already have established strong trade secret protection (Wang & Chang 2019). Wang and Chang (2019) conducted a quantitative analysis of the legislation, enforcement, and actual protection of trade secrets in China, which is the only empirical study addressing trade secret's civil protection in China. They found the protection's paradox. On the one hand, their data suggest that the legislation of the first version of the AUCL in 1993 was perfect regarding trade secret protection in the view of the TRIPS and the enforcement of the law was increasingly strengthened between 1993 and 2014. During this period, the quality of judicial decisions was high and stable. On the other hand, because China was at a stage of imitation innovation, the enforcement of trade secret protection was poor, especially when firms need to learn advanced technology through trade. However, the U.S. does not positively view China's legislation on trade secret protection in the same way as Wang and Chang (2019). Even after the latest revision of the AUCL in 2019, the U.S.-China Phase One Agreement ("Phase-One deal") formed after the revision repetitively emphasized its concerns about trade secret protection in China.

Because of the controversial preference for trade secret protection in China's market and China's positive attitude toward strengthening the protection, it is necessary to develop an empirical study on how Chinese courts enforce the protection in judicial practice. Therefore, this study reviews 399 public judgments that were extended between January 2013 and December 2021 for the claims of the misappropriation of technical secrets, especially the 68 of them that include detailed judicial opinions.

Following the adjudication patterns of Chinese courts, it evaluates the judicial enforcement of trade secrets in China and explores the obstacles impeding effective trade secret protection there. First, the application of the AUCLs shows that courts struggled to understand the legal elements of trade secret misappropriation regardless of the clarification and specification of the statutory language by legal revisions. One reason is that the concepts of trade secrets are still ill-defined in the AUCLs. Another reason is that judges are still on the path of strengthen-ing the understanding of the protection of trade secrets. Courts treated trade secrets as a type of intellectual property ("IP") rights but faced difficulties to distinguish them from other types of IP rights (e.g., patents and copyright) when applying the AUCLs. Second, the lack of transparency and judicial autonomy makes the problem even worse. Third, strong deference to criminal investigations is another problem of civil proceedings for trade secret protection. Overall, there is still room for China to improve civil protection for trade secrets from legisla-tion and judicial performance.

Section 2 examines the statutory history of AUCLs and the criminal code governing trade secret issues in China and introduces the research question based on the interests and problems raised in the statutory history. Section 3 introduces the empirical study design, including data, coding strategy, methodology, and the limitations of the data. Section 4 deploys the data to show how courts decided upon trade secret misappropriation. Section 5 digs into the cases finding the misappropriation and explores how courts awarded compensation for trade secret right holders. Section 6 discusses implications and Section 7 delivers the conclusion.

2.   THE DEVELOPMENT OF THE LAW OF TRADE SECRET PROTECTION

2.1   The 1993 AUCL

The law regulates the problems of trade secret misappropriation within the AUCL in China. China first introduced the AUCL in 1993. On the one hand, the goal of its enactment was to coordinate the market (Wu & Liu 2020) and attract foreign investment by improving the investment environment (Yu 1994). On the other hand, the AUCL and other amendments to patent law and trademark law were the fruits of the negotiations between the U.S. and China for preventing a potential trade war by signing the Memorandum of Understanding on the Protection of Intellectual Property (Yu 2021). For protecting trade secrets, Article 10 of the 1993 AUCL prohibited trade secret misappropriation and provided a definition for trade secrets.

> Art. 10 A business operator shall not use any of the following means to infringe upon trade secrets:[1]
> (1)   obtaining an obligee's trade secrets by stealing, luring, intimidation or any other unfair means;
> (2)   disclosing, using or allowing another person to use the trade secrets obtained from the obligee by the means mentioned in the preceding paragraph; or
> (3)   in violation of the agreement or against the obligee's demand for keeping trade secrets, disclos-ing, using or allowing another person to use the trade secrets he possesses.
> Obtaining, using or disclosing another's trade secrets by a third party who clearly knows or ought to know that the case falls under the unlawful acts listed in the preceding paragraph shall be deemed as infringement upon trade secrets.
>   [']Trade secrets['] mentioned in this Article refers to any technology information or business oper-ation information which is unknown to the public, can bring about economic interests to the obligee, has practical utility and about which the obligee has adopted secret-keeping measures.

---

[1]   In some versions of translation of the 1993 AUCL, trade secrets were translated as business secrets.

The 1993 AUCL, however, attracted many complaints from scholars and practitioners for its deficiencies. The primary problem is that it was too ambitious to be clear or detailed for effectively instructing its enforcement by courts or administrative agencies (Wu & Liu 2020). For example, its language was not clear whether or not employees and former employees can be deemed as a defendant for trade secret misappropriation because they may not constitute "a business" that Article 10 of the 1993 AUCL addresses; nevertheless, courts usually believe that employees and former employees constitute "a business" for practical purposes (Kong 2018). Moreover, as the market is being constructed and modernized in China, the statutes in the 1993 AUCL cannot govern the modern problems effectively (Wu & Liu 2020) and guide the market competition to an efficient approach. For example, in Article 25, the statutory damages for trade secret misappropriation were set from 10,000 yuan to 200,000 yuan, which was about 1,429 dollars to 28,571 dollars.

2.2 The 2017 AUCL

The 1993 AUCL was not amended until 2017, while the revision was launched by the State Administration for Industry and Commerce of the PRC in 2003. On the one hand, the 2017 AUCL in general responded to practical problems in China's emerging market (Chai 2018). On the other hand, it was a quick response to the U.S.–China negotiation in November 2016 regarding the U.S. complaints about China's weak trade secret protection and other market order concerns (Luo 2018), especially the former part (Chai 2018).

Compared to the rules on trade secret protection in the 1993 AUCL, there were five main changes in the 2017 AUCL. Three changes referred to the definition of trade secret misappropriation, which was moved from Article 10 of the 1993 AUCL to Article 9 of the 2017 AUCL; the other two changes referred to statutory damages and fines for trade secret misappropriation. First, "bribery and fraud" were added as a type of misappropriating act, and "luring" was specified as "bribery." Second, the liability of a third party and employees was further clarified. The written law directly indicates that acts of authorizing others to use the trade secrets obtained through the employees and former employees of the right holders, other firms, or individuals are prohibited. Third, the elements of "utility" and "economic interests" for establishing the existence of trade secrets were removed; instead, having "commercial value" replaced those elements. Fourth, the cap of statutory damages for trade secret misappropriation was clarified as 3 million yuan. Fifth, the fines entitled for the misappropriation were enhanced from between 10,000 yuan to 200,000 yuan to between 50,000 yuan to 500,000 yuan. Besides posting the fines, the State Administration for Industry and Commerce ("SAIC") and its local branches were extended new administrative investigative powers in trade secret cases, such as the ability to "conduct on-site inspection and dawn raids, sealing and seizure of property related to the illegal acts, and access to and inquiry concerning bank accounts of the infringer" (Ran, Huang, &Williams 2018).

Beyond the above advancement, the 2017 AUCL was still not ideal for most legal practitioners and scholars. First, the statute's language is still vague about whether employees and former employees constitute "a business" that is liable to trade secret misappropriation (Kong 2018). Moreover, some plaintiff-friendly changes in the draft amendment to the 1993 AUCL were not reflected in the final version of the 2017 AUCL. For example, the draft "initially contemplated a provision permitting the inference of misappropriation and a concomitant shift of the burden of proof" (Ran, Huang, & Williams 2018). Under this draft rule of burden-shifting, plaintiffs only need to establish the substantial similarity between their invention and the information used by the defendants, and then the defendants need to prove that the information is acquired from a legitimate source. However, it was not adopted by the 2017 AUCL.

Overall, at this stage, trade secret protection was still considered as ruling on competition orders in China (Kong 2017). Under the framework of unfair competition, the government intervention strengthened in the 2017 AUCL may improve the effectiveness of trade secret protection (Ran, Huang, & Williams 2018). However, the limited view on protecting trade secrets within that framework may result in little change in reality without treating trade secrets as a type of intellectual property (Lin 2018).

2.3   The 2019 AUCL

The 2017 AUCL did not relieve the concerns of foreign companies regarding trade secret misappropriation (Lee 2019). The Office of the United States Trade Representative ("USTR") 2018 Special 301 Report repeatedly expressed concerns about the leakage of trade secrets and confidential information. One particular concern in the Report was about cyber intrusion and consequent trade secret misappropriation.

In April 2019, another amendment to the AUCL was passed, which improved the 2017 AUCL regarding trade secret protection from at least six directions. First, the 2019 AUCL responded to the cyber intrusion concern addressed in the USTR by stipulating "electronic intrusions" as a type of act of trade secret misappropriation. Second, it stipulates the definition of trade secret further as "technical, operational or other commercial information." Third, whether a "business" constituting trade secret misappropriation in the 1993 AUCL and 2017 AUCL includes employees and other individuals has been fixed in the 2019 AUCL: "Natural persons, legal person, or unincorporated organization" are independently regulated in Article 9.2 to follow the rules for the "business" in Article 9.1. Fourth, the cap of statutory damages for trade secret misappropriation was enhanced from 3 million yuan to 5 million yuan. Fifth, punitive damages for malicious infringement are allowed under the 2019 AUCL. Sixth, in Article 32, the 2019 AUCL, shifting the burden of proof is not only realized but also strengthened further to favor plaintiffs compared to the draft amendment to the 2017 AUCL.

> Art. 32 In a civil proceeding on the infringement of trade secret, the lawful holder of the trade secret shall submit prima facie evidence to prove that it has taken confidentiality measures for the claimed trade secret, and to reasonably indicate that the trade secret has been infringed upon. The alleged infringer shall then prove that the trade secret claimed by the lawful holder does not constitute a "trade secret" under this Law. The alleged infringer shall prove the absence of the infringement, if the lawful holder of a trade secret submits prima facie evidence reasonably indicating that the trade secret has been infringed upon, and submits any of the following evidence:
> (1) Evidence indicating that the alleged infringer has the method or opportunity to obtain the trade secret, and the information it used is substantially the same with such trade secret;
> (2) Evidence indicating that the trade secret has been disclosed or used, or is at risk of disclosure or use, by the alleged infringer; or
> (3) Other evidence indicating that the trade secret has been infringed upon by the alleged infringer.

Again, the quick movement of amending the AUCLs was part of an outcome of the U.S.–China trade war to respond to the U.S. concerns (e.g., Lu 2019; Lee 2019; Beconcini 2020). However, some scholars believe that this revision did not mollify the U.S. effectively (e.g., Lee 2019). For example, China committed again to enumerating the acts of "electronic intrusions" constituting trade secret misappropriation in the "Phase-One deal" formed in December 2019, which the 2019 AUCL had addressed. By contrast, some scholars believe that the "Phase-One deal" ignored the 2019 AUCL, which fully addressed the primary concerns over the effectiveness of trade secret protection in China (e.g., Beconcini 2020). For example, the deal restates the draft rule on burden-shifting which the 2019 AUCL had addressed and the draft judicial interpretation for the 2019 AUCL complemented (Beconcini 2020). However, the concerns expressed in the deal still matter because Article 24 of the formal judicial interpretation for the 2019 AUCL did not update the rule on shifting the burden of proof but only repeated the evidence list that plaintiffs need to fulfill.

2.4   Criminal Law Doctrines

In addition to perfecting the civil law to strengthen trade secret protection in China, the "Phase-One deal" pushed China to relive the "actual losses" requirement to initiate a criminal investigation for trade secret misappropriation and clarify the "great loss" threshold for criminal enforcement under the trade secret provision (Beconcini 2020). The trade secret provision refers to Section 219 of China's criminal law, which was embraced into criminal law in 1997. The language of Section 219 of the 1997 Criminal Law is consistent with the 1993 AUCL on the definitions of trade secrets and the misappropriation of trade secrets.

After the "Phase-One deal," both of the requirements were removed in the Eleventh Amendment to Criminal Law, which was published in December 2020 and promulgated in March 2021. In the amended Section 219, definitions of trade secrets and the misappropriation of trade secrets are consistent with the language in the 2019 AUCL (e.g., listing "electronic intrusions," "bribery," and "fraud" as types of misappropriating acts). In addition, the maximum penalty for trade secret misappropriation is enhanced to 10 years from seven years, suggesting a stronger penalty for stealing or leaking trade secrets in China.

After the above legal changes, Chinese legal practitioners and scholars are struggling with the nexus and coherence between civil and criminal proceedings. On the one hand, some scholars suggest a "criminal-first, civil second" model, which means to initiate a civil proceeding after the completion of the corresponding criminal proceeding to authorize trade secret right holders' strong monopoly rights (e.g., Wang & Zhang 2020). On the other hand, some lawyers remind that this "criminal-first, civil second" model may harm the rights and privileges of the accused (e.g., Li & Ling 2019).

Before digging into the nexus, however, a fundamental question that foreign companies and legal practitioners care about is whether those laws can be enforced in China to protect trade secrets effectively as the strengthened protection of other IP rights, such as patents (e.g., Beconcini 2020). Therefore, this study takes the judicial cases under the complaints of technical secret misappropriation as examples to review the logic and standard of Chinese courts adjudicating trade secret misappropriation issues. When reviewing those judgments, this study particularly focuses on the concerns addressed in the "Phase-One agreement," such as burden-shifting from plaintiffs to defendants (i.e., Art. 1.5), the scope of actors liable for trade secret misappropriation (i.e., Art. 1.3), the scope of misappropriating acts (i.e., Art. 1.4), and availability of permanent and preliminary injunctions as legal reliefs for the misappropriation (i.e., Art. 1.6).

3.   EMPIRICAL STUDY DESIGN

3.1   Data

3.1.1   Sample selection

This study selects the judgments over the civil cases addressing the claims of technical secret misappropriation. There are two types of trade secret misappropriations in claim records: One refers to the misappropriation of technical secrets; the other refers to the misappropriation of commercial secrets. Technical information can be strategically protected under patents or trade secrets. An invention should fulfill the requirements of utility, novelty, and non-obviousness to acquire patent rights or only novelty and confidentiality to construct trade secret rights. Compared to the detailed guidance on patent examination, the standards of establishing the existence of trade secrets are more uncertain, especially when utility is an element of trade secrets under the 1993 AUCL. Thus, it is meaningful to scrutinize the process of adjudicating technical secret misappropriation cases for designing legal advice and IP strategies around patents and trade secrets.

The database of judicial cases includes the 46 judgments published on China Judgments Online, which is run by the Supreme People's Court, and another 22 judgments revealed by the Peking University (PKU) Law database for supplementing the former cases. The judgments were decided between January 2013 and December 2021, which is the longest window of judicial disclosure regarding the claims and judicial discussions of technical secret misappropriation on China Judgments Online. For constructing the database, this study reviews all of the 381 judicial outcomes published on China Judgments Online before March 2022 and supplements the results with additional substantive judicial opinions during the same period included in the PKU Law database. The 46 judgments are the only documents that include some legal opinions regarding the claim of trade secret misappropriation regardless of that they are substantive results or procedural results. The judgments that only discussed about personal jurisdiction or both discussed personal jurisdiction and standing (N=1) are excluded for constructing the database. Within the 68 judgments, five judgments are further excluded for repetitive information.[2]

Therefore, this study analyzes 63 judgments in detail, which is also the maximum number of public judgments that discussed about the claims of technical secret misappropriation in China. In those 63 judgments, eight cases include two judgments each at two levels of adjudication proceedings and the rest (47 cases) only have one level of adjudication proceedings available to the public. The two levels of judgments for those eight cases are retained in the database for analysis because the logic and the process of law application could be very different.

3.1.2   Characteristics of the samples

Before analyzing the characteristics of the judicial reasoning in the sample judgments, this subsection portrays the sample judgments with some background information about the courts and the connections between the disputing parties. Among the 63 judgments for the 55 cases,

---

[2]   The four judgments were results of the retrial proceeding in two cases, which were initiated by defendants for consistent reasons and decided by the courts with the same language. Only one retrial judgment regarding the same case was kept as the latest record for the empirical analysis in this study.

29 judgments were first trial decisions, 24 were appellate decisions, and 10 were court opinions of retrial. Only two judgments involved foreign companies as the accusing party.

Most defendants in trade secret misappropriation cases were the plaintiffs' former employees or associated with the plaintiffs' former employees. The disputes in 45 judgments were raised based on former employment relationships. 82.22% of those 45 judgments (N=37) involve a company as a co-defendant. 8.06% of the judgments (N=5) refer to the disputes between employers and independent contractors. Moreover, the disputes in seven judgments were raised between competitors, taking 11.29% of the 63 judgments. In those seven judgments, six judgments upheld trade secret misappropriation and the trade secrets were revealed by former employees and five of the judgments had preceding criminal proceedings. There was only one judgment in which the competitor defendant did not have any connections with the plaintiff's former employees and prevailed based on reverse-engineering.[3]

Besides employment or competition relationships, business allies or potential business allies also sue each other under the claim of trade secret misappropriation. They have agreements of technology transfers, technology licensing, or co-invention or are negotiating for the agreements. Even though some plaintiffs argued that the defendants acquired the accused information through the plaintiffs' employees or former employees, the plaintiffs did not sue those employees in their claims.

3.2   Coding Strategy and Methodology

This study hand-codes the substance of the sample judgments from five directions. First, it covers the background information of the parties and their connections, including (1) whether a foreign company is involved as a party; (2) what is the relationship between the parties; and (3) if an employee or a former employee is accused, whether there is an associated company accused simultaneously. Second, it codes the results of the judgments, including whether the court finds (1) secrecy and (2) misappropriation. Third, the study codes the acts of the plaintiffs and the defendants and how courts treat the acts, including (1) the confidentiality manners adopted by the plaintiffs; (2) the reasons for finding those manners effective or ineffective; (3) the conduct by the defendants; and (4) the reasons for defining or rejecting those conducts as misappropriation of trade secrets. Fourth, the study codes (1) the evidential sources and (2) the burden of proof. Fifth, it codes the results of the judgments, including (1) the availability of adjunctive reliefs and (2) damages extended to injured parties.

Based on the above variables, this study conducts descriptive statistics to review the background information of the disputing parties and judicial proceedings, as shown in the judgments. By descriptive statistics, this study explores common characteristics of judicial decision-making in trade secret civil disputes shared by the sample judgments, which may be consistent with other countries or unique to China. It also picks up some unique characteristics suggesting some judicial preferences or judicial biases in some Chinese courts.

---

[3]   Sike Test v. Languang Mechanical, (Sup. People's Ct. 2020) (China).

3.3   Limitations of the Data

The primary limitation of the study is the data's completeness. Between January 2013 and December 2021, there are another 50 judgments and 31 settled agreements the substance of which is hidden from the public. Thus, this study cannot access to the information of those 81 cases. Moreover, judicial transparency is always a serious problem in China, even though it is agreed upon to disclose judicial decisions in the TRIPS Agreement Article 63. In this study, about 32% of the judgments (N=22) in the database are from the private database—PKU Law. It is unlikely the quantity of the missing cases and the adjudication logic behind those cases can be estimated. On the one hand, in this study's database, the judicial history of 55 cases cannot be traced as separate public judgments. On the other hand, taking 2019 as an example, among the 12 cases substantively decided by the Supreme People's Court in total (The Intellectual Property Court of the Supreme People's Court 2020), only four cases' judgment records can be traced in judicial case databases by May 2022, including but not limited to China Judgments Online and the PKU Law. Therefore, it is inevitable that the missing cases may lead biases to understand the adjudication in the empirical analysis based on those public judgments.[4]

The published judgments could be assumed to be those with fewer flaws and those less critical or controversial compared to the hidden ones (Versteeg 2020). It means many flaws in practice may not be exposed in public judgments, which will be inevitably overlooked by this study. The empirical findings only relying upon public judicial opinions are biased for lack of those flaws. However, assuming the public judicial decisions this study observes present the relatively high-quality adjudication in China, it is a unique opportunity to expose the efforts of Chinese courts to strengthen trade secret protection and inspect the true defects of judicial proceedings for the protection.

4.   THE STANDARDS OF TRADE SECRET MISAPPROPRIATION

4.1   Trade Secrets

Recall the elements to establish a trade secret under the protection of the AUCLs. An ideal situation is that a trade secret right holder can prove that the technical information (1) is unknown to the public ("UKP"), (2) can produce economic interests, (3) has utility, and (4) is protected under confidentiality measures for the disputes raised before the 2017 AUCL. The elements of "utility" and "economic interests" are replaced by "commercial value" in the 2017 AUCL and the 2019 AUCL. Moreover, based on the rule of shifting the burden of proof in the 2019 AUCL, the plaintiff may only need to establish prima facie evidence on the element of confidentiality measures, and the defendant should prove the technical information does not constitute a trade secret under Article 9. Therefore, this Section reviews how parties establish the above elements and what standards those courts adopt to adjudicate upon those elements.

---

[4]   While 30% of IP cases were filed with the Supreme People's Court and settled (the Intellectual Property Court of the Supreme People's Court 2020), there were still cases adjudicated by the Court without public access.

4.1.1 Confidentiality measures

Table 7.1 displays the confidentiality measures adopted by right holders in the 55 cases covered by this study. There are four primary confidentiality measures—non-disclosure agreements ("NDAs"), covenants of non-compete ("CNCs"), physical security measures, and confidential management schemes. CNCs can only be applied to employee- or former employee-defendants. NDAs and other confidentiality measures can be applied to allies and competitors in addition to employees and former employees. The confidentiality measures are displayed by the success of establishing the existence of trade secrets and by the relationships between the plaintiffs and the defendants. In the cases with multiple defendants, if a defendant constitutes the plaintiff's employee or former employee, the relationship is defined as an employment relationship.

Table 7.1   Statistics of plaintiff's confidentiality measures

	no	NDAs only	other	NDAs+ other	NDAs+ CNCs	NDAs+CNCs +other	blank	Total
Court opinions								
No TSs	4	5	6	2	2	1	7	27
TSs	0	9	5	9	2	3	0	28
Relationships								
Employment	2	12	7	7	3	4	4	39
Strategic cooperator	0	0	0	1	0	0	0	1
Supplier and long-term client	0	0	1	0	0	0	0	1
Licensor and licensee	0	0	1	0	0	0	0	1
Independent contractor	1	0	1	0	1	0	0	3
Co-invention	0	0	0	0	0	0	1	1
Competitors	1	2	1	3	0	0	0	7
Potential cooperator	0	0	0	0	0	0	1	1
Total	4	14	11	11	4	4	7	55

The distribution of cases by confidentiality measures and the final court decisions regarding the establishment of trade secrets is shown in Figure 7.1. 87% of the 55 cases disclose the confidentiality measures adopted by the right holders. For the remaining 14% of the cases with undisclosed confidentiality measures, the plaintiffs all failed in establishing the existence of trade secrets. It is not possible to tell whether their claims of holding trade secrets were foundationless or they failed to design effective confidentiality measures for the disputed technical information.

Figure 7.1 shows that courts considered NDAs a strong confidentiality measure in China. NDAs can be strengthened further by other confidentiality measures, such as physical security measures or a confidential management scheme. 7.3% of the right holders did not have any confidentiality measures, which unsurprisingly resulted in failing to show a protectable trade secret by the accused technical information. Most plaintiffs only adopted NDAs as a single strategy to protect the disputed technical information. About 64% of those plaintiffs successfully established trade secrets by this single measure, which is a level much higher than the effectiveness of NDAs in the U.S. (Almeling et al. 2010; Almeling et al. 2011). Of the plaintiffs who adopted additional physical security measures or a confidential management scheme, 80% achieved success in establishing the existence of trade secrets in court.

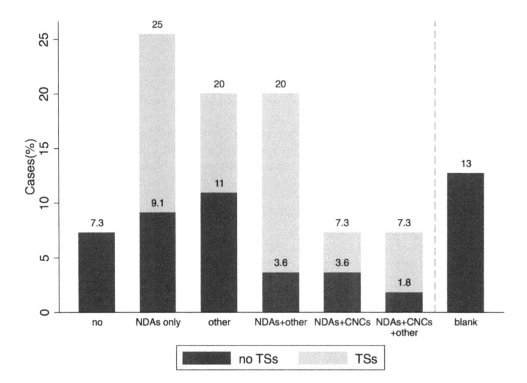

*Figure 7.1   The distribution of the cases by confidentiality measures and the secrecy
results from courts*

By contrast, CNCs did not lead right holders to a higher level of trade secret protection in court, compared to NDAs and other confidentiality measures. None of the plaintiffs treated CNCs as a sole confidentiality measure. In order to establish strong confidentiality, in *Guo v. Jieshi Tech.,*[5] while the accused party is an independent contractor developing technologies for the plaintiff, rather than the plaintiff's employee or former employee, the plaintiff still shows the CNCs it signed employees for showing it has consistent and strong confidentiality measures. Overall, Figure 7.2 shows among the plaintiffs who signed both NDAs and CNCs with employees, the ones who succeed in establishing the existence of trade secrets were at a lower level than the plaintiffs who adopted NDAs only or having other confidentiality measures.

The primary problem of the failure to establish the existence of trade secrets, however, may not be ineffective confidentiality measures. Figure 7.2 shows how courts judged the confidentiality measures in the 31 judgments of 27 cases, in which the plaintiffs failed to establish the existence of trade secrets. In 45% of the 31 judgments, courts did not discuss the effectiveness of confidentiality measures because they believe this element was needless to be considered in those situations. For example, the information is commonly known in the field or is too vague to be defined as an eligible subject matter. Six judgments of five cases reject the existence of trade secrets for weak security measures, which only takes 9.5% of the 63 judgments in total.

---

[5]   (Beijing High People's Ct. 2017) (China).

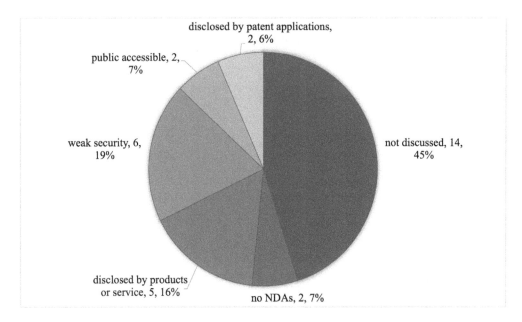

Figure 7.2 Judicial reasons for the failure of confidentiality measures

Moreover, courts in two judgments rejected the existence of trade secrets for lack of effective NDAs. Compared to the lack of effective confidentiality measures, plaintiffs were more likely to fail to establish the existence of trade secrets for voluntary disclosure in products, services, or patent applications, which suggests ineffective confidentiality strategies.

4.1.2 Commercial value, economic value, or utility

Economic value or commercial value is not a material bar to the existence of trade secrets. Among the 63 judgments, courts have never rejected a trade secret claim for lack of economic value or commercial value. Table 7.2 shows some economic values or commercial values which were sufficient or insufficient to support the existence of trade secrets. Courts usually upheld commercial or economic value due to having competitive advantages. More frequently, courts directly express that the accused information is useful for innovation, production, or management, which suggests commercial values.

There were only three judgments in which the courts rejected trade secrets for not fulfilling the element of economic value, commercial value, or utility. The primary reasons for the

Table 7.2 Accept or reject economic or commercial value by courts

	No TSs	TSs	Total
Value-related discussions			
Determined as no value	3	0	3
Established value by utility	1	13	14
Established value by competitive advantages	1	8	9
Mentioned with no explanation	0	1	1
Not mentioned	26	10	36
Total	31	32	63

rejection were the lack of utility in one judgment[6] and the lack of concrete contents subject to trade secret protection in the other two judgments.[7] The vagueness of the accused information hardly generated potential profits or obtained competitive advantages, which resulted in that the plaintiff failed to establish value for the information.[8] Two of those three judgments were written by Guangzhou IP Court, which may suggest that the court is aggressive on applying the value element to rejecting trade secrets.

4.1.3   Unknown to the public

UKP is the most significant and tough element for parties to establish or rebut the existence of trade secrets in court. Figure 7.3 shows the distribution of the primary judgments by the reasons given by courts for sustaining or rejecting the existence of trade secrets. In ten judgments, courts rejected or upheld the existence of trade secrets by investigating one side's evidence and arguments. Those judgments were reasoned as that the other side lacked evidence to prove UKP or known to the public ("KP") or debunk UKP.

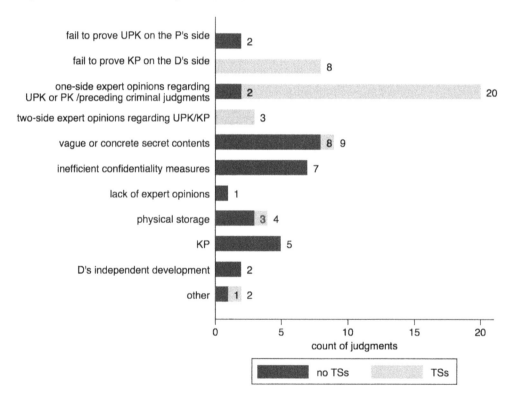

Figure 7.3   *The distribution of the judgments by the primary reasons for sustaining or rejecting the existence of trade secrets*

[6]   Hongcheng Mechanical v. Yiren Mechanical, (Guangzhou Intell. Prop. Ct. 2018) (China); Biaoji Packaging v. Song, (Guangzhou Intell. Prop. Ct. 2017) (China).
[7]   Tailong Youye Ltd. v. Song, (Sichuan Chengdu Intermediate People's Ct. 2018) (China); Hongcheng Mechanical v. Yiren Mechanical, (Guangzhou Intell. Prop. Ct. 2018) (China).
[8]   Hongcheng Mechanical v. Yiren Mechanical, (Guangzhou Intell. Prop. Ct. 2018) (China).

To plaintiffs, the failure of showing UKP was not a material bar. In eight of those ten judgments, defendants bore the negative consequence of the failure of proof of KP. Among the eight judgments, the proof of having concrete secret contents or taking confidentiality measures for some technical information triggered the shift of the burden of proof from plaintiffs to defendants. In two judgments regarding one case, the Beijing IP court and its retrial court—Beijing High People's Court—directly explained that UKP is a negative fact that should not be proved by plaintiffs.[9] This reasoning was given before the enactment of the 2019 AUCL which embraced the rules on shifting the burden of proof. Nevertheless, the remaining two of those ten judgments suggested that the inherent reason for courts to conclude in the failure of showing UKP was the plaintiffs failed in distinguishing the accused information from the common knowledge or technologies in the field. The two judgments were decided by the Guangzhou IP Court, which also believed the plaintiffs did not adopt effective confidentiality measures.[10]

Figure 7.4 digs into the application of the burden of proof among the courts across the three versions of the AUCLs.[11] The strength of the burden of proof on the side of plaintiffs is from high to low as the bar grows. Most courts have believed that defendants have the burden of proof of KP since their application of the 1993 AUCL. This attitude was gradually increasing across the changes of AUCLs, even though the 2017 AUCL had not adopted the rules on shifting the burden of proof.

The accused parties in five judgments established KP under various standards. The most direct way for the accused parties was to show the accused technical information was obtainable from public access. Courts also explained that the information addressed in a patent application or copyrightable design constitutes KP. Moreover, the Beijing IP court categorized the information widely known by the experts in the field as a type of the situations of KP.[12] Alternatively, it is enough to rebut the plaintiff's claim on trade secrets if the accused party can show they developed the information prior to the plaintiff, as shown in *Sainuo Phar. v. Dali University.*[13]

Instead of investigating the evidence by courts, most courts directly relied on expert opinions or criminal judgments, as shown in Figure 7.3. Among the 20 judgments in which only one side provided expert opinions regarding UKP or KP or had a preceding criminal judgment, courts followed the expert opinions or the criminal judgments. Some preceding criminal judgments also went through expert opinions. There were three judgments in which both disputing parties showed expert opinions. As a result of the judgments, UKP and the existence of trade secrets were upheld.

There was one unique judgment, in which judges rejected the existence of a trade secret, reasoning lack of expert opinions submitted by the plaintiff.[14] Even though the Supreme People's Court rejected this reasoning in retrial, the plaintiff still failed to establish the existence of

9   Jieshi Zhongkun Tech. v. Jieshi Tech., (Beijing Intell. Prop. Ct. 2017) (China); Guo v. Jieshi Tech., (Beijing High People's Ct. 2017) (China).
10   Hongcheng Mechanical v. Yiren Mechanical, (Guangzhou High People's Ct. 2018) (China).
11   The samples exclude the judgments that do not indicate the cited version of the AUCLs.
12   Weizi Hengtong Tech. v. Datang Telecom, (Beijing Intell. Prop. Ct. 2018) (China).
13   Sainuo Phar. v. Dali University, (Yunnan High People's Ct. 2017) (China); Sainuo Phar. v. Dali University, (Sup. People's Ct. 2017) (China).
14   Hongzhuo Robots v. Tianying Defense, (Shanxi Xian Intermediate People's Ct. 2019) (China).

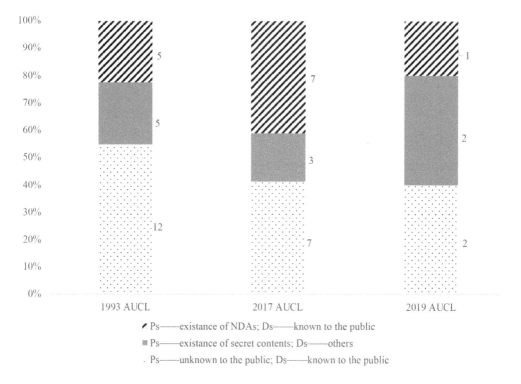

Figure 7.4   Shifting burden of proof regarding the existence of trade secrets

a trade secret.[15] Moreover, in another judgment, the court upheld the existence of a trade secret because the defendant failed to prove KP.[16] The court found the failure of the defendant after the plaintiff applied for a technical investigation and received expert opinions.

4.1.4   Other reasons for the failure of trade secrets

Besides the elements written in the AUCLs, there are scattered reasons for courts to reject the existence of trade secrets. The specification of the accused information or showing its concrete contents is a critical reason to establish or reject the existence of trade secrets. Among the 63 judgments, the most frequently cited reason to reject the existence of trade secrets by courts was lack of concrete contents, as shown in the eight judgments in Figure 7.3. Consistently, the Supreme People's Court in *Tianci High-Tech Corp. v. Wu*[17] directly reasoned the existence of trade secrets for the specification of the accused technical information based on expert opinions, even though an inherent reason could be that the defendant failed to show KP. By contrast, a concrete description of some technical information may result in the failure of UKP determined by courts, as suggested in *Weizi Hengtong Tech. v. Datang Telecom.*[18]

---

[15]   Hongzhuo Robots v. Tianying Defense, (Sup. People's Ct. 2020) (China).
[16]   Ruichang Environment v. Yuanming Chemical, (Sup. People's Ct. 2020) (China).
[17]   (Sup. People's Ct. 2019) (China).
[18]   (Beijing Intell. Prop. Ct. 2018) (China).

In addition, physical storage was a reason for courts to uphold or reject the existence of trade secrets in four judgments, even though the statutory language of the AUCLs never requires it as the Defend Trade Secrets Act ("DTSA") in the U.S. For example, the Guangzhou IP Court directly rejected the plaintiff's claim of the existence of trade secrets based on lack of physical storage in *Tianwei New Material v. Aoxin Material*.[19] Correspondingly, the judicial reason supporting the plaintiff holding effective rights was the existence of physical storage for secret information in *Jieli Chemical v. Shen*.[20]

There are also unique reasons for courts to support or reject the existence of trade secrets. For example, the plaintiff in *Tailong Youye Ltd. v. Song* (2018) failed to deem its technical information as trade secrets because the court believed that abstract ideas that lack technical solutions and equipment are not an eligible subject matter under trade secret protection. Moreover, preemption can be an effective defense. The Guangzhou IP Court refused to protect trade secrets in addition to copyrights in *Yiyong Design v. Sandian Yiwu Design*.[21] By contrast, the Shanghai IP Court upheld the existence of trade secrets directly by reasoning that the information is customized to be trade secrets in *Shubei Information v. Shuyuan Information*.[22]

4.2   Misappropriation

The judgment on misappropriation is highly relevant to the judgments on the existence of trade secrets. Misappropriation should be an element independent from secrecy for courts to decide. However, besides one judgment in which the existence of trade secrets was established but misappropriation was rejected, in all other 31 judgments in which courts found the existence of trade secrets, courts found misappropriation simultaneously. This Section shows how courts determined the misappropriation of trade secrets.

4.2.1   Acts of misappropriation and non-misappropriation

As the revisions of the AUCLs increasingly specify the list of the acts that constitute misappropriation of trade secrets, what are the acts captured by courts for finding the misappropriation in adjudication? Figure 7.5 lists the diverse primary reasons for courts to determine the misappropriation of trade secrets. The subfigure on the left refers to the judgments finding the misappropriation. The subfigure on the right refers to the judgments rejecting the claims of trade secret misappropriation.

In the 32 judgments finding misappropriation, the acts constituting the misappropriation can be categorized as disclosure and acquisition. Regarding disclosure, courts had three primary expressions. First, the defendant has access to the accused information, which was shown in 14 judgments. The access can be direct access acquired based on the identity of an employee or a former employee and the nature of his or her work contents. Alternatively, the access can be indirect access acquired through a shareholder or a former employee with direct access. Second, the defendant who has access to the accused information could not show a legitimate source for the information it uses, which was found in seven judgments. Third, the duty to maintain secrecy of trade secrets extends after the termination of NDAs, which leads to dis-

[19]   (Guangzhou Intell. Prop. Ct. 2019) (China).
[20]   (Zhejiang Yuyao Intermediate People's Ct. 2016) (China).
[21]   (Guangzhou Intell. Prop. Ct. 2018) (China).
[22]   (Shanghai Intell. Prop. Ct. 2018) (China).

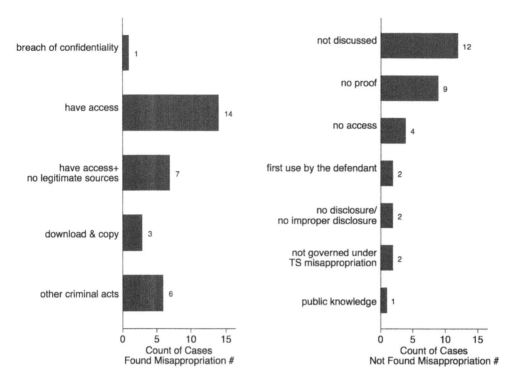

Figure 7.5   Reasons for the determination of the misappropriation of trade secrets

closures after the termination of the misappropriation. This explanation was provided in seven judgments and was the only reason for finding the misappropriation in one judgment.

Moreover, courts explored improper measures of acquisition in nine judgments other than the acquisition based on the disclosure. In three judgments, courts captured the improper measures of unauthorized download and copy, as shown in the plaintiff's physical record or expert opinions, which were costly. Comparatively, it was easier for courts to capture the improper measures in the other six judgments, which were associated with preceding criminal proceedings. The acts constituting the misappropriation are consistent under civil statutes and criminal codes.

By contrast, there are three conducts indicating no misappropriation of trade secrets, suggested by the 31 judgments not finding the misappropriation. In four judgments, the accused party prevailed for lack of access to the accused information. In two judgments, the courts did not find the misappropriation because of the lack of disclosure or improper disclosure of the accused information. In two judgments, the accused parties did not only show that they independently invented the accused information but also built the first use of the information prior to the use by the plaintiffs. However, if the plaintiffs failed on establishing the existence of trade secrets, the defendants did not need to be tense about the elements of misappropriation.

Among the 22 judgments with the failure of the existence of trade secrets, courts in 12 judgments did not discuss misappropriation. Alternatively, courts simply commented on the plaintiffs' no proof in nine judgments or held the discussion by commenting that the accused information was public knowledge. In one unique case, the Supreme People's Court found that the defendant unfairly set a lower price for the products invented by the plaintiff in *Lanxing Business v. Wangmao Property*,[23] but it did not link the suspicious act with the misappropriation because the plaintiff failed to show the secrecy of the accused information. Finally, the suspicious act led the plaintiff to recover under an unfair competition claim.

4.2.2 Access and substantial similarity

"In judicial practice, the determination on trade secret misappropriation needs to consider 'access and substantial similarity.'"[24] The elements of access and substantial similarity were commonly discussed by experts and courts for finding misappropriation of trade secrets in the 63 judgments, even though they have not become the elements mentioned in any versions of the AUCLs or their interpretation by the Supreme People's Court. The expressions regarding substantial similarity can be "no substantial difference," "the same," "high similarity," "highly the same," "substantially the same," and "identity" in addition to "substantial similarity." The underlying goal is to find the use by the accused party by comparing the accused information and the information used by the accused party. The expression of "substantially the same" plus "access" has been formally adopted in Article 32 of the 2019 AUCL and the judicial interpretation for it. Furthermore, the judicial interpretation excludes "substantially the same"

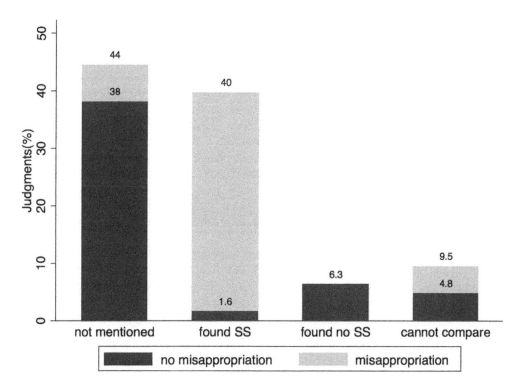

Figure 7.6   *Results of comparison for substantial similarities by misappropriation*

---

[23]   (Sup. People's Ct. 2017) (China).
[24]   Biaoji Packaging v. Song, (Guangzhou Intell. Prop. Ct. 2017) (China).

by "substantial differences." Those changes in the statutory language introduced a uniform expression in the judgments that came afterward.

Substantial similarity was discussed more than access in the judgments, regardless of the new requirements in the 2019 AUCL and its interpretation by the Supreme People's Court regarding trade secret protection. Recall Figure 7.5: 39.68% of the 63 judgments (N=25) discussed the establishment of access, which the courts applied to find the misappropriation. By contrast, 46.3% of the 63 judgments (N=29) discussed substantial similarity ("SS") or similarity, as shown in Figure 7.6. A primary reason is that substantial similarity is more difficult to be found than access. Substantial similarity usually was explored and investigated by experts. Compared to substantial similarity, access could be found more easily when there was an employment relationship between the right holder and those who disclosed the trade secrets.

Substantial similarity is a critical element to find misappropriation. In about 77.42% of the 31 judgments (N=24) finding the misappropriation established the substantial similarity. By contrast, there is one judgment that established substantial similarity but concluded no misappropriation of trade secrets because the plaintiff failed to establish the existence of trade secrets. There are also 6.3% of the 63 judgments (N=4) that found no substantial similarity so as to conclude no misappropriation of trade secrets. In about 9.5% of the 63 judgments (N=6), the courts attempted to compare for substantial similarity but failed for lack of enough information or believed it was unnecessary to compare.

Without a comparison for substantial similarity, three judgments deduced that the accused parties must have used the trade secrets based on superficial comparisons or some suspicious acts done by the accused parties. For example, in *Zhonghua Chemical v. Wang*, the accused party could not provide any proper reason why some marks on its technical documents are the same as the trade secrets in the form of the plaintiff's physical records.[25] In *Qianyou Tech. v. Xu*,[26] the Guangdong High People's Court found substantial similarity without comparison. The accused party developed the game faster than the market on average but did not explain the process of its independent development. Thus, the finding of substantial similarity was a punitive outcome to support the plaintiff's argument based on the evidence rules interpreted by the Supreme People's Court because the accused party refused to provide its source code for the comparison.[27] Similarly, the Supreme People's Court in *Zhenghai Bio v. Shenyang Chemical Corp.*[28] upheld the plaintiff's expert opinions of the existence of substantial similarity without comparison because the accused party did not initiate such a comparison or provide any opposite expert opinions at trial.

By contrast, courts in the other three judgments did not compare or refused to compare due to the fault of the plaintiffs. In *Yinghou Mechanical v. Hewei Mechanical*,[29] the plaintiff brought many documents to the court and asked for a comparison. The accused party refused to show its own technical documents to compare because it argued that the contents embedded in the plaintiff's documents were not concrete to establish the existence of trade secrets. This

---

[25]   (Sup. People's Ct. 2020) (China).
[26]   (Guangdong High People's Ct. 2019) (China).
[27]   Some Provisions of the Supreme People's Court on Evidence in Civil Procedures (2019). Art 95. If one party contains the evidence and refuses to submit it without justifiable reasons, and the party who bears the burden of proving the facts of the evidence claims that the content of the evidence is unfavorable to the controller, the people's court may determine that the claim is valid.
[28]   (Sup. People's Ct. 2016) (China).
[29]   (Zhejiang Hangzhou Intermediate People's Ct. 2020) (China).

argument prevailed, so the lack of comparison did not result in a negative consequence to the side of the accused party. Similarly, the plaintiff in *Sainuo Phar. v. Dali University*[30] tried to pursue the comparison, which was refused by the accused party for protecting its own trade secrets. The courts supported the accused party and believed that it is not reasonable to make the comparison when the accused party applied the accused information independently from the plaintiff.

The application of the element of substantial similarity has a difference in whether there were expert opinions among the judgments finding the misappropriation (X^2 (4, N=31)= 7.84, p=0.098<0.1). The difference can be directly observed in Figure 7.7. In most judgments, substantial similarity was established by expert opinions and then adopted by courts. Without expert opinions, courts relied on the preceding criminal investigations or investigated the substantial similarity at trial to find the misappropriation. In other words, expert opinions and the investigation in preceding criminal proceedings supplemented the judgment on substantial similarity for finding the misappropriation. Courts never found the misappropriation without consulting expert opinions, preceding criminal proceedings, or the standard of substantial similarity, even though courts may have failed in processing the comparison for similarities if defendants did not cooperate.[31]

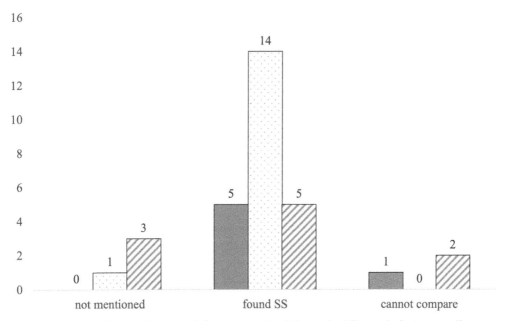

Figure 7.7   *Judgment distribution of substantial similarity addressed in expert opinions*

---

[30]   Sainuo Phar. v. Dali University, (Yunnan High People's Ct. 2017) (China); Sainuo Phar. v. Dali University, (Sup. People's Ct. 2017) (China).
[31]   *E.g.*, Qianyou Tech. v. Xu, (Guangdong High People's Ct. 2019) (China).

4.2.3   Subjective state of mind

Even though the state of mind of the accused parties is not an element for determining misappropriation in China, courts in 25.4% of the 64 judgments (N=16) mentioned it and found the misappropriation. In nine of those judgments, courts claimed that the accused party had knowledge about the misappropriation. In seven judgments, courts defined the accused party as bad faith. Among the 47 judgments which do not address state of mind, courts found the misappropriation in 31.9% of those judgments (N=15).

5.   REMEDIES FOR TRADE SECRET MISAPPROPRIATION

5.1   Damages

There were 27 cases that found trade secret misappropriation and conferred damages for right holders. Courts did not change the amount of the damages for any of those cases if the cases experienced appellate or retrial proceedings, even though the amount of damages was a critical issue for appealing or raising a retrial. The latest judgments for those cases show the plaintiffs received damages between 0.15 million yuan to 159.32 million yuan. The mean is 10.21 and SD=30.56 (measure: million yuan). In other words, the variability of damages, which are case by case, was high. The damages include three main parts—lost profits, attorney's fees, and expert fees for the experts directly hired by the parties. Courts considered expert fees for the experts they hired for the parties as a part of judicial costs rather than damages, which were usually borne by the losing party.

Attorney's fees and expert fees are usually considered in the judgments, even though the fees might not get fully reimbursed.[32] Those fees are called "reasonable expenses" or "reasonable expenses of legal acts." On the one hand, the minimum coverage for the expenses was 0.02 million yuan. The covered expenses in an amount of below 0.1 million were common for the cases having a preceding criminal judgment. On the other hand, the maximum coverage for the expenses was 3.49 million yuan.[33] It was a unique situation because the court believed the accused party acted in bad faith. In another case where the court found bad-faith acts based on long-lasting misappropriation, the court extended one million yuan of reasonable expenses according to the circumstance.[34] Alternatively, the amount ordered by the court could be about 200,000 to 600,000 yuan, regardless of the actual expenses.[35]

A state of mind matters to the amount of damages. Figure 7.8 shows the means of damages awarded to plaintiffs by states of mind.[36] Trade secret right holders on average received damages of 3.89 million yuan more in the judgments defining accused parties as having

---

[32]   The amount of recovered attorney's fees cannot be calculated precisely because many judgments only extended a lump-sum amount for lost profits, attorney's fees, and expert fees.
[33]   Zhonghua Chemical v. Wang, (Sup. People's Ct. 2020) (China).
[34]   Youkai Mechanical v. Cao, (Sup. People's Ct. 2019) (China).
[35]   E.g., Zhonghua Chemical v. Wang, (Sup. People's Ct. 2020) (China). The plaintiff spent 3,49 million yuan on attorney's fees but got reimbursed for 300,000, which was 91.4% less than its actual expenses.
[36]   The samples exclude *Zhonghua Chemical v. Wang* (2020) in which the court awarded the maximum of the damages, which is much higher than other situations and treated as an outlier in the group of bad-faith actors.

knowledge (N=7) than in the judgments not mentioning a state of mind (N=41). The difference was at a statistically significant level (F(1, 46)=3.33, p=0.074<0.1). Consistently, the courts finding the accused parties in bad faith (N=6) on average awarded trade secret right holders 3.86 million yuan more than the courts not mentioning a state of mind in the judgments (N=41). The difference was also at a statistically significant level (F(1, 45)=3.28, p=0.077<0.1). There was no statistical significance in damages between the defendants having knowledge and the bad-faith defendants (F(1, 11)=, p=0.992). In addition to the high reimbursement for attorney's fees resulting from acts in bad faith, in *Tianci High-Tech Corp. v. Wu*,[37] the court awarded punitive damages at a ratio of 5:1 against the bad-faith defendants, which were 30 million yuan damages for 6 million yuan lost profits.[38]

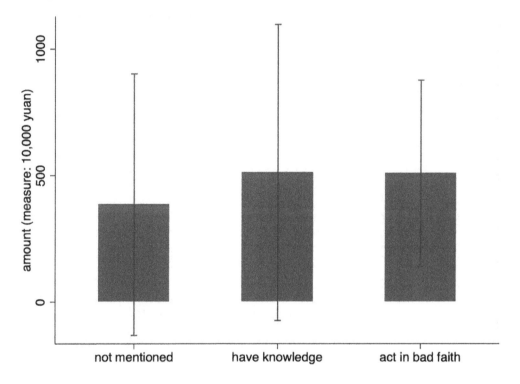

Figure 7.8   *Means of damages by state of mind*

Among the 41 cases in which states of mind were not addressed by courts at any stage of the judicial proceedings, two situations are remarkable. First, six cases had preceding or accompanied criminal proceedings but the courts did not mention the state of mind of the accused parties. In two of those six cases, courts decided the damages by deferring to the amount that experts found for criminal proceedings. Second, lack of use may result in limited reim-

---

[37]   (Sup. People's Ct. 2019) (China).
[38]   It is still arguable in China whether the ratio of punitive damages is 5:1 or 4:1 (Liang, Su, and Liang 2021).

bursement. In *Sun v. Ingersoll-Rand Industrial U.S.*,[39] the plaintiff sued before any use of the trade secrets by the accused party after his acts of download and copy. The court awarded the reasonable expenses at an amount of 0.3 million yuan. Even though it only covered 21.69% of the plaintiff's attorney fees and ignored its expert expenses, a lump sum of 0.3 million yuan was common based on judicial discretion.[40] The court also assigned one-third of the judicial expenses to the plaintiff after a plea of relieving judicial costs raised by the defendant, even though the losing party usually pays the total amount of the judicial expenses.

5.2   Equitable Remedy

Compared to the diversity in awarding damages, courts were consistently extending permanent injunctions. In the 31 judgments finding the misappropriation of trade secrets, courts extended a permanent injunction in 83.87 of them (N=26). In the remaining five judgments, it was unnecessary for courts to extend injunctions. Some accused parties voluntarily stopped using the technology which triggers the trade secret rights. Alternatively, some accused parties (i.e., individuals and firms) were seized, it was not practical for them to continue the misappropriating acts.

6.   IMPLICATIONS

6.1   Mixed Elements for Finding Trade Secrets

The application of the AUCLs in courts suggests that trade secrets are ill-defined in China, regardless of the two revisions. Having confidentiality measures is the least controversial element compared to other elements to establish the existence of trade secrets. The elements of "commercial value" and UKP are confusing to both courts and experts.

First, even though the element of economic interests or commercial value is not a challenging threshold for right holders, the judicial explanation of the failure of economic interests or commercial value suggests how courts may get muddled in interpreting and applying this element. For example, Guangzhou IP Court, the most aggressive court on applying economic interests to reject trade secrets explained the failure from multiple directions without clear instructions. In *Biaoji Packaging v. Song*,[41] the Court believed the accused information did not fulfill the value requirement for no sales and lack of utility, even though the plaintiff was issued a utility model and a utility patent for the invention associated with the accused information. The interpretation implies that the Court may set a higher threshold of "utility" when interpreting it with the 1993 AUCL compared to the "utility" requirement in patent law. However, the interpretation may not be justified. First, the Court explained that the accused information, which is a technical solution, can be directly observed from its usage in the plaintiff's potential products, which leads to obvious, valueless, and open to the public. Second, the

---

[39]   (Sup. People's Ct. 2020) (China).
[40]   The number of reasonable expenses could be set based on the experience of judges, which was suggested in an interview with Zhihan Liu on July 12, 2022. Ms. Gao is a lawyer particularly practicing in the area of business law at Hengdu Law Firm Beijing.
[41]   (Guangzhou Intell. Prop. Ct. 2017) (China).

Court believed that the accused information was only the description of some technical functions rather than being functional by itself, so it is odd to define such information to be useful. Overall, economic or commercial value per se would not result in the failure of showing the existence of trade secrets in China.

Second, the UKP element is confusing both in terms of the burden of proof and standards. Figure 7.3 and Figure 7.4 show plaintiffs constantly bore the burden to show the prima facie evidence of having effective confidentiality measures, which enables the burden-shifting regarding UKP or KP. However, besides confidentiality measures, what else constitutes the prima facie evidence that blocks the plaintiffs from burden shifting? The failure of the plaintiffs to shift the burden suggests at least two reasons. One refers to whether the accused information is concrete and the other refers to whether the accused information is physically stored.

Moreover, regardless of burden-shifting, a critical barrier concerning UKP and KP to the disputing parties, their experts, and courts is who constitutes the public. The easiest way is to show open access to the accused information. Furthermore, with expert opinions, KP can be established if the technical information is or should be known to the experts in the field. Even though such a standard avoids the concerns of a broad protection of trade secrets (Hrdy 2019), which harms innovation and employee mobility, experts and courts struggle with the question whether the technical information constitutes general knowledge in the field. For example, Guangdong High People's Court rejected the UKP of the accused information because the plaintiff failed to show it was better than other technologies in *Hongcheng Mechanical v. Yiren Mechanical* (2018). This reasoning suggests confusion over the standards of novelty and non-obviousness in patent law and the standard of UKP for protecting trade secrets in adjudication.

The above problems in the interpretation of those elements by courts and experts expose a critical missing part in the AUCLs—the subject matter of trade secrets. The DTSA in the U.S. defined trade secrets not only with the fundamental elements of secrecy, economic value, and security measures but also with specifications of the types of information and the forms of the information which is subject to trade secret protection.[42] Compared to the precise statutory language in the DTSA, the AUCLs and its judicial interpretation in 2020 are too broad and less instructive.

6.2   Strong Deference to Expert Opinions

The judgments suggest constantly strong deference to expert opinions, especially when the opinion directly came from an administrative agency or a criminal judgment or was assigned by an administrative agency. Expert opinions were all given by state-owned expertise centers, which were more powerful than individual expert witnesses who testified in court. In *Tianxiang Jiantai Phar. Mechanical v. Dongfulong Tech. Corp.*,[43] the Shanghai IP Court rejected the opinions from the expert witness who testified in court. In appeal, the Shanghai

---

[42]   18 U.S. Code § 1839 . ("…(3) the term 'trade secret' means all forms and types of financial, business, scientific, technical, economic, or engineering information, including patterns, plans, compilations, program devices, formulas, designs, prototypes, methods, techniques, processes, procedures, programs, or codes, whether tangible or intangible, and whether or how stored, compiled, or memorialized physically, electronically, graphically, photographically, or in writing if—…").

[43]   (Shanghai Intell. Prop. Ct. 2016) (China).

High People's Court did not give the defendant another chance to acquire expert opinions from an expertise center.

Expert opinions deal with two primary issues. One issue refers to the existence of trade secrets. Having concrete content and finding UKP or KP are the key sub-issues in those expert opinions. The other issue refers to the substantial similarity between the information raised by the right holder and the information used by the defendant for misappropriation of trade secrets.

The strong deference to expert opinions by courts, however, is problematic. Courts testified expert opinions regarding substantial similarities more than the existence of trade secrets (e.g., *Libang Instruments v. Mairui Bio*[44]). However, the lack of testifying expert opinions could not be a prevailing argument in appeals. For example, in *Jieshi Zhongkun Tech. v. Jieshi Tech*,[45] the Beijing IP Court ignored the argument that the defendant raised about the lack of testifying of the plaintiff's expert witness for substantial similarity. It is very unlikely to overcome expert opinions finding substantial similarity, as suggested by the comparison between Figure 7.6 and Figure 7.7. Among the four judgments in which courts rejected substantial similarity as shown in Figure 7.6, there were only two judgments in which courts decided on the misappropriation after testifying the expert opinions at court. By contrast, even though an accused party testified in court and attempted to overcome the existence of substantial similarity suggested by the expert opinions provided by the plaintiff, the Supreme People's Court believed that the difference in technology indicators in the same field did not sufficiently overturn the expert opinions.[46]

Without clear instructions to technical experts, both the reasonableness and the fairness of trade secret judgments relying on expert opinions raise concerns and result in negative consequences on innovation. Not only will the weakness of technical experts in the expertise centers be inherited by judges, but the intervention of expert opinions also manipulates the standards of trade secret protection. On the one hand, when injunctions are extended without independent judicial decisions, trade secrets could be overprotected, which suggests strong subsidies to plaintiffs (Wang 2020). On the other hand, the confusion of experts in deciding UKP may also result in the under-protection of valuable technical secrets.

6.3   Ex-Ante Criminal Intrusions

The judgments reviewed by this study show that courts had strong deference to criminal investigations or criminal judgments. In all of the 55 public civil cases, whenever police or prosecutors intervened, a full-scaled criminal intrusion with a full-blown evidentiary search and an arrest happened before civil proceedings. Moreover, whenever there was a corresponding criminal proceeding, the police investigation supported the civil investigation. In six cases, courts found the existence of trade secrets and the misappropriation of trade secrets based on expert opinions or the preceding criminal judgments. The evidence to find the acts of the misappropriation could be derived only from the defendant's confession during the custodial

---

[44]   (Guangzhou High People's Ct. 2014) (China).
[45]   (Beijing Intell. Prop. Ct. 2017) (China).
[46]   Sanyou Lvjian Ltd. v. Shenyang Chemical Corp., (Sup. People's Ct. 2016) (China).

interrogation. The two stages of judgments for *Hengchang Mechanical v. Liu*[47] are the only judgments where courts determined the misappropriation by independent expert opinions after consulting the criminal judgments. By contrast, even though there were another two cases in which the misappropriation of trade secrets failed after criminal intrusions, the civil decision was made based on the criminal investigation results regarding UKP and substantial similarity.

The empirical evidence supports the practical legal strategy that criminal intrusions are a critical and effective strategy in pursuing the protection of trade secrets under the AUCLs. In practice, criminal claims are pushed ahead of civil claims as a litigation strategy by the lawyers of trade secret right holders for forcing a settlement with the accused party (e.g., Yuan 2019) or enhancing the damages awarded by courts.[48] The strategy of enhancing the damages for trade secret misappropriation is reliable, as suggested by the data. Courts awarded 6.12 million yuan of damages in the cases with preceding criminal procedures (N=9) more than the cases without an accompanying criminal investigation at a statistically significant level (N=17)[49] ($t(24)=2.34$, $p=0.028<0.05$).

Regardless that trade secret right holders may receive effective protection under strong policing intervention, however, it raises justice concerns when criminal procedures precede civil procedures and civil courts defer to the criminal prosecutors in finding the existence of trade secrets and the misappropriation of trade secrets. The insufficient due process and fairness in criminal proceedings in China (Lu 2021; Whitfort 2005) may result in the misuse of the claims of trade secret misappropriation. Even though the accused parties and courts may be able to recognize bad-faith trade secret claims (e.g., Katyal & Graves 2021) and have refused to over-subsidize some plaintiffs in some existing judgments, it is inevitable that improper interventions or over-interventions of policing power harms the fairness of trade secret civil litigations, especially when courts are confused about the application of the elements of trade secret misappropriation. Some accused parties may lose their own trade secrets for showing their innocence or get forced to settle under custody.

7.   CONCLUSION

This study explored the adjudication of trade secret misappropriation in China by reviewing all the judgments available to the public between January 2013 and December 2021 that address issues about the misappropriation of technical secrets. It reveals deficiencies of Chinese civil courts when adjudicating trade secret disputes. First, the broad language of the AUCLs suggests a lack of clear guidance and instructions for courts, technical experts, and parties in trade secret disputes. Second, judicial autonomy is vulnerable due to the strong deference to expert opinions and ex-ante criminal intrusions. Moreover, this study shows that Chinese courts are treating trade secrets as a type of IP rights, even though trade secret law has not been established in China. Courts are paying efforts to avoid the overprotection of trade secrets by distinguishing them from patents, copyrights, or general knowledge in the field. However,

---

[47]   Hengchang Mechanical v. Liu, (Anhui Hefei Intermediate People's Ct. 2017) (China); Hengchang Mechanical v. Liu, (Anhui High People's Ct. 2018) (China).

[48]   The strategy is suggested in an interview with Zhihan Liu on Jan. 20, 2022. Mr. Liu is a lawyer particularly practicing in the area of trade secret misappropriation at Yingke Law Firm Beijing.

[49]   The judgment awarding the maximum damages at 159.32 million yuan is excluded as an outlier.

the above deficiencies in practice prohibit the courts from effectively adopting the statutes governing trade secret protection as innovation policies.

REFERENCES

Almeling, David S, Darin W Snyder, Michael Sapoznikow, Whitney E Mccollum, and Jill Weader. 2010. "A Statistical Analysis of Trade Secret Litigation in Federal Courts." *Gonzaga Law Review* 45 (2): 291–334. http://www.fas.org/irp/ops/ci/docs/2002.pdf.%0Ahttps://www.tradesecretsandemploy eemobility.com/files/2014/05/Statistical-Analysis-of-Trade-Secret-Litigation-in.pdf.
Almeling, David S, Darin W Snyder, Michael Sapoznikow, Whitney E Mccollum, and Jill Weader. 2011. "A Statistical Analysis of Trade Secret Litigation in State Courts." *Gonzega Law Review* 46 (1): 57–101.
Beconcini, Paolo. 2020. "The State of Trade Secret Protection in China in Light of the U.S.–China Trade Wars: Trade Secret Protection in China Before and After the U.S.–China Trade Agreement of January 15, 2020." *UIC Rev. Intell. Prop. L.* 20: 108–144.
Chai, Yaotian. 2018. "The New Anti-Unfair Competition Law of the People's Republic of China 2018." *Journal of Intellectual Property Law and Practice* 13 (12): 998–1008. https://doi.org/10.1093/jiplp/jpy158.
German, Michael, and Alex Liang. 2022. "Amid New Trial, End of Chinese Espionage 'Initiative' Brings Little Relief to US Academics Caught in Net of Fear." Just Security. https://www.justsecurity.org/80780/amid-new-trial-end-of-chinese-espionage-initiative-brings-little-relief-to-us-academics-caught-in-net-of-fear/.
Hrdy, Camilla A. 2019. "The General Knowledge, Skill, and Experience Paradox." *Boston College Law Review* 60 (1): 1–66.
Katyal, Sonia, and Charles Graves. 2021. "From Trade Secrecy to Seclusion." *The Georgetown Law Journal* 109: 1137–1420. https://doi.org/10.2139/ssrn.3760123.
Kong, Xiangjun. 2017. "Discussing the New Role of Anti-Unfair Competition Law." *Peking University Law Journal* 29 (3): 736–57.
Kong, Xiangjun. 2018. "Explanations and Evaluations for New Amendments on Anti-Unfair Competition Law." Judicial Protection for Intellectual Property. https://www.chinaiprlaw.cn/index.php?id=5390.
Lee, Jyh-an. 2019. "Shifting IP Battlegrounds in the U.S.–China Trade War." *Colum. JL & Arts* 147 (43): 147–95.
Li, Chunxuan, and Rui Ling. 2019. "Respond to the 'Criminal First, Civil Second' Model in Trade Secret Misappropriation Cases." Lifang & Partners. http://www.lifanglaw.com/plus/view.php?aid=1780.
Liang, Sisi, Heqin Su, and Zhechen Liang. 2021. "Study on the Application Problems of the 'Ratio' of Punitive Damages." IPLead. https://www.zhichanli.com/p/1379643830.
Lin, Wei. 2018. "The Research on Connductor of Trade Secret Misappropriation—Under the Background of the Amendment on Anti-Unfair Competition Act." *University of International Business and Economics Legal Studies* 3: 52–68.
Lu, Tian. 2019. "China Amends Trade Mark and Unfair Competition Law to Tackle Trade Mark Squatting and Enforcement Issues." The IKPat. https://ipkitten.blogspot.com/2019/04/china-amends-trade-mark-and-unfair.html.
Lu, Yuguang. 2021. "Comparative Research of the Plea Leniency System of China." Indiana University.
Lucas, Ryan. 2022. "The Justice Department Is Ending Its Controversial China Initiative." *NPR KQED*. The U.S.: NPR KQED. https://www.npr.org/2022/02/23/1082593735/justice-department-china-initiative.
Luo, Mozi. 2018. "US China Trade Dispute Over Intellectual Property." San Jose State University.
Office of the United States Trade Representative. 2018. "2018 Special 301 Report."
Pooley, James. 2020. "Has China Finally Embraced Robust Trade Secret Protection?" IPWatchdog. https://ipwatchdog.com/2020/06/14/china-finally-embraced-robust-trade-secret-protection/id=122471/.

Ran, Ruixue, Sheng Huang, and Robert Williams. 2018. "Trade Secret Law in China: 3 Highlights from 2017." Law360. https://www.cov.com/-/media/files/corporate/publications/2018/01/trade_secret_law _in_china_3_highlights_from_2017.pdf.

The European Commission. 2021. "Report on the Protection and Enforcement of Intellectual Property Rights in Third Countries."

The Intellectual Property Court of the Supreme People's Court. 2020. *Annual Report of the Intellectual Property Court of the Supreme People's Court*. People's Court Press. https://www.court.gov.cn/zixun -xiangqing-225861.html.

Versteeg, Mila. 2020. "Making Chinese Court Filings Public? Some Not-So-Foreign American Insights." *Harv. L. Rev.* 133: 1728–49.

Wang, Limei, and Junqiang Zhang. 2020. "Revisit the Interacted Court Proceedings Between Criminal and Civil Trade Secret Cases." *Jianghuai Tribune* 299 (1): 116–23.

Wang, Lina, and Kuoping Chang. 2019. "A Quantitative Study of Trade Secrets Protection in China." *Science Research Management* 40 (9): 65–74.

Wang, Runhua. 2020. "Judicial Reward Allocation for Asymmetric Secrets." *Pace Law Review* 40 (2): 226–87.

Whitfort, Amanda. 2005. "The Right to a Fair Trial in China: The Criminal Procedure Law of 1996." *Hong Kong Law Journal* 695: 141–51.

Wu, Taixuan, and Yang Liu. 2020. "The Perfection of Local Legislation against Unfair Competition in China." *Journal of Southwest Petroleum University (Social Science Edition)* 22 (2): 78–84.

Yu, Peter K. 2021. "Legal Studies Research Paper Series US-China Intellectual Property Trade Wars." Research Paper No. 21–28. Legal Studies Research Paper Series. https://deliverypdf.ssrn .com/delivery.php?ID=16612108410108410801107510907600903103702003405201005002806 8 01112712500307610102610105500512303612105911603110408208811908412610303207405508 01170061011170650940260360770800241060990291250660980920060011000261 17.

Yu, Tianlong. 1994. "An Anti-Unfair Competition Law Without a Core: An Introductory Comparison Between U.S. Antitrust Law and the New Law of the People's Republic of China." *Indiana International & Comparative Law Review* 4 (3): 315–38. https://doi.org/10.18060/17540.

Yuan, Li. 2019. "How Huawei Lost the Heart of the Chinese Public." *The New York Times* https://www .nytimes.com/2019/12/04/technology/huawei-china-backlash.html.

PART III

COPYRIGHT

8.   A survey of empirical analysis of U.S. copyright law

Ben Depoorter

1.   INTRODUCTION

Empirical scholarship in copyright law can be grouped into the following categories: (1) the analysis of doctrinal issues; (2) the description of the litigation process, remedies, and the enforcement of copyrights; and (3) the examination of judicial motivations and potential bias in copyright disputes.

2.   NON-LITERAL COPYRIGHT INFRINGEMENT

Determining whether a copyright has been infringed is usually straightforward in cases involving literal copying. But when an allegedly infringing work contains few literal similarities (verbatim copying, sampling), rulings on copyright infringement claims are plagued by a lack of coherence and consistency (Samuelson, 2013). For instance, the Second and Ninth Circuits have developed five parallel tests to decide disputes involving nonliteral copyright infringements. As a result, the doctrine of substantial similarity remains one of the most elusive concepts in copyright law.

The various similarity tests employed across jurisdictions (ordinary observer, more discerning ordinary observer, total concept and feel, extrinsic/intrinsic, and abstraction/filtration/comparison) create a complex legal landscape. This legal backdrop raises an important empirical question: do plaintiffs fare better under some tests than others? If the varied substantial similarity tests give rise to differences in outcomes, copyright plaintiffs might seek to engage in forum-shopping.

The first set of empirical studies of substantial similarity case law (Lippman, 2013; Rogers, 2013) use a dataset of 234 published Court of Appeals decisions. Twelve variables were coded for each case: (1) type of injunction sought in the lower court (preliminary, permanent, or none); (2) subject-matter category (literary works and movies; pictures, sculptures, clothing, toys; factual works; songs and music; computer software; and architecture); (3) the method upon which the lower court decided the case (bench trial on the merits, dismissed, judgment as a matter of law, JNOV, jury trial, preliminary injunction, or summary judgment); (4) deciding circuit; (5) which party won at the trial; and (6) circuit court levels and binary identifiers for the test variant(s) the court purported to use in deciding the case: (7) ordinary observer; (8) more discerning ordinary observer; (9) total concept and feel; (10) extrinsic/intrinsic; (11) intended audience; and (12) abstraction/filtration/comparison. The plaintiff win rate is employed as the dependent variable at both the appellate and trial levels against three independent variables: deciding circuit, the substantial similarity test used by the deciding circuit, and the subject matter of the copyrighted work.

Lippman (2013) finds that the three main groupings of substantial similarity tests (ordinary observer; extrinsic/intrinsic; and abstraction/filtration/comparison) provide no statistically significant difference regarding the plaintiff win rate. Instead, Lippman observes a high degree of variation between the plaintiff win rates across the various subject matters. Overall, the odds in copyright substantial similarity litigation were found to be overwhelmingly against plaintiffs.

Rogers (2013) finds that, across the various substantial similarity tests, a plaintiff has the same chances of winning if either the ordinary observer or the extrinsic/intrinsic test are applied. However, a plaintiff is statistically less likely to win on appeal if a circuit applies the filtration/comparison test than the ordinary observer or extrinsic/intrinsic tests. Roger's interpretation is that the filtration/comparison test regime is unfriendly to plaintiffs because it involves a more salient separate step dedicated entirely to removing material from the plaintiff's work that is classified as "unprotectable". Rogers finds that forum shopping is a viable litigation strategy, as the Second and Ninth Circuits favor plaintiffs more than the Eleventh Circuit. Moreover, a plaintiff has a better chance (+13%) of prevailing if his or her copyrighted work is high-tech in nature, but the use of expert testimony by the trier of fact may not necessarily aid the plaintiff's case.

The findings in Lippman (2013) and Rogers (2013) are limited, of course, by the focus on Circuit court decisions. Given that appeals decisions are not necessarily representative of the average copyright dispute (for instance, appealed cases might have higher stakes or present more difficult legal questions), it would be unwise to extend the finding that "the odds are overwhelmingly against plaintiffs in substantial similarity cases" to district court cases.

In this regard, Asay's study (2022) of substantial similarity opinions from district courts is a valuable addition to the literature. His study uses a random sample of over 1,000 decisions in every circuit between 1978 and 2020 to code the subject matter and copyright rights in dispute; procedural posture; opinion date; the subtests, expert evidence, and copyright limitations used in the opinion; the sources of authority that courts rely on in their opinions; and outcomes for each part of the test and the case overall.

Asay finds that defendants win substantial similarity cases only slightly more frequently than plaintiffs. Courts typically spend little time assessing whether a defendant copied from the plaintiff's work. Courts mostly look at whether a defendants had access to the plaintiff's work and tend to favor plaintiffs on the issue of access. Contrary to conventional wisdom, courts rarely rely on expert evidence to assess whether two works are so similar that independent creation is unlikely. Although plaintiffs enjoy significantly greater success on the first part of the test, it is largely inconsequential for the overall success rate of copyright infringement decisions.

The second part of the test, where courts assess whether the defendant's copying amounts to improper appropriation, is characterized by significant heterogeneity. In any given opinion, a court typically uses multiple subtests and copyright limitations to decide this inquiry. Courts use expert evidence more frequently under this prong of the infringement test. The data also suggest that one of the keys to winning, for either defendants or plaintiffs, is the extent to which the court engages with and discusses copyright limitations.

Two experimental studies examined the copyright infringement test in music copyright.

Music recordings copyright consists of separate rights in the underlying composition and the sound recording. One item of contention on the application of infringement tests to music is that copyright law's lay listener test often involves jurors listening to sound recordings to evaluate a potential infringement of a plaintiff's composition. This makes it challenging to prevent jurors from focusing on unprotected sound recording elements. Lund (2011) conducted several experiments that replicated the copyright infringement from litigated infringement suits in a controlled setting where participants assessed the similarity of compositions. One set of participants heard two pairs of music that were performed similarly (timbre, orchestration, tempo, key, and style). The other group of participants heard identical compositions that were performed differently (different timbre, orchestration, tempo, key, and style). When asked whether they thought the songs were "substantially similar," based on an ordinal scale finding of similarity (1–5 scale), participants were much more (less) likely to find substantial similarity when the songs were played similarly (differently). Participants consistently rated compositions performed similarly as being more compositionally similar than identical compositions played dissimilarly. Lund's findings suggest that although the method of performance strongly influences a finding of substantial similarity with two songs that are neither strongly similar nor dissimilar, there is more room for gamesmanship for a plaintiff to prove infringement in copyright litigation when the songs are more different than there is room for creative tactics by a defendant to avoid liability when two songs are more identical. In a follow-up paper, Lund (2013) suggests that musicians are better suited to serve as jury members in composition infringement litigation.

Lee and Moshirnia's (2020) experimental evidence suggests that music industry defendants make a strategic mistake when they fail to pursue fair use as a defense, as observed in many music infringement disputes. Participants were presented with two scenarios involving a possible infringement of a musical work by a subsequent musical work. Each scenario laid out a brief description of the facts of the dispute and provided an audio file for a synthesized piano instrumental performance of each work in the musical pair. Participants were provided a legal rule (substantial similarity or fair use) to apply when deciding the dispute. Subjects were then asked to determine if the subsequent work (1) infringed the prior work's copyright or (2) made a fair use of the work, depending on the legal rule at issue. Subjects then reassessed the outcome and confidence for the same music pair under the different legal rule. After analyzing this music pair twice (once for each legal rule), subjects were asked to resolve a similar dispute with a different music pair. The legal rule (fair use versus substantial similarity) was found to have a significant impact on findings of no liability. Subjects in both cases involving low similarity and high similarity between songs returned higher no liability rates under a fair use analysis than a substantial similarity analysis. Notably, the legal rule had a larger impact on cases involving high similarity. Fair use was of assistance more to defendants in cases of high similarity, and especially when participants had a background in law or music.

3.   FAIR USE

Legal systems employ different approaches to copyright exemptions. Many countries, including the United States, employ open-ended exemptions that provide judges with broad discretion to excuse unauthorized copying. Other countries, such as European Union member states, utilize enumerated copyright exceptions that are provided by statute.[1] The unpredictable and fast changing nature of technologies that are impacted by copyright law arguably makes

---

[1]   *See* Article 5(2) of the EU Copyright Directive. 2001 O.J. (L167) at 10–19.

open-ended standards more suited for copyright law (Burk, 1999, 140; Depoorter, 2009; Sag, 2005, 435). Precise legal rules, by contrast, are more quickly outdated by innovative applications of copyrighted works. As a downside, the flexibility of open standards increases legal indeterminacy. For instance, the U.S. doctrine of fair use has been criticized for being "notoriously difficult" to predict (Liu, 2008) and infusing significant uncertainty into copyright law. In fact, the doctrine of fair use is so widely debated that it has been observed that there have been extended periods where there are more law review articles published on the topic in any given year than there are fair use judicial opinions reported in the same year.[2] It comes as no surprise then that the scholarly fascination with the fair use doctrine has spilled over into the sphere of empirical research.

The fair use defense enables uses of copyrighted material that would otherwise violate copyright law. In determining whether an unauthorized use of a work is a fair use, courts consider the following four factors: (1) the purpose and character of the use, including whether such use is of a commercial nature or is for nonprofit educational purposes; (2) the nature of the copyrighted work; (3) the amount and substantiality of the portion used in relation to the copyrighted work as a whole; and (4) the effect of the use upon the potential market for or value of the copyrighted work (Copyright Act of 1976, 17 U.S.C. §107 (2007)).

The empirical analysis of fair use case law got underway in earnest with Barton Beebe's (2005) pioneering study of judicial fair use case law. Beebe analyzed 306 reported judicial opinions on fair use between 1978 and 2005, examining correlations between fair use findings and each of the four fair use factors. Additionally, a regression analysis isolates subfactors that drive the assessment of each individual fair use factor.

One of the major findings is that the market impact of an unauthorized use on the copyrighted work (factor four) is most highly correlated with a fair use verdict. Similarly, but to a lesser extent, the purpose and character of the use (factor one) also correlate with high overall fair use determination for alleged infringers. Factors two and three were found to be less decisive in fair use determinations by courts. Beebe's analysis of subfactors shows that the concept of "transformative use" can have a decisive impact on the outcome with respect to both factor one and the overall fair use decision. Interestingly, Beebe also finds that most opinions examine each factor independently. Courts do not let a finding of fair use under one factor dictate the court's decisions under other factors. Even if, as the study finds, a finding of fair use under factors one or four (or both) ultimately helps persuade the court to find fair use overall, courts appear to assess the individual factors of the fair use test on the merits for each individual factor.

Three years following Beebe's groundbreaking research, Netanel (2011) published a follow-up study focusing on the 2006-to-2010 time window. Netanel's study chronologically sorts opinions to avoid bundling cases that apply different Supreme Court guidelines. When lumping together case law over extended periods that cover dramatic shifts in the fair use doctrine and the factor test, as articulated by the Supreme Court, one is bound to observe greater variance across the case law. For instance, the U.S. Supreme Court redirected the fair use doctrine to a significant extent in its *Campbell v. Acuff Rose* decision. As the Supreme Court's teachings in *Campbell* had become established in his 5-year period, Netanel finds that the application of the fair use test by courts is far more consistent and predictable than

---

[2]   Beebe, 2008, 565 n.64.

conventional wisdom suggests. Along the same lines, Samuelson (2009) employed a method of clustering fair use cases by type of use (rather than time period) to reveal a more predictable landscape of fair use case outcomes than previously assumed. While Beebe's study reported that a significant percentage of fair use opinions did not employ the transformative use concept in those prior years, Netanel's analysis of subsequent case law shows that the transformative use concept was emerging more frequently in fair use examinations and informed outcomes more overall in this time period.

Two subsequent studies analyzed the increased role of the transformative nature of an unauthorized use as a consideration in fair use decision-making. Liu (2019) examines all 260 reported transformative use decisions in the U.S. copyright law from 1978 to 2017, accounting for 51.7% of all fair use decisions. Liu reports that the share of transformative use decisions in fair use decisions jumped from 8% to 41% one year after the Supreme Court endorsed the consideration of transformative use in *Campbell v. Acuff-Rose* in 1994. Liu finds that the percentage of cases featuring prominent discussion of the transformative nature of an infringing use further increased in fair use analysis from 60% to 90% around 2007 to stabilize at 90%. In addition to becoming almost a universal feature in fair use analysis, findings of transformative use (63.3% of transformative use defenses overall after 2010) have a dispositive effect on fair use case outcomes. Of all decisions that upheld transformative use, 94% eventually led to a finding of fair use. The study performs a series of correlation coefficients and logistic regressions that reveal the overshadowing impact of transformative uses on the four factors and their subfactor. A finding of transformative use casts aside circumstances that otherwise would undercut a fair use finding, including the commercial purpose (a finding of transformative use consistently overrode a finding of commercial purpose in 91.5% of the decisions where the two pointed to opposite directions), verbatim copying, and the evidence of damage to the primary or derivative market. These profound findings primarily are most pertinent in visual art industries, including photographs, as well as fine arts, literary works, and audiovisual works.

The powerful impact of the transformative use analysis on fair use decisions is also confirmed in Asay, Sloan and Sobczak (2020). The authors collected data from all district and appellate court fair use opinions from 1991 through 2017. Among other variables, the dataset includes how frequently courts apply the doctrine, how often they deem a use transformative, win rates for transformative users, the types of uses courts are most likely to find transformative, what sources courts rely on, and how frequently the transformative use doctrine spills over into and influences other parts of the fair use test. The results show overwhelmingly that the transformative use concept is front and center in fair use analysis. A vast majority of both appellate and district courts apply the transformative use concept in their opinions. District courts apply the transformative use concept in about 91% of their opinions since 2011. Moreover, winning the transformative use argument is essential to be granted a fair use: "Of all opinions that discuss transformative use, only about half of defendants win the transformative use inquiry. But when they do, those defendants nearly always succeed on their fair use defense. And when they do not, they nearly always lose." The authors conclude that transformative use affects the resolution of other factors within the fair use inquiry more than any other subfactor or factor.

The findings in Liu (2019) and Asay, Sloan and Sobczak (2020) align with a pattern previously revealed in Sag (2012). Coding the characteristics of the purported fair use (as opposed to the judicial determinations) and the parties involved in all district court disputes between

1978 and 2011, Sag observes that uses involving a "creative shift"—a partial proxy for transformative use—have significant predictive power as to whether courts will find a fair use.[3]

4.   COPYRIGHT REMEDIES

Questions of substantive rights are front and center in legal scholarship. But legal remedies are key to enforcing those rights, of course. The availability and types of remedies deeply affect the incentive effects of the legal system. In the area of copyright law, the application of injunctions (Blair and Cotter, 2005), statutory damages (Samuelson and Wheatland, 2009), and the disgorgement of profits (Samuelson, Golden and Gergen, 2020) are fascinating topics that have been explored in depth by leading commentators. Increasingly, scholars are also deploying empirical methods to shed light on the role of copyright remedies.

4.1   Statutory Damages

Article 504 of the American Copyright Act provides that once infringement has been established, a plaintiff is at liberty to elect a statutory-damage award. In this manner, the Copyright Act unburdens copyright holders from providing evidence of actual harm. In recent years statutory damage awards have become controversial, however. Due to the sheer amount of infringed works in online settings, critics observe that the statutory damage framework is utilized by plaintiffs opportunistically as a scare tactic when filing sometimes dubious infringement claims. Others maintain that statutory damages serve the beneficial role of increasing access to justice for cash-strapped copyright plaintiffs.

Depoorter (2019) examines the role of statutory damages in the copyright arena based on an in-depth empirical analysis of docket records and case law study. The docket study uses Cotropia and Gibson's (2014) collection of docket entries from 2005–2008, which includes complaints and pertinent documents from approximately 1,000 copyright disputes. Additionally, all 102 judicial decisions where courts addressed a claim of willful copyright infringement from the same time period were coded to identify the arguments raised by the plaintiffs, and the definition and application of enhanced damages for willful infringement by courts. This case law analysis included new coding of (1) subject-matter area; (2) a description of the defendant's allegedly infringing actions; (3) a plaintiff's proposed definition of willfulness; (4) the definition of willfulness employed by the court; (5) any additional considerations of culpability withheld by the court; (6) the remedial outcome (including damage award numbers); (7) the description of the express calculation of the statutory award; (8) whether the court awarded enhanced damages; (9) the number of infringing works; (10) the amount sought per infringing work/the total amount requested; (11) the amount awarded by the court for each infringing work/total award; and (12) any policy objectives that the court considered in awarding willful damages.

---

[3]   On the transformative nature of works, a prior study by Reese (2015) reviewed all published circuit court opinions applying the statutory fair use analysis between the Supreme Court's decision in *Campbell* and the end of 2007. His study concluded that judicial fair use findings focused on whether the purpose of the defendant's use is transformative. Courts did not view the preparation of any derivative work as (1) necessarily transformative, (2) crucial to a finding that a defendant's use is transformative.

The findings reveal that statutory-damages claims are commonplace in virtually all areas of copyright law. Plaintiffs in copyright litigation request statutory damages in 90% of pleadings. Instead of seeking compensation for the actual harm suffered from infringement, a large majority of plaintiffs turn to statutory awards. Even in industries that enjoy only weak copyright protection, copyright holders almost universally claim that they are entitled to enhanced statutory damages due to willful infringement. Courts rarely grant enhanced damages, however. Plaintiffs sought enhanced damages for willful infringement in 81% of all copyright disputes in the examined period, yet courts awarded enhanced damages in less than 2% of all cases that moved to verdict. The striking gap between the demand and supply of statutory damages and several additional factors relating to the nature of claims and subject-matter areas undermine the credibility of the nearly ubiquitous claims of willful infringement by plaintiffs.

4.2   Injunctive Relief

In the landmark *eBay v. MercExchange* decision, the U.S. Supreme Court held that courts should apply the four-factor test under traditional principles of equity before awarding plaintiffs an injunction in patent cases. At the time, there was an extensive policy debate in patent law about the excessive threat that injunctive relief imposed on defendants in patent disputes and the ability of plaintiffs to extract royalties that are grossly disproportionate to the value of the allegedly infringed patents.

Questions emerged in copyright scholarship about whether the *eBay* holding would have the same influence in copyright law as it did in patent law. Some were skeptical that the denial of permanent injunction despite liability would become a common feature in copyright law, especially since, as it was argued, injunctive relief has been routinely available to copyright owners who succeed on the merits. Liu (2012) conducted an empirical study based on all 506 reported copyright-injunction decisions during the period from the issuing date of the *eBay* decision in 2006 to mid-2010. Liu reports that the *eBay* decision had no deterrent effect on the use of injunctions in copyright cases. There has been no decline in the number of motions filed for copyright injunctions and plaintiffs succeeded in obtaining copyright injunctions in 82.8% of these decisions. Only 16.9% of cases referred to the four-factor test. By contrast, 37.3% of the decisions acknowledged the traditional test that a copyright plaintiff is entitled to a permanent injunction when liability has been established and there is a threat of continuing violations.

In a more recent study, Sag and Samuelson (2022) examine a longer timeline of cases, distinguishing between default judgments and contested cases. They find evidence to the contrary: the *eBay* equity rule has become very influential when courts decide on injunctive relief in copyright disputes. This finding is based on the number of citations to *eBay* and related cases, as well as an examination of the language judges use to discuss the need to balance hardships to plaintiffs and defendants when considering whether to grant injunctive relief. The authors observe that injunctions have become more difficult to obtain in the aftermath of *eBay*. Sag and Samuelson suggest that early impressions that *eBay* had little impact in copyright cases can be ascribed to a time lag between the initial resistance to and the eventual embrace of the *eBay* ruling, especially following support for *eBay* at the circuit court level.

5.   IDEOLOGY IN COPYRIGHT LITIGATION

There is a clear division in academic scholarship between commentators that favor strong copyright protection, on the one hand, and scholars that are more skeptical of the impact of copyright law on creativity and welfare. Yet very little theoretical writing has been devoted to prevailing ideological viewpoints among judges. Here, empirical work has done most of the lifting.

In his pioneering study, Beebe (2008) examined over 200 fair use decisions between 1978 and 2005 and found no significant relationship between the ideology of the judges and their adjudication of the fair use defense.

By contrast, on the level of the U.S. Supreme court, Sag, Jacobi and Sytch (2009) found that judicial ideology is a significant determinant of voting in intellectual property cases. The authors examined the effect of ideology on the voting behavior of individual justices of the U.S. Supreme Court in intellectual property decisions from 1954 to 2006. The more conservative a justice is, the more likely he or she is to vote in favor of recognizing and enforcing rights to intellectual property. Notably, the findings suggest that the size of the effect of ideology in intellectual property cases was significantly smaller than in some other categories of cases involving prominent social issues. Across areas of intellectual property law, justices were significantly more likely to vote for the intellectual property owner in copyright cases than patent cases.

6.   COPYRIGHT ENFORCEMENT

The online digitization of copyrighted content opened new modes of digital distribution and novel business avenues for copyright holders. Yet the online setting also presented unique enforcement challenges to owners of copyrighted content. The emergence of peer-to-peer file sharing protocols, which allowed users to share access to files and data over the Internet, brought about decentralized piracy on an unprecedented scale. The exponential rise of digital piracy presented copyright industries with a Hobson's choice: either aggressively ramp up enforcement against all infringers—despite the widespread public condemnation of the practice—or face potentially devastating losses in revenue.

The massive infringement of songs and movies ultimately prompted copyright owners to file infringement suits against thousands of individuals, sometimes in the same lawsuit. These "John Doe" copyright infringement lawsuits (to obtain via subpoena the personal identifying information associated with an IP-address that shared copyrighted content on a file-sharing platform) featured prominently in the litigation campaign by the Recording Industry Association of America (RIAA) from 2004 to 2008 and the BitTorrent monetization effort by individual right holders and private enforcement entities from 2010 to 2014.

Matthew Sag (2015) has comprehensively documented the evolution of John Doe lawsuits in U.S. courts, from its inception in the recording industry lawsuit campaign in 2003 to its evolution to the private enforcement model, in the context of piracy of pornography works in 2010–2014. Sag systematically reviewed all copyright owner lawsuits against "John Doe" or "unknown" or otherwise unidentified defendants between 1994 and 2014 to determine which of those cases related to pornography. The data shows that the nature of John Doe litigation initially operated on permissive mass joinder suits. As District Court judges became resistant to this type of enforcement, the model had shifted to law suits against unnamed individual defendants by a few very active plaintiffs. For instance, the pornography producer Malibu Media was the plaintiff in over 41.5% of all copyright suits nationwide in 2014.

In a series of survey experiments Depoorter et al. (2006; 2011) examined the influence of various copyright enforcement measures on file-sharers' (1) self-reported attitudes about copyright law in the first phase and (2) intended download behavior when the probability of detection falls to zero in the second phase. The experimental findings indicate that punitive enforcement creates a backlash effect by strengthening prior anti-copyright positions among frequent copyright offenders. The results suggest that offenders, when able to circumvent enforcement measures through technological means, will download illegally more than if they were faced with punitive enforcement measures. Because technological innovations reduce the efficacy of enforcement in online settings, the content industries cannot afford to neglect public attitudes. A follow-up experimental study by Depoorter and Van Hiel (2015) examined reactions to the U.S. copyright alert system. Interestingly, the findings from this experimental scenario study suggest that, perhaps due to perceived privacy intrusions, even a very moderate graduated response system (as opposed to France's more aggressive three-strikes regime) elicits negative reactions that are almost on a level with the adverse response to the recording industry litigation campaign.

BIBLIOGRAPHY

Asay, Clark D. 2022. "An Empirical Study of Copyright's Substantial Similarity Test", 13 *U.C. Irvine L. Rev.* 35.

Asay, Clark D., Arielle Sloan and Dean Sobczak. 2020. "Is Transformative Use Eating the World?", 61 *B.C. L. Rev.* 905.

Barnes, Jeffrey Edward. 2000. "Comment: Attorney's Fee Awards in Federal Copyright Litigation after Fogerty v. Fantasy: Defendants Are Winning Fees More Often, but the New Standard Still Favors Prevailing Plaintiffs", 47 *UCLA L. Rev.* 1381.

Beebe, Barton. 2006. "An Empirical Study of the Multifactor Tests for Trademark Infringement", 94 *Calif. L. Rev.* 1581.

Beebe, Barton. 2008. "An Empirical Study of U.S. Copyright Fair Use Opinions, 1978–2005", 156 *U. Penn. L. Rev.* 549.

Blair, Roger and Thomas F. Cotter. 2005. *Intellectual Property: Economic and Legal Dimensions of Rights and Remedies*, Cambridge University Press.

Burk, Dan L. 1999. "Muddy Rules for Cyberspace", 21 *Cardozo L. Rev.* 121, 140.

Carroll, Michael W. 2007. "Fixing Fair Use", 85 *N.C. L. Rev.* 1087.

Cotropia, Christopher A. and James Gibson. 2014. "Copyright's Topography: An Empirical Study of Copyright Litigation", 92 *Texas Law Review* 1981.

Depoorter, Ben. 2009. "Technology and Uncertainty: The Shaping Effect on Copyright Law", 157 *U. Pa. L. Rev.* 1831 (2009).

Depoorter, Ben. 2019. "Copyright Enforcement in the Digital Age: When the Remedy is the Wrong", 66 *UCLA L. Rev.*

Depoorter, Ben and Alain Van Hiel. 2015. "Copyright Alert Enforcement: Six Strikes & Privacy Harms", 39 *Columbia J. L. & Arts* 233.

Depoorter, Ben and Sven Vanneste. 2006. "Norms and Enforcement: The Case Against Copyright Litigation", 84 *Oregon L. Rev.* 1127.

Depoorter, Ben and Alain Van Hiel. 2011. "Copyright Backlash", 84 *Southern California Law Review* 1251.

Favale, Marcella, Martin Kretschmer and Paul C. Torremans. 2016. "Is There a EU Copyright Jurisprudence? An Empirical Analysis of the Workings of the European Court of Justice", 79 *Mod. L. Rev.* 31–75.

Ford, William K. 2006. "Judging Expertise in Copyright Law", 14 *J. Intell. Prop. L.* 1.

Gerhardt, Deborah R. 2011. "Copyright Publication: An Empirical Study", 87 *Notre Dame L. Rev.* 135.

Rogers, Eric. 2013. "Substantially Unfair: An Empirical Examination of Copyright Substantial Similarity Analysis among the Federal Circuits", 2013 *Mich. St. L. Rev.* 893.

Landes, William M. 2004. "An Empirical Analysis of Intellectual Property Litigation: Some Preliminary Results", 41 *Hous. L. Rev.* 749.

Lee, Edward and Andrew Moshirnia. 2020. "Does Fair Use Matter? An Empirical Study of Music Cases (March 26, 2020)", 94 *Southern California L. Rev.* Available at SSRN: https://ssrn.com/abstract= 3579383 or http://dx.doi.org/10.2139/ssrn.3579383 .

Lippman, Katherine. 2013. "The Beginning of the End: Preliminary Results of an Empirical Study of Copyright Substantial Similarity Opinions in the U.S. Circuit Courts", 2013 *Mich. St. L. Rev.* 513.

Liu, Jiarui. 2012. "Copyright Injunctions After eBay: An Empirical Study", 16 *Lewis & Clark L. Rev.* 215.

Liu, Jiarui. 2019. "An Empirical Study of Transformative Use in Copyright Law (February 6, 2019)", 22 *Stan. Tech. L. Rev.* 163.

Liu, Joseph P. 2008. "Two-Factor Fair Use?", 31 *Colum. J.L. & Arts* 571.

Lund, Jamie. 2011. "An Empirical Examination of the Lay Listener Test in Music Composition Copyright Infringement", 11 *Va. Sports & Ent. L.J.* 137.

Lund, Jamie. 2013. "Fixing Music Copyright", 79 *Brook. L. Rev.* (2013).

Netanel, Neil Weinstock. 2011. "Making Sense of Fair Use", 15 *Lewis & Clark L. Rev.* 715.

Nimmer, David. 2003. "Fairest of Them All and Other Fairy Tales of Fair Use", 66 *Law & Contemp. Probs.* 263.

Priest, George L. and Benjamin Klein. 1984. "The Selection of Disputes for Litigation", 13 *J. Legal Stud.* 1.

Reese, R. Anthony. 2015. "How Much Is Too Much? Campbell and the Third Fair Use Factor", 90 *Wash. L. Rev.* 755.

Sag, Matthew. 2005. "God in the Machine: A New Structural Analysis of Copyright's Fair Use Doctrine", 11 *Mich. Telecomm. & Tech. L. Rev.* 381, 435.

Sag, Matthew, Tonja Jacobi and Maxim Sytch. 2009. "Ideology and Exceptionalism in Intellectual Property: An Empirical Study", 97 *Cal. L. Rev.* 801.

Sag, Matthew. 2012. "Predicting Fair Use", 73 *Ohio St. L.J.* 47.

Sag, Matthew. 2013. "Empirical Studies of Copyright Litigation: Nature of Suit Coding 7", *Loyola Univ. Chi. Sch. of Law Pub. Law & Legal Theory*, Research Paper No. 2013-017, 2013. Available at http:// ssrn.com/abstract=2330256.

Sag, Matthew. 2015. "Copyright Trolling, An Empirical Study", 100 *Iowa L. Rev.* 1105.

Sag, Matthew. 2016. "IP Litigation in United States District Courts: 1994 to 2014", 101 *Iowa Law Review* 1065.

Sag, Matthew and Pamela Samuelson. "Discovering eBay's Impact on Copyright Injunctions Through Empirical Evidence (January 28, 2022)".

Samuelson, Pamela. 2009. "Unbundling Fair Uses", 77 *Fordham L. Rev.* 2537.

Samuelson, Pamela and Tara Wheatland. 2009. "Statutory Damages in Copyright Law: A Remedy in Need of Reform", 51 *Wm. & Mary L. Rev.* 439.

Samuelson, Pamela, John M. Golden and Mark P. Gergen. 2020. "Recalibrating the Disgorgement Remedy in Intellectual Property Cases", 100 *Boston University L. Rev.* 1999.

Samuelson, Pamela. 2013. "A Fresh Look at Tests for Nonliteral Copyright Infringement", 107 *Nw. U. L. Rev.* 1821.

Case List

Campbell v. Acuff-Rose Music, Inc. (1994), 510 U.S. 569.

eBay Inc. v. MercExchange, L.L.C. (2006), 547 U.S. 388.

Fogerty v. Fantasy, Inc. (1994), 510 U.S. 517.

Legislative Materials

The Copyright Act of 1976, 17 U.S.C. 101 et seq.
The Copyright Act of 1976, 17 U.S.C. 505.

9. An empirical defence of expanded fair dealing in UK copyright law

Emily Hudson

1. INTRODUCTION

In this chapter, I draw from my empirical work with cultural institutions to present some thoughts on the drafting and interpretation of copyright exceptions in the UK in a post-Brexit world.[1] My research with cultural institutions began in 2003 when I commenced work on a project that examined the impact of copyright on the digitisation practices of Australian institutions.[2] This project included fieldwork in metropolitan and regional locations and sought to understand how institutions were using digitisation and how copyright was handled within such projects. Since that time, I have undertaken further empirical work with leading institutions in Australia, Canada, the United Kingdom and the United States in order to investigate decision-making in relation to copyright. This research was never intended to focus on exceptions, and indeed interviewees have always been asked a range of questions about their copyright practices. However, exceptions turned out to be particularly interesting due to the divergence in practices between countries and the change in practices over time. As such, many of the outputs from this research, including this chapter, explore questions about exceptions.[3]

In the first part of the chapter, I provide some background to my research, including an overview of my interview methodology and some of the key observations and themes to come from this work. One theme is the importance of using empirical methodologies in IP scholarship.[4] There can be a vast gap between the 'law in books' (statutes, cases, commentary and other materials written by legal experts) and the 'law in action' (the law as understood and practised by everyday users). This is significant for copyright exceptions, as much of the literature on the role and adequacy of such provisions has focused heavily or exclusively on the law in

---

[1] This chapter builds on a presentation given as part of the CREATe Public Lecture Series 2020–2021: Emily Hudson, 'An Empirical Perspective on Drafting Copyright Exceptions', 24 March 2021. I also wish to thank Tanya Aplin, Robert Burrell and Michael Handler for their comments on a draft of this chapter.

[2] This project is described in detail in Emily Hudson and Andrew Kenyon, 'Digital Access: The Impact of Copyright on Digitisation Practices in Australian Museums, Galleries, Libraries and Archives' (2007) 30 *University of New South Wales Law Journal* 12.

[3] Particularly relevant for this chapter are Emily Hudson, *Drafting Copyright Exceptions: From the Law in Books to the Law in Action* (Cambridge University Press, 2020) and Michael Handler and Emily Hudson, 'Fair Use as an Advance on Fair Dealing? Depolarising the Debate' in Shyamkrishna Balganesh, Ng-Loy Wee Loon and Haochen Sun (eds), *The Cambridge Handbook of Copyright Limitations and Exceptions* (Cambridge University Press, 2021).

[4] The 'empirical turn' in IP scholarship is discussed in Emily Hudson and Andrew Kenyon, 'IP & Empirical Research' in Graeme Austin, Andrew Christie, Andrew Kenyon and Megan Richardson (eds), *Across Intellectual Property: Essays in Honour of Sam Ricketson* (Cambridge University Press, 2020).

books.[5] While such doctrinal analysis is an indispensable part of any evaluation of the law, we risk misdiagnosing problems and recommending ineffective solutions if we proceed without any consideration of user behaviour.

In the second two parts, I elaborate on what the UK might do with the law-making freedoms that Brexit is said to bring. In the copyright context, these freedoms come from (1) the UK no longer being bound by EU copyright directives or by new decisions of the Court of Justice of the European Union (CJEU),[6] and (2) the Withdrawal Agreement and post-Brexit free trade agreements (FTAs) not (currently) prescribing the form of exceptions.[7] I will focus on the question of whether the UK should introduce fair use, a reform that is seen as precluded, in EU copyright law, by Article 5 of the Information Society Directive.[8] I will argue that fair use is

---

[5]   See Hudson (n 3), pp. 3–4. Recent empirical studies that focus on or have particular relevance to copyright exceptions include: Kris Erickson and Martin Kretschmer, '"This Video is Unavailable": Analyzing Copyright Takedown of User-Generated Content on YouTube' (2018) 9 *Journal of Intellectual Property, Information Technology and E-Commerce Law (JIPITEC)* 75; Christian Handke, Lucie Guibault and Joan-Josep Vallbé, 'Copyright's impact on data mining in academic research' (2021) 42 *Managerial and Decision Economics* 1; and Bartolomeo Meletti and Stef van Gompel, 'Issue reports on how copyright exceptions and other permitted uses that are relevant for documentary filmmakers and immersive digital heritage practitioners are understood in the Netherlands and the UK' (2021), at https://zenodo.org/record/5070427.

[6]   The general approach of Brexit has been to avoid the creation of massive gaps in UK law. Following expiry of the transition period on 31 December 2020 (during which EU law continued to apply), the starting point was that EU-derived domestic legislation was saved. For copyright, this meant that reforms that implemented EU directives did not automatically disappear, although some EU-related copyright initiatives have been repealed (such as the orphaned works exception under the Orphan Works Directive) or been reformed (such as eligibility for the *sui generis* database right): The Intellectual Property (Copyright and Related Rights) (Amendment) (EU Exit) Regulations 2019 (SI 2019/605), regs. 11, 12 and 23 (omitting ss. 44B and 76A and Schedule ZA1 from the Copyright, Designs and Patents Act 1988 ('CDPA')), regs. 28(3) and 38 (amending the qualification requirements in reg. 18 of the Copyright and Rights in Databases Regulations 1997, but not for existing databases). We also have guidance in relation to the status of retained EU case law. The starting point is that judgments handed down before the end of the transition period remain binding, whilst those handed down after that point are not binding. That said, judges may consider these non-binding EU developments; plus it is possible for the Supreme Court and the Court of Appeal to depart from retained EU case law: European Union (Withdrawal) Act 2018, s. 6; European Union (Withdrawal) Act 2018 (Relevant Court) (Retained EU Case Law) Regulations 2020 (SI 1525/2020), reg. 3(b).

[7]   The Withdrawal Agreement included only a limited number of provisions in relation to IP, and only one specifically directed to copyright, being the *sui generis* database right: *Agreement on the withdrawal of the United Kingdom of Great Britain and Northern Ireland from the European Union and the European Atomic Energy Community* (2019/C 384 I/01), Title IV (Intellectual Property). In contrast, the UK and EU reached more detailed agreement about IP in the *Trade and Cooperation Agreement between the European Union and the European Atomic Energy Community, of the one part, and the United Kingdom of Great Britain and Northern Ireland, of the other part* (30 April 2021, L 149/10), Part Two, Title V. Article 233 deals with exceptions and limitations, and adopts the three-step test: '[e]ach Party shall confine limitations or exceptions to the rights set out in Articles 225 to 229 to certain special cases which do not conflict with a normal exploitation of the work or other subject-matter and do not unreasonably prejudice the legitimate interests of the right holders'. So far, post-Brexit free trade agreements also use the three-step test, and indeed the FTA with Australia refers to the need for balance in copyright law: *Free Trade Agreement Between the United Kingdom of Great Britain and Northern Ireland and Australia* (signed 17 December 2021), Articles 15.62 (three-step test), 15.63 (balance).

[8]   See, e.g., Ian Hargreaves, *Digital Opportunity: A Review of Intellectual Property and Growth* (May 2011), [5.12]–[5.19] (review of UK copyright law proceeding on the basis that fair use is

the wrong question in the UK, at least for now, and at least in isolation. There are a number of reasons for this, including lack of legislative bandwidth and the political challenges in implementing what would be regarded as a highly contentious reform. But more fundamentally, if we are to campaign for fair use, we need to be clear about the problems we believe need to be addressed, how fair use will help solve these problems, and the risk that advocating for fair use may concede (implicitly or otherwise) that the changes to UK exceptions in 2014 were inadequate. My argument is *not* that fair use is an undesirable reform option. On the contrary, there are many compelling arguments in favour of a fully open-ended exception. However, I do not see fair use as the endpoint of a mature copyright system, and believe that empirical analysis helps demonstrate the merits of other approaches. This chapter draws from UK experiences to present the case for expanded fair dealing, however its lessons are applicable to other jurisdictions that are considering ways to open up exceptions.

This chapter is structured as follows. As noted above, in Part 2, I provide further background to my empirical work into copyright and cultural institutions. In Part 3, I discuss the 'fair use panacea': the proposition that there are problems with exceptions in countries such as the UK; that these problems are a function of the existing, closed-ended approach to drafting in those jurisdictions; and that the only viable, long-term solution is to introduce a fully open-ended exception such as fair use.[9] In that part, I draw from my empirical work to explain why fair use is an attractive reform option, but also why change to the 'law in books' does not necessarily lead to, and is not necessarily a pre-condition for, change to the 'law in action'. In Part 4, I explore the proposition that the UK already has the foundations of a well-functioning suite of exceptions, in particular given the expansion of fair dealing in 2014. If this is right, rather than focusing on wholesale legislative change, we might instead ask how to support users in harnessing the existing flexibilities in the UK system – although targeted reforms may also be desirable. In my short concluding remarks, I consider what this chapter means for the EU copyright system, given the closed list approach in Article 5.

2.   EMPIRICAL WORK

The analysis in this chapter draws from my research on the copyright management practices of cultural institutions. During a period spanning over 14 years, I conducted fieldwork with hundreds of staff of cultural institutions and other allied bodies in Australia, Canada, the United States and the United Kingdom. My empirical work involved semi-structured interviews supplemented with review of any interviewee-supplied internal documents (such as pro forma copyright licences) and publicly available information (for instance, copyright information on

---

not a reform option, given EU copyright law) https://www.gov.uk/government/publications/digital-opportunity-review-of-intellectual-property-and-growth; *Spiegel Online GmbH v Beck* (C-516/17) [2019] ECDR 24 (Grand Chamber), [40]–[49] (the list of exceptions and limitations in Article 5 is exhaustive; Member States may not extend the scope of those exceptions and limitations, for instance by reference to fundamental rights).

⁹   For discussion of the fair use panacea, see especially Robert Burrell, 'Reining in Copyright Law: Is Fair Use the Answer?' [2001] *Intellectual Property Quarterly* 361; Robert Burrell and Allison Coleman, *Copyright Exceptions: The Digital Impact* (Cambridge University Press, 2005), chapter 9.

institution websites).[10] In addition to producing a case study on copyright experiences in the cultural institution sector, this work was also relevant to broader questions about legislative drafting, social norms, the interpretative practices of everyday legal actors, and why people obey the law. On the other hand, the fieldwork was never intended to be a comprehensive survey of institutional practices. Much of my work was with major institutions, as judged by collection size and significance, staff numbers, and so forth. I focused on these institutions for a number of reasons, including because they were more likely to be (1) thinking about copyright, and (2) the origin of norms and interpretations that might ripple throughout the sector.[11]

I have described my interview methodology in detail elsewhere.[12] As such, I focus in this part on the headline statistics, the content of each tranche of interviews, and the key ideas to arise from those interviews. The fieldwork can be divided into three stages. The first stage took place as part of a project on copyright and digitisation at the University of Melbourne.[13] The fieldwork for that project (2004–2005) had two parts. During the first part, 94 people at six major institutions were interviewed to obtain a detailed understanding of institution missions, the mechanics and use of digitisation, and each institution's approach to and experiences with copyright. In the second part, interviews were conducted with a further 40 people from 32 metropolitan and regional institutions in order to get a sense of issues and trends across the sector. The Australian experiences raised a number of questions, including in relation to the relevance of free exceptions and whether those provisions were narrow and underutilised, such that they might benefit from reform.

The second stage of empirical work took place as part of my doctorate, and involved fieldwork in the United States and Canada (2007–2009), thus allowing comparisons to be made between these countries and (using the earlier research) Australia. The US and Canada were selected for study for several reasons.[14] One was that institutions in these countries were, like those in Australia, being encouraged to develop virtual as well as physical spaces, and might therefore face similar challenges in relation to their use of digital and online technologies. Doctrinally, whilst the three countries had broadly similar copyright regimes, including special accommodations for cultural institutions via libraries and archives provisions,[15] there were

---

[10]   There were a number of reasons for using interviews rather than other techniques, such as written surveys: Hudson (n 3), pp. 341–342. One was that the research aimed to explore decision-making processes in relation to copyright. It was thought that this would be best achieved through structured discussions in which participants could fully explain their institution's processes and the thinking behind them.

[11]   Ibid pp. 342–343.

[12]   Ibid pp. 65–70; 339–348. Interviews typically lasted 1–2 hours, were conducted face-to-face where possible, and were audio-recorded (where consent was given) in addition to notes being taken by hand or on a computer. To encourage free and frank disclosure, all interviews were conducted anonymously.

[13]   See, in particular, Hudson and Kenyon (n 2).

[14]   Hudson (n 3), pp. 340–341.

[15]   Provisions directed to the activities of libraries, archives and museums are now found in Copyright Act 1968 (Cth) ('Australian Act'), ss. 48–53, 110A, 113G–113M, 200AB; the Copyright Act (RSC 1985, c C-42) ('Canadian Act'), ss. 30.1, 30.4; and Copyright Act of 1976 (Title 17, US Code) ('US Act'), s. 108. Other exceptions are also relevant to cultural institutions, for instance in relation to institutional liability for the use of patron-operated machines on the premises (Australian Act, ss. 39A, 104B; Canadian Act, s. 30.3), and fair dealing and fair use exceptions.

also differences, for instance in relation to the open-ended fair use exception in US law,[16] and the emphasis in Canada on collective licensing.[17] Canada was also attractive for empirical study due to the Supreme Court's 2004 decision in *CCH v Law Society*, where it was held that a custom photocopying service at a law library was research-based and fair.[18] This case was immediately heralded in the academic literature as a 'landmark' due to the Court's insistence on a large and liberal interpretation of research and its description of exceptions as 'users' rights'.[19] With over four years having elapsed since *CCH* was handed down, might Canadian experiences with fair dealing differ from those in Australia?

During this second stage, I visited 44 cultural institutions and 17 related bodies such as peak associations. During each visit I typically conducted one or two interviews, with 114 people interviewed in total. The interviews adopted the same ethical and procedural framework as the Australian fieldwork, although the questions were updated to focus less on technical aspects of digitisation and more on copyright.[20] For fieldwork with institution staff, interviewees were asked to describe whether their institution digitised or otherwise copied collection items for any of the following purposes: internal administration and collection management; preservation; supplying external requests; providing onsite access (for instance in exhibitions); and providing offsite access (for instance in publications or on institution websites). For each sphere in which they were digitising or otherwise copying collection items, they were asked whether copyright was considered and, if so, how it was handled. This aspect of the interviews therefore included discussion of negotiation-based strategies such as licensing, and institutional reliance on exceptions. Finally, the interviews included general questions about the resources dedicated to copyright, risk preferences, orphaned works, and so forth.

Despite differences between the law in Australia, Canada and the US, there was much in common in reported experiences in relation to copyright management, for instance regarding the benefits and challenges of licensing,[21] and the preference for using public domain works in large-scale digitisation projects.[22] Despite this historical focus in Canada on licensing,

---

[16]   US Act, s. 107.

[17]   For a discussion of the history of the Canadian Act, see Hudson (n 3), pp. 317–323. In essence, when copyright law was being reformed in Canada in the 1980s and 1990s, one of the key organising principles was that licensing should be the main mechanism for allowing access to and re-use of copyright works, with exceptions playing a much smaller role. Legislation to facilitate collective licensing (in the late 1980s) pre-dated legislation that expanded exceptions (in the late 1990s). One observation from the Canadian fieldwork was the degree to which norms that arose during that period were difficult (although as it turns out, not impossible) to dislodge.

[18]   *CCH Canadian Ltd v Law Society of Upper Canada* [2004] 1 SCR 339.

[19]   *CCH* (n 18), [51] and [48], respectively. For the language of 'landmark', see Parveen Esmail, '*CCH Canadian Ltd v Law Society of Upper Canada*: Case Comment on a Landmark Copyright Case' (2005) 10 *Appeal* 13. Other contributions to emphasise the importance of *CCH* included Teresa Scassa, 'Recalibrating Copyright Law? A Comment on the Supreme Court of Canada's Decision in *CCH Canadian Limited et al v Law Society of Upper Canada*' (2004) 3 *Canadian Journal of Law & Technology* 89; Daniel Gervais, 'Canadian Copyright Law Post-*CCH*' (2004) 18 *Intellectual Property Journal* 131; Abraham Drassinower, 'Taking User Rights Seriously' in Michael Geist (ed), *In the Public Interest: The Future of Canadian Copyright Law* (Irwin Law, 2005); and Giuseppina D'Agostino, 'Healing Fair Dealing? A Comparative Analysis of Canada's Fair Dealing to UK Fair Dealing and US Fair Use' (2008) 53 *McGill Law Journal* 309.

[20]   For further detail in relation to the interview questions, see Hudson (n 3), pp. 344–346.

[21]   Hudson (n 3), pp. 74–84.

[22]   Ibid pp. 71–74.

interviewees in that country did not report new or innovative licensing strategies when compared with their Australian and US colleagues. However, there was considerable divergence in reported experiences in relation to exceptions. Interviewees in the US reported relying on fair use for a broad range of institutional uses, and indeed the fieldwork hinted at an emerging trend of invoking fair use for some online uses.[23] In Australia and Canada, on the other hand, interviewees described a far less prominent role for fair dealing,[24] and noted that sector-specific exceptions tended not to extend to public-facing activities (and certainly not online use).[25]

In thinking about why this was the case, a key conclusion was that this was *not* just a product of the law in books. For instance, academic commentary following *CCH* argued that Canadian fair dealing and US fair use were more closely aligned following the Supreme Court's decision, including because they use similar fairness infrastructure; the Court's liberal interpretation of 'research' opened up the scope of fair dealing; and its user rights language likewise provided unambiguous guidance as to how exceptions should be applied.[26] Despite this, at the time of the Canadian fieldwork, *CCH* had received an extremely muted response within participating institutions, with very few changes in practice attributable to the case. This chapter will return, in Part 4, to why this was the case. As will be discussed, many of these reasons related to the challenges in displacing institutional attitudes and workflows in which exceptions played only a marginal role.

In the third stage of fieldwork (2012–2019), I completed a number of batches of empirical work. The fieldwork used largely the same methodology and interview structure as the US and Canadian interviews, and turned out to be very important to illustrate another feature of the 'law in action': that although norms can be sticky, at other times there is considerable dynamism in practices. The first batch of fieldwork took place in Australia in 2012–2013, supplemented with follow-up interviews in 2016.[27] It included institutions and even interviewees that had participated in the earlier fieldwork in 2004 and 2005, and enabled me to (1) explore whether there had been any changes to views and practices over time, and (2) evaluate the success of 2006 reforms to Australian exceptions, including new section 200AB, an exception for cultural and educational institutions intended to capture some of the benefits of fair use.[28] As discussed in Part 3, while interviewees reported very low uptake of section 200AB, they also described numerous instances of digitising items for public-facing activities, having 'risk managed' such uses.[29] To be clear, Australian interviewees did not describe a free-for-all. Risk management was used thoughtfully. However, this raised the question of why risk manage-

---

[23] Ibid pp. 175–191. This is discussed further in Part 3 of this chapter.

[24] Ibid pp. 232–235 (Australia), 252–261 (Canada). The Canadian experiences are discussed further in Part 3.

[25] Ibid chapter 4. By public-facing, I mean activities in which the institution makes an item generally accessible, for instance in an exhibition, publication or online database. Although sector-specific exceptions include copying services for researchers, these services are not 'public-facing' under this definition.

[26] See especially Gervais (n 19) and d'Agostino (n 19).

[27] The Australian fieldwork involved interviews with 77 interviewees at 21 cultural institutions, and five interviewees from four related bodies. The follow-up interviews in 2016 were with seven institutions that participated in 2012/2013, often with the same interviewees as previously. These institutions and participants are not double-counted in the fieldwork statistics.

[28] Second reading speech of the Attorney-General: Commonwealth, *Parliamentary Debates*, House of Representatives, 19 October 2006 (Philip Ruddock). Section 200AB is discussed in Hudson (n 3), chapter 6.

[29] Hudson (n 3), pp. 88–92, 220–222.

ment had grown in Australian institutions, and why the factors that informed a risk-managed decision were not considered relevant to section 200AB.

In this final phase of fieldwork, I also undertook targeted interviews with North American participants, especially in relation to developments in educational copying in Canada;[30] and added the UK as a jurisdiction, with some initial interviews in 2014 (around the time of a major liberalisation of UK exceptions) and a bigger tranche of fieldwork a few years later, in which the impact of those changes could be assessed (2017–2019).[31] As will be discussed in Part 4, the 2014 reforms included the expansion of fair dealing to cover three new sets of purposes: quotation; caricature, parody and pastiche; and illustration for instruction.[32] The UK fieldwork revealed some similar trends to those in Australia, for instance in relation to interviewees reporting far greater comfort with risk than might be expected (or was hitherto the case) for a sector that is often described as conservative.[33] However, there were also signs that institutions were embracing and were keen to further embrace the new fair dealing exceptions, with quotation seen as particularly relevant.[34] Thus, although the fieldwork in Canada and Australia had initially painted a gloomy picture for fair dealing, the later work illustrated the capacity for the doctrine to play a more meaningful role in the copyright system. In the remainder of this chapter, I provide an empirical defence of expanded fair dealing as an attractive model for countries that wish to open up exceptions using less prescriptive drafting.[35] To set the scene, I shall start in Part 3 by discussing the reasons for ongoing interest in the 'fair use panacea', and why we should be cautious about viewing fair use as clearly superior to all other drafting options.

3.   THE FAIR USE PANACEA

Anyone who researches on UK exceptions often gets asked whether UK copyright law would benefit from fair use. This interest in fair use is not specific to the UK,[36] and can be seen in other jurisdictions with a closed-list approach to exceptions, that is, 'an exhaustive set of exceptions in which each provision focuses on a specific act or is otherwise limited in scope,

---

[30]   The targeted fieldwork included six Canadian interviewees, being five librarians and one person from a related body.

[31]   The UK fieldwork involved interviews with 27 interviewees at 18 cultural institutions, and five interviewees from five related bodies. A small number of participants in the 2014 work were re-interviewed in the main UK fieldwork, and are not double-counted in these statistics.

[32]   CDPA ss. 30(1ZA), 30A, 32, respectively.

[33]   Hudson (n 3), pp. 88–92, 297–301.

[34]   Ibid pp. 275–292.

[35]   I have also discussed the merits of expanded fair dealing in Handler and Hudson (n 3).

[36]   As seen in, for example, Carys Craig, 'The Changing Face of Fair Dealing in Canadian Copyright Law: A Proposal for Legislative Reform' in Michael Geist (ed), *In the Public Interest: The Future of Canadian Copyright Law* (Irwin Law, 2005); Alexandra Sims, 'The case for fair use in New Zealand' (2016) 24 *International Journal of Law and Information Technology* 176; P. Bernt Hugenholtz, 'Flexible Copyright: Can the EU Author's Rights Accommodate Fair Use' in Ruth Okediji (ed), *Copyright Law in an Age of Limitations and Exceptions* (Cambridge University Press, 2017); Peter K. Yu, 'Customizing Fair Use Transplants' (2018) 7 *Laws* 1; Christophe Geiger and Elena Izyumenko, 'Towards a European "Fair Use" Grounded in Freedom of Expression' (2019) 35 *American University International Law Review* 1.

especially through being restricted to a particular purpose'.[37] One of the central propositions to underpin the fair use panacea is that closed-list systems are inherently prone to numerous drafting problems: exceptions tend to be over- and under-exclusive due to the use of rule-like language; this specificity also limits their ability to self-update in response to technological and other change; and specificity does not necessarily result in certainty or clarity for users, for instance when the legislative language does not map onto industry practices.[38] Closed-list systems, it is said, often require constant legislative tinkering to correct these faults. This, in turn, raises issues with legislative resources and statutory complexity, the latter being a particular issue where such tinkering favours the addition of detail rather than unnecessary elements being taken away.

Introducing a fully open-ended exception is said to deal with these drafting issues by replacing rule-like language with that of a standard. The essence of a standard (as defined in the legal rulemaking literature) is that the application of a legal regulation to a particular scenario is determined by a judge or other adjudicator *after* that scenario occurs.[39] To illustrate, consider a prohibition against 'excessive speed' (a standard) versus one against driving above 50km/h (a rule).[40] For the rule, the questions for the judge are largely factual, and revolve around how fast the defendant was driving. For the standard, the judge must also consider the content of the law, in this case, what factors are relevant to excessiveness. Fair use in US law is a multi-factor standard.[41] The kernel of the provision is that a fair use of a work is not an infringement of copyright. The statute also sets out some illustrative fair use scenarios and lists four factors that judges shall consider when determining whether a use is fair. This provides greater constraint on judicial decision-making than a pure standard, which would lack these indications. In addition, some standards can become more rule-like in countries with a system of precedent, where interpretations in earlier cases may need to be applied in subsequent ones, thus creating judge-made sub-rules.[42]

In a post-Brexit world, fair use is once again an open question for the UK.[43] I am on record as supporting fair use, for reasons I will elaborate on in this chapter.[44] But even as such a person, I think that for the UK, fair use is the wrong question to focus on, at least for now, and at least in isolation.

---

[37]   Handler and Hudson (n 3), p. 140. Under this model, fair dealing, although more standard-like than many other exceptions, is a closed exception.

[38]   These concerns accord with many of the problems said to arise for legal commands that are drafted as rules. For an overview of the standards and rules literature, with a particular focus on copyright exceptions, see Hudson (n 3), chapter 2; Handler and Hudson (n 3), pp. 151–153.

[39]   Louis Kaplow, 'Rules versus Standards: An Economic Analysis' (1992) 42 *Duke Law Journal* 557. Other scholars use the 'degree of precision' to capture the difference between standards and rules: see, e.g., Isaac Ehrlich and Richard A. Posner, 'An Economic Analysis of Legal Rulemaking' (1974) 3 *Journal of Legal Studies* 257, 258.

[40]   This is a very common example in the literature: see, e.g., Ehrlich and Posner (n 39), p. 257; Kaplow (n 39), p. 560; Russell Korobkin, 'Behavioral Analysis and Legal Form: Rules vs. Standards Revisited' (2000) 79 *Oregon Law Review* 23, 23.

[41]   See Hudson (n 3), pp. 36–37.

[42]   Ibid pp. 38–40.

[43]   See n 6 to n 8 and surrounding text.

[44]   See, e.g., Emily Hudson, 'Implementing Fair Use in Copyright Law: Lessons from Australia' (2013) 25 *Intellectual Property Journal* 201; Handler and Hudson (n 3), p. 142.

Some of the reasons for this view relate to the political realities of introducing fair use. First, such a reform requires legislative bandwidth. Leaving aside the question of whether UK copyright law would benefit from fair use, there is the question of how to do it. This is not just a matter of writing a new section 28AA into the CDPA. There are questions about the form of words one would use: section 107 of the US Copyright Act?[45] An extended version of fair dealing, where the words 'such as' make the purposes illustrative?[46] Some other home-spun language?[47] There are also questions about consequential amendments: would all the fair dealing provisions be repealed? What about other exceptions? In short, implementing fair use is not a small project, and the evidence at the moment suggests that copyright law is not a priority for the UK government.

In addition to issues with legislative bandwidth, there are also issues with the political attractiveness of fair use. Even if the bandwidth to undertake large-scale copyright reform were to emerge, we need to be cognisant that there would likely be a highly polarised review process in which certain respondents would argue emphatically against fair use.[48] In the face of such resistance, the government may be reluctant to adopt fair use if other, intermediate, positions are available. This is what has happened in Australia, where a number of major law reviews have recommended the introduction of fair use.[49] When draft legislation was finally released by the (then) federal government, it contained interventions within the existing closed-list model, including a quotation exception that is limited in numerous ways.[50]

Another reason to be cautious about the fair use panacea is that it can rest on over-simplified critical analysis.[51] To understand this concern, it is useful to start by expanding on some of the arguments in favour of fair use. One such argument draws from the standards and rules

[45]   This was the approach in Sri Lanka and Israel: see Intellectual Property Act, Act No. 36 of 2003, s. 11 and Copyright Act 2007, art. 19, respectively.

[46]   This was the approach initially taken in Singapore: see Copyright Act 1977 (Sing), ss. 35(1) and 109(1) (as amended by the Copyright (Amendment) Act 2004 (Sing)). Since that time, Singapore has updated its 'permitted uses' to include a fair use provision modelled on the language of the US statute: see Copyright Act 2021 (Sing), ss. 190 and 191.

[47]   This was the approach in Australia with 'flexible dealing' for cultural and educational institutions: see Australian Act, s. 200AB.

[48]   See, e.g., Handler and Hudson (n 3), pp. 142–146.

[49]   Australian Law Reform Commission (ALRC), *Copyright in the Digital Economy* (Report No 122, November 2013); Productivity Commission, *Intellectual Property Arrangements* (Report No 78, September 2016), chapter 6; and note Ernst & Young, *Cost Benefit Analyais of Changes to the Copyright Act 1968* (2016), at https://www.infrastructure.gov.au/media-centre/publications/cost-benefit-analysis -changes-copyright-act-1968.

[50]   Exposure draft of the Copyright Amendment (Access Reform) Bill 2021 and *Discussion Paper—Exposure Draft Copyright Amendment (Access Reform) Bill 2021 & Review of Technological Protection Measures Exceptions* (Department of Infrastructure, Transport, Regional Development and Communications, December 2021), both at https://www.infrastructure.gov.au/have-your-say/have -your-say-draft-copyright-reform-legislation. The government ran a consultation process in relation to this draft legislation; for a response focusing on the proposed quotation exception, see Tanya Aplin, Lionel Bently and Emily Hudson, *Submission to Australian Government: Department of Infrastructure, Transport, Regional Development and Communications on the Discussion Paper – Exposure Draft Copyright Amendment (Access Reform) Bill 2021* (24 February 2022), at https://ssrn.com/abstract= 4043190. There was a change of government in Australia in May 2022, and at the time of writing the fate of this legislation remains to be seen.

[51]   See also Handler and Hudson (n 3), pp. 149–157.

literature: that fair use is desirable as a matter of legislative efficiency.[52] We cannot expect the legislature to have the time and foresight to articulate, in advance, a series of rules that deal with every possible contingency. Copyright cases are characterised by highly variable fact patterns in which the question of whether a use ought to be infringing can depend on a nuanced analysis. For instance, we might agree that it is appropriate for an exception to apply to the reproduction of text and images as part of publishing works of biographical scholarship, but not in all cases – we might think differently about a glossy image on the cover of a book compared with a small illustration on the inside.[53] In the face of highly variable fact patterns, the most efficient form of legal drafting may be to enact a standard like fair use, rather than try to draft a huge list of detailed rules. Because the application of the law in any given case is determined by judges, fair use is less likely to be under-inclusive or prone to redundancy. Introducing fair use might also prevent the need for endless rounds of law reform, because it can better respond to changes in user practices and technology.

A second reason for introducing fair use is that it could have a strong signaling effect and be well adapted to comprehensively 'reboot' the copyright system. One concern about reform to exceptions is that the effects can be extremely muted in the absence of changes to judicial interpretations, legal advice and user behaviours.[54] It may be that fair use would be more likely to send the message that existing approaches need to be revisited. Using language modelled on section 107 of the US Copyright Act might also help address the concern that a new open-ended provision would introduce a great deal of uncertainty into UK law, because such a provision would not be an unknown quantity.[55]

A final argument in favour of fair use is that empirical evidence from the US suggests that it works, that is, that it has predictable content and is invoked by users in a variety of circumstances.[56] This is seen not only in systematic analysis of judicial interpretations.[57] In my research with US cultural institutions, interviewees reported relying on fair use for all manner

---

[52]   This is developed in detail in Hudson (n 3), pp. 42–58.

[53]   See, e.g., *Bill Graham Archives v Dorling Kindersley Limited*, 448 F 3d 605 (2nd circuit, 2006) (use of small scale images of concert tickets and posters in an illustrated biography on musical group, The Grateful Dead, held to be a fair use).

[54]   This was one of the concerns raised by Burrell and Coleman in relation to the fair use panacea: Burrell and Coleman (n 9), pp. 256–264. They observed that UK judges considering the fair dealing exception of the Copyright Act 1911 often preferred narrow interpretations, despite there being no suggestion that fair dealing was intended to have a limited operation. This trend continued with the Copyright Act 1956, where fair dealing was revised in a way that reflected those readings. Burrell and Coleman asked whether fair use would reverse the trend of judges reading down exceptions.

[55]   Handler and Hudson (n 3), p. 156. As noted there, one argument against this approach is that it might be undesirable in the long term if US law shifts in a direction that is objectionable or unsuited to UK conditions.

[56]   The importance of empirical study is recognised in the legal rulemaking literature, which suggests that whilst predictions can be made about the characteristics of different forms of legal drafting, much turns on the interpretations of experts and users: see especially Cass Sunstein, 'Problems with Rules' (1995) 83 *California Law Review* 953, 959.

[57]   See, e.g., Barton Beebe, 'An Empirical Study of US Copyright Fair Use Opinions, 1978–2005' (2008) 156 *University of Pennsylvania Law Review* 549; Pamela Samuelson, 'Unbundling Fair Uses' (2009) 77 *Fordham Law Review* 2537; Matthew Sag, 'Predicting Fair Use' (2012) 73 *Ohio State Law Journal* 47; Barton Beebe, 'An Empirical Study of U.S. Copyright Fair Use Opinions Updated, 1978–2019' (2020) 10 *NYU Journal of Intellectual Property and Entertainment Law* 1.

of institutional activity, reflecting confidence that fair use had discernible content.[58] Fair use was seen as relevant in situations where there was no applicable specific exception for cultural institutions (such as collection management),[59] or where there were limits in the coverage of such an exception (such as preservation and fulfilling external requests).[60] Participants also reported that fair use was invoked regularly for onsite activities, such as including images on explanatory panels and playing film extracts in exhibitions.[61] Two ideas seemed to inform this application of fair use: first, that the institutional mission of providing access to the collection requires educational, contextual and wayfinding information if that access is to be meaningful; and second, that the key economic interest of copyright owners is not controlling copying *per se*, but authorising and receiving an income from commercialisation and distribution. The fact that access was limited to the premises was therefore important to the fair use analysis. That said, interviewees also described offsite uses that were undertaken by reference to fair use, including in the online world: at around half of participating institutions, fair use had been applied to online uses, in particular with thumbnail images.[62]

Indications since the fieldwork suggest that this emerging norm of online fair use has continued, and that institutional interpretations are consistent with the direction of the case law.[63] This includes a lawsuit brought against the Metropolitan Museum of Art in relation to its use of a 1982 photograph of Eddie van Halen playing his 'Frankenstein' guitar on a website for the exhibition, *Play it Loud: Instruments of Rock & Roll*. In April 2021, the Court of Appeals for the Second Circuit held that the Met's use was a fair use.[64]

However, empirical evidence also shows that legislative reform and landmark cases do not necessarily lead to a change in practices, raising the question of whether UK fair use would suffer a similar fate. In Canada, for example, the fieldwork in 2008/2009 suggested very little movement amongst participating institutions in response to *CCH* despite that case relating to a photocopying service at a library, and the Supreme Court stating, in the strongest possible terms, that fair dealing should have a meaningful operation. Reports from interviewees suggested that *CCH* had fortified some institutions in their existing approach to researcher requests (in which some copies were supplied in the absence of permission) and had encour-

---

[58]   Hudson (n 3), pp. 175–191.

[59]   Ibid pp. 177–179. This must be understood in light of the strong norm of collection management, which was often described in ways that seemed 'before' copyright law. That is, numerous interviewees said that institutions have a duty to care for collections and that they would undertake acts such as record photography irrespective of what the law said. As such, many had not thought in detail about a fair use analysis, but – when asked to elaborate on the copyright status of internal management acts – seemed confident that fair use would apply. For analysis agreeing with this view, see Marie C Malaro and Ildiko Pogány DeAngelis, *A Legal Primer on Managing Museum Collections*, 3rd edition (Smithsonian Books, 2012), p. 187.

[60]   Ibid pp. 180–182. Fair use was particularly important for museums, as those institutions are not covered by the libraries and archives provisions in section 108 of the US Act.

[61]   Ibid pp. 182–183.

[62]   Ibid pp. 184–189.

[63]   Ibid pp. 191–205, discussing, in particular, *Authors Guild, Inc v HathiTrust*, 902 F Supp 2d 445 (SDNY, 2012), 755 F 3d 87 (2nd circuit, 2014) and the *Georgia State* litigation, the final opinion of which was *Cambridge University Press v Becker* (ND Georgia, 2 March 2020).

[64]   *Marano v The Metropolitan Museum of Art*, 472 F Supp 3d 76 (SDNY 2020); 844 F App'x 436 (2nd circuit, 2021).

aged some academic libraries to move to digital delivery for requests.[65] However, interviewees did not, subject to an important caveat I'll return to shortly, seem to consider that fair dealing might have relevance elsewhere, especially for public-facing uses, despite indications in the post-*CCH* case law that judges were willing to consider fair dealing for multiple copying and even online use.[66]

As mentioned earlier, Australia experimented with 'flexible dealing' for educational and cultural institutions when it introduced section 200AB into the Copyright Act in 2006.[67] This provision was intended to capture, for those users, some of the benefits of fair use. However, rather than using a standard like 'fairness' or language modelled on the US statute, section 200AB was drafted in a very different and more complex way, including using phrases said to have the same meaning as the three-step test in Article 13 of TRIPS.[68] In interviews in 2012/2013 and 2016, the consensus was that section 200AB had marginal relevance to practices, and to the extent it was used, operated mostly as a de facto orphaned works exception. A number of reasons were given for this state of affairs. One was the words of section 200AB, which institutions and their legal advisors struggled to interpret. Interviewees saw section 200AB as convoluted, technical, full of legalese and yet also lacking authoritative guidance. They were concerned that the 'special cases' limb of section 200AB effected a significant narrowing of the scope of the provision. Even amongst interviewees who felt confident in applying section 200AB, they found it hard to make a clear and compelling case to those higher up in their institutions.

The experiences with *CCH* and section 200AB demonstrated that change to the law in books does not necessarily have any meaningful effect on the law in action. However, the fieldwork also demonstrated how norms and practices can change because of *other* events and imperatives. In the discussion of *CCH*, I noted an important caveat to the proposition that the case received an extremely muted response. At the time of the fieldwork, there were reports that a handful of universities had added fair dealing to their copyright policies for creating electronic reserves.[69] This was a 'hot button' issue,[70] especially given the likely resistance from Access Copyright, the collective that licenses educational copying in Canada. However, events from 2010 resulted in a major shift in practices in Canadian universities, with many

---

[65] Hudson (n 3), pp. 252–261.
[66] *Statement of Royalties to be Collected by SOCAN for the Communication to the Public by Telecommunication, in Canada, of Musical or Dramatico-Musical Works*, Tariff 22A (Internet – Online Music Services) 1996–2006, Copyright Board of Canada, 18 October 2007 (fair dealing for the purpose of research applies to previews (i.e., short extracts) provided by online music sellers to help consumers identify the music they wish to purchase); and note *Euro-Excellence Inc v Kraft Canada Inc* [2007] 3 SCR 20, per Bastarache J (taking seriously, in a case on secondary infringement, the idea of copyright as a balanced right).
[67] See Hudson (n 3), chapter 6.
[68] For a use to be covered by section 200AB, it is necessary that the 'the circumstances of the use … amount to a special case'; 'the use does not conflict with a normal exploitation of the work or other subject-matter'; and 'the use does not unreasonably prejudice the legitimate interests of the owner of the copyright': Australian Act, s. 200AB (1)(a), (c), (d). For cultural institutions, additional conditions for a use to fall within section 200AM include that the use 'is made by or on behalf of the body administering a library or archives'; 'is made for the purpose of maintaining or operating the library or archives …'; and 'is not made partly for the purpose of the body obtaining a commercial advantage or profit': s. 200AB(2).
[69] See Hudson (n 3), pp. 257–259, 268.
[70] To use the words of interviewee 117L.

opting out of Access's blanket licence and instead expanding their own in-house licensing efforts.[71] Relevantly, this new paradigm also involved copying by reference to fair dealing, as the resourcing of copyright offices meant that there was now the time, expertise and authority to implement fair dealing arguments.

There were a number of matters that encouraged this shift, including from the law in books: in 2012, the Supreme Court confirmed the *CCH* approach in *Alberta v Access Copyright*,[72] a case that concerned multiple copying for secondary school students; and in that same year, the Canadian legislature added education as a fair dealing purpose,[73] thus removing doubts about the degree to which research and private study could extend to instructor-led copying.[74] However, the immediate impetus for change was Access Copyright's application to the Copyright Board to approve a new tariff in relation to copying by post-secondary institutions.[75] The headline figure in that application was so high that universities decided to overhaul their workflows, having been satisfied, up until that point, with rolling over Access licences. To the extent some university staff had already been arguing for a greater role for fair dealing, it was this change to copyright resourcing (by bringing licensing in-house) that allowed these arguments to be implemented. Access pushed back strongly against these developments, including by bringing litigation in which it argued that its Board-approved tariff was mandatory.[76] Despite initial success in the Federal Court, this argument was rejected by the Supreme Court in 2021.[77]

In Canada, the impetus for a new role for fair dealing in universities was therefore perceived over-reaching by a copyright collective. In Australia, on the other hand, changes to practices occurred against the backdrop of long-standing legislative inertia. The 2012/2013 fieldwork was conducted around the same time as a review into exceptions in which many cultural institutions advocated in favour of fair use.[78] By that point, there had been long-standing concerns about orphaned works and the management of copyright within large-scale digitisation

---

[71]   See Hudson (n 3), pp. 269–275.

[72]   *Alberta (Education) v Canadian Copyright Licensing Agency (Access Copyright)* [2012] 2 SCR 345.

[73]   Copyright Modernization Act (SC 2012, c 12) (assented to 29 June 2012).

[74]   In *Alberta v Access Copyright* (n 72), it had been accepted by the parties that the copying fell within the allowable purposes of research and private study.

[75]   *Statement of Proposed Royalties to Be Collected by Access Copyright for the Reprographic Reproduction, in Canada, of Works in its Repertoire: Post-Secondary Educational Institutions (2011–2013)*, Supplement, *Canada Gazette*, Part I (12 June 2010).

[76]   *Canadian Copyright Licensing Agency ("Access Copyright") v York University* [2018] 2 FCR 43.

[77]   *York University v Canadian Copyright Licensing Agency (Access Copyright)*, 2021 SCC 32. This case also included a counter-claim by York seeking declarations in relation to its fair dealing policies. Those declarations were not made. It has been questioned (rightly, in my view) whether York should have counter-claimed in relation to fair dealing: see discussion in Hudson (n 3), p. 302. Not only was it unnecessary to win the case, but there were no specific allegations of infringement against which fair dealing could be judged: see also SCC, [83] (noting that Access did not have standing to bring infringement proceedings, and that '[t]he undesirable consequence of assessing fair dealing guidelines in the absence of a genuine dispute between proper parties is that the analysis is inevitably anchored in aggregate findings and general assumptions without a connection to specific instances of works being copied'). The Supreme Court nevertheless made some comments on fair dealing, as the judgments from the Federal Court, which were critical of York's approach to fair dealing, contained 'some significant jurisprudential problems': [87].

[78]   See ALRC (n 49).

projects. And yet the Australian fieldwork suggested that some of these problems, especially around orphaned works, had become less of an issue, largely due to changed attitudes to risk.[79] In the absence of legislative change, Australian institutions experimented with risk management, creating a positive feedback loop: if a digitisation project included some orphaned works and there were no complaints and indeed only positive responses, the next project might include more orphaned works and/or more risky ones. Whilst (the right) legislative intervention would still be welcome, and may be important for other sectors and for uses where risk management is less viable, it may operate to affirm existing approaches rather generate new ones.

A final example of an external event spurring new copyright understandings is the Covid-19 pandemic. In the UK, for example, many universities and libraries rethought how they might apply fair dealing to educational uses, for instance in relation to the use of film and audiovisual content in online teaching.[80] These understandings built on, but also accelerated, existing approaches to the new fair dealing exception for illustration for instruction. Prior to the pandemic, university users were confident about using this exception for in-classroom uses, but less so for digital ones.[81] With the pandemic necessitating a shift to online platforms for teaching and access to library collections, at times to the exclusion of *any* in-person contact, institutions were forced to confront these copyright questions. It is likely that many of the practices introduced in response to the pandemic will remain in place, as many of the factors relevant to fairness are not dependent on pandemic circumstances.[82]

In sum, I have argued in this part that while fair use is attractive as a reform option, a change to the law in books does not necessarily lead to new practices, and is not essential for new practices to emerge. In thinking about why we might be attracted to the fair use panacea (or other reforms), we need to consider our goals: to broaden the existing provisions? Clarify their scope? Encourage use? It may be that some of these goals can be achieved without any legislative change, or through a less comprehensive amendment than fair use, by instead focusing on strategies or interventions that might help change existing interpretations and behaviours. I shall expand on this in Part 4, where I will discuss reported UK experiences in relation to expanded fair dealing.

---

[79] See also Emily Hudson, 'Copyright and Invisible Authors: A Property Perspective' in Andrew Johnston and Lorraine Talbot (eds), *Great Debates in Commercial and Corporate Law* (Macmillan, 2020), pp. 118–119 (noting that with changed approaches to risk management in Australia and the UK, orphaned works may be less of a problem, although other issues may be coming into sharper focus, such as non-responsive copyright owners).

[80] See, e.g., Emily Hudson, 'Copyright Guidance for Using Films in Online Teaching During the COVID-19 Pandemic' (6 August 2020), at https://ssrn.com/abstract=3667025; Emily Hudson and Paul Wragg, 'Proposals for copyright law and education during the COVID-19 pandemic' (2020) 71 *Northern Ireland Legal Quarterly* 571.

[81] CDPA s. 32; for these existing approaches, see, eg, Hudson (n 3), pp. 284–287; Chris Morrison, 'Illustration for Instruction and the UK Higher Education Sector' (MA dissertation, King's College London, 2018), at https://kar.kent.ac.uk/73310/.

[82] See, e.g., Emily Hudson, 'Updated Copyright Guidance for Using Films, Audiovisual Works and Images in Online Teaching: Beyond the Covid Pandemic' (24 February 2022), at https://ssrn.com/abstract=4042770.

4.   EXPANDED FAIR DEALING

In 2014, the UK government made a series of reforms to exceptions in the CDPA. This was the culmination of discussions that had taken place over the preceding decade.[83] The government added three new sets of fair dealing purposes,[84] amended existing exceptions (for instance, by expanding the scope of exceptions for disabled persons),[85] and introduced new exceptions (including for non-commercial text and data mining, and the making available of works on dedicated terminals by cultural and educational institutions).[86] In 2014, the UK also implemented the EU Orphan Works directive.[87] Although that directive is often described as containing an exception for cultural and educational institutions, the provision is functionally more like a remedies limitation.[88] This provision was repealed following Brexit.

One question for my empirical work was the reception of the 2014 reforms, including whether expanded fair dealing had received a more enthusiastic reception than *CCH* and section 200AB. The headline message is that the UK fieldwork pointed to many reasons to be positive about expanded fair dealing and the ability of cultural institutions to embrace those provisions. This was most obviously the case for quotation. Despite it being relatively early days for this exception, UK interviewees described quotation in a manner reminiscent of how US interviewees discussed fair use. The inclusion of concepts such as 'a quotation'[89] and that 'the extent of the quotation is no more than is required by the specific purpose'[90] was not seen as problematic or as rendering the exception unknowable (as was the case for the three-step test language in section 200AB). Instead, interviewees seemed confident in giving content to these concepts (despite the lack of case law[91]), and saw benefits in the breadth of drafting and the use of language that was 'nicely nondescript'.[92] Quotation was being applied to a variety of public-facing contexts – including some online uses – leading to an incremental expansion of the circumstances in which cultural institutions would undertake public-facing uses without a licence.

In saying this, I should note that UK interviewees did not speak in one voice in relation to their applications of quotation. Furthermore, the uses they described typically involved literal copying of discrete parts, such as reproducing a block of text or playing part of a sound

---

[83]   Especially Andrew Gowers, *Gowers Review of Intellectual Property* (HM Treasury, 2006); Hargreaves (n 8).

[84]   CDPA ss. 30(1ZA) (quotation), 30A (caricature, parody and pastiche) and 32 (illustration for instruction).

[85]   Ibid ss. 31A–31F.

[86]   Ibid ss. 29A, 40B, respectively.

[87]   Ibid Schedule ZA1.

[88]   See Hudson (n 79), p. 117. This is because a resurfacing copyright owner could obtain compensation, the amount being set (in the absence of agreement) by the Copyright Tribunal.

[89]   CDPA s. 30(1ZA) ('Copyright in a work is not infringed by the use of a quotation from the work (whether for criticism or review or otherwise) …').

[90]   Ibid s. 30(1ZA)(c).

[91]   The fieldwork was completed prior to the three CJEU judgments on quotation in July 2019: *Pelham GmbH v Hütter* (C-476/17) [2019] ECDR 26, *Funke Medien v Germany* (C-469/17) [2019] ECDR 25 and *Spiegel Online v Beck* (C-516/17) [2019] ECDR 24. Prior to that, CJEU guidance on quotation was limited, with perhaps the main indications appearing in *Painer v Standard Verlags GmbH* (C-145/10) [2012] ECDR 6.

[92]   Interviewee 313M.

recording in an exhibition. There has been some suggestion, in particular from Tanya Aplin and Lionel Bently, that the quotation exception extends well beyond this, including because it is not limited to particular purposes, does not require quotations to be identified as such, and can tolerate quotations being modified.[93] So far, the CJEU has not understood quotation in such broad terms. Although the Information Society Directive speaks of 'quotations for purposes such as criticism or review',[94] the CJEU has confined quotation to uses 'for the purposes of illustrating an assertion, of defending an opinion or of allowing an intellectual comparison between that work and the assertions of that user';[95] plus its analysis suggests that the exception may run out where quotations are modified.[96] To the extent there remains debate amongst copyright experts about the scope of the quotation exception, this may, however, be less relevant for cultural institutions, as their uses will often fall within the CJEU's narrower definition of quotation.

The interviews also suggested that participating institutions were using the new exception for illustration for instruction in section 32. Amongst non-university participants, it was clear that institutions had internalised (correctly) the fact that section 32 is not limited to acts by traditional educational establishments. Further, they did not understand the exception to require a traditional classroom-style setup, although some genuine instruction was necessary. That is, illustration for instruction was being used for educational programmes and not as a catch-all for public-facing uses, for instance on the basis that people visit institution websites for the purpose of learning. Amongst university participants, there were a number of questions about the ambit of section 32, in particular its application to online teaching and posting content on virtual learning environments. Whilst interviewees were confident about staff using section 32 in the classroom, they were still finding their way in relation to the online sphere. As noted earlier, there has been a significant raising of awareness of section 32 with the Covid-19 pandemic, resulting in universities becoming far more confident that illustration for instruction applies to online uses. As noted earlier, I anticipate that these understandings will continue.

Finally, there was less discussion of fair dealing for caricature, parody and pastiche in the UK interviews, perhaps because institutions are not typically understood to undertake acts for these purposes.[97] That said, a number of interviewees asked whether an institution might

---

[93]   Especially in Tanya Aplin and Lionel Bently, *Global Mandatory Fair Use: The Nature and Scope of the Right to Quote Copyright Works* (Cambridge University Press, 2020), pp. 69–71, 114–128.

[94]   Information Society Directive, Art. 5(3)(d).

[95]   *Pelham v Hütter* (n 91), [71].

[96]   Ibid [74] (the quotation exception 'does not extend to a situation in which it is not possible to identify the work concerned by the quotation in question'). For discussion, see Aplin and Bently (n 93), pp. 212–214; James Parish, 'Sampling and copyright – did the CJEU make the right noises?' [2020] 79 *Cambridge Law Journal* 31.

[97]   Hudson (n 3), pp. 288–289. Pastiche is not defined in the CDPA. In guidance released by the IPO in 2014, pastiche was defined as 'musical or other composition made up of selections from various sources or one that imitates the style of another artist or period': Intellectual Property Office, *Exceptions to Copyright: Guidance for Creators and Copyright Owners* (IPO, 2014), p. 6. This broadly accords with definitions in the Oxford English Dictionary and in specialist texts, in which pastiche has two forms, being works made using parts drawn from other works or sources, and works that imitate the style of someone or something else: Emily Hudson, 'The Pastiche Exception in Copyright Law: A Case of Mashed-Up Drafting?' [2017] *Intellectual Property Quarterly* 346 (arguing that the applications of pastiche include mash-ups, fan fiction, music sampling, collage, appropriation art, medleys, and many other forms of homage and compilation). This dual definition of pastiche, and that pastiche does different

expose itself to risk through dealings with parodic or pastiche works if the artist has not cleared any rights. My view is that to be workable, fair dealing for parody or pastiche must apply not only to the initial act of creation but to downstream acts in which such works are publicly distributed or presented.[98] Consider a television station that broadcasts a satirical talk show that includes excerpts from programmes on rival networks. The station's purpose in broadcasting the show is unlikely to be parody – rather, it will have commercial goals of attracting an audience and raising revenue from advertising. However, judges in fair dealing cases do not tend to make distinctions between the purposes of the presenters on the show, the writers, the production company, and the broadcaster.[99] Similarly, there are good arguments that if the creation of a work falls within the pastiche exception, there will be no infringement of copyright in the source works by a museum showing or playing the pastiche work, although the museum would obviously need to consider what licences are required from the pastiche artist.

In sum, the research discussed in this chapter suggests that, at least for cultural institutions, expanded fair dealing is not some undesirable, merely second-best alternative to fair use.[100] If we are serious about making expanded fair dealing work in the UK, it would be valuable to conduct empirical work with other copyright stakeholders for whom fair dealing might also be relevant, in order to understand their copyright practices and fair dealing's actual and potential role within them.[101] It may be that some targeted reforms to fair dealing would be useful, such as removing any unnecessary requirements (for instance, that research or private study be non-commercial, and that criticism or review must relate to 'that or another work') and updating language that might appear to be limited (for instance, replacing the purposes of 'illustration for instruction' and 'reporting current events' with 'education' and 'reporting news', respectively). With reports that access and copy controls are preventing users from undertaking fair dealings with digital works, it may also be desirable to change the approach to technological protection measures that prevent users from carrying out permitted acts, as the current procedure for resolving such conflicts, which involves an application to the Secretary of State,[102] is not fit for purpose.

---

work to parody and may apply in these situations, was accepted in *Shazam Productions Ltd v Only Fools the Dining Experience Ltd* [2022] EWHC 1379 (IPEC).

[98]   Hudson (n 3), pp. 288–289; Jani McCutcheon and Simon Holloway, 'Whose fair dealing? Third-party reliance on the fair dealing exception for parody or satire' (2016) 27 *Australian Intellectual Property Journal* 54.

[99]   See especially *TCN Channel Nine Pty Ltd v Network Ten Pty Ltd* (2001) 108 FCR 235, (2002) 118 FCR 417 (in considering whether fair dealing applied in this very scenario, the purposes of Network Ten, the defendant, were not understood as different to the panellists who were making the commentary).

[100]   This language of a 'second-best' option is taken from Handler and Hudson (n 3), pp. 146–149. In Australia, the ALRC supported fair use, with the alternative approach of expanded fair dealing presented as a 'pragmatic second-best option': ALRC (n 49), [6.40].

[101]   A number of such projects are in progress. For instance, Tanya Aplin and I are working on a project examining how third-party text and images are dealt with in the publishing industry, including the relevance of the quotation exception: Emily Hudson, 'An Empirical Study of Quotation Norms in the Publishing Industry' (UK Launch of Fair Dealing Week, Institute of Advanced Legal Studies, February 2022). A team of researchers from Learning on Screen, CREATe, University of Kent, and City, University of London, are examining how audiovisual materials are used in teaching: Bartolomeo Meletti, 'Copyright and Fair Practice in Film Education' (ICEPOPS conference, Oxford, September 2022).

[102]   CDPA s. 296ZE.

However, a major lesson from the empirical work is that meaningful changes to copyright interpretations and practices can often be achieved without *any* change to the law. For cultural institutions in the UK and elsewhere, there are numerous strategies that might facilitate greater use of exceptions. One is to resource copyright appropriately, in terms of expertise, time, budget, workflows and authority.[103] These qualities were seen in the UK institutions that reported greater engagement with new fair dealing purposes. Resourcing was also one explanation for the gulf in experiences between the US and Canada in the 2007–2009 fieldwork. Whilst copyright knowledge was variable amongst interviewees in both countries, in the US it tended to be higher, and in Canada it tended to be lower. Copyright management in US institutions was often overseen in centralised units and/or by specialist copyright officers; this was much less common amongst equivalent institutions in Canada. When there was a major change to fair dealing approaches amongst Canadian universities from 2010 onwards, this was linked to new copyright offices that were intended primarily for licensing, but which could also turn their expertise to fair dealing. In Australia, too, changes in practices from the first phase of fieldwork to subsequent batches coincided with much greater interviewee familiarity with copyright law and with cooperation across the sector.

A second strategy for increasing the use of exceptions is to reconsider the approach to risk and how copyright 'problems' are viewed. Increasing legal knowledge can help with this, as risk aversion is often a product of fear of getting the law wrong. But staff also need to understand that standards like 'fair dealing' are intended to be vague (to use the language of Timothy Endicott and Michael Spence),[104] in order to give judges the freedom to ensure legal outcomes respond appropriately to the facts. This means that there will almost inevitably be some uncertainty involved in a fair dealing analysis. In thinking about whether an institution is willing to bear those risks, it may be useful to consider not only legal aspects (such as the likelihood of complaint and options for resolution without litigation) and non-legal ones (such as reputational concerns), but also the risks of *not* doing the act. Often times, discussions are framed around whether such-and-such may create copyright problems, and this encourages managers to say no, just to be on the safe side. Might a different answer emerge by framing copyright questions in a different way, for example by saying that showing entire films in a film studies class is a mission-critical activity that has to take place – how can we do it in a way that minimizes our exposure to risk?

Much of the above has focused on well-resourced institutions. A final strategy to encourage greater use of exceptions is to engage in sector-wide discussions and information-sharing (especially to support colleagues in smaller institutions) and to explicitly encourage the use of exceptions by others (for instance by including information about exceptions on institution websites). In suggesting this, I recognise that such discussions are not always straightforward, as institutions may be reluctant to speak publicly about copyright for fear of attracting attention and becoming 'the test case'. As such, it may be useful for some discussions to take place in closed meetings or through other informal networks. There may also be benefits in guidance coming from those who do not directly share this risk, such as representative bodies and copyright academics.

---

[103]   Hudson (n 3), pp. 294–296, 315–316.
[104]   Timothy Endicott and Michael Spence, 'Vagueness in the Scope of Copyright' (2005) 121 *Law Quarterly Review* 657.

5.   CONCLUDING REMARKS

This chapter has argued that expanded fair dealing is not a mere 'second-best' alternative to a fully open-ended fair use provision. In doing so, it has drawn from research with cultural institutions in three fair dealing jurisdictions: Australia, Canada and the UK. However, many of the lessons in this chapter are also applicable to jurisdictions that do not use fair dealing. This includes the need for empirical analysis in our consideration of exceptions reform. What does such evidence suggest are the problems faced by users in that country? Bearing in mind those problems, to what extent is statutory reform part of the solution, and to what extent should we focus on the interpretative practices of users and copyright experts? The latter is particularly significant when the options for wholesale reform are limited. Consider, for example, EU copyright law, and in particular the quotation exception in Article 5(3)(d) of the Information Society Directive. It has been observed by Aplin and Bently that there is considerable variation in the form of quotation exceptions within EU countries, with some enacting an exception that is written in terms far narrower than the language of Article 5(3)(d).[105] If our goal is to liberalise exceptions, it may be that these provisions need to be revised. But for those countries that have implemented Article 5(3)(d) as fully as possible, the only option, if quotation is believed to be under-utilised, may be to analyse the impediments that are stopping users from invoking that exception in a full and robust way. This may involve a focus on judges, whose interpretative practices can both read away flexibility or emphasise its existence. But it is likely that a lot will come from work with users themselves, to understand the matters that drive their decisions, and to identify what might need to change – both at the individual or institutional level, and in the broader legal, social, political and economic climate – to facilitate a meaningful role for copyright exceptions.

---

[105]   Aplin and Bently (n 93), pp. 204–208.

10. Empirical methods for researching copyright in Australia

Kylie Pappalardo[1]

1. INTRODUCTION

In this chapter, I use two case studies of empirical projects in copyright law – one qualitative and one quantitative – to demonstrate how empirical data can both illuminate and fill the gaps in existing copyright theory and policy. I argue, first, that grounded research, particularly in-depth interviews with creators, can disrupt economic justifications for copyright rules. Qualitative research, both mine and others', shows that creators are motivated by creative challenges, building their professional reputations, and deepening their relationships with their audiences and other creators at least as much as – and often more than – any promise of economic returns.[2] My work (with colleagues at the Queensland University of Technology and American University) has also found that the copyright system is as likely to hinder creative production as it is to incentivise it.[3] Creators can feel more constrained by the risk of inadvertently infringing copyright in their own recombinant creations than by concerns that others will infringe their work.[4] Second, I discuss how large-scale quantitative datasets can provide insights into the functioning of copyright media markets at a national and international level. For us, quantitative data has been critical in understanding how Australian audiences fare as compared to North American audiences, when measuring the availability and cost of media content such as film, television and music. My experience is particularly within the Australian legal and political context, and these examples provide a small demonstration of some of the empirical legal work being undertaken in Australia. Finally, I outline some reflections on the importance of empirical data to copyright research in general. In particular, I suggest that the ability to bring qualitative and quantitative data together into mixed-method approaches will be fundamental to the ongoing agenda to make *good* copyright law and policy that meets the needs of creators, producers, distributors, consumers and users.

[1] Senior Lecturer, School of Law, Queensland University of Technology. Kylie is a Chief Investigator with the Digital Media Research Centre and an Associate Investigator with the ARC Centre of Excellence for Automated Decision Making and Society. Kylie is the recipient of an Australian Research Centre (ARC) DECRA Fellowship (DE210100525), and she works on Turrbul and Yugara lands. Thanks to Lucinda Nelson for research assistance and Nicolas Suzor for comments on an earlier draft.
[2] Jessica Silbey, *The Eureka Myth: Creators, Innovators and Everyday Intellectual Property* (Stanford University Press, 2014); Kylie Pappalardo et al, *Imagination Foregone: A Qualitative Study of the Reuse Practices of Australian Creators* (Report, November 2017).
[3] Kylie Pappalardo et al, *Imagination Foregone: A Qualitative Study of the Reuse Practices of Australian Creators* (Report, November 2017).
[4] Jessica Silbey, *The Eureka Myth: Creators, Innovators and Everyday Intellectual Property* (Stanford University Press, 2014); Kylie Pappalardo et al, *Imagination Foregone: A Qualitative Study of the Reuse Practices of Australian Creators* (Report, November 2017).

2.   QUALITATIVE RESEARCH: UNDERSTANDING WHAT CREATORS WANT FROM THE LAW

Copyright is a monopoly right granted by the government for a limited time to a creator of a work. The best-known rationale for copyright protection – incentivising creation – lends itself to economic explanation.[5] A work can take many years and significant time and labour to produce; creating can be long and hard, copying is quick and easy. A monopoly right allows the creator to be the sole exploiter of the work for a sufficient time to recoup their costs and perhaps make a profit. In theory, the monopoly grant means that many creators undertaking a costs-benefit analysis will determine that it is worth the time and labour to create, and thus society in general gains (in time) the fruits of this productive labour.[6]

Copyright law limits access so that a creator can price their goods sufficiently to incentivise creation in the first place. In their influential 1989 article, Landes and Posner explain, "For a new work to be created, the expected return…must exceed the expected cost."[7] They express this as a mathematical formula:[8]

$$\text{II} = (p - c)x - e(z)$$

In English, this means: profit = (price per copy – production cost per copy) multiplied by the number of copies produced, minus the cost of creation. So, for instance, if I were to write a paperback novel and sell this for $30 per copy (a standard price in Australia), assuming that each copy costs $5 to produce, $10 to distribute, and my costs of creation were $20,000,[9] I would need to sell more than 1300 copies to make a profit:

$$\text{Profit} = (\$30 - \$15)1333 - \$20,000$$

Landes and Posner's analysis of copyright law includes many more mathematical equations, all of greater complexity than the one I have extracted here. I have personally never connected with economic accounts of copyright law, probably, in all honesty, because I am not great with figures. But also because there are elements missing from economic analyses that mean that we are not getting the full, messy, human picture of why people create and how they manage their creations. As a rough approximation for how copyright incentives work at scale, particularly for publishers, economic theory works relatively well. But it works better in abstraction than in the detail. As both David McGowan and Jessica Litman have argued, "the economic justification for any particular copyright rule rests on instinct and guesswork".[10] Litman goes

---

[5]   William M Landes and Richard A Posner, 'An Economic Analysis of Copyright Law' (1989) 18(2) *Journal of Legal Studies* 325, 325 ("Intellectual property is a natural field for economic analysis of law").

[6]   Mark Lemley, 'Ex Ante versus Ex Post Justifications for Intellectual Property' (2004) 71(1) *University of Chicago Law Review* 129, 129–31.

[7]   William M Landes and Richard A Posner, 'An Economic Analysis of Copyright Law' (1989) 18(2) *Journal of Legal Studies* 325, 327.

[8]   Ibid 333–4.

[9]   On the assumption that I take six months to write the novel, with my time costed at minimum wage rates in Australia.

[10]   Jessica Litman, 'Real Copyright Reform' (2010) 96 *Iowa Law Review* 1, 29, citing David McGowan, 'Copyright Nonconsequentialism' (2004) 69 *Missouri Law Review* 1, 2–7.

further, stating that within copyright jurisprudence, "the economic rationale for copyright law [has] ascended to the status of an article of faith in the absence of any empirical validation".[11] Empirical research, especially rich, qualitative work, can help to round out economic assumptions by providing the missing stories of how creators engage in the process of creation and how they interact with copyright law. The qualitative work that I recount in this chapter is an example of how the insights gained by talking to people whose lives and livelihoods are conducted within the structures of copyright regulation really ought to change the way we think about copyright incentives and access to copyright works.

Many scholars before me have pointed out the problems with a purely economic view of copyright.[12] For one, a focus on price and profit begets a trade-off with access, particularly for those consumers who cannot afford the price of a copy. In economic terms this is a "deadweight loss" – the gap in the market between what a product costs and what some consumers are willing to pay. In a rational market, this gap is minimised through competition. But in copyright, the deadweight loss is exacerbated by several realities, including that true competition is difficult in markets characterised by monopoly rights and artificial scarcity,[13] that the content industries have evolved to wield considerable power and engage in rent seeking,[14] and that lack of access can be an equity concern with respect to content such as educational material.

An economic approach treats copyright material as a commodity, and this leads to arguments that intellectual property should be treated like other forms of property under law – that is, subject to robust protection, potentially in perpetuity,[15] with few exceptions. As Neil Netanel explains, neoclassical economics favours "expansive, exclusive proprietary rights that are concentrated, at least as an initial matter, in a single owner"[16] to efficiently manage the copyright resource. The "economic logic of real property"[17] can be tempting in the context of intellectual property, because it gives courts and commentators a way to talk about the production, ownership and licensing of intellectual creations in a way that can be visualised. But property rhetoric can lead to the idea that an IP owner "is entitled to capture the full social

---

[11]   Jessica Litman, 'Real Copyright Reform' (2010) 96 *Iowa Law Review* 1, 29.

[12]   See, e.g. Nicolas Suzor, 'Free-riding, Cooperation and "Peaceful Revolutions" in Copyright' (2014) 28(1) *Harvard Journal of Law and Technology* 137; Brett M Frischmann, 'Evaluating the Demsetzian Trend in Copyright Law' (2007) 3(3) *Review of Law and Economics* 649; Mark Lemley, 'Property, Intellectual Property, and Free Riding' (2004) 83 *Texas Law Review* 1031; Brett M Frischmann and Mark Lemley, 'Spillovers' (2007) 107 *Columbia Law Review* 257; Eric Johnson, 'Intellectual Property and the Incentive Fallacy' (2012) 39 *Florida State University Law Review* 612.

[13]   See Mark Lemley, 'Property, Intellectual Property, and Free Riding' (2004) 83 *Texas Law Review* 1031, 1059–60.

[14]   Jessica Litman, 'The Politics of Intellectual Property' (2009) 27(2) *Cardozo Arts & Entertainment Law Journal* 313, 314–15; Jessica Litman, *Digital Copyright* (Prometheus Books, 2001); Neil Weinstock Netanel, 'Why has Copyright Expanded? Analysis and Critique' in Fiona Macmillan (ed), *New Directions in Copyright Law* (Edward Elgar, 2005–2007) vol 6, 3–4.

[15]   See Neil Weinstock Netanel, 'Why has Copyright Expanded? Analysis and Critique' in Fiona Macmillan (ed), *New Directions in Copyright Law* (Edward Elgar, 2005–2007) vol 6, 3, 20, discussing William M Landes and Richard A Posner, 'An Economic Analysis of Copyright Law' (1989) 18(2) *Journal of Legal Studies* 325.

[16]   Neil Weinstock Netanel, 'Why has Copyright Expanded? Analysis and Critique' in Fiona Macmillan (ed), *New Directions in Copyright Law* (Edward Elgar, 2005–2007) vol 6, 3, 18.

[17]   Mark Lemley, 'Property, Intellectual Property, and Free Riding' (2004) 83 *Texas Law Review* 1031, 1033.

value of her right",[18] which in turn leads to attitudes that most, if not all, unlicensed uses are wrongful and that copyright enforcement mechanisms must be continuously strengthened. Yet as Mark Lemley has argued, not even in real property do we allow owners to internalise the full positive externalities of their property.[19] They cannot, for instance, capture the value that passers-by may experience in appreciating the beauty of an architecturally designed house or a garden of vibrant flowers.[20] Lemley writes, "The assumption that intellectual property owners should be entitled to capture the full social surplus of their invention runs counter to our economic intuitions in every other segment of the economy."[21]

Copyright goods are *cultural* goods, with the potential to enrich lives far beyond the commercial realm. Focusing too heavily on economics obscures the cultural in favour of the commercial. Cultural economist Ruth Towse has argued that "most of the standard economic literature on copyright…ignores a number of aspects that have considerable significance for cultural production in general and for artists in particular".[22] These aspects include the importance of moral rights for creators, and whether and how creators are able to earn a living from their work. Towse continues, "most writers assume that the interests of creators and performers are in perfect harmony with those of publishers, sound recording makers, broadcasters and all the other businesses that process and distribute their work as if there were no contractual problems between them over property rights".[23] Indeed, despite the prevalence of property rights rhetoric (which tends to be individual rather than collective), we see remarkably little of individual creators in copyright discourse and policy – except, of course, when certain high-profile creators are trotted out by the content industries to advocate for expanded rights or against broader copyright exceptions.[24]

For many creators, it is questionable whether copyright actually provides the economic security blanket that it is supposed to. Let's return to my hypothetical in the equation above – that even on a conservative estimate of my creation and production costs, I would need to sell 1333 copies of my paperback novel to recoup my investment. Writing in 2006, Chris Anderson noted that the average book in America sells about 500 copies.[25] He elaborated that in 2004, of the 1.2 million titles tracked by Nielsen Bookscan, 950,000 titles – just under 80% – sold fewer than 99 copies.[26] This is far short of the hundreds of sales needed to incentivise creation according to classic economic theory. Of course, markets have changed significantly since

---

[18]   Ibid.
[19]   Ibid, 1046.
[20]   Ibid, 1048.
[21]   Ibid, 1046.
[22]   Ruth Towse, 'Copyright and Artists: A View of Cultural Economics' (2006) 20(4) *Journal of Economic Surveys* 567, 568.
[23]   Ibid.
[24]   See, for example, the #freeisnotfair campaign <https://www.copyright.com.au/2017/06/creative -organisations-launch-freeisnotfair-campaign/> and <https://www.copyright.com.au/2016/12/australian -celebrities-share-life-changing-stories-to-protect-creative-rights/> in opposition to the Australian Law Reform Commission's recommendation that Australia adopt a fair use exception (ALRC, *Copyright and the Digital Economy* (ALRC Report 122) February 2014) and the Productivity Commission's support for that recommendation (Australian Government Productivity Commission, *Intellectual Property Arrangements,* Final Report, December 2016).
[25]   Chris Anderson, 'A Bookselling Tail', *Publishers Weekly*, 14 July 2016.
[26]   Ibid.

2004, notably with the introduction of e-books[27] and the rise of online retailing.[28] *Publishers Weekly* recently reported that in 2021, unit sales of print books were the highest recorded by NPD BookScan since 2004.[29] Copyright production is a gamble, and the chances of any one work becoming a major commercial success are exceedingly slim. The risk involved means that for productions of any significant size, the expected profits for highly successful works need to be so high that they cover the costs of producing all those that make only moderate returns. It is publishers who can generally afford to take these gambles; it is rare for creators to be able to support themselves from their creative income alone.[30]

In 2016–2017, a team of researchers at Macquarie University in Australia, led by Professor David Throsby, conducted a survey of professional creators across Australia.[31] The researchers surveyed a random sample of participants from 35,940 identified creators across all artforms;[32] the final surveyed number was 823 creators (2.3% of the whole).[33] Participants were asked to respond to a list of questions, and researchers then used those responses to draw inferences about the broader population of creators.[34] The survey focused only on "serious, practising professional artists", which the researchers explained as:

> The seriousness is judged in terms of a self-assessed commitment to artistic work as a major aspect of the artist's working life, even if creative work is not the main source of income. The practising aspect means that we confine our attention to artists currently working or seeking to work in their chosen occupation. The term professional is intended to indicate a degree of training, experience or talent and a manner of working that qualify artists to have their work judged against the professional standards of the relevant occupation.[35]

The data showed that only 23% of the practising professional artists surveyed were able to spend all their working time on creative work. The vast majority had to supplement their creative work with either arts-related work, such as teaching, or non-arts work in order to make a living.[36] The data also showed that "artists' income from creative work in their chosen profession is far below that earned by similarly qualified practitioners in other professions".[37] When asked what was preventing them from spending more time at their creative practice, most artists pointed to economic factors, including inadequate financial return for work sold and insufficient markets for their work.[38]

---

[27] Amazon released its Kindle e-book reader in 2007.

[28] Kristen McLean, 'Book Sales in the U.S. Are Stronger Than Ever', *Publishers Weekly*, 19 April 2022.

[29] Ibid.

[30] Australia Council for the Arts, *Making Art Work: A Summary and Response by the Australia Council for the Arts*, November 2017, 5.

[31] David Throsby and Katya Petetskaya, *Making Art Work: An Economic Study of Professional Artists in Australia*, 2017.

[32] The artforms were: writers, visual artists, craft practitioners, actors and directors, dancers and choreographers, musicians, composers, and community cultural practitioners.

[33] David Throsby and Katya Petetskaya, *Making Art Work: An Economic Study of Professional Artists in Australia*, 2017, Appendix I.

[34] Ibid, 21.

[35] Ibid, 20.

[36] Ibid, 67.

[37] Ibid, 78.

[38] Ibid, 70.

We know by now that many people create without the promise of economic return.[39] Indeed, there are entire creative industries that seem to operate with no or minimal reliance on intellectual property rights to incentivise production or facilitate transactions.[40] Other industries seem to be highly profitable for a small proportion of highly successful creators while providing little monetary benefit to the majority. So it is worth asking how well copyright law is actually working for creators on the ground. In truth, we know remarkably little about what creators think about copyright. What role does it play in their motivations to create? Do they think of their creations as property to be exploited? Does copyright law work in their interests or against them? Questions like these were the impetus for a 2017 project on the reuse practices of Australian creators, funded in part by the Australian Digital Alliance,[41] which I led at the Queensland University of Technology (QUT).[42]

In designing this project, I was heavily inspired by the work of Professor Jessica Silbey in the United States, who has conducted in-depth, face-to-face interviews with artists, scientists and engineers, and their lawyers, agents and business partners, to understand their lived experiences with creating and innovating, and how intellectual property law intervenes in their lives.[43] Silbey's work found that creators tend to value their relationships with other creators and their audiences more than they worry about small-scale infringements of their work by those people.[44] Silbey reports that creators often acknowledge that their own creative processes involve a complex mix of originality and reuse, sometimes through infringement, and so they seem to have a degree of tolerance for small or creative acts of copyright infringement.[45]

---

[39]   Nicolas Suzor, 'Free-riding, Cooperation and "Peaceful Revolutions" in Copyright' (2014) 28(1) *Harvard Journal of Law and Technology* 137, 144–5; Jessica Silbey, 'Harvesting Intellectual Property: Inspired Beginnings and "Work-Makes-Work", Two Stages in the Creative Processes of Artists and Innovators' (2011) 86 *Notre Dame Law Review* 2091, 2110; Rebecca Tushnet, 'Economies of Desire: Fair Use and Marketplace Assumptions' (2009) 51 *William & Mary Law Review* 513, 515–6; Raymond Shih Ray Ku et al, 'Does Copyright Promote Creativity? An Empirical Analysis of Copyright's Bounty' (2009) 62 *Vanderbilt Law Review* 1669, 1675.

[40]   See Kal Raustiala and Christopher Sprigman, *The Knockoff Economy: How Imitation Sparks Innovation* (OUP, 2012).

[41]   The Australian Digital Alliance (ADA) is a non-profit organisation and advocacy body. It is Australia's peak body representing copyright users and innovators, with the mission to promote the public interest in copyright. Its membership is primarily made up of universities and libraries, but does include Google and Facebook. It is important to note that no party outside of the research team, including the ADA and its members, exercised any control over the design of our research project or our findings and analysis, and no external party had the power to prevent or otherwise control the publication of our project report. The research team was at all times strongly committed to independence and integrity in research and the ethical norms of funded research in intellectual property: Robin Feldman et al, 'Open Letter on Ethical Norms in Intellectual Property Scholarship' (2016) 29(2) *Harvard Journal of Law & Technology* 1.

[42]   The research team was made up of four researchers: Dr. Kylie Pappalardo, Jessica Stevens (now Jessica Thiel) and A/Prof Nicolas Suzor from the QUT School of Law and Prof Patricia Aufderheide from the School of Communication at American University. At the time of our research, A/Prof Suzor was the recipient of an ARC DECRA Fellowship (DE160101542) and Prof Aufderheide was a Fulbright Commission senior research fellow at the Digital Media Research Centre at QUT.

[43]   Jessica Silbey, *The Eureka Myth: Creators, Innovators and Everyday Intellectual Property* (Stanford University Press, 2014).

[44]   Ibid, 153.

[45]   Ibid, 45–6; Jessica Silbey, 'Fairer Uses' (2016) 96 *Boston University Law Review* 857, 859–61.

Our project at QUT, though much smaller in scope than Silbey's research, corroborates her findings.

Our project had two components. The first was a small-scale study designed to explore how a sample of Australian creators understand, use, and manage copyright work. The methods were qualitative – over a period of three months, between January and April 2017, my team and I interviewed 29 creators from across Australia. We did not focus on any particular artform in recruiting participants. Instead, the parameters we drew around this study focused on creators' experiences with licensing content and their understanding and use of legal exceptions to infringement. Thus, we spoke to creators who had, at some time in their career or creative practice, used the copyright work of another in their creations.[46] We started with creators whose work incorporating third-party material came to our attention because of news articles, presentations at conferences, or personal contacts. We then used snowball sampling to recruit further participants through word-of-mouth and email.

We ended up with 29 interviewees from a variety of artforms. Ten participants identified as documentary filmmakers; nine identified as writers, including book authors and screen writers; eight participants identified as musicians, including composers, DJs and sampling artists; eight participants were online content creators, including YouTube creators and game developers; and four participants identified as visual artists. The number of participants in each artform, added up, comes to a greater number than the total number of participants. This is because some of the interviewees worked across multiple artforms. The interview participants had various levels of expertise in their fields – seven participants had less than five years' experience (which we called 'emerging'), nine had between five and ten years' experience (which we called 'experienced'), and thirteen had more than ten years' experience ('veterans'). Ten participants identified as female and nineteen identified as male. None identified as Aboriginal or Torres Strait Islander. Participants hailed from Brisbane, Sydney, Melbourne, Perth and rural townships around Australia.

Each participant was interviewed in-depth. Interviews ran for between 40 and 90 minutes and were conducted either in-person or over Skype. We asked participants semi-structured, open-ended questions about their creative practice, whether and how they thought about copyright law, and their experiences with seeking permission to reuse the content of another. We asked about how participants responded if they were denied permission. We asked participants about how they felt if someone else used their work – what did they expect in terms of requests, acknowledgements, payment? Interviews were recorded and professionally transcribed. We then conducted thematic analysis of the data collected. We coded for themes around participants' understanding of copyright law, practices of reuse, experience with copyright licensing, reliance on copyright exceptions, problems encountered in reuse, and responses to problems encountered.

These in-depth interviews were supported by another component of the project, involving a survey instrument, led by University Professor Patricia Aufderheide. The online survey asked just under 50 questions, in yes/no, multiple-choice, and free-text formats. For example, questions included:

Q14　When you use copyrighted works of others how often do you seek permission?

---

[46]　For example, including existing audiovisual material in a documentary, sampling music, remixing artistic or musical works, quoting from literary works.

Q15   Have you ever had to get permission when you thought you should not have to?
Q16   Can you tell us more about that?[47]

The survey link was distributed in a variety of ways. We used announcements on social media, including Facebook and Twitter, to share the link, and we publicised the survey in presentations at conferences and events,[48] and in op-eds in *Inside Story* and *The Saturday Paper*. We asked colleagues at universities around Australia to distribute the survey link through their networks and we asked arts organisations to share the link with their members. The creator associations we contacted included the National Association for the Visual Arts, the Australian Arts & Cultural Management Network, and Screen Australia.

Our survey drew 476 responses from Australian creators. Respondents worked in a range of artforms including filmmakers (35%), writers (27%) and musicians (11%). There was a roughly even gender split – 52% identified as female and 48% as male. Almost one-third of respondents had more than 20 years' experience in their field (31%). Our respondents were highly professionalised – 60% reported making a living from their creative work.

Our findings from this project have been detailed in other publications,[49] and I won't repeat them in full here. In short, however, many of the creators that we surveyed and interviewed found the law unhelpful and difficult to understand. Their confusion about copyright law was compounded by jurisdictional differences between legal systems but jurisdictional collapse on the internet. For instance, many creators thought that Australia had a fair use exception to copyright infringement. We don't – in Australia, our exceptions are the more limited fair dealing exceptions. But Australian creators had learnt of the US fair use exception on the internet and had not understood that it was anchored to a place. Nevertheless, creators did their best to abide by the law and seek permission for reuse, but they found the process of clearing rights time-consuming, expensive, frustrating and sometimes demeaning. Overwhelmingly, creators discussed norms and values of fairness and respect, and they were guided by these norms and values rather than by legal rules. Except when they had to comply with the administrative burdens imposed by copyright (such as completing online forms to request permission to reuse content), creators didn't think about the law much at all.

The very human stories told through our empirical data are very different to the ones told through economic theory. Our data suggests that the legal realm of copyright and the realm of creative practice are two very different places. We found that the law does influence creative behaviour, but not in the ways it is intended. The creators we spoke to were not incentivised by copyright protection to create; they did not seem to think about their creations as property

---

[47]   Full survey protocol in appendix of Patricia Aufderheide et al, 'Calculating the Consequences of Narrow Australian Copyright Exceptions: Measurable, Hidden and Incalculable Costs to Creators' (2018) 69 *Poetics* 15.

[48]   Presentations at MuseumNext, Australian International Documentary Conference, Vivid Sydney and Fulbright TedX incorporated announcements of the survey.

[49]   Kylie Pappalardo et al, *Imagination Foregone: A Qualitative Study of the Reuse Practices of Australian Creators* (Report, November 2017); Patricia Aufderheide et al, 'Calculating the Consequences of Narrow Australian Copyright Exceptions: Measurable, Hidden and Incalculable Costs to Creators' (2018) 69 *Poetics* 15; Kylie Pappalardo and James Meese, 'In Support of Tolerated Use: Rethinking Harms, Moral Rights and Remedies in Australian Copyright Law' (2019) 42(3) *University of New South Wales Law Journal* 928; Kylie Pappalardo and Patricia Aufderheide, 'Romantic Remixers: Hidden Tropes of Romantic Authorship in Creators' Attitudes about Reuse' (2020) 12(1) *Cultural Science Journal* 1.

or commodities to be exploited. Of course, they were delighted when they could earn money from their creative labour, but this was generally not at the forefront of their minds. Many told us that they would create – and had created – anyway, even when the prospects of commercial gain were very low. Our data corroborated Towse's observations that the interests of creators and the interests of commercial copyright owners are often not aligned. In our interviews, the most commonly expressed frustration was with commercial copyright owners from whom creators sought permission to sample or reuse content. Copyright owners often failed to respond to these permission requests, denied permission, charged what the creators felt were exorbitant licensing fees, or otherwise made the licensing process difficult. And here is where we found that copyright law influenced creative practice – instead of incentivising creation, it hindered it. Creators reported having to abandon, delay or alter projects because of difficulties with obtaining licences for existing works.

Sometimes, what we discovered through our data was surprising. Creators were more law-abiding than I expected – they went to great lengths to ensure that they did right by other artists. Going into the project, I had expected to hear more views that I might describe as territorial. I had previously worked for several years in a community legal centre that provided pro bono legal advice to artists and creators. My notion, from my time there, was that creators could be possessive about their work – I had seen artists get extremely upset when they thought that someone else had drawn from their work without permission. But what we saw reflected back to us in interviews was a spirit of sharing. Participants told us that they were happy for others to reuse parts of their work; they said they would be "honoured" and "flattered".[50] What was important to them was that reuse was done respectfully. Sometimes "respect" involved asking permission, but often it simply required acknowledgement and attribution. Our data indicated that moral rights were extremely important to creators.

Interestingly, while copyright law did not determine a great deal of what our participants did in practice, the idea of what copyright conveys about the social significance of creativity was something they held dear. We found that the rhetoric of romantic authorship was incredibly pervasive, even amongst creators heavily involved with recombinant reuse. Participants used copyright notions of originality to measure the worth of their creations – they saw original work as more creative than recombinant work, and they often internalised the barriers generated by copyright law, such as licensing constraints, as being about their own creativity. As we have previously written:

> Yet often creators did not experience this frustration as a problem with copyright policy, but as a natural feature of the creative process. They thus reclaimed agency from frustration by perceiving second-best solutions as creative, often heroically creative, acts. In various ways, they expressed the belief that being told "no" actually spurs creativity, by forcing a creator to be more ingenious in devising workarounds.[51]

Our empirical work was able to provide us with insights that simply would not have been possible without qualitative data. Our research took place at a time in Australia when copyright policy was highly polarised. The government was contemplating amendments to our

---

50   Kylie Pappalardo et al, *Imagination Foregone: A Qualitative Study of the Reuse Practices of Australian Creators* (Report, November 2017).

51   Kylie Pappalardo and Patricia Aufderheide, 'Romantic Remixers: Hidden Tropes of Romantic Authorship in Creators' Attitudes about Reuse' (2020) 12(1) *Cultural Science Journal* 1.

Copyright Act to provide greater scope for reuse of creative works. The proposal was for a new exception to copyright infringement that more or less mirrored US fair use. The response from the copyright industries was swift and fierce. Fair use would decimate Australia's content industries, they claimed, and Australian creators would suffer.[52] Individual creators lobbied against exceptions that would, in fact, help them in their creative practice by streamlining their ability to reuse content. Our observations about the persistent influence of romantic authorship on how creators saw themselves and their work helps to explain why creators might speak out against their own interests in copyright policy. The economic realities of copyright are not distinct from the more emotional concerns about what it means to be a creative person, and each muddies our understandings of the other.

There are, however, ways forward, and again the empirical research offers new ways to think about the role of copyright law. For instance, a law that gave proper credence to creators' emphasis on attribution would likely place greater significance on moral rights and would adjust remedies for infringement accordingly.[53] It might also prompt us to reconsider how the law treats remixes and mash-ups.[54] These are not conclusions that can be reached by relying only on neoclassical economic theory.

3.   QUANTITATIVE DIGITAL METHODS: MAPPING DIGITAL MEDIA MARKETS

Empirical research can shed light on how the law impacts on and is impacted by global changes in technology and business practices. Australia has long been a mass importer of copyright goods, primarily from the United States. For as long as content was delivered on physical media, Australians had to get used to "the tyranny of distance".[55] Media titles premiered in Australia later than in other parts of the world and were more expensive to purchase. These delays and costs were attributed to the peculiarities of the Australian market – supply chain costs to get content to Australia were higher, and distributing content within Australia was also more expensive due to Australia's relatively small and geographically sparse population and because wages for distribution and retail staff are higher in Australia than the United States.[56] However, as more and more content became available in digital form and delivered over the internet, the reasons for delayed and higher-cost distribution began to fall away. Prices,

---

[52]   Kim Williams, 'Safeguarding Australian Creativity – What's Really at Stake over Copyright Reform', speech delivered at the Melbourne Press Club, Thursday 17 August 2016; Patricia Aufderheide and Dorian Hunter Davis, 'Contributors and Arguments in Australian Policy Debates on Fair Use and Copyright: The Missing Discussion of the Creative Process' (2017) 11 *International Journal of Communication* 522.

[53]   Kylie Pappalardo and James Meese, 'In Support of Tolerated Use: Rethinking Harms, Moral Rights and Remedies in Australian Copyright Law' (2019) 42(3) *University of New South Wales Law Journal* 928.

[54]   Alan Hui, 'Mashup Music as Expression Displaced and Expression Foregone' (2021) 10(4) *Internet Policy Review* 1; Yahong Li, 'The Age of Remix and Copyright Law Reform' (2020) 12(1) *Law, Innovation and Technology* 113.

[55]   Tama Leaver, 'Watching Battlestar Galactica in Australia and the Tyranny of Digital Distance' (2008) 126(1) *Media International Australia* 145, 153.

[56]   Standing Committee on Infrastructure and Communications, Parliament of Australia, *At What Cost? IT Pricing and the Australia Tax* (Report, July 2013).

however, did not fall. Media companies continued to engage in price discrimination based on geographic regions, and were able to enforce market segmentation through a technological process known as geoblocking.[57] Prices for media content continued to be higher in Australia, based not on any logistical reason but simply because that was what content companies had determined that the Australian market would bear.[58] Australians grew resentful of this practice. They could not see why digital goods delivered online should be more expensive in Australia than in the United States, and why they were being treated like "second class" media citizens.[59]

In 2017, colleagues and I decided to gather data about the extent to which this divide continued to exist between Australia and the United States. We obtained funding from the Australian Communications Consumer Action Network (ACCAN)[60] to investigate the availability of digital media content to Australian consumers, the price of that content, and the choice in formats for that content, as compared to the options available to US consumers.

This project involved collecting quantitative data. We decided to focus on popular media titles in the categories of movies, television, music and games. For each category, we created a list of the most popular titles for the five years preceding 2017. We then checked the availability, price and available formats for those titles with Australian and American digital content providers over one month in early 2017.

We created our lists of popular titles from data from the following sources:[61]

- Music: Billboard 200 – Top 200 albums based on radio airplay, sales data and streaming figures collected in the US by online music stores and ranked and published by Nielsen Music.
- Film: Box Office Mojo – Weekly box office releases, ranked by gross worldwide takings. For previous years (2012–2016), rankings are collected only annually.
- Television series: IMDB Top 250 television titles, ranked by user search behaviour on the IMDB website. For previous years (2012–2016), rankings are collected only annually.
- Console computer games: Weekly global top video game sales (Microsoft Xbox One and Sony PlayStation 4 titles). No historical ranking data was collected for this category, so the number of console game titles reflects titles detected on the charts in 2017 only.

For this project, we ended up tracking 6118 music albums, 3880 films, 1298 television series and 346 console games. We gathered data on pricing and availability of titles through public Application Programming Interfaces (APIs), supplemented with standard web scraping tech-

---

[57] 'Geoblocking' refers to the use of technology to identify a consumer's geographical location and prevent them from accessing digital goods being sold in another region. See Nicolas Suzor et al, *Australian Consumer Access to Digital Content* (Report, August 2017) 6.

[58] Standing Committee on Infrastructure and Communications, Parliament of Australia, *At What Cost? IT Pricing and the Australia Tax* (Report, July 2013).

[59] Ibid.

[60] The Australian Communications Consumer Action Network (ACCAN) is Australia's peak body for consumer representation in communications. It is a not-for-profit organisation. ACCAN runs a small grants program which funds research, education or representation projects that address issues for telecommunications consumers in Australia. More information available at <https://accan.org.au/grants/grants-program-overview>. Our project was funded in the 2016 grant round for $59,860. See <https://accan.org.au/grants/grants-projects/1254-access-digital-media>.

[61] List is taken verbatim from Nicolas Suzor et al, *Australian Consumer Access to Digital Content* (Report, August 2017) 9.

niques. For films and television titles to purchase, we collected data across major distributors in Australia and the US including Google, Apple, Microsoft, Amazon and PlayStation.[62] For film and television streaming, we collected data from major subscription streaming services, including Netflix, Foxtel, Stan, Amazon and Hulu.[63] We did not collect data for free-to-air television channels or their catch-up services, or for US cable television. For music to purchase, we compared album prices on the iTunes stores in the United States and Australia. For music streaming, we collected data across Spotify, Deezer and Tidal. A limitation of our study was that we were unable to collect data for Apple Music. For console games, we collected data for Microsoft Xbox One and Sony Playstation 4. We developed filters to identify the key variables within the results, including availability, price, and quality and format options for the titles. We used data from the Reserve Bank of Australia for currency exchange rates between the Australian dollar and the US dollar. We then used standard statistical software as well as data visualisation packages like Tableau and R to analyse and visualise the results.

Our detailed findings are available in our full report, which includes our data visualisations.[64] Overall, we found that as at early 2017, Australian consumers were disadvantaged compared to American consumers across all four media categories. For film and TV purchasing, Australians had access to about 65% of movie titles and 75% of TV titles that were available to their US counterparts, although the price to purchase titles was the same. Australians fared worse in film and TV streaming markets – more than half of the television series and close to two thirds of the films available to stream in the US were not available in Australia.[65] Australians paid around 25% more than American consumers to purchase music and game titles, though their access to titles was on par. The only case where Australian consumers were in a better position was music streaming, where consumers had access to approximately the same number of titles for slightly cheaper subscription fees.

Data about availability and pricing in media markets helps us to understand the conditions under which content companies and copyright owners distribute their products in a global marketplace. Just as intellectual property law creates artificial scarcity, market segmentation creates artificial barriers for digital distribution, enabling price discrimination based in geographical region. Price discrimination is not uniformly bad – it can facilitate cheaper pricing for consumers in developing nations, for example. But better data about how market segmentation occurs in copyright markets and its impact on consumers can shed light on some of the pervasive issues of copyright policy.

One such issue is that of "piracy" – or large-scale unlicensed downloading and sharing of media content. Commercial copyright owners and their lobbying groups tend to paint piracy as a kind of existential threat to creative production.[66] Piracy has long been seen as a problem that is particularly acute in Australia. Australians have been accused of being amongst the most

---

[62] Full list in Nicolas Suzor et al, *Australian Consumer Access to Digital Content* (Report, August 2017).
[63] Ibid.
[64] Nicolas Suzor et al, *Australian Consumer Access to Digital Content* (Report, August 2017).
[65] Australians did, however, have access to about 90% of the Top 50 most popular films available in the US.
[66] See, for example, the websites of the Motion Picture Association of America (MPAA) and the Recording Industry Association of America (RIAA).

prolific unlawful downloaders in the world.[67] But as journalist Mark Serrels wrote in 2016, "Australia doesn't have a piracy problem. Australia has a distribution problem."[68] Most of the reports about piracy in Australia from that time focused on the paradigmatic image of ordinary Australians illicitly downloading episodes of *Game of Thrones*. Legitimate access to *Game of Thrones* had always been limited in Australia, largely because the show was exclusive to Foxtel, Australia's only cable subscription service. For most Australians, Foxtel is not cheap; the subscription plans range from AUD $25/month to AUD $104/month. Australia also has a relatively low rate of cable television subscribers compared to the US. At the same time, Australians were exposed to reviews, media reports, social media buzz, memes and discussions about *Game of Thrones* whenever they went online. For engaged and globally connected media consumers, this discrepancy seemed deeply unfair.[69]

Despite the rhetoric around piracy that frames it as impulsive, reckless and selfish behaviour, research has shown that consumers, in general, will try to do the right thing.[70] For example, before the streaming platform Netflix was launched in Australia in 2015, it was not uncommon for Australians to use technological workarounds to evade geoblocking technologies so that they could pay to access the platform.[71] This required Australian consumers to appear to geoblocking software as though they were US consumers, in order to subscribe to Netflix. These were consumers who were attempting to *pay* for access to content, not to pirate content for free. Even after Netflix launched in Australia, many users reportedly continued to use the same methods to access the US Netflix catalogue, rather than the much more limited Australian catalogue.[72]

Thus, empirical data of the kind collected in this project is able to cast the problem of copyright piracy in a different light, at least in some circumstances. It suggests that piracy might be better dealt with as an issue of access and distribution, rather than through the criminalisation of such behaviour.

Large scale quantitative datasets speak to a different aspect of copyright law and policy than the detailed qualitative work discussed earlier in this chapter. This project considers the *distribution* function of copyright; unlike the messages that came from individual creators in our qualitative work, the quantitative research paints a strongly commercial picture of copyright management. The copyright owners and distributors are mostly large commercial entities; the consumer interests that we consider are very different to the reuse interests of recombinant creators. That both of these projects have relevance to copyright policy demonstrates just how complex copyright is and the extent to which its impacts can vary. The economic theory

---

[67]   See Paula Dootson and Nicolas Suzor, 'The Game of Clones and the Australia Tax: Divergent Views about Copyright Business Models and the Willingness of Australian Consumers to Infringe' (2015) 38(1) *University of New South Wales Law Journal* 206, 206.

[68]   Mark Serrels, 'I Refuse to Feel Guilty for Torrenting Game of Thrones', *Kotako* (online, 27 April 2016) <https://www.kotaku.com.au/2016/04/i-refuse-to-feel-guilty-for-downloading-game-of-thrones/>.

[69]   See Tama Leaver, 'Watching Battlestar Galactica in Australia and the Tyranny of Digital Distance' (2008) 126(1) *Media International Australia* 145, 145–54; Paula Dootson and Nicolas Suzor, 'The Game of Clones and the Australia Tax: Divergent Views about Copyright Business Models and the Willingness of Australian Consumers to Infringe' (2015) 38(1) *University of New South Wales Law Journal* 206.

[70]   See Paula Dootson and Nicolas Suzor, 'The Game of Clones and the Australia Tax: Divergent Views about Copyright Business Models and the Willingness of Australian Consumers to Infringe' (2015) 38(1) *University of New South Wales Law Journal* 206.

[71]   Ibid, 225–6.

[72]   Nicolas Suzor et al, *Australian Consumer Access to Digital Content* (Report, August 2017) 3.

discussed earlier can be both true and false for copyright, depending on the context and the stakeholders involved. For copyright researchers, this means examining both the big picture and the finer detail – the forest and the trees – in order to make any convincing claims about the impacts of copyright law and policy.

4.   A MIXED METHODS APPROACH TO RESEARCHING AUSTRALIAN SCREEN CONTENT

My ongoing work for the next few years is to examine how copyright structures and influences the distribution of screen content (film and television) in Australia.[73] In particular, I am investigating how copyright policy and practice can be improved to facilitate ongoing access and reuse of screen content in a converged media environment.

Screen industries have gone through a massive period of disruption over the last decade, as internet-enabled television has flourished.[74] While in many ways subscription video-on-demand services (SVODs) have been a boon for consumers, the market for audiovisual content is still grossly inefficient. Unlike the music and book industries, which have evolved into competitive markets that allow for efficient distribution of copyrighted content, access to screen content is highly segmented across multiple providers. For music, most commercially produced songs are available to purchase or stream through a range of different digital channels – a consumer need only subscribe to Spotify or Apple Music, for example, to access a broad catalogue of music.[75] Book publishers also routinely license to multiple distributors, including all major lending services.[76] In the digital environment, where storage and distribution are cheap, we should expect a successful copyright market to enable seamless access to almost the entire wealth of recorded cultural production.[77] Yet this has not been the case in the screen industries. In Australia, at least, there is very little overlap in the catalogues of major SVODs (see Figure 10.1). This means that for Australians to access a full spectrum of television and movie content, they need to subscribe to upwards of six services (Netflix, Stan,[78] Amazon Prime Video, Binge,[79] Disney+, Apple TV+) each costing approximately AUD $15 per month. While each subscription is affordable on its own, the combined cost of multiple subscriptions can take broad access to audiovisual content outside of the reach of many Australians.

Additionally, there is audiovisual content that is not easily accessible at all. In 2019, Lobato and Scarlata found that most Australian content on Netflix and Stan is less than five years

---

[73]   I am funded to undertake this work by the Australian Government, under the Australian Research Council (ARC) Discover Early Career Researcher Award (DECRA) scheme (Project ID: DE210100525).
[74]   Additionally, the global COVID pandemic has presented extra challenges for cinema release films.
[75]   Nicolas Suzor et al, *Australian Consumer Access to Digital Content* (Report, August 2017).
[76]   Rebecca Giblin, Jenny Kennedy, Kimberlee Weatherall, Daniel Gilbert, Julian Thomas, and François Petitjean, 'Available, but not accessible? Investigating publishers' e-lending licensing practices', (2019) 24(3) *Information Research* <http://informationr.net/ir/24-3/paper837.html>.
[77]   This is the utopian ideal of the 'universal library': Adrian Johns, *Piracy: The Intellectual Property Wars from Gutenberg to Gates* (University of Chicago Press, 2010) or the 'celestial jukebox': Paul Goldstein, *Copyright's Highway: From Gutenberg to the Celestial Jukebox* (Stanford University Press, rev ed, 2003).
[78]   Stan is Australia's national SVOD.
[79]   Binge is owned by Streamotion, which is a wholly owned subsidiary of the Foxtel Group.

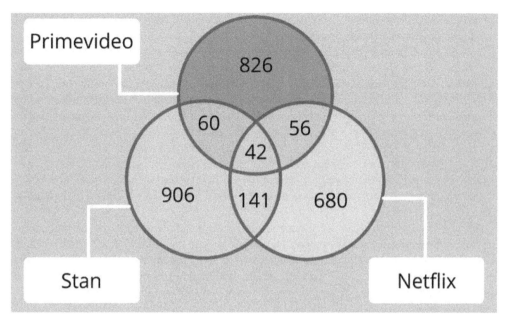

Note: Based on our ongoing data collection, this shows that as at the first quarter of 2021, there was very little overlap in the film catalogues of Netflix, Stan and Prime Video for popular titles in Australia. Only 42 films from our list of thousands of popular titles were available on all three platforms. Overwhelmingly, films were available only on one SVOD.

Figure 10.1   Recent and historical films in Australian streaming services, 2021 Q1

old.[80] The risk here is that there is significant culturally and historically important Australian material that is simply not available. The Australian Government has noted that broadcasters, cultural institutions and government bodies hold "significant archive[s] of past program material" in their physical shelves and digital archives,[81] but much of this is not available to the public online.

In intricate markets like audiovisual production and distribution, where there are many rightsholders connected through complicated webs of contracts, there is good reason to think that the high transaction costs of negotiating licences results in the under-distribution of a great deal of valuable material.[82] This complexity, combined with heavy vertical integration in screen production and distribution,[83] means that the industry's response to digital disruption is

---

[80]   Ramon Lobato and Alex Scarlata, *Australian Content in SVOD Catalogs: Availability and Discoverability* (Report, 2019).

[81]   Department of Broadband, Communications and the Digital Economy, *ABC and SBS: Towards a Digital Future* (Discussion Paper, October 2008) 7.

[82]   Emily Hudson and Andrew T Kenyon, 'Digital Access: The Impact of Copyright on Digitisation Practices in Australian Museums, Galleries, Libraries, and Archives' (2007) 30(1) *University of New South Wales Law Journal* 12; Sally McCausland, 'Getting Broadcaster Archives Online: Orphan Works and Other Copyright Challenges of Clearing Old Cultural Material for Digital Use' (2009) 14(2) *Media Arts Law Review* 142.

[83]   Kathy Bowrey, 'What are You Missing Out on? Big Media, Broadcasting, Copyright and Access to Innovation' in Andrew T Kenyon (ed), *TV Futures: Digital Television Policy in Australia* (Melbourne

far from uniform, continuously evolving, and falls far short of the vision of universal access that digital distribution makes possible.

Historically, broadcast policy has been used to ensure broad and equitable access to screen content, as part of the regulatory obligations that accompany the use of public spectrum. Broadcast regulation, for example, sets quotas for local content on free-to-air television.[84] Broadcasting rules also explicitly override parts of copyright law, allowing the retransmission of signals to improve reach in rural and regional Australia.[85] Especially for small communities in rural Australia, where physical access can be difficult, infrastructure is poor, and people can be isolated from the rest of the country, television has long been recognised as an important source of news, education, connection, identity building and social cohesion.[86] Subscription Video on Demand services have become critical to how Australians watch screen content,[87] but the broadcast era rules that promote access to screen content do not extend to digital distribution over the internet.[88]

The first stage of this project is to understand the scale and significance of the problem of the lack of availability of screen content. The only way to do this is through empirical research methods. The digital infrastructure that we built to gather quantitative data about digital media markets (detailed above) is still running, which will enable me to conduct a longitudinal study of the availability of film and television content on streaming services, as well as when titles move from one SVOD to another (or disappear from catalogues altogether). We have improved and added to our infrastructure over time, so that we now gather data not only from streaming services like Netflix, but the catch-up TV services of Australia's free-to-air channels. We currently track approximately 16,500 television and film titles, including both new releases and historical content. The list of titles tracked is automatically expanded each week from publicly available lists of box office and television releases. Once a title is added to the list, we track its ongoing availability in perpetuity, allowing us to eventually develop a strong longitudinal data set over time. This infrastructure provides, to our knowledge, the only comprehensive mechanism to examine exactly what titles are available through digital channels in Australia, and the only longitudinal evidence of how licensing and distribution decisions impact the ongoing availability of titles over time.

A key advantage of this empirical data is that it enables analysis of the availability of niche content and older "back catalogue" screen content. It will also allow me to examine the patterns of availability for content of cultural significance – including Indigenous stories, historical material, Australian drama, sports, children's programming, and culturally and linguistically diverse content. This analysis will enable me to better understand the scope of the access problem in audiovisual content and to identify categories of content that are not well served by current distribution arrangements.

University Press, 2007) 135.

[84]   *Broadcasting Services (Australian Content) Standard 2005.*

[85]   *Broadcasting Services Act 1992* (Cth).

[86]   Andrew T Kenyon and Robin Wright, 'Television as Something Special? Content Control Technologies and Free-to-Air TV' (2006) 30(2) *Melbourne University Law Review* 338.

[87]   Ramon Lobato, *Netflix Nations: The Geography of Digital Distribution* (New York University Press, 2019); Stuart Cunningham and Alexa Scarlata, 'New Forms of Internationalisation? The Impact of Netflix in Australia' (2020) 177(1) *Media International Australia* 149.

[88]   Jason Bosland, 'Regulating for Local Content in the Digital Audiovisual Environment – A View from Australia' (2007) 18(3) *Entertainment Law Review* 103.

The next stage is to understand what can be done to improve access to content and, again, empirical research is key. We already have some idea of why access might be compromised, and it is largely because of the dominant conceptual framework of copyright as property. As Patterson and Lindberg note: "If a television station regularly erases video tapes of its news broadcasts, the public domain is defeated, but the station has a right to do with its property as it pleases".[89] This is a long-standing tension in copyright law that has not been resolved with the obsolescence of video tapes: the promise of digital technologies to deliver access to knowledge and culture can be frustrated by a property-model of copyright, if licensing markets are not working efficiently.

In this stage, I focus on understanding the legal challenges that prevent the successful negotiation of licences to distribute content, of which there are many. Audiovisual copyright is substantially more complex than other areas of copyright law.[90] Screen productions are extremely expensive and involve many different people with potentially conflicting rights, including rights that apply to underlying dramatic works, films, broadcasts and performances, as well as moral rights and performers' rights, each of which have to be negotiated through complex contractual arrangements. The many potential rightsholders can create a "gridlock" situation, where one "no" can block use despite other granted permissions.[91] At times, iden-tifying or locating the appropriate rightsholder is impossible, and the work is effectively "orphaned".[92] In copyright parlance, "orphan works" are those works for which the copyright owner is unknown or can no longer be identified or located. This is more common than one might think – creators working in collaboration may fail to accurately record each person's contribution to the final product; corporate copyright owners may go out of business, or merge or be acquired, and records can be lost. Where copyright owners cannot be found, they cannot be asked for permission to use the content. The content then falls into a kind of limbo, where it cannot be shared or used until a sufficiently long amount of time has passed that it can be presumed that the copyright term has lapsed and the content is now in the public domain. For a great deal of content, this can require waiting close to 100 years.[93]

Even where a distributor has acquired rights for broadcast in the past, they may not have acquired the rights for digital distribution in the future. Broadcasters, especially public service

---

[89] L Ray Patterson and Stanley W Lindberg, *The Nature of Copyright: A Law of Users' Rights* (University of Georgia Press, 1991) 141.

[90] Emily Hudson and Andrew T Kenyon, 'Digital Access: The Impact of Copyright on Digitisation Practices in Australian Museums, Galleries, Libraries, and Archives' (2007) 30(1) *University of New South Wales Law Journal* 12; Michael Handler, 'Continuing Problems with Film Copyright' in Fiona Macmillan (ed), *New Directions in Copyright Law* (Edward Elgar, 2005–2007) vol 6, 173; Kimberlee Weatherall, 'Culture Clash: The Australian Law Reform Commission's Discussion of Retransmission and the World of Broadcast' (2014) 24(4) *Australian Intellectual Property Journal* 202.

[91] Sally McCausland, 'Getting Broadcaster Archives Online: Orphan Works and Other Copyright Challenges of Clearing Old Cultural Material for Digital Use' (2009) 14(2) *Media Arts Law Review* 142; Michael A Heller, 'The Tragedy of the Anticommons: Property in the Transition from Marx to Markets' (1998) 111(3) *Harvard Law Review* 621.

[92] Matthew Rimmer, 'Robbery under Arms: Copyright Law and the Australia-United State Free Trade Agreement' (2006) 11(3) *First Monday*, https://doi.org/10.5210/fm.v11i3.1316.

[93] In Australia, the length of copyright for most works (literary, dramatic, artistic and musical works) is the life of the author plus 70 years: *Copyright Act 1968* (Cth), s. 33. For sound recordings and cinematograph films, the duration of copyright is generally 70 years from the date of first publication: *Copyright Act 1968* (Cth), ss. 93 and 94.

broadcasters with acute budget constraints, tend to only acquire the rights they need for the immediate purpose of broadcasting, and these rights are unlikely to extend to future uses or new technology formats.[94] Where licences exist, their terms may be unclear, particularly if the licences have not been drafted by lawyers,[95] have mischaracterised the scope of rights granted under copyright law, or are a standard-form agreement being used in a non-standard setting.[96] With all of these challenges, negotiating new licences can be prohibitively difficult and expensive.[97]

The second stage of my project develops a series of in-depth qualitative interviews to better understand the challenges that screen distributors are facing in negotiating copyright licences. It examines the legal factors that contribute to the different gaps in distribution identified from the quantitative data. Through detailed semi-structured interviews with content production and acquisition managers at Australian television networks, and both Australian and international SVOD services, I will examine how licensing decisions are made and what challenges different stakeholders face in making content available. I will interview production industry representatives, including producers, directors, managers and union representatives, in order to better understand any supply-side challenges to selling rights to distribute content through digital channels. I will work with broadcasters and national archive bodies to better understand the particular copyright and licensing challenges they face in making historically and culturally significant content available in a digital form. Finally, I will interview documentarians, filmmakers and producers about the particular issues they have experienced in sourcing, accessing and licensing existing audiovisual content, how they negotiated licences to use this content, and what constraints were placed on their use.

A rigorous understanding of the challenges that hinder licensing and distribution is crucially important to identify practical improvements and potential legal reforms that could reduce the transaction costs of negotiating agreements and improve the distribution of screen content. From this combination of quantitative and qualitative data, I hope to develop guidelines to address certain key problems and low hanging fruit for copyright management within the screen industries. For instance, I think that greater clarity is needed around:

• Providing for the distribution of screen content into the future, noting that the commercial life of content is often much shorter than the copyright term. This may include exploring the potential reversion of rights to creators and producers once the material is no longer commercially distributed.
• How orphan works may be utilised, including developing clear procedures for identifying potential orphan works, conducting a diligent search for the copyright owner, and making orphan works available with appropriate disclosures.

---

[94]   Sally McCausland, 'Getting Broadcaster Archives Online: Orphan Works and Other Copyright Challenges of Clearing Old Cultural Material for Digital Use' (2009) 14(2) *Media Arts Law Review* 142.
[95]   Emily Hudson and Andrew T Kenyon, 'Digital Access: The Impact of Copyright on Digitisation Practices in Australian Museums, Galleries, Libraries, and Archives' (2007) 30(1) *University of New South Wales Law Journal* 12.
[96]   Michael Handler, 'Continuing Problems with Film Copyright' in Fiona Macmillan (ed), *New Directions in Copyright Law* (Edward Elgar, 2005–2007) vol 6, 173.
[97]   Kylie Pappalardo et al, *Imagination Foregone: A Qualitative Study of the Reuse Practices of Australian Creators* (Report, November 2017).

- Assisting documentarians and filmmakers to navigate the permissions thicket for reusing audiovisual clips in future works and clarifying sector agreement on the possible application and scope of the fair dealing exceptions for reporting the news and for criticism and review.
- How screen archives can make use of existing copyright exceptions to provide greater public access to archival content.

Empirical data can help to illuminate how these issues might be addressed within the existing regulatory environment without the need for law reform. The international treaty framework and national legal and political structures make copyright law reform painfully slow and exceedingly difficult, sometimes impossible.[98] There is potential to improve the operation of copyright law by working within its boundaries to improve practice,[99] such as through developing best practice guides in collaboration with industry stakeholders.[100]

However, copyright law reform may be needed to improve distribution where copyright licensing markets are not working well and where improvements to licensing practices are insufficient or impossible. Again, empirical data can help to identify where the sticking points are in the law for those who have to work within the structures created by copyright law in their everyday practice. We can start with the qualitative stories told to us by people on the ground and combine this with doctrinal legal knowledge to extrapolate out about how the law could develop – indeed, ought to develop – to work better in practice. This is the heart of evidence-based policy.

The trouble with approaching policy issues *without* qualitative work is that we end up with laws that do not make sense on the ground. We could probably draw examples of this occurrence from most jurisdictions around the world, but one example in the Australian context is the copyright exception in s 200AB *Copyright Act 1968* (Cth). This provision applies only to libraries or archives, educational institutions, and users assisting persons with a disability. It purports to provide a more generalised "flexible dealing" exception to those entities, so that their uses of copyright works will not amount to infringement even if they do not fall within Australia's specific fair dealing exceptions which apply only to uses for discrete purposes.[101] However, the application of s 200AB is limited by several factors including that the use must not be made "partly for the purpose of the body obtaining a commercial advantage or profit".[102] Most significantly, the provision explicitly incorporates the three step test from Article 13

---

[98]   Rebecca Giblin and Kimberlee Weatherall, 'A Collection of Impossible Ideas' in Rebecca Giblin and Kimberlee Weatherall (eds), *What if We Could Reimagine Copyright?* (ANU Press, 2017) 315; Sam Ricketson, 'The International Framework for the Protection of Authors: Bendable Boundaries and Immovable Obstacles' (2018) 41(3) *Columbia Journal of Law and the Arts* 341.

[99]   Rebecca Giblin, 'A New Copyright Bargain? Reclaiming Lost Culture and Getting Authors Paid' (2018) 41(3) *Columbia Journal of Law and the Arts* 369.

[100]   See e.g. Patricia Aufderheide and Peter Jaszi, *Reclaiming Fair Use: How to Put Balance Back in Copyright* (University of Chicago Press, 2011).

[101]   Australia's fair dealing exceptions are for: research or study (*Copyright Act 1968* (Cth) ss. 40 and 103C), criticism or review (ss. 41 and 103A), parody or satire (ss. 41A and 103AA), reporting the news (ss. 42 and 103B), judicial proceedings or the giving of professional legal advice (ss. 43 and 104), and providing access to a person with a disability (s. 113E).

[102]   *Copyright Act 1968* (Cth), ss. 200AB (2)(c), (3)(c), (4)(c).

TRIPS[103] that the use must be a special case, must not conflict with a normal exploitation of the work or subject-matter, and must not unreasonably prejudice the legitimate interests of the copyright owner.[104] It is probably evident already that the language of this provision was not grounded in the needs of the sector and instead came about through political lobbying and compromise.[105] The provision was enacted in 2006 and has rarely been used since, largely because the very people it was intended to help have absolutely no idea about its scope or how to apply it.[106] It is not clear to users when they can rely on the provision, because it is not clear to them what a "special case" is, or what it means to "prejudice the legitimate interests" of a copyright owner.[107]

Indeed, qualitative work undertaken by Emily Hudson in 2013 demonstrates this very point. Hudson interviewed 66 staff members across 21 cultural institutions (libraries, museums, galleries and archives) and four industry bodies.[108] The interviews were conducted individually or in small groups and followed a semi-structured list of questions about copyright compliance and copyright management practices, including use of s 200AB.[109] Hudson's data revealed that s 200AB "failed to emerge as a meaningful exception for cultural institutions" because it was "overly complex and ambiguous".[110] When Hudson undertook her study in 2013, more than five years had passed since the provision was enacted. Yet interviewees reported using the provision only sporadically, if at all.[111] The main reason they gave for avoiding s 200AB was that it was incomprehensible, both to them and their legal advisors.[112] Hudson concludes that far from supporting cultural institutions to make use of copyrighted works, s 200AB had the opposite effect. She writes, "the particular drafting of s 200AB has served to oust intuitive understandings and industry norms, and put in their place a series of concepts that neither institutional users nor their professional advisors feel confident to interpret".[113]

As this example makes clear, we cannot separate policy decisions about the shape and structure of the law from what our culture looks and sounds like and how it is experienced. Copyright is fundamental to how our cultural industries produce and distribute content; any changes to the law are likely to have a marked impact on how those industries operate and what gets produced and shared. We should, therefore, be guided by the needs of those industries on the ground – through rich, empirical data – and not by assumptions that are divorced

---

[103]   Agreement on Trade Related Aspects of Intellectual Property – available at <https://www.wto.org/english/docs_e/legal_e/27-trips_01_e.htm>.

[104]   *Copyright Act 1968* (Cth), ss. 200AB (1), (7).

[105]   Emily Hudson, 'Fair Use and Section 200AB: What Overseas Experience Teaches Us about Australian Copyright Law' (Conference Paper, VALA2010 Conference, February 2010).

[106]   Australian Law Reform Commission, *Copyright and the Digital Economy* (Discussion Paper 79, May 2013) 222–4 [11.16]–[11.21]; Emily Hudson, 'Fair Use and Section 200AB: What Overseas Experience Teaches Us about Australian Copyright Law' (Conference Paper, VALA2010 Conference, February 2010).

[107]   Ibid.

[108]   Emily Hudson, 'Implementing Fair Use in Copyright Law: Lessons from Australia' (2013) 25(3) *Intellectual Property Journal* 201, 222.

[109]   Ibid.

[110]   Ibid, 223, 225.

[111]   Ibid, 223.

[112]   Ibid, 226.

[113]   Ibid, 227.

from lived experiences, or by mistaken notions that law somehow operates separate to the people and industries it governs.

Copyright law (and the judges who apply it) have always been extremely reluctant to make value judgements about art and about what creations are worthy of protection; on these questions they claim to be agnostic.[114] But in truth, copyright law has value *impacts*, because it structures the market for copyright works.[115] This affects what gets produced and distributed, by whom and to whom, where and how and for what price. This, in turn, affects the shape of our culture and the voices that it represents. Much of what we, as audiences, understand to be important or "natural" in our society, what we care about, and how we construct our social identities is shaped by the stories told through media objects, particularly film and television.[116] This gives narrative power to those whose stories are told most frequently or most strongly (white, cis-gendered, heterosexual, western) at the expense of those whose voices and stories are marginalised (black, blak, brown, Asian, LGBTIQ+, etc.). A recent example of the power of representation is the celebration from dark-skinned South Asian women at finally seeing themselves represented – and represented as beautiful and desirable – in Season Two of Netflix's period drama, *Bridgerton*.[117] If we approach copyright problems purely, or even predominantly, as matters of legal interpretation or abstract economic analysis, it is possible to overlook copyright's impacts on culture and diversity. With empirical research, especially grounded research, it is far more difficult to miss these nuances of the ripple effects of copyright law, because it is precisely *the point* of the empirical work – to understand, in all its complexity, how law and legal structures affect the day-to-day lives and lived experiences of individuals.

5.   CONCLUSION

In this chapter, I have sought to show how detailed qualitative research can disrupt economic assumptions about the role of copyright law, and how large-scale quantitative analysis can provide critical insights into the functioning and evolution of media distribution markets. The most important point, however, remains to be said: that to properly understand the full scope of copyright law, we need to be able to do *both*. We must be able to see, at close range, how the law works in practice (which is different to the law on the books), how market forces

---

[114]   The principle that persons trained only in law cannot be judges of artistic merit was most famously expressed in the US case of *Bleistein v Donaldson Lithographing Co.* 188 U.S. 239, 251–252 (1903). For commentary, see for example, Robert Kirk Walker and Ben Depoorter, 'Unavoidable Aesthetic Judgments in Copyright Law: A Community of Practice Standard' (2015) 109 *Northwestern University Law Review* 343.

[115]   See Julie E Cohen, 'Copyright and the Perfect Curve' (2000) 53(6) *Vanderbilt Law Review* 1799.

[116]   Dwight E Brooks and Lisa P Hébert, 'Gender, Race, and Media Representation' in Bonnie J Dow and Julia T Wood (eds), *The SAGE Handbook of Gender and Communication* (SAGE Publications, 2006) Chapter 16, 297–317.

[117]   Furvah Shah, '"Finally characters in a period drama who look like me": South Asian women celebrate Bridgerton's representation', *Independent*, 6 April 2002 <https://www.independent.co.uk/life-style/bridgerton-charithra-chandran-kate-sharma-asian-b2050649.html>; Mia Raja, 'South Asian representation has long been full of lazy stereotypes – then came Bridgerton', *The Tab*, April 2022 < https://thetab.com/uk/2022/04/05/south-asian-people-have-long-been-misrepresented-on-tv-then-came-bridgerton-season-two-representation-netflix-246105>.

impact on individuals, and how the law is felt and experienced by creators and consumers. Qualitative work allows us to test the theories and assumptions underlying the law. But we must also be able to abstract out from the detailed, rich, qualitative stories in order to model how the law might or should develop. This becomes a process of theory building rather than theory testing, and it is critical to law and policy reform. Quantitative data can help us to see the bigger picture.

Copyright law and regulation, copyright industries, copyright markets, and cultural policies shaped by copyright law are far-reaching and diverse. They touch individuals, local organisations, companies, global conglomerates and national economies. They affect creative projects that cost nothing and reap nothing, through to multi-million-dollar productions. Copyright has relevance to economic interests, but also to culture, to diversity and representation, to how we communicate with one another. Policy made in one area of copyright, for one set of purposes, can have unintended consequences in another area. There is a great deal to understand. To make good law and good policy, we must be able to examine the impacts of copyright both from above (top-down) and from below (bottom-up). This examination is likely to take many years of dedicated work by a collective of scholars from around the world. But we can do none of it without empirical research.

11. Public views on disgorgement of profits in copyright law

A role of harm and wrongful gain

Branislav Hazucha[1]

1. INTRODUCTION

Over the last two decades, several social networks,[2] such as YouTube,[3] Instagram[4] and TikTok,[5] have become hubs for social communities built upon the sharing of user-generated content not only among relatives, friends, colleagues and other acquaintances, but also with millions of strangers. Such networks have even expanded to allow for the emergence of several new social phenomena such as vlogging, amateur content creation and influencer marketing.[6] Online communities have thus become important venues for marketing and advertising, hence also for the commercialization of user-generated content, which presents a crucial source of income for a number of social-network members.

Although a portion of user-generated content is highly original and unproblematic from the perspective of copyright law, much of it contains, in part or entirely, other people's copyrighted works such as music, photographs and videos. In some cases, content creators are permitted to use other people's copyrighted works without the need for a licence or other permission from the concerned copyright holders,[7] but in other cases, they are required by

---

[1] The content of this chapter has been presented on several occasions and I am very thankful to Yoshiyuki Tamura, Christophe Geiger, Estelle Derclaye, Toshiya Kaneko, Sunimal Mendis, Yukari Hira, Johanna Robinson, and the participants of both the 2022 *Annual Conference of EPIP*, held at the University of Cambridge (14–16 September 2022) and the intellectual property law workshop organized by the University of Tokyo (7 March 2020) for their valuable feedback on early drafts of the chapter and on the study upon which it is based. My thanks also go to a number of persons, including Noriko Shimizu, Cédric Baptendier-Santiquet, Clara Ducimetière, Christelle Traband and Stefan Wrbka, who kindly helped me with translations of questionnaires into different languages. The research which is presented in the chapter was supported by the JSPS KAKENHI grant No JP18KK0356.
[2] See, eg, José van Dijck, *The Culture of Connectivity: A Critical History of Social Media* (OUP 2013).
[3] www.youtube.com.
[4] www.instagram.com.
[5] www.tiktok.com.
[6] See, eg, Graeme Turner, *Ordinary People and the Media: The Demotic Turn* (SAGE 2010); Alice E Marwick, *Status Update: Celebrity, Publicity, and Branding in the Social Media Age* (Yale UP 2013); Duncan Brown and Nick Hayes, *Influencer Marketing: Who Really Influences Your Customers?* (Routledge 2016).
[7] See, eg, Lionel Bently, Brad Sherman, Dev Gangjee and Phillip Johnson, *Intellectual Property Law* (5th edn, OUP 2018) 226–83; Paul Goldstein and P Bernt Hugenholtz, *International Copyright:*

law to acquire the necessary copyright licence for their activities.[8] Many creators on social networks, however, seldom or never attempt to obtain such a licence.

In order to deal with copyright issues, online service providers operating social networks have designed a number of measures that allow copyright holders to request the blocking or demonetization of user-generated content in certain circumstances specified in the providers' terms of use and content monetization policies.[9] In many cases, providers are even required to implement those measures by law, although individual conditions can vary between jurisdictions.[10]

A range of stakeholders can be affected by the implementation of such measures, and various controversies have already emerged in this respect.[11] This chapter therefore examines both how the use of those measures can be justified and how they are perceived by the general public. For this purpose, the chapter relies upon an empirical cross-cultural study conducted in four countries over three continents, namely France, Germany, Japan and the US. The study examines how the public views the use of other people's copyrighted works in the case of user-generated content shared on social networks. It also analyses whether the public deems demonetization of such content, in the form of partial or complete transferal of revenues gained from it to the concerned copyright holders, as a fair measure, or entirely inadequate. The study also scrutinizes whether copyright law and its remedies are only constructs of law or whether they have any foundations in social norms recognized by the public.

The chapter is divided into three sections. The first section outlines an array of issues that occur on online social networks with regard to sharing of user-generated content. Several copyright-related issues arise when one person's copyrighted work is used by someone else in the creation of their content, which is then shared with other internet users. These issues are magnified by the fact that certain social networks allow monetization of such content. At the same time, in cases of alleged copyright infringements, online service providers can

---

Principles, Law, and Practice (4th edn, OUP 2019) 349–81; Stavroula Karapapa, *Defences to Copyright Infringement: Creativity, Innovation, and Freedom on the Internet* (OUP 2020).

[8]   See, eg, Bently, Sherman, Gangjee and Johnson (n 7) 141–80, 307–13; Goldstein and Hugenholtz (n 7) 283–336.

[9]   See, eg, Google, 'YouTube Channel Monetization Policies' (2022) <https://support.google.com/youtube/answer/1311392?hl=en> accessed 21 October 2022; Meta, 'Instagram Content Monetization Policies' (2022) <https://help.instagram.com/2635536099905516> accessed 21 October 2022; TikTok, 'Monetize on TikTok' (2022) <https://support.tiktok.com/en/business-and-creator> accessed 21 October 2022.

[10]   See, eg, Directive (EU) 2019/790 of the European Parliament and of the Council of 17 April 2019 on copyright and related rights in the Digital Single Market and amending Directives 96/9/EC and 2001/29/EC (DSM Directive) [2019] OJ L130/92, art 17(4); US Copyright Act 1976, s 512; Japanese Law on the Limitation of Liability for Damages of Specified Telecommunications Service Providers and the Right to Demand Disclosure of Identification Information of the Senders 2001, art 3. See also European Commission, *Guidance on Article 17 of Directive 2019/790 on Copyright in the Digital Single Market* (Communication from the Commission to the European Parliament and the Council, COM(2021) 288 fin).

[11]   See, eg, Tom Gerken, 'YouTube's Copyright Claim System Abused by Extorters' (*BBC News*, 14 February 2019) <https://www.bbc.com/news/technology-47227937> accessed 21 October 2022; Isaiah Colbert, 'YouTuber Hit with Ungodly Number of Anime Copyright Strikes Gets a Win for Everyone' (*Kotaku*, 27 January 2022) <https://kotaku.com/anime-youtube-toei-copyright-strike-fair-use-totally-no-1848432919> accessed 21 October 2022.

execute a form of demonetization by which revenues collected by those who have posted copyrighted content are partially or completely transferred to the copyright holders concerned. This measure may, however, be deemed by some as a windfall for copyright holders. Hence, its implementation in practice tends to cause tensions between affected persons.

The second section then examines how such measures can be justified. Demonetization is, to a degree, comparable with restitutionary (ie, gain-based) damages in tort law,[12] and this section enquires how that remedy can be justified, by employing deontological as well as utilitarian arguments that can be found in present legal scholarship.

Although the use of this remedy can be justified by legal theory in several ways, the question is to what extent it is recognized by the general public. The third section thus scrutinizes how the public perceives the disgorgement of profits in several possible scenarios where another person's copyrighted work is used to create further user-generated content shared on online platforms. It also examines why it is important to study public perceptions of legal norms, and it explains online survey design and data collection. At the end, key findings and their implications for our understanding of copyright law and policy are presented.

2.   SHARING OF USER-GENERATED CONTENT ON SOCIAL NETWORKS

Social networks, such as YouTube, TikTok and Instagram, allow their users not only to interact and communicate between each other but also to share diverse digital content which can range from photos to music and videos. Much of that content is generated by individual internet users. Countless members of social networks enjoy showing photos of their appearance, clothes, meals, travels or other leisure activities to friends, classmates, colleagues and various online acquaintances.[13]

In many cases, the content shared among social-network members can raise a range of copyright-related questions, because its uploaders can, intentionally, knowingly or sometimes even without having any actual knowledge, use the whole or part of other people's copyrighted works without having obtained a licence or other permission from the concerned rightholders. Copyrighted works can consist of photographs, music or movies. Consequently, users of such content can share copyrighted photographs of their favourite actors, singers or music group, can incorporate copyrighted music as soundtracks into their video footages, or can produce video summaries of copyrighted movies they like.

---

[12]   For analysis of restitutionary remedies in intellectual property law, including copyright law, see, eg, Ralph S Brown, 'Civil Remedies for Intellectual Property Invasions: Themes and Variations' (1992) 55 Law & Contemp Probs 45, 66–70; Dane S. Ciolino, 'Reconsidering Restitution in Copyright' (1999) 48 Emory LJ 1; Pamela Samuelson, John M Golden and Mark P Gergen, 'Recalibrating the Disgorgement Remedy in Intellectual Property Cases' (2020) 100 Boston U L Rev 1999.

[13]   See, eg, Charissa Coulthard, 'Self-Portraits and Social Media: The Rise of the "Selfie"' (*BBC News*, 7 June 2013) <https://www.bbc.com/news/magazine-22511650> accessed 21 October 2022; Leo Kelion, 'Posting Children's Photos on Social Media Divides Nation' (*BBC News*, 3 August 2017) <https://www.bbc.com/news/technology-40804041> accessed 21 October 2022; Sarah Lee, 'Picture Perfect? How Instagram Changed the Food We Eat' (*BBC News*, 29 December 2017) <https://www.bbc.com/news/uk-england-london-42012732> accessed 21 October 2022.

The specific use of third parties' copyrighted works also varies significantly from case to case. Sometimes, copyrighted works are used without any modification having been made to them, and such use can be classified in copyright law as literal copying.[14] Other times, users make minor or more notable changes to copyrighted works.[15] Depending upon the level and manner of transformation, such uses can lead to the creation of derivate works,[16] which might fall within a copyright exception, such as in the cases of parody, satire, caricature, pastiche, review or quotation.[17]

Recently, several well-reported cases have engendered controversy on social networks that allow the sharing of user-generated content. In many cases, the shared content was demonetized due to copyright claims raised by concerned copyright holders.[18] In some cases the copyright holders even requested the posted content to be partially or completely blocked.[19]

Another controversial issue lies in the use of automated systems for detecting and reporting acts of copyright infringement.[20] Although such systems can employ diverse methods for detecting the use of copyrighted works, copyright holders tend to design their crawlers so that any, even very minor, uses of their works, including parts of works, can be detected. Crawlers, however, rarely analyse whether a particular use of copyrighted work is covered by any of the copyright exceptions. This leads to massive overclaiming in relation to the original creator's exclusive rights and to the switching of the burden to other involved parties, which are often the affected internet users (ie, content creators).[21]

Moreover, there can be notable differences between jurisdictions as to the scope of individual copyright exceptions. Certain uses of copyrighted works by third parties may be allowed in some countries and restricted or completely banned in others. For instance, under US copyright law an act of parody must target the respective copyrighted works or its author.[22] On the other hand, the parody exception under EU copyright law is somewhat

---

[14]   See, eg, Bently, Sherman, Gangjee and Johnson (n 7) 199–215; Goldstein and Hugenholtz (n 7) 286–88.

[15]   See, eg, Bently, Sherman, Gangjee and Johnson (n 7) 215–22; Goldstein and Hugenholtz (n 7) 299–301.

[16]   See, eg, Sam Ricketson and Jane C Ginsburg, *International Copyright and Neighbouring Rights: The Berne Convention and Beyond* (2nd edn, OUP 2006) vol 2, 645–56; Pamela Samuelson, 'The Quest for a Sound Conception of Copyright's Derivative Work Right' (2013) 101 GeoLJ 1505.

[17]   See, eg, Bently, Sherman, Gangjee and Johnson (n 7) 226–83; Goldstein and Hugenholtz (n 7) 349–81; Karapapa (n 7).

[18]   cf, eg, Tom Gerken, 'YouTuber in Row over Copyright Infringement of His Own Song' (*BBC News*, 5 July 2018) <https://www.bbc.com/news/technology-44726296> accessed 21 October 2022.

[19]   See, eg, Tom Gerken, 'YouTubers Face £4,600 Bill over Copyright Claims' (*BBC News*, 13 January 2020) <https://www.bbc.com/news/blogs-trending-51090857> accessed 21 October 2022; Colbert (n 11).

[20]   See, eg, Jennifer M Urban, Joe Karaganis and Brianna L Schofield, 'Notice and Takedown: Online Service Provider and Rightsholder Accounts of Everyday Practice' (2017) 64 J Copyright Soc'y 371, 382, 384–89.

[21]   See, eg, Google, 'Youtube Copyright Transparency Report H1 2021' (June 2021) 11, <https://storage.googleapis.com/transparencyreport/report-downloads/pdf-report-22_2021-1-1_2021-6-30_en_v1.pdf> accessed 21 October 2022 (reporting that in the first half of 2021 60% of 3,698,019 disputes were resolved in favour of uploaders).

[22]   See, eg, *Campbell v Acuff-Rose Music, Inc* [1994] 510 US 569, 580–81 (Sup Ct) (US) ("Parody needs to mimic an original to make its point, and so has some claim to use the creation of its victim's (or

broader. It permits the use of other people's copyrighted works when targeting any social phenomenon, which do not need to be related to the work being used at all, on the condition that such use is humorous.[23] In Japan, the parody exception is, to a certain degree, comparable to the EU approach. It, however, seems that it requires the higher level of transformation or lower degree in which essential characteristics of the used work are copied. Otherwise, there is a high risk of interfering with the concerned author's moral right of integrity.[24]

In some cases, copyright holders' claims have even led to more severe sanctions being imposed upon internet users who have shared such works. For example, several online channels on social networks, which can often represent valuable assets and important sources of income, have been restricted, to make them inaccessible from certain jurisdictions.[25] This happens when the content which is legitimate in one jurisdiction can be considered copyright infringement in the other.

In the cases of some repeat copyright infringers, their channels have even been completely terminated.[26] As channels with a couple of million subscribers can generate considerable amounts of revenue for their owners,[27] such measure can have a significant impact on channel owners.

This brings us to the issue of why copyright holders should be entitled to control diverse transformative uses of their copyrighted works by third parties and why those sharing such works should be obliged to transfer gained profits to the concerned copyright holders. Why should copyright holders be allowed to claim profits gained by other people who share user-generated content created by using other people's copyrighted works? The next section will therefore examine how the use of such a restitutionary remedy, often called "gain-based damages",[28] "disgorgement of profits"[29] or "restitution for wrongs",[30] can be justified.

---

collective victims') imagination, whereas satire can stand on its own two feet and so requires justification for the very act of borrowing.").

[23]   See Case C-201/13 *Johan Deckmyn and Vrijheidsfonds VZW v Helena Vandersteen and Others* ECLI:EU:C:2014:2132 (CJEU) (EU).

[24]   See *Montage photo* [1980] 1976 (O) No 923, [1980] 34(2) Minshu 244 (Sup Ct) (JP).

[25]   See, eg, Colbert (n 11); Timothy Geigner, 'YouTube Dusts Off Granular National Video Blocking to Assist YouTuber Feuding with Toei Animation' (*techdirt*, 1 February 2022) <https://www.techdirt.com/2022/02/01/youtube-dusts-off-granular-national-video-blocking-to-assist-youtuber-feuding-with-toei-animation/> accessed 21 October 2022.

[26]   See, eg, Gerken (n 11); Gerken (n 18).

[27]   See, eg, Amanda Perelli, 'How Much Money YouTubers Make, According to Dozens of Creators' (*Insider*, 3 September 2022) <https://www.businessinsider.com/how-much-money-youtube-creators-influencers-earn-real-examples-2021-6> accessed 21 October 2022; Sona Hakobyan, 'How Much do YouTubers Make in 2022?' (*Renderforest*, 20 September 2022) <https://www.renderforest.com/blog/how-much-do-youtubers-make> accessed 21 October 2022.

[28]   See, eg, James Edelman, *Gain-Based Damages: Contract, Tort, Equity and Intellectual Property* (Hart Pub Ltd 2002).

[29]   See, eg, Peter Jaffey, 'Restitutionary Damages and Disgorgement' (1995) 3 RLR 30; Ewoud Hondius and André Janssen (eds), *Disgorgement of Profits: Gain-Based Remedies throughout the World* (Springer 2015).

[30]   See, eg, Daniel Friedmann, 'Restitution of Benefits Obtained through the Appropriation of Property or the Commission of a Wrong' (1980) 80 Colum L Rev 504; Ian M Jackman, 'Restitution for Wrongs' (1989) 48 CLJ 302; Daniel Friedmann, 'Restitution for Wrongs: The Measure of Recovery'

3.   JUSTIFICATION OF THE DISGORGEMENT OF PROFITS

The aim of tort law is to deal with externalities of human activities within society. Many activities result in some people gaining advantages, while others are left worse off. However, this does not mean that compensation will always be due to the latter, nor that the gains of the former ought to be transferred to the latter. Conversely, the fundamental principle in law is that each person should bear harm suffered by them, just as they are entitled to keep their gains, unless any special reason exists for the redistribution of wealth between individual members of society.

An exception to this principle is that the burden of bearing harm can be moved to another person, if the harm was caused intentionally, negligently by a breach of duty of care, if the duty was owed to the injured person and the harm caused was foreseeable and not too remote, or there were other specific conditions required by law.[31]

The main remedy used in such situations is compensation in the form of damages. However, when and why should gains obtained by a wrongdoer as a result of committing a wrong be transferred to the injured person? The conventional answer is that nobody should gain profit from wrongs.[32]

Gains acquired by a wrongdoer might be considered wrongful gains, because they have acquired them by committing a wrong. Had they not committed that wrong, they would not have obtained the respective gain. At the same time, the wrongdoer has acquired the gain at the expense of another person.

In addition, it might be deemed that the wrongdoer has gained an unfair advantage against other members of society, who follow and obey the rules. Moreover, if wrongdoers were allowed to benefit from wrongs, this would undermine the normative power of legal rules. A part of society might be thus encouraged to disregard rules and to commit wrongs in order to gain benefits, unless there is a measure in place that requires any wrongful gains to be disgorged.

This brings us to another question. To whom should such gains be transferred? One option is presented by the confiscation of profits by a public authority. Another option is to transfer it to the injured person. However, this raises a further issue, because such transfer could be considered a windfall obtained by the injured person, because they would gain benefits in addition to the full compensation for their harm.[33] This might even encourage a portion of society to litigate wrongs in order to receive such windfalls.

In legal scholarship, it is possible to find several ways of justifying the disgorgement of profits. On the one side are views which rely upon deontological theories of corrective or

---

(2001) 79 Tex L Rev 1879; Craig Rotherham, 'The Conceptual Structure of Restitution for Wrongs' (2007) 66 CLJ 172; Francesco Giglio, 'Restitution for Wrongs: A Structural Analysis' (2007) 20 Can J L & Jurisprudence 5.

[31]   See, eg, Konrad Zweigert and Heinz Kötz, *An Introduction to Comparative Law* (3rd edn, OUP 1998) 595–708; John CP Goldberg, 'Tort' in Peter Cane and Mark Tushnet (eds), *The Oxford Handbook of Legal Studies* (OUP 2003) 21, 22–35; Cees van Dam, *European Tort Law* (2nd edn, OUP 2013).

[32]   See, eg, Andrew Burrows, *The Law of Restitution* (Butterworths 1993) 376, 395–96.

[33]   See, eg, Ernest J Weinrib, 'Restitutionary Damages as Corrective Justice' (2000) 1 Theoretical Inq L 1, 2–3; Rotherham (n 30) 191.

distributive justice.[34] On the other are those which employ utilitarian and consequentialist arguments.[35]

3.1 Deontological Justifications

The disgorgement of profits has been developed by courts as a remedy in cases where they felt it was unfair for wrongdoers to benefit from wrongs. However, its case law is frequently seen as perplexing and inconsistent. There have therefore been several attempts to clarify and simplify it.[36] One such attempt led Lord Goff and Gareth Jones to come up with a radical proposal to allow restitution for all wrongful gains.[37] They formulated it into the following simple rule: "[I]f it can be demonstrated that a tortfeasor has gained a benefit and that benefit would not have been gained but for the tort, he should be required to make restitution."[38]

Nevertheless, this proposal has faced harsh criticism, especially from scholars who advocate that private law, and particularly tort law, is based upon principles of corrective justice.[39] Supporters of corrective justice arguments criticize this proposal as being "insensitive to the limited significance of factual causation and to the need to forge a normative link between the wrong and the gain".[40]

At the same time, those critics point out that corrective justice can help us to create such a link, because it "discloses the normative nature of the nexus between the two parties",[41] that is, between the wrongdoer and the injured person, and so "highlights the correlativity of right and duty that characterizes the norms connecting the parties".[42] This normative correlativity upon which private law is deemed to rest allows us, according to corrective justice arguments, "to conceive of private law as a coherent moral system".[43]

Regarding the disgorgement of profits, those supporters of corrective justice arguments stress the normative and not merely historical connection between a wrong and gained benefits.[44] They emphasize that in the case of an interference with property rights the main feature of the wrong is "the materialization of a possibility – the opportunity to gain – that

---

[34] See, eg, Weinrib (n 33); James Gordley, 'The Purpose of Awarding Restitutionary Damages: A Reply to Professor Weinrib' (2000) 1 Theoretical Inq L 39; Rotherham (n 30) 186–87; Layne S Keele, 'Copyright Infringement's Blurred Lines: Allocating Overhead in the Disgorgement of Profits' (2017) BYUL Rev 1059.

[35] See, eg, Saul Levmore, 'Probabilistic Recoveries, Restitution, and Recurring Wrongs' (1990) 19 J Legal Stud 691; A Mitchell Polinsky and Steven Shavell, 'Should Liability Be Based on the Harm to the Victim or the Gain to the Injurer?' (1994) 10 J L Econ & Org 427; Robert Cooter and Ariel Porat, 'Disgorgement Damages for Accidents' (2015) 44 J Legal Stud 249.

[36] See, eg, Daniel Friedmann, 'Restitution of Benefits Obtained through the Appropriation of Property or the Commission of a Wrong' (1980) 80 Colum L Rev 504; Edelman (n 28); Rotherham (n 30); Giglio (n 30).

[37] Lord Goff of Chieveley and Gareth Jones, *The Law of Restitution* (5th edn, Sweet & Maxwell 1998).

[38] ibid 781.

[39] Weinrib (n 33) 7–12.

[40] ibid 11.

[41] ibid 3.

[42] ibid 37.

[43] ibid 3.

[44] ibid 8.

rightfully belonged to the plaintiff".[45] As the owner has the right to profit from dealings with her property and "the potential for gain is an incident of the right that the wrongdoer violated",[46] any gains resulting from the misappropriation of property should necessarily be subject to restitution.[47]

Accordingly, proponents of the corrective justice approach underline that "[b]ecause it is an incident of the plaintiff's entitlement that the defendant has wrongfully infringed, the gain is not merely the result of a wrongful act, but is the continuing embodiment of the injustice between the parties".[48] They add that "the point of a legal remedy is to undo that injustice, and so the remedy must mirror the structure of the injustice".[49] It is therefore apparent that "the disgorgement of these proprietary gains fits readily within the correlativity of corrective justice".[50]

To sum up, the approach based upon corrective justice relies upon the argument that when a wrongdoer gains profits by unlawfully using an incident of the property right belonging to another person, she should be obliged to hand over such profit to the property rightholder in question. In this way, the profit is not deemed a windfall for the rightholder, but is rather viewed as something that has been generated by the use of that incident of her exclusive right granted by copyright law, and so the rightholder should have the right to claim for its restitution, that is, the transfer of the profit from the wrongdoer to the rightholder.

3.2   Utilitarian Justifications

On the other hand, law-and-economics scholars have attempted to justify the disgorgement of profits by its deterrence effect.[51] The issue is that not all wrongdoings are detected and successfully litigated. Hence, the deterrence effect of any compensation in the form of damages is reduced by the low probability of catching the wrongdoer and the rightholder successfully claiming the compensation from them.[52]

Moreover, the deterrence effect is further reduced when gains acquired by the wrongdoer from a wrongdoing are higher than the actual damage inflicted upon a third person.[53] If wrongdoers could keep the benefits gained from their wrongs in such cases, they would be encouraged to commit wrongs, because such activities would be always profitable for them, even in the cases where they were caught.

Law-and-economics scholars therefore argue that there are two options to increase the deterrence effect of any remedy. The first potential measure is to increase the likelihood that wrongdoers will be caught and injured persons properly compensated. The second measure is to increase the extent of sanctions that the wrongdoer should bear once caught.

---

[45]   ibid.
[46]   ibid 37.
[47]   ibid 12.
[48]   ibid 8.
[49]   ibid 37.
[50]   ibid 12.
[51]   See, eg, Levmore (n 35); Polinsky and Shavell (n 35); Cooter and Porat (n 35).
[52]   See, eg, Gary S Becker, 'Crime and Punishment: An Economic Approach' (1968) 76 J Pol Econ 169.
[53]   See, eg, Polinsky and Shavell (n 35) 428, 436.

One way to boost potential sanctions would be the imposition of punitive or quasi-punitive damages,[54] with the disgorgement of profits being considered a form of quasi-punitive damages. Threat of disgorgement of profits could then notably strengthen the deterrence effect of remedies in tort, because wrongdoers would not only be unable to keep their profits gained from committed wrongs, but would also have to compensate the persons concerned for any harms suffered. Supporters of deontological justifications, however, criticize utilitarian approaches for "treating the plaintiff merely as a convenient conduit of social consequences rather as someone to whom damages are owed to correct the wrong suffered".[55]

4.   PUBLIC VIEWS ON DISGORGEMENT OF PROFIT

As presented above, legal scholarship can justify the disgorgement of profits in several ways. This brings us to the question whether and how internet users really perceive such measures. Do they find them appropriate and adequate, or do they deem them unreasonable and unfair?

The importance of public perception of the disgorgement of profits is reflected by the fact that the law is a system of norms which should have expressive power,[56] that is, any subject who is targeted by norms should follow them because the subject has internalized the norms and based their behaviour on them.[57] At the same time, when a norm has no or minimal expressive power, any subjects targeted and regulated by such a norm tend to behave in a way that leads them to pay little attention to it or even completely disregard it. This issue has been addressed in more detail by the author and several other scholars elsewhere.[58]

For our discussion here, it is important that internalization of legal norms leads to the reduction of enforcement costs.[59] Legal norms that are recognized by the general public are on average obeyed without any special need to use power in order to force individuals to comply with them. On the other hand, legal norms that go against social norms established within society tend to be disregarded by the public and so it can be costly to implement them in practice.

Consequently, the question remains whether the general public perceives it as reasonable and fair that someone who has shared another's copyrighted work without the requisite licence should be required to transfer her gains to the affected rightholder. To examine how the public sees the disgorgement of profits, an online survey was conducted in four countries

---

[54]   See, eg, A Mitchell Polinsky and Steven Shavell, 'Punitive Damages: An Economic Analysis' (1998) 111 Harv L Rev 869.

[55]   See Weinrib (n 33) 6.

[56]   See, eg, Cass R Sunstein, 'On the Expressive Function of Law' (1996) 144 U Pa L Rev 2021; Richard H McAdams, 'Focal Point Theory of Expressive Law' (2000) 86 Va L Rev 1649.

[57]   See, eg, Robert Cooter, 'Do Good Laws Make Good Citizens? An Economic Analysis of Internalized Norms' (2000) 86 Va L Rev 1577, 1593–94; Lawrence Lessig, *Code: Version 2.0* (Basic Books 2006) 344–45.

[58]   See, eg, John N Drobak (ed), *Norms and the Law* (CUP 2006); Branislav Hazucha, Hsiao-Chien Liu and Toshihide Watabe, 'Private Ordering and Consumers' Rights in Copyright Law: A View of Japanese Consumers' in Graeme B Dinwoodie (ed), *Intellectual Property and General Legal Principles: Is IP a Lex Specialis?* (EE Pub 2015) 119, 137–40; Richard H McAdams, *The Expressive Powers of Law: Theories and Limits* (HUP 2015).

[59]   See, eg, Sunstein (n 56) 2032–33; Cooter (n 57) 1590.

with different legal, social and cultural environments and traditions. The survey's aim was not only to study social norms universally recognized by people around the world, but also to observe any cross-cultural differences.

4.1   Survey Design and Execution

The online survey was designed so that several potential biases were limited as much as possible. Four countries with different cultures and traditions were selected so that cultural variations between respondents could be measured. In addition, the survey relied upon coded vignettes in order to measure how specific factors influence respondents' decision-making in terms of the appropriateness of the disgorgement of profits as remedy in the cases of transformative uses of other people's copyrighted works on online social networks. Finally, the survey questionnaire also contained a number of control questions and used the randomness of individual vignette variants so as to minimize possible biases on the part of respondents as well as those that could occur due to the survey design itself.

4.1.1   Selection of studied countries

The countries studied were carefully selected, and consisted of Germany, France, Japan and the US. Each country has its own specificities. Moreover, when the position of an individual and the role of social norms within society are taken into consideration, the countries can be ordered into a spectrum of different cultures.

The two extremes in that spectrum are presented by the US and Japan. The former is commonly characterized by strong individualism and emphasis upon personal freedom.[60] The latter's society is regularly seen as communitarian, where membership of social groups plays an important role, to the degree that social duties can significantly restrict the personal freedom of individual members.[61]

The other selected countries, France and Germany, can be located somewhere between those two extremes. Like the Japanese people, the Germans are typically considered to strictly obey legal rules.[62] On the other hand, France has a long tradition of republicanism and emphasis on personal freedom.[63]

4.1.2   Vignettes and coded factors

In order to study how respondents perceive diverse uses of other people's copyrighted works, which they may routinely encounter on social networks, several vignettes were designed. Individual vignettes were inspired by judicial cases that occurred in the studied countries.

---

[60]   See, eg, V Lee Hamilton and Joseph Sanders, *Everyday Justice: Responsibility and the Individual in Japan and the United States* (Yale UP 1992) 49–51.

[61]   ibid 49, 51–58; and John Owen Haley, *Authority without Power: Law and the Japanese Paradox* (OUP 1991) 190–91.

[62]   See, eg, Joe Baur, 'What Makes Germans So Orderly?' (*BBC*, 2 June 2020) <https://www.bbc.com/travel/article/20200531-what-makes-germans-so-orderly> accessed 21 October 2022.

[63]   See, eg, Michèle Lamont, *Money, Morals, and Manners: The Culture of the French and the American Upper-Middle Class* (U Chi P 1992) 136–39.

In the first vignette, one person rewrote the story of a book originally published by another person.[64] The former's main aim was to present the original story in a different context. The vignette stems from the US and French cases in which Margaret Mitchell's saga *Gone with the Wind* was parodied by different authors.[65] Similar situations frequently happen in the cases of fanfiction, where fans retell their favourite literary story, fill its gaps, or narrate its prequels, sequels, or alternative endings.[66]

The second vignette dealt with the use of a cartoon character, designed by another person, to create a new cartoon strip.[67] This vignette took inspiration from the *Deckmyn* case,[68] which was decided by the Court of Justice of the European Union. In that case, the composition used in the copyrighted cartoon was slightly modified and reused so as to criticize a local Belgian politician.[69] Similar cases, where famous cartoon characters were used without obtaining a copyright licence from the copyright holder, can also be found in both France[70] and Germany.[71]

The third vignette depicted the sampling of a popular song composed by another person.[72] This situation is quite common in the genre of rap and hip-hop music. It is not surprising, then, that the highest judicial institutions in several jurisdictions (eg, in the US,[73] EU[74] and Germany[75]) have already expressed their views on copyright issues raised by such uses of copyrighted works.

---

[64] This fanfiction vignette began as follows: "Without obtaining any prior permission, John X has written and published a book that retold in new way a story previously written and published by Michael Y."

[65] See *SunTrust Bank v Houghton Mifflin Co* [2001] 268 F3d 1257 (11th Cir) (US) (examining Alice Randall's 2001 parody *The Wind Done Gone*); *Sté Trust Company Bank v Régine Deforges* [1992] D JP 182 (Cass civ 1) (Fr) (dealing with the book *La Bicyclette bleue* written by Régine Deforges).

[66] See, eg, Rebecca Tushnet, 'Legal Fictions: Copyright, Fan Fiction, and a New Common Law' (1997) 17 Loy LA Ent L Rev 651.

[67] This cartoon character vignette stated as follows: "John X has drawn and published a new cartoon strip. Without obtaining any prior authorization, the strip used a cartoon character previously designed and published by Michael Y, but its story was different from Michael Y's cartoons."

[68] *Deckmyn* (n 23).

[69] ibid, paras 8–9.

[70] See, eg, *Sté Moulinsart v Xavier Marabout* [2021] 17/04478 (TJ Rennes) (Fr).

[71] See, eg, *Alcolix* [1993] I ZR 263/91 (BGH) (Ger); *Asterix-Persiflagen* [1993] I ZR 264/91 (BGH) (Ger); *'Gies-Adler'* [2003] I ZR 117/00 (BGH) (Ger).

[72] This music sampling vignette was described as follows: "John X is a rapper. He copied a 10-second music track from Michael Y's recorded song without asking for the latter's permission. John X looped it many times throughout his 3-minute song, while the copied part remained clearly noticeable. He then added his rapping over this music background."

[73] See, eg, *Campbell* (n 22).

[74] See, eg, Case C-476/17 *Pelham GmbH and Others v Ralf Hütter and Florian Schneider-Esleben* ECLI:EU:C:2019:624 (CJEU) (EU).

[75] See, eg, *Metall auf Metall IV* [2020] I ZR 115/16 (BGH) (Ger). See also Bernd Justin Jütte and João Pedro Quintais, 'The *Pelham* Chronicles: Sampling, Copyright and Fundamental Rights' [2021] 16 JIPLP 213.

In the fourth vignette, a photograph taken by another person was modified or otherwise distorted.[76] The vignette is based upon a German case,[77] where the photo of an attractive actress was distorted to make her look significantly fatter. Comparable disputes, where the copyrighted work in question was a photograph, can also be found in other jurisdictions.[78]

The fifth vignette outlined a video collage composed of humorous accidents which had happened during live TV broadcasts.[79] This scenario was inspired by videos of this kind, which are abundantly available on social networks allowing sharing of user-generated content.

Several factors were encoded into individual vignettes.[80] The factors were selected from the reasons given by courts in the four countries in deciding parody cases. Accordingly, they consisted of circumstances under which such uses of copyrighted works had occurred, that is, parody's humorousness[81] and creativity,[82] the target of its criticism,[83] how well known the used work of another author was[84] and the parodist's intent to harm the author of the

---

[76]   This photograph distortion vignette was depicted as follows: "Without any prior authorization, John X digitally distorted the photo of a handsome male fashion model taken by Michael Y so that the model looked more ordinary, fatter and less manly."

[77]   See, eg, *Auf fett getrimmt ('Trimmed to the fat')* [2016] I ZR 9/15 (BGH) (Ger).

[78]   See, eg, *Montage photo* (n 24); *Leibovitz v Paramount Pictures Corp* [1998] 137 F3d 109 (2d Cir) (US). See also Mariko A Foster, 'Parody's Precarious Place: The Need to Legally Recognize Parody as Japan's Cultural Property' (2013) 23 Seton Hall J Sports & Ent L 313.

[79]   This video collage vignette read as follows: "John X has made and uploaded a 10-minute video online so that anyone could watch it via the internet. Without obtaining any prior permission, the video consisted of funny incidents which had occurred to Michael Y as a television host during live TV broadcasting."

[80]   For the methodology of coded vignettes, see, eg, Hamilton and Sanders (n 60) 89–90.

[81]   See, eg, *Deckmyn* (n 23) [20] (stating that "the essential characteristics of parody are, first, to evoke an existing work while being noticeably different from it, and, secondly, to constitute an expression of humour or mockery"); *Suntrust Bank v Houghton Mifflin* (n 65) 1269 n 23 (pointing out that the Court is not required to assess whether a work is humorous, because it 'would always be a wholly subjective inquiry'). The humorousness factor was coded into the video collage vignette by the following two alternatives: unhumorous ("The retold version was not funny at all.") and humorous ("The retold version was hilariously funny."). Other vignettes contained comparable clauses.

[82]   The creativity factor was coded into the video collage vignette by the following two alternatives: non-creative ("The order of the individual parts was random." and creative ("The individual parts were ordered so as to make the final video even funnier.").

[83]   See, eg, *Campbell* (n 22) 580–81. The targeting factor was coded into the fanfiction vignette by the following two alternatives: no targeting ("It criticized political and social views prevailing in the current society. This criticism was, however, not aimed at the original story.") and targeting ("It criticized political and social views presented in the original story."). Other vignettes contained comparable clauses.

[84]   See, eg, *Jean-François Bauret and others v Jeffrey Koons and others* [2019] 17/09695 (CA Paris); *Jeffrey Koons and others v FD and others* [2011] 19/09059 (CA Paris). The fame factor was coded into the fanfiction vignette by the following two alternatives: unfamous ("Before publishing this book, only a few people were aware of Michael Y's original story, because it had never been very successful commercially.") and famous ("Before publishing this book, Michael Y's original story was quite famous and very successful commercially."). The music sampling vignette contained comparable clauses.

reproduced work.[85] In addition, the factors contained aspects such as gained profit,[86] type of caused harm, that is, material[87] or reputational[88] harm, and causal nexus.[89]

Into individual vignettes five factors were coded, producing 32 variations for each.[90] For instance, one variation of fanfiction vignette read as follows:

> Without obtaining any prior permission, John X has written and published a book that retold in new way a story previously written and published by Michael Y. The retold version was hilariously funny. It criticized political and social views prevailing in the current society. This criticism was, however, not aimed at the original story.
>
> John X earned $50,000 from publishing his book. This happened only because he had retold that original story. Before publishing this book, Michael Y's original story was quite famous and very successful commercially.

4.1.3   Questionnaire

The questionnaire was composed of several question types. The first group of questions examined the demographics of respondents, that is, age, gender, place of residence, education, occupation and income.

The second group consisted of control questions that aimed to control for possible biases, such as intensity of internet use as well as passive and active participation in online social networks where user-generated content is generally shared among their members. Furthermore, several questions examined the respondents' attention. One of them asked

---

[85]   See, eg, *SNC Prisma Presse and EURL Femme v Charles V and Association Apodeline* [2001] 00/16766 (TGI Paris) (Fr) 5 ("La parodie suppose l'intention d'amuser sans nuire."); *Moulinsart v Marabout* (n 70) 12 ("à la condition qu'il n'existe pas de volonté de nuire"). The intent factor was coded into the cartoon character and photograph distortion vignettes by the following two alternatives: no intent ("John X had no intention of causing any such harm to Michael Y.") and intent ("John X had intended to cause such harm to Michael Y.").

[86]   The benefit factor was coded into the fanfiction vignette by the following two alternatives: no profit ("John X earned no money from publishing his book.") and profit ("John X earned $50,000 from publishing his book."). Other vignettes contained comparable clauses.

[87]   The material harm factor was coded into the cartoon character vignette by the following two alternatives: no material harm ("no negative economic impact on the marketing of Michael Y's cartoons featuring the cartoon character could be perceived either") and material harm ("Michael Y's cartoons featuring the cartoon character could not be marketed anymore and that loss amounted to $50,000."). The photograph distortion and video collage vignettes contained comparable clauses.

[88]   The reputational harm factor was coded into the cartoon character vignette by the following two alternatives: no reputational harm ("As a result of John X publishing the strip, Michael Y, the author of the original cartoon character, experienced no harm to his professional reputation") and reputational harm ("As a result of John X publishing the strip, Michael Y, the author of the original cartoon character, experienced significant harm to his professional reputation."). The photograph distortion and video collage vignettes contained similar clauses.

[89]   The causal nexus factor was coded into the fanfiction vignette by the following two alternatives: no causal nexus ("As a result of John X publishing the strip, Michael Y, the author of the original cartoon character, experienced no harm to his professional reputation") and causal nexus ("This happened only because he had retold that original story."). The music sampling vignette contained comparable clauses.

[90]   The humorousness, targeting, benefit, causal nexus and fame factors were coded into the fanfiction and music sampling vignettes; the humorousness, intent, benefit, and reputational and material harm factors into the cartoon character and photograph distortion vignettes; and the criticism, creativity, benefit, and reputational and material harm factors into the video collage vignette.

for the capital of the respondent's country and instructed the respondent upon its correct answer so as to avoid any possible confusion in its answering.[91] All respondents who answered this question incorrectly were excluded from the sample. In addition, a minimal response time condition was added for the inclusion into the sample.[92]

The third group of questions measured respondents' views on the presented vignettes. Each respondent randomly received one variation of each vignette. Vignettes were followed by questions on appropriate sanctions (if any) and the wrongfulness of the presented vignette variant.

When respondents answered that the depicted activity should be sanctioned in some way, they were asked to specifically identify suitable sanctions. They had several predefined options, such as an order to apologize to the concerned copyright holder, to terminate such conduct, to transfer any gained profit, to compensate for harm caused and to impose a small or substantial fine and imprisonment. In addition to these predefined options, respondents could freely identify other suitable measures. This open-answer option was used only by a small proportion of respondents.[93]

With regard to the cartoon character and photograph distortion vignettes, the respondents were asked two additional questions dealing with details of the presented stories, in order to control for their attention and comprehension. They were asked about the degree of harm suffered and the profits gained in the presented vignettes.

4.1.4   Data collection

The survey was conducted online through Cross Marketing Inc in the summer of 2020.[94] In total, 500 responses were collected from each country, 2,000 responses in total. The respondents ranged from 15 to 49 years old, and their composition reflected sampled

---

[91]   Question 29 in the questionnaire for the US respondents stated as follows: "What is the current capital city of the United States of America? As you know, the correct answer is Washington, D.C. This question is designed to filter out mechanical responses. We deeply appreciate your cooperation."

[92]   In order to include a response into the collected sample, its respondent had to spend at least 3.5 minutes in the case of Japanese respondents and at least 5 minutes as to the other respondents. The difference in minimal response time is justified by the fact that the Japanese script allows for faster reading.

[93]   Open-ended option "others" was used 41 times (3.04%) in 1,348 responses that found it appropriate to impose some sanction in the fanfiction vignette; 35 times (2.19%) in 1,598 responses concerning the cartoon character vignette; 37 times (2.47%) in 1,495 responses concerning the music sampling vignette; 22 times (1.38%) in 1,594 responses concerning the photograph distortion vignette; and 13 times (1.01%) in 1,289 responses concerning the video collage vignette. This option was used the most often by the German and US respondents (respectively, up to 7.07% and 3.55% in the fanfiction vignette).

[94]   The data collection started on 30 July 2020, and it was completed by 17 August 2020 in Japan, by 27 August 2020 in the US, by 23 August 2020 in France and by 26 August 2020 in Germany.

populations in the four countries as to their age and gender. They were also spread across individual territories,[95] social groups[96] and educational backgrounds.[97]

4.2 Survey Findings and Implications

Analysis of collected data brought several interesting findings, which can help us to better understand how the general public perceives the disgorgement of profits in the cases of using another person's copyrighted works. Data show that the harm caused and the profit gained are important factors for determining whether any sanction should be imposed in a particular case. Respondents plainly recognized the disgorgement of profits as an adequate remedy, but only in certain circumstances. The data analysis also pointed to several important cross-cultural differences between the countries in terms of respondents' approaches towards sanctioning and individual types of sanctions. Despite those national differences, the findings of this study undoubtedly demonstrate that copyright law is not only a construct created by law but also has deep roots in moral foundations.

4.2.1 Harm as an important factor for sanctioning

Collected data shows that respondents evidently accepted that it is wrong when someone uses another person's work of authorship without obtaining permission for doing so from the concerned person. This was reflected in the respondents' views on the need to impose some forms of sanctions for such usage, which could range from an apology, through to compensation, restitution and injunction, to criminal sanctions, such as fines and imprisonment.

The majority of respondents perceived an acute need to provide affected persons with remedies in two vignettes where it was expressly mentioned that such persons suffered harm, whether material or reputational. Those vignettes dealt with the use of a cartoon character[98] and photographic distortion.[99] These were then followed by vignettes which were silent on any harm and only mentioned whether the user gained any profit by using

---

[95] The US respondents were distributed among 50 federal states and District of Columbia; the Japanese respondents 47 prefectures, the French respondents 12 regions in mainland France and the German respondents 16 federal states.

[96] Respondents' composition as to their annual income was as follows: 438 (21.90%) out of 2,000 respondents earned less than EUR10,001; 297 (14.85%) respondents earned from EUR10,001 to EUR20,000; 315 (15.75%) respondents earned from EUR20,001 to EUR30,000; 245 (12.25%) respondents earned from EUR30,001 to EUR40,000; 192 (9.60%) respondents earned from EUR40,001 to EUR50,000; 154 (7.70%) respondents earned from EUR50,001 to EUR60,000; 172 (8.60%) respondents earned from EUR60,001 to EUR80,000; 88 (4.40%) respondents earned from EUR80,001 to EUR100,000; 51 (2.55%) respondents earned from EUR100,001 to EUR120,000; and 48 (2.40%) respondents earned more than EUR120,000.

[97] As to the highest level of achieved education, respondents were distributed as follows: 8 (0.4%) out of 2,000 respondents had completed only elementary school; 186 (9.30%) middle school; 581 (29.05%) high school; 425 (21.25%) vocational school; 506 (25.30%) a bachelor's degree; 223 (11.15%) a master's degree; 40 (2.00%) a doctorate; and 31 (1.55%) respondents used open-answer option "others".

[98] Overall, 79.9% of respondents deemed it necessary to impose some sanction in the cartoon character vignette.

[99] Overall, 79.7% of respondents considered it necessary to impose some sanction in the photograph distortion vignette.

another person's work of authorship. Those were the fanfiction and music sampling vignettes.[100]

Respondents were the least sensitive in the case of the video collage vignette.[101] Although it was explicitly stated in that vignette that the affected person suffered material or reputational harm, not as many respondents as in the two abovementioned vignettes perceived it necessary to impose any sanction in the case of such activity.

Two possible explanations arise for this difference. The first might be that video collage is quite a common activity in commercial TV broadcasting as well as on social networks and thus respondents might not have felt it to be as harmful as the two other vignettes where the harm factor was also encoded. This is also expressed in the lower level of wrongfulness perceived by respondents in this vignette.[102]

The second possible explanation might be that, in contrast to those two vignettes, the user's intention to achieve the presented consequences of their activities was not encoded into the video collage vignette. However, the soundness of this reason is undermined by the fact that the intention factor did not yield statistically significant results, except for the French respondents with regard to the photograph distortion vignette.[103]

4.2.2   Cross-cultural differences in sanctioning

Another aspect observed from the collected data regarding respondents' perception of the need to impose some form of sanctions for using another person's works of authorship is that there were considerable differences between individual countries. The Japanese respondents were most open to sanctioning,[104] followed by the French[105] and German[106] ones. At the other end of this spectrum were respondents from the US.[107]

---

[100]   Overall, 74.75% of respondents viewed it necessary to impose some sanction in the music sampling vignette, and 67.4% of respondents in the fanfiction vignette.

[101]   Overall, 64.45% of respondents perceived a need to impose some form of sanction in the video collage.

[102]   The respondents valued the wrongfulness of the video collage vignette on average as -0.431 ± 0.028 on a 5-point Likert-type scale from wrongful (-2) to rightful (2).

[103]   In France, difference in means regarding the intention factor in the photograph distortion vignette was statistically significant in the t-test, with its value being 0.138 ± 0.038 (N=500, $t(498)=3.6445$, $p<0.0005$).

[104]   In Japan, 435 (87.00%) out of 500 respondents deemed it necessary to impose some sanction in the presented variant of the fanfiction vignette; 448 (89.60%) respondents in the cartoon character vignette; 411 (82.20%) respondents in the music sampling vignette; 444 (88.80%) respondents in the photograph distortion vignette; and 419 (83.80%) respondents in the video collage vignette.

[105]   In France, 320 (64.00%) out of 500 respondents viewed it as necessary to impose some sanction in the presented variant of the fanfiction vignette; 390 (78.00%) respondents in the cartoon character vignette; 374 (74.80%) respondents in the music sampling vignette; 379 (75.80%) respondents in the photograph distortion vignette; and 328 (65.60%) respondents in the video collage vignette.

[106]   In Germany, 311 (62.20%) out of 500 respondents considered it necessary to impose some sanction in the presented variant of the fanfiction vignette; 393 (78.60%) respondents in the cartoon character vignette; 355 (71.00%) respondents in the music sampling vignette; 399 (79.80%) respondents in the photograph distortion vignette; and 280 (56.00%) respondents in the video collage vignette.

[107]   In the US, 282 (56.40%) out of 500 respondents deemed it necessary to impose some sanction in the presented variant of the fanfiction vignette; 367 (73.40%) respondents in the cartoon character vignette; 355 (71.00%) respondents in the music sampling vignette; 372 (74.40%) respondents in the photograph distortion vignette; and 262 (52.40%) respondents in the video collage vignette.

These differences might be explained by different approaches towards personal freedom of individuals and their position within society in the studied countries. As mentioned above, the US is commonly characterized by strong individualism and importance of personal freedom. It was thus anticipated that, unlike respondents from other countries, those from the US would be quite cautious in accepting the need to impose sanctions in the individual vignettes.

On the other hand, Japan is ordinarily viewed as a country with long and strong traditions of communitarianism, where membership of social groups and obedience towards an array of social norms are deemed to be vital. It was then expected that, contrary to other respondents, the Japanese participants would perceive many presented variants of vignettes as unacceptable conduct that would require some form of remedy.

Accordingly, respondents from France and Germany were somewhere in between those two extremes. In contrast to the US respondents, they accepted in more cases that restrictions should be imposed upon the personal freedom of individuals where another person's works have been used, but they were not as open to extensive constraints as the Japanese respondents were.

Furthermore, in the US, the respondent's age and gender was relevant in deciding whether any sanction should be imposed in the presented scenarios. These findings are consistent with previous studies from the US.[108] Differences in responses due to respondents' gender were also sometimes observed in Germany and Japan.

Older respondents in the US[109] were more inclined than younger ones to perceive the need to impose sanctions where another person's works have been used. In literature, an explanation for this is usually that younger respondents are not yet fully socialized.[110] Moreover, young people habitually challenge any established orders and institutions, including social norms.

In addition, as mentioned above, male respondents in the US[111] and, in certain circumstances and to an extent in Germany[112] and Japan,[113] also had a lower tendency to perceive

---

[108] See, eg, Eric Chiang and Djeto Assane, 'Software Copyright Infringement among College Students' (2002) 34 Appl Econ 157, 161–62.

[109] In the US, differences in means between those respondents who were under 30 years old and the others in the case of sanctioning were statistically significant in the *t*-test with regard to three vignettes, with their values as follows: 0.164 ± 0.040 (N=500, $t(498)=4.0686$, $p<0.0005$) in the music sampling vignette; 0.103 ± 0.039 (N=500, $t(498)=2.6305$, $p<0.01$) in the photograph distortion vignette; and 0.108 ± 0.045 (N=500, $t(498)=2.4047$, $p<0.05$) in the video collage vignette.

[110] See, eg, Chiang and Assane (n 108) 161–64; Rajiv K Sinha and Naomi Mandel, 'Preventing Digital Music Piracy: The Carrot or the Stick?' (2008) 72 J Mark 1, 12.

[111] In the US, differences in means regarding respondents' gender in the case of sanctioning were statistically significant in the *t*-test, with their values as follows: 0.126 ± 0.044 (N=500, $t(498)=2.8478$, $p<0.005$) in the fanfiction vignette; 0.078 ± 0.039 (N=500, $t(498)=1.9677$, $p<0.05$) in the cartoon character vignette; 0.101 ± 0.040 (N=500, $t(498)=2.5003$, $p<0.05$) in the music sampling vignette; 0.082 ± 0.039 (N=500, $t(498)=2.1022$, $p<0.05$) in the photograph distortion vignette; and 0.117 ± 0.044 (N=500, $t(498)=2.6226$, $p<0.01$) in the video collage vignette.

[112] In Germany, several differences in means regarding respondents' gender in the case of sanctioning were statistically significant in the *t*-test, with their values as follows: 0.111 ± 0.040 (N=500, $t(498)=2.7593$, $p<0.01$) in the music sampling vignette; and 0.169 ± 0.044 (N=500, $t(498)=3.8543$, $p<0.0005$) in the video collage vignette.

[113] In Japan, difference in means regarding respondents' gender in the case of sanctioning was statistically significant in the *t*-test only in the music sampling vignette, with its value being 0.070 ± 0.034

the need to impose any sanction for using another person's works. This can be explained by the fact that males tend to be more disagreeable[114] and inclined to commit more violent criminal acts than females.[115] They might be therefore more sensitive to restrictions on their personal freedom and to the imposition of sanctions.

However, no comparable correlations could be observed in other studied countries. There are two possible explanations for this finding with regard to respondents' gender. The first reason might stem from the fact that individualism and personal freedom play a more important role in the US than in the other countries, with males potentially more sensitive to any interference with their personal freedom. The second reason might be that males' sensitivity is increased by the level of inequality within society, this being another crucial difference between the studied countries.[116]

4.2.3   Moral foundations of copyright law

Despite the abovementioned differences between the four countries, it is evident that in each, various uses of another person's works of authorship are viewed, in certain circumstances, as wrongs and thus they might require some remedies to re-establish the original balance of interests between the concerned parties. Copyright law is therefore clearly based upon moral foundations in social norms recognized by the general public,[117] and is not only a construct created by law in order to generate a social bargain between creators and the users of their literary and other artistic creations.[118] Apparently, the public perceives that it is wrong to use another person's work of authorship unless there are certain mitigating circumstances, such as in cases of parody or criticism.[119]

(N=500, $t(498)$=2.0598, $p<0.05$).

[114]   See, eg, Alan Feingold, 'Gender Differences in Personality: A Meta-Analysis' (1994) 116 Psychol Bull 429, 446–50; Paul T Costa Jr, Antonio Terracciano and Robert R McCrae, 'Gender Differences in Personality Traits across Cultures: Robust and Surprising Findings' (2001) 81 J Pers Soc Psychol 322, 328.

[115]   See, eg, Richard B Freeman, 'Why Do So Many Young American Men Commit Crimes and What Might We Do about It?' (1996) 10 J Econ Perspect 25; Satoshi Kanazawa and Mary C Still, 'Why Men Commit Crimes (and Why They Desist)' (2000) 18 Sociol Theory 434.

[116]   Income inequality Gini coefficients of equivalized disposable income in the studied countries were in the year of 2020 as follows: 46.9 in the US; 33.4 in Japan; 30.5 in Germany; and 29.3 in France. See also Robert de Vries, Samuel Gosling and Jeff Potter, 'Income Inequality and Personality: Are Less Equal U.S. States Less Agreeable?' (2011) 72 Soc Sci Med 1978, 1983–84 (finding that "populations of states with a greater degree of income inequality have significantly lower average levels of Agreeableness").

[117]   For different ways in which intellectual property rights can be justified by deontological theories, see, eg, Justin Hughes, 'The Philosophy of Intellectual Property' (1988) 77 Georgetown LJ 287; Wendy J Gordon, 'A Property Right in Self-Expression: Equality and Individualism in the Natural Law of Intellectual Property' (1993) 102 Yale LJ 1533, 1540–83; Peter Drahos, *A Philosophy of Intellectual Property* (Routledge 1996); William Fisher, 'Theories of Intellectual Property' in Stephen R Munzer (ed), *New Essays in the Legal and Political Theory of Property* (CUP 2001) 168, 184–92.

[118]   For ways in which intellectual property rights can be justified by utilitarian theories, see, eg, Fisher (n 117) 177–84; William M Landes and Richard A Posner, *The Economic Structure of Intellectual Property Law* (Belknap Press 2003) 11–24; Mark A Lemley, 'Ex Ante versus Ex Post Justifications for Intellectual Property' (2004) 71 U Chi L Rev 129.

[119]   Difference in means regarding the humorousness factor in the cases of wrongfulness of the fanfiction vignette was statistically significant in the t-test, with its value being 0.220±0.052 (N=2,000, $t(1,998)$=4.2374, $p<0.0005$) with regard to the fanfiction vignette.

This understanding is also reflected in another finding obtained by analysing the collected data. When it was mentioned that the user of another person's work had gained some profit, there was a higher chance that respondents found it appropriate to impose some form of sanction. But this was only one of several factors.

The strongest factor was whether respondents considered the presented activities to be wrongful. Although there might be a certain overlap between respondents' answers about sanctioning and wrongfulness of the presented scenarios, each decision correlated with partially different variables. For instance, while humorousness of the user's derivative work was a mitigating factor for both decisions, the gained benefit factor correlated mainly with a tendency to favour the imposition of remedies.[120] Respondents thus tended to answer that a remedy is necessary, if they perceived the use of another person's work as wrongful and if the user gained profit by such activity. Consequently, they clearly deemed that wrongdoers should not benefit from their wrongs and so this rule also has strong moral foundations.

4.2.4 Disgorgement of wrongful gains

Collected data demonstrate that although respondents deemed disgorgement of profits an appropriate remedy in certain cases,[121] it was not as important as several other remedies. A significant difference was observed between disgorgement of profits and a triad of most appropriate remedies, that is, damage compensation,[122] injunction[123] and apology.[124]

Respondents plainly considered that when an author of the copyrighted work, or another concerned copyright holder, sustains harm when their work is used by a third party, they should be compensated for such harm. In addition, the respondents deemed that nobody

---

[120] Differences in means regarding the benefit factor in the cases of sanctioning were statistically significant in the *t*-test, with their values as follows: 0.096±0.021 (N=2,000, $t(1,998)$=4.6030, $p<0.0005$) with regard to the fanfiction vignette; 0.041±0.018 (N=2,000, $t(1,998)$=2.2814, $p<0.05$) with regard to the cartoon character vignette; 0.111±0.019 (N=2,000, $t(1,998)$=5.7619, $p<0.0005$) with regard to the music sampling vignette; 0.056±0.018 (N=2,000, $t(1,998)$=3.1175, $p<0.005$) with regard to the photograph distortion; and 0.073±0.021 (N=2,000, $t(1,998)$=3.4220, $p<0.001$) with regard to the video collage vignette.

[121] In all the studied countries, 362 (26.85%) out of 1,348 respondents, who deemed it necessary to impose some sanction in the presented variant of the fanfiction vignette, found disgorgement of profits an appropriate remedy; 493 (30.85%) out of 1,598 respondents in the cartoon character vignette; 484 (32.37%) out of 1,495 respondents in the music sampling vignette; 544 (34.13%) out of 1,594 respondents in the photograph distortion vignette; and 422 (32.74%) out of 1,289 respondents in the video collage vignette.

[122] In all the studied countries, 818 (60.68%) out of 1,348 respondents, who deemed it necessary to impose some sanction in the presented variant of the fanfiction vignette, found compensatory damages an appropriate remedy; 961 (60.14%) out of 1,598 respondents in the cartoon character vignette; 835 (55.85%) out of 1,495 respondents in the music sampling vignette; 982 (61.61%) out of 1,594 respondents in the photograph distortion vignette; and 728 (56.48%) out of 1,289 respondents in the video collage vignette.

[123] In all the studied countries, 638 (47.33%) out of 1,348 respondents, who deemed it necessary to impose some sanction in the presented variant of the fanfiction vignette, found injunction an appropriate remedy; 871 (54.51%) out of 1,598 respondents in the cartoon character vignette; 787 (52.64%) out of 1,495 respondents in the music sampling vignette; 995 (62.42%) out of 1,594 respondents in the photograph distortion vignette; and 861 (66.80%) out of 1,289 respondents in the video collage vignette.

[124] In all the studied countries, 730 (54.15%) out of 1,348 respondents, who deemed it necessary to impose some sanction in the presented variant of the fanfiction vignette, found apology an appropriate remedy; 924 (57.82%) out of 1,598 respondents in the cartoon character vignette; 855 (57.19%) out of 1,495 respondents in the music sampling vignette; 987 (61.92%) out of 1,594 respondents in the photograph distortion vignette; and 795 (61.68%) out of 1,289 respondents in the video collage vignette.

should be allowed to continue to carry out wrongful activities. Moreover, they perceived the importance of apology in such interactions.

On the other hand, although respondents recognized that disgorgement of profit might be an appropriate remedy, its use was considered to be limited to certain circumstances. Its use in individual scenarios did not, however, correlate with the benefit factor coded into individual vignettes.[125] Respondents did not feel that any profit gained by using another person's work of authorship should be transferred to the copyright holder concerned.

Conversely, disgorgement of profits was correlated with the respondents' perception of the wrongfulness of the presented scenarios.[126] The more wrongful the presented vignette was perceived by a respondent, the higher was the chance that disgorgement of profits was deemed a suitable remedy. It should be noted here that when a respondent actively participated in social networks, that is, they shared their photos, music or videos with others via social networks, they tended to consider disgorgement of profits as a less appropriate measure.[127]

In addition, notable differences between approaches towards disgorgement of profits in the studied countries were observed. The most open towards this form of remedy were respondents from the US,[128] followed by those from Germany[129] and France.[130]

---

[125] Differences in means regarding the benefit factor in the cases of imposing the disgorgement of profits were not statistically significant in the t-test, except for the following results: 0.101 ± 0.050 (N=320, $t(318)=2.0026$, $p<0.05$) with regard to the fanfiction vignette in France; 0.109 ± 0.051 (N=311, $t(309)=2.1306$, $p<0.05$) with regard to the fanfiction vignette in Germany; and 0.227 ± 0.050 (N=372, $t(370)=4.5221$, $p<0.0005$) with regard to the photograph distortion vignette in the US.

[126] Differences in means between those, who found presented variants of vignettes at least a bit wrongful, and the other respondents were statistically significant in the t-test, with their values as follows: 0.147 ± 0.027 (N=1,348, $t(1346)=5.4766$, $p<0.0005$) in the fanfiction vignette; 0.081 ± 0.028 (N=1,598, $t(1,596)=2.8651$, $p<0.005$) in the cartoon character vignette; 0.104 ± 0.027 (N=1,495, $t(1,493)=3.8492$, $p<0.0005$) in the music sampling vignette; 0.090 ± 0.029 (N=1,594, $t(1,592)=3.1410$, $p<0.005$) in the photograph distortion vignette; and 0.096 ± 0.029 (N=1,289, $t(1,287)=3.3393$, $p<0.001$) in the video collage vignette.

[127] Differences in means between those, who never uploaded any video to YouTube or similar online platforms, and the other respondents were statistically significant in the t-test, with their values as follows: 0.103 ± 0.027 (N=1,598, $t(1,596)=3.8825$, $p<0.0005$) in the cartoon character vignette; 0.112 ± 0.027 (N=1,495, $t(1,493)=4.1224$, $p<0.0005$) in the music sampling vignette; and 0.097 ± 0.030 (N=1,289, $t(1,287)=3.2627$, $p<0.005$) in the video collage vignette.

[128] In the US, 97 (34.40%) out of 282 respondents, who deemed it necessary to impose some sanction in the presented variant of the fanfiction vignette, found disgorgement of profits an appropriate remedy; 160 (43.60%) out of 367 respondents in the cartoon character vignette; 152 (42.82%) out of 355 respondents in the music sampling vignette; 162 (43.55%) out of 372 respondents in the photograph distortion vignette; and 105 (40.08%) out of 262 respondents in the video collage vignette.

[129] In Germany, 88 (28.30%) out of 311 respondents, who deemed it necessary to impose some sanction in the presented variant of the fanfiction vignette, found disgorgement of profits an appropriate remedy; 132 (33.59%) out of 393 respondents in the cartoon character vignette; 126 (35.49%) out of 355 respondents in the music sampling vignette; 154 (38.60%) out of 399 respondents in the photograph distortion vignette; and 100 (35.71%) out of 280 respondents in the video collage vignette.

[130] In France, 88 (27.50%) out of 320 respondents, who deemed it necessary to impose some sanction in the presented variant of the fanfiction vignette, found disgorgement of profits an appropriate remedy; 123 (31.54%) out of 390 respondents in the cartoon character vignette; 124 (33.16%) out of 374 respondents in the music sampling vignette; 123 (32.45%) out of 379 respondents in the photograph distortion vignette; and 107 (32.62%) out of 328 respondents in the video collage vignette.

The most limited acceptance was witnessed in Japan.[131]

This demonstrates there are notable cultural differences between the four countries in terms of understanding the role of individual remedies. While disgorgement of profits, which allows the redistribution of wealth between concerned parties, was viewed as appropriate by more respondents from the US than those from other countries studied, remedies such as apology, termination of wrongful activities and compensation, which reconstitute the original state, peace and harmony between the parties, were important to more of the respondents from Japan.[132] As expected, respondents from both European countries were found somewhere between those two extremes.

To sum up, despite national differences between the studied countries, respondents clearly recognized disgorgement of profits as an appropriate remedy in addition to damages, injunction and apology, but only when a particular scenario was deemed by them to be wrongful.

5. CONCLUSION

As previous analysis showed, the general public undoubtedly recognizes that nobody should benefit from wrongs, that is, if a person gains profit from wrongfully using another person's work of authorship, the former should be obliged to transfer such profit to the latter. However, it does not mean that any profit gained from the use of another person's copyrighted work should be automatically subject to the disgorgement of profits. Here, the triggering moment is the commission of a wrong and not just any use of a copyrighted work without the appropriate licence.

Consequently, the general public also plainly deems it possible to use other people's works freely without the need to obtain any prior permissions from, and to share any gained profits with, the concerned persons in certain circumstances. The public evidently distinguishes between public and private uses on the one hand and between literary copying and transformative uses on the other. While the public undoubtedly perceives that the former uses in those two sets are wrongful activities, the latter are viewed as less wrongful and as not requiring the imposition of any sanctions.

Finally, as expected, several important differences between the four studied countries were observed. The differences appear to stem from distinctive approaches towards personal freedom and the role of an individual within society in those countries. While respondents from countries valuing individualism stress the importance of personal freedom and min-

---

[131] In Japan, 89 (20.46%) out of 435 respondents, who deemed it necessary to impose some sanction in the presented variant of the fanfiction vignette, found disgorgement of profits an appropriate remedy; 78 (17.41%) out of 448 respondents in the cartoon character vignette; 82 (19.95%) out of 411 respondents in the music sampling vignette; 105 (23.65%) out of 444 respondents in the photograph distortion vignette; and 110 (26.25%) out of 419 respondents in the video collage vignette.

[132] In Japan, 282 (64.83%), 266 (61.15%) and 264 (60.69%) out of 435 respondents, who deemed it necessary to impose some sanction in the presented variant of the fanfiction vignette, found apology, injunction and compensation, respectively, as appropriate remedies; 311 (69.42%), 281 (62.72%) and 263 (58.71%) out of 448 respondents in the cartoon character vignette; 281 (68.37%), 269 (65.45%) and 192 (46.72%) out of 411 respondents in the music sampling vignette; 315 (70.95%), 318 (71.62%) and 269 (60.59%) out of 444 respondents in the photograph distortion vignette; and 217 (64.68%), 325 (77.57%) and 229 (54.65%) out of 419 respondents in the video collage vignette.

imize any possible restrictions, those from countries in which communitarianism prevails emphasize the role of an individual within society and the need to maintain social order and harmony.

PART IV

TRADEMARKS

12. The story of USPTO trademark data

Deborah R. Gerhardt and Jon J. Lee

The great advantage of empirical research is that it shows patterns. Instead of hearing one voice, empirical research features the chorus of all voices (or a representative sample) together. A single voice may be typical or extraordinary—we cannot know without listening to it in relation to others. Empirical studies offer this high-level perspective. The entire chorus offers a blend of the entire population, and by pulling out some sections we can see patterns in discrete categories. Applying this strategy to new datasets can help us discern trends. By learning which variables are linked to success and failure, research can prompt conversations that drive policy decisions.

Over the past decade, United States federal trademark prosecution data has made it possible to meaningfully inform intellectual property scholarship, law, and policy. This chapter begins with an overview of the dual state and federal protection schemes for trademarks in the United States, explains the significant benefits of federal trademark registration, and then shares discoveries found through empirical research since the United States Patent and Trademark Office ("USPTO") made its trademark application and registration data available in 2010.

This chapter first sets the foundation for understanding empirical trademark research. We begin with the basic contours of U.S. trademark protection and then describe the USPTO, its trademark registration process, and the benefits gained by applicants who secure trademark rights through federal registration. Next, we survey prior empirical research conducted on trademark registration and litigation. Finally, using a newly released USPTO dataset, we empirically analyze trademark registration data to update the prior research and clarify some of the important variables that correlate with success in trademark prosecution.

The USPTO is a federal government agency that issues U.S. patents and registers trademarks. Congress authorized the USPTO to administer patents to further the goal in Article I, Section 8, Clause 8 of the United States Constitution, of promoting "the Progress of Science and useful Arts, by securing for limited Times to Authors and Inventors the exclusive Right to their respective Writings and Discoveries." Trademark registration is premised on Congressional power to regulate interstate commerce under Article I, Section 8, Clause 3 of the Constitution. Pursuant to these powers, Congress created the USPTO as a division of the Department of Commerce.

In addition to administering patents and trademarks, the USPTO advises the President of the United States, the Secretary of Commerce, and other U.S. officials on intellectual property law and policy to promote innovation through stronger and more effective IP protection. On its website (http://www.uspto.gov) the agency states that it "furthers effective IP protection for U.S. innovators and entrepreneurs worldwide by working with other agencies to secure strong IP provisions in free trade and other international agreements. It also provides training, education, and capacity building programs designed to foster respect for IP and encourage the development of strong IP enforcement regimes by U.S. trading partners."[1]

The USPTO employs more than 10,000 people. Its main offices span multiple interconnected buildings in Alexandria, Virginia. These offices house administrative staff, patent and trademark examiners, engineers, scientists, economists, analysts, librarians, and computer scientists. On its ground floor, one can visit a small museum and a gift shop with merchandise for patent and trademark fans. The USPTO also has regional offices in Dallas, Denver, Detroit, and San Jose. At the end of the 2021 fiscal year, the USPTO employed 8,073 patent examiners, 662 trademark examining attorneys, and 27 administrative trademark judges.

1.   OVERVIEW OF UNITED STATES TRADEMARK LAW

A trademark is a symbol that identifies a product or service as coming from a particular source in a way that distinguishes that source from its competition. A symbol may be protected as a trademark only if it is distinctive enough "to identify and distinguish" goods or services, "from those manufactured or sold by others and to indicate the source of the goods, even if that source is unknown."[2] Distinctiveness works as follows. When we see a shoe marked with the word "Nike" or its iconic swoosh, we understand that the shoe comes from Nike, Inc. and not one of its competitors. In addition to words and logos, U.S. law recognizes that nontraditional subject matter, such as product design, décor, color, and sound, may also serve as trademarks.

Trademarks are an especially durable form of intellectual property in the United States. Most forms of intellectual property have set end dates. All copyrights and patents enter the public domain after their term of protection expires, and trade secrets lose their protection upon disclosure. Trademarks are different. Trademark rights last as long as a mark's owner continues to use the symbol in commerce.[3] While steps must be taken to secure other forms of intellectual property, trademark rights arise through use in commerce, even if the holder does not seek registration.[4] While patent and copyright law is exclusively federal, for trademarks, federal and state statutes and common law protect mark owners against infringement, unfair

---

[1]   *About Us*, U.S. PATENT & TRADEMARK OFFICE, https://www.uspto.gov/about-us (last visited June 13, 2022).

[2]   15 U.S.C. § 1127.

[3]   15 U.S.C. § 1064 (stating when a trademark may be cancelled); *id.* §§ 1058–59 (laying out the duration and renewal terms that govern federal trademarks); McAirlaids, Inc. v. Kimberly-Clark Corp., 756 F.3d 307, 310 (4th Cir. 2014) (stating that trademark law can provide indefinite protection unlike patent law which provides protection for only a limited period); W.T. Rogers Co. v. Keene, 778 F.2d 334, 337 (7th Cir. 1985) (explaining that, upon certain conditions, trademarks may provide "an indefinite term of protection"); Saratoga Vichy Spring Co. v. Lehman, 625 F.2d 1037, 1043–44 (2d Cir. 1980) (discussing the abandonment of a trademark); King-Seeley Thermos Co. v. Aladdin Indus., 321 F.2d 577, 579 (2d Cir. 1963) (noting that, through the holder's lack of care, the trademark "Thermos" became a generic term and entered the public domain); Bayer Co. v. United Drug Co., 272 F. 505, 510–15 (S.D.N.Y. 1921) (finding that the trademark "Aspirin" fell into the public domain due, in part, to the trademark holders' actions). Trademark owners must take some additional steps, such as periodically certifying continued use, in order to maintain federal registration. 15 U.S.C. §§ 1058–59.

[4]   15 U.S.C. § 1125 (providing a federal cause of action for infringement and dilution for all marks, including those not having federal registration).

competition, dilution, false advertising, use of their marks in domain names, and harm to business reputation.[5]

The common law of trademarks is founded on both the idea of protecting business investment in reputational symbols and minimizing consumer deception.[6] Depending on the jurisdiction, state trademark protection is limited to the state or geographic area of use within it.[7] At common law, trademark rights attach when one first uses a mark in commerce.[8] If two U.S. businesses develop the same mark in good faith on similar products but in different locations, each may have rights to the mark in their respective geographic territory.[9] As soon as the two uses overlap, conflicts may arise over who has superior rights. Generally, the first user in the market has priority and may exclude the later user.[10] Local or regional brand owners may register their marks in individual states, but state trademark registration provides little value beyond common law protection obtained automatically through use in commerce.[11]

Although the first federal trademark law was enacted in 1870, the current statutory scheme, known as the Lanham Act, was enacted in 1946. The Lanham Act does not exclude any subject matter that may function as a mark on account of its nature. The definition states that a mark may consist of "*any* word, name, symbol, or device, or any combination" of these elements.[12] While not limited in subject matter, the definition narrows protectible marks to symbols that are distinctive, used in commerce, and not barred by the Lanham Act. This use in commerce requirement differentiates United States law from many other nations that extend trademark rights to entities on a first to file basis (like internet domain names) regardless of whether a mark has ever been used in commerce.

---

[5]   *See id.* (providing for various federal causes of action); *see also* J. THOMAS MCCARTHY, 3 MCCARTHY ON TRADEMARKS AND UNFAIR COMPETITION § 22:1.50, Westlaw (5th ed. database updated Jun. 2022) (discussing state law causes of action and their relationship to Lanham Act).

[6]   *See* J. THOMAS MCCARTHY, 1 MCCARTHY ON TRADEMARKS AND UNFAIR COMPETITION § 2:1, Westlaw (5th ed. database updated Jun. 2022) (discussing the dual goals of trademark law).

[7]   15 U.S.C. § 1065 (noting the existence of state trademarks); Dorpan, S.L. v. Hotel Melia, Inc., 728 F.3d 55, 62 (1st Cir. 2013) ("Trademark users may still gain state law rights to use a trademark either through registration with a state government or through use in that state"); MCCARTHY, *supra* note 5 (explaining that the protection extended by state trademarks is limited to the boundaries of the state or the geographic region of the mark's use).

[8]   *See* United Drug Co. v. Theodore Rectanus Co., 248 U.S. 90, 100 (1918) ("Undoubtedly, the general rule is that, as between conflicting claimants to the right to use the same mark, priority of appropriation determines the question"); *see also* Emergency One, Inc. v. Am. Fire Eagle Engine Co., 332 F.3d 264, 267 (4th Cir. 2003).

[9]   *See* Hanover Star Milling Co. v. Metcalf, 240 U.S. 403, 415 (1916) ("But where two parties independently are employing the same mark upon goods of the same class, but in separate markets wholly remote the one from the other, the question of prior appropriation is legally insignificant; unless ... the second adopter has selected the mark with some design inimical to the interests of the first user ..."); *see also* J. THOMAS MCCARTHY, 5 MCCARTHY ON TRADEMARKS AND UNFAIR COMPETITION § 26:3, Westlaw (5th ed. database updated Jun. 2022).

[10]   *See* Emergency One, 332 F.3d at 267 ("When more than one user claims the exclusive right to use an unregistered trademark, priority is determined by 'the first actual use of [the] mark in a genuine commercial transaction'"); *see also* MCCARTHY, *supra* note 5.

[11]   McCarthy, *supra* note 5.

[12]   15 U.S.C. § 1127 (emphasis added).

Federal trademark applicants must complete a multi-page online form and pay an application fee.[13] An applicant must identify the specific symbol it plans to use in connection with a concrete set of goods and services. Legal counsel experienced with navigating the USPTO registration system may be especially helpful in selecting a mark that meets the statutory requirements and completing the application in a way that minimizes the chance that the application will prompt an objection from a USPTO trademark examiner.

Applicants may choose among one of five filing bases. Section 1(a), known as "use or use-based," is for applicants who have already used their mark in commerce when the application is filed.[14] Section 1(b), the "intent to use" or "ITU" basis, was added as part of the Trademark Law Revision Act of 1988 for applicants who have a bona fide intent to use a mark in commerce but have not yet done so.[15] Although at first glance the addition of this filing basis might appear to extend trademark protection to marks prior to their use, that is not the case because the mark cannot be registered until the applicant presents evidence of use.[16] The advantage of an ITU filing is that it enables applicants to receive nationwide priority for the mark as of the filing date even if use has not yet begun.

The other three filing bases may be used by applicants who have applied to register their marks abroad. Section 44(e), referred to as "foreign registration," may be selected by applicants who obtain an earlier trademark registration in another country.[17] When an application is based on a foreign registration, USPTO registration may be obtained without proof of use in United States commerce if the applicant expresses a bona fide intent to do so in the future.[18] If foreign registration is secured in a country that does not have a use in commerce requirement, the applicant may avoid demonstrating use to the USPTO until they are required to file a Section 8 declaration of use, which is not due until a mark has been registered in the United States for five years.[19]

Section 44(d), referred to as "foreign priority," may be used by applicants who previously applied for trademark registration in another country.[20] If the USPTO application was filed within six months of the foreign application filing date, the applicant will have nationwide priority from the date on which the foreign application was filed.[21] Because Section 44(d) is not an independent basis for registration, applicants must include another filing basis prior to registration.

Section 66(a), referred to as "Madrid," became available in 2003 to bring the United States in compliance with the Madrid Protocol and allows marks protected by international trade-

---

[13] *Trademark Process*, U.S. PATENT & TRADEMARK OFFICE, https:// www .uspto .gov/ trademarks -getting -started/trademark-process (last visited June 13, 2022). The fee ranges from $100 to $500 for each mark in each class of goods and services. *USPTO Fee Schedule*, U.S. PATENT & TRADEMARK OFFICE, https:// www .uspto .gov/ learning -and -resources/ fees -and -payment/ uspto -fee -schedule #Trademark %20Fees (last visited June 13, 2022).
[14] 15 U.S.C. § 1051(a).
[15] *See generally* Pub. L. No. 100-667 (Nov. 16, 1988) (Trademark Law Revision Act).
[16] *See* 15 U.S.C. § 1051(b)(3).
[17] 15 U.S.C. § 1126(e).
[18] *Id.*
[19] *See* 15 U.S.C. § 1058(a). A trademark registered pursuant to Section 44(e) could not be enforced until it had been used in commerce, however, and three years of nonuse would constitute prima facie evidence of abandonment. *See id.* § 1127.
[20] 15 U.S.C. § 1126(d).
[21] *Id.*

mark registrations to have that protection extended to the United States.[22] As with the foreign registration filing basis, applicants relying on Madrid need not demonstrate use in the United States prior to registration if they attest to a bona fide intent to commence use in the near future.[23] Unlike the other filing bases, the Madrid basis cannot be combined with any of the other four,[24] which means that scope of the protection will mirror that conferred by the other country.[25]

To register a trademark, applicants must overcome two hurdles: examination by the USPTO and potential opposition by third parties. After an application is submitted, the USPTO assigns it a serial number and uploads the applicant's information into the USPTO's publicly available USPTO online database, the Trademark Electronic Search System ("TESS").[26] Once an application appears in TESS, any member of the public can follow its progress. Next, a USPTO trademark examiner is assigned to review the application, identify any defects, and search for confusingly similar pending or registered marks that may have priority.[27] In addition to establishing use, an applicant must provide additional information required by Section 1 of the Lanham Act which identifies the necessary components of a trademark application. These include "specification of the applicant's domicile and citizenship, the goods in connection with which the application has a bona fide intention to use the mark, and a drawing of the mark."[28]

If an applicant fails to satisfy any requirement, the trademark examiner will issue an office action and afford the applicant time to remedy the defect.[29] Before proceeding to registration, the applicant must amend the application or explain why the examiner's objection was unwarranted.[30] If the applicant provides no response or an unsatisfactory one, the application will not proceed further. If the applicant satisfies the trademark examiner, which may involve multiple rounds of office actions and responses, the mark is published in the USPTO's Official Gazette.[31]

Publication marks success in the USPTO's examination of the application but opens the second window of vulnerability.[32] Once a mark is published, third parties have thirty days in which to oppose the application. Any third party who thinks it may be harmed if the mark is registered may initiate an opposition proceeding. While most applications receive at least one office action, only about 3% are challenged through opposition proceedings.[33] If no opposition is filed (or if the applicant responds, and the USPTO agrees with the applicant), marks filed on a use basis may proceed immediately to registration.[34] ITU applicants must complete an

---

[22]   15 U.S.C. § 1141e(a).
[23]   *See* 15 U.S.C. § 1141f(a).
[24]   37 C.F.R. §§ 2.34(b), 2.35(a).
[25]   *See* John M. Murphy, *Demystifying the Madrid Protocol*, 2 Nw. J. Tech. & Intell. Prop. 2, 15 (2004) (discussing the advantages and disadvantages of Madrid filings).
[26]   *Trademark Electronic Search System (TESS)*, U.S. Patent & Trademark Office, https://tmsearch.uspto.gov/bin/gate.exe?f=login&p_lang=english&p_d=trmk (last visited Jun. 7, 2022).
[27]   *Trademark Process, supra* note 13.
[28]   15 U.S.C. § 1051(a)(2).
[29]   *Trademark Process, supra* note 13.
[30]   *Id.*
[31]   *Id.*
[32]   *Id.*
[33]   Deborah R. Gerhardt & Jon P. McClanahan, *Do Trademark Lawyers Matter?*, 16 Stan. Tech. L. Rev. 583, 620 (2013).
[34]   *See* 15 U.S.C. § 1058.

additional step. After publication, the USPTO will issue a "Notice of Allowance," indicating that registration will occur once the applicant submits evidence of use in commerce.[35] That evidence will be reviewed before a registration certificate is issued to make sure the use matches the claims in the application and that an appropriate specimen supports the use.[36] The registration process is illustrated in Figure 12.1.

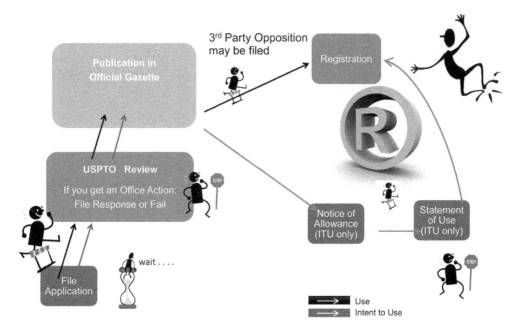

Figure 12.1   *USPTO trademark registration process*

Section 2 of the Lanham Act contains substantive limits on trademark protection, by enumerating a list of bars to registration. For example, Section 2(a) prohibits registration of deceptive marks.[37] Deceptiveness may not always be as straightforward as one might imagine because a symbol's meaning may change over time. For example, environmental friendliness was not always an important consideration to American consumers. In the twentieth century, a "green" designation for lawn care may have been deemed merely descriptive, and registrable in connection with other distinctive words. The meaning of "green" services evolved to connote special attention to environmental sustainability, and the USPTO may flag a mark as deceptive if it includes the word "green" but does not offer products or services designed to protect the environment.[38] Similarly, Section 2(e)(3) prohibits the registration of trademarks

---

[35]   *See* 15 U.S.C. §§ 1051(b), 1063(b)(2).
[36]   15 U.S.C. § 1051(d).
[37]   15 U.S.C. § 1052(a).
[38]   *See* David E. Adelman & Graeme W. Austin, *Trademarks and Private Environmental Governance*, 93 Notre Dame L. Rev. 709, 742–43 (2017) (discussing TTAB's refusal to register "GREEN SEAL" as a trademark "because the applicant did not provide any evidence that the products were environmentally friendly").

that are primarily geographically misdescriptive, a statutory bar that was added in connection with implementation of the North American Free Trade Agreement (NAFTA).[39] Section 2(d) is one of the most common bars used to thwart registration and is cited if an examining attorney views an applicant's mark as confusingly similar to another already present in the USPTO trademark database.[40]

Some registration bars were recently declared unconstitutional. Until 2017, the Lanham Act prohibited registration of any mark that "may disparage ... persons ... or bring them into contempt, or disrepute."[41] In *Matal v. Tam* an Asian-American electronic dance band sought to register the "THE SLANTS" for entertainment services. The USPTO refused registration after concluding that "slants" may disparage people of Asian descent. Tam's appeal ultimately made its way to the United States Supreme Court which unanimously held in his favor. In ruling that the disparagement clause violated the First Amendment, the Supreme Court found that "trademarks are private, not government speech," and viewpoint-based limits on federal registration are impermissible.[42] Soon afterwards, the Supreme Court held that barring registration of "immoral" and "scandalous" marks also violated an applicant's First Amendment right to freedom of expression and invalidated that portion of Section 2(a) as well.[43]

2.   BENEFITS OF FEDERAL TRADEMARK REGISTRATION

Brand owners can significantly expand the geographic scope, means for maintaining market distinctiveness, and economic value of their marks through federal registration. Although registration is not necessary to have trademark protection, mark owners often seek to buttress their rights by registering their marks with the USPTO.[44] Once registration is achieved, it must be renewed regularly with payment of a fee and a Section 8 declaration attesting to continued use.[45] Federal registration confers significant benefits on mark owners by augmenting protection, minimizing costs, and strengthening the economic value of a mark.

Nationwide protection is one of the primary benefits of federal trademark registration. Federal registration confers priority throughout the United States, even if the mark is not

---

[39]   15 U.S.C. § 1052(e)(3); *see also* In re California Innovations, Inc., 329 F.3d 1334, 1337–39 (Fed. Cir. 2003) (discussing revisions to the Lanham Act due to NAFTA and their impact on the geographic misdescriptiveness determination).

[40]   *See* Possible Grounds for Refusal of a Mark, U.S. PAT. & TRADEMARK OFF., https://www.uspto.gov/trademark/additional-guidance-and-resources/possible-grounds-refusal-mark, https://perma.cc/6E3L-BJ85, accessed 6 April 2021.

[41]   *See* 15 U.S.C. § 1052(a); Stephen R. Baird, *Moral Intervention in the Trademark Arena: Banning the Registration of Scandalous or Immoral Trademarks*, 83 TRADEMARK REP. 661, 663 (1993); *see also* Rosemary Coombe, *Marking Difference in American Commerce: Trademarks and Alterity at Century's End*, 19 POL. & LEGAL ANTHROPOLOGY REV. 105, 109–12 (1996).

[42]   Matal v. Tam, 137 S. Ct. 1744, 1748 (2017).

[43]   Iancu v. Brunetti, 139 S. Ct. 2294, 2302 (2018).

[44]   *See, e.g.*, 15 U.S.C. § 1057(b) (presumption of validity); *id.* § 1065 (incontestability); *id.* § 1117; *id.* § 1121; B & B Hardware, Inc. v. Hargis Indus., Inc., 575 U.S. 138, 142 (2015) ("Registration is significant. The Lanham Act confers 'important legal rights and benefits' on trademark owners who register their marks") (internal citations omitted); *In re* Brunetti, 877 F.3d 1330, 1344 (Fed. Cir. 2017), *aff'd sub nom.* Iancu v. Brunetti, 139 S. Ct. 2294 (2019) (listing benefits).

[45]   *See* 15 U.S.C. §§ 1058–59; *Trademark Process*, *supra* note 13.

being used nationwide.[46] In this way, it streamlines priority battles by giving the first registrant nationwide priority without having to prove first use in a particular geographic market. Therefore, federal registration may be more cost effective and efficient than securing rights through actual expansion into new territories. A limited area exception provides some protection to mark users who do not seek registration.[47] For example, when two firms develop the same mark in different locations and one applies to register the mark, if its registration succeeds, the registrant generally will have nationwide priority except in geographic locations where the other business had used the mark in good faith prior to the registrant's application date.[48] Although federal law provides protections to these users who fail to seek federal registration, it effectively locks them into their common law territories, giving the users who registered priority in the rest of the nation, regardless of their current geographic scope of business.[49] Beyond these limited protections, federal registration empowers the registrant to seek an injunction requiring other later adopters to stop using any confusingly similar symbols when the registrant expands into their geographic territory.[50] Therefore, the possibility of securing nationwide priority is a strong incentive for seeking federal registration.

Registration also constitutes prima facie evidence of the validity of the mark and the identity of the owner.[51] Owners can attach a statutory registration notice to their marks,[52] signaling that they own intellectual property rights and may be prepared to assert them. Federal registration also enables mark owners to obtain enhanced statutory damages for counterfeiting.[53]

Additional benefits from registration result from the mark's presence in TESS, the USPTO online database.[54] New entrants seeking to determine if a word is available for registration often search TESS to see if someone has already secured rights in that word. If the word or a confusingly similar word has already been registered for similar goods or services, the USPTO will block a later application while that mark is live on the Register. If a new entrant sees the conflict, it may avoid an inevitable office action by choosing another word with no obvious conflicts in the TESS data. In this way, a mark's presence in TESS can serve as a powerful deterrent to new entrants who might otherwise adopt it. If a new entrant misses a confusingly similar registration and files an application to register the word, the trademark

---

[46]   15 U.S.C. §§ 1072, 1057(c); *see also* Zirco Corp. v. Am. Tel. & Tel. Co., 21 U.S.P.Q.2d 1542 (T.T.A.B. 1991) (discussing constructive use and priority for intent-to-use filings).

[47]   15 U.S.C. §§ 1052, 1057(c).

[48]   *See id.* §§ 1052, 1057(c); *see, e.g.,* Dudley v. Healthsource Chiropractic, Inc., 883 F. Supp. 2d 377, 389 (W.D.N.Y. 2012) ("Federal registration, however, does not give priority over persons who had used and had not abandoned the mark prior to filing. A senior user retains common law rights to exclusively use the mark within its territory of prior use") (internal citations omitted).

[49]   *See id.* §§ 1052, 1057(c); *Dudley,* 883 F. Supp. 2d at 389.

[50]   *See, e.g.,* Dawn Donut Co. v. Hart's Food Stores, Inc., 267 F.2d 358, 365 (2d Cir. 1959) (denying injunctive relief after finding no likelihood of confusion but clarifying that "the plaintiff may later, upon a proper showing of an intent to use the mark at the retail level in defendant's market area, be entitled to enjoin defendant's use of the mark").

[51]   15 U.S.C. § 1057(b).

[52]   15 U.S.C. § 1111.

[53]   4 J. THOMAS MCCARTHY, MCCARTHY ON TRADEMARKS AND UNFAIR COMPETITION § 25:15, Westlaw (5th ed. database updated Jun. 2022) ("[A] counterfeit of a mark that is registered on the principal register in the United States Patent and Trademark Office for such goods or services sold, offered for sale, or distributed and that is in use, whether or not the person against whom relief is sought knew such mark was so registered").

[54]   *Trademark Electronic Search System (TESS), supra* note 26.

examiner will likely identify the conflict during its initial examination and deny the new entrant's application. In this way, the USPTO confers an additional benefit on registrants, as it protects their mark from confusingly similar registrations, without the registrant taking any action or perhaps even knowing of the conflict.[55]

The USPTO maintains two registers: the Principal Register, for marks that comply with all statutory requirements, and the Supplemental Register, for marks that are not yet distinctive. If a mark is capable of acquiring distinctiveness, it may be placed on the Supplemental Register until its owner gathers evidence of secondary meaning and reapplies for admission to the Principal Register.[56] Supplemental registration does not confer enforceable trademark rights, but it does permit the mark owner to use the symbol "®" to indicate its mark is registered with the USPTO.[57] This notice, as well as the mark's presence in the TESS data, may provide some deterrent value, but the other benefits of principal registration are not conferred on marks on the Supplemental Register.[58]

Since the USPTO made its trademark data available for public research, scholars from multiple disciplines have discovered many patterns revealed in the data. The following section provides an overview of this emerging field of research.

3.   PRIOR EMPIRICAL TRADEMARK RESEARCH

The team of economists at the USPTO publish data affirming the substantial influence that IP-intensive industries have on the U.S. economy and employment.[59] Their 2021 Report on Intellectual Property and the U.S. Economy found that trademarks "enhance the value of both patented and unpatented innovations, as well as reputation, by identifying a good's or service's source of origin."[60] In evaluating output, the study reports that in 2019, the group of IP-intensive industries accounted for $7.8 trillion of the GDP. Although industries may fit within more than one area of IP, trademark-intensive industries led the pack at $7.0 trillion, patent-intensive industries accounted for nearly $4.5 trillion, and copyright-intensive industries accounted for just under $1.3 trillion.[61]

In 2010, the USPTO posted bulk data containing information from decades of trademark registration applications making it possible for scholars to analyze hundreds of variables without filing a FOIA request. Since then, United States trademark registrations have attracted significant scholarly attention.[62] In an earlier study, we found that trademark applicants were

---

[55]   *See* Gerhardt & McClanahan, *supra* note 33, at 578.

[56]   *See* 15 U.S.C. § 1091.

[57]   *See* 15 U.S.C. § 1111 (providing that all registrants can provide statutory notice, which includes marks on the Supplemental Register).

[58]   *See* Gerhardt & McClanahan, *supra* note 33, at 587–88 (comparing and contrasting the principal and supplemental registers).

[59]   ANDREW A. TOOLE ET AL., INTELLECTUAL PROPERTY AND THE U.S. ECONOMY: THIRD EDITION, at ii (U.S. Pat. & Trademark Off. ed., 2021).

[60]   *Id.* at 1.

[61]   *Id.* at 3.

[62]   Rebecca Tushnet, *Registering Disagreement: Registration in Modern American Trademark Law*, 130 HARV. L. REV. 867, 875–78 (2017) (explaining the benefits of trademark registration and calling for renewed attention to the importance of trademark registration, explaining why trademark registration decisions make important distinctions between types of marks, and suggesting improvements that could

more likely to succeed to publication and registration if they were assisted by legal counsel, and that the success rates were even higher if the applicant's lawyer had prosecuted more than thirty applications.[63] Below, we update those findings with more recent data and greater granularity in attorney experience levels. Beebe and Fromer analyzed the availability of marks to new applicants and found that the supply of desirable trademarks is not inexhaustible[64] and that the Principal Register has become so cluttered with word marks[65] that new applicants in many fields must overcome depletion and congestion barriers.[66] We reached the opposite conclusion in our study of color marks, finding that colors—apart from other indicia—are claimed as marks much less frequently than their expressive potential might suggest.[67] Bitton, Schuster, and Gerhardt analyzed marks prosecuted by individuals and found significant disparities in success rates correlating with race and gender.[68] One of the surprising findings from this research is that although women are underrepresented in the population of individual trademark applicants, their publication and registration rates exceed those of men.[69]

Additional empirical trademark research has also focused on data outside the registration context. Some studies show a correlation between trademarks and entrepreneurial success. Trademarks, for example, have been found to provide competitive advantages[70] and promote informational and economic efficiency.[71] Scholars have also shown that firm sur-

---

benefit trademark owners, their competitors, and consumers); Shukhrat Nasirov, *The Use of Trademarks in Empirical Research: Towards an Integrated Framework*, SSRN (November 20, 2018) https://ssrn.com/abstract=3296064 at 11–36, accessed 11 April 2023.

[63]   *See* Gerhardt & McClanahan, *supra* note 33, at 622 (finding that trademark lawyers have a significantly higher likelihood of prosecuting successful trademark applications and successfully rebutting office actions and opposition than pro se applicants).

[64]   *See* Barton Beebe & Jeanne Fromer, *Are We Running Out of Trademarks? An Empirical Study of Trademark Depletion and Congestion*, 131 Harv. L. Rev. 945, 1041 (2018) (finding that firms will likely always find at least some minimally communicative unregistered mark, but that increasing depletion and congestion will impose greater costs and less benefits on firms and increase consumer search costs).

[65]   *See id.*

[66]   *Id.* at 950–51 (defining "trademark depletion" as "the process by which a decreasing number of potential trademarks remain unclaimed by any trademark owner," and defining "trademark congestion" as "the process by which an already-claimed mark is claimed by an increasing number of different trademark owners").

[67]   *See* Deborah R. Gerhardt & Jon J. Lee, *Owning Colors*, 40 Cardozo L. Rev. 2483, 2546–47 (2019) (citing support for the powerful cognitive signals that colors are capable of imparting on consumers and finding 221 registrations of color as a trademark alone out of millions registered since the U.S. Supreme Court ruled color alone trademarkable in 1995).

[68]   Miriam Marcowitz-Bitton, Deborah R. Gerhardt & William Michael Schuster, *An Empirical Study of Gender and Race in Trademark Prosecution*, 94 S. Cal. L. Rev. 1407, 1459–60 (2022); *see also* Emma Williams-Baron, Jessica Milli & Barbara Gault, Innovation and Intellectual Property Among Women Entrepreneurs, at ii, 12 (Inst. Women's Pol'y Rsch. ed., 2018) (finding that male-owned businesses are 7.0% likely to hold a trademark registration and female-owned businesses are only 6.1% likely).

[69]   *Id.*

[70]   *See* Richard Hall, *The Strategic Analysis of Intangible Resources*, 13 Strategic Mgmt. J. 135, 143 (1992) (finding that trademarks, among other intangible assets such as company reputation and employee know-how, are sources of sustainable competitive advantages).

[71]   *See* William M. Landes & Richard A. Posner, *Trademark Law: An Economic Perspective*, 30 J.L. & Econ. 265, 268–73 (1987) (arguing that trademark law works to promote economic efficiency through a reduction of consumer information costs and incentivizing expenditures to maintain the high quality of goods and services).

vival, performance-related metrics, and other innovation measures correlate with trademark registration.[72]

Empirical studies of judicial opinions have also contributed to a better understanding of infringement and dilution litigation. In the United States, proof of trademark infringement is established by showing that consumers are likely to be confused by another's use of an identical or similar mark.[73] Each of the federal circuits employs a multi-factor test to determine the likelihood of confusion.[74] Beebe employed correlation and logistic regression analysis on over 300 judicial opinions issued from 2000–2004 to determine the impact of these factors.[75] He found that senior trademark litigants seeking to stop another's use must win in proving its mark is strong and that the junior's mark is confusingly similar. Proof of an infringer's bad faith, evidence of actual confusion, and proximity of the goods and marketing channels are also significant.[76] A more recent study by Lim also noted that similarity, actual confusion, and proximity were among the most important factors to courts evaluating likelihood of confusion.[77] He further found that courts engage in "factor folding," a process by which they "combine factors and analyze them together," and "tend to start limiting the factors that they choose to consider when confronted with complex decision processes."[78]

4.   METHODOLOGY FOR CURRENT EMPIRICAL STUDY

Although the TESS website is an excellent resource for searching individual applications and registrations, it does not work well for conducting longitudinal research and analyzing trends. To conduct our empirical study of trademark application and registration data, we relied on the USPTO's Trademark Case Files Dataset ("TCF dataset") released by the Office of the Chief Economist to facilitate academic research and transparency.[79] Although the bulk trademark application data used in much of the earliest empirical research is still available, the TCF dataset is significantly more streamlined. It includes a primary table that contains one record for each trademark application along with seventy-nine variables.[80] This primary table

---

[72]   *See* Christine Greenhalgh & Mark Longland, *Running to Stand Still? – The Value of R&D, Patents and Trade Marks in Innovating Manufacturing Firms*, 12 INT. J. ECON. BUS. 307, 310 (2005) (finding that, due to depletion and inability to stave off imitation, firms must continually renew IP assets to maintain market position).

[73]   15 U.S.C. § 1114.

[74]   *See* J. THOMAS MCCARTHY, 4 MCCARTHY ON TRADEMARKS AND UNFAIR COMPETITION § 24:30, Westlaw (5th ed. database updated Jun. 2022).

[75]   Barton Beebe, *An Empirical Study of the Multifactor Tests for Trademark Infringement*, 94 CAL. L. REV. 1581, 1584, 1600 (2006).

[76]   *Id.* at 1607–14.

[77]   Daryl Lim, *Trademark Confusion Revealed: An Empirical Analysis*, 71 AM. UNIV. L. REV. 1285, 1338–39 (2022).

[78]   *Id.* at 1345.

[79]   *See Research Datasets*, U.S. PATENT & TRADEMARK OFFICE, https://www.uspto.gov/ip-policy/economic-research/research-datasets (last visited June 13, 2022) (describing the various research datasets and providing links to download them).

[80]   *USPTO Trademark Case Files 2020 Variable Tables*, U.S. PATENT & TRADEMARK OFFICE, https://www.uspto.gov/sites/default/files/documents/2020-tm-case-files-variable-tables.pdf, accessed 13 June 2022.

is linked to thirteen additional tables through the application's serial number, which serves as a unique identifier for each application. Given the one-to-many relationship between the primary table and several additional tables, hundreds of information points may be gleaned for each application. The USPTO periodically releases updated versions of this dataset with new information the USPTO continuously enters into TESS.

In early 2022, the USPTO released a new version of the TCF dataset that contained all information it maintained on trademark applications filed between 1870 and early 2021. Due to data limitations, the following analysis is based on applications filed in the forty-year period between January 1, 1981, and December 31, 2020. As first noted by Barton Beebe, the number of unsuccessful applications is exceedingly low before 1981, suggesting that prior to that year, the USPTO may have purged unsuccessful applications.[81] Other empirical studies of trademark data have employed similar types of date limitations as well.[82] For these reasons, our analysis of trademark applications relies on forty years of trademark data beginning in 1981.

Success for any trademark applicant is not immediate as each application can take months or even years to make its way through the registration process. Therefore, in analyzing publication and registration success rates, we limited our inquiry to applications filed between January 1, 1981, and December 31, 2018 that had reached a final disposition of registration or abandonment. As noted above, the prosecution of a trademark application can take several years, especially if an examiner issues multiple office actions. ITU applications may also sit for years between publication and registration. Once the notice of allowance issues, ITU applicants are given six months to file a statement of use. But even after that initial period expires, applicants may seek several additional six-month extensions of time.[83] In order to ensure that our reported success rates were not skewed by these prosecution delays, we excluded from those calculations all applications filed during the final two years of the study (2019–2020) along with any earlier applications that were still pending.

We then determined whether any additional records should be excluded. Although the TCF dataset appears to be reliably coded and maintained, we excluded a small subset. For example, each record contains a current status code, indicating whether a mark is "live" or "dead" in the USPTO system. A record is deemed "live" if the application is pending or the registration has issued and is still active; a record will be considered "dead" if the application failed to register or if the registration issued but was later cancelled. While nearly all records fit neatly into one of the two categories above, some status codes for the "dead" category signal that the record contains invalid or incorrect data. Given that the USPTO itself flagged this set as erroneous or incomplete, we excluded 2,709 records (0.03% of all applications) from our analysis.

A final set of issues arises in the examination of the data on attorneys who assisted with the filing of trademark applications. First, the attorney data fields are inconsistently populated on applications filed prior to 1983; therefore, we shortened the time frame for the analysis of attorney representation accordingly. Second, both the fact of attorney assistance and the name of the attorney are self-reported by the person who filed the application. Although the field ordinarily includes the lawyer's name and in theory would be blank if the applicant is pro se, some applicants entered information such as a question mark or the word "none." We

[81] *See* Barton Beebe, *Is the Trademark Office a Rubber Stamp?*, 48 HOUS. L. REV. 751, 760 (2011).
[82] *See, e.g.*, Beebe & Fromer, *supra* note 64 (limiting empirical study to applications filed since 1985); Gerhardt & Lee, *supra* note 67 (limiting empirical study to applications filed since 1987).
[83] *See* 15 U.S.C. § 1051(d).

recoded these records as pro se because although the attorney field was not blank, the written text suggested the application was prosecuted without the assistance of counsel. On the flip side, some applications filed by major corporations with a suite of in-house counsel may file multiple applications through an experienced paralegal on behalf of the company.[84] Although these applications would be coded as pro se, the applicant in fact may be assisted by lawyers in selecting the brand, preparing the application, or responding to office actions.[85] Third, when an applicant hires or changes counsel after the initial filing, the new attorney's name may appear in the TESS data even if that lawyer was not originally involved. Fourth, because the USPTO does not maintain a registration system for trademark attorneys who appear before it,[86] one cannot know for certain the number of applications a particular attorney has filed. For example, an attorney who uses a middle initial when filing some but not all applications will appear as two different individuals in the dataset, as will an attorney who has changed their last name. Although we implemented some measures to more accurately match attorney names (e.g., removing non-alphabetic characters), we acknowledge that this method of tracking attorneys is a conservative approach that may overestimate the success rates for less experienced attorneys and underestimate the findings of higher success rates for experienced attorneys. Finally, all the applications for an attorney who files more than 100 applications will be counted as highly experienced even though those lawyers were novices early in their careers. Counting their earlier applications (when they did not have experience) with the rest of the experienced filings again serves to underestimate the success of only those applications filed by experienced counsel.

After identifying the records within the time period of interest and scrubbing the data, 9,189,498 applications remained for our longitudinal analysis. Because this study examines the entire population rather than a sample, computing statistical significance is inapposite. As there is no risk of variation between a selected sample and the population of trademark applications, we are able to describe with certainty the observations set forth below.

5.   EMPIRICAL STUDY RESULTS

As of May 2022, there were 3,784,721 live marks on the Principal Register and another 107,633 on the Supplemental Register. While these total numbers are substantial, they do not capture the growth in trademark applications and registrations over the last four decades. The number of live marks in the TESS data changes daily as new applications are filed and marks no longer in use are abandoned. To illustrate how the dataset grew over time, Figure 12.2 shows the annual number of applications filed between 1981 and 2020.

Figure 12.2 shows a dramatic increase in trademark applications filed over the past forty years. The annual number of applications jumped from under 50,000 per year in 1981 to over 650,000 in 2020—a 1,274% increase. The spike in 1989 coincides with the year when intent to use was first available as a filing basis. Although an ITU application cannot mature to

---

[84]   Gerhardt & McClanahan, *supra* note 33, at 609.
[85]   *See id.* at 612–14.
[86]   Jon J. Lee, *Double Standards: An Empirical Study of Patent and Trademark Discipline*, 61 B.C. L. Rev. 1613, 1678–80 (2020) (noting deficiency and suggesting that the USPTO develop a registration system to better track trademark attorneys who practice before it).

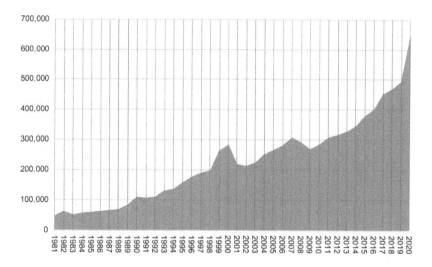

Figure 12.2   Trademark applications over time

registration until the applicant submits proof of use, the applicant can secure priority from the date the application is filed, and as illustrated in Figure 12.3, applicants quickly began to take advantage of this opportunity and stake their claim to marks that they had not yet begun using in commerce.

The dramatic increase around 2000 may be attributed to the availability of electronic filing beginning in late 1998 and the Internet bubble phenomenon.[87] The most recent surge in trademark applications was fueled by a sudden rush of applications from China. Between 2013 and 2019, applications from China jumped from 4,706 to 76,566, far outpacing the increase in applications from those domiciled in the United States.[88] Because the increase corresponded with a flood of fraudulent specimens and other indications that the marks may not be related to genuine businesses, the USPTO amended its regulations to require that all applications from entities domiciled in other countries be prosecuted by an attorney licensed to practice in the United States.[89] That change became effective in August 2019, and therefore, data in future years will reveal the extent to which it has an impact on filing and success rates.

Figure 12.3 documents changes in filing basis trends. To create this figure so that the categories were mutually exclusive, we limited the universe to the vast majority of applications (96%) claiming a single filing basis.

The great majority of applications filed prior to 1989 were based on use in commerce. Once intent to use became an option for applicants on November 16, 1989, it quickly gained popularity. By 1993, ITU applications exceeded those filed based on use. In 2017, use-based

---

[87]   *See* Beebe, *supra* note 81, at 761 (discussing Internet Bubble); Gerhardt & McClanahan, *supra* note 33, at 602–03 (noting connection with introduction of online filings).

[88]   *Trademarks and Patents in China: The Impact of Non-Market Factors on Filing Trends and IP Systems*, U.S. PATENT & TRADEMARK OFFICE (Jan. 2021), https://www.uspto.gov/sites/default/files/documents/USPTO-TrademarkPatentsInChina.pdf, accessed 11 April 2023.

[89]   *See* Requirement of U.S. Licensed Attorney for Foreign Trademark Applicants and Registrants, 84 Fed. Reg. 31498 (July 2, 2019) (to be codified at 37 C.F.R. pts. 2, 7, & 11).

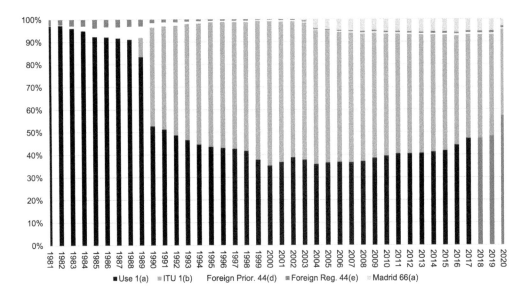

Figure 12.3   Application filing basis over time

applications once again regained the lead. The spike in applications from Chinese-domiciled entities likely contributed to this shift, as a large percentage of those applications were based on alleged use.[90]

Figure 12.3 also displays shifting trends for applications originating outside the United States. In the 1980s, foreign registration and foreign priority filings constituted nearly 10% of all single-basis applications, but by 1990, that percentage declined significantly and remained relatively low for the next decade. Madrid filings, first available in 2003, quickly became the most popular basis for USPTO registration of marks originating abroad. Although the percentages look small relative to other filing bases, applicants are still filing a significant and increasing number of trademark applications based on foreign registration and foreign priority. In fact, the number of applications in each category doubled over the last eight years.

Because Figure 12.3 is limited to applications claiming only one filing basis, it does not fully capture how foreign priority is being used in combination with other filing bases. Although relatively few applications claim more than one basis (4%), 62% of those that do claim foreign priority. The prevalence of foreign priority among multiple-basis filings is a logical one, because applicants cannot rely on foreign priority as a standalone basis for registration; they need to add another basis for registration. A closer look at foreign priority applications reveals that they are most often coupled with ITU filings; 86% of multi-basis filings claiming foreign priority include ITU as an additional basis. This finding is consistent with the hypothesis that some businesses strategically leverage foreign priority to secure early nationwide priority for marks they have not yet used in the United States.[91] An empirical study by Carsten Fink et

---

[90]   *See Trademarks and Patents in China: The Impact of Non-Market Factors on Filing Trends and IP Systems*, *supra* note 88.

[91]   *See* Carsten Fink et al., *Submarine Trademarks* 12 (J. Econ. & Mgmt. Strategy Working Paper No. 51, 2018).

al. named them "submarine trademarks" because large corporations often use this strategy to secretly secure early filing dates for trademarks related to new products or services.[92]

In addition to choosing a filing basis, each trademark applicant must specifically identify the classes of goods and services it uses (or intends to use) in connection with the claimed mark. Overall, most trademark applications (60%) are claimed in connection with goods. One third (33%) are for service marks, and 7% claim use in connection with both goods and services. Figure 12.4 illustrates some modest variation in filings within class types over time.

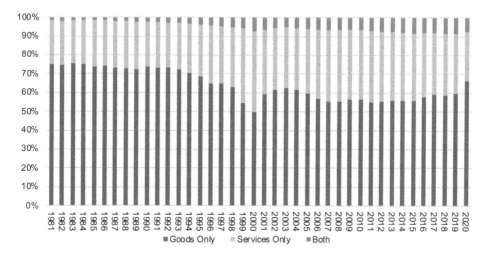

Figure 12.4   Applications for goods and/or services over time

Figure 12.4 shows that in the 1980s, goods accounted for over 75% of applications. The percentage of services (either alone or in connection with goods) began to increase beginning in the 1990s. Once, in 2000, applications filed in connection with goods accounted for fewer than 50% of applications. Since then, the percentage has generally hovered between 55% and 60%. The most recent filing data from 2020 reflects the highest percentage (66%) of applications filed since 2000 in connection with goods alone. This upturn may have resulted from the Covid-19 pandemic as businesses may have delayed launching new services. Data from future years will bear out whether this finding is a temporary blip or a pivot point.

Figure 12.5 shows the percentage of marks registered in each of the international goods and service classes. Goods classes are depicted in the darker shade of grey, and service classes are in the lighter shade.

Interestingly, three of the four most popular classes are for services. This finding is not surprising given that there are fewer service classes, and some classes for goods, such as yarns and threads or musical instruments, are rather narrow.

In addition to protecting use in connection with a wide variety of goods and services, U.S. trademark law generally does not exclude a symbol from serving as a mark on account of its nature. To facilitate efficient searching, the USPTO codes marks for multiple elements, includ-

---

[92]   *Id.* at 32.

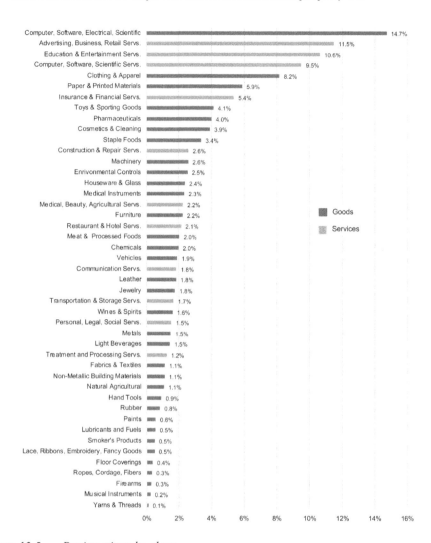

Figure 12.5   Registrations by class

ing the use of words, designs, shapes, colors, and non-visual elements, such as scent or sound. The TCF dataset sorts all marks into four basic categories based on its content: (1) text only, (2) design only, (3) text and design, and (4) other marks that cannot be visually represented by a drawing (e.g., sound or scent marks). In our analysis below, we use "text" and "design" to describe marks that contain only those elements exclusive of any other, and we use the term "nontraditional" to describe the fourth nonvisual category.

Because the USPTO permits applicants to seek registration of a trademark in multiple formats, an applicant seeking strong protection may register multiple versions of their mark. For example, the Coca-Cola Company has registered the word "Coca-Cola," a text and design mark for "Coca-Cola" written in its classic script font, and a design mark for its classic glass bottle shape, all in connection with its beverage products.[93]

Figure 12.6 depicts the percentage of applications within each content category over the past forty years. At 0.01%, nontraditional marks constitute such a miniscule percentage that, although their slice is represented in Figure 12.6, it cannot be seen by the naked eye.

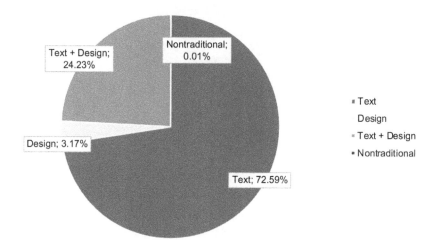

Figure 12.6   Content of marks submitted for registration

Although trademark law permits applicants to seek registration for any symbol that identifies and distinguishes a business from its competition, the data reflects an overwhelming preference for textual marks. More than 96% of applications are filed for marks containing text; 73% of the total include no design element, and 24% seek registration of text and design. Only 3% of applications seek registration of marks that consist solely of a design, but in terms of absolute numbers that category is still substantial, containing more than 290,000 applications.

For trademarks that consist of elements other than design or text, the USPTO data does not contain codes that easily identify and distinguish them. For example, marks claiming a single color are included as one of the design codes, and the USPTO has not consistently coded them in the TCF dataset in such a way to facilitate reliable analysis. Our prior empirical research, which required manual review and coding of application data, revealed that there had been 1,237 applications for color alone filed between 1987 and 2017, a relatively small number.[94] Yet, as described in further detail below, applications for color are more popular than the other nontraditional marks prosecuted before the USPTO.

Figure 12.7 illustrates the distribution of the 813 nontraditional trademark applications (excluding color) filed between 1981 and 2020. We reviewed each application to verify the nature of the claimed mark.

---

93 Registration Nos. 3,252,896, 0238145, 0238146 and 0696147.
94 Gerhardt & Lee, *supra* note 67, at 2532.

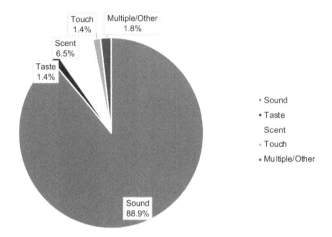

Figure 12.7   Nontraditional marks

Of these nontraditional marks, the vast majority (89%) were for sound. These were followed by scent marks (7%), and then by equally small percentages (1% each) of taste and touch marks.

Marks shared among a group with common interests constitute another subcategory of marks with interesting variation over the duration of the study, as illustrated in Figure 12.8. This subcategory includes certification and collective marks. Certification marks are unusual in that they are owned by an organization that sets standards for use in connection with a mark but does not use the mark itself. Certification marks may be used "to certify, regional or other origin, material, mode of manufacture, quality, accuracy, or other characteristics of such person's goods or services or that the work or labor on the goods or services was performed by members of a union or other organization."[95] Collective marks, which may be used by their owners, are for "members of a cooperative, an association, or other collective group or organization" to indicate "membership in a union, an association, or other organization." [96]

Figure 12.8 shows that the filing trends in shared marks have shifted over time. Applications in the 1980s most often sought protection for collective marks. That trend changed in 1993 when applications for certification marks took the lead and began an upward trajectory that peaked in 2008. One reason for the increase in certification mark applications relative to collective marks during this time period is that the former are more likely to be filed on an intent-to-use basis, which became available in 1989. Indeed, the increase in certification mark applications followed a similar trajectory to that for the total universe of trademark applications between 1981 and the early 2000s. While there is not an apparent trademark law reason for the steep increase between 2005 and 2008 followed by a sharp drop and levelling off, one hypothesis is that the desire for such marks roughly follows the broader U.S. economic trends.

---

95   15 U.S.C. § 1127.
96   *Id.*

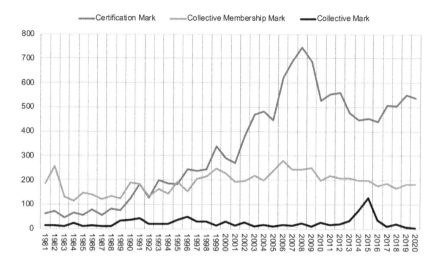

Figure 12.8   Certification and collective mark applications over time

Time will tell if that is the case. Nevertheless, in the past decade certification mark applications have been filed twice as often as all three types of collective marks combined.

6.   APPLICATION SUCCESS RATES

Trademark examination practices differ considerably by country. In some nations, trademark filings get scant oversight, and once filed, pass immediately to registration. Other nations have more stringent review and other procedural hurdles that may delay or hinder protection.[97] The U.S. falls into the more stringent side of that spectrum. USPTO trademark applications are examined by specialized trademark attorneys, and many fail to survive that process.

Once trademark applications are filed with the USPTO, they follow one of multiple paths. Figure 12.1 illustrates the differences in ITU and use-based application procedures. Some applications will publish and be put on the Principal Register with little additional work on the part of the applicant. Others may have to respond to office actions, provide additional evidence, or defeat an opposition proceeding. Still others that fail to publish on the Principal Register may be placed on the Supplemental Register until they acquire sufficient distinctiveness to reapply for inclusion on the Principal Register.

Figure 12.9 depicts the success rates over time for all trademark applications filed with the USPTO between 1981 and 2018.

The top trend line represents the relatively steady publication rate which has generally fluctuated between 70–79%, though it dipped to 67% in 2000. However, in most years, the rate has hovered within three percentage points of the 76% overall rate. Similarly, the bottom

---

[97]   See *Filing a Trademark Application Outside the United States*, INTERNATIONAL TRADEMARK ASSOCIATION, https://www.inta.org/fact-sheets/filing-a-trademark-application-outside-the-united-states/ (last visited June 13, 2022).

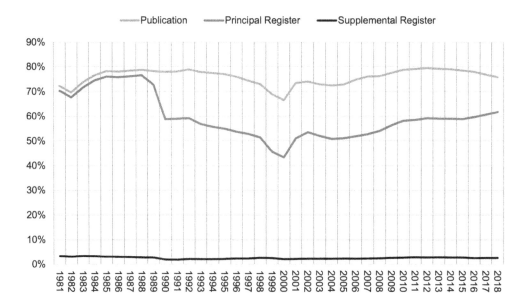

Figure 12.9   Application success rates over time

trend line shows that the percentage of marks placed on the Supplemental Register has held steady around 3%.

By contrast, the middle line, representing the registration rate, shows more variation. The Principal registration and publication rates were nearly identical until 1989, when the registration rate dropped precipitously and has remained around 20 percentage points lower since that time. Although one might question whether this drop resulted from a change in USPTO practices, no substantial administrative changes have been shown to have caused this effect. Therefore, like other scholars, we surmise that this decline is due to the simultaneous introduction of intent to use as a filing basis.[98] As noted earlier, ITU applications may publish prior to the applicant's use of the mark in commerce, but they cannot register until the applicant demonstrates use. Some applicants may make a business decision not to use the mark following publication or to abandon the application for other reasons.

To better understand the decline in principal registration rates depicted in Figure 12.9, we examined success rates by filing basis. The results are depicted in Figure 12.10, which is limited to applications initiated with a single basis. For the rest of this chapter, "registration" will refer to placement on the Principal Register.

Figure 12.10 confirms that much of the difference between publication and registration rates is attributable to intent to use applications, for which the gap is between 37 and 38 percentage points. The differences in rates for each of the other filing bases are between one percentage point (Madrid) and three percentage points (foreign priority).

Figure 12.10 highlights that trademark applicants who rely on registrations secured from other countries succeed at the highest rates. Indeed, the registration rates for Madrid and

---

[98]   *See, e.g.,* Beebe, *supra* note 81, at 762–63 (cataloguing the decline in registration rates and linking it to the introduction of the intent-to-use basis).

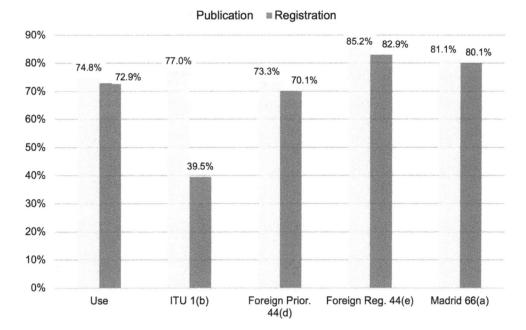

Publication ■ Registration

Figure 12.10   Success rates by filing basis

foreign registration filings exceed 80%. These statistics underscore the potential advantage to businesses who opt to seek trademark protection in another country before filing an application with the USPTO.

Even though Figure 12.6 showed that textual marks are the most popular in terms of application filings, that popularity does not equate to having the greatest success before the USPTO. Figure 12.11 depicts the success rates for each of the four basic content types. It indicates that applications for marks claiming design but not text have the highest rates of publication and registration.

Applications for marks claiming only design have an 83% publication rate and a 68% registration rate, clearly the highest among all categories. Text marks and applications claiming text and design have similar publication rates (75% versus 77%), though the registration rate for text is considerably lower than the rate for applications containing both text and design (54% versus 63%). Nevertheless, it is notable that the success rates for applications claiming text and design do not match or exceed those claiming only design since they contain different types of elements that could theoretically increase their distinctiveness. The reasons for this phenomenon may be fertile ground for further research. One possible explanation is that some applicants who think their textual mark may be initially unprotectable, perhaps because it is descriptive, might attempt to obtain registration for a design used in connection with the descriptive term. Nontraditional marks publish at a 68% rate. Although this rate is the lowest among the four categories, it indicates that many nontraditional marks are just as capable of distinctive source identification as traditional text and design marks.

To understand why trademark applications fail to register, we took a closer look at each unsuccessful application. Nearly every failed application has a current status code that identifies its fatal stumbling block. Occasionally, an application will include a current status code

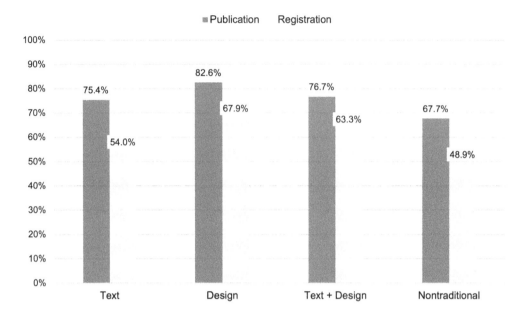

Figure 12.11   Success rates by content of mark

that reflects a subsequent event (e.g., petition to revive) or that is otherwise inapposite (e.g., internal shifts in data storage). This small set of records for which the failure could not be pinpointed were excluded from Figure 12.12, which depicts the reasons why the bulk of failed applications met their demise.

Most unsuccessful trademark applications (51%) were thwarted by an office action, 49% before publication and 2% afterwards. The substantive reason, however, may have some overlap. Post-publication office actions for ITU applications may be due to a problem with a specimen submitted after the mark published and received a notice of allowance. The same flaw for a use-based application would occur prior to publication.

There are many reasons why a trademark application may be abandoned following an office action. Some applicants may perceive the examiner's objection as insurmountable. Others, especially pro se applicants, may be unsure how to respond or miss the deadline due to inattention. Future research delving into these reasons is an important area of inquiry because the data unequivocally shows that office actions are the primary reason that marks fail to register.

The next most common stumbling block is failure to file a proper statement of use (40%). These applications already succeeded in overcoming USPTO review and obtaining publication. Indeed, if a published mark fails to register, 84% of the time the progress halts from not filing a proper statement of use. Examining these applications more closely, it became clear that in virtually all cases the applicant did not submit any statement of use, perhaps because the applicant decided against using the mark in commerce. These results further confirm that the decline in registration rates around 1989 (as seen in Figure 12.9) likely was due to the introduction of the intent to use filing basis, when filing a statement of use after USPTO approval became an administrative step many applicants would not take.

Express abandonment occurs approximately 5% of the time, with relatively more occurring before publication (3% of total) than after (2% of total). Unfortunately, the status codes

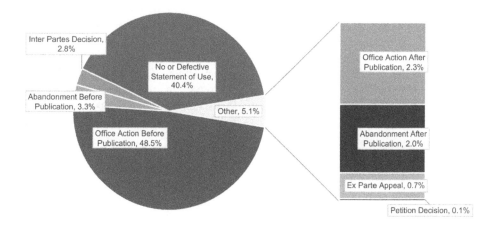

Figure 12.12   Reasons for unsuccessful applications

associated with express abandonment do not provide additional insight into why the applicant decided not to continue with prosecution. Some applicants may have made a business decision to abandon the mark, apart from any issues related to its protectability. Alternatively, an applicant who received an office action may have filed an express abandonment rather than respond—even though not responding at all would have led to the same result. We also suspect that some applicants filed an express abandonment to settle threatened litigation from another trademark holder who asserted superior rights.

The remaining reasons for unsuccessful applications involved higher-level USPTO decisionmakers or other proceedings, but they individually and collectively represent a small percentage of the total. Although opposition proceedings provide an opportunity for third parties to thwart trademark registration, they only account for 3% of unsuccessful applications. Even when combined, adverse petition decisions and ex parte appeals account for less than 1% of the total.

7.   SUCCESS RATES AND THE PRESENCE OF COUNSEL

Trademark prosecution is generally much less expensive than patent prosecution but moderately more costly than registering a copyright. A separate fee must be filed for each class of goods and services claimed in an application and hiring trademark counsel can bring the cost over $1,000, even for a single class. The costs can be far higher if the applicant confronts multiple office actions, an opposition proceeding, or litigation by a well-funded opponent. While filing a trademark application may be less expensive than patent prosecution, the costs are not negligible, especially for small businesses or low wealth entrepreneurs. Therefore, empirical data indicating whether assistance of counsel is advantageous can help applicants decide whether to invest scarce resources in hiring legal counsel or to take a risk by filing an application pro se.

Historically, trademark applicants all had the choice of prosecuting their application without the assistance of counsel. As mentioned earlier, the USPTO now requires all foreign applicants, registrants, or parties to a proceeding to be represented by an attorney who is admitted to practice in a U.S. state. By contrast, U.S. applicants may still file trademark applications pro se.

Figure 12.13 depicts the annual percentages of applications filed by legal counsel. This percentage steadily declined from over 90% in 1985 to 64% in 2017, when it rose again. The requirement that foreign applicants file through a U.S.-licensed attorney took effect in August 2019 and may account for some of the increase (from 65% to 75%) between 2018 and 2020.

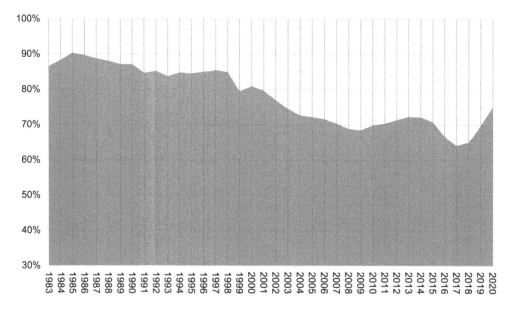

Figure 12.13   Percentage of applications prosecuted by legal counsel over time

Given that a substantial percentage of trademark applications are filed pro se (and even more could be if applicants chose to do so), one may question whether the presence of counsel impacts success rates. Figure 12.14 provides insight into the answer, depicting the publication and registration rates for applications filed by attorneys and pro se. It unequivocally indicates that applications filed by counsel are associated with higher success rates.

While 63% of pro se applications succeed to publication, the publication rate jumps to over 80% for those filed by legal counsel—a 28% increase. The difference in registration rates is also substantial. While 46% of pro se applicants succeed in registering their marks, the registration rate jumps to 60% for those represented by counsel—a 31% increase.

In addition to increasing their chance of success, applicants may experience additional benefits when they hire experienced trademark counsel. Trademark specialists can assist clients in selecting strong, distinctive marks to meet the Lanham Act's requirements. They also know how to navigate the application process and overcome office actions, which, as shown in Figure 12.12, is the most common barrier to registration.

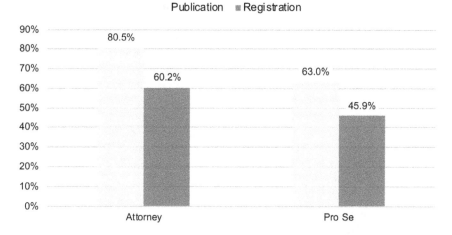

Figure 12.14   Success rates for applications filed pro se and with counsel

Of the trademark applications that could not overcome a final office action, 44% were filed pro se, even though only 26% of all applications from that time period were pro se. This data shows that office actions are upending a higher proportion of pro se applications than those filed by counsel. Aware that U.S.-based applicants with scarce resources may choose to navigate the selection and application process pro se, the USPTO periodically updates its online application platform to be more user friendly.

While having the assistance of any attorney correlates with greater success before the USPTO, a deeper dive into the data shows that more experienced lawyers have even higher success rates than their less experienced peers. Figure 12.15 depicts the publication and registration rates for pro se applicants as the baseline, and then it breaks out the success rates of applications filed by counsel by the attorney's experience. We defined an attorney's level of

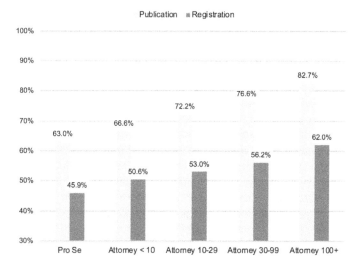

Figure 12.15   Success rates for pro se applicants and attorneys by experience level

experience by the number of applications naming that attorney as counsel between 1983 and 2020.

The pair of bars on the far left depicts the percentage of pro se applications that succeeded first to publication, and second to registration. Fewer than two thirds of pro se applications (63%) publish, and fewer than half (46%) mature to registration. The remaining pairs show the success rates for applications filed by counsel. These success rates increase modestly to 67% and 51% for the least experienced attorneys, but they steadily increase as the experience level of the attorney increases. For attorneys who prosecuted 100 or more applications, the success rates jump to 83% for publication and 62% for registration. These success rates substantially exceed the rates for pro se applicants and less experienced attorneys. Based on these results, applicants who are seeking legal counsel to help them register a trademark may have a greater chance of success if they hire experienced counsel. Although there are limits in the quality of the attorney data, as detailed in the methodology section these results likely underestimate the true impact of hiring experienced counsel.

Some additional context will be helpful to fully understand the attorney experience data. Figure 12.16 shows the attorney experience categories broken out in two ways: first by the percentage of attorneys having various experience levels, and second, by the percentage of applications filed by attorneys at each level. Figure 12.16 reflects the fact that although the group of most experienced attorneys (those filing 100 or more applications) is relatively small at 5% of all lawyers who have filed trademark applications during the time period of interest, that cohort prosecutes 79% of all applications filed by counsel.

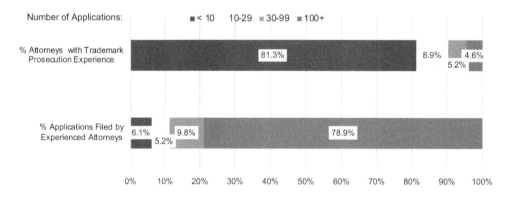

Figure 12.16   Attorney experience categories

Despite the popular notion that "anyone" can file a trademark application, trademark prosecution has become a specialized field, largely comprised of a relatively small percentage of attorneys who have the most experience and the most success before the USPTO. The USPTO has begun to recognize the important role that trademark attorneys play, both in requiring that foreign entities have legal representation and disciplining trademark attorneys who fail to meet their ethical obligations. Recent empirical research conducted by Lee confirms that the USPTO does exercise its disciplinary authority against both trademark attorneys and patent practitioners, though it still sanctions trademark attorneys less often and less severely than their patent counterparts.[99]

8. CONCLUSION

Over the past forty years, the annual number of trademark applications filed with the USPTO has increased dramatically. Despite a multitude of efforts by the USPTO to make the application process more accessible, the process still poses many challenges to applicants. Every year, thousands of applications fail to publish and register. While publication and supplemental registration rates have held rather steady, principal registration rates dropped dramatically after the introduction of the intent to use filing basis. While use-based and ITU applications have similar publication rates, they differ dramatically with regard to registration because many ITU applicants do not complete the application process by filing a statement of use. Overall, applicants relying on a registration from another country navigated the registration process more successfully than U.S. applications. While the foreign registration and Madrid filing bases are far less common than use and intent to use, they have higher USPTO registration rates.

Success rates also vary by mark category. Textual marks are by far the most popular yet they are not the most successful. That distinction goes to applications claiming design only. Both registration and publication rates are higher for design marks than those comprising only text. Nontraditional trademarks are the rarest category, and they publish and register at the lowest rates among all categories, but those rates are not dramatically lower than marks claiming text and/or design.

Another important dynamic revealed in the data is that office actions present the most formidable barriers to federal trademark registration. Another substantial percentage are thwarted between publication and registration because the applicant did not file a statement of use.

Finally, recent data emphasizes that the presence of counsel makes a big difference. When it comes to success before the USPTO, applications filed by attorneys are more likely to publish and register than those that are filed pro se. Despite the USPTO's efforts to make the application process run smoothly for pro se applicants, specialized skills are often required to successfully navigate the process. The data also unequivocally shows that attorneys with higher levels of prosecution experience have the highest success rates.

While this study focused on the past forty years, this chorus of data foretells signs of change on the horizon. Given concerns about clutter and depletion, the dramatic increase in applications from those domiciled outside of the United States, and concerns about fraudulent applications, the USPTO recently has implemented new opportunities to challenge registrations and a requirement that foreign applicants retain U.S. counsel.[100] Future studies will reveal

---

[99]   Lee, *supra* note 86, at 1663.
[100]   *See generally* Changes To Implement Provisions of the Trademark Modernization Act of 2020, 86 Fed. Reg. 64,300 (Nov. 17, 2021) (to be codified at 37 C.F.R. pts. 2 & 7) (summarizing USPTO's new expungement, reexamination, and cancellation procedures related to nonuse); Requirement of U.S. Licensed Attorney for Foreign Trademark Applicants and Registrants, 84 Fed. Reg. 31498 (July 2, 2019) (to be codified at 37 C.F.R. pts. 2, 7, & 11).

whether these policy changes impact the quantity or quality of future applications as well as the integrity of marks that populate the Principal Register.

13. An empirical study of the basis of refusal of EU trade marks for 3D marks

Ilanah Fhima

1.   BACKGROUND

This research investigates the conditions under which three-dimensional (3D) shape marks are refused registration by the EU Intellectual Property Office (EUIPO). It forms part of a larger empirical project being completed by the author investigating the registration of 3D shape marks under EU trade mark law.[1]

The registration of shape marks is controversial.[2] Until EU harmonisation in the 1990s, shape marks could not be registered in a number of jurisdictions in Europe,[3] and even today, there remain calls for an end to, or limitation of, their protection under trade mark law.[4] The purpose of registration is to protect the role that trade marks have of indicating the commercial origin of goods and services. While shapes are capable of performing this function, consumers are not always accustomed to deriving messages about origin from the shape of product or their packaging, rather than, for example, words or logos that they may also feature.[5] Moreover, product and packaging shapes may have other functions too. In protecting shapes of products in particular, the fear is that trade mark owners will end up with a monopoly on how

---

[1]   Currently, Directive (EU) 2015/2436 to approximate the laws of the Members States relating to trade marks, OJ L 336/1 (23 December 2015) (EUTMD) and Regulation (EU) 2017/1001 of the European Parliament and of the Council of 14 June 2017 on the European Union trade mark (codification), OJ L 154/1 (16 June 2017) (EUTMR).

[2]   See, e.g. Graeme Dinwoodie, 'Non-Traditional Marks in Europe: Conceptual Lessons from their Apparent Demise?', NYU Colloquium, Draft of 4 February 2019, available at <http://www.law.nyu.edu/sites/default/files/upload_documents/Graeme%20Dinwoodie.pdf> accessed 27 May 2022, p. 3; also Irene Calboli and Martin Senftleben (eds), *The Protection of Non-Traditional Trademarks: Critical Perspectives* (OUP, 2018).

[3]   Annette Kur, 'Yellow Dictionaries, Red Banking Services, Some Candies, and a Sitting Bunny: Protection of Color and Shape Marks from a German and European Perspective' in Irene Calboli and Martin Senftleben, *Non-Traditional Trademarks*, n 2, p. 89 mentions Germany, Italy, Austria and Greece. The same was true of product packaging in the UK – see *In re Coca-Cola Co.* [1986] 1 WLR 693.

[4]   Particularly in the USA – see e.g. Christopher Buccafusco and Mark Lemley, 'Functionality Screens' (2017) 103(7) *Virginia Law Review* 1293, 1373; Robert Bone, 'Functionality Reexamined' (2015) 7(1) *Journal of Legal Analysis* 183; Caitlin Canahai and Mark McKenna, 'The Case Against Product Configuration Trade Dress' in Graeme Dinwoodie and Mark Janis (eds), *Research Handbook on Trademark Reform* (Edward Elgar, 2019), though this would not be permitted under the TRIPs agreement – see Annette Kur, 'Too Common, Too Splendid or "Just Right"? Trade Mark Protection for Product Shapes in the Light of CJEU Case Law' (2014) Max Planck Institute for Innovation and Competition Research Paper No 14-17, p. 27.

[5]   *Henkel* v *OHIM* (Joined Cases C-456/01 P and 457/01 P) [2004] ETMR 87, ECLI:EU:C:2004:258, [38].

a particular product works, or on product features that otherwise appeal to consumers,[6] thereby overlapping with (and potentially duplicating/undercutting) the existing protection that is offered by the patent, design and copyright systems[7] and making it impossible for competitors to compete effectively.[8]

Nevertheless, under European trade mark law, *any* sign can be registered as a trade mark as long as it is capable of distinguishing and of being represented on the Trade Mark Register. This explicitly includes the shape of goods and their packaging.[9] However, there are a number of reasons why this presumption of registrability may not apply, and hence why marks may be refused registration. Of particular relevance to 3D marks are the exclusions from registration found in Article 7(1)(e) EUTMR (corresponding to Article 4(1)(e) EUTMD). Indeed, until relatively recently these exclusions were limited to signs consisting exclusively of the shape of goods,[10] though this has recently been expanded to include non-shape characteristics. For shape marks, the Article 7(1)(e) exclusions apply to signs which consist exclusively of: shapes which result from the nature of the goods themselves (also known as 'the first indent'),[11] shapes which are necessary to obtain a technical result ('the second indent')[12] and shapes that add substantial value to the goods ('the third indent').[13] These exclusions are particularly

---

[6]   Under Art.7(1)(e)(iii) EUTMR – see Ilanah Fhima, 'Consumer Value as the Key to Trade Mark Functionality' (2022) 85(3) *Modern Law* Review 661, 669–670.
[7]   *Koninklijke Philips Electronics NV* v *Remington Consumer Products Ltd* (Case C-299/99) [2002] ETMR 81; ECLI:EU:C:2002:377, [82]; *Lego Juris* v *OHIM* (Case C-48/09 P) [2010] ETMR 63; ECLI:EU:C:2010:516, [46].
[8]   *Philips* v *Remington*, n 7, [78]; *Lego Juris*, n 7, [46]. On the policies underlying Art.7(1)(e)(ii) see further Apostolos Chronopoulos, 'De Jure Functionality of Shapes Driven by Technical Considerations in Manufacturing Methods' [2017] *Intellectual Property Quarterly* 286, 291–293. Thus, scholars have identified a common competition-based policy underlying the various Art.7(1)(e) exclusions – see Uma Suthersanen and Marc Mimler, 'An Autonomous EU Functionality Doctrine for Shape Exclusions' (2020) 69(6) *GRUR International* 567; Antoon Quaedvlieg, 'Shapes which give substantial value to the goods: Towards a systematic and homogeneous protection of designs in the EU' in Marie-Christine Janssens and Geertrui van Overwalle (eds), *Harmonisation of European IP Law: From European Rules to Belgian Law and Practice: Contributions in Honour of Frank Gotzen* (Bruylant/Larcier, 2012), 202; Eleonora Rosati, 'The absolute ground for refusal or invalidity in Article 7(1)(e)(iii) EUTMR/4(1)(e) (iii) EUTMD: in search of the exclusion's own substantial value' (2020) 15(2) *Journal of Intellectual Property Law & Practice* 103, 107.
[9]   EUTMR Art.4.
[10]   EUTMD replaces Directive 2008/95/EC of the European Parliament and of the Council of 22 October 2008 to approximate the laws of the Member States relating to trade marks [2008] OJ L 299/25, which in turn replaced the First Council Directive 89/104/EEC of 21 December 1988 to approximate the laws of the Member States relating to trade marks [1989] OJ L 40/1. There have been three versions of the Regulation governing pan-EU trade marks: Council Regulation (EC) 40/94 of 20 December 1993 on the Community trade mark [1994] OJ L 11/1 was amended by Council Regulation (EC) 207/2009 of 26 February 2009 on the Community Trade Marks [2009] OJ L 78/1, which was amended by Regulation (EU) 2015/2424 of the European Parliament and of the Council of 16 December 2015 [2015] OJ L 341/21. The latter was repealed by EUTMR which took effect from 1 October 2017.
[11]   Art.7(1)(e)(i). The reference to 'indents' originates from the unnumbered provisions of Art.3(1) (e) of the original Trade Mark Directive of 1989, which was cited in the early case law relating to these exceptions.
[12]   Art.7(1)(e)(ii).
[13]   Art.7(1)(e)(iii).

designed to take into account the fact that registering the shape of goods – even one serving as a distinctive trade mark – brings with it the risk to competition, as mentioned above.[14]

In addition to the Article 7(1)(e) exclusions, shape marks may also encounter difficulties relating to whether they are distinctive.[15] The position adopted by the CJEU is that, while the standard of distinctiveness required is the same for all forms of marks, in practice consumers are not used to inferring messages concerning the origin of goods from their shape.[16] Consequently, shape marks will only be viewed as inherently distinctive if they depart significantly from the norms of the sector concerned. It should be noted though that under EU law (and unlike in the USA[17]), there is no *a priori* bar on shape marks being considered inherently distinctive, and so some shape marks can be registered without evidence of acquired distinctiveness.

The other grounds for refusal of registration may apply to shape marks, in the same way that they would apply to any form of mark. In particular, a shape may be viewed as descriptive.[18] Descriptiveness may also come into play where there is an attempt to register a non-distinctive shape with a descriptive term printed or embossed upon it. Shape marks may also be barred from registration under the relative grounds if they are confusingly similar to, dilute or take advantage of an earlier mark.[19]

2.   AIMS OF THIS RESEARCH

This project aims to understand which factors are driving the refusal of registration of 3D marks in Europe with a view to commenting on whether the approach to 3D marks gives rise to significant competition concerns. Given the fact that the Article 7(1)(e) ground was originally included in the Regulation as a competition-saving measure for 3D marks,[20] it might be assumed that it should play the leading role in the refusal of registration of such marks. However, the provision has been criticised as difficult to understand.[21] The scope of the natural shape exclusion remains murky. Also, evidencing technical function or substantial value can be complicated, requiring technical expertise and evidence gathering. It is evident from the CJEU's case law that lack of distinctiveness also plays an important role in relation to the registrability of product shapes. Thus, this research seeks to determine whether it is

---

[14]   *Philips v Remington*, n 7, [78]; *Lego Juris*, n 7, [46]. See Ilanah Fhima, 'Technical functionality in European trade mark law' (2021) 137 *Law Quarterly Review* 113 for more commentary on the policies that underlie the shape exclusions.

[15]   Art.7(1)(b) EUTMR.

[16]   *Henkel v OHIM*, n 5, [39]; *Mag Instrument Inc v OHIM* (Case C-136/02 P) [2005] ETMR 46; ECLI:EU:C:2004:592, [31]; *Linde AG, Winward Industrie Inc and Rado Uhren AG v Deutsches Patent-und Markenamt* (Joined Cases C-53/01 to C-55/01) [2003] ETMR 78; ECLI:EU:C:2003:206, [69].

[17]   In the USA, product design (termed 'product configuration') can only be protected on proof of acquired distinctiveness (termed 'secondary meaning') whereas product packaging may be protected as 'inherently distinctive', see *Wal-Mart Stores, Inc. v Samara Bros.* 529 U.S. 205 (2000), 213–216.

[18]   Art.7(1)(c).

[19]   Arts 8(1)(a), 8(1)(b) and 8(5).

[20]   Although Art.7(1)(e) now applies to any characteristic of the goods, as discussed above, following the updating of the law in the EUTMR and EUTMD.

[21]   See, e.g. Annette Kur's detailing of the various uncertainties in the provision in 'Too Common', n 4, especially pp. 14–25; also Dinwoodie, *Conceptual Lessons*, n 2.

functionality or lack of distinctiveness that is playing the more prominent role in the refusal of registration. This is particularly important given that the Max Planck Institute, in its 2011 report on the trade mark system, argued that the substantial value exclusion in particular could be abandoned as the same result would be achieved by employing the distinctiveness and descriptiveness exclusions.[22] Thus, this research seeks to determine the extent to which these two provisions overlap with 3D shape marks being refused on both functionality and on distinctiveness grounds.

On the issue of distinctiveness, while shape marks can be inherently distinctive in principle, in practice, few pure product shapes are held to deviate sufficiently far from 'the norm' to satisfy the CJEU's test. Thus, we might expect that applicants for registration who face an Article 7(1)(b) objection will try to provide evidence of acquired distinctiveness, if the shape mark in question has been in use for a period prior to filing.[23] Indeed, providing such evidence of secondary meaning would be the standard practice in the USA. Thus, this research investigates how often acquired distinctiveness was claimed in relation to refused marks.

Finally, this project investigates whether any particular characteristics of shape marks lead to marks being refused more frequently. It considers whether the shape of products or of packaging are refused registration most often. Additionally, it considers the impact that adding additional potentially distinctive matter, such as a colour, word mark or trade dress might have in overcoming objections to registration.

3.   EXISTING LITERATURE

There is now a distinct and growing literature on the empirical analysis of intellectual property in the UK and EU investigating not only the substantive law,[24] but also which factors and actors[25] influence the development of that law.

However, empirical studies of trade mark law are relatively few in number. There are a number of studies examining the reasoning of courts in trade mark cases. Jane Cornwell[26] has

---

[22]   Max Planck Institute for Innovation and Competition, *Study on the Overall Functioning of the European Trade Mark System* (Munich, 2011), [2.34].

[23]   On the importance of acquired distinctiveness in relation to non-traditional marks, see Dinwoodie, *Conceptual Lessons*, n 2, pp. 4–5.

[24]   See, for example, Marcella Favale, Martin Kretschmer and Paul Torremans, 'Is There an EU Copyright Jurisprudence? An Empirical Analysis of the Workings of the European Court of Justice' (2016) 79(1) *Modern Law Review* 31; Oliver Church, Estelle Derclaye and Gilles Stupfler, 'An Empirical Analysis of the Design Case Law of the EU Member States' (2019) IIC 50 685.

[25]   See, for example, Estelle Derclaye, 'The multifaceted influence of the Advocates General on the Court of Justice's copyright case law: legal secretaries, literature and language' in Eleonora Rosati (ed), *Routledge Handbook of EU Copyright Law* (Routledge, 2021); Marcella Favale, Martin Kretschmer and Paul Torremans, 'Who is steering the jurisprudence of the European Court of Justice? The influence of Member State submissions on copyright law' (2020) 83(4) *Modern Law Review* 831; Oliver Church, Estelle Derclaye and Gilles Stupfler, 'Design litigation in the EU Member States: Are overlaps with other intellectual property rights and unfair competition problematic and are SMEs benefitting from the EU design legal framework?' (2021) 46(1) *European Law Review* 37; Emily Hudson, *Drafting Copyright Exceptions* (CUP, 2020).

[26]   Jane Cornwell, 'Playing by its own rules? A quantitative empirical analysis of justificatory legal reasoning in the registered trade mark case law of the European Court of Justice' (2021) 46(5) *European Law Review* 647.

studied modes of legal reasoning in the CJEU's trade mark jurisprudence, dividing them into literal, systemic and purposive reasoning. She finds that systemic rather than purposive reasoning dominates, but that in a significant number of cases, the reasoning is 'missing', calling into question the transparency of the Court's decision making. Inspired by Barton Beebe's study of infringement factors in the USA,[27] this author[28] has conducted a study considering which factors were most influential in finding likelihood of confusion in the General Court's trade mark jurisprudence, and which, despite being part of the confusion test formulated by the CJEU, had little impact.

A recent addition to the literature uses empirical methodology not to analyse the jurisprudence of which trade marks have been refused or allowed registration, but rather as a practical tool to estimate market power derived from different forms of trade dress in an attempt to allow courts to quantify competitive effects in applying the aesthetic functionality doctrine in the USA.[29] Xiaoren Wang's study uses data on the frequency with which particular colours of goods are stocked on Amazon as a proxy for their desirability to consumers.

There are also a number of empirical studies of aspects of trade mark registration in the European Union. One line of research examines whether there are so many trade marks registered that registration impedes, rather than promotes, competition. Barton Beebe and Jeanne Fromer, having analysed the entirety of the body of trade marks applied for before the EUIPO, argue that there is a problem of trade mark depletion which forms a significant barrier to entry for new businesses because all of the suggestive, or otherwise 'useful' brand names are already owned.[30] This builds on their similar study in relation to the US Trademark Register.[31] Georg von Graeventiz[32] studies the registration of pharmaceutical names, finding that EU enlargement in 2004 led to a greater risk of those names being unregistrable because of conflicts with an increased number of earlier marks, and also the added risk of the mark being objectionable in the language of one of the accession states. Thus von Graeventiz concludes that the number of suitable trade marks is not infinite and congestion effects are possible. Problems of congestion certainly form the backdrop to this piece of research with the fear that if it is too easy to register shape marks, not only will it be difficult to register shapes as *marks*, but it will also be impossible for competitors to offer the *product* embodied as the mark to consumers, i.e. clutter on the market and not just on the register.

Closer to this research is Mitchell Adams and Amanda Scardamaglia's twenty-year study of the registration of non-traditional trade marks.[33] Their research is of significantly wider geographical scope, covering the registers of the EUIPO, the United Kingdom (UK), Singapore,

[27] Barton Beebe, 'An Empirical Study of the Multifactor Tests for Trademark Infringement' (2006) 94(6) *California Law Review* 1581.
[28] Ilanah Simon Fhima and Catrina Denvir, 'An Empirical Analysis of the Likelihood of Confusion Factors in European Trade Mark Law' (2015) 46(3) IIC 310.
[29] Xiaoren Wang, 'Trade Dress Protection and Its Impact on Competition: An Attempt at an Empirical Approach' (2022) 112(3) *Trademark Reporter* 644.
[30] Barton Beebe and Jeanne Fromer, 'The Future of Trademarks in a Global Multilingual Economy: Evidence and Lessons from the European Union' (2022) 112 *The Trademark Reporter* 902.
[31] Barton Beebe and Jeanne Fromer, 'Are We Running Out of Trademarks? An Empirical Study of Trademark Depletion and Congestion' (2018) 131(4) *Harvard Law Review* 945.
[32] Georg von Graeventiz, 'Trade Mark Cluttering – Evidence from EU Enlargement' (2013) 65(3) *Oxford Economic Papers* 721.
[33] Mitchell Adams and Amanda Scardamaglia, 'Non-Traditional Trademarks: An Empirical Study' in Calboli and Senftleben, *Non-Traditional Trademarks*, n 2, pp. 37–58.

Japan and Australia. They found that of all non-traditional marks, shape marks dominate. They also track the number of applications over time, finding that the number has decreased following an initial flurry of activity following the opening of the EUIPO, as well as which classes the marks were applied for. This study is of particular interest in the context of this research because, as the authors note, Australia does not have a functionality exclusion.[34] We might therefore expect a disproportionately large number of shape applications in Australia compared to other jurisdictions. Yet, Australia has in fact experienced negative growth in terms of non-traditional trade marking activity.[35]

Also allied to this research is Carolina Castaldi's study of non-traditional marks registered in the USA up to 2016.[36] She examines which of these marks have been registered, and also by whom. It should be noted though that the US context is different to that in the EU, since US law requires marks comprising of product shape alone to have acquired a secondary 'trade mark' meaning, whereas in the EU, inherent distinctiveness can suffice. This poses particular challenges in relation to empirically analysing the protection or otherwise of 3D marks in the US. The US system is use-based, and marks are protected in the absence of registration. Given the difficulty and cost of demonstrating secondary meaning, the risk of having to demonstrate that one's mark is not functional and the fact that unregistered protection is broadly comparable, many would-be mark owners will wait to establish the scope of their rights through litigation if faced with a copyist. Thus, the US Register is not wholly reflective of which 3D shape marks actually would be protected in the USA. For good measure, where such marks are registered, the US Patent and Trademark Office search facility does not include a category for 3D marks, making the identification of such marks challenging.[37]

The focus of this research is somewhat different to those detailed above. This project and the preceding studies have empirical methodology in common, and indeed in the case of many of those detailed, a focus on registration. However, this project specifically examines which marks have been *refused* registration, rather than the whole universe of those applied for. In particular, and unlike previous studies, this project also considers the reasons for those refusals in detail.

4.   HYPOTHESES

To examine which marks are being refused registration at the EUIPO and why, the following hypotheses will be considered:

1. **More product shapes have been refused registration than shapes of packaging** – we might expect more product shapes have been refused registration because packaging has traditionally served a role in distinguishing between like goods from different sources, whereas the shape of a product is more likely to embody what consumers are seeking in

---

[34]   Ibid, 42.
[35]   Ibid, 57.
[36]   Carolina Castaldi, 'The Economics and Management of Non-Traditional Trademarks: Why, How Much, What, and Who?' in Calboli and Senftleben, *Non-Traditional Trademarks*, n 2, pp. 227–270.
[37]   I am grateful to Jeanne Fromer for these observations.

a good and/or how the goods function, and so the registration of products is more likely to have a negative effect on competition.

2. **More black and white marks have been refused registration than colour marks** – registration of a black and white mark grants protection against use of that mark in every colourway. Thus, a black and white registration will have a greater impact on availability, and hence competition, and so we might expect it to be more difficult to register such a mark, than one filed in a specific colour or combination of colours.

3. **More marks without additional non-3D characteristics have been refused registration than those with** – similarly, a mark consisting exclusively of the shape of a product would grant its owner the ability to block third parties from using the product itself, whereas the addition of non-shape matter, such as wording, a logo or other decorative elements might suggest that the owner's claim is limited to that specific qualified embodiment of the product.

4. **Functionality plays a significant role in 3D marks being refused registration** – since Article 7(1)(e) was originally a bespoke exclusion created for shape marks, and given the important competition-protecting function that the CJEU has found that the provision has, we might expect the provision and its subcategories to play a prominent role in 3D shape marks being refused registration.

5. **Lack of distinctiveness is the most common reason for marks to be refused** – nonetheless, given the complications involved in demonstrating functionality, we might expect lack of distinctiveness to play an important role blocking the registration of shape marks that might interfere with competition.

6. **Acquired distinctiveness is frequently argued in order to overcome an objection that a shape mark is devoid of distinctiveness** – the CJEU has held that many shape marks will be non-distinctive because consumers are not used to viewing the shape of goods in particular as indicative of origin.[38] However, the legislation allows for a lack of inherent distinctiveness to be overcome by evidence of acquired distinctiveness.[39] Given that the registration of the mark is otherwise doomed to certain failure, we might expect that applicants for shape marks which have been refused for lack of inherent distinctiveness will have frequently tried to demonstrate acquired distinctiveness, as is the required practice in the USA, given that product shapes there can *only* be registered on proof of secondary meaning.[40]

5.   METHODOLOGY

To test these hypotheses, an original dataset was created, including all 3D shape European Union Trade Marks (EUTMs) filed during the five-year period 1 January 2017 to 31 December 2021 that were refused registration. These marks were located using the EUIPO's 'Advanced Search' function on 'eSearch Plus'.[41] To locate just the 3D shape marks, '3D shape' was

---

[38]   *Linde AG*, n 16, [69].
[39]   Article 7(3) EUTMR.
[40]   See n 17.
[41]   See <https://euipo.europa.eu/eSearch/#advanced/trademarks> accessed on 30 May 2022.

chosen in the 'Trade mark type' field. This field is selected by trade mark applicants on their application forms. Such marks are defined in the EUIPO Guidelines as a:

> mark consisting of, or extending to, a three-dimensional shape, including containers, packaging, the product itself or its appearance. The term 'extending to' means that shape marks cover not only shapes per se, but also shapes that contain other elements, such as word elements, figurative elements or labels.[42]

The fact that it is the applicant who decides whether the mark fits in this category means that there are some atypical examples which go beyond the shape of goods and their packaging, such as logos with shading that makes them appear three-dimensional. Nonetheless, it was decided to retain those marks in the dataset because (a) that is how they are categorised within the EU Register and (b) the EUIPO has the power to demand that marks be recategorized, but has chosen not to do so in relation to these marks.[43]

'Application Refused' was selected for 'Trade mark status (EUTM)' and '01/01/2017' to '31/12/2021' were entered into the 'Filing date' field. It would have produced a more stable dataset if refusal date could have been used as the chronological limit of the study. However, while refusal dates are visible in the timelines included as part of the official record of individual marks, the EUIPO does not index marks according to refusal dates, and therefore there is no way of searching for refusals dated according to a specific period. The challenge with using filing dates is that the size of the dataset changes over time because each refusal takes a different amount of time to issue, depending on the nature of the objection, etc. Thus, the study was limited to all marks with a filing date falling within the aforementioned range that had been refused as of 1 May 2022.

These parameters produced a dataset of 294 refused applications. To put this number into perspective, in total 2024 3D shape marks were applied for during the five-year period of this study, of which 1462 had proceeded to registration at the time of writing.[44]

Details of the refused marks were initial coded in Excel. Data was collected in relation to the following:

- the trade mark number,
- the description of the mark,
- whether it was for a product or packaging or other,
- whether it was colour or black and white,
- which Nice Classes had been designated,
- the filing and refusal dates,
- the presence and nature of any non-shape elements of the sign,
- whether acquired distinctiveness had been considered and whether it had been found,
- the grounds for the refusal of registration, in particular lack of distinctiveness, descriptiveness, the three Article 7(1)(e) grounds for refusal, relative grounds and any other ground.

---

[42]   EUIPO Guidelines for Examination of European Union Trade Marks, Part B, Section 2, Ch. 9.3.3, (March 2022 version).
[43]   See Art.3(3)(c) EUTMIR – for an example see EUTM No. 018458471 (LA MILANESINA), Decision of 26/04/2021.
[44]   As of 13 July 2022. The remaining marks were either withdrawn, still subject to examination or appeal, or were cancelled or surrendered.

This information was gathered by the author from the EUIPO's electronic record for each of the refused trade marks. Most of the information could be found on the file record itself. However, the grounds on which the mark was refused, as well as whether acquired distinctiveness had been argued, were derived by the author from reading the Ruling on Opposition (or appeals where appropriate) included within the file record.[45] It should be noted though that in 43 cases, this ruling was missing,[46] making it impossible to determine why the mark was refused registration. For these signs, only the data regarding the mark itself and the relevant dates were recorded.

The dataset was then imported into SPSS[47] for statistical analysis to test the hypotheses. Bar and pie charts were generated in Excel.

It should be noted that we cannot deduce from the data used in this chapter which types of mark are more likely to be refused registration than others. Rather, this data shows us in absolute terms how many product shapes and how many packaging shapes were refused registration, and the same for colour versus black and white marks and those with or without non-3D shape matter. This is because the data set includes refused marks only. To tell how *likely* it is that one form of mark versus another would be refused registration, we would need to examine both those marks which are refused registration *and* those which were applied for. Only by knowing, for example, the percentage of product and packaging shapes *applied for* that result in refusals could we conclude that product shapes are more likely to be refused registration than packaging if equal numbers of shapes of products and shapes were applied for. This would be even more true if fewer product shapes than packaging shapes were applied for, and yet more product shapes were refused. Equally, if far more product shapes are applied for than packaging shapes, it would not be surprising that there were more product shape refusals in absolute terms. The same would be true in relation to colour and non-3D matter. Thus, further research (which is planned to form part of the wider project), is required to understand the relative likelihood of each of these characteristics of shape marks being refused registration. It should further be noted that what this study cannot capture is information regarding shape mark applications which have been withdrawn prior to refusal to prevent the grounds for a likely refusal from being made public.

6. RESULTS

This next section tests the hypotheses by reference to the data gathered and analysed.

---

[45] In fact, the file record also details the provision under which the mark was refused registration. However, the author found that this information did not always capture the full reasons, particularly where there were multiple reasons for refusal. Additionally, it did not always document when acquired distinctiveness was argued unsuccessfully.

[46] Attempts were made to secure these missing decisions from the EUIPO, this was successful for some, but not all, of the marks.

[47] SPSS – standing for 'Statistical Package for the Social Sciences' – is data analysis software, acquired by IBM, and now officially known as IBM SPSS Statistics.

6.1   Are More Product Shapes Refused Registration than Packaging?

It was hypothesised that more product shapes would be refused registration than packaging. Descriptive statistics were used to test this hypothesis. As can be seen below, this hypothesis was proven to be correct. 65%[48] (n.191) of 3D marks refused registration consisted of the 3D shape of products while less than half of this, 28.9% (n.85), consisted of the shape of packaging. It should be noted that there were a small number of refused marks that did not fit neatly into either category. There were two logo marks, consisting of words and devices which presumably were labelled as 3D shape marks because they had shading that made them appear 3D. There were also seven marks which I classed as 'other'. These tended to be marks for services, rather than goods, where the shape depicted was for subject matter related to the service (e.g. the shape of a glass of Martini for services in Class 43[49]). Finally, there were a small number of marks which covered a range of goods meaning that it was potentially the shape of the product for some, but the shape of packaging for others. For example, the shape of an inhaler[50] was registered for both inhalers (product) and pharmaceutical preparations (packaging). See Table 13.1 and Figure 13.1 for an overview of these findings.

Table 13.1   Refusals by mark type in relation to products and packaging

		Frequency	Percent	Valid Percent	Cumulative Percent
Valid	Logo	2	0.7	0.7	0.7
	Other	7	2.4	2.4	3.1
	Packaging	85	28.9	28.9	32.0
	Product	191	65.0	65.0	96.9
	Product and Other	2	0.7	0.7	97.6
	Product and Packaging	7	2.4	2.4	100.0
	Total	294	100.0	100.0	

6.2   Are More Black and White Marks Refused Registration than Colour Marks?

It was hypothesised that more black and white marks would be refused registration than colour marks. Descriptive statistics were used to test this hypothesis. As Table 13.2 and Figure 13.2 show, this hypothesis was proven to be correct: 185 of the refused marks were black and white, equating to 62.9% of the sample. This is considerably more than the 109 colour marks (37.1%) which were refused.

6.3   Are More Marks without Additional Non-3D Characteristics Refused Registration than Those With?

It was hypothesised that more signs which consisted only of the 3D shape would be refused registration than those which had additional non-3D characteristics (such as logos, wording,

---

[48]   Note that because 43 decisions were missing, SPSS generates percentages in terms of the absolute numbers of marks refused, and 'valid percentages', excluding the marks where the reasons for refusal were missing. References herein will be to valid percentages.

[49]   EUTM No. 018049127.

[50]   EUTM No. 018172665.

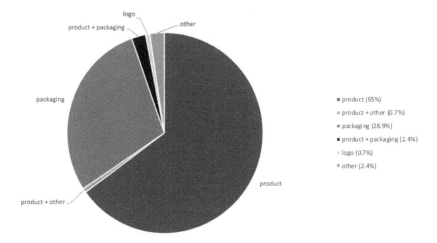

Figure 13.1   Percentage of refusals by mark type

Table 13.2   Refusals by colour of trade mark

		Frequency	Percent	Valid Percent	Cumulative Percent
Valid	Black and white	185	62.9	62.9	62.9
	Colour	109	37.1	37.1	100.0
	Total	294	100.0	100.0	

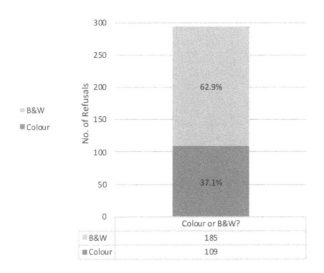

Figure 13.2   Number/percentage of refusals by colour claim

Table 13.3   Refusals by presence/absence of non-3D features

		Frequency	Percent	Valid Percent	Cumulative Percent
Valid	Absent	235	79.9	79.9	79.9
	Present	59	20.1	20.1	100.0
	Total	294	100.0	100.0	

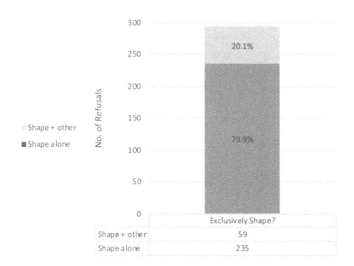

Shape + other	59
Shape alone	235

Figure 13.3   Number/percentage of refusals by presence/absence of non-3D features

getup etc.). This was proven to be correct using descriptive statistics: 79% (n.235) of the refused marks featured no non-3D characteristics (see Table 13.3 and Figure 13.3).

However, 20.1% (n.59) of the refused marks did have non-3D characteristics which were insufficient to overcome the objection to registration. One might expect the addition of non-3D characteristics to overcome any objection based on lack of distinctiveness. It was therefore further hypothesised that, for those marks which included non-3D features, the ground for refusal was likely to be something other than lack of distinctiveness, e.g. the relative grounds for refusal. Crosstabulation[51] was used to test this hypothesis. See Tables 13.4–13.7 for more detail.

First, it should be noted that, as described above, the ground for refusal is not available for some of the marks. The grounds were available for 45 of the 59 marks which had non-3D features but were nonetheless refused registration.

- 29 of those marks lacked distinctiveness.
- 0 were technically functional.
- 3 added substantial value to the goods.
- 13 were rejected based upon relative grounds.

---

[51]   A crosstabulation, or contingency, table shows the relationship between two or more variables by recording the frequency of observations that have multiple characteristics.

Table 13.4   *Crosstabulation of presence of non-3D features and refusal on basis of Art.7(1)(b) (Lack of distinctiveness)*

| | | Art.7(1)(b) | | Total |
		Not raised	Raised	
Presence of non-3D features	Absent	3	203	206
	Present	16	29	45
Total		19	232	251

Table 13.5   *Crosstabulation of presence of non-3D features and refusal on basis of Art.7(1)(e)(ii) (Second Indent)*

| | | Art.7(1)(e)(ii) | | Total |
		Not raised	Raised	
Presence of non-3D features	Absent	193	13	206
	Present	45	0	45
Total		238	13	251

Table 13.6   *Crosstabulation of presence of non-3D features and refusal on basis of Art.7(1)(e)(iii) (Third Indent)*

| | | Art.7(1)(e)(iii) | | Total |
		Not raised	Raised	
Presence of non-3D features	Absent	199	7	206
	Present	42	3	45
Total		241	10	251

Table 13.7   *Crosstabulation of presence of non-3D features and refusal on basis of relative grounds*

| | | Relative Grounds | | Total |
		Not raised	Raised	
Presence of non-3D features	Absent	205	1	206
	Present	32	13	45
Total		237	14	251

Thus, the further hypothesis was proven to be incorrect, and the majority of those marks which feature non-3D characteristics but were nonetheless refused registration were refused because of a lack of distinctiveness. An objection based on relative grounds was the next most common ground for refusal. None of the examples of this category of marks were found to be technically functional under the second indent.

6.4   Does Functionality Play a Significant Role in 3D Marks Being Refused Registration?

It was hypothesised that, Article 7(1)(e), as the provision created originally to consider the particular dangers to competition posed by shape marks, would play a major role in the ground for which 3D shape marks were refused. However, using descriptive statistics to track the frequency with which each of the Article 7(1)(e) grounds was relied upon as a ground for refusal suggests that this hypothesis is *untrue*.

Table 13.8   Refusals on basis of Art.7(1)(e)(ii) (Second Indent)

		Frequency	Percent	Valid Percent	Cumulative Percent
Valid	Art.7(1)(e)(ii) not raised	238	81.0	94.8	94.8
	Art.7(1)(e)(ii) raised	13	4.4	5.2	100.0
	Total	251	85.4	100.0	
Missing		43	14.6		
Total		294	100.0		

Table 13.9   Refusals of basis of Art.7(1)(e)(iii) (Third Indent)

		Frequency	Percent	Valid Percent	Cumulative Percent
Valid	Art.7(1)(e)(iii) not raised	241	82.0	96.0	96.0
	Art.7(1)(e)(iii) raised	10	3.4	4.0	100.0
	Total	251	85.4	100.0	
Missing		43	14.6		
Total		294	100.0		

Table 13.10   Refusals on basis of Art.7(1)(e)(i) (First Indent)

		Art.7(1)(e)(ii)		Total
		Not raised	Raised	
Art.7(1)(b)	Not raised	18	1	19
	Raised	220	12	232
Total		238	13	251

Table 13.11   Crosstabulation: refusals on basis of Art.7(1)(b) (lack of distinctive character) and refusals on basis of Art.7(1)(e)(ii) (Second Indent)

		Frequency	Percent	Valid Percent	Cumulative Percent
Valid	Art.7(1)(e)(i) not raised	251	85.4	100.0	100.0
Missing		43	14.6		
Total		294	100.0		

The second indent (characteristics which are necessary to obtain a technical result) relates to how things work, and therefore perhaps is the ground that is most protective of competition, and is what is commonly thought of as functionality. However, as can be seen in Table 13.8, it was raised in just 4.4% (n.13) of refusals studied.

The third indent (characteristics which add substantial value to the goods) was relied on in even fewer instances – 3.4% (n.10) of the refusals studied (Table 13.9).

Finally, the first indent (characteristics resulting from the nature of the goods themselves) was not raised in *any* of the refusals studied (Table 13.10).

Given the surprising lack of reliance on the Article 7(1)(e) grounds for refusal, it was decided to explore how many examples there were of functionality alone serving as the ground for refusal of registration. This was considered via a cross tabulation with the ground for refusal most likely to overlap with Article 7(1)(e), lack of distinctive character. The results demonstrate that technical functionality and substantial value were the sole ground for the

Table 13.12   *Crosstabulation: refusals on basis of Art. 7(1)(b) (lack of distinctive character) and refusals on basis of Art. 7(1)(e)(iii) (Third Indent)*

		Art.7(1)(e)(iii)		Total
		Not raised	Raised	
Art.7(1)(b)	Not raised	18	1	19
	Raised	223	9	232
Total		241	10	251

refusal of registration in just one decision each.[52] This means that in every other functionality case, the Article 7(1)(e) grounds overlapped with the devoid of distinctive character grounds (see Tables 13.11 and 13.12).

6.5   Is Lack of Distinctiveness the Most Common Reason for Marks to be Refused?

It was hypothesised that lack of distinctiveness would be the most common reason for marks to be refused registration. Descriptive statistics were used to analyse which ground was most commonly used as the basis of marks being refused. It should be remembered that a mark can be refused for more than one reason.

The data below demonstrates that lack of distinctiveness was by far the most common reason for marks to be refused registration in 92.4% of decisions for which the reasons are present (n.232). Thus, the hypothesis was proved to be correct. Next were the relative grounds, raised in just 5.6% decisions (n.14). The second indent (5.2%, n.13) and third indent (4.0%, n.10) came next. Descriptiveness was raised in only 2.4% (n.6) of cases. Other reasons (such

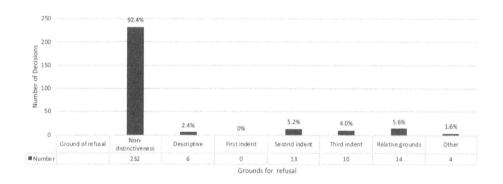

Figure 13.4   *Frequency/percentage of the different grounds for refusal*

---

[52]   It will be remembered that the EUIPO did not raise the 'natural shapes' exclusion of the first indent in relation to the cases in the dataset, and so this ground did not form part of this crosstabulation.

as problems with the representation of the mark) were present in just 1.6% (n.4) of cases and there were no decisions refused under the first indent. See Figure 13.4 and Tables 13.13–13.19.

Table 13.13   Refusals based on Art.7(1)(b) (lack of distinctiveness)

		Frequency	Percent	Valid Percent	Cumulative Percent
Valid	Art.7(1)(b) not raised	19	6.5	7.6	7.6
	Art.7(1)(b) raised	**232**	**78.9**	**92.4**	100.0
	Total	251	85.4	100.0	
Missing		43	14.6		
Total		294	100.0		

Table 13.14   Refusals based on Art.7(1)(c) (descriptiveness)

		Frequency	Percent	Valid Percent	Cumulative Percent
Valid	Art.7(1)(c) not raised	245	83.3	97.6	97.6
	Art.7(1)(c) raised	**6**	**2.0**	**2.4**	100.0
	Total	251	85.4	100.0	
Missing		43	14.6		
Total		294	100.0		

Table 13.15   Refusals based on Art.7(1)(e)(i) (First Indent)

		Frequency	Percent	Valid Percent	Cumulative Percent
Valid	Art.7(1)(e)(i) not raised	**251**	**85.4**	**100.0**	100.0
Missing		43	14.6		
Total		294	100.0		

Table 13.16   Refusals based on Art.7(1)(e)(ii) (Second Indent)

		Frequency	Percent	Valid Percent	Cumulative Percent
Valid	Art.7(1)(e)(ii) not raised	238	81.0	94.8	94.8
	Art.7(1)(e)(ii) raised	**13**	**4.4**	**5.2**	100.0
	Total	251	85.4	100.0	
Missing		43	14.6		
Total		294	100.0		

Table 13.17   Refusals based on Art.7(1)(e)(iii) (Third Indent)

		Frequency	Percent	Valid Percent	Cumulative Percent
Valid	Art.7(1)(e)(iii) not raised	241	82.0	96.0	96.0
	Art.7(1)(e)(iii) raised	**10**	**3.4**	**4.0**	100.0
	Total	251	85.4	100.0	
Missing		43	14.6		
Total		294	100.0		

Table 13.18   Refusals based on Art.8 (Relative grounds)

		Frequency	Percent	Valid Percent	Cumulative Percent
Valid	Art.8 not raised	237	80.6	94.4	94.4
	Art.8 raised	**14**	**4.8**	**5.6**	100.0
	Total	251	85.4	100.0	
Missing		43	14.6		
Total		294	100.0		

Table 13.19   Refusals based on other reasons

		Frequency	Percent	Valid Percent	Cumulative Percent
Valid	Absent	247	84.0	98.4	98.4
	Present	**4**	**1.4**	**1.6**	100.0
	Total	251	85.4	100.0	
Missing		43	14.6		
Total		294	100.0		

6.6   Is Acquired Distinctiveness Argued in the Majority of Shape Mark Refusal Cases to Overcome Prejudices Regarding the Distinctiveness of Shape Marks?

Descriptive statistics demonstrated that acquired distinctiveness was argued in only 8.8% (n.26) of the refusal proceedings surveyed, meaning that the hypothesis that acquired distinctiveness would be argued in the majority of shape refusals was false (see Table 13.20 and Figure 13.5).

It should be noted that acquired distinctiveness was not demonstrated in *any* of the 294 refusal decisions surveyed. This is not entirely surprising. If the marks in question had acquired distinctiveness, they probably would not have been refused registration given that it appears to be lack of distinctiveness, rather than functionality (which cannot be overcome by acquired distinctiveness), that is driving shape refusals.

Table 13.20   Refusals where acquired distinctiveness was claimed

		Frequency	Percent	Valid Percent	Cumulative Percent
Valid	No	225	76.5	89.6	89.6
	Yes	26	8.8	10.4	100.0
	Total	251	85.4	100.0	
Missing		43	14.6		
Total		294	100.0		

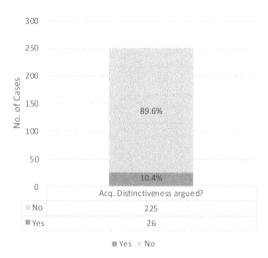

Figure 13.5   Number/percentage where acquired distinctiveness was argued

7.   DISCUSSION AND NEXT STEPS

Certain of the results in this study confirm empirically what trade mark lawyers already suspect. It is little surprise that more black and white marks are refused registration than colour marks and likewise that more marks without non-3D features are refused registration than those with. This is because both colour and non-3D features – providing they are non-trivial – can contribute to making the mark different from those already on the market, and so less likely to be considered devoid of distinctive character. Likewise, we might instinctively expect more product shapes to be refused registration than packaging shapes given that these are likely to have the greatest effect on competition. Additionally, undertakings have always used product packaging to convey information about goods (whether or not that packaging was allowed to be registered) and so consumers are arguably more likely to derive messages about origin from packaging than the shape of the product itself. What is perhaps challenging is that, according to the CJEU's jurisprudence,[53] competition concerns are only meant to be considered directly at least as part of the Article 7(1)(e) analysis. Yet we might suspect from these results that, as Dinwoodie has previously suggested,[54] effect on competition might be being indirectly considered through Article 7(1)(b) given that more of the forms of marks that are likely to restrict competition are being refused registration.

However, a limitation of this study is that, as mentioned, because only refused marks were examined, we cannot prove from this data that black and white, product shapes or marks

---

[53]   *Henkel* v *OHIM*, n 5, [45]–[46]; *SAT.1 SatellitenFernsehen GmbH* v *OHIM* (Case C-329/02 P) [2005] ETMR 20: ECLI:EU:C:2004:532, [23]–[27].
[54]   Dinwoodie, *Conceptual Lessons*, n 2, pp. 24–25: 'Although concerns for competition have nominally been pushed (in large part) into assessments of descriptiveness and the requirement of a sign capable of graphic representation, the settled approach to assessing the distinctive character of shapes and colors is, I would suggest, a normative rule embedded in what is supposedly simply an empirical assessment.'

without non-3D matter are more likely to be refused registration as we do not know in what proportion such marks were applied for, compared to colour marks, packaging shapes and marks with non-3D matter. Further research (which is part of this author's wider project) is needed to determine which forms of shape marks are most likely to be refused registration by contextualising this data against the universe of all 3D shape marks applied for and ultimately registered in the relevant period.

In terms of *why* marks are being refused, here the results are more surprising. This study has shown that functionality has had only a very small role in shape marks being refused over the past five years and almost no independent role. This is important for a number of reasons.

The first question to ask is *why* is functionality being sidelined? Ramírez Montes[55] suggests that there is a reluctance on the part of examiners to apply functionality because it is perceived as 'harsh' due to its inability to be overcome with evidence of acquired distinctiveness. Other possibilities include it being too complicated to apply,[56] requiring too much evidence or that it is just much less challenging to demonstrate a lack of distinctive character. These are not questions that a study of this nature can answer, though there is future scope for asking the actors involved in the system, particularly those examining marks, why this state of affairs may have arisen.

The next question we might ask is, if functionality has such a limited independent role, is it worth even having it as a ground for the refusal of registration? The Max Planck Report[57] suggested that the first indent (shapes resulting from the nature of the goods) overlapped with lack of distinctive character, and so it could safely be removed from the Directive and Regulation. Given the results of this study we might ponder whether the same is true of the second or third indent too, given that they have been shown, in this dataset, to overlap almost entirely with distinctiveness. However, a change to the legislation is unlikely at this point in time. More importantly, the empirical data for which marks are being refused does not tell us whether the presence of the functionality grounds deters applicants from applying for marks which would be competitively harmful in the first place. It is very possible that the existence of the functionality exclusions is having a deterrent effect against the registration of functional marks. The existence of the functionality exclusions also sends a powerful signal that marks that have a negative effect on competition should not be registered, even if the ultimate ground on which they are refused registration may well be lack of distinctiveness. Functionality should also prevent the registration of marks which may have only acquired a distinctive character because they have enjoyed a monopoly through patent or design protection, which has

---

[55]   César Ramírez-Montes, 'Proving inherent distinctiveness of trade dress marks: does European Union law depart significantly from the norm? Part 1' [2019] *Intellectual Property Quarterly* 224, 236 onwards.

[56]   The various steps that need to be undertaken to show technical functionality are detailed in Ilanah Fhima, 'Functionality in Europe: When do Trademarks Achieve a Technical Result?' (2020) 110(3) *The Trademark Reporter* 659.

[57]   *Max Planck Report*, n 22. Though in later writing, 'Aesthetic functionality in EU law – should it be deleted?' in Dinwoodie and Janis, *Research Handbook*, n 4, pp. 188–191, Kur has clarified that it was never the intention to grant registration to the sorts of marks that might fall under the third indent and that it was always the intention to ensure that competition was protected. While the Max Planck Report suggests that distinctiveness and descriptiveness might be the vehicles for providing this competition, in later writing she suggests a US-style exclusion merging technical and aesthetic functionality with protection of competition as the ultimate goal behind both.

prevented competitors from offering goods having a similar appearance. An example would be the three-headed shaver which was the subject of *Philips v Remington*.[58] It should be noted though that, given that no marks were found to have acquired distinctiveness in the five-year period studied, there were no examples of functionality playing such a role in this study. While removing the functionality exclusion is unlikely, and on balance ultimately undesirable, the fact that this study demonstrates that it is seldom relied on when marks are refused does suggest that the time is ripe for an examination of whether the exclusion is doing what it is meant to do particularly in terms of protecting competition. If it is not, we need to ask why.

A further concern is that the grounds for refusal are meant to be considered in the light of the public policy underlying them. In the case of functionality, this policy is based on the access needs of competitors. However, for marks which are devoid of distinctive character, competition concerns are *not* meant to be considered and instead the examination is meant to be limited to the ability of the mark to function as a trade mark. If functionality is routinely not being considered, this means that the opportunity for competition issues to be considered during the examination of shape marks has all but disappeared. This is problematic, particularly given the impact that registering product features that make a good work can have on competition. In the light of this finding, there may be an argument for revisiting Kur's recommendation[59] that shape marks should be considered a special category with competition concerns forming part of the distinctiveness analysis, in the same way as availability to competitors forms part of the distinctiveness analysis for colour marks.[60] While it is true that competition concerns may alternatively be considered as part of the consideration of whether a mark is descriptive, the data shows that descriptiveness plays very little role in the shape mark cases, being raised only six times, and in a number of those cases, the descriptiveness arose from the wording on the label applied to the shape, rather than the shape mark itself.

It is also worth noting Adams and Scardamaglia's finding that, despite the lack of a functionality ground for refusal in Australia, there has been negative growth in the registration of non-traditional marks. While it might be tempting to assume that a lack of a functionality ground would lead to it to being much easier to register shape marks in Australia than in the EU, the research in this study suggests that functionality is doing very little work before the EUIPO in terms of blocking shape marks anyway, with lack of distinctiveness, a ground that Australia shares, playing the leading role instead. This, combined, with Adams and Scardamaglia's finding regarding the diminishing number of shape marks, suggests that further research might usefully explore whether the Australian approach to shape marks, and any lessons therein, is more similar than we might otherwise have assumed.[61] In particular, further research might examine whether Australia has managed to incorporate competition concerns into its distinctiveness analysis and if so, whether Europe could do the same.

Finally, this study has shown a seeming reticence by those who are applying for shape marks to argue that their marks have acquired distinctiveness. Acquired distinctiveness was

---

[58]   *Philips v Remington*, n 7.
[59]   Kur, 'Too Common', n 4, pp 29–30.
[60]   *Libertel Groep BV v Benelux-Merkenbureau* (Case C-104/01) [2003] ETMR 63: ECLI:EU:C:2003:244, [60].
[61]   However, see Michael Handler, 'Disentangling Functionality, Distinctiveness and Use in Australian Trade Mark Law' (2018) 42(1) *Melbourne University Law Review* 15. The author paints a bleak picture, arguing that the lack of a functionality doctrine has meant that functionality concerns have not been properly considered, and the operation of the distinctiveness exclusion has been distorted.

argued in only 8.8% of refusals. We might expect that number to be higher. It is acknowledged that proving acquired distinctiveness requires the gathering of a substantial amount of evidence, and is particularly challenging given the requirement that, for an EUTM, the mark must have acquired distinctiveness throughout the whole EU.[62] However, once the mark is set to be refused, acquired distinctiveness is the only chance to 'save' the mark. Yet in most cases it just is not argued. This is despite the fact that in the overwhelming majority of cases, the data has shown that the reasons for the refusal of the mark is a lack of inherent distinctiveness which acquired distinctiveness can solve, rather than functionality which acquired distinctiveness would not 'cure'. Why acquired distinctiveness is not argued more often is, at this point, a matter for speculation. Difficulties in gathering sufficient evidence may play a role, though it is worth noting that, unlike in the use-based US system, marks, including shape marks in Europe, can be applied for before they are used,[63] meaning that at least some of the marks may have never had the opportunity to acquire distinctiveness. However, if the difficulty is that it is just too difficult to demonstrate acquired distinctiveness across the EU we might ask if the standard is correctly calibrated. Given that the possibility of showing acquired distinctiveness was included in the EUTMR, to have a standard that is so unattainable that trade mark owners faced with the loss of their marks do not even try to demonstrate it is problematic.[64]

AUTHOR NOTE

The author would like to thank Professor Nigel Balmer for his assistance with understanding the hidden depths of SPSS, Professor Jeanne Fromer and Professor Phillip Johnson for helpful comments and Dr Lynne Chave for excellent research assistance.

---

[62]   For 3D marks held to lack inherent distinctiveness, this objection applies throughout the EU territory. In such cases, the CJEU has confirmed that an applicant must demonstrate acquired distinctiveness throughout the EU too; *Société des Produits Nestlé SA* v *Mondelez UK Holdings & Services Ltd (formerly Cadbury Holdings Ltd)* (Case C-84/17 P) [2018] ETMR 38; ECLI:EU:C:2018:596. In that case, although Nestlé – seeking to register the shape of a four-fingered Kit Kat bar – had been selling the product in many EU member states for decades, the application failed because there had been no assessment of whether the shape had acquired a distinctive character in Ireland, Belgium, Luxembourg, Portugal or Greece. Although these countries represented only 10% of the EU population, lack of distinctiveness in some parts of the EU territory could not be offset by a higher level of awareness in others.

[63]   Pursuant to EUTMR, Arts 18 and 58(1)(a), EUTMs can be registered for up to five years before they are liable for revocation on the grounds of non-use.

[64]   For a detailed discussion on the application of acquired distinctiveness to non-traditional marks see Luis Porangaba, 'Acquired Distinctiveness in the European Union: When Nontraditional Marks Meet a (Fragmented) Single Market' (2019) 109(3) *Trademark Reporter* 619.

14. Trade marks law of Thailand and certain empirical incongruities

Piani Nanakorn

1. INTRODUCTION

In Thailand, trade marks law has gained momentum. The significantly rising number of applications for registration of trade marks has resulted in an enormous backlog of work at the Department of Intellectual Property of Thailand. Although mechanisms for the protection of trade marks under the Trade Marks Act, B.E. 2534 (1991) are, overall, in line with the international obligations in the Agreement on the Trade-Related Aspects of Intellectual Property Rights (the TRIPS Agreement), meticulous analysis of this Act reveals certain ineptness calling for appropriate amendment. Indeed, a perusal of rulings of authorities bring to light the interpretation of law in a way much impeding registration of trade marks in this jurisdiction.

This work portrays reality surrounding the current trade marks legislation of Thailand. It will, first, provide a brief account of evolution of trade marks law in this country from days of yore up to the present. A summary of contents of each legislation dealing with trade marks will be explicated. The next part will discuss key contents of the Trade Marks Act, B.E. 2534 (1991) which is currently in force. This will be followed by analysis of certain problematical issues residing in, or generated by inept interpretation of, this legislation. The concluding part suggests solutions to such incongruities.

2. HISTORICAL EVOLUTION OF TRADE MARKS LAW IN THAILAND

Legal recognition of trade marks in Thailand came into sight in 1907 during the late reign of King Rama V. Under the then subsistence agriculture economy, the use of trade marks for commercial purposes was uncommon for Thai people and, rather, concentrated amongst foreign expatriates. Trade marks protection operated under the umbrella of criminal law rather than *sui generis* legislation. The Penal Code of 1907[1] introduced certain offences relating to trade marks. Culpable acts included unduly using another person's or firm's name with goods, packaging or price labels,[2] counterfeiting or imitating another person's or firm's trade mark[3] and importing goods known to carry a name or mark unlawfully used as aforesaid.[4] Although this Code was replaced by the current Penal Code of 1957, offences concerning trade names

---

[1] This Penal Code is known as the Penal Code, R.E. (*Rattanakosin* Era) 127, which is equivalent to B.E. 2450 or A.D. 1907.

[2] S. 235 of the Penal Code, R.E. 127.

[3] SS. 236–237 of the Penal Code, R.E. 127.

[4] S. 238 of the Penal Code, R.E. 127.

and trade marks are retained, with modification. In 1910, despite no concepts regarding registrability of trade marks, the Trade Marks Register Office was established within the Ministry
of Agriculture for registering trade marks typically for agricultural produce. Later, specific
legislation on trade marks emerged, as will be discussed shortly.

2.1   Trade Marks and Trade Names Act, B.E. 2457 (1914)

The Trade Marks and Trade Names Act, B.E. 2457 (1914) appeared as the first *sui generis*
trade mark legislation of the country. Despite its emergence as specific law, legal concepts
appeared rather undeveloped. The Act dealt with registration of trade marks and trade names
without modern notions concerning registrability and invalidity of trade marks. Following
this enactment, too little registration of trade marks was witnessed and, indeed, registration
of trade names was unheard of. However, efforts in facilitating registration of trade marks for
commercial purposes transpired. The Ministry of Commerce was established in 1920. Shortly
afterwards, in 1923, the Commercial Registration Department was founded within this new
Ministry and took over trade marks registration tasks from the Ministry of Agriculture.

2.2   Trade Marks Act, B.E. 2474 (1931)

The Trade Marks Act, B.E. 2474 (1931) (the "Act of 1931") is the first trade marks legislation
of its kind which introduced modern legal concepts. Although Thailand, at that time, did not
join the Paris Convention for the Protection of Industrial Property, modern concepts in this
Act were attributable to its being framed along the line of the Trade Marks Act 1905 of the
United Kingdom. Under this Thai Act, a trade mark was registrable if it possessed a distinctive
character. The Act provided a list of four essential particulars for establishing distinctiveness:
(1) the name of a company, individual, or firm, represented in a special or particular manner,
(2) the signature of the applicant for registration or some predecessor in his business, (3) an
invented word or invented words and (4) a word or words having no direct reference to the
character or quality of the goods, and not being according to its ordinary signification a geographical name or a surname.[5] A trade mark containing none of those listed particulars was
registrable only if proven, upon evidence, to possess distinctiveness,[6] which was defined to
be what could be adapted to distinguish the goods of the mark's owner from those of others.[7]
A trade mark possessing any of prohibited components (including official flags, royal arms,
royal names, royal effigies, official emblems and any mark contrary to public policy or morality) was outright unregistrable.[8]

 The Act, for the first time in Thailand, introduced classification of goods and allowed
application for registration to be made for the whole class of goods or for particular goods in
each class.[9] Legal concepts concerning identical or similar trade marks also unprecedentedly

---

   [5]   S. 4 (1) to (4) of the Act of 1931, exactly replicating s. 9 (1) to (4) of the Trade Marks Act 1905 of
the U.K.
   [6]   S. 4 (5) of the Act of 1931, adopting, with some modification, s. 9 (5) of the Trade Marks Act 1905
of the U.K.
   [7]   S. 4 para. 2 of the Act of 1931, couched along the lines of the definition in s. 9 of the Trade Marks
Act 1905 of the U.K.
   [8]   S. 5 of the Act of 1931.
   [9]   S. 8 of the Act of 1931.

came forward in this Act, as to which a trade mark identical with a registered trade mark or so similar to a registered trade mark as to deceive the public would be unregistrable, provided that such identity or deceptive similarity occurred in respect of goods of the same class.[10] However, the Act allowed registration by different owners of identical or nearly identical trade marks for the same goods or description of goods in the case of honest concurrent use or special circumstances.[11] Further, the Act introduced the concept of disclaimers. Where a trade mark contained a matter common to the trade or a non-distinctive part, the registrar was empowered to order the applicant to disclaim the exclusive use of that part or to make any other disclaimer.[12]

Detailed registration procedures were formulated by this Act. These included procedures for publication of applications and for opposition,[13] but legal grounds for opposition were not specified. With respect to effects of registration, an owner of a registered mark had the exclusive right to use it for the goods of the class or classes for which registration was made.[14] Protection of a registered trade mark commenced as from the filing date, which was deemed to be the registration date,[15] and took effect for all colours if no colour limitation was made.[16] Protection was for a renewable period of ten years.[17] The Act made clear that no legal proceedings were allowed for preventing, or recovering damages for, infringement of any unregistered trade mark, but a legal action against passing-off was not precluded.[18]

The Act empowered the Court to cancel a trade mark registration where the claimant had a better right, the registered trade mark subsequently became a common matter in the trade or the registered trade mark was devoid of distinctiveness or was a prohibited mark.[19] Non-use of a registered trade mark constituted a ground for cancellation where its owner had no *bona fide* intention to use it and actually never *bona fide* used it or where, over the past five years, there was no *bona fide* use by its owner.[20]

Statutory protection did not extend to service marks, certification marks or collective marks and the notion of particular protection of well-known marks was non-existent. Also, concepts as regards licensing were not found in this Act; the Act permitted a transfer of a registered trade mark only together with a transfer of the business concerned in the goods for which the trade mark was registered.[21] The Act failed to lay down clear powers of registrars. At its initial enactment, the Act made no provision for appealing against registrars' orders to a non-judicial appellate body. It only allowed registrars' refusal orders to be reviewed by the Minister.[22] The appellate tribunal called the Trade Marks Board was subsequently set up by the amending Act in 1961. In effect, although this Act was repealed by the Trade Marks Act, B.E. 2534 (1991), several modern concepts have been carried into the new Act with refinement.

---

[10]   S. 16 of the Act of 1931.
[11]   S. 18 of the Act of 1931.
[12]   S. 19 of the Act of 1931.
[13]   SS. 21 and 22 of the Act of 1931.
[14]   S. 27 of the Act of 1931.
[15]   S. 24 of the Act of 1931.
[16]   S. 28 of the Act of 1931.
[17]   SS. 35–37 of the Act of 1931.
[18]   S. 29 of the Act of 1931.
[19]   S. 41 of the Act of 1931.
[20]   S. 42 of the Act of 1931.
[21]   S. 31 of the Act of 1931.
[22]   S. 16 para. 2 of the Act of 1931.

2.3   Trade Marks Act, B.E. 2534 (1991)

The Trade Marks Act, B.E. 2534 (1991) has, at the time of its drafting, been framed much in imitation of the Trade Marks Act 1938 of the United Kingdom. As its preparation and legislative process occurred while negotiations of the WTO Agreement, including the TRIPS Agreement, were in progress, certain concepts in the subsequently finalised TRIPS Agreement and in some provisions of the Paris Convention as incorporated into the TRIPS Agreement have been implanted into this new legislation. However, in the same way as the Trade Marks Act 1938 of the U.K. refined legal notions enshrined in the Act of 1905, the Trade Marks Act, B.E. 2534 (1991) of Thailand has made further development from the former Act of 1931 in several aspects.

3.   KEY CONTENTS OF THE CURRENT TRADE MARKS ACT

The Trade Marks Act, B.E. 2534 (1991) (the "Act of 1991" or the "current Act") is the *sui generis* legislation presently in force and, as hitherto mentioned, has put forth amelioration in furtherance of the Act of 1931. A plethora of legal concepts which had no recognition in the preceding Act are put in place in this new Act with a view to spawning betterment and, upon its subsequent amendment, implementing the TRIPS Agreement as well.

3.1   General Statutory Details

The sentiment against outmoded notions in the Act of 1931 after six decades of its life led to new enactment in 1991. In effect, with a high degree of complication, the preparation of this new Act consumed a period of almost ten years. Before discussing registration procedures under this Act, its general details should be brought out here.

3.1.1   Extension of protection to services marks and certification marks
The Act extends protection to service marks. As such, this Act ameliorates classification of "goods and services" and empowers the Minister to make subordinate legislation on this matter.[23] Provisions on trade marks apply to service marks *mutatis mutandis*.[24] (As such, discussions on trade marks in this work entirely apply to service marks and a mention of "goods" refers to "services.) Moreover, certification marks are brought into the protective net under this Act, as the Act directs the application of provisions on trade marks to certification marks as well, with certain additional requirements as regards, in particular, the owners' regulations on the use of the marks for certification purposes.[25]

---

[23]   S. 9 of the Act of 1991. The current classification has been made along the Nice Agreement (Nice Agreement Concerning the International Classification of the Registration of Marks) and now embodied in the Notification of the Ministry of Commerce on Classification of Goods and Services, in force as from 1st July 2017.
[24]   S. 80 of the Act of 1991.
[25]   SS. 81–93.

3.1.2   'Distinctiveness' requirement

Major improvement has been made on the distinctiveness issue. The specific provision on distinctiveness defines a distinctive character as one "by which members of the public or users of the goods know and apprehend that the goods for which the trade mark is used are distinguished from other goods".[26] The Act provides a list of essential particulars deemed to constitute distinctiveness of a trade mark. The listed particulars are much larger than the four items in the Act of 1931.[27] Included in the list are, *inter alia*, invented letters or numerals, the applicant's photograph and an invented picture. This list has undergone further enhancement upon the amendments in 2000 and 2016. The amendment in 2000 was intended to implement the TRIPS Agreement, under which trade marks include figurative elements and combinations of colours.[28] As such, combinations of colours represented in a special manner have been brought into the list following the amendment in 2000, whilst figurative elements appear in the list upon the amendment in 2016.[29] Actually, the amendment in 2016 has substantially streamlined listed matters. The current list embraces a sound, provided that it has no direct reference to the character or quality of the goods and is not naturally produced from the goods or their operation.[30]

A trade mark devoid of any of such distinctive particulars as statutorily listed is registrable if shown to have been widely used for distribution, dissemination or advertisement of goods in accordance with the rules prescribed, by Notification, by the Minister.[31] Registrability on such basis of "distinctiveness acquired through use" indeed follows the TRIPS Agreement.[32] In such a scenario, the trade mark in question has derived a secondary meaning perceived by consumers at large.

3.1.3   Prohibited marks

A list of trade marks prohibited from registration has been expanded from the list in the Act of 1931. Notably, the list includes a trade mark which is "contrary to public order or good moral or public policy".[33] Such wordings have been re-couched from "contrary to public policy or morality" as used in the preceding Act.[34] Although it is sound to include a mark "which is contrary to public order or good moral or public policy" in the statutory list of prohibited marks, practical application of this listed item has brought about conceptual incongruity, as discussed later in this work. Indeed, the Act also empowers the Minister to prescribe, by Notification, other prohibited marks in addition to those listed in the Act.

3.1.4   Identity, similarity and *bona fide* concurrent use

Another refined aspect lies in the issue of identity or similarity of trade marks. Whilst the preceding Act of 1931 prevented registration of a trade mark identical with or deceptively similar to another person's trade mark already registered for "*goods of the same class*", the

---

[26]   S. 1 para. 1 of the Act of 1991.
[27]   See *supra* 2.2.
[28]   Article 15 para. 1 of the TRIPS Agreement.
[29]   S. 7 para. 2 (5) and (10) respectively of the Act of 1991.
[30]   S. 7 para. 2 (11) of the Act of 1991.
[31]   S. 7 para. 3 of the Act of 1991.
[32]   Article 15 para. 1 of the TRIPS Agreement.
[33]   S. 8 (9) of the Act of 1991.
[34]   S. 5 (7) of the Act of 1931.

new Act of 1991 lays down the concepts corresponding to the requirements in the TRIPS Agreement; the owner of a registered trade mark has the exclusive right to prevent anyone else from using in the course of trade identical or similar marks for *identical or similar goods*, where such use would result in a likelihood of confusion.[35] Notably, in the current Act, the expression "whether it [the trade mark] is intended to be used for goods of the same class or a different class considered by the registrar to exhibit a similar nature"[36] depicts identical or similar goods as envisaged by the parallel provision of the TRIPS Agreement. With respect to the likelihood of confusion, whilst the TRIPS Agreement presumes such likelihood of confusion in case of the use of an identical sign for *identical* goods, the presumption in the Thai Act is of the greater compass, given that the likelihood of confusion is presumed when the trade mark intended to be registered is identical with another person's registered trade mark in respect of *identical goods or similar goods*.[37] Thus, in Thailand, an application for registration of a trade mark identical with another's registered identical trade mark for identical or similar goods will *simpliciter* be rejected without any need for finding the likelihood of confusion, as it is already presumed by the Act. Notwithstanding, as with the former Act, the current Act allows *bona fide* concurrent use by different owners of identical or similar trade marks in respect of identical or similar goods. Further, registration is permitted for identical or similar trade marks intended to be used for identical or similar goods where it is justified by special circumstances. The registrar may impose appropriate conditions or limitations, in particular, on the mode and scope of use.[38]

3.1.5 Well-known marks protection
Another first-time creature in the current Act dwells in special protection dedicated to well-known marks. This protection is even broader in scope than required by the TRIPS Agreement. The TRIPS Agreement, as with the Paris Convention, protects well-known marks, whether registered or not, but the TRIPS Agreement extends protection to services.[39] Also, whilst the Paris Convention protects a well-known mark against being reproduced, imitated or translated for use by another, in a manner liable to create confusion, for identical or similar goods only,[40] the TRIPS Agreement protects a well-known mark against such conduct even in the case where the conduct befalls in relation to unassociated goods or services if such well-known mark is registered.[41] Thus, an unregistered well-known mark is protected against its confusion-generating use by another for associated, whether identical or similar, goods or services whilst a registered well-known mark enjoys greater protection against confusing use by another for related or even unrelated goods or services.

Thailand's Act of 1991 far more generously guards well-known marks in that protection is given regardless of their registration and regardless of association between the goods or services of the mark-owners and those of others. Protection of well-known marks is, however, placed under the umbrella of the "prohibited marks" – registration of a trade mark is prohibited

---

[35] Article 16 para. 1 of the TRIPS Agreement.
[36] S. 13 of the Act of 1991.
[37] S. 13 (1) of the Act of 1991.
[38] S. 27 of the Act of 1991.
[39] Article 16 para. 2 of the TRIPS Agreement.
[40] Article 6*bis* para. 1 of the Paris Convention.
[41] Article 16 para. 3 of the TRIPS Agreement.

if it is "a trade mark which is identical with a well-known mark … or so similar to such mark as to be liable to create public confusion as to the owner or origin of the goods, whether it has been registered or not".[42] In effect, the Act empowers the Minister to prescribe, by Notification, rules on well-known marks. At present, the relevant Notification[43] sets forth two requirements, in line with the TRIPS Agreement,[44] for considering a well-known mark: (1) it has been used, regularly and in good faith, for distribution or advertisement of goods or services, or by any means so widely as to cause its knowledge amongst the public or the relevant sector of the public in Thailand and (2) it has gained acceptable repute amongst consumers. Such wide use may also be through the owner's representatives or licensees.[45]

3.1.6   Disclaimers
The Act of 1991 retains the concept as regards disclaimers. As with the predecessor Act, the current Act authorises registrars to order disclaimers where a trade mark contains any part which is a matter common to the trade for certain goods or classes of goods such that exclusive right thereto should not be granted to any particular person or where any part is of a non-distinctive character. In such a case, the registrar may require the applicant to disclaim any right to the exclusive use of the part concerned or make such other disclaimer as the registrar may consider necessary for defining rights under the registration.[46] In effect, numerous disclaimers have voluntarily been declared by applicants with a view to securing registrability of their composite marks.

3.1.7   Effects of registration
The Act of 1991, retaining major legal effects proclaimed by the preceding Act, grants the owner of a registered trade mark the exclusive right to its use for the goods to which the registration relates.[47] Registration is valid for a renewable period of ten years as from the registration date.[48] The filing date is regarded as the registration date,[49] but the Act accords a priority right in certain cases, along the line of the provisions of the Paris Convention[50] as incorporated into the TRIPS Agreement. In this connection, a person who, with the required qualifications regarding nationality, a domicile or an industrial or commercial establishment, has duly filed an application elsewhere and subsequently files an application in Thailand within six months as from the first filing abroad enjoys a right of priority to the effect that the date of such first filing abroad is deemed to be the date of filing in Thailand so that legal protection runs from such date.[51] In effect, a right of priority extends to the case where an international exhibi-

---

[42]   S. 8 (10) of the Act of 1991.
[43]   Notification of the Ministry of Commerce Re: Rules for the Consideration of Well-Known Marks, B.E. 2547 (2004).
[44]   Article 16 para 2 of the TRIPS Agreement.
[45]   Clause 2 (1) and (2) of the Notification of the Ministry of Commerce Re: Rules for the Consideration of Well-Known Marks, B.E. 2547 (2004).
[46]   S. 17 of the Act of 1991, essentially replicating s. 14 of the Trade Marks Act 1938 of the U.K. which served as a model for the Thai Act at that time.
[47]   S. 44 of the Act of 1991.
[48]   S. 53 of the Act of 1991.
[49]   S. 42 of the Act of 1991.
[50]   Article 4 of the Paris Convention.
[51]   S. 28 of the Act of 1991. Although the "right of priority" concepts were earlier found in s. 20 of the Act of 1931, their details appeared scant.

tion of goods bearing a trade mark is officially organised.[52] Legal treatment of unregistered trade marks follows the predecessor Act; an unregistered trade mark gives rise to no right to a lawsuit for preventing infringement or claiming compensation therefor, but its owner is not precluded from pursing an action in passing off.[53]

3.1.8   International registration of marks
Thailand has acceded to the Protocol Relating to the Madrid Agreement Concerning the International Registration of Marks concluded in 1989 and the accession has taken effect as from 7th November 2017. In preparation for joining this Madrid System, a new set of provisions[54] has been inserted, by the amending Act of 2016,[55] into the Act of 1991 to accommodate international registration of marks under the said Protocol, pursuant to which a person (with the required qualifications concerning nationality, a domicile or an industrial or commercial establishment) who applies for registration, or has already secured registration, of a mark in one Contracting State may also file an international application and designate other Contracting States in which the same mark is intended to be registered. As a result of this scheme, the Department of Intellectual Property of Thailand has thenceforth embarked on its sturdy mission involving international applications.[56]

3.1.9   Transfers and licensing
The Act of 1991 allows transfers of trade marks both by way of assignment and by way of inheritance. The restriction, in the predecessor Act, that a transfer of a trade mark was permissible only together with a transfer of the business has now been eliminated. The current Act even permits an assignment in respect of all or some goods for which a trade mark has been registered.[57] As regards licensing, whilst the preceding Act made no provision on this matter, the current Act takes full recognition of the owner's right to authorise the use of his registered trade mark and allows licensing for all or certain goods covered by the registration. The law requires licensing to be in writing and registered with the registrar[58] and, in addition, the use by the licensee in a manner repugnant to public order or good morals or public policy or the licensee's inability to control the quality of the goods for which the licensing is granted constitutes a ground for cancellation of the registered licensing.[59] Also, licensing is not prejudiced by assignment or inheritance of the licensed trade mark.[60]

3.1.10   Trade Marks Board
The Act of 1991 establishes the Trade Marks Board as a quasi-judicial appellate body for reviewing registrars' orders in specified cases of importance, in particular, for the review of

---

[52]   S. 28*bis* of the Act of 1991.
[53]   S. 46 of the Act of 1991.
[54]   See Chapter 1/1, ss. 79/2 to 79/15, of the Act of 1991.
[55]   The Trade Marks Act (No. 3), B.E. 2559 (2016).
[56]   For further discussion, see O Panuspatthna, 'The Revision of the Thai Trade Marks Act in Compliance with the Madrid System' (2010) Special Issue J Intel Prop and Int'l Trade L 194.
[57]   SS. 48 and 49 of the Act of 1991.
[58]   S. 68 of the Act of 1991.
[59]   SS. 72–75 of the Act of 1991.
[60]   S. 79/1 of the Act of 1991, as inserted by the amending Act in 2016.

registrars' orders on these matters: refusal of registration,[61] disclaimers,[62] *bona fide* concurrent use[63] and opposition following publication of applications.[64] In addition, the Board possesses competence to cancel registration of trade marks in certain cases. The Board's decisions are merely of administrative finality and subject to judicial review.

3.2   Registration Procedures

The Act of 1991 prescribes detailed procedures concerning applications for registration. Once an application is filed for registering a trade mark, the registrar will examine its registrability. This involves ascertainment that the trade mark possesses a distinctive character, free from statutorily prohibited matters and is neither identical with another person's registered trade mark nor so similar to such mark as to cause public confusion as to the owner or origin of the goods, in respect of associated goods ("goods of the same class or a different class considered by the registrar to exhibit a similar nature").[65] Where deficiency occurs in an immaterial part of a trade mark, the registrar may order amendment of the application in the interest of registrability of that mark.[66] Also, the registrar may, as earlier explained, order an appropriate disclaimer against a portion constituting a matter common to the trade or a portion devoid of a distinctive character.[67]

An application which passes the registrar's investigatory muster will undergo its publication process.[68] At this stage, any person whose better right (earlier right) is found or who considers that the published trade mark is unregistrable on statutorily specified grounds (lack of distinctiveness, statutory prohibitions, identity or similarity) or that the application proceedings have failed to conform to the Act may file the opposition to the registrar.[69] The applicant is then allowed to file a counter-statement to remonstrate the opposition. Where no opposition is filed or where the opposition is unsuccessful, registration will be effected.[70] On the contrary, the successful opposition leads to removal of the application from the register. Indeed, the applicant's failure to file a counter-statement also results in his application being considered as abandoned.[71]

4.   CERTAIN PROBLEMATICAL ISSUES

A glimpse of a historical account of the trade mark legislation of Thailand and key principles in the Trade Marks Act, B.E. 2534 (1991) provides sufficient ingredients for critical explora-

---

[61]   S. 16 in conjunction with s. 18 of the Act of 1991.
[62]   S. 17 in conjunction with s. 18 of the Act of 1991.
[63]   S. 27 paras. 2 and 3 of the Act of 1991.
[64]   S. 37 para. 2 of the Act of 1991.
[65]   However, the statutory leeway for registration in the case of *bona fide* concurrent use of identical or similar trade marks, as explained at 3.1.4, should be recalled.
[66]   S. 15 of the Act of 1991.
[67]   S. 17 of the Act of 1991. See *supra* at 3.1.6.
[68]   S. 29 of the Act of 1991.
[69]   S. 35 of the Act of 1991.
[70]   S. 40 of the Act of 1991.
[71]   S. 36 para. 3 of the Act of 1991.

tion of problematical issues dwelling in the Act. Given space limitation, analysis in this part merely embraces two main points at which difficulties lie – (1) the obstructive interpretation of distinctiveness and (2) the prevention of registration in bad faith prejudicial to earlier rights. Much discussion avails itself of empirical rulings of the Trade Marks Board as well as judicial decisions on the issues concerned. Indeed, certain deficiencies reside in the provisions of the Act itself whilst some incongruities appear to have stemmed from interpretation of statutory provisions. All this will be dealt with *seriatim*.

4.1 Obstructive Interpretation of "Distinctiveness"

It should be recalled that the Act of 1991 requires distinctiveness for registrability of a trade mark and defines a distinctive trade mark as one possessing "a character by which members of the public or users of the goods know and apprehend that the goods for which such trade mark is used are distinguished from other goods".[72] Despite its harmony with universal conceptions, interpretation of distinctiveness is, in practice, fraught with difficulty and has, to a large degree, impeded registration of trade marks. Such an enormous number of trade marks have been, and will be expected to be, refused for registration despite their successful registration elsewhere. Empirical evidence reveals at least a couple of manners of obstructive interpretation.

4.1.1 Extraordinarily broad perception of genericness
Trade marks laws around the world share rather universal perception as regards generic terms. Given that a generic term merely refers to the genus of the goods or services, it fails to perform a distinguishing function; that is to say, it does not, in any way, enable users of the goods or services to distinguish them from those of others. As such, a generic term can never possess a distinctive character, with the immediate result that when a generic term is used as a trade mark, such mark is outright devoid of distinctiveness and *simpliciter* unregistrable. However, tenacious incongruity found in Thailand is the eccentric breadth of the genericness as interpreted by Thai authorities. This actuality is reflected in a plethora of decisions of registrars and the Trade Marks Board.

A long line of rulings wherein marks comprising a non-generic word or words have somehow been found unregistrable in Thailand constitute persistent astonishment. Registrars and the Trade Marks Board, more often than not, use the language "generally expressed words" as a reason for refusing registration and, in doing so, seem to have perceived that such words would succumb to the same fate as generic words. For instance, **PLATFORM**, sought to be registered for the services involving compilation of goods for convenience in Class 35, has been found devoid of distinctiveness because: "It has been used as a general expression and thus incapable of distinguishing the services."[73] By parity of reason, the Board found **ART COLLECTION** unregistrable for goods in Class 21 including combs and brushes[74] and also refused registration of **WIDER WORLD** for services in Class 42 relating to evaluation of technological specialisation.[75] In some cases, words which merely "come close to being

---

[72] See *supra* at 3.1.2.
[73] Trade Marks Board's Decision No. 2191/2562 (2019) for the Application No. 170102920. In this work, a decision of the Trade Mark Board shall hereinafter be cited as "TMB Decision".
[74] TMB Decision No. 123/2561 (2018) for the Application No. 899717.
[75] TMB Decision No. 2566/2562 (2019) for the Application No. 170121468.

generic" rather than being generic *per se* have unfortunately been ruled unregistrable for want of distinctiveness. An illustration can be afforded by the case concerning the word **TV** as an essential part of the trade mark **AWESOMENESS TV** intended to be registered for goods in Class 9 including downloadable software for computer games and smart phones. The Trade Marks Board found this mark ineligible for protection, *inter alia*, because the word **TV** was "a generally expressed word" (apart from the reason that the word **AWESOMENESS** was descriptive).[76] In reality, the word **TV** in this case did not refer to the genus of the goods for which registration was sought. It should be said, for comparison purposes, that several foreign decisions reveal opposite outcomes.[77]

The use of a phrase or long statement as a trade mark in Thailand has encountered a similar unpleasant fate. Tenacity of the Trade Marks Board's perception of a general expression as incapable of indicating the origin of the goods or services and thereby devoid of distinctiveness has ousted a massive number of trade marks from legal protection, albeit their registrability in other jurisdictions where distinctiveness receives reasonable interpretation. Again, the common language uttered by the Board is that: "It is a general expression and, therefore, fails to distinguish the goods (or services) from those of others." A list of rulings in this direction has grown over the years. The following trade marks were found non-distinctive on the basis that they were merely general expressions: **WHY WAIT** for services of providing telecommunication data (Class 38),[78] services relating to online journals and online-education programmes (Class 41)[79] and services of designing software for wireless communication (Class 42);[80] **OPPORTUNITY DAY** for advertising and business counselling services (Class 35),[81] security data services (Class 36),[82] radio and television broadcasting services (Class 38),[83] services involving radio and television programmes production (Class 41)[84] and services

---

[76]   TMB Decision No. 704/2561 (2018) for the Application No. 929797.
[77]   See *In re American Online, Inc.*, 77 USPQ2d. 1618 (TTAB 2006) where the TTAB ruled that **INSTANT MESSENGER** intended to be registered for services in Class 38 (telecommunication services), Class 39 (electronic storage of data) and Class 42 (computer services, including computer networks) was non-generic, simply because members of the relevant public did not primarily understand such term as referring to the genus of the services concerned. The Board relied on the two-step inquiry established in *H. Marvin Ginn Corp.* v. *International Association of Fire Chiefs, Inc.*, 782 F. 2d. 987 where the Court of Appeals for the Federal Circuit has addressed: "Determining whether a mark is generic therefore involves a two-step inquiry: First, what is the genus of goods or services at issue? Second, is the term sought to be registered or retained on the register understood by the relevant public primarily to refer to that genus of goods or services?" The Court found that **Fire Chief** used for the monthly circulated fire-fighting magazine was, at best, descriptive rather than generic. Similarly, in *In re Mine Safety Appliances Company*, 66 USPQ2d. 1694 (TTAB 2002), the Board concluded that **Workmask**, for safety equipment (self-contained breathing apparatus), was merely descriptive rather than generic but acquired distinctiveness through extensive use. Indeed, where it remains doubtful whether the term in question has widely been perceived of as describing the genus of the goods or services, rulings are likely to be in applicants' favour, as illustrated in *In re Trek 2000 International Ltd.*, 97 USPQ2d. 1106 (TTAB 2010) where **THUMBDRIVE** was not considered as a generic term for portable digital electronic devices for data storage.
[78]   TMB Decision No. 179/2560 (2017) for the Application No. 882127.
[79]   TMB Decision No. 180/2560 (2017) for the Application No. 882128.
[80]   TMB Decision No. 181/2560 (2017) for the Application No. 882129.
[81]   TMB Decision No. 126/2560 (2017) for the Application No. 878314.
[82]   TMB Decision No. 127/2560 (2017) for the Application No. 878315.
[83]   TMB Decision No. 128/2560 (2017) for the Application No. 878316.
[84]   TMB Decision No. 129/2560 (2017) for the Application No. 878317.

of computer software design and development (Class 42)[85] and **CHASE YOUR DREAM** for machines (Class 7),[86] tyres and parts of vehicles (Class 12),[87] certain goods made of rubber and plastics (Class 17)[88] and building materials (Class 19).[89] General expressions found by the Board as registrable are indeed rare, as epitomised by the mark **28ᵗʰ SEAGAMES Singapore 2015** for printed matters and stationery (Class 16).[90]

Adversely sweeping interpretation of genericness pursued by the Trade Marks Board has not gone unnoticed by the Courts in judicial review of the Board's orders. The Supreme Court of Thailand, in one case,[91] reversed the Trade Marks Board's ruling that **madame FIGARO** for goods in Class 16 (including books and magazines) was generic and unregistrable. The Supreme Court graphically explained that the word **madame** did not signify the genus of the intended goods. Similarly, in another case,[92] the Supreme Court has found **OK!** distinctive and registrable for goods in Class 16 (magazines). The Supreme Court has, again, brought home that although the term **OK** is a general word in a dictionary, it is not generic for magazines. Further, **4 SEASONS** has been ruled to be far from generic in respect of building paint (and also far from common to the trade).[93] In effect, many of these decisions come close to affirming registrability of what is known as an "arbitrary mark" – a mark which has, in the ordinary language, a common meaning not related to the goods or services concerned – as seen, for example, in the case of the use of **APPLE** for computers or **CAMEL** for tobacco products.

Thai Courts have also overturned the Board's refusals to register marks comprising general statements or expressions. The Supreme Court has allowed registration of **HAVE IT YOUR WAY** for restaurant services (Class 43).[94] A similar judgment has been rendered in favour of **TMB Make THE Difference** for banking services (Class 36), where the Supreme Court disapproved the ruling that the phrase **Make THE Difference**, as the essential part of this mark, lacked distinctiveness because it was a mere general statement.[95] Likewise, **Dream, Believe and Achieve …** written in handwriting format, has judicially been found to be inherently distinctive and thus registrable for services in Class 35 (business management of department stores).[96] In another case,[97] the Central Intellectual Property and International Trade Court has pointed out that the registrar and the Trade Marks Board erred in finding **Orchestrating a brighter world** devoid of distinctiveness on the ground of "being a mere general expres-

---

[85]   TMB Decision No. 130/2560 (2017) for the Application No. 878318.
[86]   TMB Decision No. 1328/2560 (2017) for the Application No. 1013360.
[87]   TMB Decision No. 1329/2560 (2017) for the Application No. 1013361.
[88]   TMB Decision No. 1330/2560 (2017) for the Application No. 1013362.
[89]   TMB Decision No. 1331/2560 (2017) for the Application No. 1013363.
[90]   TMB Decision No. 1684/2560 (2017) for the Application No. 945892. However, the words "28ᵗʰ" and "2015", which formed part of this trade mark, were ordered to be disclaimed for want of distinctiveness.
[91]   Supreme Court's Decision No. 2592-2593/2553 (2010).
[92]   Supreme Court's Decision No. 1141/2553 (2010).
[93]   Supreme Court's Decision No. 4811/2559 (2016).
[94]   Supreme Court's Decision No. 5448/2554 (2011). It was also held that this trade mark was not descriptive *vis-à-vis* restaurant services.
[95]   Supreme Court's Decision No. 2587/2559 (2016).
[96]   Supreme Court's Decision No. 15017/2558 (2015). The Supreme Court, in its Decision No. 5332/2558 (2015), also reversed the Board's finding that **Wear Your Attitude**, for similar services in Class 35, was a general phrase and thus devoid of distinctiveness.
[97]   Central Intellectual Property and International Trade Court's Decision No. IP 119/2564 (2021).

sion". Despite judicial determinations, registrars and the Trade Marks Board, by and large, remain inclined to maintain their own line of rulings at odds with internationally recognised perception. Authorities of the Department of Intellectual Property, called upon as witnesses in judicial review, have usually testified that different rulings are an inevitable upshot of different proclamation in Thai law. In effect, as the distinctiveness requirement has an international origin, the different treatment found on Thai soil has stemmed from impeding interpretation of law rather than the law itself. Furthermore, the Department of Intellectual Property's most recent Manual of Trade Marks Registration, as effective as from 17th January 2022, directs refusal of registration of general statements or expressions.[98] Such treatment largely rests upon the thinking that words or expressions of general use should not be monopolised by anyone. Although this concern has some merit, it needs particular proclamation outside the boundary of distinctiveness.[99]

Notably, in other jurisdictions, genericness, for satisfying statutory distinctiveness, has not undergone such lamentably extensive interpretation as to oust a gigantic number of trade marks from legal protection. One has witnessed a long list of registered trade marks comprising general words or expressions as long as they do not refer to the genus of the intended goods or services and do not describe any character or quality of such goods or service.

As a matter of global practice, trade marks are typically classified into five categories on a spectrum of distinctiveness, from the strongest to the weakest, for the purpose of determining their strength: (1) fanciful marks, (2) arbitrary marks, (3) suggestive marks, (4) descriptive marks and (5) generic marks. Fanciful marks are formed by invented words not generally found in dictionaries whilst arbitrary marks comprise terms that have a common meaning unconnected with the goods or services for which the marks are used.[100] Suggestive marks merely suggest certain characters or qualities of the goods or services (simply because a strong degree of consumers' imagination is required for perceiving those characters or qualities)[101] whilst descriptive marks make immediate description thereof without consumers' much imag-

---

[98]   This Manual states that "generally used words, that is to say, words of general signification capable of use by every sector of the public, every business or every group of persons" are "devoid of a distinctive character". Apart from generic terms, the Manual provides the following items as examples: words depicting internationality (e.g. **International Global**), colours (e.g. **Dark Silver**) and counting numbers or numerals (e.g. **One**, **Two**, **First**, **Second** or **46**). In addition, the said Manual, having pointed out that general expressions exhibit no distinctiveness, provides the following as illustrations: proverbs, greetings, phrases (e.g. **Buckle up first**), abbreviations (e.g. **LOL** for Laugh Out Loud), mottos or slogans. Notably, numerous items in the list are not generic but treated by the Manual in the same way as generic terms. See Trade Marks Division, *Manual of Trade Marks Registration 2022* (Department of Intellectual Property 2022) 30–33.
[99]   The current Act also addresses this concern in section 17 in which a part, of a composite mark, which is a matter common to the trade can be ordered to be disclaimed and in section 66 under which a trade mark can be judicially cancelled if it has subsequently become a matter so common to the trade as to lose significance as a trade mark.
[100] See, for example, *Palm Bay Imports, Inc.* v. *Veuve Clicquot Ponsardin Maison Fondee En 1772*, 73 USPQ2d. 1689 (Fed. Cir. 2005), where the French word **VEUVE** (meaning Widow in English) was used as a trade mark for champagne and sparkling wine.
[101] An example can be drawn from *In Re Vienna Sausage Mfg. Co.*, 156 USPQ 155 (TTAB 1967), in which **FRANKWURST** was held suggestive, as the combination of the words "frank" (meaning "wiener") and "wurst" (synonymous with "sausage") was incongruous.

ination to gain their understanding.[102] Generic marks are those comprising words employed for designating the genus of the goods or services for which the marks are used. Encumbering rulings by Thailand's registrars and Trade Marks Board have resulted in putting non-generic marks into the category of generic marks and thereby preventing their registrability at variance with treatment elsewhere.

In effect, such tenacious line of hindering rulings leading to an extraordinarily high number of trade marks being refused for registration has personally been witnessed by the author in the course of the author's discharge of duties as a member of the Trade Marks Board of Thailand. Although no statistical fact sheet indicating trade marks refused for registration for want of distinctiveness over a certain period of time, as compared to those allowed to be registered, has officially been prepared by Thailand's Department of Intellectual Property, the truism as regards hostile interpretation of law by registrars and the Trade Marks Board on this genericness-related issue has long been felt by legal practitioners in Thailand. Despite several judicial decisions, including those of the Supreme Court, against obstructive decisions by the Trade Mark Board as described above, this trend of judicial rulings may possibly vary in view of the fact that the doctrine of binding precedent has no legal room in Thai law. As such, decisions of trial courts at variance with those of the Supreme Court are, at times, heard of. This remark indeed applies to the issue of distinctiveness in the light of sequences of letters and numerals, which will shortly be discussed, as well.

4.1.2   Improper interpretation of the statutory list of particulars deemed distinctive

Further hindrance to registrability of trade marks in Thailand has constantly been engendered by the interpretation of the list of particulars statutorily deemed distinctive. As earlier alluded to, the law requires a trade mark to be distinctive and the relevant provision (section 7 paragraph one) defines a distinctive trade mark as one having a character by which the goods (or services) can be distinguished from those of others. The Act provides, in paragraph two of the same section, a list of several particulars deemed to make a trade mark distinctive. Indeed, this list is the heritage from the preceding Act of 1931, which in turn owed its origin to the

---

[102]   Illustrations of descriptive marks as provided by the USPTO are insightful: **Creamy** for yogurt, **Apple Pie** for potpourri or **Bed & Breakfast Registry** for accommodation booking services: see USPTO, *Trademark Basics*, at https://www.uspto.gov/trademarks/basics (accessed 15 May 2022). The demarcation between a suggestive mark and a descriptive mark is sometimes difficult to be drawn, as reflected in *In re Pennwalt Corp.*, 173 USPQ 317 (TTAB 1972), where **DRI-FOOT** was held merely suggestive of anti-perspirant deodorant for feet, as it was not usual to describe anti-perspirant deodorant for "foot" rather than "feet": see Stephen Reed and Esther Barron, *Entrepreneurship: Cases and Materials* (2nd edn, Aspen Publishing 2021), 141. Indeed, rulings in Thailand have come upon comparable difficulty. Thai Courts have reversed numerous findings of the Trade Marks Board, as exemplified by the Supreme Court's Decision No. 3543/2545 (2002) where **TRUSTY** for animal foodstuffs (Class 31) was found not descriptive, Decision No. 9466/2554 (2011) where **BIOFRESH** for refrigerating apparatus was found merely suggestive, Decision No. 4676/2558 (2015) in which **LIVE WITH CHIVALRY** for non-alcoholic beverages (Class 32) and alcoholic beverages (Class 33) was held non-descriptive and Decision No. 3753/2558 (2015) wherein the Board's finding that **VFLEX** described the flexible nature of the goods (instruments for protection against pollution, Class 9) was judicially overturned. In some cases, courts seem to sound an alarm on unusual sensitivity of registrars and the Board, as envisioned in the Supreme Court's Decision No. 2557/2558 (2015) where the Court disagreed that the word **SCOTCH** would, for scissors (Class 8), convey an act of cutting and Decision No. 8762/2555 (2012) where the Court quashed the finding that the French word **ARMURE** for herbicides (Class 5) was descriptive.

Trade Marks Act 1905 of the United Kingdom. Whilst the Act of 1931 limited the list to four essential particulars,[103] Thailand's current Act has expanded the list to embrace more items and, after its amendments in 2000 and 2016, has subsequently systematised the list with the addition of further particulars deemed distinctive.

The present list, after all amendments, contains the following: (1) a natural person's name or a natural person's surname not importing ordinary signification or a juridical person's full name or a trade name, where it is represented in a special manner and makes no direct reference to the character or quality of the goods,[104] (2) a word or expression making no direct reference to the character or quality of the goods and not being a geographical name prescribed by the Minister,[105] (3) an invented word,[106] (4) invented letters or numerals,[107] (5) a combination of colours represented in a special manner,[108] (6) a signature of the applicant for registration or of the predecessor of his business or a signature of another person with such person's permission,[109] (7) a photograph of the applicant for registration or of another person with such person's permission or, where such person is dead, with permission of his ascendant, descendant and spouse, if any,[110] (8) an invented picture,[111] (9) a picture making no direct reference to the character or quality of the goods and not being a picture of a map or of a geographical site prescribed by the Minister,[112] (10) a shape or figurative element, not being the natural feature of the goods or not being a shape or figurative element which is necessary for technical functionality of the goods or not being a shape or figurative element which gives added value to the goods[113] and, finally, (11) a sound making no direct reference to the character or quality of the goods or a sound not being the natural sound of the goods or a sound not resulting from the functionality of the goods.[114] A trade mark which is devoid of any of these listed items can also acquire distinctiveness through its widespread use (distribution, dissemination or advertisement) in accordance with the rules prescribed, by Notification, by the Minister.[115]

The list above would pose no practical impediment to registrability if properly interpreted as a mere non-exhaustive list. Although its historical investigation reveals that all the listed items are merely intended to be illustrative without precluding matters not listed there from constituting distinctiveness if the statutory generality under section 7 paragraph one (i.e. the ability to be adapted to distinguish the goods or services from those of others) is satisfied, this list has largely been construed as exhaustive. Any trade mark comprising a particular contrary to what is addressed in the list has been, and will normally be, found to be unregistrable for want of distinctiveness unless its acquired distinctiveness or secondary meaning is proven.

---

[103] See *supra* at 2.2.
[104] S. 7 para. 2 (1).
[105] S. 7 para. 2 (2).
[106] S. 7 para. 2 (3).
[107] S. 7 para. 2 (4).
[108] S. 7 para. 2 (5).
[109] S. 7 para. 2 (6).
[110] S. 7 para. 2 (7).
[111] S. 7 para. 2 (8).
[112] S. 7 para. 2 (9).
[113] S. 7 para. 2 (10).
[114] S. 7 para. 2 (11).
[115] S. 7 para. 3. See *supra* at 3.1.2.

A striking illustration of such encumbering interpretation can be afforded by the use of a sequence of letters or numerals. As previously explicated, the statutory list includes "invented letters or numerals". It has been interpreted that when a trade mark takes the form of unembellished letters or numerals, it is outright non-distinctive and unregistrable simply because such plain letters or numerals are not "invented letters or numerals" as mentioned in the list. On this footing, applications for registering the following marks comprising a sequence of non-stylised letters have been rejected: **ABS** for drilling and polishing tools (Class 7),[116] **IMS** for certain goods including computer software and discs for analysing pharmaceutical, medical and health data (Class 9)[117] and **RCI TILE** for ceramic tiles (Class 19).[118] Indeed, where a sequence of unembellished letters or numerals forms a minor part of a trade mark whilst other components are distinctive, that part is usually ordered to be disclaimed on the asserted ground of non-distinctiveness.[119] Contentions that the use of an unusual sequence of letters or numerals, albeit unembellished, makes the entire mark distinctive in view of its performing the function of distinguishing the origin of the goods or services have a very sparing chance of success. Thus, trade marks comprising a sequence of unadorned letters or numerals are ineligible for protection. This discernment, despite some support by local academic writings,[120] runs counter to modern treatment.[121] Notably, in certain jurisdictions, such conventional thinking has been replaced by modern insight.[122]

---

[116] TMB Decision No. 858/2561 (2018) for the Application No. 949424.

[117] TMB Decision No. 730/2561 (2018) for the Application No. 882336.

[118] TMB Decision No. 860/2561 (2018) for the Application No. 941728. The Board refused registration because, first, the letters **RCI** were not embellished and, secondly, **TILE** was descriptive.

[119] See, for example, TMB Decision No. 10180/2559 (2016) for the Application No. 808108 (in which the letters **PS** in **PSVITA**, intended to be registered for games and playthings (Class 28), were ordered to be disclaimed) and TMB Decision No. 1379/2559 (2016) for the Application No. 868624 (where a disclaimer of the numeral 100 in the trade mark, for plant-nourishing materials (Class 1), was ordered). Such rulings may run counter to the so-called "anti-dissection" rule internationally recognised.

[120] See What Tingsamitr, *Text on Trade Marks Law* (Nititham 2002), 19 and Tatchai Supapholsiri, *Text on Trade Marks Law* (Nititham 1993), 33. But see the opposing view in Nandana Indananda, 'Roles of Courts in Interpreting and Formulating Rules on Distinctiveness of Trade Marks', at https://ipitc.coj.go.th/th/file/get/file/202005159fad647db18e718a999cef7e2c546cd7095117.pdf?fbclid= IwAR3Gq8iOJuJGB_IjRmnWg2QlBOI2A0CgwZtp6QyyC2zqBOuygdDgqh6YG74 (accessed 20 May 2022).

[121] For instance, **BGW** has been registered in Germany for goods and services in Classes 16, 35 and 41. In *Baroness Small Estate, Inc.* v. *American Wine Trade Inc.*, 104 USPQ2d. 1224 (TTAB, 2012), **CMS** was held inherently distinctive for red wine and the argument that **CMS** was generally understood as an acronym descriptive of a blend of "cabernet", "merlot" and "syrah" was untenable. Cases involving refusal of a sequence of letters for registration are undeniably witnessed but the refusal in those cases is based upon the fact that the sequence of letters in question are abbreviations or acronyms known to describe certain characters of the goods or services, as illustrated in *In re Pre-Paid Legal Services, Inc.*, Serial No. 86423483 where the TTAB, in 2017, refused to register **PPL** for the services featuring "pre-paid legal" expense plans and *In re Thomas Nelson, Inc.*, 97 USPQ 2d. 1712 (TTAB, 2011) where **NKJV**, applied for registration for bibles (Class 16), was found to be an abbreviation known to describe the "NEW KING JAMES VERSION" bibles and thus non-distinctive (but this mark was held to have acquired distinctiveness through use).

[122] The change is at least visualised in the United Kingdom. The treatment, as guided by the Trade Marks Registry Works Manual (1989 revision), of unpronounceable three-letter marks as *prima facie* devoid of distinctiveness has now been substituted by the guidance in the 1999-revision Manual under which three-letter marks should *prima facie* be accepted "unless they are objectionable in their own right as well known acronyms, etc". The Court has noticed such change in *Financial Systems Software (UK)*

Thai Courts have voiced concerns over the wide interpretation. Whilst a single letter or number or a sequence of letters and/or numbers arranged in normal order (e.g. **ABC** or **123**) may reasonably be treated as devoid of distinctiveness,[123] the Supreme Court has taken a dissimilar perception *vis-à-vis* letters or numbers arranged in rather uncommon order. It has been held that **A380**, as placed in plain character, duly rendered the mark distinctive and registrable for games, playthings and gymnastic and sporting articles in Class 28.[124] Likewise, the Supreme Court found registrable, opining that **NTT**, as a word sequence, formed an essential part and perfectly constituted a distinctive character although the letters were not stylised.[125] A similar finding was reached for **DR PEPPER**, written in standard character, wherein the Supreme Court opined that the plain letters **DR**, forming this trade mark for beverages in Class 32, were not an abbreviation of the word **Doctor** and constituted a distinctive character needing no disclaimer therefor.[126] In another striking decision, the Supreme Court found **PRO V1**, used for golf balls in Class 28, satisfactorily distinctive.[127] The Supreme Court has graphically expounded that distinctiveness needs consideration in the entirety of the mark. In the Court's view, although the letters and Arabic numeral were not stylised, their combination has constituted distinctiveness when viewed in totality. Notably, the fact that the letters and Arabic numeral were in a capsule-like rectangle has added to the finding of the overall distinctiveness. Nevertheless, the main judicial reason seemingly rests upon the overall distinctiveness formed by the combination of the letters and numeral. More recently, the Court has gone far towards proclaiming that letters, arranged in a sequence, can form "invented letters" mentioned in the statutory list of particulars deemed distinctive.[128]

An alarm judicially uttered has led to the Department of Intellectual Property varying its treatment regarding a sequence of letters or numbers. The current version of its Manual of Trade Marks Registration describes that at least three letters or numerals which are placed in a sequence not following alphabetical or normal order can sufficiently constitute distinc-

---

Ltd. v. *Financial Software Systems Inc.* [2001] EWCA Civ 386, concerned with the **FSS** mark. However, as the determination of distinctiveness in this case was based upon the Act of 1938 rather than the Act of 1994, the Court followed the previous-revision Manual.

[123]   See the Supreme Court's Decision No. 4326/2561 (2018), in which the trade mark W Hotels was held unregistrable because **W**, as the essential part, was in a standard-character form and thereby made the entire mark devoid of distinctiveness. The Supreme Court reached the same finding in its Decision No. 7358/2561 (2018).

[124]   Supreme Court's Decision No. 936/2561 (2018).

[125]   Supreme Court's Decision No. 2465-2469/2563 (2020). However, the Court concurred with the Trade Marks Board in ordering a disclaimer against the word **DaTa** as it described the goods or services concerned, including smart phones and data carriers (Class 9), advertising services (Class 35) and telecommunications services (Class 38).

[126]   Supreme Court's Decision No. 5400/2553 (2010).

[127]   Supreme Court's Decision No. 1447/2560 (2017).

[128]   Specialised Cases Appellate Court's Decision No. 2544/2563 (2020), allowing registration of **BOE**. However, the judicial reasoning is rather dubious. The Court has explained that the term "invented letters" under the Act connotes an arrangement of letters in an unusual pattern rather than signifying stylised letters. In fact, stylised letters have long been regarded, practically, academically and judicially, as "invented letters" under the Act. An uncommon sequence of letters can be viewed as an additional stance of "invented letters". Alternatively, and more conceptually, if the interpretation of "invented letters" remains conventionally confined to stylised or embellished letters, letters arranged in an uncommon sequence can be distinctive, without falling in the non-exhaustive list provided by the Act, on the ground that they can perform the distinguishing function.

tiveness.[129] Indeed, the Manual makes direct reference to two decisions of the Supreme Court to that effect.[130] In these cases, the Supreme Court has elucidated that the use of an unusual sequence of letters produces no effect of precluding others from using each of the letters as a trade mark.

4.2   Prevention of Registration in Bad Faith Prejudicing Earlier Rights

Given the protection upon registration, a trade mark first registered is afforded protection in preference to identical or similar trade marks in respect of identical or related goods or services. As the filing date is regarded as the registration date, a registered trade mark is protected as from the filing date. However, trade marks legislation around the world prevents any use of trade marks in bad faith. An act of registering any trade mark that, in contravention of bad faith, reproduces, imitates or translates another trade mark earlier used by its legitimate owner must be prohibited. An application for registration of a trade mark constituting such dishonest manifestation must, therefore, be rejected and, if such trade mark has been registered, it is subject to cancellation. Indeed, registration in bad faith is typically envisioned in the case where the applicant has been a distributor of the goods supplied by a foreign owner of a trade mark unregistered in the country of the application.

Prohibition of registration of a trade mark in bad faith in a manner hitherto described has found recognition in the current Act of Thailand but legal thoughts therein appear unsystematically postulated. Well-thought prevention of bad faith conduct detrimental to earlier rights necessitates candid proclamation by the law to that effect at two stages – the application stage and the cancellation stage. At the application stage, the law must state clearly that an application for registration of a trade mark in which another person has an earlier right is to be absolutely refused, when evidence shows the applicant's bad faith. At the cancellation stage, the law must likewise have an unequivocal provision for cancelling a trade mark erroneously registered in bad faith prejudicing another person's existing right. Undoubtedly, proof of bad faith is necessary. The fact that the goods or services are identical or related, coupled with some unscrupulous conduct, is likely to evince bad faith. To appreciate ineptitude in the law, discussion can be presented in relation to the two aforesaid stages.

4.2.1   Application stage

The application stage may be split into two junctures – first, the registrar's initial consideration and, secondly, the opposition following publication of a trade mark approved by the registrar. Unlike elsewhere, the current Act of Thailand does not forthrightly pronounce registration in bad faith as an absolute ground for refusing registration. Registrars, in considering registrability, prevent dishonest registration by resorting to the "prohibited marks" notion. As earlier explained, a list of prohibited trade marks includes a trade mark "contrary to public order or

---

[129]   Trade Marks Division (n 98), 30–33.

[130]   Supreme Court's Decisions No. 9480/2552 (2009) concerning the use of **TCL** for washing machines and other apparatus in Class 7 and No. 13879/2556 (2013) relating to the use of **htc** for smart phones and related goods in Class 9. Actually, there exist other decisions of the Supreme Court not cited in the Manual, including the Decision No. 5432/2551 (2008) wherein **BDF**, with four black-surfaced cycles, was found distinctive.

good moral or public policy".[131] When it appears that the mark for which registration is applied reproduces or imitates another person's mark in bad faith, registrars avail themselves of the "prohibited marks" provision in declaring that such devious mark is contrary to *public policy*. This approach has gained endorsement by the Trade Marks Board, as reflected in a long line of its decisions.

The perception that a trade mark which, at the time of application for registration, reproduces or imitates another person's mark in bad faith is contrary to public policy is fraught with difficulty in the context of the Thai Act. A meticulous perusal of the "prohibited marks" provision (viz., section 8) reveals that all prohibited items target the *appearance* of the mark in question rather than the *conduct* as regards its use. To name a few, the prohibitions embrace State arms, royal arms, the national flag, official flags, flags of foreign States or international organisations, royal names, royal effigies, official emblems, emblems of the Red Cross and official emblems of foreign States or international organisations. Indeed, the opening wording of this provision ("*A trade mark containing or comprising any of the following characteristics shall be prohibited from registration ... *") makes it most conceivable that the prohibition is triggered by the outward appearance of the mark – a mark whose appearance tallies any of the listed items is outright unregistrable. Interpreting the expression "a mark which is contrary to public order or good moral or public policy", in section 8 (9) of the Act, to denote dishonest conduct is far from reasonable and comes close to contradicting the *ejudem generis* rule of interpretation. Logical thinking simply leads to the conclusion that a trade mark is "contrary to public order or good morals or public policy" when its appearance is objectionable as such.[132]

When it comes to the opposition juncture, the Act candidly thwarts registration dishonestly disturbing earlier rights. An application for registration, upon approval by the registrar, is published. At this point, the Act allows anyone to raise an opposition when he "*considers that he has a **better right** than the applicant for registration of such trade mark or that such trade mark is unregistrable under section 6 [i.e. lacking distinctiveness, constituting prohibited items or possessing identity or similarity] or that the application therefor fails to comply with the provisions of this Act*".[133] Notably, the mention, in the Act, of "better right" ("earlier right") as a distinct ground for an opposition in separation from the ground that the trade mark comprises a prohibited item is a sturdy indication that prohibited marks statutorily listed do not extend to a mark sought to be registered in bad faith to the detriment of another person's earlier rights. If the Act intends the boundary of prohibited marks to reach dishonest conduct involving registration prejudicing earlier rights, the "better right" standpoint simply needs no repetition as a distinct ground.

The fact that the Act directly brings up the "better right" stance as an individual ground for raising an opposition to a trade mark considered by the registrar as registrable but fails to mention "better right" as an absolute ground for refusing registration at the stage where the registrar initially determines registrability of a trade mark (prior to the publication procedure)

---

[131] S. 8 (9) of the Act of 1991. See *supra* at 3.1.3.
[132] The following marks provide illustrations: **nudie** (TMB Decision No. 1251/2549 (2006)), **Gulongdu** literally meaning "I try", with **"Gu"** being a coarse pronoun in the Thai language (TMB Decision No. 181/2552 (2009)) and the mark designed to resemble a fish with a penis-like head (TMB Decision Nos. 733-735/2554 (2011)). Notably, assessment of "public order, good morals or public policy" hinges upon domestic values including the cultural background.
[133] S. 35 of the Act of 1991.

portrays uneven thinking, which should be put right through legislative amendment.[134] It should further be noted that although the Act allows an opposition on the individual ground of better rights, no opposition has thus far been raised on such specific ground. In practice, those alleging that applications are made in bad faith to the detriment of their existing rights have always formulated their oppositions on the basis of the "prohibited mark" provision – contending that the mark constituting *mala fide* reproduction or imitation prejudicial to the opposers' earlier rights is contrary to public policy and thus prohibited from registration. This odd practice has enduring life as registrars and the Trade Marks Board have invariably pursued this track, despite judicial cautions that "prohibited marks" point to an exterior look rather than conduct. In a leading case,[135] the Supreme Court found that the plaintiff acted in bad faith in applying for registration of a trade mark nearly identical with the trade mark earlier registered by the defendant in several countries although unregistered in Thailand. The finding of bad faith concentrated on the facts that both parties' trade marks were prominently designed in an image of a bulldog with almost identical posture and the plaintiff was a director of a company authorised to distribute the goods manufactured and supplied by the defendant. To the Court, the plaintiff must have known of the defendant's mark; hence, its registration in Thailand by the plaintiff for identical products constituted the exercise of a right in bad faith. The defendant was found to have better rights. Notably, the contention that registration in bad faith would render the mark "contrary to public policy" and tantamount to a "prohibited mark" under section 8 (9) of the Act was markedly responded by the Court's pronouncement that such dishonest conduct could never result in the mark being contrary to public policy (an item of prohibited marks), as prohibited marks would be determined by their sole look.[136]

---

[134] The drafting history reveals that the early draft prepared by the Ministry of Commerce contained a provision empowering registrars to refuse registration of a trade mark when the applicant "has exercised the right in bad faith": see Office of the Council of State of Thailand, Official Case File No. 244/2528 (1985), 710039. Unfortunately, this candid provision was, during scrutiny by the Council of State, expunged because it was felt that registration in bad faith would normally occur amongst well-known marks and would thus be handled by the well-known marks provision subsequently added to the draft: *ibid.*, 710567 and 710602-13. Such view seems fallacious, as dishonest registration was not limited to well-known marks.

[135] Supreme Court's Decision No. 7203/2554 (2011), followed by the Central Intellectual Property and International Trade Court's Decision No. IP 209-211/2560 (2017). *Cf.* the opposing view by the same trial court in its Decision No. IP 219/2560 (2017).

[136] In fact, before the Supreme Court's Decision No. 7203/2554 (2011), the Supreme Court took a different view in its Decision No. 310/2550 (2008) in which a trade mark registered by the defendant was cancelled on the ground of its repugnance to "public policy" when, on the facts, the defendant knew of (through his father who used to work for the plaintiff) the plaintiff's unregistered trade mark and dishonestly registered the defendant's trade mark in imitation of the plaintiff's mark. Given the order of time, the Decision No. 310/2550 (2008) may be perceived of as superseded by the Decision No. 7203/2554 (2011). However, simply because no *stare decisis* doctrine *per se* exists in Thai law, courts may feel free to decide cases differently. A firm judicial trend on the issue concerning the application of the "public policy" provision is, therefore, hardly predictable. Notably, although these decisions concerned the cancellation stage, the judicial reasoning on s. 8 (9) could equally apply to the application stage. It should also be mentioned that, in Thailand, decisions of trial courts are not open for public access, statistical analysis of trends of judicial decisions as a whole appears far from attainable.

4.2.2   Cancellation stage

The Act specifies several grounds for cancelling trade mark registration. Apart from the two cases unconnected with erroneous registration (the "non-use" case[137] and the case where the registered mark subsequently becomes a matter so common to the trade as to lose its signification as a trade mark),[138] the Act allows cancellation of incorrectly registered trade marks on the following grounds: (1) lack of distinctiveness,[139] (2) prohibited marks,[140] (3) identity,[141] (4) similarity,[142] (5) repugnance to public order, good morals or public policy[143] and (6) better rights.[144] Noticeably, the fact that the Act places the case involving repugnance to public order, good morals or public policy and the "better right" case (inextricably entwined with the "bad faith" standpoint) as separate grounds for cancellation most perceivably bespeaks the statutory perception that the former is limited to objectionable appearance. It is unlikely that the Act intends a case concerning registration in bad faith to trigger both grounds for cancellation (i.e. the "public policy" ground and the "better right" ground), since each of these two grounds falls within jurisdiction of different bodies (the Trade Marks Board for the former and the Court for the latter). *Travaux préparatoires* reveal that drafters have intended the "better right" merit to be judged solely by the Court in view of, in particular, the judiciary's greater competence to hear evidence as contrasted with that of the Board.[145] The Act allows "better right" claims to be brought before the Court within five years as from the date of the registration order.[146] Despite such manifest spirit of the law, the Trade Marks Board remains active in cancelling *mala fide* registered trade marks on the misconceived basis that they are "contrary to public policy".

5.   CONCLUDING REMARKS

Thorough exploration of trade marks legislation of Thailand portrays gradual advancement satisfying international obligations and in consonance with global recent developments. Unfortunately, there remain certain incongruities in the law itself and in the interpretation of law. In particular, a huge number of trade marks successfully registered elsewhere without legal hindrance have, in Thailand, regrettably been considered devoid of any distinctive character and unregistrable because registrars and the Trade Marks Board have consistently clung to such remarkably obstructive interpretation of distinctiveness that numerous trade marks not exhibiting genericness are treated in the same way as generic marks. As ineptitude on this point stems from inappropriate interpretation of law rather than defect in the law itself, regis-

---

[137]   S. 63 of the Act of 1991.
[138]   S. 66 of the Act of 1991.
[139]   S. 61 (1) of the Act of 1991.
[140]   S. 61 (2) of the Act of 1991.
[141]   S. 61 (3) of the Act of 1991.
[142]   S. 61 (4) of the Act of 1991.
[143]   S. 62 of the Act of 1991. In effect, given that the "prohibited marks" ground under s. 61 (2) also includes a trade mark which is contrary to public order or good moral or public policy under s. 8 (9), petitions for cancellation of trade marks on the ground of public order or good moral or public policy are in practice made both under s. 61 (2) in conjunction with s. 8 (9) and under s. 62.
[144]   S. 67 of the Act of 1991.
[145]   Office of the Council of State of Thailand, (n 134), 711758-9.
[146]   S. 67 of the Act of 1991.

trars and the Board may simply rectify their interpretation and take heed of the alarm sounded by the Courts on such hindering rulings.

Another incongruity lies in disorganised conceptions concerning the prevention of registration in bad faith detrimental to earlier rights. Thailand's current Act contains no candid provision stating registration in bad faith as an absolute ground for refusal or cancellation of registration. Authorities have, therefore, attempted to prevent *mala fide* registration by calling into play the "public policy" provision – rationalising that marks sought to be registered in bad faith are "prohibited marks" because they are "contrary to public policy" under section 8 (9) of the Act and that their incorrect registration, if any, can be cancelled. Given that this reasoning is hardly defensible when the "prohibited marks" notion most perceivably directs at their appearance rather than conduct in their use, this incongruity should be eviscerated by legislative amendment to the effect of introducing a provision directly proclaiming bad faith as an absolute ground for refusal and cancellation of registration, as envisioned elsewhere.[147] Indeed, the Trade Marks Board should, where registration is alleged to have been made in bad faith, respect the legislature's intention by allowing such bad faith claims (essentially correlated with "better rights") to be adjudicated by the Court only. It is also suggested that the five-year limitation period statutorily attached to court litigation for cancelling dishonest registration prejudicing earlier rights finds too little justification and should, therefore, be removed in fairness to rightful owners.

---

[147] See ss. 3 (6) and 47 (4) (bad faith) and ss. 3 (3)(a) and 47 (1) (public policy and accepted principles of morality) of the Trade Marks Act 1994 of the United Kingdom and s. 8 (2) nos. 5 and 14 and s. 50 (3) of the German Act on the Protection of Trade Marks and Other Signs 1994.

15. Empirical experiences in IP – conducting qualitative empirical research in law and regulation

William van Caenegem

1.   INTRODUCTION

What is the place of empirical research in legal scholarship? Who can conduct legitimate empirical research? What can we actually learn from empirical research in law and regulatory studies? Who has the requisite training to undertake such research? Is it real legal research or sociological study, or some other discipline, and therefore beyond legal academics' ken? What inferences can we safely draw from empirical data? What distinguishes good from bad empirical work? What techniques should we use?

Legal academics face so many questions when they take an interest in gathering information other than by 'desktop' research. They can be so daunting as to deter anybody from undertaking such research or participating in it. The work itself also requires more resources than standard legal research, which these days usually requires little more than some extra time. What I describe below is partially intended to nonetheless encourage empirical research, which from my perspective has been very enriching and informative, despite the difficulties that attend it.

How did I come to undertake empirical work, and then in particular qualitative, interview-based research? The first such project I was involved with related to how legal restraints on the mobility of employees impacted on innovation performance. My interest in innovation was by that time longstanding and the factors that trigger innovation remained intriguing, and as is well known, still up for debate[1]. However, colleagues Arup, Dent, Howe and I shared a well-informed sense that when it comes to employee mobility, important dynamics that influence employees' decisions are simply not revealed by the explicit settings and considerations of the law that underlies those decisions[2]. Prior research suggested that employers and employees act in certain ways in the shadow of non-compete law. Trying to reveal how and why seemed important in a competitive economy. The only way to find that out was by asking the actors involved, and that is what we set out to do.

My own 'philosophy' faced with the many questions listed above when embarking on this research, was that whatever the methodological difficulties, whatever the doubts about legit-

---

[1]   See e.g. William van Caenegem (2007) *Intellectual Property Law and Innovation*, Cambridge: CUP; William van Caenegem (2003) 'Intellectual property law and the idea of progress' 3 Intellectual Property Quarterly 237–256.

[2]   Chris Arup is now a Professor Adjunct to the Department of Business Law and Taxation at Monash University: https://research.monash.edu/en/persons/christopher-arup; John Howe is now Director of the Melbourne School of Government and Director of the Centre for Employment and Labour Relations Law at the University of Melbourne: https://law.unimelb.edu.au/about/staff/john-howe; Chris Dent is now Associate Professor at Murdoch University: http://profiles.murdoch.edu.au/myprofile/christopher-dent/.

imacy and our ability to draw inferences, it was worth gathering and publishing information gleaned from the actors involved. If the method is well explained and the difficulties we encountered were explicitly recounted in our published work, others would be able to form their own opinions about the empirical data, and the legitimacy and universal application of our conclusions. They could then undertake more or better work or critique our work as they saw fit. But at least some interesting and rich information would be 'out there'. I was also interested in going beyond mere technical legal ('black letter') and descriptive work, and in attempting to better inform important policy debates about the settings of the relevant law and regulation.

That has remained my approach throughout the multiple empirical research projects that I have undertaken or been involved with since. Below I describe some of the particular issues that arose in the qualitative interview-based research that I have since undertaken.

2. EMPLOYEE MOBILITY – HOW THE LAW CASTS ITS SHADOW

This project was funded by the Australian Research Council and was based at the University of Melbourne, involving John Howe (initially Colin Fenwick) and Chris Dent, then of the Law Faculty there, Chris Arup (Chief Investigator) of Monash and myself[3]. As indicated above, my own interest stemmed from a realisation derived from some prior research, that tacit knowledge is important to innovation[4], and that the degree of mobility of such knowledge, of necessity fixed in the minds of employees, was a crucial policy issue. If the law forces employees to remain at their present employment and denies them the freedom to move, that could have an adverse impact. But so could excessive mobility which might lead firms to underinvest in knowledge acquisition and development by their employees[5]. To cut to the heart of the issue, we knew that the prevalence of non-competes in knowledge intensive industries was a significant determinant of mobility. We discovered extensive US (but not Australian) scholarship and policy debate on what the law of non-competes says or should say.

But we did not know or find much from public sources, about how employees and employers actually acted post-employment in the face of non-competes. Did they take them seriously? Did they anticipate trouble if they changed jobs, and therefore stay put? How did they evaluate the real effects of breaching (e.g. being sued) or complying (e.g. missing a real job opportunity) with a non-compete? All these questions seemed only to be resolvable by speaking with

---

[3]   Australian Research Council, 'Nothing can be created out of nothing: workers, their know-how and the employment relationships that support them' [Arup, Christopher (Primary Chief Investigator (PCI)); Dent, Chris (Chief Investigator (CI)); Fenwick, Colin (Chief Investigator (CI); later Howe, John); van Caenegem, William (Chief Investigator (CI))]. Subsequently published in Christopher Arup, Chris Dent, John Howe and William van Caenegem (2013) 'Restraints of Trade: The Legal Practice' 36(1) University of New South Wales Law Journal 1–29. See also Chris Dent (2014) 'Unpacking Post-Employment Restraint of Trade Decisions: The Motivators of the Key Players' 26 Bond Law Review 1–26.

[4]   Michael Polanyi (1967) *The Tacit Dimension*, New York: Anchor Books.

[5]   Issues further considered in William van Caenegem (2013) 'Employee know-how, non-compete clauses and job mobility across civil and common law systems' 29(2) International Journal of Comparative Labour Law & Industrial Relations 219–238.

– interviewing – actual employers and (ex-)employees. The cases did not reveal what happens in situations where the matter does not end up in court, which we considered must be most instances by far. But how to get at the interviewees, how to select them and persuade them to be interviewed? That was a crucial difficulty the import of which is obvious, and we did not really resolve it. We considered trying to identify and reach out to HR managers in firms etc, and which organisations might assist us to find and contact such individuals, but they proved too difficult to identify and hence access. Speaking to employees randomly would not be necessarily productive – how to locate ones that had actually experienced non-competes in action?

In the final analysis we solved this dilemma by adopting an alternative method which we realised had shortcomings but was still an acceptable (or perhaps the best real) option to get at information which otherwise would remain hidden. We thus interviewed a selection of 'intermediaries': lawyers involved in the practice of labour law and non-competes in particular, including solicitors, barristers and judges, in state jurisdictions in Australia. We learned how many disputes about compliance are resolved without access to the courts but informed by the law – in particular by the uncertainty surrounding the enforceability of non-competes. We learned how and why 'boilerplate' non-complete clauses are so prevalent, and about the practice of 'undertakings' being entered into where employers had taken issue with the new activities of a departed employee. There was much that we knew we could not learn by interviewing only intermediaries and not the employees themselves, e.g. how the latter made decisions about moving, or not, without recourse to lawyers or advice about the terms they had signed up to, and whether employees perceived non-competes as 'not worth the paper they are written on'. Nonetheless we agreed that the information we did obtain was consistent enough in vital aspects to support a conclusion that the settings of the law of non-competes (or 'restraints of trade') in employment matters risked deterring movement to a degree that was not optimal in terms of knowledge mobility. Suffice it to say here, without going into the detail, which we published[6], that we gathered a mass of information not revealed in any other sources (including published cases and academic work). That material justified, in our opinion, the conclusion that the issue of non-competes deserved more attention from policymakers in Australia. It justified us reinforcing the significance of decisionmakers (judges and others involved in the employment law system) adhering strictly to their aversion to non-competes and not allow a softening in the application of the rules and principles that shackle such agreements and protect job mobility and competition[7].

On a final point, we started our work with a research-based intuition derived from what we already knew, which was by and large confirmed by our interviews. Although that intuition was tested in our team discussions (a combination of labour lawyers' and IP lawyers' views), we were therefore conscious of the risk of 'confirmation bias' and the importance of remaining alert to the competing interests at stake (not just those of employees who want to jump ship whenever and however they like, free to use whatever they have learned). Our

---

[6]   See above at n 3.

[7]   Non-competes are a controversial legal device and a more acute policy issue in some other jurisdictions, in particular the US; see for instance more recently Orly Nobel and Mark Lemley (2021) 'Supporting Talent Mobility and Enhancing Human Capital: Banning Noncompete Agreements to Create Competitive Job Markets', Day One Project, January, available at https://law.stanford.edu/wp-content/uploads/2021/01/Supporting-Talent-Mobility-and-Enhancing-Human-Capital-Banning-Noncompete-Agreements-to-Create-Competitive-Job-Markets-Jan2021.pdf.

conclusions therefore tended towards the 'subtle' – we did not call for a wholesale abolition of non-competes (along the lines of Californian law[8]) but some more limited measures and the continued vigilance referred to above. We were conscious that our interview sample was relatively limited, intermediate, and suffering from various biases – for instance that by speaking with lawyers of their experiences with non-competes, we were to a degree addressing a self-selecting sample with heightened and vested interests. All respondents had considered our issues with great care before. However, where the consistency of the responses to particular questions that we obtained was overwhelming, we decided those responses made a valid basis for drawing inferences. Readers can make what they wish from the publications drawing on our interview data[9].

We early on decided against the alternative methods of surveys and more quantitative methods, because of the above mentioned difficulty in identifying and reaching a sufficiently large sample of targets, the enormous diversity of those targets and the difficulties of selection, because of anticipated low response rates, and because single question/answer items would not allow us to obtain sufficiently 'rich' and subtle information. Interviews allow a particular line of questioning to be pursued in more depth, and also allow some direct human assessment by the interviewers of how honest, considered and uncontaminated answers are. Coupled with what we knew about the 'busyness' of our putative targets, we therefore ruled out a survey approach. We also were fortunate that some of our team had previous experience with qualitative interviewing and related methodological issues and were well acquainted with the relevant literature. We were therefore well informed on method.

3.   EMPIRICAL WORK ON GEOGRAPHICAL INDICATIONS OF ORIGIN

My second experience with empirical research related to the then still emerging topic of geographical indications of origin ('GIs'). At the time there was, and this continues today, a lively debate about the desirability of a *sui generis* GI regulatory system for food in Australia. We already have such a system for wines[10]. Jen Cleary, Peter Drahos and I concluded that because this issue was so commonly seen in the context of trade negotiations and Australia's positioning in relation to European demands and initiatives in particular[11], insufficient attention had been devoted to the question whether the 'system' might have policy advantages for Australian agriculture *per se*. In particular, could food GIs assist producers (farmers) to capture a larger slice of the value-adding pie, and promote accuracy in consumer messaging around

---

[8]   See Ronald J. Gilson (1999) 'The Legal Infrastructure of High Technology Industrial Districts: Silicon Valley, Route 128, and Covenants Not to Compete' 74(3) New York University Law Review 575–629.

[9]   See inter alia Arup et al at n 3, Dent at n 3 and Chris Arup (2012) 'What/Whose Knowledge? Restraints of Trade and Concepts of Knowledge' 36(2) Melbourne University Law Review 369–414.

[10]   Administered by Wine Australia, see https:// www .wineaustralia .com/ labelling/ register -of -protected-gis-and-other-terms/geographical-indications.

[11]   Peter Drahos is Professor at ANU: see https://regnet.anu.edu.au/our-people/academic/peter-drahos; Jen Cleary is a part-time researcher at the Centre for Global Food and Resources at the University of Adelaide and a geographer specialising in RRR communities, and presently CEO of Centacare SA.

provenance? There was in fact no previous research conducted in this space in Australia[12]. We obtained funding from what was then the Rural Industries Research and Development Corporation (RIRDC) for our empirical project and wrote a report that was subsequently published by the RIRDC (which later became AgriFutures Australia)[13]. The principal costs that RIRDC met were of travelling around Australia to six different locations (some quite remote, such as Kununurra in the far north of Western Australia) to conduct interviews with farmers and others in the value chain of agricultural food production.

There were again numerous methodological issues we had to tackle· but fortunately my two colleagues Drahos and Cleary had extensive experience with qualitative and empirical research methodology in the social sciences[14]. We intended to conduct interviews across the value chain, from farmers to wholesalers to processors to supermarkets and other retailers, and we wanted a sufficiently large and diverse sample. The cost of the project was thus considerable, also because we decided that it was optimal if all three of us undertook every interview. That was partly because we brought varied skills and experience, because the interviews required a lot of subtlety and sensitivity, and because we intended to conduct quite a lot of interviews on any given interviewing day. Interviewing is tiring and requires great focus and travelling from interview to interview every day is also challenging. It was important to us to be consistent in the questioning between interviewees and having three of us present helped to ensure this. The ultimate interview sample was quite large, with 170 or so interviews conducted for the project, each of about 1 hour.

The qualitative method adopted called for 'semi-structured' interviews[15]. In essence these are interviews in which planned and consistent issues are addressed through a series of predetermined questions[16], but room is left for responsiveness to interviewees and the information, issues and questions they have during the interview[17]. We determined from desktop research what the relevant issues and questions had to be and made sure they were raised in every interview. We shared the actual questioning and dialogue with interviewees, and each of us took written notes (having decided against recording interviews, so as to elicit the frankest answers), which we then consolidated and cross-checked after each day or period of interviewing. One critical issue was that interviewees faced a fairly steep learning curve, as we needed

---

[12]   About provenance branding, see William van Caenegem (2015) 'Quality local food products – some aspects of trademarks law and GIs' Corporate Governance eJournal, Paper 35; the project was pre-described in William van Caenegem, Jen Cleary and Peter Drahos (2014) 'Pride and Profit: Geographical Indications as Regional Development Tools in Australia' 16(1) Journal of Economic and Social Policy 1–25.

[13]   William van Caenegem, Peter Drahos and Jen Cleary (2015) *Provenance of Australian food products: Is there a place for geographical indications?* Rural Industries Research and Development Corporation, https://www.agrifutures.com.au/wp-content/uploads/publications/15-060.pdf.

[14]   As reflected for instance in Peter Drahos (ed.) (2017) *Regulatory Theory: Foundations and Applications*, ANU, Canberra ePress; and Jen Cleary (2014) 'Cultural Icons and Cash Commodities: The Two-World Story of Australian Bush Foods', available at https://www.nintione.com.au/resource/ClearyJ_CulturalIconsAndCashCommodities_PhD.pdf.

[15]   In effect a case study method: see M.J. Hird, 'Case Study', in R.L. Miller and J.D. Brewer (eds) (2003) *A-Z of Social Research*, London: Sage.

[16]   See T.R. Lindlof and B.C. Taylor (2002) *Qualitative Communication Research Methods*, 2nd edn, California: Sage Publications.

[17]   See M. Leonard, 'Interviews', in R.L. Miller and J.D. Brewer (eds) (2003) *A-Z of Social Research*, London: Sage.

to explain how a hypothetical GI system might work in Australia and how it was situated in the legal landscape of passing off, trade marks, branding and provenance. This involves sometimes subtle legal distinctions. However, we found that by and large interviewees already had some grasp of the essence of provenance branding, of generating a 'back story' for their products, and of the relationship between the particularities of their location and the individual character of their local food products[18]. They were generally aware of the limitations of what the law could do for them. The answers we got therefore tended to be reasonably astute, and we were generally confident that they were given with a sufficient understanding of the issues we were pursuing. We also conducted a pilot project[19], and from our preliminary research were aware of the impact of deregulation and demutualisation on the balance between cooperation and competition among farmers.

Our critical aspiration was to determine whether across the wide range of interviews (as mentioned, about 170 in total)[20], certain consistent themes emerged from responses that would allow us to formulate persuasive conclusions and then make policy recommendations. Some but not all of our intuitions were confirmed but we also learned a great deal more about agricultural production, competition and collaboration between farmers, previous attempts at collaboration around region branding, interactions between farmers and processors etc than we had anticipated or tentatively predicted. In other words, we derived a wealth of information from the interviews[21], in some respects far more than we anticipated, and also suggestive of other issues and research targets worth pursuing later[22]. This was a great additional benefit of the semi-structured interview approach.

Our recommendations were not uncontroversial and attracted support but also some fairly vigorous opposition. But without a doubt it put the whole issue of the policy goals of GIs and adaptation of their regulatory design to Australian conditions up for debate. Our work shifted the focus from solely international trade to also include domestic Rural Regional and Remote (RRR) development policy[23]. To enhance the credibility of our publications in that context, we were explicit about methodology, about the factual elements of our research strategy and

---

[18] GIs are a particular form of provenance branding, very different from standard or certification trade marks. The TRIPS definition of a GI requires that they are 'indications which identify a good as originating in the territory of a Member, or a region or locality in that territory, where a given quality, reputation or other characteristic of the good is essentially attributable to its geographical origin' (article 22(1)).

[19] Described in 'Pride and Profit...', above n 12.

[20] So-called 'thematic analysis'; for a recent overview, see Lorelli S. Nowell, Jill M. Norris, Deborah E. White and Nancy J. Moules (2017) 'Thematic Analysis: Striving to Meet the Trustworthiness Criteria' 16 International Journal of Qualitative Methods 1–13.

[21] One of the critical advantages of the semi-structured interview technique is exactly the richness and contextuality of the information gained from interviews.

[22] Some of which was undertaken with further funding from Agrifutures – see below at 4. See also William van Caenegem and Jen Cleary (eds) (2017) *The Importance of Place: Geographical Indications as a Tool for Local and Regional Development*, Springer, Heidelberg, Ius Gentium series; Peter Drahos, 'Sunshine in a Bottle? Geographical Indications, the Australian Wine Industry and the Promise of Rural Development', in Irene Calboli and Ng-Loy Wee Loon (eds) (2017) *Geographical Indications at the Crossroads of Trade, Development, and Culture: Focus on Asia-Pacific*, Cambridge: CUP (at pp.259–280).

[23] The issue is very much alive in the context of FTA negotiations between Australia and the EU; in that regard see IPAustralia, Australia-European Union Free Trade Agreement: Consultation on a Possible New Geographical Indications Right, available at https://consultation.ipaustralia.gov

interviews, about how we drew conclusions and how firmly we supported them. We also identified questions that remained to be addressed so did not lay claim to having somehow, in the one project, provided all the answers. GIs are after all a complex matter that resides at the confluence of many different policy spheres: agriculture, IP, international trade, competition, regulatory design etc.

As far as I personally was concerned, this empirical research project opened my eyes to the realities of agriculture in Australia, both in terms of the challenges faced, the flexibility and innovation in the sector, its rapid evolution over time, the entrepreneurialism and constant search for innovative solutions of many of its participants, and the structural elements of the competitive landscape. In other words, it was a learning experience that garnered knowledge and information that has been very valuable to me as a researcher. The vigorous debates within our small team around policy and inferences to be drawn from what we were learning were also very rewarding. Having three well-informed and interested researchers involved improved the rigour of our conclusions. It felt like every possible angle was exhaustively debated before any conclusions were committed to paper for our report.

4.   INTERVIEWING IN NON-ENGLISH SPEAKING COUNTRIES

This first empirical research project into GIs in Australia funded by RIRDC/AgriFutures pointed us to many more deserving questions, one of which was whether an Australian food GI system, if it were to be introduced, could result in benefits for farmers not just in the domestic market (which the first project focused on) but in export markets as well. If agricultural products were to be de-commodified by provenance branding them, and having the provenance brand protected as a GI, would that impact on the opportunities for Australian agriculture to derive more value from its exports into foreign markets? A principal issue with a high-quality, local value added, provenance branding strategy for particular agricultural food products is that the risk of free riding is so great that it disincentivises investment. In other words, free riding undercuts quality producers who rely on provenance and deprives them of the potential surpluses generated by their strategy. We had, for instance, incidentally picked up that Mangoes from Mareeba (in North Queensland) had developed a quality reputation in parts of China, but that unscrupulous providers there would simply fill genuine 'Mareeba Mango' boxes with cheaper imports from Thailand, undercutting the real fruit from Queensland. We had also heard that there was a similar problem, for instance, with Tasmanian cherries which are sold at a very high premium in the Chinese market (at particular times of year especially). In terms of protecting brands from imitation, GIs differ from corporate trade marks (and also from certifications trade marks) because they are not private property, but either collectively owned or simply a regulatory system. It thus falls to government authorities to enforce GIs. They can and are also the subject of mutual protection through state-to-state trade negotiations[24]. We therefore were interested to know whether, if there were, hypothetically, Australian

---

.au/ policy/ geographical-indications/; see also Kana Nakano and William van Caenegem (2020) 'An Australian GI system made from local ingredients' 43(1) European Intellectual Property Review 16–33.

[24]   This is exemplified for instance by the Agreement between the European Community and Australia on trade in wine (2009); available at https://eur-lex.europa.eu/legal-content/en/TXT/PDF/?uri =CELEX:22009A0130(01)&rid=1), which requires GI style protection of European wine indications,

registered food GIs in the future, this would afford greater and more direct protection to our so registered provenance brands in overseas markets. If so, the case for a local food GI registration system was strengthened; even if not, there remained the purely domestic policy goals to consider. Our empirical research into this issue was again funded by the RIRDC/Agrifutures[25].

We settled on Japan and China as crucial markets for Australian agricultural exports. However, up to date and accessible literature on provenance brand protection in those jurisdictions either by GIs or certification trade marks or in any other way was very limited. We did not know with sufficient precision what the regulatory structures in those countries were, how the different regimes might interact, what the impact of trade negotiations present and future might be, what influence the two big GI contestants, the US and the EU, had on policy thinking in those countries etc[26]. We felt that to have sufficient information to assess our research question required work on the ground in the two target markets. Only with direct interaction with, on the one hand, students and users of the GI system, in the form of academics and practitioners, and on the other hand, officialdom, would we be able to develop a sufficiently subtle picture to allow us to answer our research question[27]. Whereas the previous GI project aimed to develop a picture of the situation at the grassroots level, this project aimed to fill out the poor information we had about the regulatory situation and policy landscape in the targeted jurisdictions.

My colleague Lucie Tréguier and I were thus able to visit Japan for one week and then China for a further week, to conduct interviews[28]. Neither of us spoke either language, so we had to rely on interpreters to a certain degree. Most respondents were sufficiently well versed in English, but that was not the case with officialdom in China in particular.

These interviews were more information-focused than those described above for our first project: to find out the precise nature of the existing regulatory landscape (complex in particular in China); how it might evolve; how much the GI system was supported by government; what role international relations and connections played in the policy and regulatory choices made; and how existing and future regulations could affect Australian importers who might rely on provenance branding. Again, we used semi-structured interviews, but in this case the interviewees had all been selected for their prior knowledge about GIs.

Although we were thus not required to explain the nature of GIs to respondents, we did encounter other challenges. Interpretation requires the interpreter to have a good understanding

---

and reciprocal protection of Australian wine GIs in the EU; see also the current debate about food GIs in the EU-Australia FTA negotiations: Ian Zhou and Rob Dossor (2021) 'Geographical indications and the Australia-EU Free Trade Agreement' 2 July, Economic Policy Section, Parliament of Australia, available at https://www.aph.gov.au/About_Parliament/Parliamentary_Departments/Parliamentary_Library/pubs/rp/rp2122/AustraliaEUFreeTradeAgreement.

[25]   Our report on these issues, funded by RIRDC/Agrifutures was published as William van Caenegem, Jen Cleary and Lucie Tréguier (2016) *Local to Global: Provenance Branding and Farmer Co-operation for High Value Export Markets*, available at https://www.agrifutures.com.au/wp-content/uploads/publications/16-068.pdf.

[26]   The EU has been actively promoting its GI regulatory model in Asia: see Fe Emmanuelle Panlilio and William van Caenegem (2019) 'An Australian anomaly? Sui generis GIs in Australia and the Asia Pacific region' 41(10) European Intellectual Property Review 628–638.

[27]   In terms of directly interviewing farmers, we determined that there were too many practical impediments, although we did conduct interviews at one farming cooperative outside Tokyo.

[28]   Jen Cleary, the third member of the team, was not able to travel at the relevant time. Lucie Tréguier is now a solicitor with Deprez Guignot in Paris, France: https://en.ddg.fr/equipe/lucie-treguier.

of the subject matter – they need to be able to 'translate' the interviewers' questions in more than a literal sense, and relay responses while including contextual understandings that underly what the interviewee says. It is an advantage if interpreters can respond to initial follow-up questions from targets with some further explanation without having to refer back to the interviewer every time. We therefore briefed in some detail in relation to our subject matter, until we were confident in the interpreter's ability to explain the goals of our interviews. Further, we had to rely on the interpreter to explain to us some of the subtleties and nuances involved in the answers to questions and in the interview dynamics. However, too much reliance on contextualisation by the interpreter risks them simply reinterpreting the interviewer's questions and also risks them being biased towards interpreting answers in a manner they think the interviewer wishes to hear. Alternatively, it puts too much of their personal stamp on the content of an interview. A very clear understanding and very capable interpreters are therefore really essential. Although we were seeking 'information' rather than opinion, in fact some of our questions also required evaluation from our interviewees, a degree of subtlety and personal interpretation of what we wanted to know and of what was happening in the regulatory and policy environment in their country. The interpreter needed to understand properly what was required in this regard.

Another particular issue with our interviews lay with the nature of officialdom, and then maybe particularly so in China. There seemed to be an official line to follow, which is uncontroversial, but this line was often not made explicit, nor apparently followed with any rigidity or even clearly known to interviewees. There were evident and sometimes perplexing inconsistencies between answers emanating from different departments, in part because of failing coordination but also because of inter-departmental rivalries. Thorough and broad background research is essential, and there is a certain amount of care required in the questioning and then unpacking of answers, with due regard for underlying relationships. These might for instance be between different individuals in the hierarchy, or between departments, where jockeying for power and influence over particular portfolios is a significant dynamic that might skew answers. Our strategy of not interviewing only officials, but backing up with practitioners and academics, assisted us to develop a fairly consistent picture in the face of the sometimes contradictory or unclear accounts from officials, and to test our interpretation and understanding of what they said. But across the board a different interview style is required in countries such as Japan and in particular China: contradicting or appearing to take issue with what interviewees in high positions maintain is far less acceptable and if it happens (sometimes unwittingly) is liable to result in subsequent unresponsiveness. In other words, there are cultural differences at play which influence interviewing technique; a skilled interpreter and cultural preparation with trusted interlocutors can assist to bridge the gap.

Interviews were also complicated by the fact that, although in Japan there was a clearly developed and consistent government position on GIs which officials understood and clearly shared, in China that was less the case. Policy goals were various or not developed, and there was less consistency, enhanced by the above-mentioned inter-agency rivalry and a lack of clear direction 'from the top'. The information we obtained from prior research and non-official sources allowed us to navigate and interpret this landscape, but we were nonetheless on guard against presenting too much as certain and clear in our reporting. However, there was a lot that we could learn and safely unpack from our interviews, and that we felt confident to include in our report and use to formulate conclusions. Again, we did not underplay these systemic issues so that readers can make up their own minds in an informed manner about our conclusions.

5. EMPIRICAL WORK INVESTIGATING COMPETITION AND REGULATION IN AGRICULTURE

As indicated above, interviewing agriculturists about GIs revealed many underlying structural issues. This triggered a broader interest in the dynamics of competition and collaboration in agriculture, and the impact of various forms of regulation on that particular sector. This broad interest resulted in a number of other externally funded research projects. One undertaken with Brenda Marshall, Jen Cleary and Madeline Taylor, and also funded by RIRDC/AgriFutures, related to collective bargaining in agriculture[29]. The project sat within the competition policy sphere, in particular the regulation of bargaining between initial producers (farmers) and processors and others further up the 'value chain' (including wholesalers and the very powerful retail chains that exist in Australia, predominantly Coles and Woolworths). The issue is most simply explained by reference to the dairy sector, but it is repeated time and again in relation to other product categories. The dairy farmer supplies a largely undifferentiated product into what is essentially a commodity market. There is a substantial number of such suppliers in the market but a very small number of dairy processors (those who process and package milk for the drinking market but also for processed products such as cheese and dairy drinks etc). This leads to a substantial imbalance of market power where the processors have an overwhelming ability to set prices autonomously and play off individual suppliers against each other. Those suppliers are then pushed into a cycle of smaller margins which can only be made profitable by economies of scale – in other words, fewer dairy farms with larger herds[30]. The consequences for the life and vitality of rural communities dependent on agriculture are easy to imagine.

However, the Australian legislator has provided for an exemption to the competition law which allows suppliers in such a situation to bargain collectively – in other words there is an exception to the normal prohibition on collusion (in particular over price)[31]. To put it simply, normally it is illegal for a group of dairy farmers to agree, for instance, to supply their milk only at or above a certain price to a particular processor. But the Australian Competition and Consumer Commission (ACCC) can grant an exemption for such collective bargaining. The central question we wanted to investigate is why there seemed to be so little take-up of this exemption opportunity at the time, not only in dairy but also in other sectors of food production (such as for instance chicken farming). Our interest in collaboration vs competition was reignited: why did farmers seemingly prefer to compete individually and thereby suffer

---

[29] The RIRDC report resulting from this project, *Collective Bargaining in the Agricultural Sector*, by William van Caenegem, Madeline Taylor, Jen Cleary and Brenda Marshall is available at https://www.agrifutures.com.au/wp-content/uploads/publications/15-055.pdf. Brenda Marshall is Professor of Law at the Faculty of Law, Bond University and Madeline Taylor is now Senior Lecturer at Macquarie University: https://researchers.mq.edu.au/en/persons/madeline-taylor.

[30] The Australian Competition and Consumer Commission investigated some of these issues in the Dairy Inquiry, which reported in 2018, see https://www.accc.gov.au/focus-areas/inquiries-finalised/dairy-inquiry-0.; see also in relation to Collective Bargaining Class exemptions: https://www.accc.gov.au/public-registers/class-exemptions-register/collective-bargaining-class-exemption; and https://www.accc.gov.au/system/files/public-registers/documents/Collective%20bargaining%20class%20exemption%20consultation%20-%20Submission%20by%20Prof%20Dr%20William%20van%20Caenegem%3B%20Dr%20Madeline%20Taylor%3B%20Dr%20Jen%20Cleary%3B%20Dr%20Brenda%20Marshall%20-%2025.09.18%20-%20PUBLIC%20VERSION.pdf.

[31] See n 29 and 30 above in relation to the conditions that apply to the grant of such exemptions.

price pressure that they could potentially avoid by cooperating? In the final analysis, through conducting interviews, we identified difficulties with the regulatory and administrative structure of the collective bargaining provisions which were an impediment to their uptake[32]. But we also realised that the interests of primary producers were not necessarily sufficiently aligned, and that the underlying structures and relationships for collaboration (in the era of demutualisation) were often not present. Farmers were also time-poor, doubtful about the law, and worried about the consequences of being perceived to 'gang up' on vital processors. Also at the heart of the problem lay the reluctance of some farmers, who saw themselves as highly efficient, to throw in their lot with others whom they regarded as inefficient, perhaps old-fashioned, not sufficiently astute etc. They felt in other words that existing practices worked for them, and that they had nothing to gain from dragging up their less competent competitors (as milk suppliers for instance) through collective bargaining. They also tended to find that other suppliers would perhaps play along with efforts to organise a collective approach, only then to agree individually on a price with the processor which was lower than the target price set by the group – a problem of blind negotiation which the law was powerless to prevent or render unattractive at the time. This systemically important information would be almost impossible to obtain other than by the interviewing method that we deployed.

However, the interviews were not without their challenges. One of these was that many farmers or primary producers operated in a context of distrust of each other and fear of the market power of the processors. How best to overcome this apprehension, obtain frank answers and reduce interviewee self-censorship proved to be a major question. The issue highlighted the need for confidentiality and anonymity in reporting. The standard way of dealing with this is that interviewees are only identified in the report (which in this case was to be published by RIRDC) as 'Respondent No 1...' etc. Only the researchers have a list that matches the Respondent numbers to particular interviewees, and the researchers operate under the confidentiality conditions imposed by their University Ethics Committee clearance. Where the number of interviewees is relatively small (e.g. within a given geographical area, or in an industry with few actors) additional care has to be taken to draft the resulting report or publication in a manner that does not allow readers to sheet home particular information or contents to particular interviewees. Naturally not all respondents are concerned by these matters, but in the case of our collective bargaining research, some certainly were. It takes some care also to ensure that in successive interviews, one does not inadvertently refer to other or previous interviewees in a manner that identifies them. Nonetheless it is sometimes useful to put to one interviewee, under the cover of anonymity, what another interviewee has said and obtain a reaction.

In particular where the empirical research is conducted in a limited geographical area, as was the case for some of our collective bargaining interviews, and for instance also later in our King Island GI research (see further below), we had to tread carefully. In a small area word quickly spreads that some researchers are 'doing the rounds' and asking about certain issues. We found interviewees who were thus already informed of the topics, beyond what we had shared in the preliminary stage by way of email and telephone conversations. It was always our practice to arrange interviews by first communicating by email and explaining our topic and interests, and then if necessary backing this up with conversations by phone. In any case

---

[32]   Some of these impediments have now been addressed, see above n 30.

our ethics approval required consent to be obtained prior to conducting interviews. We found it passing rare that individuals refused to be interviewed, or were unhappy to be approached, or took a dislike to the way we framed or were interested in a particular issue. In our GI research we did encounter a (very few) who were *au fait* with the issue and very much opposed to the whole notion – but only one or two refused to speak with us about it. However, in particular where interviewees had become more informed about our topics, the challenge was sometimes to maintain focus on what we wanted to hear about, rather than on what some interviewee wanted to talk about!

One aspect of our interviewing strategy that bears mention here is the selection of respondents. This relied on preliminary research conducted via the internet, to identify targets, in almost every case within a particular geographical area and industry. They might be particular producers with their own websites, or ones reported on in media stories, or members of associations that could be so identified, or sometimes an initial approach was required to a particular organisation to identify individuals to speak with. Very important was then a second layer of cross-referrals – interview targets, either before the actual interview or during it, would identify others who they thought would be useful to interview. Almost always that proved to be the case, and not infrequently it was possible to arrange such interviews at short notice. Naturally there was an inherent risk of selection bias – that interviewees would recommend others who were of a like mind. But we often tracked down outliers or individuals with an opposing view, because they *were* in fact mentioned by other targets. We made a point of asking whether interviewees were aware of those who disagreed with them, or had differing views or were 'outliers' in terms of industry practices, collegiality and business approaches. Further, because we were interviewing across the value chain (from primary producers to processors to retailers etc) we tended to come to identify the principal divergent viewpoints and points of contestation. In other words, a variety of strategies and alertness to the risk of reinforcement of one's own biases built a buffer against one-sidedness or against merely setting out to confirm what we already suspected. We were of course also as well informed as possible of the contested issues and discordant views from a preliminary strategy of comprehensive desktop research, which included access to media accounts. In most industries and in relation to most topics, there are at least some published sources to draw on. However, as mentioned above, not infrequently important information was entirely hidden from view until revealed by interviewees[33]. It sometimes became apparent throughout a series of interviews that we had somewhat misconceived a target issue and had to adapt and ask additional or different questions. Again, it is an advantage of the qualitative approach that this is an option.

Further research projects that I managed, related to agriculture and regulation, and consisting of externally funded qualitative research by way of interviews, regarded on the one hand the regulation of other aspects of the dairy industry and, on the other, the abovementioned case study of the provenance branding landscape on King Island (KI). The former project conducted with Madeline Taylor and funded by the Australian Specialist Cheesemakers' Association was intended to investigate why there was so little production of raw (unpasteur-

---

[33]   A striking example of this related to previous attempts at provenance branding of King Island dairy products and in particular producing Tetra packed milk on the Island; see William van Caenegem, and Kana Nakano (2020) 'Standard trade marks, geographical indications and provenance branding in Australia: What we can learn from King Island' 23(5-6) Journal of World Intellectual Property 632–657.

ised) milk cheese in Australia[34]. We had learned during GI research that the fact most cheese in Australia is purely imitative in style, utilising European varieties and cultures[35], was exactly due to the exclusive use of pasteurised milk in production. Milk so treated does not have the same biodynamic characteristics resulting from interaction with the immediate environment as exist in Europe, where raw milk cheeses are many and varied. While Australia imported a substantial amount of such cheeses, we produced vanishingly little of it. Why was this so? Why was there not a thriving artisanal cheesemaking culture as in Europe, contributing to the local economy of Rural Regional and Remote (RRR) communities?

At least in part, the answer seemed to lie in the very demanding regulations concerning production, based on sanitary prescriptions inspired by health concerns[36]. The rules here appeared to be much more far-reaching, uniform and inflexible than in Europe, and in particular in France. We therefore devised an interview strategy that targeted specialty or artisanal cheesemakers in Australia, with the aim of discovering what impact health regulations had on their production decisions. A very few cheesemakers did already produce raw milk cheeses. We learned how the regulations posed challenges for small operators, and the economics which steered them away from raw milk cheese production. Ultimately, we recommended a more modulated approach to small scale raw milk cheese production allowing for artisanal processes whose safety was in fact well documented in other jurisdictions such as France. A regulatory regime more adapted to small-scale production was in our view essential to reduce costs and thus result in variety that consumers would appreciate, and economic activity that would contribute to communities.

In terms of the challenges of empirical research, what we experienced as a real difficulty in this project was the overweening influence of dairy industry associations that dominated regulatory policy[37]. We discovered from published sources, but also from sometimes difficult interviews, that there was very determined opposition to the use of raw milk in dairy production at any level. To some extent this was understandable, but it also seemed to us a policy stance skewed in favour of large producers and an industry driven by economies of scale. The great danger seemed to be perceived as being the risk of outbreaks of for instance salmonellosis in the context of raw milk cheese production[38]. Yet our research told us that this was actually a very low risk when some basic rules, and ordinary cheese-making practices were observed. The real risk seemed to be more reputational, and therefore to concern the industry as a whole rather than small individual producers alone. However, we found it difficult to precisely pinpoint the risks of raw milk use as apparently perceived by the 'big end of town'.

---

[34]   See the resulting article: William van Caenegem and Madeline Elizabeth Taylor (2017) 'Real Deal or No Deal? A Comparative Analysis of Raw Milk Cheese Regulation in Australia and France' Vol. 2017, No. 1, pp. 1–19, 2017, International Journal of Rural Law and Policy 1. For the Australian Specialist Cheesemakers Association see https://australiancheese.org/pages/meet-our-members.

[35]   In the biological sense: see e.g. https://australiancheese.org/collections.

[36]   Addressed by HACCP food safety plans: see https://www.foodsafety.com.au/blog/everything-you -need-to-know-about-haccp and https://www.foodstandards.gov.au/industry/safetystandards/documents/ Guide%20321%20FoodSafetyPrograms-WEB.pdf.

[37]   In particular Dairy Australia: see https://www.dairy.com.au/.

[38]   Our research on French practices and regulations, and on the relevant scientific literature, did not support a view that raw milk cheese production was unacceptably dangerous; see above n 34. The article cited contains all the relevant data.

Effectively we ran up against one of the potential limitations of our type of very open interview strategy – that some respondents would not be fully prepared to 'tell the whole story', or perhaps were also deterred from interacting with us. Apart from the resulting risk of obtaining skewed information, a danger is that the interviewer by insisting on trying to find out more, becomes seen as an advocate for a particular cause, which for us was not actually the case. On a final note concerning interview dynamics, the picture can also be clouded by other loosely related issues, which are difficult to avoid and steer clear of in interviews: here that was the controversy concerning raw milk for drinking[39]. This has fanatical supporters and is part of a lively debate in some quarters – it was at times difficult to steer clear of it and to get interviewees to focus on the quite different topic of making cheese with unpasteurised milk.

Some similar issues were to the fore in the King Island provenance branding study undertaken with external funding in collaboration with Kana Nakano[40]. This study was a fieldwork examination of provenance branding *in situ* and attempted to answer the hypothetical question what a food GI option, if it were feasible, would contribute to economic development of the island. We also wanted to test some preconceptions about the regulatory design of a putative food GI system in Australia. We interviewed targets in the dairy, beef and lobster industries. Each of these has an established 'King Island' provenance reputation in Australia. In particular in relation to beef there are many accounts of free-riding on the quality image of the KI product[41]. The Island presented us with a unique opportunity to gather information about three different industries at once. For each industry, the branding landscape and market conditions were very different, which added to the interest. We were therefore able to concentrate many interviews within a relatively short period on the island.

In some ways this also presented challenges, as the word soon spread about our presence and our interests, a difficulty I referred to above. The risk was that future interviewees would get a skewed or inaccurate idea about what we really wanted to know, or would 'get ready' to tell us about something that galled or fascinated them but was not necessarily what we wanted to know, or would worry that information they shared would get passed on. However, we found interviewees largely very robust, knowledgeable and unconcerned about differing views of other interviewees they knew we would or had spoken with. They were largely alive to critical issues, networks and relationships, and the pitfalls and potential of provenance branding in the industries concerned. We also learned that knowledge and experience have many initially hidden layers that are not apparent from published sources which have been scanned prior to the fieldwork. Interviews revealed a lot of hidden history and connections, in a manner that vindicated the time and resources expended upon them. This also meant that, apart from using interviewees to identify other targets as is a well-known and accepted strategy, we also could use information gleaned from interviewees (about things that had happened in the past, commercial initiatives taken, plans for instance for the erection of a new abattoir on the Island) to inform our questions in later interviews.

---

[39] See Food Standards Australia for an objective appraisal: https:// www .foodstandards .gov .au/ consumer/safety/Pages/Raw-drinking-milk.aspx; see, for instance, for proponents' views: https://www .ausrawmilk.org/regulating-rm.

[40] See above n 33 for the ensuing article.

[41] See for instance 'ACCC swoops on King Island beef brand claims', Beef Central (2012) available at https://www.beefcentral.com/news/accc-swoops-on-king-island-beef-brand-claims/; see also https:// www.accc.gov.au/media-release/accc-acts-to-protect-consumers-and-king-island-producers.

One critical issue which again presented a strategic challenge, and kept us alert to the fact that it is important to cross-verify interview data and rely only on consistent themes in interviews to found conclusions, was the fact that Saputo[42], a multinational dairy company based in Canada, is owner of the King Island Dairy processing facility and trade marks (in itself perhaps controversially) and as the only processor on KI, had disproportionate market power there. In some way its strategies and negotiating tactics were determinative of the economic future of local dairy farmers. The fortunes of the latter have long been in steady decline, favouring conversion of their lands to beef production. Again, issues of confidentiality of interviews were to the fore, as was trying to fully understand and interpret sometimes guarded answers. Posing certain questions (the answers to which might reflect adversely on certain industry players) was somewhat confronting and had to be done delicately, while still trying to get at the underlying facts, and the levers of decision-making. To our regret we were unsuccessful in obtaining interviews with the Saputo or King Island Dairy companies, perhaps because they were aware of the tendency of our questions, and that what we had in mind concerning GIs was not necessarily in line with their perceived interests. However, the King Island Dairy company was in a stage of transition to a new owner (Saputo) with perhaps new branding strategies, which may well (and understandably) explain their reluctance to communicate with us. Whatever the case may be, it alerts researchers in our position to the risks that we are being gamed, or that we are getting less than reliable or clear answers because of the influence of certain actors, in our case in particular markets. Again, the key is to be open about what we know and limitations encountered, and understand about this when writing up and publishing the research, to carefully devise an interviewing strategy, and also to have a certain degree of scepticism and care about one's own conclusions.

6.   STAYING ON TARGET – INTERVIEWS WITH FASHION DESIGNERS

A recently concluded externally funded empirical project concerned a wholly different subject matter, related to a long-standing interest of mine, and of my doctoral student Violet Atkinson, in fashion and IP[43]. We were intrigued by some of the writing of Sprigman and Raustialia concerning the need for IP protection in the fashion industry[44]. They basically argued that there was a very high level of innovation (even 'churn') in the fashion industry in the United States, in the virtual absence of IP protection. That naturally gives rise to some interesting questions about the role of and need for (high levels of) IP protection more generally. Yet

---

[42]   See https://www.saputodairyaustralia.com.au/en/our-products/consumer-brands.
[43]   As reflected in some publications, see for instance, Violet Atkinson, Viviane Azard, Julien Canlorbe and William van Caenegem (2018) 'A comparative study of fashion and IP: Trade marks in Europe and Australia' 13(3) Journal of Intellectual Property & Law Practice 194–211; William van Caenegem, Violet Atkinson, Jacopo Ciani and Gustavo Ghidini (2019) 'A Comparative Study of Fashion and IP: Non-traditional Trademarks in Italy and Australia' 50(9) IIC – International Review of Intellectual Property and Competition Law 1101–1130.
[44]   See Kal Raustialia and Christopher Sprigman (2006) 'The Piracy Paradox: Innovation and Intellectual Property in Fashion Design' 92 Virginia Law Review 1687–1777, 1691; and (2021) 'Faster Fashion: The piracy paradox and its perils' 39(2) Cardozo Arts and Entertainment Law Review 535, available at https://cardozoaelj.com/wp-content/uploads/2021/11/1.-Raustiala-Sprigman-ARTICLE.pdf.

we were also aware through our comparative work in this sphere, that in Europe the opposite view holds sway – that IP protection is very important to value creation in original fashion design. This stretches from copyright to designs to trade marks law, but we were particularly interested in copyright. Some of our research with French and Italian colleagues tended to indicate that the standard of originality, which is critical to the vesting of copyright in fashion, was approached quite differently in those jurisdictions, and perhaps in a manner that was more favourable toward authors of such designs. We learned that French courts regularly focus their inquiry on what exactly the creative process of a design author consisted of in a particular case. By contrast in Australian law, that issue was approached (in our tentative view) in a more abstract manner and with a certain tendency to oppose the vesting of copyright in practical and mass-produced items such as fashionable clothing[45].

We therefore concluded that when considering optimal IP protection in fashion (an issue that was also 'live' in the context of reforms to designs law in Australia)[46], it would be inform-ative to know how the creative processes of fashion designers actually operated. What were their sources of inspiration, how did they work practically (drawing, mood boards, pinning, photography etc), and how constrained did they perceive their own imagination, freedom to create and originality to be? We approached these questions from the standpoint of examining certain tropes or preconceptions about fashion design as a creative pursuit – were they accurate or at odds with the creative practice and self-perception of designers[47]?

We obtained some funding from the Australian Fashion Council to conduct interviews with fashion designers, which we undertook in Sydney, Melbourne and the Gold Coast[48]. Here we did encounter serious practical issues, because fashion designers are extremely busy people and it was difficult to tee up interview times. Eventually we succeeded with a small sample of 13 designers – in other words, this was a pilot project, and we were alert to the critical question of scale: how many interviews are required to discern themes with sufficient consistency, to warrant broad conclusions and recommended translation into policy prescriptions? Another difficulty was segregating what we were ultimately interested in (what position IP law should take concerning imitation) from what interviewees often wanted to talk about, and despite our alerts, often initially thought we were researching: the apparent prevalence of counterfeiting and piracy in the fashion industry. As with the raw drinking milk issue mentioned above, we had to explain clearly what our question was, and then also how copyright works in its basic principles, and in particular the test of 'originality'. Interviewees were overwhelmingly quick to understand the parameters of our research, but at times we had to lead them back to the

---

[45]   See Violet Atkinson and William van Caenegem (2019) 'The fashion sector: copyright, designs or unfair competition?' 14(3) Journal of Intellectual Property Law & Practice 214–222; and William van Caenegem and Violet Atkinson (2015) 'Creativity in fashion: the complex effects of IP' 28(6) Australian Intellectual Property Law Bulletin 150–155.

[46]   See IPAustralia (2021) 'New changes to the Designs Act make it easier for designers to protect their IP', available at https://www.ipaustralia.gov.au/about-us/news-and-community/news/new-changes -designs-act-make-it-easier-designers-protect-their-ip.

[47]   Our findings were published in the form of an article: William van Caenegem and Violet Atkinson (2021) 'Observing creativity in fashion: implications for copyright' 16(12) Journal of Intellectual Property & Law Practice 1398–1414.

[48]   For information about the Australian Fashion Council see https://australianfashion.org/?gclid= EAIaIQobChMIoLz_xcPA-AIVrJpmAh2LpQMCEAAYASAAEgKzk_D_BwE.

core issue of their own practice, and away from their concerns and occasional outrage about 'rip-offs'.

Given our relatively small interview sample, the critical question of what inferences were justified was in part answered by skewing our reporting more towards simply relaying to readers what we learned about creative practice. We found (and that was interesting in and of itself) that the individual practices of our interviewees were very varied indeed. Their sources of inspiration were different, their practices were different, their training was different, their self-perception varied, their backgrounds and the nature of their businesses was inconsistent. However, they were keen to share the details of their creative processes in operation, which we were able to reflect in our report and subsequent article. We were conscious of the fact that the fashion industry is highly reliant on promotion and advertising, and that projecting an image of creativity and originality is significant. We were therefore on the lookout for accounts that were perhaps too self-serving and inclined to promote the idea that the fashion design industry is highly creative and individual, as opposed to cyclical, highly predetermined by function and trend, limited in its options etc. Our judgement was that the accounts we were given were overwhelmingly frank and not contrived. Interviewees were interested and sometimes somewhat perplexed about their own creativity and imagination, the source of their ideas, about the endless choices they perceived to be still available for fashion despite its long history and technical/functional constraints. We put both sides of the argument concerning more or less protection into our report and subsequent article, to demonstrate that we are fully conscious of the fact that there are reasonably persuasive arguments going both ways. At the very least, the information we provided about what creativity means for fashion designers can help to inform the debate about copyright in that industry.

On a final note, in this fashion context we had a lot of difficulty obtaining a small amount of funding to defray travel costs for interviewing. The fashion design industry in Australia seemed to have difficulty developing policy positions relating to IP protection, although that has now improved, the industry taking an active role in relation to designs reform[49]. Whereas there is little controversy about fighting counterfeiting, there is much more ambivalence about combatting (or not) imitation and certain forms of derivation. There is after all a 'top end' of the design spectrum, which emphasises originality, non-trend dependency and IP protection, and another which emphasises the need for trendiness, the freedom to imitate, and the advantages of providing consumers with cheap imitations of more high-end style. Both have a point, and since our report was more aimed at the technical copyright question of originality, we focused our interviews on fashion houses (some very small and some quite substantial) that invest in original design rather than mass-market derivations[50]. For us the project shows the importance of 'knowing your limitations' when devising an empirical research strategy, and not overclaiming on the basis of the empirical data actually acquired. It is critical to address the limitations inherent in a particular study explicitly, such as the selection and nature of the sample interviewed, and alert the reader to the inherent limitations of any conclusions drawn.

---

[49]   See Justin Cudmore (2021) 'New law passed to give Australian designers greater legal protection', AFC, available at https://ausfashioncouncil.com/new-law-passed-to-give-australian-designers-greater -legal-protection/.

[50]   For the most part, our interviewees had deliberate strategies in place to combat trend-dependency; see further above n 47.

Despite these reservations, publishing the rich information obtained in interviews is in any case worthwhile and promotes informed debate, as already stressed above.

7.   CONCLUSIONS

On a personal level my empirical research, which consisted exclusively of interviews, has been very enriching for me as a researcher. It has taken me away from my desk and expanded my knowledge in relation to particular industries. I understand the operation of certain markets better and have developed a deeper understanding of policy issues that they face. I have obtained information that has informed my ideas and policy thinking, and understand better the distinction between what the law says and what actors perceive it to say. Most importantly, I have gained access to information and knowledge that was otherwise simply not available.

Was the empirical research important? I think it did usefully inform policy analysis, and in relation to issues that I do consider significant, not only in and of themselves, but because of their broader implications. For instance the interviews conducted in relation to GIs richly informed us interviewers about the real issues that agricultural producers face: their time-poverty; their sense of powerlessness in the face of competitive practices that breach complex laws (as for instance passing off or competition law); the risks and power relationships they have to deal with; and the reality of their personal experience of the impact of the economy and business on community life and health. Conducting interviews has layered my understanding because of the way it personalised and made more immediate the impact of policies and legal issues that we were considering. For instance, the position of dairy farmers *vis à vis* processors and the prices they can command in a competitive environment has a real impact on family life, and particularly continuity and trans-generational prospects in the industry. My sense is that much was revealed by way of empirical research that would otherwise have remained in the shadows, and that what was revealed was relevant and helpful to know. The information gleaned certainly highlighted important issues or failings of regulatory policy that would otherwise have remained in the dark, and suggested further research directions and more effective prioritisation of research time and investment.

All the empirical research described above was also collaborative, involving a number of other researchers and research assistants. Whatever conclusions were generated were the result of very active and often very rigorous discussion – any conclusion was usually subjected to opposing views and an active process of attempting to find fault, generate opposing interpretations and properly informed discussion. Therefore the resulting conclusions were often more strenuously tested than commonly occurs in traditional legal research, which still, in contrast with other sciences, is an often solitary pursuit.

That is not to say that conclusions resulting from interview data are attended by absolute certainty. Perhaps in the social sciences, conclusions rarely are, but obviously although the system of multiple interviews and identification and analysis of common themes gives rise to reasonably confident conclusions, there is still variety and density to deal with. That then leads to the question of how and at what level of generality to formulate conclusions that are useful – i.e. that are not so equivocal as to be of little use for policymakers or decisionmakers. We had most difficulty in that regard where the interview sample was the smallest, in regard to the fashion industry, as described above. However, numbers can't always be high, as for instance in some industries there are few participants – that should not prevent qualitative research in that particular sphere.

Another issue is that empirical research usually requires some external funding. That means applications with all that entails. Often the question is whether the game is worth the candle. In Australian terms the main source of funding for empirical research is the Australian Research Council (ARC), and then in particular Discovery grants[51]. There is no doubt that this system has many drawbacks. It requires enormous application documents, and the period of assessment and ARC decision-making is very long. There is little flexibility in terms of what is asked for, and there are odd restrictions on budget items. Strangely enough, there is little effective follow-up in terms of whether the goals and commitments of grantees have been met by the actual work produced. There is no system of reporting back on this to the ARC, with a review and a feedback loop or any type of repercussion for substandard performance. I was fortunate to have the alternative option of obtaining funding from the RIRDC/Agrifutures, which has a far more manageable two-step application system and also requires the actual provision of reports to the funding body, with feedback and analysis from the experts it retains. However, the touchpoint between IP research and that particular organisation, concerned as it is with agriculture, is relatively small.

On the point of legitimacy of conclusions derived from relatively small samples of interviewees, as explained above, there are well-accepted techniques that allow the triaging of persuasive conclusions from doubtful inferences. Further, explicitness in the reporting on interviews and the information gained allows readers to draw their own conclusions about the validity of the associated recommendations. This remains a useful alternative or addition to surveys, which can be difficult to adapt to the needs of certain social science research questions, to structure properly and to use to obtain information about questions that require preliminary explanation and engagement[52]. The rich, targeted, multi-dimensional data gained from interviewing and made explicit in reports commonly provides a very useful informational resource for all.

---

[51]   See https:// www .arc .gov .au/ grants/ discovery -program/ discovery -projects #: ~: text = Grants %20from%20the%20ARC%20are,up%20to%20five%20consecutive%20years.
[52]   They are often plagued by low response rates leaving a difficult question as to what conclusions can still be safely drawn; see Richard C. Stedman, Nancy A. Connelly, Thomas A. Heberlein, Daniel J. Decker and Shorna B. Allred (2019) 'The End of the (Research) World as We Know It? Understanding and Coping with Declining Response Rates to Mail Surveys' 32(10) Society & Natural Resources 1139–1154.

PART V

DESIGNS

16. A qualitative method for investigating design

Mark P. McKenna and Jessica Silbey

Intellectual property scholarship has recently taken notice of the increasing legal and economic importance of design. Once a relatively minor focus, especially as compared to the other objects of intellectual property and technology law, design is now on many scholars' radar, particularly following the multi-billion dollar global dispute between Apple and Samsung.[1] But despite design's growing legal and economic significance, relatively little is known (by legal scholars and policymakers) about designers or the design process.

That lacuna is particularly striking in light of the empirical turn in modern intellectual property scholarship. Legal scholars have studied a number of creative communities in recent years in order to understand the economic and structural factors that shape the nature and direction of those communities' creative practices and the role of intellectual property and other legal regulation in shaping output. But those studies ignored designers and focused on communities and practices relating to the types of innovation or creative output that we typically associate with either utility patents or with copyright. This chapter describes our study of designers, which we recently carried out to fill that scholarly void. We particularly focus here on our qualitative interview methodology, which allowed us to shed light on some of the persistent puzzles in design law.

One obvious challenge to a study of "designers" is the difficulty of determining how that category should be defined. That challenge presented our first line of inquiry. The design literature generally identifies certain design disciplines (traditionally focusing on industrial design and graphic design, and later user-interface/user-experience design (UI/UX)), and a few design fields that are defined by industry (automobile design and fashion design, primarily). But our sense from our initial research, which our interviews have confirmed, was that those categories are no longer exhaustive and are evolving. As we describe more below in our methods section, identifying the relevant categories of designers and design work is essential for stratifying our interview data set and selecting interviewees. Only by doing that could we produce a thick description of the field on which to base hypotheses about, for example, the communities' motivations, values, and structural mechanisms as they relate (or do not relate) to design law.

Relatedly, our initial research suggested that "design" work was taking place in increasingly diverse contexts, and as a result, "designers" held a wider range of positions within organizations. We hypothesized that understanding the status of designers within their organizations and the changing nature of their roles within their places of employment would help to further identify and explain the various roles of design and designers in complex production chains, and thus also the role (or absence) of design law in that structure.

---

[1]   In the United States, that litigation included a trip to the Supreme Court on an issue having to do with the calculation of design patent damages. Samsung Elecs. Co. Ltd. v. Apple Inc., 580 U.S. 53 (2016) (holding that "article of manufacture," as used in a Patent Act provision governing damages for design patent infringement, encompasses both a product sold to a consumer and a component of that product).

Our second line of inquiry focused on the design process itself. Design literature commonly refers to that process in terms of problem solving. We sought to understand from the designers whether the literature reflected their understanding of the process and if so, what "problem solving" means. Because intellectual property law tends to highlight certain types of problems (particularly "technical" or "utilitarian" ones), and to associate those kinds of problems uniquely with utility patent law, we wanted to understand how designers conceptualized "problems" and what it means to them to solve those problems. We also hypothesized that designers' self-conception as "problem solvers" might help define their professional identities, the roles they perform in companies and for clients, and the institutional or legal help or hurdles they faced while pursuing their work.

Further to the question of professional identity, we wondered how, if at all, designers' understanding of the problems to be solved would map onto the relevant legal categories, or to the conceptions of other actors whose professional and institutional contexts are influenced by intellectual property regulation (e.g., entertainment industries, pharmaceutical companies, the computer industry). Intellectual property's typical protagonists are "writers," "musicians," "sculptors," "scientists," or "engineers." But those identities are rapidly changing, and many "sculptors" today call themselves "designers," many "writers" describe their work as "information architecture," and visual artists are "graphic designers." New forms of creativity and innovation are constantly emerging in the digital age. We were therefore interested in how old and new professional identities within the design fields were interacting with more typical understandings of intellectual property laws as a plausible way to understand the origins of (and possible solutions for) the problems of overlapping IP rights.

Our third line of inquiry followed from the second. Design literature commonly identified the integration of form and function as a primary goal of design. We aimed to learn from designers and their organizations what "integration" means in this sense. This is a particularly important line of inquiry because intellectual property doctrine attempts in various ways to *separate* form from function, precisely to allocate different aspects of design to different intellectual property regimes. And as any student of these doctrines is well aware, they are among the most difficult in all of intellectual property law. We sought to understand the relationship between "integration" and the goals and outputs of design practice as partially coincident with, or possibly resistant to, intellectual property law rules. We thought better understanding what "integration of form and function" means to designers might illuminate some of these trenchant doctrinal puzzles that IP lawyers face.

Finally, we hoped to learn what designers and the organizations they work for regard as successful (or even "excellent") design. At the doctrinal and institutional level, intellectual property law claims to abjure qualitative standards beyond the low metrics required for protection.[2] But in studying design literature, we understood that design practice (like many professional fields) has its own standards driven by field leaders, educational institutions, and market trends. We sought to understand from designers what those standards are and how they are measured and evolve. To our mind, this line of inquiry seemed essential to understanding how to evaluate the success of design regimes themselves, which purportedly exist to promote the progress of design. Relatedly, we sought to better understand how the metrics for evaluating good design compare to those used to evaluate more conventional subject matter of utility

---

[2]   Originality and fixation for copyright; novelty, non-obviousness, and utility for patent law; distinctiveness for trademark; and non-obviousness, novelty, and ornamentality for design patents.

patent and copyright. We thought doing so would tell us something about the plausibly unique (or overlapping) role design patent law might play in our intellectual property regimes.

1.   OUR METHOD

1.1   Why Qualitative Research

Our qualitative empirical study of "design" is based on a semi-structured interview method. Although our four lines of inquiry are informed by legal and design literature, court cases, and statutory law, our original contribution derives from the empirical data we collected and analyzed using a non-representative sampling of interview subjects stratified among variables relevant to the questions under investigation, which we describe in more detail below.[3] This qualitative empirical analysis complements any legal doctrinal or policy analyses. Our aim was to broadly investigate the legal and popular meaning of "design" outside "intellectual property law," for example, other than through court decisions and statutes. This method presumes that relevant creative communities engaging in "design" can help situate and maybe also give insight into the legal categories and doctrinal rules by grounding an explanation of "design practice" in their lived experience.

Generally, lawyers, legislators, and legal scholars are more familiar with textual and doctrinal analyses and close readings of cases and statutes. Qualitative empirical research is less familiar as a method of analysis and way of producing knowledge about law because it remains rare in legal studies. And collecting the data is time-consuming and costly. Nonetheless, qualitative research is vital for understanding the significance and variation of lived experience that law affects. It complements and enriches (and can be especially useful when combined with) quantitative research, which remains the dominant empirical research method in legal scholarship today. Qualitative methods:

> develop insights about the underlying forms and dynamics of the phenomenon under study. Unlike quantitative research in which researchers seek to generate precise estimates based on a sample that can be generalized with estimated degrees of error to a larger population, qualitative researchers seek "analytic generalizations" that attach meaning, rather than measurement, to the phenomena observed.[4]

In other words, qualitative research is useful to identify and explain situated knowledge (i.e., actors' experiences and interpretations) about a particular object, practice, or field. For example, "what is design work for which companies are hired?" and "what is design excellence that companies seek to achieve?" Qualitative studies identify variations in these interpretations, events, and behaviors through data that is "densely textured, locally grounded, meaningful to the subjects themselves."[5] A hallmark of qualitative research is the development

---

[3]   *See* Jan E. Trost, "Statistically Nonrepresentative Stratified Sampling: A Sampling Technique for Qualitative Studies," *Qualitative Sociology* 9 (1986): 54–57.

[4]   Pamela Stone, *Opting Out: Why Women Really Quit Careers and Head Home* (Berkeley, California: University of California Press, 2007), 243, 248.

[5]   Jack Katz, "Ethnography's Warrants," *Sociological Methods and Research* 25 (1997): 391–423, 392.

of categories and their explanations from within the narrative structures that interviewees provide and that can be further analyzed in other studies, both qualitative and quantitative.

Another reason to use a qualitative research method is that narratives and popular concepts are explanatory and justificatory tools in the constitution of law and culture. Qualitative field research collects actors' accounts of their lived experiences, which in this study reveals how designers develop and make sense of their professional identity and the role of "design" work in the larger context of creative and innovative business ecosystems. A systematic analysis of the data offers explanations of what counts as "design," what is a "problem" to be solved, what is "excellent design" and how that definition and standard has evolved over time. If we are interested in understanding or more precisely defining design work as it relates to the legal regulation of designed objects and the structure of firms that engage in design, these interviews provide direct and varied evidence from the individuals whose businesses and professional practice are implicated by the law of design. Understanding the diversity in the field and the themes that might connect or explain the variations within the field is a critical first step to evidence-based lawmaking and law reform.

1.2   The Qualitative Research Method for Investigating Design

Qualitative research starts with hypotheses based on lines of inquiry, which we outlined above in section 1.1. Those hypotheses are grounded in the literature and a general understanding of the field. They are also necessary to structure the initial stratification of interviews and selection of categories of questions.

The qualitative researcher aims to identify a comprehensive set of relevant variations in the studied experience or practice that relate to the practice's functions or roles in the lives of those under study. They do so in order to test the hypotheses and generate alternative ones.[6] To get there, the researcher identifies the population to be studied and the key dimensions that are likely to generate distinctions in the experience under analysis. This "stratifies" the population into relevant sub-groups within those dimensions. Talking with people across many sub-groups increases the chances of identifying relevant variations and achieving comprehensiveness in the explanation of the phenomena. Having a complete set of variations may be impossible, but the goal is to discern as full a set as possible. The researcher has done so when they reach "saturation" – the point when the most recent interviewees are providing accounts that align with previous accounts.[7]

Qualitative work will not lead to a statistical measure of correlations among variables or a mathematical test of causal inference. But a core benefit of qualitative interview-based research, and the key reason qualitative methods are superior for the questions we explore in this study, is the ability to generate diverse, multifaceted variables relevant to study and nuanced explanations of those variables that aggregate and interact to form the basis of complex social phenomena.

For the design case study, we interviewed twenty-four designers between 2018 and 2020. We began our interviews with designers who had a long history in the field and could tell us

---

[6]   Mario Luis Small, "How Many Cases Do I Need?," *Ethnography* 10 (2009): 5–38. In contrast to quantitative methods, interview research does not use a random sample nor does it provide a measure of the frequency that variations appear.
[7]   *See* Small, *supra* note 6, at 25–28 (explaining the concept of saturation).

about their experience of the changing nature of the design profession and design work. This helped us identify and clarify as foundational particular design disciplines (industrial design and graphic design, for example) and settings in which designers worked (legacy design firms or "consultancies," such as IDEO and FROG, and early in-house design teams, such as in the automobile industry). Those initial interviews led to others (in the "snowball" sampling method) and the categories began to grow and evolve.

We sought to interview designers with experience in a range of different industries and who designed for different markets. We ultimately interviewed designers with experience in at least eight different contexts: automotive, household goods, user-interface, fashion, graphic design, medical and technological devices, service-based design, and landscape design. We also interviewed designers who were working in different organizational settings. Some were in-house at firms that have major design components (such as OXO, Facebook, and Whirlpool); others were solo designers with their own brands and products. We also interviewed designers who work (or have worked) in design consultancies. As is common, many people had diverse experiences in different work settings – moving from consultancies to in-house, and vice-versa – and so they could compare these settings. Designers with decades of experience could also describe changes in design practice over time. We sought to interview both young, emerging professionals as well as experienced designers.

As it turned out, many designers work across the disciplinary categories or have developed expertise in more than one area. Some started in graphic design, for example, but are now focusing on UI/UX and "motion design." Others started in industrial design but primarily work on branding strategies and service-based design. We learned that many designers today consider interdisciplinarity and boundary blurring essential to excellence in design and thus, despite expertise in a particular sub-field (in medical devices, for example, or user-interface design), many reject disciplinary categories, although not all do. Automotive designers tended to identify most strongly with their category, though even some auto designers had applied their skills in other industries. For example, one of the automotive designers we interviewed ultimately left that industry and worked designing appliances. Identifying variation like this – starting with common themes and then hypothesizing the existence of exceptions to the themes – is part of the rich generativity of qualitative research.

By about the fifteenth interview, after speaking with designers from all the categories at various stages of their career, we were hitting the saturation point. The same themes were arising in each interview; we were hearing very similar accounts of disciplinary boundary crossing and the centering of design work in more and more diverse businesses. Designers were using the same words to describe the nature and practice of design work, and the designers started even referring to each other and to the firms or businesses we had already visited. For legal scholars, it resembled to us the point at which the case law research starts becoming self-referential. There were exceptions, of course. We had a sense that automotive designers would stand out, and they did, because they were some of the first high-status designers in the design field. But even they provided accounts of design practice generally that resembled in meaningful ways the professionals at Whirlpool and IDEO, for example.

We kept interviewing, however, well past this saturation point. We stopped at twenty-four, although we would happily do more (and may still!). Based on the qualitative methods research, however, we believe we have enough cases to defend the validity of the variables we assert are relevant to understanding what "design" means to designers and how that explanation implicates the questions with which we are concerned to better understand and help inform the evolution of intellectual property law.[8]

2.   THE INTERVIEW PROCESS AND DATA ANALYSIS

Most interviews lasted between one and two hours. Each relied on an approved Institutional Research Board (IRB) protocol for the semi-structured interview, which allowed us to standardize across all the interviews. But the protocol also allowed deviation and follow-up when necessary to clarify potential contradictions or dig deeper into apparent idiosyncrasies or parallels. Interviewees could elect to be on or off the record. We use pseudonyms when quoting off-record interviews, and the biographical details for confidential interviews are more generalized to protect anonymity. All of the interviews were recorded and transcribed by a professional transcriber. We conducted most of the interviews in person until the COVID pandemic lockdown in March 2020, when we finished the last few interviews over Zoom.

We are happy to share our interview protocol with readers who seek more detail than is provided below. But, in general, we asked questions centering on the four lines of inquiry described above. Our interview outline was organized by themes, with both open-ended and specific, fact-based questions. It is important when doing interview-based qualitative work to ask both open-ended and specific questions to generate the variability that qualitative research seeks. So, for example, we asked questions such as "how did you become a designer" and "what kind of educational or work background is typical for a designer today?" We asked about how designers are situated within their firms, how they understand the role of design within their organization, with whom they interact collaboratively and at what stage of the organization's productivity.

We also asked questions about the sorts of projects and problems designers understand themselves to be addressing. We asked about client relations, both actual and ideal. And, crucially, we asked for specific examples that would ground the more general and abstract discussions, which often added nuance and complication to their statements about design work. We probed success stories and some more difficult or less successful relationships (asking why they were difficult or unsuccessful). We asked especially about each interviewee's specific design process: what are their steps, are the steps the same for any client or project, how do they build teams and why, and how do they know when they are done?

We heard a lot about background field research, which was often observational (sitting in restaurants or watching people use kitchen utensils), and about looking for inspiration in adjacent or far-flung spaces. We followed up with questions about copying and influence, seeking to understand what kind of borrowing and iteration was expected and whether novelty or originality was a relevant standard. We asked questions about how designers add value to the overall project and what skills are particular to designers that complement the other professionals on the team, always asking for examples as we probed the answers. We were particularly interested here in the ways the designers characterized the value they added to the process, as distinct from the value added by other skilled professionals (e.g., management consultants, lawyers, finance or business developers).

---

[8]   *See* Small, *supra* note 6, at 25–28 (explaining the concept of saturation).

We were also very interested in the designers' perceptions of the relative roles of aesthetics and functional utility in their design work, and so whenever those concepts came up, we would ask for clarification and examples. We also asked about what kinds of problems were *not* design problems – for example, which problems would be sent to engineering, or to business.

We asked many questions about change over time, asking the designers to reflect on past practices and educational models and how those are the same or have changed. We sought explanations for the centrality of design to so many fields today, and of the goals of designers both for clients specifically and for themselves as professionals. We asked each of our interviewees what counts as "design" and how they evaluate the quality of design – and in particular, how they identify "excellent design." As the design field is evolving, are the metrics for excellence also changing? If so, how? Were those metrics for excellence part of how designers discuss their work? Where do these metrics come from, if they exist? Near the end, we always asked if there were impediments to doing excellent work and what, if anything, they would change about the design profession. We also always asked them to describe the cutting edge of design work today: where is design innovation and where is it headed?

As we conducted interviews and read transcripts, and then re-read and analyzed the transcripts, we revised our understandings and interpretations of the phenomena under study. Interview analysis follows several steps. First, after each interview, we wrote a two- to three-page memo summarizing the interview. The memo included any notes we made during the interview, a description of notable stories or quotations from the interviewee, and a list of overarching themes from the interview. Memos are often co-drafted and shared to produce a common framework of the ongoing analysis. As often as possible, we endeavored to write these memos together at the end of an interview day.

Second, we both read the interview transcripts closely. We studied the interviews at the level of language (word choice, narrative structure, and content) and at the level of conceptual themes, which are drawn from reading across the transcripts and from the literature in the relevant fields (photography or design practice, for example). We then generated a list of code words developed deductively from preliminary findings and inductively from the emergent language, repetitions, narrative structure, and conceptual themes contained in the interviews.

Third, we read the transcripts again to code them, first by hand and then using a system developed as a team using Excel. (At this point our team included a research assistant who was also a law student with both qualitative and quantitative coding skills from her undergraduate studies. Brittany Von Rueden was an essential member of our coding team with whom we discussed the codes, their application, and their analysis using the Excel software. She developed the Excel coding tables that allowed us to analyze the transcripts as an entire data set.) Coding allowed us to search and sort the data by code or any other category we establish. Coding together and interpreting the interviews as a research group enhances intercoder reliability, which is critical to the descriptive and interpretive validity of qualitative empirical analysis.[9] Where we coded differently because of differences in interpretation, we discussed and resolved the differences. By its very nature, working with qualitative data is an interpretive process. Nonetheless, strong consensus can be achieved by regularly sharing coding on a common text and thus collectively developing common parameters for interpretation. The

---

[9]   For a discussion of intercoder reliability, see Joseph A. Maxwell, "Understanding and Validity in Qualitative Research," *Harvard Educational Review* 62 (1992): 279–300, 287–291.

coding software allow for combining, segregating, and sorting of all three data sets according to chosen categories.

In the end, a qualitative study must respect (through close reading and interpretation) the language used in interviews as a source of meaning and purpose. The validity of the interview data depends on how much the interview responses reliably describe recognizable practices, whether the descriptions are sufficiently thick to be credible, and whether the theoretical interpretations are sufficiently grounded in these and comparative data.[10] For this reason, quoting the interviews at length is necessary for final publications, so that readers can assess the interpretation of the accounts for themselves.

We did our best to emulate the methods of well-regarded and robust qualitative interview studies in order to assure optimal validity. Quality of interviewing matters a lot. We conducted all the design interviews as a team to facilitate careful listening and questioning in a conversational style building from a trustworthy context.

> The more discursive, conversational style of the interview affords opportunities to prompt respondents to explain seeming oversights and inconsistencies, which serve as consistency or reliability checks of sorts. These same in-depth techniques are also well suited for getting underneath the superficial, socially desirable, or conventional responses people give when accounting for their behavior because the depth of information generated allows the researcher to detect deeper levels of meaning that the respondent herself may not be aware of, but which reveal underlying motivations that conventional or initial accounts belie.[11]

Despite our confidence that the interviews were robust and probing, our interpretations are necessarily suggestive rather than exhaustive. Qualitative work by its nature generates hypotheses about social phenomena. We have written one article so far with preliminary interpretations of the data.[12] Based on feedback we have received on that article, we are working on additional papers that will look more deeply into some of the other variables within the data that we think offer insight into the complex and evolving phenomenon of design's ascendancy in the digital age. What follows is a loosely organized list of some of those variations already described in our publication, and some that we have not yet analyzed in depth but plan to explore in future articles.

3.   EMPIRICAL FINDINGS

The below-listed items are illustrative and not exhaustive. We aim here only to provide examples of the textured data and sample analyses to demonstrate early output of the above-described methodology.

---

[10]   Matthew Miles and A. Michael Huberman, *Qualitative Data Analysis* (Thousand Oaks, California: Sage Press, 1994), 245–285.
[11]   Pamela Stone, *supra* note 4, at 254.
[12]   "Investigating Design," *University of Pittsburgh Law Review* 84 (forthcoming 2023).

3.1   Professional Identity: Who Is a Designer?

In our interviews, we asked questions about design education, career trajectories (planned and unplanned), and the distinction between designers and other skilled professionals. Older designers described design school as competitive and grueling, with focus on renderings (form giving), where the premium outcomes were jobs in automotive or industrial design. Some older designers also started out in graphic design and developed skills in marketing. The educational trend over the decades, however, was to move away from these disciplinary categories and to focus instead in both design education and skill-building on research methods, interdisciplinarity, and working in teams. Being a "designer" has more to do with *how* you work than what you make. That way of thinking affects the shape of firms, the place of designers in firms, and the nature of clients. What follows are two examples from the data.

Here is one explanation of this phenomenon from an IDEO executive who preferred to stay anonymous:

> There's a deliberate sort of shifting of realizing that as we can incorporate different types of people and different disciplines, we can tackle different types of problems, so originally like we're hired to like design the thing, you know, the product, and we team up to be able to do that, and that's a subset of like, you can imagine, engineer, designer, electrical engineer, a software engineer, but as we start to realize that we can actually have a bigger impact if we can also think about, you know, the brand, we can also think about the packaging, we can also think about the website and the communications and the app and all the other things that surround the experience, then we can design a more holistic experience and therefore have a broader impact, right? So that's how it's, in my sort of experience, that's how we went from sort of designing things to designing experiences, right? Holistic experiences. Because, and then, you know, the next part of it was then, oh, and are the organizations that we're working with capable of sustaining, maybe going into a new, completely new business, or a new way of working? Like our work maybe creates, the outcome of our work could be a new product or service, but it could also be sort of launching a completely new business that the organization is not necessarily capable of doing as they exist today.

A different design leader provides another variation on how design education has morphed to become more interdisciplinary or "blurry" and has produced new specializations within businesses. Here, Michael Rock is responding to our question "where do you think the design field is going, if you had to predict?"

> I think this blurriness is the condition that we're gonna live in now, and what I predict is that there won't be a kind of central activity. And so an example I would use is that in some ways if I went to business school in 1950, I'd do very little math when I was there. I would be doing management theory, and HR theory, and a whole bunch of things like that. Sometime starting in the '70s, business school co-opted math, and it became a kind of major part of their program, right? I find the same thing's happening with design now.
>
>   I think design's being folded into the language of business, and I think that they're probably more quick to capitalize on it to a certain extent. ... So I think that in some ways I see it just being absorbed into these, that it becomes software, or a kind of part of the language of these different activities somewhat, and therefore the individual components of graphic design will start to exist as kind of proficiencies in themselves. So, and we already see it happening, like so there's a whole very robust profession of font designers, for instance, who are doing digital font design for all different kinds of things, right? And that's become a subset of graphic design, which is very specialized, and has its own set of softwares as tools, own set of contractual relationships, own set of kinds of clients, challenges they're dealing with, something like that, and that's now become very specialized. I think each one of these things will start to have its own, you know, organization somehow. ... [And] I think it's gonna

make [design] difficult to teach ..., because you have to say what's the value of a general education in design anymore? Like do you, is getting a graphic design degree meaningful at this point? Or would you just go immediately into one of the other things, and I think you see that right now, where people are going into UX design, or something like that, you know, it's really a standalone profession now, you know, and it has its own kind of curriculum and pedagogy and way of thinking about it, and it's starting to have its own history.

The increasingly common definition of design and designers in methodological terms generates an optimism and open-endedness to the professional identity, so much that some designers talk about "design futures" or "speculative design" as a field (where designers are imagining things and processes of the future in a utopian kind of way). And other designers describe designers, and especially the movement toward "human-centered" design, as an essential antidote to late-stage capitalism and environmental destruction.

Here is Laura Forlano, who describes an evolution of design practice this way:

[When] I first arrived in 2011, the majority of the projects were communication design of some sort. So they would take complex problems, like a health care system, or whatever, and then they would go do the user research, and then they would visualize and map and represent those things in a way that helped make sense of it, right? So that was very common. Now in more recent [years] we've had a lot more projects that are physical prototypes, partially because ... I've been trying to get people to do these more speculative projects, and speculative design, which is a different field of design that overlaps much more with art ... there's an overlap between the design and the futuresism space. So then there are others that are arguing for like futures and design. ... speculative design is intended to be a critical practice. So it's a critique of the world. And it's posing different kinds of questions towards alternative possible futures.

More often, the designers were not describing "speculative future" practice in the way Laura does, but instead were explicitly describing ethical design practices and ways in which the work one does as a designer and for a client actually improves human welfare in light of challenging materialities of everyday life, such as unsustainable waste production, poverty, and health outcomes. Here is Jay Newman of Jump Associates describing that process as pursuing the "big why" for his company and his client's company.

Now we happen to like, as a conscious capitalist company, right? like, we happen to love the fact that like growth has two meanings in our world, there's deep economic growth that is interconnected to like the growth that comes at the individual level, and certainly like a billion dollars of value might mean like big returns, but it also might mean a billion dollars of impact on a local community, right? Or, you know, a billion people lifted out of poverty. So these things are all interconnected into each other, I think. That's the place we start our..., we start with that bigger why for the organization, like who are you and why do you exist? And we often hope to bring our clients along the same types of questions.

Importantly, designers are not management consultants or finance executives. Neither are they marketing professionals, although designers commonly work with all of those people. Designers have common backgrounds in design research and industrial design, and to some extent in traditional and modern aesthetic practices. But the precedent for their contemporary work is broader, and constraints on their work less than might be expected. This leads to very wide impact for clients.

3.2   The Evolution of Design Work

The designers in our study described an earlier time in which designers primarily conceived of themselves as form-givers, skilled artists or sculptors who would create models of a new car, washing machine, or font type. Today, the designers describe their work much more holistically. As is evident from the above quotes, modern designers consider themselves to be designing "experiences." And, importantly, human-centered design work begins not with the object but with the lives of the real people who will be using the object or the service. This means that designers learn to act like anthropologists and sociologists, studying people and situations as much as they study form and utility. They don't know what they are going to produce because their research into the situation their client has asked them to study may turn up creative solutions or responses that are surprising. This kind of human-centered research is grounded in sociality and emotion as well as feasibility.

   Michael Kahwaji, at Whirlpool, talks about the move from being a "form-giver" to understanding human needs.

> People think industrial designers are form-givers, and that's all we do. 'Oh, here, can you make this look pretty?' No, we believe that we're connected directly to the consumer. We understand their needs, their emotions, so it's psychology, it's marketing, it's engineering. So the engineering part of industrial design is not necessarily solving the exact functional mechanics of it, although some of our designers are tilted towards that, and others are tilted more towards the sensory experience they want. So I don't know how I'm going to make this shelf work, but the action that this shelf needs to do is slide back, move up, and then slide back again, because that's what my consumer needs.

Ann-Marie Conrado, who teaches and practices design, describes this human-centered approach in terms of her work for the U.S. dairy industry. Seeking to promote the consumption of milk in particular, Ann-Marie explains that her job was to first understand the culture of milk consumption.

> I went in, we spent time with people, you know. And so the first part of the design process now is driven by ethnography. Right? … it's go where people are, go where people are doing the things, observe them, engage them in the process of eating and drinking or preparing food. We went to five different metropolitan areas that had close relationships with the outer suburbs, so we could go to rural and metropolitan within a short drive. We went to each of those places, we talked to people in every one of those places. We had a sit-down interview like this followed by a second visit with some sort of engagement. … with one person, we watched him like smoke meat for four hours, because that was his passion. Another person, I got up and I was there at 6 am so she could make five different lunches for all her kids, and make all these mini meals for the whole day. Another person, I went with her to our coop, because that's her favorite place in the world. I wanted to see the activities around food and drink that excited them, you know, that they were passionate about.

Understanding the consumer or the culture and activities surrounding the human phenomenon sought to be "designed" is critical to the success of the outcome. So when Lee Moreau, a designer then at Continuum, describes the success of the Swiffer, a newly designed object, he characterizes the success in terms of the experience it produced through its designed form.

> We are creating new experiences. The Swiffer is … what the Swiffer does, which is magical, is it creates a new behavior, and the new behavior is, instead of every six weeks, I mean everybody says they clean their kitchen floor once a week, they fucking don't. They fucking don't. They do it once every six weeks if they have to, if it's that bad, and if they have company coming. What it does is it

changes the behavior. It enables a behavior, which is I'm just gonna, once or twice a week, tidy up a bit, it actually cleans the stuff off your floor, because it has the technology in those towelettes, ... so it's very effective, and you feel a sense of accomplishment. You take that dirty thing off, and you're, "Ewww," and you put it in the trash, and you know it works. It shows you that. So that behavior change is really what the Swiffer enables. It's just that to get that feeling you have to buy a Swiffer, and you have to do it, but the product is just enabling this feeling of accomplishment, and what we're enabling is the sense that people who value the cleanliness of their floor because they feel it's a reflection of themselves...

George Aye, one of the most senior and well-known designers we interviewed, describes the evolution in design work "away from the tangible." He describes moving from tangible materials to digital materials, and ultimately to people.

I'd say it [design work] moves away from the tangible. The value of aesthetics is still present, no matter, I haven't found it to be diminished. But the material choice and the execution is very, very different. So instead of executing on the finish of let's say, how smooth or rough the product is, literally, like the surface texture, it's going to be completely different of a question if it's only pixels on a screen, versus whether it's a product you hold in your hand. ... it's just a completely different language, and there was an emerging practice around how did you design screens and interactions alongside how do you design people interacting with other people, which is service design. So you break it down to say what are the materials that I have control of as a designer? It used to be plastic and metal, plastic, metal, wood. Then it became pixels and their movement. And then you end up with people, which I think is the hardest one. Designing people and their behaviors.

One way designers conceptualize this way of thinking about who designers are and what designers do is that they are "problem finders" not "problem solvers." Based on the fluidity and hybridity in their skills and teams, designers spend more time defining and understanding "the problem" as a way of understanding the people and the situation their client has hired them to address. There were many examples of this process throughout the interviews, but here are just two: A brand and design professional at OXO said the company's "true magic ... is when we solve problems people don't realize are problems until we solve them."[13] Alissa Rantanen, a young designer at a medical device company, explains the process of opening up of the "problem" to reveal new opportunities in the context of medical devices in the following way.

Out of research we have opportunities that are not prescriptive, they don't say "You should do this solution." They're much more open-ended, of "The opportunity is better traceability." And then the design staff takes a look at that says, "Ok. How do we improve traceability? Well, we can look at grocery stores and see how they do that. We can look at how other people handle inventory management." We can leverage all this, come up with a bunch of ideas ... bounce ideas off of each other with the client, and then ultimately filter out what doesn't align with the client's capabilities or vision.[14]

Critical to the design "problem finding" process is going outside the narrowly-defined particular field (here medical devices) and locating analogous systems or solutions in unrelated places, such as in grocery stores or factories. This broad search for problems and their solu-

---

[13] Interview with "Kate," Marketing and Design Professional, OXO, in N.Y.C. N.Y. (December 11, 2018).
[14] Interview with Alissa Rantanen, Design Manager, Insight Product Development, in Chi., Ill. (February 5, 2018).

tions expands the scope of design practice and expertise and resists compartmentalization and hierarchy.

3.3   Design Work Today: The What, How, and Who For?

Because designers see themselves and their work in these unique, methodological terms, design has extremely broad application. Indeed, from the designers' perspective, there are virtually no limits in terms of what designers do and who they do it for. We interviewed landscape architects who consider themselves environmental impact designers; we interviewed web designers who consider themselves designers and facilitators of better communities and family relations. We even interviewed designers at a legacy design firm who were hired to redesign the first-year curriculum at Boston College.

Designers may be more ubiquitous today than in decades past, and their clients more diverse. But they are also careful to explain how they are not engineers, or business consultants, or marketing professionals. The design method – the way they work with iterative prototyping and qualitative research, the interdisciplinary teams and hybrid skill-building across aesthetics, social science, engineering or manufacturing, and business strategy – is what makes designers designers. Even those designers who made household objects of beauty (like drinking glasses or lamps) in studios under their own names described their work in this way.

We were intrigued by the desire of most of the designers to describe an ethics or value-centered approach to design work that they say also distinguishes their work from other professionals. (Whether this is true as a matter of fact is another question.) The designers believe they are addressing real human needs, and they seek to have meaningful impact. We probed these answers with some skepticism because, we thought, how do they know they aren't just manufacturing and selling new desires rather than addressing true needs? The responses were illuminating and varied. Some of the answers follow:

A younger designer working in-house developing medical devices explains:

> I really appreciate aesthetics, and look and feel, and beautiful things, and that's part of my passion. But I do not want to do something superficial. Because I don't think this world needs more junk, for lack of a better word. ..., the ideal is some balance ... and something that I know will have a real impact.[15]

A more seasoned designer working at a small consultancy said that for him "the main anchor of solving the problems is we go find the needs that people have, we don't go look for wants that people have."[16]

But others were a bit more skeptical and self-critical. Here is George Aye again, perhaps the most critical within our interview data.

> Designers have a unique ability to address a need, ... or, and maybe in my case, driven by discovering needs. When you present the thing that you think is valuable, ideally being paid for it, it makes people go "Huh, I didn't know I needed that, but now I want it." Now what's been troubling about it for a long time is that ability to identify a need and then visualize this thing that you found to be really

---

[15]   Interview with Alissa Rantanen, Design Manager, Insight Product Development, in Chi., Ill. (February 5, 2018).
[16]   Interview with Mike Smith, Designer, Jump Assocs., in Redwood City, Cal. (February 26, 2020).

compelling was mostly in service of corporations, ... a client who says, "We need to sell more here." Right? ... I'm over it, and I think it's a house of cards, because the people who are describing those needs are perversely incentivized to benefit from the need response, I'm gonna discount the validity of that need. So it tends to be true that people's needs have been met as in like, "I feel bad about myself, and now through this product, I feel slightly better," whether the product is Instagram, or that product is, you know, a new iPhone. I certainly appreciate all the things that I've bought, has met those mostly I'd say needs that were about self-perception, or even just, even something that's more practical, just like, it's more convenient to do it this way. ... I'm not denigrating making beautiful things, there's so much value in that. ... Where it bothers me is when you present design as saving the world, when that is patently untrue, you're actually destroying it in many cases.

When we asked George to describe work he thought was adhering to a more ethical design practice, or at least the kind of design work he preferred to pursue, he described his evolution from "form-giving" to service design in the following way:

> What I found in my experience was that it was like one in ten or one in twenty projects, and until that tenth or twentieth project would come by, I was mostly making plastic injection-molded objects. And when I was there, and while I was a participant of it, I loved it. I was so excited that I could make something that would then become real. I have, I think it's like five or six design patents, and I have probably about half a dozen products that are sold to market. And you know, I only say that as like one tiny piece in the machinery. Whole design teams, you know, were involved in making it from the client team to the manufacturing and engineering, but to see something on the shelf that you've contributed to is mind-blowing. There's such a satisfying feeling. And then I got over it, because I started realizing, "I don't get the satisfaction I used to from that feeling," and I realized ... "I'm not sure if I can do this any longer." So those projects of one in ten that I felt ecstatic about, probably the most memorable one was working on a hospital complex, a patient experience for young people with chronic diseases ... That project was so exciting. ... it was really satisfying. ... rather than being a regular healthcare experience, this was designed very much around a patient-centered, versus what is typical, which is designed around a doctor-centered [system]. So really rad.

Lee Moreau puts this critique of avoiding making "more stuff" and instead doing good in the world in terms of a pitch to clients. He says this is what he says to his clients:

> "This is what your consumer's doing now. We did this qualitative research. This is what they value, and what they aspire to, and this is a new behavior that we believe they will have in the future. Nobody else is giving them this behavior. Nobody else is forcing them to do this, but if they do it, they're gonna want it more and more." And so that's where the ethics come in, is, is this actually something that's good for the world?

The principles of ethical design varied from avoiding waste, making sure real human needs are met, to ensuring everyone feels like they are loved and they belong. Here are partners in a landscape design firm describing their ethical goals for their design practice.

> Michelle Crowley: Our big thing, which has to do with love, is accessibility, and getting people in the front door equitably? Like forever it was, "You can go around the back, and there's a ramp in the back to the loading dock, and you can take some freight elevator up," right? I mean everything now is changing, which is great, ... we want everybody going in the front door. So we integrate all of our accessibility as best as we can into the landscape so that anyone who is disabled feels like they belong in there. ...

> Naomi Cottrell: I believe that designed landscapes, especially in the urban or suburban environment, where we've lost our connection to nature, is an essential part of humanity. And will save the world. Quote me on that.

4.   CONCLUSION

Thus far, we have only superficially mined the data. The coded data contains many more ways to isolate and compare other categories and variables. For example, our code book includes codes relating to the qualities of design work, such as "simple," "coherence," "beauty," "hierarchy," and "utility." Other codes relate to business strategy and client demands, including "growth," "feasibility," "sustainability," and "disruption." We coded for ways of working in or for companies, including "freelance," "collaboration," "team," "constraint-role," and "constraint-legal." Our data analysis includes codes relating to ethics, professional organizations, employment status, and broader social and legal issues, including wealth inequality, the climate crisis, and intellectual property law. We have only scratched the surface in our analysis of the data. But the above description and analysis of some of the data demonstrates the richness and textured nature of the empirical data, which we anticipate will be useful for others who seek to better understand the relationship between any one particular variable and other existing legal or institutional mechanisms.

17. Re-engaging with concerns over latent design invalidity: examination and invalidation of registered Community designs at the EUIPO

Jane Cornwell

1. INTRODUCTION

There has been little legal empirical research to date examining the EU design legal framework.[1] This chapter addresses the important but under-explored issue of latent invalidity among registered Community designs ('RCDs') and related questions over the utility of increased *ex ante* examination of RCD applications by the EU Intellectual Property Office ('EUIPO') in light of the European Commission's review of EU design law.[2]

One of the issues considered in the Commission's review is whether the RCD application process should be reformed by increasing the scope of *ex ante* examination to include mandatory examination for novelty/individual character.[3] The Commission has concluded against this, taking the view that the currently very limited pre-grant examination of RCD applications 'seems to work well in practice'.[4] In essence, three main contentions are relied upon to support this view: first, that the low cost and speed of the RCD application process should not be jeopardised; second, that there is no evidence of widespread RCD invalidity; and third, that examination cannot in any event exhaustively identify all relevant prior art.[5]

This chapter explores the second and third of these contentions. Section 2 sets out the legal and policy background, and section 3 outlines the methodology used. Section 4 examines the evidence relied upon by the Commission to support its views on RCD invalidity, and compares this to data on RCD invalidation rates in EUIPO invalidity proceedings before the Invalidity Division and Board of Appeal. Section 5 turns to the issue of examination and prior art searching, and – in the absence of any evidence on this from the EU design law review process – presents and analyses a new dataset of Invalidity Division invalidation decisions compiled for this chapter investigating the prior art relied upon to invalidate contested RCDs, particularly the extent to which that prior art took the form of IP filings which could have been located through IP register searches. Section 6 considers the broader implications. I argue that the data pre-

---

[1] Oliver Church, Estelle Derclaye and Gilles Stupfler, 'An Empirical Analysis of the Design Case Law of the EU Member States' (2019) 50 IIC 685, 686.

[2] Outlined as at the time of writing in Henning Hartwig, 'Evaluation of EU legislation on design protection' (2022) 17 JIPLP 107.

[3] European Commission, *Evaluation of EU legislation on design protection* (Brussels, 6 November 2020, SWD(2020) 264 final), 45–47; see also the earlier *Legal review on industrial design protection in Europe* (April 2016, MARKT2014/083/D <https://op.europa.eu/en/publication-detail/-/publication/43fd4a5c-6c26-4639-ac9a-281ab57687de> accessed 25 May 2022, 108–109.

[4] Commission, *Evaluation*, n 3, 45.

[5] Commission, *Evaluation*, n 3, 45–46.

sented here adds to concerns that latent RCD invalidity may be more widespread than has been accepted by the Commission. While not underplaying the considerable challenges of design searching, this chapter also takes an exploratory first step in testing the perceived limitations of *ex ante* RCD examination, the data analysed here providing at least tentative evidence that increased *ex ante* examination of RCD filings may in fact have greater potential to assist in pre-empting the grant of invalid RCDs than has been acknowledged. This chapter concludes with a call for the Commission to engage more fully than it has done to date with concerns about the potential extent of latent RCD invalidity and to consider more comprehensively the steps required to evaluate and address this issue. Given the scale of uptake of the RCD system since its launch approaching 20 years ago, the concerns discussed in this chapter have considerable practical and commercial import; the findings discussed here are also of interest to other jurisdictions debating the preferred approach to design examination.

2.   BACKGROUND: *EX ANTE* EXAMINATION IN THE RCD SYSTEM

After checking formalities pursuant to Article 45 of the Community Designs Regulation ('CDR'),[6] *ex ante* examination of RCD applications by the EUIPO is extremely limited. Article 47(1) CDR provides simply:

> If the Office, in carrying out the examination pursuant to Article 45, notices that the design for which protection is sought –
> (a)   does not correspond to the definition under Article 3(a); or
> (b)   is contrary to public policy or accepted principles of morality, it shall refuse the application.[7]

There is no examination of novelty or individual character, the two core substantive requirements for valid registration which test whether a design is sufficiently different to earlier designs to merit protection.[8] There is also no examination of the exclusions from protection for design features solely dictated by function or must-fit interconnections.[9] RCDs are routinely granted very quickly, sometimes on the day they are filed.[10] Whether an RCD is valid will only be tested post-grant in an invalidity application to the EUIPO or a counterclaim in infringement proceedings before one of the Community design courts.[11]

---

[6]   Council Regulation (EC) 6/2002 on Community designs [2002] OJ L3/1.
[7]   Although Article 47 suggests that examination of these matters is optional, the EUIPO's guidelines state that applications 'must be' examined *ex officio* for these deficiencies: EUIPO, *Designs Guidelines – Examination of Applications for Registered Community Designs* (2022 edition, entry into force: 31 March 2022) <https://euipo.europa.eu/ohimportal/en/guidelines> accessed 25 May 2022, para 1.2.4.
[8]   CDR, Arts 4–6.
[9]   CDR, Art 8.
[10]   David Stone, *European Union Design Law – A Practitioners' Guide* (2nd edn, OUP, 2016), para 15.06. The EUIPO 'Fast Track' service aims to register designs within two working days, and accounts for around 30% of all RCD filings: see EUIPO, *EUIPO Statistics for Community Designs – 2003-01 to 2022-04 Evolution* <https:// euipo .europa .eu/ tunnel -web/ secure/ webdav/ guest/ document_library/ contentPdfs/about_euipo/the_office/statistics-of-community-designs_en.pdf> accessed 25 May 2022, Table 3.2.1.
[11]   CDR, Art 24.

Although many jurisdictions with design registration systems do not conduct substantive *ex ante* examination, some do – including important jurisdictions such as the US and Japan.[12] There are also hybrid systems which require examination in certain circumstances.[13] Debates remain live over the optimal approach – at the time of writing, for example, the UK Intellectual Property Office ('UK IPO') has recently consulted on re-introducing examination for novelty and individual character for UK national registered designs, and plans to consider further options and to consult again on this issue.[14] The design of the RCD system is driven by the 'fundamental objective' that the procedure for obtaining an RCD 'should present the minimum cost and difficulty to applicants'.[15] This reflects a policy stance in favour of speedy and cheap registration that predominated from the very inception of the RCD system, the Commission having argued from the outset that it was an 'essential element' of the RCD system that the registration procedure should be 'as easy and expedient as possible'.[16]

However, the lack of *ex ante* examination also brings with it significant underlying policy challenges. The recitals to the CDR talk of the 'greater legal certainty' that registration confers compared to unregistered protection,[17] but in reality an RCD is 'little more than a self-serving claim fixed on paper'.[18] The current set-up also passes the burden of locating and dealing with invalid RCDs onto third parties – a particularly acute consideration given that RCDs enjoy up to 25 years of absolute monopoly protection against even independently created designs, backed up by a statutory presumption of validity.[19] The effect of the absence of substantive examination at the EUIPO is 'to remove a filter against the registration of obviously invalid designs' and 'transfer the burden of removing them onto trade competitors who will need to commence invalidation proceedings'.[20] This is not a small-scale issue: across intellectual property offices worldwide, the EUIPO receives the second highest volume of global design filings every year; it registered over 90,000 RCDs each year from 2017 to 2020, and granted

---

[12]   For an overview of different approaches, see: Australian Government Advisory Council on Intellectual Property, *Review of the Designs System – Issues Paper*, September 2013 <https://www .ipaustralia.gov.au/sites/default/files/issues_paper_on_designs_review.pdf> accessed 25 May 2022, 12–13 (Table 2.5). Within the EU, examination of national design applications has been retained in a small number of Member States: see Commission, *Evaluation*, n 3, 46 (Czechia, Finland, Hungary, Romania and Slovakia).

[13]   For example, in Australia design registrations must be examined ('certified') before they can be enforced: ACIP, *Issues Paper*, n 12, 24–25.

[14]   UK IPO, 'Call for views on designs', 25 January 2022 <https://www.gov.uk/government/consultations/reviewing-the-designs-framework-call-for-views/call-for-views-on-designs> accessed 25 May 2022; UK IPO, 'Call for views on designs: Government response', 12 July 2022 <https://www .gov.uk/government/consultations/reviewing-the-designs-framework-call-for-views/outcome/call-for -views-on-designs-government-response> accessed 19 July 2022. The UK had previously examined UK national design applications, but dropped this in 2006 to harmonise practice with the EUIPO.

[15]   CDR, Recital 24; see also Recital 18.

[16]   European Commission, *Green Paper on the Legal Protection of Industrial Design* (Brussels, June 1991, III/F/5131/91-EN), 108.

[17]   CDR, Recitals 16 and 21.

[18]   Annette Kur, 'The Design Approach and procedural practice – mismatch or smooth transposition?' in Annette Kur, Marianne Levin and Jens Schovsbo, *The EU Design Approach – A Global Appraisal* (Edward Elgar, 2018), 173.

[19]   CDR, Arts 12, 19 and 85.

[20]   Martin Howe, *Russell-Clarke & Howe on Industrial Designs* (10th edn, Sweet & Maxwell, 2022), para 2-273.

over 100,000 RCDs in 2021 alone.[21] It cannot be assumed that the third parties who find themselves at the sharp end of tackling invalid RCDs will be able to afford the cost, time or risk of mounting invalidation challenges or running invalidity counterclaims needed to clear the way for legitimate competitive activity.

3.   METHODOLOGY

This chapter uses data on RCD invalidation proceedings at the EUIPO accessible via the 'eSearch Case Law' tool on the EUIPO website.[22]

First, data on the outcomes of RCD invalidation proceedings at the EUIPO was compiled using that tool's search functions for each year from the launch of the RCD system in 2003 through to the end of the calendar year 2020.[23] This covered decisions at first instance before the Invalidity Division and on appeal to the EUIPO Third Board of Appeal.[24]

Second, to allow investigation of the invalidating prior art relied upon in the EUIPO's invalidation decisions, the 'eSearch Case Law' tool was used to form a sample of all Invalidity Division decisions published in English in which the contested RCD was invalidated over the 10-year period from 2011 to 2020.[25] This gave a sample of 1,103 Invalidity Division decisions: removing a small number of what, on review, turned out to be erroneous entries in the search results,[26] this gave a dataset of 1,086 findings of invalidity for analysis. Although the need to focus on decisions handed down in English meant that random sampling could not be used in a way that might make the data more broadly generalisable, it nonetheless represents a substantial and useful body of Invalidity Division invalidations: English is the most common

---

[21]   World Intellectual Property Organization, *WIPO IP Facts and Figures* series 2017–2021 <https://www.wipo.int/publications/en/details.jsp?id=4577> accessed 25 May 2022; EUIPO, *EUIPO Statistics for Community Designs*, n 10, Table 5.

[22]   At <https://euipo.europa.eu/eSearchCLW/> accessed 25 May 2022.

[23]   Using the 'Designs decisions' tab at the 'Advanced search' option, selecting 'Invalidity decisions' or 'Board of Appeal decisions', entering a date range between 1 January and 31 December for each year and using the drop-down options at the 'Outcome of invalidity'/'Outcome of BoA appeal' search boxes.

[24]   Which hears all RCD appeals. Its decisions may deal with more than just invalidity: the focus here was on substantive invalidity appeal decisions with outcomes recorded at the 'Outcome of BoA appeal' search box as 'RCD invalidated', 'RCD partially invalidated' or 'Invalidity application rejected'. At first instance, there were no Invalidity Division decisions with the outcome 'RCD partially invalidated'. There were two decisions recorded with this outcome on appeal: on review, the first of these (R-2703/2004-3) in fact upheld the first instance decision invalidating the contested design in its entirety for lack of novelty and this was therefore included in the data as an invalidation of the contested RCD; the second (R-2449/2018-3) resulted in the contested design being upheld in amended form pursuant to Art 25(6) CDR – as this meant that RCD protection was not lost, this was included in the data as a case in which the invalidity application was ultimately unsuccessful.

[25]   Formed as set out at n 23, selecting 'English' as the language of the proceedings at the 'Language' drop-down search box and selecting the option 'RCD invalidated' at the 'Outcome of invalidity' drop-down search box.

[26]   Four decisions were not published in English, three were duplicates of other entries and ten decisions in fact involved the validity of the RCD being upheld. Particulars are provided along with the dataset at https://doi.org/10.7488/ds/3485.

language of RCD invalidity proceedings,[27] and the dataset represents 66.5% of all findings of invalidity by the Invalidity Division in the 10-year period reviewed. Each decision in the dataset was reviewed to identify the ground of invalidity upon which the contested RCD was invalidated and, for all invalidations based on lack of novelty or individual character, whether the invalidating prior art relied upon by the Invalidity Division included some kind of IP filing. For each such IP filing,[28] data was collected on its type (for example, whether an earlier design, trade mark, patent or utility model), jurisdiction, and whether its classification matched or was equivalent to the Locarno classification of the contested RCD.[29] For prior art design filings, this was done by comparing the Locarno classifications of the contested RCD and earlier design; for prior art trade marks, patents and utility models, this was done by comparing the Nice or International Patent Classification (IPC) classification.[30]

4.   LATENT RCD INVALIDITY: EXPLORING RCD INVALIDATION RATES AT THE EUIPO

A public consultation carried out in 2018–19 as part of the EU design law review process high-lighted concerns among some respondents that too many designs lacking novelty or individual character were being registered, leading to legal uncertainty and 'unjust situations' in court.[31] However, the Commission has rejected these concerns on the basis that they 'do not seem to be reflected in the total number of disputes'.[32] The Commission relies on the statistic, supplied by the EUIPO, that on average less than 0.05% of all RCDs are declared invalid each year.[33] This figure can be found in an earlier EUIPO report where it is noted that 'no more than 0.05% of the total in force population' of RCDs was declared invalid each year from 2010 to 2019.[34] There are, however, limits to what can be inferred from this figure: this low percentage could, in particular, be driven just as much by an unduly low rate of challenge against invalid RCDs

---

[27]   EUIPO, *EUIPO Design Focus – 2010 to 2019 Evolution* <https:// euipo .europa .eu/ tunnel -web/ secure/ webdav/ guest/ document _library/ contentPdfs/ news/ EUIPO _DS _Focus _Report _2010 -2019_Evolution_en.pdf> accessed 25 May 2022, 25.

[28]   This was captured in the dataset for up to three invalidating prior art IP filings per decision, noting one (exceptional) further case in which the Invalidity Division based its ruling on a total of nine prior art IP filings. All nine prior art RCDs in that case are taken into account in the data presented here.

[29]   Locating the relevant prior art IP filing from the details given by the Invalidity Division and check-ing online databases such as eSearch plus, DesignView, TMView or Espacenet. In some instances, the prior art IP filing had to be located using details such as filing, publication or registration dates, where there appeared to be a typographical error in the filing or registration number given by the Invalidity Division. Some contested designs covered more than one Locarno class or sub-class: the relevant prior art was coded as having the same Locarno or an equivalent Nice/IPC classification where there was at least one match.

[30]   For the Nice comparison, using the Nice-Locarno concordance table in *The CITMA & CIPA Community Designs Handbook* (Sweet & Maxwell, 2022), para 2-021. The IPC classification was consulted at: <https://www.wipo.int/classifications/ipc/en/> accessed 25 May 2022, comparing the class and sub-class descriptors for the Locarno classification of the contested RCD against the IPC section and class titles for the prior art patent/utility model.

[31]   Commission, *Evaluation*, n 3, 46.

[32]   Commission, *Evaluation*, n 3, 46.

[33]   Commission, *Evaluation*, n 3, 46.

[34]   EUIPO, *EUIPO Design Focus*, n 27, 27.

as by anything inherent in the quality of RCD filings themselves. The earlier EUIPO report alludes to this when it mentions the 'relatively low annual volume' of RCD invalidity filings and subsequent decisions.[35]

The Commission also cites research by Church *et al* analysing decisions of EU Member States' courts on various types of design right, including RCDs.[36] According to the Commission, this research shows that 'the absence of a full-blown substantive examination does not mean that designs are more likely to be declared invalid'.[37] Church *et al* do conclude from their dataset that 'courts are more likely to find designs valid than invalid': for RCDs in particular, in their sample (consisting, for RCDs, of 591 court decisions) 81.4% of RCDs were found valid.[38] However, their findings are subject to the explicit caveat – highlighted at the start of their paper, but not mentioned by the Commission – that conclusions based on litigated cases 'cannot be extrapolated with certainty beyond such litigated cases, as litigation is only the tip of what could be termed "the dispute iceberg"'.[39] This caveat rightly acknowledges the selection bias inherent in any dataset based on court rulings. Only a proportion of all IP disputes will result in court proceedings and only a smaller proportion yet will reach trial or, after that, a decision by the court.[40] It is to be expected that a rightholder will not choose to put into litigation an RCD the validity of which they regard as potentially questionable; if doubts arise as to validity during the course of litigation, given the broader implications of losing the RCD beyond the individual dispute in hand, the rightholder's interest will also be in favour of settling the litigation before it reaches a decision on the merits.[41] It is therefore likely that, given their particular research focus, Church *et al*'s dataset and findings were directed towards those designs which rightholders regarded as the most robust.

Neither of the pieces of evidence relied upon by the Commission can support with confidence its somewhat brisk dismissal of concerns over potentially widespread latent RCD invalidity. A useful counterpoint can be obtained by looking at rates of RCD invalidation before the EUIPO. EUIPO invalidity proceedings are the only way in which third parties can, of their own motion, challenge the validity of an RCD, and they offer a large pool of RCD invalidity determinations for analysis. Table 17.1 sets out the data compiled as noted in section 3 above on the outcomes of RCD invalidation proceedings before the Invalidity Division and Board of Appeal from the launch of the RCD system in 2003 to the end of the calendar year 2020, incorporating minor adjustments for the small number of erroneous entries in the EUIPO database identified during data collection on invalidating prior art.[42] Figures 17.1 and 17.2 illustrate the total number of Invalidity Division and Board of Appeal decisions on RCD validity each

[35]   EUIPO, *EUIPO Design Focus*, n 27, 27.
[36]   Church *et al*, n 1, 686. Their research did not cover decisions of intellectual property offices such as the EUIPO: 687 and 692.
[37]   Commission, *Evaluation*, n 3, 46.
[38]   Church *et al*, n 1, 700 and 703 (Table 2).
[39]   Church *et al*, n 1, 687.
[40]   See Jane Cornwell, 'Between the formal and the informal: "repeat players", "one-shotters" and case trajectories in intellectual property infringement litigation at the Scottish Court of Session' (2017) 36 CJQ 441, 457–458 and the literature cited there.
[41]   See, for example, in relation to patents: Joachim Henkel and Hans Zischka, 'How many patents are truly valid? Extent, causes, and remedies for latent patent invalidity' (2019) 48 *European Journal of Law and Economics* 195, 200, 203, 207 and 210.
[42]   See n 26 above.

Table 17.1   RCD invalidity determinations at the EUIPO

Year	Invalidity Division			Board of Appeal		
	Total decisions on RCD validity	RCD invalidated	Invalidity application rejected	Total decisions on RCD validity	RCD invalidated	Invalidity application rejected
2003	0	-	-	0	-	-
2004	14	10 (71.4%)	4 (28.6%)	0	-	-
2005	43	24 (55.8%)	19 (44.2%)	0	-	-
2006	143	84 (58.7%)	59 (41.3%)	3	0 (0.0%)	3 (100.0%)
2007	109	73 (67.0%)	36 (33.0%)	21	18 (85.7%)	3 (14.3%)
2008	94	65 (69.1%)	29 (30.9%)	17	11 (64.7%)	6 (35.3%)
2009	50	26 (52.0%)	24 (48.0%)	31	28 (90.3%)	3 (9.7%)
2010	128	79 (61.7%)	49 (38.3%)	16	9 (56.3%)	7 (43.8%)
2011	172	118 (68.6%)	54 (31.4%)	21	16 (76.2%)	5 (23.8%)
2012	299	142 (47.5%)	157 (52.5%)	37	27 (73.0%)	10 (27.0%)
2013	268	180 (67.2%)	88 (32.8%)	51	33 (64.7%)	18 (35.3%)
2014	262	154 (58.8%)	108 (41.2%)	56	31 (55.4%)	25 (44.6%)
2015	230	138 (60.0%)	92 (40.0%)	53	28 (52.8%)	25 (47.2%)
2016	178	139 (78.1%)	39 (21.9%)	76	37 (48.7%)	39 (51.3%)
2017	200	144 (72.0%)	56 (28.0%)	65	43 (66.2%)	22 (33.8%)
2018	309	201 (65.0%)	108 (35.0%)	50	32 (64.0%)	18 (36.0%)
2019	357	219 (61.3%)	138 (38.7%)	62	31 (50.0%)	31 (50.0%)
2020	330	197 (59.7%)	133 (40.3%)	89	49 (55.1%)	40 (44.9%)
Total	3,186	1,993 (62.6%)	1,193 (37.4%)	648	393 (60.6%)	255 (39.4%)

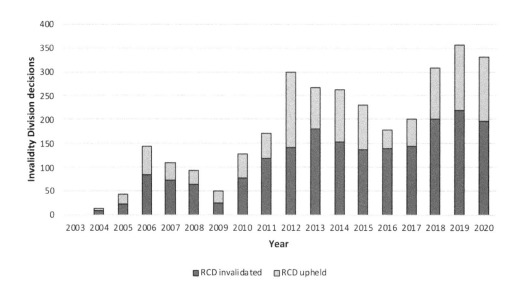

Figure 17.1   Invalidity Division decisions on RCD invalidity 2003–2020

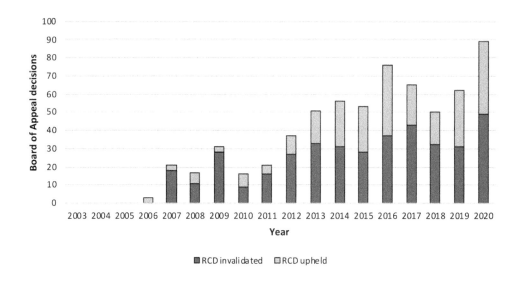

Figure 17.2   Board of Appeal decisions on RCD validity 2003–2020

year, contrasting those decisions in which the contested RCD was invalidated and those in which it was upheld.

As the data shows, when RCDs have been contested before the EUIPO the rate of invalidation has been high. In every year bar one, over 50% of Invalidity Division decisions resulted in the contested RCD being invalidated; at first instance, the rate of invalidation reached over 70% in some years, with an overall invalidation rate of 62.6% across the time period reviewed.[43] Subject to the inevitable time lag as disputes found their way to appeal, the picture is also similar at the Board of Appeal. On appeal, the invalidation rate was also 50% or more in all bar one of the years reviewed, reached highs of over 80% in some earlier years in particular and sat overall at 60.6%.

There is a striking comparison to be made with recently published empirical data on post-grant US design patent invalidations – the US being a jurisdiction which does conduct substantive *ex ante* examination. Confounding some long-standing preconceptions on how well US design patents hold up under post-grant challenge, Burstein and Vishnubhakat have found that, in cases filed between 2008 and 2020, US district courts making post-grant determinations of validity upheld the contested US design patent 88.4% of the time and that, in the period from 2012 to August 2020, the overall survival rate of US design patents in post-grant validity challenges before the US Patent Trial and Appeal Board (PTAB) was 79%.[44] Burstein and Vishnubhakat caution against assuming that the high rate at which the US design patents are upheld necessarily reflects high quality prosecution and examination; an alternative explanation may be that Federal Circuit case law tests for design patentability are relatively easy to satisfy in practice.[45] From a European perspective, however, the marked divergence in survival rates for RCDs at the EUIPO and US design patents at the PTAB in particular should at least give pause for thought.

The data on RCD invalidation rates before the EUIPO Invalidity Division and Board of Appeal sit uneasily with the Commission's conclusion that there is no evidence to support concerns over potentially widespread RCD invalidity. What might it mean in practice if the rates of RCD invalidation at the EUIPO were actually replicated across the whole population of RCDs? As at 1 January 2020, there were more than 813,000 in-force RCDs:[46] on these invalidation rates, this would translate into around half a million latently invalid RCDs sitting on the Community design register. Of course, potential selection bias means that we cannot extrapolate from EUIPO invalidation rates to the whole of the RCD population: just as we can expect designs asserted in litigation to be those which the rightholder regards as the most robust, designs attacked in invalidation proceedings may be those that the challenger feels most confident of successfully invalidating.[47] That said, given the particular challenges of design searching, this selection effect may not be that strong: as an image- rather than text-based exercise, design searching is notoriously difficult,[48] and there may be more invalid RCDs on the register than potential challengers have simply been able to locate. Even if the overall rate

---

[43] Similar invalidation rates are given for 2010–2019 in the EUIPO's 'Design Focus' report: EUIPO, *Design Focus*, n 27, 26–27. There are some differences between Table 17.1 and that report's data, although this is hard to pin down precisely as the figures in the EUIPO report are not complete.

[44] Sarah Burstein and Saurabh Vishnubhakat, 'The Truth about Design Patents' (2022) 71 Am UL Rev 1221, 1271–1272, 1274 and 1282–1283. Burstein and Vishnubhakat also look at validity determinations before the US International Trade Commission, although the number of such determinations was small: ibid, 1273.

[45] Burstein and Vishnubhakat, n 44, 1279.

[46] EUIPO, *Design Focus*, n 27, 4.

[47] By way of parallel, in the patent context Henkel and Zischka note that, in the German bifurcated patent litigation system, alleged infringers will be more likely to challenge patents via validity challenges the less robust those patents are perceived to be: Henkel and Zischka, n 41, 202.

[48] Burstein and Vishnubhakat, n 44, 1249 and the literature cited there.

of latent RCD invalidity was half the rate in EUIPO invalidation proceedings, this would still translate into around a quarter of a million currently registered but invalid RCDs. This does not just have implications within the EU: with the wholesale cloning of RCD registrations onto the UK design register that has taken place as part of the post-Brexit arrangements for continuing protection of EU IP rights in the UK, any existing issue of widespread RCD invalidity will now be replicated on the UK design register as well.

5.   THE LIMITATIONS OF *EX ANTE* EXAMINATION: INVESTIGATING THE INVALIDATING PRIOR ART

The data set out above on RCD invalidation rates at the EUIPO suggests that the Commission's dismissal of stakeholder concerns over latent RCD invalidity warrants re-evaluation. What of the Commission's position on the second major issue considered in this chapter, namely the limitations of *ex ante* RCD examination?

Alongside broader policy points around cost and time implications, the Commission has offered two particular arguments on the limitations of prior art searching to support its conclusion against introducing increased *ex ante* examination for RCDs. First, it is noted that examination of RCDs 'would not be exhaustive', since 'any earlier design in the world (registered or not) can be novelty-destroying'.[49] Second, the Commission has also asserted that searching by product class is 'not possible', given that neither product indication nor classification affects the scope of protection of a Community design as such.[50] However, it does not necessarily follow from either of these propositions that *ex ante* examination must be *per se* ruled out. The inherent incompleteness of any examination process is not in and of itself a conclusive argument for not carrying out any examination at all: after all, patent examination is also inherently non-exhaustive, but nonetheless plays an important role in the checks and balances of the patent system.[51] While RCD examination would, of course, not be able to locate *all* relevant prior art, it could undoubtedly locate *some*. A more nuanced way of reflecting on the utility of increased *ex ante* examination for RCDs is to explore its potential usefulness as a matter of degree: just how complete, or incomplete, might the process actually be?

Neither the Commission nor the earlier Legal Review has offered any reflection or data on this. It is beyond the scope of this chapter to model up and test a full process of search and examination. However, it is possible to take an exploratory first step in examining this issue empirically through analysis of the dataset on invalidating prior art compiled for this chapter as described above: taking a sample of RCDs known to have been found invalid by the Invalidity Division and analysing the characteristics of the prior art known to have formed the basis for that invalidation, we can at least start to investigate how far that was prior art of a kind that could have been located during pre-grant examination had such a system been in place.

As explained in section 3 above, the first data point captured for all findings of invalidity included in the dataset was the ground upon which the contested RCD was invalidated by the Invalidity Division. As Table 17.2 shows, most invalidations in the dataset were based on lack

---

[49]   Commission, *Evaluation*, n 3, 45; see also the earlier *Legal review*, n 3, 109.

[50]   Commission, *Evaluation*, n 3, 45–46.

[51]   And as the literature notes, patents are often revoked in light of prior art not identified by the examiner: see, for example, Henkel and Zischka, n 41, 228 and 230.

Table 17.2   Invalidity Division invalidations: Article 25 CDR grounds

Ground of invalidation		No. of decisions	% of decisions in dataset
Article 25(1)(a)	RCD not a 'design'	1	0.1
Article 25(1)(b)	Lack of novelty[a]	337	31.0
	Lack of individual character[b]	629	57.9
	RCD wholly comprised of component parts not visible in normal use[c]	13	1.2
	RCD wholly dictated by technical function/must-fit[d]	37	3.4
	RCD contrary to public policy/morality[e]	0	0.0
Article 25(1)(c)	RCD holder not entitled to design	0	0.0
Article 25(1)(d)	Conflict with a prior unpublished design filing	12	1.1
Article 25(1)(e)	Use of an earlier distinctive sign	56	5.2
Article 25(1)(f)	Unauthorised use of a copyright work	0	0.0
Article 25(1)(g)	Improper use of Paris Convention Art 6ter rights	0	0.0
Other	Other[f]	1	0.1
	Total	1,086	

Notes:
[a] CDR, Arts 25(1)(b) and 5.
[b] CDR, Arts 25(1)(b) and 6.
[c] CDR, Arts 25(1)(b) and 4(2).
[d] CDR, Arts 25(1)(b) and Article 8.
[e] CDR, Arts 25(1)(b) and Article 9.
[f] One invalidation decision addressed whether a previously challenged RCD could be maintained in amended form pursuant to Article 25(6) CDR.

of novelty or individual character, the two core substantive requirements for valid registration testing the contested RCD against the publicly available prior art.[52]

Lack of novelty and individual character were often pleaded together but, in the interests of procedural economy, the Invalidity Division often only considered individual character (the more demanding of the two criteria, and thus the more likely to be determinative): we cannot therefore read too much into the figures for lack of novelty and individual character as individual categories in Table 17.2. Together, however, decisions based on lack of novelty and lack of individual character accounted for 88.9% of the findings of invalidity in the dataset.

Focusing from here on these invalidations for lack of novelty or individual character, it is useful to break down the data between, on the one hand, those invalidations that were based on some form of IP filing and, on the other, invalidations based on non-IP-based forms of prior art. IP filings should, in particular, be the most readily searchable forms of prior art, and it is prior art IP filings on which this chapter is particularly focused.

Prior art other than IP filings played a large role: 58.5% of invalidations for lack of novelty or individual character were based on non-IP-based prior art. This included online disclosures, disclosures via print media such as product catalogues or brochures, exhibition at trade fairs and evidence of actual sales. However, IP filings were also important. Some form of invali-

[52] In almost all cases, the Invalidity Division decided the dispute on the basis of one or other of these grounds. In three decisions, the Invalidity Division found the contested RCD invalid for both lack of novelty and lack of individual character: for present purposes, these three decisions have been coded as invalidations for lack of novelty given that, after the novelty conclusion, the finding on individual character was strictly extraneous.

dating prior art IP filing was relied upon by the Invalidity Division as the basis for its decision in 41.5% of the invalidations for lack of novelty or individual character in the dataset.[53] If anything, this figure is likely to underrepresent the potential role of IP filings as invalidating prior art: for reasons of procedural economy, the Invalidity Division typically focused its decision on only a single prior art disclosure, but 7.8% of invalidations disposed on the basis of non-IP-based prior art also featured submissions by the invalidity applicant citing an IP filing not considered by the Invalidity Division.[54]

Focusing on the invalidating prior art IP filings that were relied upon by the Invalidity Division in its invalidations for lack of novelty or individual character, Figure 17.3 shows that the vast majority of these (81.8%) were design filings,[55] followed by trade marks (11.0%), patents (4.2%) and utility models (3.0%).[56]

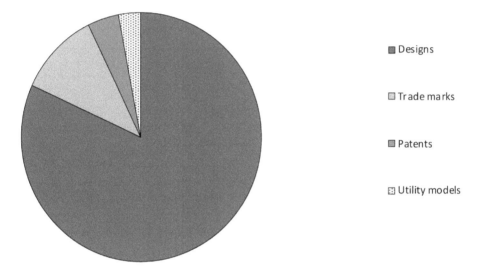

Figure 17.3   *Invalidity Division findings of lack of novelty/individual character: invalidating prior art IP filings – by IP type*

The invalidating prior art IP filings came from a wide range of jurisdictions, but categorising the data by the major jurisdictional groupings evident from the dataset, Figure 17.4 shows that far and away the largest body of prior art filings relied upon for invalidations for lack of novelty or individual character were prior RCDs.

---

[53]   The IP filing in question was typically the sole item of prior art relied upon by the Invalidity Division; occasionally, it was relied upon alongside some other non-IP-based form of prior disclosure, typically evidence of the sale or marketing of the product embodied in the IP filing.

[54]   Not including IP filings cited by the invalidity applicant for purposes other than as invalidating prior art (for example, as evidence of the general state of the design corpus or design freedom).

[55]   Including all forms of registrable design protection, including *sui generis* registered designs such as the RCD and designs protected via sub-categories of patent law, such as US design patents.

[56]   In most instances (95.5%), the invalidation decision was based on a single prior art IP filing, with a small proportion (4.5%) based on two or more IP filings.

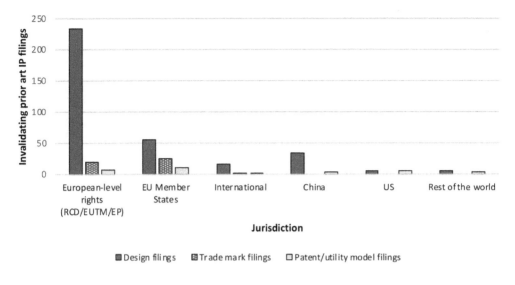

Figure 17.4   *Invalidity Division findings of lack of novelty/individual character:*
invalidating prior art IP filings – by IP type and jurisdiction

Among invalidating prior art design filings, 66.9% were RCDs, 15.7% were design filings at EU Member States, 9.7% were Chinese design patent filings, 4.6% International design filings, 1.4% US design patent filings and 1.7% design filings made elsewhere in the world. The importance of EU- or European-level IP filings and IP filings in EU Member States was also evident for trade marks and patents/utility models, albeit on a smaller scale: 42.6% of trade mark filings relied upon by the Invalidity Division for lack of novelty or individual character were EUTMs and 53.2% were trade mark filings at EU Member States; 22.6% of patent or utility model filings relied upon were European patents and 32.3% were patent or utility model filings at EU Member States.[57]

Finally, looking at the data in terms of product classification, Table 17.3 breaks down the invalidating IP filings relied upon by the Invalidity Division in its findings of lack of novelty and individual character by IP type and by alignment with the Locarno classification of the contested RCD.

As Table 17.3 shows, 90.0% of the invalidating IP filings relied upon for lack of novelty or individual character were from the same Locarno class as that of the contested RCD, or a Nice or IPC classification equivalent.[58] Within the category of prior art design filings in particular (where the classification comparison is at its most straightforward), 93.5% were from the same Locarno class as the disputed RCD and 86.8% were also from the same Locarno sub-class. Focusing further on prior art RCDs, 94.5% were within the same Locarno class and 88.5% within the same Locarno sub-class.

---

[57]   Including the UK, given the pre-Brexit time period under review.

[58]   This rises to 92.1% if contested RCD Locarno classifications in class 9 (packaging and containers) and class 19 (for 'labels') are treated as catch-all equivalents to all of the Nice trade mark classes in the same way that Locarno class 32 (logos) is so treated in the Nice-Locarno concordance table at n 30.

Table 17.3   Invalidity Division findings of lack of novelty/individual character:
invalidating prior art IP filings – by IP type and classification

IP type/classification	No. of invalidating prior art IP filings	% of invalidating prior art IP filings by IP type	% of all invalidating prior art IP filings[a]
Designs			
Same Locarno class and sub-class	296	86.8	70.6
Same Locarno class, different sub-class	23	6.7	5.5
Different Locarno class	22	6.5	5.3
Trade marks			
Nice equivalent class	35	74.5	8.4
Nice non-equivalent class	12	25.5	2.9
Patents/utility models			
IPC equivalent class	23	74.2	5.5
IPC non-equivalent class	8	25.8	1.9
Total	419		

Note:
[a] In a small number of cases (9 prior design filings), the classification of the earlier design could not be established, either because the relevant online record was not complete or because no online database entry could be located, in some cases possibly because of typographical errors in the Invalidity Division decision. These cases are not included in the data in Table 17.3.

What can we take from all of this? Although exploratory in nature, the data presented here does suggest at least tentatively that the limitations of *ex ante* examination highlighted by the Commission and the earlier Legal Review may not be so categorically insurmountable as the EU design law review process has perhaps implied. Many invalidations in the dataset were not based on any kind of prior IP filing, but it cannot be assumed that all of that prior art was by definition unidentifiable – it is beyond the scope of this chapter to test empirically how readily searchable (and datable) this non-IP-based evidence of prior art would have been in *ex ante* examination, but at least some of it is likely to have been capable of identification with the use of appropriate search techniques. Either way, 41.5% of the invalidations for lack of novelty or individual character in the dataset were based on some form of invalidating prior IP filing which was – assuming availability of appropriate search technologies – capable of being located through IP register searches.

   This chapter has not assessed how quickly those prior art IP filings could have been located by an RCD examiner or how readily the necessary legal evaluation could have been undertaken without additional evidence or input. What the data discussed here does at least provisionally suggest, however, is that – even without exploring the position on non-IP-based prior art – a meaningful proportion of invalid RCDs could have been pre-emptively weeded out through a fuller process of examination than is currently in place by searches on a relatively focused set of IP registers, and even limiting those searches by product classification, if the examiner were equipped with sufficiently effective search tools. As Figure 17.4 in particular shows, most of the invalidating prior art IP filings relied upon in the findings of lack of novelty and individual character in the dataset were clustered within a limited number of IP registers. Indeed, 54.7% were RCDs and 4.7% were EUTMs, meaning that 59.4% of all invalidating IP filings relied upon by the Invalidity Division for lack of novelty or individual character in the dataset were IP rights administered by the EUIPO itself. This covers almost a quarter (24.4%)

of all findings of lack of novelty or individual character reviewed. At least as far as can be seen from the evidence presented here, the assertion that it is 'not possible' to search for prior art by classification also seems overstated: at least 90.0% of all prior art IP filings relied upon for lack of novelty or individual character were in the same or an equivalent Locarno, Nice or IPC class as the contested RCD, that figure rising to 93.5% for alignment in Locarno class among prior art designs and 94.5% among prior art RCDs. This is without even considering possible cross-search strategies between Locarno classes. These findings accord with the intuition that, notwithstanding the unlimited theoretical scope of RCD protection and prior art, in reality many cases are likely to revolve around the same or related products.

6.   DISCUSSION

Among the top four jurisdictions in the world for volume of design filings each year,[59] the RCD system is alone in leaving third parties entirely responsible for all monitoring and policing of design validity, including all searching for potentially invalidating prior art. In China, which receives the greatest volume of design filings globally, design patent applications are not substantively examined, but (alongside the availability of invalidation proceedings) it is possible for design patent owners, interested third parties and alleged infringers to request a 'patent evaluation report' from the China National Intellectual Property Administration ('CNIPA') evaluating the validity of Chinese design patents on the basis of searches which the CNIPA will carry out; proposals are under consultation to open up this procedure to any third party.[60] The Republic of Korea, which handles the third highest volume of design filings, operates a hybrid examination system in which certain design applications are not substantively examined but others are.[61] In the US, the fourth most-used design registration system, design patent applications are substantively examined, including for novelty and non-obviousness.[62]

Although the data presented here is only a preliminary first step in exploring empirically the limitations of any possible system of fuller *ex ante* RCD examination, it does suggest that the Commission's review process moved on too quickly from this issue. At the time of writing, the Commission has not only effectively put aside the issue of RCD examination but is now considering moves to eliminate *ex ante* examination at the national level from those Member States which still retain such processes.[63] This is premature. Rather than writing off increased

---

[59]   See the WIPO reports at n 21.

[60]   Stefan Luginbuehl and Thomas Pattloch, 'The awakening of the Chinese patent dragon: the revised Chinese Patent Law 2009' (2011) 42 IIC 130, 137–138; Victor Guo, 'The impact of negative patent evaluation reports in China's patent infringement litigation', Managing IP, April 2022 <https://www.managingip.com/article/b1xkhw9fh370gw/the-impact-of-negative-patent-evaluation-reports-in-chinas-patent-infringement-litigation> accessed 25 May 2022. The patent evaluation report is not a binding or formal determination of validity, but can be used as evidence in court proceedings; once issued, the report is openly accessible to the public.

[61]   Robert Mirko Stutz, 'International design law policies: present and future' in Henning Hartwig (ed), *Research Handbook on Design Law* (Edward Elgar, 2021), 412; see also KIPO, 'Overview of the Design System in Korea' <https://www.kipo.go.kr/en/HtmlApp?c=93001&catmenu=ek04_01_02> accessed 25 May 2022.

[62]   USPTO, *Manual of Patent Examining Procedure* (9th edn, June 2020), Chapter 1500, 1504 Examination [R-10.2019].

[63]   Commission, *Evaluation*, n 3, 47.

ex ante RCD examination on the basis of blanket and untested assertions as to its limitations, there is scope to form a more comprehensive empirical understanding of the extent to which such examination could in fact reduce the grant of invalid RCDs, to assess different possible examination models (for example, examining just novelty or both novelty and individual character), to work up a more granular assessment of the impacts of those different models on the speed and cost of the RCD application process, and thereby to identify in a more nuanced way what the overall cost-benefit calculus of those models would be for different stakeholders – and the public interest. Even just as an initial next step, further research could explore the characteristics of the invalidating prior art successfully relied upon across all EUIPO Invalidity Division invalidations (in all languages), in findings of RCD invalidity by Community design courts and in determinations of invalidity for harmonised national registered designs, testing for the searchability of all non-IP-based prior art relied upon and for the actual speed and ease with which relevant prior art IP filings could be located via IP register searches. The extent to which effective image-based search tools are available would be central to this latter question: the UK IPO's recent consultation flagged the potential and importance of improved search technology and use of AI tools to assist search and examination,[64] but, beyond a note by the Commission on the usefulness of '[e]fforts to develop powerful and user-friendly' search tools to enable reliable searches,[65] this issue has not been discussed in detail in the EU design law review. At present, in terms of public-facing technologies at least, the availability of image-based search for designs is limited: important public-access multi-jurisdictional online design search portals (DesignView; the WIPO Global Design Database) do not use image-based search and, although the EUIPO's 'eSearch plus' tool can use uploaded images to search for similar designs, the outcome of using this tool has been described in commentary as 'somewhat disappointing'.[66] More could also be done to gather and share detailed empirical experience on how *ex ante* examination of design filings functions within those EU Member States where this is retained and elsewhere.

Given the persistent and overwhelming policy narrative that design protection is already too hard to obtain and enforce, it is perhaps unrealistic to see any policy proposals that might slow down the RCD application process or make it more expensive being politically saleable. The Commission has highlighted that a majority of respondents to its 2018–19 public consultation did not wish to introduce mandatory *ex ante* examination of RCD applications, for fear that it might put at risk the main advantage of the RCD system in the form of its quick and efficient registration.[67] The speed and cost of the RCD application process are, of course, important considerations for design applicants, particularly individual designers and SMEs. However, 10% of respondents to the Commission's consultation did favour introducing mandatory examination, and a further 62% gave responses indicative of the view that – even if introducing full mandatory *ex ante* examination is not the answer – more needs to be done to tackle issues around RCD invalidity, whether (from the options presented in the consultation ques-

---

[64]   UK IPO, 'Call for views' (January 2022), n 14; UK IPO, 'Calls for views on designs: Analysis of responses', 12 July 2022 <https://www.gov.uk/government/consultations/reviewing-the-designs-framework-call-for-views/outcome/calls-for-views-on-designs-analysis-of-responses> accessed 19 July 2022, para 15 in particular.

[65]   Commission, *Evaluation*, n 3, 47.

[66]   Mirko Stutz, n 61, 433.

[67]   Commission, *Evaluation*, n 3, 45.

tionnaire) through the creation of an optional, fee-based RCD examination service or through the provision of enhanced image-based search tools.[68]

Whether full mandatory examination is or is not the solution, the data on EUIPO invalidation rates presented in this chapter highlight the need for more rigorous engagement with concerns around the possible extent of latent RCD invalidity and the steps needed to tackle this. It is no surprise to find high rates of RCD invalidation at the EUIPO: in the absence of substantive examination, the RCD system is ripe for intentional or inadvertent misuse, and this is only magnified by the possibility of registering multiple designs per filing at increasingly low cost the more designs filed.[69] The EUIPO's own website advises that an option for would-be applicants who are aware of prior art producing the same overall impression as their design is to 'risk registration' and to 'go ahead and file your application and risk an invalidity action'.[70] Empirical work in certain sectors by Filitz *et al* has flagged evidence of '"strategic", arguably abusive' uses of the RCD system among some registrants, and called for further research into actual and potential misuse of the RCD system.[71] The UK IPO's consultation has flagged concern about 'anti-competitive registrations' by which existing designs are deliberately registered and then used to stop the legitimate activities of the original designer;[72] earlier commentary on the same practice has noted a sense among affected businesses that 'despite its laudable objectives, design registration is open to grievous abuse'.[73] Indeed, the Commission's own 2018–19 public consultation has also generated evidence of concern: responses to one question indicate that a substantial proportion of respondents had conducted no clearance searches before filing their RCDs; on another question directed to respondents who identified themselves as 'users of designs of others', 74% of respondents agreed with the proposition that design protection in the EU 'is abused to seek protection for designs that should never be registered'.[74]

While compiling the dataset of Invalidity Division decisions discussed in this chapter, it was also impossible not to notice a steady stream of decisions that seemed troubling in terms of what they might tell us about applicants' approaches to RCD filing. The dataset included cases involving RCDs filed using design representations apparently lifted from third party design filings or copied from third party product packaging,[75] RCDs based on existing third

---

[68] Commission, *Evaluation*, n 3, 115.

[69] The current combined application and publication fees in a multiple RCD filing are EUR 350 for the first design applied for, EUR 175 for the second to tenth designs and EUR 80 for the eleventh design onwards: <https://euipo.europa.eu/ohimportal/en/rcd-fees-directly-payable-to-euipo> accessed 25 May 2022. See further Rainer Filitz, Joachim Henkel and Bruce Tether, 'Protecting aesthetic innovations? An exploration of the use of registered community designs' (2015) 44 *Research Policy* 1192, 1203.

[70] Noting further that '[t]he decision to object to an RCD registration depends on many factors' and that '[t]he existence of an earlier (un)registered design does not prevent you from applying, but it does mean that you run the risk of infringing someone else's rights and the possibility of court action against you', see the 'What to do?' tab <https://euipo.europa.eu/ohimportal/en/rcd-search-availability> accessed 25 May 2022.

[71] Filitz *et al*, n 69, 1201 and 1202 in particular.

[72] UK IPO, 'Call for views' (January 2022), n 14; see also UK IPO, 'Analysis of responses', n 64, para 9 in particular.

[73] Jeremy Phillips, 'Locarno in the limelight' (2009) 4 JIPLP 1, 1.

[74] Commission, *Evaluation*, n 3, 113 and 96–97 respectively.

[75] For the former, see Case ICD 101879 *Zhejiang Luqi Intelligent Technology Co Ltd v Avaca* (Invalidity Division, 8 November 2018); for the latter, see Case ICD 107179 *LEGO Juris A/S v MAR*

party trade marks or branding,[76] attempts to register official State symbols,[77] filings for basic geometric shapes,[78] and examples of repeated invalidation decisions against the same RCD registrants.[79] Not only this, but a substantial proportion (17.2%) of all invalidations for lack of novelty or individual character in the dataset involved a comment by the Invalidity Division or admission by the RCD holder that the invalidating prior art had actually been disclosed by the holder of the contested RCD or a closely related entity.[80] This is, if anything, likely to be an undercounting of this phenomenon: the invalidity applicant alleged disclosure of relevant prior art by the RCD holder without comment from the Invalidity Division in a further 2.1% of invalidations in the dataset and there were more cases in which the prior disclosure was likely to have been by the RCD holder.[81] Whether RCD applicants may be acting strategically

---

2000 OOD (Invalidity Division, 7 May 2020), Cases ICD 107223, 107322 and 107339 *LEGO Juris A/S v MAR 2000 OOD* (Invalidity Division, 16 June 2020), Cases ICD 107161, 107163, 107239 and 107319 *LEGO Juris A/S v MAR 2000 OOD* (Invalidity Division, 18 June 2020), Case ICD 107160 *LEGO Juris A/S v MAR 2000 OOD* (Invalidity Division, 19 June 2020), and Cases ICD 107320, 107321 and 107323 *LEGO Juris A/S v MAR 2000 OOD* (Invalidity Division, 2 July 2020).

[76] For example: Case ICD 8565 *Daffy's Inc v Juan Manuel Gonzales Muriel* (Invalidity Division, 3 July 2012); Cases ICD 8705 and 8706 *GERMA-95 EOOD v Bozhentsi EOOD* (Invalidity Division, 18 September 2012); Case ICD 9024 *Top Shop International SA v SC Romarose Invest SRL* (Invalidity Division, 9 August 2013); Case ICD 9042 *Studio Moderna SA v SC Bohmann International SRL* (Invalidity Division, 30 August 2013); Case ICD 9109 *Actervis GmbH v SC Bohmann International SRL* (Invalidity Division, 9 December 2013); Case ICD 9511 *WS Invention Trade GmbH v GEO BEST SRL* (Invalidity Division, 18 November 2014).

[77] Cases ICD 8622 and 8623 *Úřad průmyslového vlastnictví v SUVENYRY.COM sro* (Invalidity Division, 16 May 2012) (Czech official state symbol).

[78] Case ICD 10266 *Unilever Polska Sp. z o.o. v Ewa Lorenc* (Invalidity Division, 31 May 2017) and Case ICD 10267 *Unilever Polska Sp. z o.o. v Ewa Lorenc* (Invalidity Division, 5 December 2016) (basic line drawings of cylinders).

[79] For example, the cases brought by various invalidity applicants against this RCD registrant: Case ICD 9038 *Thane International Inc. v Rama Star International SRL* (Invalidity Division, 6 November 2013); Case ICD 9100 *Actervis GmbH v Rama Star International SRL* (Invalidity Division, 13 December 2013); Case ICD 9098 *WS-Invention trade GmbH v Rama Star International SRL* (Invalidity Division, 16 December 2013); Case ICD 9099 *Actervis GmbH v Rama Star International SRL* (Invalidity Division, 16 December 2013); Case ICD 9663 *Etablissement AMRA v Rama Star International SRL* (Invalidity Division, 14 April 2015); Case ICD 9688 *Homeland Housewares, LLC v Rama Star International SRL* (Invalidity Division, 10 June 2015). See also n 75 above, and the multiple invalidation actions brought against this RCD registrant: Cases ICD 9289–9293, 9295–9297, 9299, 9300, 9326–9328 *Orient Home OOD v Doors Bulgaria EOOD* (Invalidity Division, 23 April 2014); Case ICD 9298 *Orient Home OOD v Doors Bulgaria EOOD* (Invalidity Division, 2 June 2014); Cases ICD 9493 and 9498 *Orient Home OOD v Doors Bulgaria EOOD* (Invalidity Division, 28 November 2014); Case ICD 9716 *Orient Home OOD v Doors Bulgaria EOOD* (Invalidity Division, 10 March 2015); Cases ICD 9729, 9731 and 9739–9740 *Sline Arc EOOD v Doors Bulgaria EOOD* (Invalidity Division, 20 July 2015); Cases ICD 10157–10160 *'Starcelikcapi' EOOD v Doors Bulgaria EOOD* (Invalidity Division, 23 November 2016); Case ICD 10114 *Star Security Door EOOD v Doors Bulgaria EOOD* (Invalidity Division, 5 December 2016); Case ICD 10111 *Star Security Door EOOD v Doors Bulgaria EOOD* (Invalidity Division, 17 January 2017); and Cases ICD 10112–10113 *Star Security Door EOOD v Doors Bulgaria EOOD* (Invalidity Division, 18 May 2017).

[80] Such as the RCD's predecessor in title or a closely linked entity such as a company of which the RCD holder was a director.

[81] For example, where it might be inferred from company names, product branding or similarity to other cases that the RCD holder and the person effecting the prior art disclosure were the same or closely related.

or are simply poorly informed or advised, all of these observed cases add to concern about the potential extent of latent RCD invalidity. Even if full mandatory *ex ante* examination were felt – after more complete appraisal – to pose too many downsides for RCD applicants, this is not the only possible solution. Possible actions stopping short of full mandatory *ex ante* examination but designed to tackle misuse of the system – such as sanctioning RCD holders whose designs are persistently invalidated by requiring a full examination of their RCD portfolio at their own expense, or removing some of the discounts for multiple design filings – have already been put forward in the literature.[82] The recent UK IPO consultation also suggested measures such as introducing a bad faith objection, or adopting an Australian-style system in which designs must be examined before they can be enforced,[83] measures which met with some support across consultation respondents.[84]

The reality is that there is good reason to suspect wide potentially high levels of latent RCD invalidity, and to be concerned about the chilling effects that this may have. Policy makers would do well to be openly live to these concerns. An RCD does not need to be successfully enforced via litigation to shut down competition or follow-on innovation. Much IP enforcement activity happens 'in the shadow of the law' without court proceedings being commenced.[85] Even if successful in RCD invalidity proceedings, the level of costs awarded has been described as 'derisory' and, if unpaid, those costs must be pursued through the 'usually uneconomic' process of suing in national courts.[86] Third parties who conduct clearance searches may decide of their own motion not to launch new designs because of apparently problematic RCDs found.[87] Lack of substantive examination may even indirectly drive some of the professed discontent with design protection that exists among designers themselves: since professional advisers must consider the risks of invalidity challenge as when advising on RCD enforcement, time and cost savings achieved by not engaging with validity during registration will be cancelled out downstream by the later necessity of addressing the issue as a precursor to RCD enforcement.[88] Adopting a policy strategy on RCD examination that places greater emphasis on quality of granted RCDs arguably has the potential not only to balance out the allocation of burdens between stakeholders in the current system and to mitigate its chilling effects, but also to improve user confidence even among RCD holders themselves.

---

[82] Filitz *et al*, n 69, 1204.

[83] UK IPO, 'Call for views' (January 2022), n 14.

[84] UK IPO, 'Analysis of responses', n 64, paras 20 and 23 in particular.

[85] See, for example: William Gallagher, 'Trademark and Copyright Enforcement in the Shadow of IP Law' (2012) 28 Santa Clara Computer & High Tech LJ 453; Jane Cornwell, 'Intellectual property litigation at the Court of Session: a first empirical investigation' (2017) 21 Edin LR 192, 199–200.

[86] Stone, n 10, paras 17.126 and 17.133–17.134.

[87] Graeme Dinwoodie, 'Federalized Functionalism: The Future of Design Protection in the European Union' (1996) 24 AIPLA Q J 611, 709–710; see also Sarah Burstein, 'Costly Designs' (2016) 77 Ohio St LJ 107, 129.

[88] As noted in the US context by D. Gerk, 'The Debate over the Preferred System for Protecting Design in the United States: Patents versus Registrations' (2008) 26 IPL Newsl 1, 18.

7.   CONCLUSION

This chapter has addressed the issue of latent RCD invalidity and the utility of increased *ex ante* examination of RCD applications by the EUIPO. Examining the evidence relied upon by the Commission in its review of EU design law and comparing RCD invalidation rates in EUIPO invalidity proceedings, I have argued that latent RCD invalidity may be more widespread than has been accepted. Presenting and analysing a new dataset exploring the invalidating prior art relied upon in Invalidity Division invalidation decisions, I have also argued that the data provides at least tentative exploratory evidence that increased *ex ante* examination of RCD filings has greater potential to assist in pre-empting the grant of invalid RCDs than has been acknowledged to date. It is argued that the Commission should re-engage with the very real concerns that have been brought to its attention over the potential extent of latent RCD invalidity and should re-open reflection on whether – through increased *ex ante* examination or other possible options – the RCD system could contain more checks and balances to avoid the wholesale granting of unmeritorious RCD registrations.

18. Empirical analysis of design litigation in Australia

Vicki Huang[1]

1. INTRODUCTION

The only constant with Australia's design law[2] is a sense of dissatisfaction and calls for reform.[3] In Australia, the turbulent history of design law has been labelled 'tortured'[4] and the regime itself the 'poor cousin'[5] of other intellectual property rights (IPRs) such as copyright, trade marks and patents. One reason (common to many countries) is the 'inevitable tension that exists between industry and art, functionality and aesthetics'.[6] Another is the ever-changing gap between the legal meaning of 'design' (historically an aesthetic addition to a functional article) and the meaning of 'design' to the modern 'design professional' with skills encompassing aesthetics, ergonomics, technology and engineering.[7] In Australia, these tensions are amplified due to a preoccupation with preventing overlapping rights, particularly lengthy copyrights which in 2004 expanded from 50 to 70 years after the death of the author.[8]

Decades of debate and discussion resulted in the new *Designs Act 2003* (Cth) (the *2003 Act*)[9] which replaced the *Designs Act 1906* (Cth) (the *1906 Act*). Under the *2003 Act*, a design registration protects the 'overall appearance of the product', where that appearance results

---

[1]   Thanks to research assistance from Eva Cotsell and Lara Ingram; many thanks to comments on earlier drafts from Estelle Derclaye, Alex Kwong and Mitchell Adams.

[2]   Collectively, the Designs Act 2003 (Cth) (2003 Act), Designs Regulations 2004 (Cth) and the Designs Examiners' Manual of Practice and Procedure. See IP Australia, Designs Examiners' Manual of Practice and Procedure <http://manuals.ipaustralia.gov.au/designs/designs_exam_manual.htm>.

[3]   S Ricketson, M Richardson, M Davison and V Huang, Intellectual Property: Cases, Material and Commentary (6th edn, LexisNexis 2019) 564, explaining that the 1906 Act was subject to only minor amendments until a major inquiry in 1973 – the Design Law Review Committee, Report on the Law Relating to Designs (1973) (Franki Report). Subsequent to that and leading up to the 2003 Act, there was also James Lahore, Inquiry into Intellectual Property Protection for Industrial Designs (Presented to Senator the Hon John Button, Minister for Industry, Technology and Commerce, Canberra, September 1991) (Lahore Report) and Australian Law Reform Commission, Designs Report, Terms of Reference (1995) 74 (ALRC Report).

[4]   Ricketson et al (n 3) 626.

[5]   Eg Christopher Sexton, 'Spotlight Focuses again on the "Poor Cousin" of Intellectual Property' (2017), June, Intellectual Property Forum 2–7.

[6]   Sam Ricketson, 'Towards a Rational Basis for the Protection of Industrial Design in Australia' (1994) 5(4) Australian Intellectual Property Journal 193, 198.

[7]   ibid 201–202 discussing Lahore Report (n 3).

[8]   Changes enacted as a result of the US Free Trade Agreement in 2004. See Copyright Act 1968 (Cth) s 34.

[9]   In force since 17 June 2004.

from 'one or more visual features',[10] but only if those features are 'new' and 'distinctive'[11] when compared with the prior art base.[12] The *2003 Act* introduced a term reduction from 16 years to 10 years (maximum),[13] addressed the copyright/design overlap issue by instituting a loss of copyright for some types of artistic works[14] and made significant changes to the laws of infringement. This chapter is the first systematic empirical study of the law of design infringement under the *2003 Act* s 71.

The next part of this chapter discusses reforms to Australia's design law and the role that empirical economic studies played in driving the reform agenda. The third part outlines the chapter's Methodology. The fourth part, Results and Discussion, sets out descriptive statistics including win rates, and tries to explain why design litigation is less common in Australian courts than under other IPRs. This involves a discussion of allied rights, and in relation to design cases, to damages, and the length of hearings. The Conclusion further argues that the cases reveal many advantages of design registration and certification, including access to additional damages and a very high win rate in courts. Publicising this could encourage designers to apply for or to certify a design registration. However, it is also argued that the nature of design law – which requires courts to craft the scope of an 'infringeable monopoly' – leads to a more involved and thus longer court process than under other IPRs such as trade mark law which may make other IPR rights more attractive.

2.   INFRINGEMENT REFORM

The current more 'rights-friendly' infringement law is a reaction to the perceived failings of the earlier *1906 Act* to protect innovative designers from copiers.[15] Under the *1906 Act* s 30, to succeed in an infringement claim the plaintiff would need to prove that the defendant had 'applied, imported, sold or hired' an article that was an 'obvious imitation' or a 'fraudulent imitation' of the registered design.[16] In addition, the scope of protection was for 'one particular

---

[10]   2003 Act s 5 (design), s 6 (definition of a product), s 7 (definition of a visual feature).
[11]   To be distinctive a design must not be 'substantially similar' in overall impression to a design that forms part of the prior art base: 2003 Act, Part 4 'Validity'.
[12]   The prior art base for a design consists of designs publicly used in Australia or published in a document anywhere in Australia or abroad: 2003 Act s 15(2).
[13]   2003 Act s 46.
[14]   For literature on the copyright/design overlap in Australia, see Isabella Alexander, 'The Copyright/ Design Interface in Australia' in E Derclaye (ed), The Copyright/Design Interface: Past, Present and Future (Cambridge University Press 2018) 226–268; Gaye Middleton, 'Copyright/Designs Overlap: The ALRC's Recommendations and the Federal Government's Response' (1999) 10 Australian Intellectual Property Journal 20; Janice Luck, 'Section 18 of the Designs Act 2003: The Neglected Copyright/Design Overlap Provision' (2013) 23 Australian Intellectual Property Journal 68; Jani McCutcheon, 'Too Many Stitches in Time? The Polo Lauren Case, Non-infringing Accessories and the Copyright/Design Overlap Defence' (2009) 20 Australian Intellectual Property Journal 39.
[15]   See eg Janice Luck, 'The Firmagroup Case: Trigger for Design Law Reform' in Andrew T Kenyon, Megan Richardson and Sam Ricketson (eds), Landmarks in Australian Intellectual Property Law (Cambridge University Press 2009) 142–159.
[16]   Designs Act 1906 (Cth) s 30.

and specific appearance'.[17] In effect, this meant that a competitor could design around that 'specific appearance' but take the inventive part of an original design.

For example, in *Firmagroup Australia Pty Ltd v Byrne & Davidson Doors (Vic) Pty Ltd*[18] (*Firmagroup trial*), the plaintiffs owned a registered design for a rectangular recessed handle and lock for shutter doors. This was lauded by the trial judge as a 'new concept of design in products of its kind'.[19] The defendants created a product with slightly different proportions but were found to have consciously copied the 'salient features' of the registered design.[20] Despite this, the trial judge found no design infringement as it was not an 'imitation' of the 'specific appearance' of the design as registered. In 1987, the High Court (Australia's apex court), affirmed this narrow construction of the infringement inquiry in *Firmagroup Australia Pty Ltd v Byrne & Davidson Doors (Vic) Pty Ltd*[21] (*Firmagroup Appeal*).

The case left many rights holders with the valid perception that 'the commercial worth of a design' could be taken without infringing it.[22] The Australian Law Reform Commission (ALRC) in 1995 captured this consternation, reporting that rights holders claimed that 'findings of infringement are made only against virtually identical designs'.[23] In this respect, the ALRC (in a footnote) cited a practitioner submission that claimed '… in 70% of design infringement trials conducted between 1980–1991 (25 reported cases), the Court did not find infringement'.[24] However, in the same footnote the ALRC noted three later cases that had been 'decided in favour of the plaintiff'.[25]

The ALRC's recommendations for reform of the infringement law were adopted in the *2003 Act*. Under the *2003 Act*, to commence infringement proceedings, a rights owner needs to have their registered design certified as valid (in Australia, approximately 15.9% of registrations are certified).[26] Under s 71, infringement is found if a person 'makes, imports or sells a product' that embodies a design that is identical to, or 'substantially similar in overall impression' to, a registered design (with more weight given to the similarities than the differences).[27] The removal of the word 'imitation' and re-orientation to focus on similarities were intended to make it easier to argue infringement under the new *2003 Act*. The reforms seemed to appease

---

[17] *Firmagroup Appeal* [1987] HCA 37, (1987) 180 CLR 483, 488.

[18] (1985) 82 FLR 311.

[19] *Firmagroup trial* (1985) 82 FLR 311, 314.

[20] *Firmagroup trial* (1985) 82 FLR 311, 319.

[21] [1987] HCA 37, (1987) 180 CLR 483.

[22] AC Archibald QC, 'Copyright Act Amendment Bill as It Affects the Designs Act and Recent Design Case Law' (1989) 8 (August) Intellectual Property Forum 4, 11 cited by Sam Ricketson (n 6) 204.

[23] ALRC Report (n 3) [6.4] <https://www.alrc.gov.au/inquiry/designs/>.

[24] ALRC Report (n 3) [6.4] footnote 370 reporting that 'LJ Dyson, Watermark Submission 211 noted that in 70% of design infringement trials conducted between 1980–1991 (25 reported cases) the court had found that differences between the articles in dispute were sufficient to avoid a finding of infringement'.

[25] ALRC Report (n 3) [6.4] footnote 370.

[26] M Falk, H Zhang, P Drake, K Lim, B Massey, B Mitra-Kahn and M Richardson, *Design Law and Practice: Design Within Australia and How Australia Compares to its International Peers* (Economic Research Paper 08, IP Australia and IPRIA 2019) <https://www.ipaustralia.gov.au/sites/default/files/reports_publications/designs_law_and_practice_0.pdf>.

[27] 2003 Act s 71. See also the exclusive rights of registered owners: 2003 Act s 10.

litigators who at the time expressed approval that under the *2003 Act* designs would be 'harder to register … but easier to protect'.[28]

2.1   Critiques of Australia's Design Law

Despite the new laws under the *2003 Act*, calls for reform were agitated a decade later[29] and again in 2019/2020.[30] These calls were energised by economic concerns, in particular the finding that Australia lags behind comparable countries in the relative use of the registered design system and concerns about the rate at which the design labour force is growing.[31] These economic studies fed into the general anxiety that Australia must 'transition to a more innovative economy'[32] and IPRs are central to this transformation.

Unfortunately, a recent 2020 economic study found 'no conclusive evidence that major changes [made by the *2003 Act*]' affected either 'demand for design rights or productivity in Australian firms'.[33] Australian design applications have been found to be small in number (2,500–3,000 applications a year between 2001 and 2017) and stagnant.[34] By contrast, the number of design applications globally has doubled each year.[35] More recent data show that design applications in Australia fell in 2019 and 2020 but grew 13% in 2021; however, this growth was attributed to applications by non-residents.[36] Indeed, non-residents constitute the majority of design applicants for Australian designs registration.[37] Among Australian designers, awareness of design rights has been found to be the lowest of all IPRs.[38]

---

[28]   See Colin Golvan, 'The Copyright/Design Overlap – An Appropriate Balance under the New Designs Legislation?' (2004) 59 Intellectual Property Forum 36, 36. See also Dale Watson, 'A New Era in Design Law' (2005) 61 Intellectual Property Forum: Journal of the Intellectual and Industrial Property Society of Australia and New Zealand 43–45.

[29]   For example, The Advisory Council on Intellectual Property (March 2015) *Review of the Designs System* <https://www.ipaustralia.gov.au/sites/default/files/acip_designs_final_report.pdf>, and The Productivity Commission (2016) *Intellectual Property Arrangements, Inquiry Report* (Final Report no 78, 23 September 2016) <https://www.pc.gov.au/inquiries/completed/intellectual-property#report>.

[30]   For example, IP Australia, 'Design Initiatives' (web page, 10 September 2021) <https://www.ipaustralia.gov.au/designs/design-initiatives>.

[31]   Falk et al (n 26) 3.

[32]   Falk et al (n 26) 22. See also, IP Australia (2020) *Valuing Designs: The Economic Impact of Design Rights in Australia* <https://www.ipaustralia.gov.au/sites/default/files/defining_design_ip _australia_report.pdf>.

[33]   T Kollmann, A Koswatta, A Palangkaraya and E Webster, *The Impact of Design Rights on Australian Firms* (Economic Research Paper 09, IP Australia and Centre for Transformative Innovation, Swinburne University of Technology 2020) <https://www.ipaustralia.gov.au/sites/default/files/reports _publications/the_impact_of_design_rights_on_australian_firms.pdf>, looking specifically at the reduction in term protection from 16 years to 10 years, the loss of copyright protection for 2-D designs and the introduction in 2013 of the Federal Circuit court.

[34]   ibid 10. Data from 2002–2017 shows a 'declining trend in the average number of design rights (applications) per employee since 2004–05 across the economy. This decline was less marked for the design rights-intensive industries'.

[35]   IP Australia, *Valuing Designs* (n 32) 7.

[36]   IP Australia (2022) *Australian Intellectual Property Report*, p 25 <https://www.ipaustralia.gov.au/ ip-report-2022>.

[37]   ibid.

[38]   IP Australia, *Protecting Designs: Design Innovation, Copying and Enforcement in Australia*, p 10 <https://www.ipaustralia.gov.au/sites/default/files/protecting_design_ip_australia_report.pdf>, finding

To address this stagnation and other perceived failures of the Australian design system, IP Australia[39] conducted an extensive holistic review which concluded in 2020.[40] Four research reports were published, including a report titled *Protecting Designs: Design Innovation, Copying and Enforcement in Australia*. That report surveyed 254 Australian designers (140 from industry, 114 from design and patent applicants) to capture their views on IP enforcement (the IP Australia survey).[41] The survey revealed that 47% of industry respondents did not typically seek any form of formal or informal design protection.[42]

For those respondents who became aware of copying, 23%–34% of respondents (applicants/ industry, respectively) reported taking no action to enforce their rights.[43] The respondents cited the high cost of enforcement as a primary deterrent,[44] but also reported feeling intimidated by the alleged copier (owing to its relative size) and fears that the case would be difficult to prove.[45] The report found that 'the estimated median financial loss from any particular design being copied was in the $50,000 to $100,000 range', with the estimated spend on enforcement being one-tenth of this at $5,000–$10,000.[46]

For those who did take action, the survey found sending a cease and desist letter or a letter of demand was the most frequent action.[47] The least frequent action was court-based litigation.[48] The next most popular action was seeking legal advice followed by social media shaming of the copier.[49] Unfortunately the most common response to such actions 'was no response from the other party'; moreover, 'fewer than one in five [designers] reported that their actions had resulted in the other party permanently stopping copying'.[50]

Although the survey reflects views of enforcement generally (ie beyond just court-based litigation), the defeatist nature of the views marks a sad contrast to the optimistic assessments expressed by litigators at the inception of the *2003 Act*. Today, some practitioners argue that the survey results suggest '... a lack of faith in the ability of the registered design system to protect and enforce Australian designs'.[51]

It is impossible to pinpoint one factor that has led to this fatalistic view. The pessimistic views of designers may even partly be a legacy of the *Firmagroup Appeal* in 1987. Regardless, economists have made interesting suggestions as to how to change course. For example, Kollmann et al suggest that negative perceptions may be influenced by a landmark case or

---

that in an industry survey, '66% reported being aware of design rights, compared with 100% for copyright, 99% for trade marks and 98% for patents'.

[39] IP Australia is responsible for the registration and administration of IP rights and legislation. See <https://www.ipaustralia.gov.au/>.

[40] IP Australia, 'Design Initiatives' (web page, 10 September 2021) <https://www.ipaustralia.gov.au/designs/design-initiatives>.

[41] IP Australia, *Protecting Designs* (n 38).

[42] ibid 4.

[43] ibid 5.

[44] ibid 5.

[45] ibid 14.

[46] ibid 5.

[47] ibid 15.

[48] ibid 15.

[49] ibid 15.

[50] ibid 15.

[51] Amelia Causley-Todd and Marina Olsen, 'Designs Act Amendments: Total Renovation or Superficial Touch-up?' (July 2021) Australian IP Law Bulletin 68, 70.

empirical evidence that counters the defeatist narrative.[52] They argue: '[I]f changes in perception are profound and widespread, it is possible that firms that otherwise would not use the design rights system can be convinced that it is worthwhile to use it'.[53] As an example, the authors highlight European research by Church et al, which found that registered rights were frequently enforced in European Union (EU) courts and that '63.5% of designs overall across Member States are infringed while 36.5% are not'.[54]

2.2   Empirical Studies of Court-Based Enforcement of Design Rights

Since then there have been further empirical studies such as Church et al who examined overlapping claims in design litigation and found that while 'the problem of genuine overlaps exists, courts overall apply the law well'.[55] In a United Kingdom (UK) context, Grist found that design rights (unregistered and registered) were enforced in UK courts with an average success rate of 66%.[56] Grist argued that the results dispel 'the myth that it is unduly difficult to succeed in design cases before the English courts'.[57] In Australia, Huang found a win rate of 71% in fashion design cases where litigation is pursued under multiple causes of action.[58]

This study can be distinguished as it focuses on enforcement of statutory design rights solely under the current *2003 Act*. This study identifies and examines all design infringement cases under the *2003 Act* since inception (17 June 2004 – 17 June 2022). It is hoped that better information about the enforcement of statutory design rights at the court level will go some way to validate or reverse the moribund view of Australia's design law at the industry and applicant level.

---

[52]   Kollmann et al (n 33) 27–28.
[53]   ibid 27.
[54]   Oliver Church, Estelle Derclaye and Gilles Stupfler, 'An Empirical Analysis of the Design Case Law of the EU Member States' (2019) 50 International Review of Intellectual Property and Competition Law 685, 704.
[55]   Oliver Church, Estelle Derclaye and Gilles Stupfler, 'Design Litigation in the EU Member States: Are Overlaps with Other Intellectual Property Rights and Unfair Competition Problematic and Are SMEs Benefiting from the EU Design Legal Framework?' (2021) 46(1) European Law Review 37, 38.
[56]   E Grist, 'Enforcing Design in the UK – Easier Than You Might Think?' (2019) <https://designwrites.law/enforcing-design-in-the-uk-easier-than-you-might-think/>. Grist examined 35 cases over 13 years to 2019.
[57]   ibid.
[58]   Vicki Huang, 'An Empirical Analysis of the Fashion Design Case Law of Australia' (2021) 52(3) International Review of Intellectual Property and Competition Law 242.

3.   METHODOLOGY

3.1   Sample and Coding

This study identified first instance decisions where there was a substantive discussion[59] of the *2003 Act* s 71 in Australian state or federal courts[60] between 17 June 2004 and 17 June 2022 (18 years). The scope was limited to reasoning of first instance decisions, irrespective of posture. Thus, the dataset included first instance decisions where the case could be an application for an interim injunction or a full trial on the merits.[61] Since this study focused on understanding infringement, the dataset included two cases in which there had been a substantive discussion of infringement, but the underlying design had been found invalid.[62] Despite this broad mandate, only 15 cases were identified for the 18-year period.

These cases were coded for descriptive information such as hearing days; and also for legal reasoning on design law or any concurrent claims. This is because Australian designers can pursue concurrent claims against an alleged infringer. This may include pressing unregistered rights under the *Copyright Act 1968* (Cth) (*Copyright Act*), the common law tort of passing off, or breach of statutory consumer protection laws.[63] They may also pursue their registered (or certified) rights under the *2003 Act, Patents Act 1990* (Cth) or *Trade Marks Act 1995* (Cth) (*Trade Marks Act*).

To obtain a comparison of win rates under the old *1906 Act*, cases of infringement under the *1906 Act* s 30 were identified for the 18-year period prior to 17 June 2004, that is, from 17 June 1986. Only descriptive data and win rates were coded for this subset.

3.2   Limitations

It is recognised that empirical studies of court-based enforcement have limitations. For example, many cases commenced in court may settle prior to a hearing.[64] Further, many disputes are pursued and settled by letters of demand.[65] It is acknowledged that court-reported cases can only represent a small fraction of disputes that occur in the marketplace.

In addition, the number of cases in the dataset is small. Descriptive statistics based on a small number of cases are sensitive to change if a small number of new cases are added to the dataset. Nevertheless, the cases cover the entire population of available cases in the period

---

[59]   As with similar empirical studies, this means 'use beyond mere citation without analysis': Vicki Huang, 'An Empirical Investigation of 20 Years of Trade Mark Infringement Litigation in Australian Courts' (2019) 41 Sydney Law Review 105.

[60]   Most IP litigation is heard in the Federal Court of Australia. Less complex cases can be heard in the Federal Circuit Court. State courts also have jurisdiction (eg 2003 Act s 73(2)).

[61]   Huang, '20 Years of Trade Mark Infringement' (n 59) 116.

[62]   Only one case under the 2003 Act: *Rosemin Pty Ltd v Gasp Jeans Chadstone Pty Ltd* [2010] FCA 228, only one case under 1906 Act: *JMVB Enterprises Pty Ltd v Camoflag Pty Ltd* [2005] FCA 1474, (2005) 67 IPR 68.

[63]   Typically s 18 of the Australian Consumer Law, Competition and Consumer Act 2010 (Cth) Schedule 2 (ACL). Formerly the Trade Practices Act 1974 (Cth) (TPA).

[64]   Kevin M Clermont and Theodore Eisenberg, 'Do Case Outcomes Really Reveal Anything about the Legal System? Win Rates and Removal Jurisdiction' (1998) 83 Cornell Law Review 581.

[65]   Michael Campbell and Lana Halperin, 'Redesigning Designs: The Future of Design Protection in Australia' (2020) 121 Intellectual Property Forum 9, 15.

of inquiry so are in this sense representative. Still, this study does not make any predictive statements and inferences are only drawn with caution.

4.   RESULTS AND DISCUSSION

4.1   What Types of Objects Are Litigated in Courts?

Table 18.1 shows the frequency of cases by Locarno class type.[66] The majority of cases related to fashion garments. Over half of the cases involved repeat plaintiffs, for example, *Review Australia Pty Ltd* (three cases), *LED Technologies* (two cases), *GM Holden* (two cases) and *Multisteps* (two cases).

Table 18.1   Design classes in litigation (2004–2022, n = 15)

Locarno Class No	Locarno Class	Number of Cases
2	Articles of Clothing and Haberdashery[a]	5
12	Means of Transport or Hoisting[b]	2
14	Recording, Telecommunication or Data Processing Equipment[c]	2
26	Lighting Apparatus[d]	2
9	Packaging and Containers for the Transport or Handling of Goods[e]	2
13	Equipment for Production, Distribution or Transformation of Electricity[f]	1
23	Fluid Distribution Equipment, Sanitary, Heating, Ventilation and Air Conditioning Equipment, Solid Fuel[g]	1

Notes:
[a] *Review Australia Pty Ltd v Innovative Lifestyle Investments Pty Ltd* [2008] FCA 74, (2008) 166 FCR 358; *Review 2 Pty Ltd v Redberry Enterprise Pty Ltd* [2008] FCA 1588, (2008) 173 FCR 450; *Review Australia Pty Ltd v New Cover Group Pty Ltd* [2008] FCA 1589, (2008) 79 IPR 236; *Rosemin Pty Ltd v Gasp Jeans Chadstone Pty Ltd* [2010] FCA 228; *Ahiida Pty Ltd v JB Trading Group Pty Ltd* [2016] FCCA 3146.
[b] *GM Holden Ltd v Paine* [2011] FCA 569, (2011) 281 ALR 406; *GM Global Technology Operations LLC v SSS Auto Parts Pty Ltd* [2019] FCA 97, (2019) 371 ALR 1.
[c] *PositiveG Trust v Li* [2020] FCCA 2548; *GME Pty Ltd v Uniden Australia Pty Ltd* [2022] FCA 520, (2022) 166 IPR 551.
[d] *LED Technologies Pty Ltd v Elecspess Pty Ltd* [2008] FCA 1941, (2008) 80 IPR 85; *LED Technologies Pty Ltd v Roadvision Pty Ltd* [2011] FCA 146, (2011) 90 IPR 532.
[e] *Multisteps Pty Ltd v Source & Sell Pty Ltd* [2013] FCA 743, (2013) 214 FCR 323; *Multisteps Pty Ltd v Specialty Packaging Aust Pty Ltd* [2018] FCA 587, (2018) 132 IPR 399.
[f] *Bitek Pty Ltd v IConnect Pty Ltd* [2012] FCA 133.
[g] *GME Pty Ltd v Uniden Australia Pty Ltd* [2022] FCA 520, (2022) 166 IPR 551.

The overall profile provided in Table 18.1 is consistent with Australian registration data that reveal 'Australians focus heavily on clothing, building units and construction elements, furnishing, and tools/hardware'.[67] These have been called 'industries with short design life-

---

[66]   Although Australia is not a signatory to the Locarno Agreement, IP Australia's Design Classification Codes adopt the Locarno classifications for product type: IP Australia, 'Classification: Classification Systems', Designs Examiners' Manual of Practice and Procedure (7 April 2022) <https://manuals.ipaustralia.gov.au/design/classification-systems>.
[67]   Falk et al (n 26) 14.

cycles'.[68] In contrast, non-resident applicants focus on 'telecommunication and computing equipment manufacturing, packaging, medical and laboratory equipment'.[69] A closer examination of the cases reveals that the 14/15 plaintiffs were Australian-based businesses.[70]

Bearing in mind the small number of cases, this latter finding may refute a prediction made by IP Australia that non-residents may have a greater appetite for legal enforcement than Australian residents. IP Australia's hypothesis was based on a finding that between 2005 and 2016, only 15.9% of registrations were certified and thus enforceable.[71] Of these, only 34.8% were from Australian residents, that is, the majority of certifications were requested by non-resident filers.[72] IP Australia proposed that non-residents pursued certification because it could 'reflect norms in their home countries, where legal action against infringement may be relatively more common'.[73] However, this is not reflected in the profile of cases pursued to judgment, in which the majority of plaintiffs were Australian. Nevertheless, this may not completely negate IP Australia's hypothesis, since it is possible that non-residents do pursue legal action but stop short of court-based enforcement.

4.2   Winning and Losing

Starting with the older statute first, Figure 18.1 below shows that from 1988, 27 infringement cases were decided under the *1906 Act* s 30, and that the last case was decided in 2013.[74] Looking at cases under the current *2003 Act*, Figure 18.1 shows that 15 infringement cases were decided under the *2003 Act* s 71, and that the first case was decided in 2008.[75] The stacked bars show the proportion of winning and losing cases for that year and under the relevant statute.

4.2.1   Infringement under the old *Designs Act 1906* (Cth)
Observing the win/loss rates under the *1906 Act*, it is evident that from 1988 there was a 70% win rate (19/27 cases). This runs counter to the sentiment reported by the ALRC in 1995 that the courts were too friendly towards alleged infringers. However, it should be noted that all 27 cases were decided after the High Court's decision in *Firmagroup*.[76] Possibly, the clear (albeit narrow) construction set down in that case led to only confident plaintiffs with strong claims bringing cases to court.

---

[68]   ibid 5.
[69]   ibid 14.
[70]   *GM Global Technology Operations LLC v SSS Auto Parts Pty Ltd* [2019] FCA 97, (2019) 371 ALR 1, although the action involved infringements against the Australian subsidiary GM Holden Ltd (Holden).
[71]   Falk et al (n 26) 14.
[72]   ibid 14.
[73]   ibid 14.
[74]   *Gram Engineering Pty Ltd v Bluescope Steel Ltd* [2013] FCA 508, (2013) 106 IPR 1.
[75]   *Review Australia Pty Ltd v Innovative Lifestyle Investments Pty Ltd* [2008] FCA 74, (2008) 166 FCR 358.
[76]   [1987] HCA 37, (1987) 180 CLR 483.

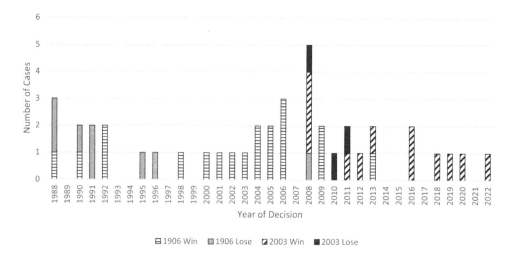

Figure 18.1   1988–2022, design infringement cases n = 42

4.2.2   Infringement under the *Designs Act 2003* (Cth)

Figure 18.1 shows that under the *2003 Act*, there were 15 cases, with an 80% win rate (12/15 cases). These win rates seem high in the context of the Priest–Klein 'divergent expectations model' of litigation, which predicts a 50/50 win/loss ratio where all parties are rational and fully informed.[77] The win rate is also high relative to other Australian empirical IPR studies that use similar methods of case coding. For example, Huang identified a win rate in trade mark litigation of 51%,[78] while Australian empirical studies of patent litigation have inferred a 48% win rate.[79]

Nonetheless, empirical studies of design litigation have also found win rates well above 50%. As discussed earlier, UK[80] and EU[81] studies found win rates above 60%. Similarly, in relation to Australia, Huang found a win rate of 71% in fashion litigation when looking across rights pursued across various causes of action.[82]

---

[77]   George L Priest and Benjamin Klein, 'The Selection of Disputes for Litigation' (1984) 13 The Journal of Legal Studies 1.

[78]   Huang, '20 Years of Trade Mark Infringement' (n 59) 119; Kimberlee G Weatherall and Paul H Jensen, 'An Empirical Investigation into Patent Enforcement in Australian Courts' (2005) 33(2) Federal Law Review 239, 280.

[79]   Weatherall and Jensen (n 78) 280. The authors coded each decision as having up to two determinations, a validity determination and an infringement determination (p 260). Looking at infringement allegations, the authors, at p 280, identified 31 original infringement determinations for 1997–2003 and found 15/31 (48%) determinations where all allegations were upheld and 16/31 (52%) where no allegations were upheld.

[80]   Grist (n 56).

[81]   Church et al, 'An Empirical Analysis' (n 54) 685.

[82]   Huang, 'Fashion Design Case Law' (n 58).

4.2.3 Winning and losing on appeal

Of the 15 cases decided under the *2003 Act*, three cases went to appeal. Of these, two appellate courts affirmed the win of the design owner[83] and one affirmed the loss of the design owner.[84] In other words, 100% of the time (n = 3) the appellate court affirmed the findings on design infringement made by the first instance court.

4.2.4 Validity

There were 8/15 cases in which validity was disputed in an infringement case. Given Australian rights holders need to have the validity of the design certified to enforce their rights,[85] it is not surprising that in the eight cases where validity was challenged, the validity of the design was upheld in seven of those cases.[86]

Bearing in mind the small dataset, the win rate of 80%, the affirmations on appeal and the positive findings on validity appear to support claims made at the inception of the *2003 Act* that infringement would be easier to prove under the new laws.

4.3 IPR Litigation Circa 2008 – Clarifying Overlaps and Other Rights

Figure 18.1 above shows that statutory design litigation peaked in 2008. Four infringement cases were decided in 2008, three of which were brought by the same plaintiff, fashion retailer Review Australia. After 2008, there were only one or two cases under *2003 Act* s 71 each year. These early cases (2008–2010) represented three wins and two losses for rights holders. These cases likely clarified the operation of the infringement provisions for future plaintiffs with only more confident plaintiffs pursuing cases in 2011–2022 (where there were nine wins and one loss).

In addition, it is proposed that around 2008–2010, several other tangential laws were being clarified by Australian courts. These cases may have influenced views on IPR litigation strategy. In relation to the copyright/design overlap, Alexander notes that in 2007 and 2008, the High Court[87] and the federal courts[88] were untangling the new and complex copyright/design overlap provisions. These cases provided greater clarity on threshold questions of functionality and whether an artistic work had become embodied in a design. In other words, courts clarified when a product 'fell out of copyright' and should (or could) have been registered as a design.

In addition to copyright/design overlaps, it is proposed that around this time greater clarity emerged over trade mark and design overlaps. For example, in relation to trade mark law and designs, in 2008 and 2009 there was a cluster of trade mark infringement decisions relating to 3D shapes. The registered shape marks were essentially the product itself, for example, a tool

---

[83] *LED Technologies Pty Ltd v Elecspess Pty Ltd* [2008] FCA 1941, (2008) 80 IPR 85; *GM Holden Ltd v Paine* [2011] FCA 569, (2011) 281 ALR 406.

[84] *LED Technologies Pty Ltd v Roadvision Pty Ltd* [2011] FCA 146, (2011) 90 IPR 532.

[85] 2003 Act (Cth) s 73(3).

[86] Validity was not found in the case of *Rosemin Pty Ltd v Gasp Jeans Chadstone Pty Ltd* [2010] FCA 228 – invalid owing to prior publication.

[87] Alexander (n 14) 261, discussing *Burge v Swarbrick* [2007] HCA 17, (2007) 232 CLR 336.

[88] ibid 262, discussing *Digga Australia v Norm Engineering* [2008] FCAFC 33, (2008) 166 FCR 268, and *Polo/Lauren Co. LP v Ziliani Holdings Pty Ltd* [2008] FCA 49, (2008) 75 IPR 143.

for a fence,[89] shoes[90] and a chair.[91] The trade mark owners lost their infringement suits in all three cases. The holdings in these cases re-emphasised that a defendant's use of the functional aspect of a plaintiff's registered trade mark is not 'use' (as a badge of origin) that can sustain an infringement action under s 120 of the *Trade Marks Act*. These cases may have instructed designers on how to future proof a 3D shape mark for enforcement purposes or convinced them that design rights would be better for their products than a 3D shape mark.

Further support for the argument that clarity was emerging around the 3D trade mark/design overlap, can be drawn from a recent empirical study of registration data by Adams.[92] Adams found that from 1996 (when shape trade marks were registrable in Australia) to 2006, nearly 20% of shape trade marks had an equivalent design on the designs register.[93] Adams found that after 2006, domestic overlap applications declined which he speculates could be due to difficulties in proving trade mark registration requirements such as the capacity to distinguish.[94] This knowledge, combined with an awareness of the outcomes of shape trade mark infringement litigation, could have provided further clarity to applicants about the poor cost/benefit ratio of holding overlapping trade mark and design rights. Clarity in the law may have encouraged candidates into submitting better quality applications to either design or trade mark registers, but not both.

Also around this time, statutory consumer law continued to play a role in IPR-related enforcement. In 2011, the Full Court of the Federal Court found in favour of Bodum, who claimed its famous coffee plunger product was being copied and imported by the defendant. In *Peter Bodum A/S v DKSH Australia Pty Ltd*,[95] the designer/plaintiff did not have a registered design or trade mark over the shape of its coffee plunger. Bodum claimed the defendant breached common law passing off and statutory consumer law provisions by importing a similar looking coffee plunger.[96] In finding for Bodum, the majority found that Bodum had a significant reputation in the features and shape of its coffee plunger, such that the defendant's absence of distinguishing labelling could mislead potential purchasers. The decision was controversial, particularly because where registered rights are available, it is assumed that courts frown upon those that fail to use them. Scardamaglia has argued that for designers with a significant reputation in a design, the application of consumer protection law provided 'another avenue of protection for traders against rivals with products using similar designs'.[97]

In summary (and bearing in mind the small dataset), the peak and subsequent fall in design infringement cases after 2008 could be explained by design infringement laws being clarified by close cases in 2008–2010 (three wins/two losses). It is argued here that contemporaneously,

---

[89] *Mayne Industries Pty Ltd v Advanced Engineering Group Pty Ltd* [2008] FCA 27, (2008) 166 FCR 312.

[90] *Global Brand Marketing Inc v YD Pty Ltd* [2008] FCA 605, (2008) 76 IPR 161.

[91] *Sebel Furniture Ltd v Acoustic & Felts Pty Ltd* [2009] FCA 6, (2009) 80 IPR 244.

[92] Mitchell Adams's thesis 'Empirical Studies of Non-Traditional Signs in Australian Trade Mark Law', chapter 5, The trade mark and design overlap, p 218 <https://researchbank.swinburne.edu.au/items/cd9df6d2-60a0-455a-a46b-990bf334462e/1/>.

[93] ibid 218.

[94] ibid 217.

[95] [2011] FCAFC 98, (2011) 280 ALR 639.

[96] At that time ss 52 and 53 of the Trade Practices Act 1974 (Cth). See footnote (n 63).

[97] Amanda Scardamaglia, 'Protecting Product Shapes and Features: Beyond Design and Trade Marks in Australia' (2012) 7(3) Journal of Intellectual Property Law & Practice 159, 161.

further clarity surrounding designs and allied rights in copyright, trade mark and consumer protection law emerged around this time. All of these factors could have impacted IPR strategies and led to only more confident plaintiffs pursuing statutory design infringement in the courts from 2011 (nine wins, one loss).

Finally, in relation to litigating under concurrent claims, only five of the 15 cases showed pursuit of concurrent claims under trade marks,[98] s 18/passing off[99] or patents,[100] but no concurrent claims under copyright. Only for the two patent cases could there be said to be a genuine overlap of rights. Design rights protect the product appearance, but a patent can protect the underlying function of the product. Where the function and form are closely related (eg ergonomic chairs), Australian law allows for overlapping rights.[101] It appears that the legislatures' efforts to demarcate design law are reflected in the singularity of design infringement litigation. The majority (10/15 cases) are determined as a single cause of action under the *2003 Act*. This contrasts with Australian trade mark[102] and copyright[103] litigation where concurrent claims are common.

4.4   Discussing Damages

The cases in the dataset also provide instruction in relation to damages. Under s 75(1) a plaintiff can elect damages or an account of profits. The latter may be unappealing if the infringer has sold a much cheaper version of the plaintiff's design. In the six cases where damages claims were reported, only one succeeded in establishing compensatory damages for lost sales.[104] The difficulty in establishing compensatory damages is because courts use a market substitutes approach. In other words, but for the existence of the infringing product would the consumer have bought the plaintiff's goods?[105] If no, then damages will be zero. This analysis is done on a product-by-product basis.

For example, Jessup J in *Review v Innovative*[106] described casual dresses as 'highly discretionary goods', refusing to accept that sales of the infringing dress represented lost sales of the plaintiff's dress.[107] This is not a blanket approach to garments. For example, Emmett J in

---

[98]   *GM Holden Ltd v Paine* [2011] FCA 569, (2011) 281 ALR 406.

[99]   *LED Technologies Pty Ltd v Elecspess Pty Ltd* [2008] FCA 1941, (2008) 80 IPR 85; *GM Holden Ltd v Paine* [2011] FCA 569, (2011) 281 ALR 406; *GM Global Technology Operations LLC v SSS Auto Parts Pty Ltd* (2019) [2019] FCA 97, 371 ALR 1.

[100]   *Multisteps Pty Ltd v Source & Sell Pty Ltd* [2013] FCA 743, (2013) 214 FCR 323; *Multisteps Pty Ltd v Specialty Packaging Aust Pty Ltd* [2018] FCA 587, (2018) 132 IPR 399.

[101]   The Productivity Commission (n 29).

[102]   Huang, '20 Years of Trade Mark Infringement' (n 59) 124, finding that 61/78 cases pleaded trade mark infringement alongside passing off and statutory consumer protection law.

[103]   Eg *Burge v Swarbrick* [2007] HCA 17, (2007) 232 CLR 336; *Polo/Lauren Co. LP v Ziliani Holdings Pty Ltd* [2008] FCA 49, (2008) 75 IPR 143; *Seafolly Pty Ltd v Fewstone Pty Ltd* [2014] FCA 321, (2014) 106 IPR 85.

[104]   For a successful claim for compensatory damages see *PositiveG Trust v Li* [2020] FCCA 2548 [81] awarding $7,175.55 for lost sales.

[105]   See eg *Review Australia Pty Ltd v Innovative Lifestyle Investments Pty Ltd* [2008] FCA 74, (2008) 166 FCR 358; see also *LED Technologies Pty Ltd v Elecspess Pty Ltd* [2008] FCA 1941, (2008) 80 IPR 85.

[106]   (2008) 166 FCR 358.

[107]   See *Review Australia Pty Ltd v Innovative Lifestyle Investments Pty Ltd* [2008] FCA 74, (2008)166 FCR 358 per Jessup [27], 365.

Ahiida[108] dealing with 'Burkinis' (Islamic swimwear sets) found that the product and market were highly specialised which favoured the plaintiff's argument for damages based on lost sales. Nevertheless, the plaintiff struggled to evidence the claim that 'but for' the sales of the defendant they 'would have sold the equivalent numbers'.[109]

Due to the difficulties with establishing compensatory damages, plaintiffs have instead put their general damages claim on other grounds such as loss of reputation with a modicum of success.[110] However, the evidentiary bar for this can be burdensome for a small business. For example, in *Ahiida*,[111] the court found no evidence of reputational damage despite agreeing that the market was unique and specialised and the defendant admitted to infringement.[112]

As general or compensatory damages have been difficult to prove, pleading 'additional damages' under s 75(3) has been important and fruitful with five out of five plaintiffs claiming additional damages being rewarded.[113] Under s 75(3), '[T]he court may award such additional damages as it considers appropriate, having regard to the flagrancy of the infringement and all other relevant matters'. Importantly, additional damages under s 75(3) have been found where the defendant has been put on notice of the plaintiff's registered design right,[114] for example, by way of letter of demand[115] or the words 'Registered Design' on packaging.[116] Additional damages have also been awarded where there was 'a history of non-response' or 'inadequate response' by the defendant.[117]

Awareness of the fact that additional damages claims are rewarded by courts – and that access to such damages comes through notice of a plaintiff's registered rights – could provide an incentive for designers to register and/or certify their design rights. Communication of this fact could balance out the more pessimistic view that claimants may have regarding the paucity of general or compensatory damages.

---

108 [2016] FCCA 3146.

109 [2016] FCCA 3146 [56].

110 Eg *Review Australia Pty Ltd v Innovative Lifestyle Investments Pty Ltd* [2008] FCA 74, (2008) 166 FCR 358 [31] awarding $7,500 for 'probable diminution of the applicant's reputation for originality'; *Review Australia Pty Ltd v New Cover Group Pty Ltd* [2008] FCA 1589, (2008) 79 IPR 236 [41]–[46] awarding $35,000 for 'diminution in the value of the design as a chose in action'; *GM Holden Ltd v Paine* [2011] FCA 569, (2011) 281 ALR 406 [89]–[93] awarding $20,000 for damage to reputation.

111 [2016] FCCA 3146.

112 [61]–[69].

113 Additional damages awarded in: *Review Australia Pty Ltd v Innovative Lifestyle Investments Pty Ltd* [2008] FCA 74, (2008) 166 FCR 358 ($10,000); *Review Australia Pty Ltd v New Cover Group Pty Ltd* [2008] FCA 1589, (2008) 79 IPR 236 ($50,000); *GM Holden Ltd v Paine* [2011] FCA 569, (2011) 281 ALR 406 ($10,000); *Ahiida Pty Ltd v JB Trading Group Pty Ltd* [2016] FCCA 3146 ($20,000); *PositiveG Trust v Li* [2020] FCCA 2548 ($25,000).

114 Under 2003 Act s 75(4): '[I]t is prima facie evidence that the defendant was aware that the design was registered if the product embodying the registered design to which the infringement proceedings relate, or the packaging of the product, is marked so as to indicate registration of the design'.

115 See eg *GM Holden Ltd v Paine* [2011] FCA 569, (2011) 281 ALR 406, [90]–[100].

116 See eg *LED Technologies Pty Ltd v Elecspess Pty Ltd* [2008] FCA 1941, (2008) 80 IPR 85, [93]. In relation to swing tags, see *Review Australia Pty Ltd v Innovative Lifestyle Investments Pty Ltd* [2008] FCA 74, (2008) 166 FCR 358; cf *Review Australia Pty Ltd v New Cover Group Pty Ltd* [2008] FCA 1589, (2008) 79 IPR 236.

117 See eg *PositiveG Trust v Li* [2020] FCCA 2548, [100]. See *Review Australia Pty Ltd v New Cover Group Pty Ltd* [2008] FCA 1589, (2008) 79 IPR 236 – New Cover's refusal to participate in the proceedings supported an award of $50,000 additional damages.

4.5   Discussion of Trial Days

The majority of design infringement cases are brought in the Federal Court of Australia (FCA).[118] From 2007, FCA registries[119] began to introduce 'Fast Track' mechanisms for 'parties to seek a quicker or truncated hearing process' of no more than five days and the use of more informal pleadings.[120] From 15 April 2013, less complex IPR matters (excluding patents) could be heard in the Federal Circuit Court (formerly the Federal Magistrates Court).[121] Of the seven cases heard after 2013, only two were brought to the Federal Circuit Court, with the balance heard by the Federal Courts of Australia.

The average length of a hearing for all 15 cases was 4.8 days. Bearing in mind the small dataset, the following cautious observations can be made. The 4.8 hearing days (n = 15) is longer than the average trade mark hearing of 3.7 days,[122] but less than estimates of patent trials, which have been found to average 11 days.[123] Six of the 15 cases were coded as 'under-contested'. In those cases, there was an admission of similarity, the sale of counterfeit products, or a default or summary judgment. These cases resolved on average within 2.3 days. In the nine cases where infringement was contested, the hearings were on average 6.7 days long.

4.5.1   Explaining the length of contested design infringement hearings

Contested design infringement hearings are comparatively long in contrast to trade marks disputes and Fast Track cases. Assuming hearing length is a proxy for the complexity of the dispute, a closer reading of the cases can reveal where litigants may face expensive hurdles. The cases show that courts are frequently engaging with witnesses and other evidence in relation to difficult questions concerning the 'informed user', the 'prior art' and the scope for innovative 'design freedom'.[124] An argument can be made that the labour of the courts is caused by the underlying policy of the *2003 Act* itself. The frequent maxim being that Australian design law does not 'prevent copying per se' but only protects demonstrable design advances over the prior art.[125]

---

[118]   Civil proceedings can also be brought in the State Supreme Court.

[119]   Eg, the 'Fast Track List' was introduced into the Victorian Federal Court Registry in 2007 and subsequently other states to 'streamline court procedures and thereby significantly reduce the costs of litigation'. See <http://www.fedcourt.gov.au/case-management-services/case-allocation/fast-track-system#key>.

[120]   P A Keane, Chief Justice, *Practice Note CM 8 Fast Track* [2.3] 'The Court expects that the Fast Track Directions will not apply to a proceeding: (a) the trial of which is likely to exceed 5 days' <http://www.fedcourt.gov.au/law-and-practice/practice-documents/practice-notes/cm8>. Note, this practice note was revoked 25 October 2016. Nevertheless, the Fast Track rules continue, but have expanded to give effect to matters beyond intellectual property and commercial cases. See, J L B Allsop, Chief Justice Federal Court of Australia, *Intellectual Property Practice Note (IP-1)*, [4.5] <www.fedcourt.gov.au/law-and-practice/practice-documents/practice-notes/ip-1>.

[121]   Formerly known as the Federal Magistrates Court.

[122]   Huang, '20 Years of Trade Mark Infringement' (n 59) 124 finding trademark litigation, including with concurrent claims, took on average 3.7 days (n = 78).

[123]   Weatherall and Jensen (n 78) 263.

[124]   2003 Act s 19 'Factors to be considered in assessing substantial similarity in overall impression'.

[125]   See eg Ricketson et al (n 3) 562, discussing the Lahore Report (n 3) 23. See also Nicholas J in *Hunter Pacific International Pty Ltd v Martec Pty Ltd* [2016] FCA 796, (2016) 121 IPR 1, [47], stating that registered designs must 'not impede the natural and ordinary growth of industry by preventing others

This policy approach manifests itself in two ways in relation to infringement. First, the court needs to construct the scope of what this article terms 'the plaintiff's infringeable monopoly'. This contrasts to trade mark law where the scope of the owner's monopoly is apparent on the face of the registration. Construction of the 'infringeable monopoly' is determined by reference to statutory factors such as the prior art (s 19(2)(a)). Under s 19, if there are 'small differences between the registered design and the prior art', then there will be 'no infringement if there are equally small differences between the registered design and the alleged infringing article'.[126] Other factors include s 19(2)(d), which requires the court to consider 'the freedom of the creator of the design to innovate'. Where there is limited scope for innovation, more weight will be given to small differences between the products.[127]

This approach contrasts with the infringement inquiry under trade mark law, where the scope of the owner's monopoly is prima facie the registration, and similarity determinations are allowed to be impressionistic. In contrast, courts in design cases reiterate that similarity cannot be 'based merely on a casual comparison between designs for a given article'.[128] Rather, the approach is 'a studied comparison based on the prescriptions of s19 of the *2003 Act*. ..., the notion of "imperfect recollection" – familiar in trade mark law – has no application when determining design similarity ...'.[129]

4.5.2   Construing the 'infringeable monopoly' – case studies

Examples illustrating the complex and nuanced approach of the courts can be seen in the contrasting outcomes in *Review 2 Pty Ltd v Redberry Enterprise Pty Ltd* (2008) 173 FCR 450 (*Redberry*) and *LED Technologies Pty Ltd v Elecspess Pty Ltd* (2008) 80 IPR 85 (*LED*).

In *Redberry*, Review Australia Pty Ltd (Review) was the owner of design registration No 307708 (the Review Design).[130] The Review Design was described as a dress design for a sleeveless, cross-over or fixed-wrap dress in an orange, brown and blue frond leaf pattern.[131]

Review alleged that Redberry's dress infringed the registered design. The Redberry dress was described as a sleeveless, cross-over or fixed-wrap dress but in chocolate brown with a 'bold floral pattern of leaves in light cream, peach and brown'.[132] Justice Kenny found

---

from making products that have features of shape and configuration that are common to a trade'. See also *Review Australia Pty Ltd v Innovative Lifestyle Investments Pty Ltd* [2008] FCA 74, (2008) 166 FCR 358 per Jessup J stating at [54], 'I must recognize that the policy of the *Designs Act* is not to prevent copying per se'.

[126]   *Hunter Pacific International Pty Ltd v Martec Pty Ltd* [2016] FCA 796, (2016) 121 IPR 1 [44].

[127]   See eg *GME Pty Ltd v Uniden Australia Pty Ltd* [2022] FCA 520, (2022) 166 IPR 551 at [37] citing the ALRC Report, [5.24]; see also *Review 2 Pty Ltd v Redberry Enterprise Pty Ltd* [2008] FCA 1588, (2008) 173 FCR 450.

[128]   Yates J in *Multisteps Pty Ltd v Source & Sell Pty Ltd* [2013] FCA 743, (2013) 214 FCR 323, affirmed by *Hunter Pacific International Pty Ltd v Martec Pty Ltd* [2016] FCA 796, (2016) 121 IPR 1, [39]; *GME Pty Ltd v Uniden Australia Pty Ltd* [2022] FCA 520, (2022) 166 IPR 551, [27].

[129]   ibid.

[130]   Infringement of this design was also the basis of the suit in *Review Australia Pty Ltd v New Cover Group Pty Ltd* [2008] FCA 1589, (2008) 79 IPR 236, where the design was found to be infringed by New Cover.

[131]   See IP Australia, Design Registration No. 307708 <https:// search .ipaustralia .gov .au/ designs/ search/details/200515441?s=de6265dc-f904-42ec-a32f-7d1ab2d02835>. For images of both dresses see, Madeleine Sy Chan and Sharon Givoni, 'Utilising Trade Mark Laws to Protect Fashion Designs' (2012) 3 Australian IP Law Bulletin 51, 53.

[132]   *Redberry* [8].

that there were 'clear similarities' between the dresses, except for the shape of the skirt and the pattern/colour of the fabric.[133] Justice Kenny pointed out that under s 19(1), similarities between the designs are to be given greater weight than differences and that 'if this were all, a finding of infringement might readily be made'.[134]

However, as stated by Justice Kenny, 'the inquiry under the Designs Act is more complex and sophisticated than this'.[135] Owing to the other statutory factors, 'the court standing in the shoes of the informed user, must also have regard to the state of the development of the prior art base for the design. The significance of the similarities and differences between these designs falls to be considered in light of the prior art'.[136] The prior art showed many cross-over or fixed-wrap dresses, which led Her Honour to conclude 'that there is limited freedom to design a cross-over [dress] ... other than by reference to the shape of the skirt ... combined with differences in the fabric pattern' (including colour).[137]

Justice Kenny therefore discounted the similarities in the bodices of the garments, which she held were common to the prior art. Finding that the skirt shape and fabric choices were the space for innovation, and that these were different between the two garments, the court held that the informed user would not find the garments substantially similar in overall impression.[138] In summary, Justice Kenny constructed the scope of the 'infringeable monopoly' from the perspective of the informed user. This monopoly was not the registered design per se, but subsets of that design – the shape of the skirt and the fabric choice.

In the second case example of *LED*,[139] the plaintiff had registered two designs for LED tail lights (Registered Design No 302359 – dual lens[140] and No 302360 – triple lens) [141] (the designs).

After reviewing the evidence, Justice Gordon held the plaintiff's design was 'a distinct advance over the prior art base in the sense that it combined various existing features in a way that had not been done before'.[142] Moreover, 'the features were the product of conscious design choice rather than compelled by industry-wide standards or technological constraints'.[143] Given the sizeable difference between the prior art and the registered design, the court construed the 'infringeable monopoly' broadly and held the defendant's product, which had taken those distinctive features (not common in the prior art), to be infringing. A similar happy result would likely have been had for Firmagroup had they litigated under the *2003 Act*.

The cases show that the inherent complexity of the infringement inquiry (shaped by the principle that design law does not protect copying per se) has meant that courts in contested cases must labour over the scope of the 'infringeable monopoly' and therefore consider

---

[133]   ibid [36].
[134]   ibid [38].
[135]   ibid [38].
[136]   ibid [39].
[137]   ibid [42].
[138]   ibid [46].
[139]   (2008) 80 IPR 85.
[140]   IP Australia, Design Registration No. 302359 <https://search.ipaustralia.gov.au/designs/search/result?s=0d4e021e-6837-4f3f-91ff-b52344da1596>.
[141]   IP Australia, Design Registration No. 302360 <https://search.ipaustralia.gov.au/designs/search/result?s=b776a831-15bd-4323-8ede-b66c643e0b33>.
[142]   *LED* [65].
[143]   ibid [65].

volumes of conflicting evidence. This includes labouring over factors such as the perception of the informed user (which had been a contested term until recent statutory amendments),[144] the interpretation of the prior art and the freedom to innovate in relation to a product. Consequently this has meant longer hearings and a more a complex case for a design rights holder to contest when compared to trade mark infringement. More complex cases typically mean increased costs.

5.   CONCLUSION

Empirical economic studies reveal low awareness and a fatalistic view of design rights enforcement in Australia. This empirical legal study complements the current body of knowledge by demonstrating that court-based enforcement of design rights typically favours the design rights holder, with an 80% win rate across the 15 cases identified since the inception of the *2003 Act*. In addition, in these 15 cases the validity of the underlying right was typically upheld, and appellate courts affirmed decisions of the lower courts (n = 3). Although these numbers are modest, they do represent the entire population of cases since the inception of the *2003 Act*. The cases reveal that having a registered and certified design can assist a plaintiff to put a defendant on notice, which will in turn enhance their ability to seek additional damages. The cases show that access to additional damages is important where compensatory damages may be hard to prove or are of low value such as for 'highly discretionary goods', for example, casual dresses.

The low number of cases after 2010 was explained by the argument that the early cases in 2008–2010 were close cases (three wins, two losses) which clarified the parameters of the new infringement legislation. This may have led to only confident plaintiffs pursuing cases in court after 2011 (nine wins, one loss). This chapter also proposes that around this time, Australian courts were crystallising the bounds of tangential IPRs, deciding important cases about the copyright/design overlap and also expanding the role of statutory consumer law in IPR litigation. This article also suggests that the (lack of) benefits to shape trade marks for design products was also clarified by trade mark infringement cases in 2008–2009 and draws further support from overlap registration studies.

These findings – that design enforcement in courts firmly favours the plaintiff – is critical to publicise. Understanding the high probability of success could affect the 'confidence rights holders and their peers have in the designs rights system'.[145] It is important for design right holders to know that win rates under the *2003 Act* are higher than under other Australian IPRs and higher than win rates in jurisdictions in the UK and Europe. These positive findings, and the knowledge that registration impacts notice and thus access to additional damages, may encourage Australian designers to participate in the registered design system.

---

[144]   *Redberry* [2008] FCA 1588, (2008) 173 FCR 450, cf Yates J in *Multisteps Pty Ltd v Source & Sell Pty Ltd* [2013] FCA 743, (2013) 214 FCR 323. The approach of Yates J in the latter was adopted by the Designs Amendment (Advisory Council on Intellectual Property Response) Act 2021 [Assented to 10 September 2021] Schedule 7 – Other amendments, Part 1: stating that the 'standard of the informed user' be substituted with the 'familiar person'. The approach to the 'informed user' in *Redberry* was that the hypothetical person needed to be a user of the product; the approach in *Multisteps* (adopted by the 2021 reforms) was that this person need only be familiar with the product.

[145]   Kollmann et al (n 33) 28.

However, while the above findings refute some of the negative perceptions of designs enforcement, this study also confirms some of the negative perceptions. In the nine cases where infringement questions were contested, the hearings were on average 6.7 days long, which is almost twice as long as the average trade mark dispute.[146] If hearing days are used as a proxy for the overall costs of the dispute, then contested design litigation may be more costly than trade mark infringement disputes. This is because unlike trade mark infringement, where the scope of the monopoly is prima facie the registration, in design law, the court must construct the plaintiff's 'infringeable monopoly' and then the overall similarity between this 'infringeable monopoly' and the impugned product. This is a complex and nuanced evaluation requiring assessment of evidence and witnesses.

The construction of the 'infringeable monopoly' is consistent with the tenets of Australian design law policy and therefore unlikely to change. Unfortunately, the nature of the infringement inquiry may not favour the types of design registrations held by Australian residents. This is because the majority of Australian design registrations are for short life cycle products such as clothing,[147] and there is a likelihood that these products come from a crowded field of prior art which shrinks the scope of the plaintiff's infringeable monopoly (eg *Redberry* dress). It is therefore unsurprising that contested infringement litigation could be viewed as a daunting task by Australian registrants. This perception may be difficult to dampen even with the knowledge that design rights holders have had frequent success in courts.

---

[146] Huang, '20 Years of Trade Mark Infringement' (n 59) 123. The author found trademark litigation, including with concurrent claims, took on average 3.7 days (n = 78).

[147] Falk et al (n 26) 5.

19. Determination of 'existing design' in Chinese patent infringement disputes

Xianwei Zhang

1. INTRODUCTION

China is a major patent filer, with up to 731,918 industrial design patents granted in 2020 alone,[1] according to publicly available data from the State Intellectual Property Office of China. Another impressive figure is that there are now over 20,000 court decisions related to industrial design in China's judgment database.[2] Part of the reason for this staggering number is that most small-to-medium enterprises in China do not yet have the capacity for independent research and development and imitating a product's design is the easiest thing to do. One issue that tends to be at the centre of design patent infringement disputes is what exactly is an 'existing design'? While some articles have been written about industrial design in general, the discussion in these articles is often not directly focused on existing designs due to the different focus. Also, information in this area is missing in the English literature. After all, even in Chinese, there are very limited papers related to industrial design — compared to other issues of intellectual property law.[3] In contrast to previous studies, this chapter attempts to provide a comprehensive overview of Chinese courts' thinking from the perspective of 'existing design' determinations, using textual comparison and identification tools. For scholars and practitioners alike, this chapter provides not only a comprehensive overview of design disputes in China but also an easy solution for quick follow-up research.

Cardozo once said, 'It is when the colors do not match, when the references in the index fail, when there is no decisive precedent, that the serious business of the judge begins'.[4] China does not have a specific industrial design law, and the rules relating to industrial design are scattered throughout different parts of the Chinese Patent Law. These provisions are very sketchy, and what this chapter attempts to show the reader is: How does China's patent law work? How does the 'serious business' of Chinese judges begin? The chapter also shows how to summarize the rules of judges' decisions, an approach that is believed to be instructive for scholars who want to study the factual binding effect of Chinese court decisions (even if they are not concerned with industrial designs).

The rest of this chapter is divided into three parts. The next part briefly introduces the rules related to existing designs in Chinese Patent Law. Part 3 presents the empirical results and

---

[1]   State Intellectual Property Office of China, 'Annual Patent Grants of Three Kinds Originated from Home and Abroad', <https://www.cnipa.gov.cn/tjxx/jianbao/year2020/b/b1.html> accessed 19 May 2022.

[2]   PKU Law, <https://www.pkulaw.com/english> accessed 19 May 2022.

[3]   In CNKI, the largest database of academic journals in China, there are a total of only 227 core journal articles on the full range of industrial design issues as of May 2022. In contrast, there are 7,289 core journal articles on copyright and 2,309 core journal articles on patent law.

[4]   Benjamin N. Cardozo, *The Nature of the Judicial Process* (Yale University Press, 1921) 21.

the corresponding analysis, and the final part is a summary. As a chapter in the *Research Handbook*, this aims to show how empirical research can help us to position the issue and, more importantly, how we can use empirical research to discover the correct meaning of the law in a given context. I hope that even if the reader is not concerned with industrial design issues or Chinese law, he or she will gain some insight through the steps and ideas provided in this chapter.

2.   EXISTING DESIGN IN CHINESE LEGAL TEXTS

An existing design is the core concept of industrial design. If a granted industrial design, or an industrial design in the application process, overlaps with an existing design, it naturally loses the legitimate basis for the exercise of property rights. In the Chinese Patent Law,[5] this concept appears in Article 23[6] and Article 67.[7] Existing designs can be used to determine whether an applicant's design is novel and defend accused infringers against infringement.

In the Patent Law of the People's Republic of China (2020 Amendment), the existing design is defined as follows: 'The term existing design as used in this Law refers to a design known to the general public both at home and abroad prior to the date of application'.[8]

The above provisions are not the only source relating to 'existing design' in the Chinese Patent Law system. What is not familiar to readers in other countries is the concept of judicial interpretations, which are issued by the Supreme People's Court of China and are binding sources of law. As the name suggests, they are 'interpretations' by the Supreme People's Court of laws enacted by the Chinese National People's Congress. Although the status of judicial interpretations is controversial in Chinese academia, in practice, 'judicial interpretations' promulgated by the Supreme Court of China are also sources of law.

In the Supreme People's Court's interpretation on several issues concerning the application of law in the Trial of Patent Infringement Dispute Cases,[9] the Supreme People's Court stated:

---

[5]   Patent Law of the People's Republic of China (2020 Amendment). Full English text can be downloaded here: <https://www.pkulaw.com/en_law/417f520f8bcb8de2bdfb.html> accessed 19 May 2022.

[6]   Article 23 reads as follows:
Any design for which a patent is granted shall not be attributed to the existing design, and no entity or individual has, before the date of application, filed an application with the patent administrative department of the State Council on the identical design and recorded it in the patent documents published after the date of application.
As compared with the existing design or combination of the existing design features, the design for which a patent is granted shall have distinctive features.
The patented design may not conflict with the lawful rights that have been obtained by any other person prior to the date of application.
The term 'existing design' as used in this Law refers to a design known to the general public both at home and abroad prior to the date of application.

[7]   Article 67 reads as follows: 'In a dispute over patent infringement, if the accused infringer has evidence to prove that the technology or design it or he exploits is an existing technology or design, no patent infringement is constituted'.

[8]   Article 23, Patent Law of the People's Republic of China (2020 Amendment). Full text can be downloaded here: <https://www.pkulaw.com/en_law/417f520f8bcb8de2bdfb.html> accessed 19 May 2022.

[9]   Interpretation of the Supreme People's Court on Several Issues concerning the Application of Law in the Trial of Patent Infringement Dispute Cases, <https:// www .pkulaw .com/ en _law/ 64d397da69a7f287bdfb.html> accessed 19 May 2022.

When determining whether designs are identical or similar, the people's court shall consider the design features of the patented design, the alleged infringing design, and the overall visual effect of the design to draw an integrative conclusion; the people's court shall not consider design features which depend on technical functions and material, internal structure, and other features of a product which have no effect on the overall visual effect.

In the following circumstances, the overall visual effect of a design is usually more affected:

(1)   The part of a product which can be easily viewed directly in the normal use of the product as opposed to other parts; or

(2)   Technical features of a patented design which are distinct from those of the existing designs as opposed to other design features of the patented design.

Where there is no difference in the overall visual effect between the alleged infringing design and a patented design, the people's court shall determine that the two designs are identical; or if there is no substantive difference in the overall visual effect between them, the people's court shall determine that the two designs are identical; or if there is no substantive difference in the overall visual effect between them, the people's court shall determine that they are similar.[10]

This interpretation is much more specific than the text of the Chinese Patent Law, and some may feel that it seems sufficient to solve the problem. After all, unlike product patents and method patents, design patents do not require claim comparison and do not require advanced technical background knowledge. Determining whether the design at issue is the same as the prior existing design is not complicated, which seems to be concluded directly by the naked eye. This view is arbitrary, as a search of China's database of decisions reveals that Articles 23 and 67 of China's Patent Law are the second and third most cited by courts in design infringement disputes. Further, by searching the typical cases published by China's Supreme Court and local courts over the past ten years, design infringement disputes have emerged almost every year. The reason for this, on the one hand, is that the number of judgments in design infringement disputes (21,738) itself is more than that in invention patent infringement disputes (10,709), and on the other hand, it shows that the trial of design infringement disputes is not as simple as it seems.

How did the Chinese courts decide over 20,000 cases just on the three provisions mentioned earlier? As Hart says, 'Sometimes, in such cases, a definition of a word can supply such a map: at one and the same time it may make explicit the latent principle which guides our use of a word and may exhibit relationships between the type of phenomena to which we apply the word and other phenomena'.[11] Thus, the determination of 'existing design' in Chinese Patent Law is really a flexible standard rather than a strict bright-line rule. Therefore, an empirical study of industrial design must not be separated from a discussion of cases that can truly explain how the idea of existing design has evolved. I will show how I extracted the appropriate judgment instruments in the following.

---

[10]   Article 11, Interpretation of the Supreme People's Court on Several Issues concerning the Application of Law in the Trial of Patent Infringement Dispute Cases, <https://www.pkulaw.com/en _law/64d397da69a7f287bdfb.html> accessed 19 May 2022.

[11]   H.L.A. Hart, *The Concept of Law* (Clarendon Press, 1994) 14.

3.   EMPIRICAL RESULTS AND ANALYSIS

3.1   Data Sources and Collection Methods

3.1.1   Data sources

The research in this paper is based on 8,242 decisions, all of which were decided directly on 'existing designs' by February 28, 2022. We did not limit the courts and districts in which they were heard. The databases we use are PKU Law[12] and IP House.[13]

Some readers may wonder whether the more than 8,000 judgments could contain many duplicate false-positive results. This chapter argues that false positives are unlikely because Chinese court decisions adhere to strict formal specifications. Imagine this scenario: You fill out a standard form in a specific order and can only get creative with the information you fill out. A Chinese court decision must include three sections: 'The court finds', 'The court considers', and 'The result of the decision'. Among them, 'the court finds' is the determination of the facts, 'the court considers' is the court's view on the application of the law, and 'the result of the decision' includes fixed terms such as 'support the plaintiff's claim' and 'reject the plaintiff's claim'.

This modular approach to judgment writing facilitates empirical research, which means we can extract and filter the judgments we need by specific keywords and filter out false positives in advance with some skill.

3.1.2   Screening and extraction methods

As mentioned above, there are more than 20,000 design infringement dispute documents in China; the list below is how the judgments were filtered.

1. I limit the keyword 'existing design' to 'the court finds' section, which means that the result must be a direct response from the court to the 'existing design'. This technique helps us to filter out false positives in cases where the parties have raised an existing design defence, but the court has not responded directly.
2. Chinese legal documents include judgments, rulings, and conciliations, and the two databases provide a function to filter the types of documents, which can help us filter out documents that do not respond to substantive issues.
3. The PKU Law Database provides a function to reverse search for judgments based on the cited legal texts. I reverse-searched all relevant judgments based on the legal provisions mentioned earlier, and these judgments could be cross-referenced with the judgments mentioned in Step 1.
4. I used optical character recognition (OCR) software[14] and a text analysis tool (Devonthink)[15] to put all judgments under one folder. Encountering duplicate judgments is a common

---

[12]   PKU Law, <https://www.pkulaw.com/> accessed 19 May 2022.

[13]   IP House, <https://www.iphouse.cn> accessed 19 May 2022.

[14]   I use Abbyy Fine Reader, but Adobe Acrobat also has OCR capabilities.

[15]   Devonthink, <https://www.devontechnologies.com/apps/devonthink> accessed 19 May 2022. Not only this tool, but any text comparison and extraction tool can do the process I described. If you are using Windows, try 'Beyond Compare'.

occurrence for bulk downloads in Chinese judicial databases. To remove duplicate documents, I used the text matching function in the software.

3.1.3   Manual processing of cases

With the above steps, we were able to get 8,242 judgments. As mentioned earlier, Chinese court judgments are in a fixed order and format, so we were able to automate the parts of trial time, court region, and judgment result through a simple text recognition script. However, this only tells us part of the findings, and manual processing/reading of the verdicts is still necessary. According to Bradford's Law[16] and Lotka's Law,[17] we do not need to read all the decisions, but only the decisions of the core district courts. The typical cases published in the core publications can help us grasp the crux of the problem — this section also ends with a textual comparison that verifies the aforementioned bibliometric laws.[18] In the IP field, the core courts in China are the Supreme Court of China and the three district courts in China's Guangdong Province (especially Shenzhen), Beijing, and Shanghai. The core decisions are the typical cases decided by the courts mentioned above. This research scans all (approximately 9,000 pages) of the 'Commentary on China IPR Guidance Cases' (7 volumes)[19] and the 'China Case Guidance' (9 volumes)[20] published annually by the Supreme Court of China to screen the typical cases. Then we use OCR technology to create a text-searchable PDF version that identifies all the decisions related to industrial design. Combined with the typical case collection issued by the court and the database cases from limited regions, 500 decisions were randomly marked using a script.[21]

How are these judgments going to help us discover and answer the questions?

We can focus on the second instance decisions judgment that rejected the first instance decisions — this can also be filtered out secondarily through a script because the second instance court has a fixed 'jargon' for expressing opinions that differ from those of the first instance court. These opposing decisions help us discover why the concept of existing design is not clear-cut, and if the legal text is the consensus of the judges, what is the nature of the disagreement in the decision?

3.1.4   Possible limitations

Although the above approach removes as many false positives as possible, there is still a limitation: this study does not specifically break down administrative and civil litigation in manual processing. Since 'existing design' can exist in both patent grant and patent infringement litigation, a subdivision might reveal more interesting findings. However, this study does

---

[16]   S.C. Bradford, 'Sources of Information on Scientific Subjects' (1934) 137 Engineering 85–86.
[17]   Alfred J. Lotka, 'The Frequency Distribution of Scientific Productivity' (1926) 16 Journal of the Washington Academy of Sciences 317–324.
[18]   Lotka's Law is one of a variety of special applications of Zipf's law. George Kingsley Zipf, *The Psycho-Biology of Language* (Houghton Mifflin, 1935).
[19]   The Intellectual Property Division of the Supreme People's Court, *Commentary on China IPR Guideline Cases Series* (China Legal Publishing House, 2011–2019).
[20]   Supreme People's Court Case Guidance Office, *China Case Guidance Series* (Law Press, 2015–2019).
[21]   This script runs in Devonthink, generates random numbers in Excel using the Rand function, and then uses Keyboard Maestro to automatically mark the files with the corresponding serial numbers.

not believe such a breakdown should be particularly meaningful since the courts review the grounds, regardless of the cause of action.

Another limitation of this study is that it does not capture the examination decisions made by Chinese patent administrative agencies on existing designs, most notably since hundreds of thousands of design patents are issued annually in China. The current database of patent administrative decisions in China does not provide an entry point from which decisions with existing design objections can be extracted. Another reason is that, even if a suitable screening method were thought of, the existing database does not have a good bulk crawl feature — perhaps precisely to prevent crawlers from crawling. I can understand the administration's concerns; the crawl limitations make it difficult to perform effective bulk analysis. It may be possible in the future to select a few dozen decisions for study by sampling — but the representativeness of the results would be difficult to ensure.

Despite these limitations, judges are expected to use the review decision of the administrative agency as a reference point when considering a case. Although a perfect situation would, of course, be to analyze the opinions of administrative organs together, I believe that focusing the study on the court decisions is sufficient to cover the problematic points in the existing design determinations.

3.2   Distribution over Time

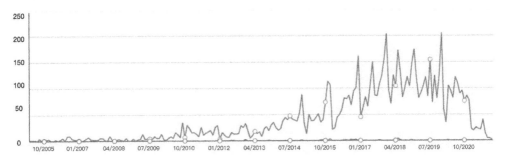

Figure 19.1   Number of industrial design cases involving existing design from 2005 to 2021

As shown in Figure 19.1, there has only been a relatively significant increase in relevant decisions since 2009 due to adding several new elements to China's design regime in 2008. The 2008 version of the patent law marked the maturation of China's patent legislation. The decline in data after 2020 is due to a delay in the inclusion of decisions in the database.

The sudden and dramatic rise in verdicts after 2014 is due to the 'Provisions of the Supreme People's Court on the Issuance of Judgments on the Internet by the People's Courts',[22] which

---

[22]   'The people's courts at all levels shall specially designate an institution to be responsible for the management of judgments released on the Internet. The institution shall perform the following duties: (1) It shall organize and upload judgments; (2) If it finds that a judgment issued on the Internet has any clerical error or is handled improperly in technical issues, it shall coordinate relevant departments for timely handling; and (3) Other relevant guidance, supervision and evaluation'. Article 3, Provisions of the Supreme People's Court on the Issuance of Judgments on the Internet by the People's Courts, <http://gongbao.court.gov.cn/Details/d0e837bbafb75a8863b4d4c407d694.html> accessed 19 May 2022.

Table 19.1   Number of granted industrial design

Year	Granted Industrial Design
1985–2014	3,083,691
2015	482,659
2016	446,135
2017	442,996
2018	536,251
2019	556,529
2020	731,918

Unit: Piece.
Source: State Intellectual Property Office Statistical Annual Report https://www.cnipa.gov.cn/tjxx/jianbao/year2020/b/b1.html.

came into effect in 2014 and requires that the effective judgment documents of the people's courts 'shall' be published on the Internet.

Of course, this does not mean there were no existing design-related decisions in China before 2009, except that Chinese courts did not produce digital versions of all patent decisions in the 1990s. Another reason is that, although the Internet in China has been popular since 2000, the mass construction of Internet applications and patent information platforms took place after 2010, and it was after 2010 that the technical strength and size of Chinese software developers rose substantially. Accordingly, the ability of accused infringers to retrieve existing designs was relatively poor prior to 2010, and these two reasons combine to limit our ability to review the judicial history through the database prior to 2010.

The number of granted industrial design patents was obtained from the statistical annual reports published by the State Intellectual Property Office of China, and the results are shown in Table 19.1.

One assumption is that there is a strong correlation between the number of patents and patent litigation. However, a comparison of Table 19.1 with Figure 19.1 does not seem to prove this assumption. While this may be because we did not count all cases, the rise in design litigation is more likely to be related to the mobile Internet only in terms of the numbers obtained for this chapter.

3.3   Distribution of Trial Courts

Of the court opinions we retrieved, there were 5,881 first instance judgments and 2,360 second instance judgments. Among these judgments, Guangdong Province and Zhejiang Province had the most design disputes. We extracted the courts responsible for the trials and listed the top five in Table 19.2. Of these top five courts, courts in Guangdong province hold three seats. Although the court in Hangzhou, Zhejiang Province, had 518 fewer judgments than the Beijing IP Court, the courts in other cities in Zhejiang Province also had 500 judgments. Thus, the courts in China's Guangdong Province and Zhejiang Province are the most experienced in China in hearing design disputes. The reason for this apparent disproportionality in peripheral

Table 19.2   Top five courts with the most cases

Guangzhou Intellectual Property Court	1,731
Guangdong High People's Court	1,186
Beijing Intellectual Property Court	757
Hangzhou Intermediate People's Court, Zhejiang Province	518
Shenzhen Intermediate People's Court, Guangdong Province	305

design disputes is that China's Guangdong Province and Zhejiang Province are the most economically developed provinces in China, with the former known for manufacturing and the latter for small goods and online shopping — thus, the designs that drive consumer purchasing decisions can trigger the most intense conflicts of interest.

3.4   Distribution of Verdict Results

When analysing the verdict, this chapter deliberately divides the verdict winning rate into two stages: the first instance and the second instance, and the lawsuit into civil and administrative (see Figures 19.2–19.5). Civil litigation is easy to understand and does not differ from patent infringement litigation in other countries. Administrative patent litigation is a special type of litigation because decisions relating to the validity of a patent in China can only be made by the China Patent Office, the licensing authority for patents. In other words, the court can only decide whether there is patent infringement. However, suppose a party is unsatisfied with the administrative authority's decision. In that case, he or she can file a patent administrative action in court against the decision itself (regardless of whether it upholds the patent's validity or invalidates the patent).

From the data, we can see that the dismissal rate in civil litigation in the first instance is 20%, meaning that the rate of cases in which the court supports or partially supports the plaintiff is 80%, and this rises to 87% when it goes to the appellate trial. In administrative litigation, the opposite picture is painted, with a 91% rate of plaintiff defeat. Therefore, we can presume that the appellants in these second instance cases are mostly plaintiffs in the first instance and that the rate of defeat of appellants in the second instance of administrative cases is 93%.

This data reflects that courts, in most cases, respect the judgment of the patent administrative authorities on the validity of patent rights. A typological analysis of a sample of 500 deci-

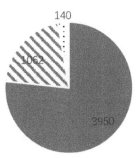

140

1062

3950

• Plaintiff's Claim Partially Supported   · Plaintiff's Claim dismissed   · Plaintiff's Claim upheld

Figure 19.2   Number of cases in first instance (civil litigation)

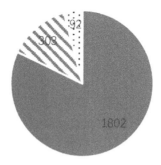

- First trial verdict affirmed
- First trial verdict reversed
- First trial verdict upheld in part and reversed in part

Figure 19.3   Number of cases in second instance (civil litigation)

- Plaintiff's claim dismissed   · Administrative decision revoked

Figure 19.4   Number of cases in first instance cases (administrative litigation)

sions found no significant correlation between the plaintiff's win rate and whether the plaintiff was a corporation or an individual. However, foreign companies had a relatively higher win rate, probably due to the higher quality of their patents and their more experienced litigation strategies. In addition, plaintiffs have a relatively higher success rate if the case goes to the court of appeal. The success rate of plaintiffs in administrative litigation cases does not differ significantly depending on whether the patent in question is also subject to civil infringement litigation.

In both civil and administrative cases, this chapter focuses on cases in which the courts of the first instance and the courts of appeal disagreed. This study finds that the courts' disagreement mainly focuses on two aspects: 1. different interpretations of 'overall visual effect'; 2. different interpretations of consumers. The chapter also finds that courts often resolve disa-

∎ The first trial verdict upheld   • The first trial verdict reversed

Figure 19.5   Number of second instance cases (administrative litigation)

greements by implicitly citing significant decisions of higher courts (or other district courts). This finding is elaborated on below in 3.6 and 3.7.

3.5   Length of Proceedings

According to China's civil procedure law, 'A people's court shall complete the trial of a case under formal procedure within six months after the case is docketed'.[23] The same provision can also be found in Administrative Litigation Law of China.[24] However, we find that some cases

Table 19.3   Length of patent litigation involving existing design determination

	Maximum	Average	Minimum
First Instance Civil Litigation	1,744	176	2
Second Instance Civil Litigation	707	75	4
First Instance Administrative Litigation	1,082	432	54
Second Instance Administrative Litigation	901	105	28

Unit: Day.

---

[23] 'A people's court shall complete the trial of a case under formal procedure within six months after the case is docketed. If an extension of the period is necessary under special circumstances, the period may be extended for six months with the approval of the president of the court; and any further extension shall be subject to the approval of the superior of the people's court'. Article 152, Civil Procedure Law of the People's Republic of China (2021 Amendment).

[24] 'A people's court of first instance shall enter a judgment within six months from the day when a complaint is docketed. Any extension of the aforesaid period as needed under special circumstances shall be subject to the approval of a Higher People's Court. Where a Higher People's Court trying a case as a court of first instance needs to extend the aforesaid period, the extension shall be subject to the approval of the Supreme People's Court'. Article 81, The Administrative Litigation Law of the People's Republic of China (2017 Revision).

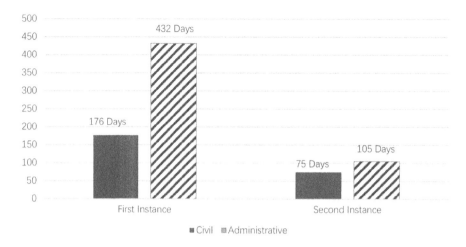

Figure 19.6   Length of trial in different instances

are far longer than this limit, both in civil and administrative cases. The longest civil cases and administrative cases exceeded 1,700 and 1,000 days, respectively. Even the median length of cases heard is very close to the maximum time limit set by civil and administrative litigation law (see Table 19.3 and Figure 19.6).

The reason for this is that, as mentioned earlier, the validity or invalidity of a patent is determined by the Chinese patent administrative agency. Therefore certain defendants will file invalidation suits with the patent administrative agency at the time of litigation, at which point the entire case will be suspended. This significantly lengthens the trial time of the case. For example, in *Alafanar Electrical Systems v. Zhejiang Lide Electric Co.*,[25] the plaintiff, Alafanar Electric Systems, sued the court on 29 August, 2007, for infringement of the design patent with the defendant, Zhejiang Lide Electric Co. The court ruled on 14 December, 2007, that the case was suspended due to the defendant's request to the State Intellectual Property Office of China to declare the patent invalid. The court resumed the case on 8 August, 2008, after the Patent Re-examination Committee of the State Intellectual Property Office issued a decision to maintain the validity of the patent right in the case. The reason that civil litigation takes significantly less time in the second instance than in the first instance is that Chinese courts do not question the factual findings of the first instance court in the second instance but only review the application of the law.

The average trial time in administrative litigation is significantly longer than in civil litigation, partly because the defendant is the patent administrative agency, and the court must respect the administrative agency's review decision. To overturn the administrative agency's decision would require very strong arguments. Of course, this does not mean the plaintiff will lose the case. For example, in a motorcycle design case, the Patent Re-examination Board in the Patent Office presumed that the 'average consumer' was the average consumer of the motorcycle product. The court held that 'average consumer' was changed to 'average con-

---

[25]   *Alafanar Electrical Systems v. Zhejiang Lide Electric Co.*, Zhejiang High People's Court (2009) ZheZhi Final Instance No. 149.

sumer of two-wheeled sport motorcycles' rather than an average consumer in the usual sense, thus overturning the previous invalidation decision.

3.6 Identification of 'Overall Visual Effect'

This chapter introduced the Chinese Patent Law on existing industrial designs in part 2. In section 3.4, we found that the courts tend to disagree on 'overall visual effect' and 'average consumer'. Just as mentioned in part 2, I read 500 randomly marked cases of disagreement and found that both the first and second instance courts focused more on differences than on similarities.

Although the judicial interpretation of the Chinese Patent Law stipulates that the principle of 'overall observation and integrative conclusion'[26] should be followed in determining the existing design, this chapter finds that the courts are more concerned with the visual difference than the common point. When comparing the granted design, the accused infringing design, and the existing design proposed by the accused infringer, most of the courts tend to identify the three different design features and do not mention the common design features between the two. Even when some courts do mention the common design features, they do not analyze the effect of the common design features on similarity.

This leads us to ask the following question: Does it meet the 'overall observation and integrative conclusion' required by the judicial interpretation if we only care about the differences and not the similarities? If the answer is yes, what are the reasons for the court's disagreement?

3.6.1 Why focus on differences

Through reading the 500 judgments, this chapter finds that, despite the different levels of detail in the courts' arguments, they follow a relatively consistent judgment step and logical sequence: 1. the distinguishing design features are the innovation of the design of the patent in question, which distinguishes the design of the patent in question from the existing design and can effectively influence the overall visual effect of the judgment. Thus, the patent in question should first be compared with the existing design to clarify the distinguishing design features; 2. the allegedly infringing product has several distinguishing design features, and the distinctive design features significantly impact the overall visual effect. Thus, the allegedly infringing product and the existing design are substantially different, and the existing design defence is not established. On the contrary, if the infringing product does not contain all the design features that distinguish the authorized design from the existing design, it is generally presumed that the infringing design is not similar to the granted design.

This approach is in line with the judicial interpretation of China's patent law. The explanation mentioned earlier: 'Technical features of a patented design which are distinct from those of the existing designs' should be more impactful. Therefore, analyzing the differences between the two is more important because determining whether there is a difference in the overall visual effect, followed by the size and nature of the difference, is the prerequisite to determining the existing design. This is different from the practice of finding common ground

---

[26] Interpretation of the Supreme People's Court on Several Issues concerning the Application of Law in the Trial of Patent Infringement Dispute Cases, <https:// www .pkulaw .com/ en _law/ 64d397da69a7f287bdfb.html> accessed 19 May 2022.

when determining trademark infringement.[27] This is because design patent infringement determinations, unlike trademark infringement determinations, do not consider whether consumers are likely to be confused about the source or provenance of the product.

3.6.2   Reasons for disagreement

Since the focus on finding differences is, in fact, consistent with the judicial interpretation of the Chinese Patent Law, why did the courts disagree? The reason for the courts' disagreement lies in their differing perceptions of the substantive impact of the 'differences'. For example, in *Honda Motor Co., Ltd. v. Patent Re-Examination Board of the State Intellectual Property Office*,[28] the Supreme People's Court held that 'the automobile headlight of this patent adopts an irregular triangular design with small teeth and a grille with a horizontal bar in the middle. The rear window of the car adopts an irregular quadrilateral design; the rear window glass is separated from the rear combination lamp by the window frame, and the smooth transition between the upper part of the car and the lower part of the car ... These differences are obvious to the average consumer of the type of car at issue in this case and are sufficient to distinguish the overall visual effect of the car design shown in this patent picture from the car design shown in Exhibit 1'.

The judge of the Beijing High People's Court, subsequently overturned by the Supreme Court, held that:

> the differences existing between this patent and Exhibit 1 are local differences, which require special attention and repeated comparison by the average consumer to distinguish, and such differences do not have a significant impact on the overall visual effect. Therefore, in the case where the overall design style, contour shape, and proportional relationship between the constituent parts of the two are similar, the combination of minor differences in several parts of the car will not produce significant visual differences.

The Beijing High People's Court judge and the Supreme People's Court judge noted the exact differences but had very different views on the differences. The Supreme Court held that the common contour features in the appearance of automobile products have a limited impact on the visual effect, while the variation of design features will attract more consumers' attention.

In a design patent relating to a fan blade,[29] the Supreme People's Court again disagreed with the Beijing High People's Court. The Beijing High People's Court held that 'to the average consumer, the difference is sufficient to make a difference in the overall visual effect'. The Supreme People's Court, on the other hand, found that the Beijing High People's Court erred in its determination of the effect of the overall visual effect: 'the difference in the thickness of the fan blades has no effect on the overall visual effect ... When in use, the protruding part is located on the side of the wind wheel mounting surface, which is difficult to be observed by the average consumer, and the overall visual effect does not have a significant impact'.

---

[27]   Yin Xintian, *Chinese Patent Law Explained* (Intellectual Property Press, 2012) 644.

[28]   *Honda Motor Co., Ltd. v. Patent Re-Examination Board of the State Intellectual Property Office*, Supreme People's Court (2010) Xingtizi No. 3.

[29]   *Zhuhai Gree Electric Appliance Co., Ltd. and State Intellectual Property Office Patent Re-examination Committee*, Administrative Dispute over Invalidation of Design Patent Rights, Supreme People's Court (2011) Xingtizi No. 1.

3.6.3 Implicit citations of typical judgments

Hart calls the ambiguities in the law 'problems of penumbra',[30] so what are the 'problems of penumbra' in existing design determinations? Before answering this question, I would like to summarize the subtleties of existing design determinations: no matter what the design, there are always existing designs that are 'common' and 'different' in some way. It is as if the water in a glass is somehow the same as the water in a river, yet it is different.[31] Despite the different perceptions of substantive impact, this chapter unexpectedly finds that the arguments in some of the decisions are consistent through the overall comparison of the texts. However, a court will often covertly cite a typical decision of the core court when it wants a similarity between the designs, which determines existing designs somewhat consistent with the development of trial practice. This author cannot help but quote Gilles Deleuze, who said: 'Coherence must not come from themselves. They must receive their coherence from elsewhere'.[32]

The word 'implicit' is used because China is a civil law country and prior court decisions are not legally binding. Of course, this does not mean that prior judgments are not binding in practice. Although many Chinese scholars have referred to judges' implicit invocation of prior decisions, this is often a reasonable inference based on human nature: Chinese judges have a heavy workload and often look to prior decisions for advice when they encounter difficult cases. However, since it is the statute that is the source of the law, the judge, even if he quotes a paragraph from a prior decision, cannot explicitly indicate the prior decision as a source, which is called 'implicit citation' by some Chinese scholars.[33]

This chapter empirically demonstrates the existence of this phenomenon by comparing the texts of the judgments.

For example, in the case of *Shanghai Chenguang Stationery Co., Ltd. v. Deli Group Co., Ltd.*,[34] the court pointed out that 'in judging whether there is a substantial difference between the infringed design and the authorized design in the overall visual effect, both the similarity and the difference between the infringed design and the authorized design should be considered. The common design features and distinguishing design features of the infringed design and the authorized design should be examined separately to determine the overall visual effect, based on the principle of overall observation and comprehensive judgment'. This passage was first made by the Shanghai IP Court in December 2016 and has been cited in 33 separate decisions since then.[35]

Additionally, in *Zhuhai Gree Electric Appliance Co., Ltd. and State Intellectual Property Office Patent Re-examination Committee*,[36] the Supreme People's Court stated the following:

[30] H.L.A. Hart, *Essays in Jurisprudence and Philosophy* (Oxford University Press, 1984) 64.
[31] Gilles Deleuze, *Difference and Repetition* (Paul Patton tr, Columbia University Press, 1995) 2.
[32] Ibid xx.
[33] Haibo Sun, 'The implicit citation of guiding cases and its correction' [2018] 40(2) Global Law Review 144.
[34] *Shanghai Chenguang Stationery Co., Ltd. V. Deli Group Co.*, Shanghai Intellectual Property Court (2016) HuMin ChuZi No. 113.
[35] For example, *Haimen Xinjia Power Tools Factory and Suzhou Baoshide Power Tools Co.*, Nanjing Intermediate People's Court (2020) Su Min Final No. 791; *Shenzhen Mike v. Suzhou GouBang*, Nanjing Intermediate People's Court (2019), Su Zhi Chu No. 666.
[36] *Zhuhai Gree Electric Appliance Co., Ltd. and State Intellectual Property Office Patent Re-examination Committee*, Administrative Dispute over Invalidation of Design Patent Rights, Supreme People's Court (2011) Xingtizi No. 1.

'Nor does the average consumer apply additional visual attention to a change in a design element based on the change in the accompanying technical effect of that design element'. The phrase was first cited on 11 November, 2011, and has been cited in full and covertly in six decisions since then (e.g. *Suqian City Yanghe Town Royal Edge Brewery v. Runchu District Made-good Snack Food Store*[37] and *Kong Wei v. Jiangsu Xuanhui New Energy Technology Co.*[38]).

We further found one of the more influential passages, this one from the *Bridgestone Corporation v. Zhejiang Huntington Bull Rubber Co.* case,[39] which identifies the object of comparison in determining an existing design. In terms of whether there is a material difference, the Supreme Court held that a simultaneous comparison of the existing design, the allegedly infringing design, and the granted design is required:

> The presence or absence of substantial differences or similarity is relative. If the allegedly infringing product design is simply compared with the existing design ... it may appear that the allegedly infringing product design, existing design and granted design are similar. In order to make accurate conclusions ... the allegedly infringing product design, the existing design, and design patents are compared with each other ...[40]

The Supreme Court finally pointed out that the original judgment held that the existing design claimed by defendant, claimant's design and the granted design are different, but the court only compared the existing design and allegedly infringing product[41] to conclude that the existing design defence was established, and the infringement comparison method was improper and should be corrected.

The court of first and second instance in this case did not think so. They held that the allegedly infringing product and the existing design constituted a similar design, because they believed that only the allegedly infringing product needs to be compared with the existing design to decide whether they are similar. The Supreme People's Court rejected this view. 'To assess the impact on the overall visual effect, attention should be paid to the difference and the similarity between the allegedly infringing product design, the existing design and the granted design ...'.[42]

The opinion of the Supreme Court of China also reveals the difference of approach when judging infringements of designs and those of patents. When judging the infringement of an invention patent, comparing the necessary technical features of the allegedly infringing patent and the granted patent one by one is crucial. Design infringement disputes are different from this; we need to carry out the three comparisons stated in the previous paragraph. This is because the Supreme Court judge held that 'when simply comparing the two, we cannot

---

[37]   Zhenjiang Intermediate People's Court of Jiangsu Province (2015) Zhen Zhi Min Chu Zi No. 73.
[38]   Zhenjiang Intermediate People's Court of Jiangsu Province (2016) Su 11 Min Chu No. 236.
[39]   Supreme People's Court (2010) Min Tizi No. 189.
[40]   Ibid.
[41]   The Beijing Second Intermediate People's Court mentioned the following arguments in its first instance judgment: 'Huntington raises the prior design defense ... if the defendant proves that the allegedly infringing product is equivalent to an existing design, then its conduct does not constitute infringement. In applying the existing design defense principle, it is only necessary to make a judgment as to whether the allegedly infringing product and the existing design adduced by the alleged infringer constitute the same'. Ibid.
[42]   Ibid.

be sure whether the conclusion that the overall visual image is similar between the existing design and the allegedly infringing design is correct'.[43] Chinese Patent Law does not specify the object of comparison of existing designs, but this decision provides guidance and has been implicitly cited in hundreds of decisions since 2010.

3.6.4 Special rules of evidence

The only way to support an infringement claim is with sufficient evidence. However, in IPR litigation, patentees often have various difficulties in adducing evidence — as part of the evidence is in the hands of the accused infringer.

In November 2020, China's Supreme People's Court issued 'Several Provisions of the Supreme People's Court on Evidence in Civil Procedures Involving Intellectual Property Rights',[44] which provides that judges are allowed to set a passive obligation to disclose evidence for the parties in order to better address the difficulty in proving evidence in intellectual property cases. Even if a party believes that the evidence is unfavourable to it and does not want to submit it, the court can urge it to actively submit the evidence through this interpretation.[45]

However, through textual comparison, this chapter finds that prior to 2020, a portion of Chinese courts had actually set part of the rules regarding the determination of existing designs in terms of proof:

> The determination of the design features shall be made by the patentee who shall adduce evidence of the design features claimed by him.[46]
> Long before the application, the design picture had been uploaded to the QQ Zone,[47] which is used as a promotion and communication platform. Also, the design picture is still available in the QQ zone in the litigation period. Thus, the design picture in the patent application can be presumed to have been in the prior art, constituting the existing design.[48]

As noted at the beginning of this section, Chinese IPR adjudication lacks specialized rules related to evidence, and IPR is one of the areas of law that places the greatest emphasis on evidence. Through textual comparison, we can assert with some confidence the proposition that in the case of difficult cases, Chinese judges consult the database and implicitly cite passages related to the validity of evidence.

---

[43]   Ibid.

[44]   Several Provisions of the Supreme People's Court on Evidence in Civil Procedures Involving Intellectual Property Rights, <https://www.pkulaw.com/en_law/61b460a9dc465f70bdfb.html> accessed 19 May 2022.

[45]   'Where a people's court requires a party to submit relevant evidence according to the law, and the party refuses to submit the evidence without any justifiable reason, submit false evidence, destroys evidence, or conducts any other act which renders evidence unusable, the people's court may presume that the opposing party's claims on the certification items relating to the evidence are tenable'. Article 25, Several Provisions of the Supreme People's Court on Evidence in Civil Procedures Involving Intellectual Property Rights, <https://www.pkulaw.com/en_law/61b460a9dc465f70bdfb.html> accessed 19 May 2022.

[46]   *Grohe Co., Ltd. v. Zhejiang Jianlong Sanitary Ware Co., Ltd.*, Supreme People's Court (2015) Min Tizi No. 23.

[47]   QQ Zone is a social network platform launched by Tencent, similar to Facebook.

[48]   *Hu Chongliang v. Dong Feng, Foshan Nanhai Dili Decoration Material Factory*, Guangdong High People's Court (2015) Min San Zhong Zi No. 517 Civil Judgment.

3.7   Identification of 'Average Consumer'

According to Article 10 of the Interpretation of the Supreme People's Court on several issues concerning the Application of Law in the Trial of Patent Infringement Dispute Cases: 'The people's court shall determine whether designs are identical or similar based on an average consumer's knowledge and cognitive ability as to a product carrying a design patent'.

We will face the same problem as assessing the 'overall visual effect' mentioned above. There is also the concept of 'consumer' in trademark law, but is it the same? The mainstream view in China is that if, as in the case of trademark law, the determination of existing designs is based on whether the average consumer would be confused between the claimant and defendant's design, the protection of design patents would be confused with the protection of trademark rights, thus obscuring the difference between design patents as creative intellectual property rights and these logo-based intellectual property rights.[49] Despite this mainstream understanding, courts are still divided because different types of products have different average consumer groups due to their different characteristics. In the decisions retrieved from this chapter, the different determinations of product type led to different determinations of 'average consumers', which directly led to opposite conclusions and outcomes. Additionally, the determination of design space limits the level of observation and ability of the average consumer. Incorrectly determining the type of product or ignoring the design space size to determine the knowledge and cognitive ability of the average consumer can also lead to different comparison results.

While the courts may be divided, is there some degree of consensus? For this study, over 8,000 design decisions that contain the words 'average consumer' and, through textual comparison, the following passages that have been implicitly cited by subsequent courts were identified:

> Functional design features are judged not by whether the design feature is not optional due to functional or technical constraints but by whether, in the eyes of the average consumer, the design feature is determined solely by a specific function and thus does not require consideration of whether the design feature is aesthetically pleasing.[50]
> For the purpose of judging design infringement, the average consumer, should have common sense understanding of the appearance of the product design and its common design techniques. In addition to minor variations, consumers should have a certain level of discernment about the differences in shape, pattern and colour.[51]
> The combination of design differences in shape and size of the components create a strong visual impact, enough to attract the attention of the average consumer.[52]
> With larger design spaces, the average consumer is usually less likely to notice smaller differences between designs.[53]

---

[49]   Yin Xintian, *Chinese Patent Law Explained* (Intellectual Property Press, 2012) 294.

[50]   *Zhang Dijun v. Patent Re-examination Board*, Cixi City Xinlong Electronics Co. Supreme People's Court (2012) Xingtizi Administrative Judgment No. 14.

[51]   *Tong Xianping v. Danyang Shengmei Lighting Equipment Co., Ltd.*, Supreme People's Court (2015) Min Shen Zi No. 633 Civil Ruling.

[52]   *Jiangling Holdings Limited and the Patent Re-examination Committee of the State Intellectual Property Office*, Beijing Intellectual Property Court (2016) Jing Xing Chu No. 4497.

[53]   *MTG Corporation v. Guangzhou Baiyun District Shengjimei Beauty Instrument Factory*, Supreme People's Court (2019) Min Zai No. 142.

If we summarize these paragraphs, we can distil the rules that Chinese courts have used in practice to identify the average consumer. Consider the product category and design space to determine the average consumer's knowledge level and cognitive ability. Furthermore, the product category should be determined by subdividing the specific product classification rather than the above broad classification to limit the object and scope of the average consumer's cognition. Determine the size of the design space, the level of observation and ability of the average consumer, and the level of attention to certain elements of change, and thus determine the need to consider the detailed design. Only when the average consumers are properly and accurately identified and their knowledge and cognitive ability clearly defined can we obtain fair and just comparison results.

4.   CONCLUDING REMARKS

In presenting the empirical data, I have already discussed the significance of the data. However, to facilitate the reader's review, a few implications are briefly reviewed and highlighted here.

This research shows how to design an empirical study for a national database of judgments and the composition of judgments. Through this study, we find that even without using any sophisticated statistical tools, meaningful investigation can be conducted with a full understanding of the structure of judgments. When we search the literature on a search engine, the best search terms are often designed only by predicting the results in advance.

Through clever keyword crafting and text extraction, we can quickly count the distribution of trial courts and make statistics on win rates. What the computer cannot do is refine the judges' reasoning. This study also demonstrates how Chinese judges have enriched the brief provisions of statutory law in practice. Chinese judges identify existing designs as John Dewey had said, 'There are in any reflective thought definite units that are linked together so that there is a sustained movement to a common end'.[54] Although the Chinese Patent Law does not provide detailed guidelines for existing industrial design determination, the text itself at least provides a basis for judges to interpret the law. This study further finds that textual matching tools can be used to verify how Chinese court decisions work. This chapter is not intended to be a comparative study, and it is not clear whether this is the case in other civil law countries. At least in the case of China, we can assume that there is a hidden 'case law' at work within the courts in determining the existing design.

If there is research focusing on Chinese 'case law' or how to distil court decisions on particular issues, the approach and implementation steps mentioned in this study may be instructive.

---

[54]   John Dewey, *How We Think* (D.C. Heath and Company, 1933) 5.

Index